Computational Retinal Image Analysis

Tools, Applications and Perspectives

THE ELSEVIER AND MICCAI SOCIETY BOOK SERIES

Advisory Board

Titles:

MICCAI

Computational Retinal Image Analysis
Tools, Applications and Perspectives

Edited by

Emanuele Trucco

Tom MacGillivray

Yanwu Xu

ACADEMIC PRESS
An imprint of Elsevier

Academic Press is an imprint of Elsevier
125 London Wall, London EC2Y 5AS, United Kingdom
525 B Street, Suite 1650, San Diego, CA 92101, United States
50 Hampshire Street, 5th Floor, Cambridge, MA 02139, United States
The Boulevard, Langford Lane, Kidlington, Oxford OX5 1GB, United Kingdom

Notices
Knowledge and best practice in this field are constantly changing. As new research and experience
broaden our understanding, changes in research methods, professional practices, or medical treatment
may become necessary.

Practitioners and researchers must always rely on their own experience and knowledge in evaluating
and using any information, methods, compounds, or experiments described herein. In using such
information or methods they should be mindful of their own safety and the safety of others, including
parties for whom they have a professional responsibility.

To the fullest extent of the law, neither the Publisher nor the authors, contributors, or editors, assume
any liability for any injury and/or damage to persons or property as a matter of products liability,
negligence or otherwise, or from any use or operation of any methods, products, instructions, or ideas
contained in the material herein.

Library of Congress Cataloging-in-Publication Data
A catalog record for this book is available from the Library of Congress

British Library Cataloguing-in-Publication Data
A catalogue record for this book is available from the British Library

ISBN 978-0-08-102816-2

For information on all Academic Press publications
visit our website at https://www.elsevier.com/books-and-journals

Publisher: Mara Conner
Acquisition Editor: Tim Pitts
Editorial Project Manager: Mariana L. Kuhl
Production Project Manager: Nirmala Arumugam
Cover Designer: Christian J. Bilbow

Typeset by SPi Global, India

Contents

CHAPTER 10 **Statistical analysis and design in ophthalmology: Toward optimizing your data** **171**

Gabriela Czanner and Catey Bunce

CHAPTER 15   Retinal biomarkers and cardiovascular disease: A clinical perspective 299

Carol Yim-lui Cheung, Posey Po-yin Wong, and Tien Yin Wong

CHAPTER 16   Vascular biomarkers for diabetes and diabetic retinopathy screening 319

Fan Huang, Samaneh Abbasi-Sureshjani, Jiong Zhang, Erik J. Bekkers, Behdad Dashtbozorg, and Bart M. ter Haar Romeny

Contributors

Samaneh Abbasi-Sureshjani
Department of Biomedical Engineering, Eindhoven University of Technology, Eindhoven, The Netherlands

Bashir Al-Diri
School of Computer Science, University of Lincoln, Lincoln, United Kingdom

Stefanos Apostolopoulos
RetinAI Medical AG, Bern, Switzerland

Antonis A. Argyros
Institute of Computer Science, Foundation for Research and Technology— Hellas (FORTH); Computer Science Department, University of Crete, Heraklion, Greece

Lucia Ballerini
VAMPIRE Project, Centre for Clinical Brain Sciences, University of Edinburgh, Edinburgh, United Kingdom

Sarah A. Barman
School of Computer Science and Mathematics, Kingston University, Kingston upon Thames, United Kingdom,

Erik J. Bekkers
Department of Mathematics and Computer Science, Eindhoven University of Technology, Eindhoven, The Netherlands

Hrvoje Bogunović
Christian Doppler Laboratory for Ophthalmic Image Analysis, Department of Ophthalmology, Medical University of Vienna, Vienna, Austria

Adrian Bradu
School of Physical Sciences, University of Kent, Canterbury, United Kingdom

Catey Bunce
Faculty of Life Sciences and Medicine, King's College London; Moorfields Eye Hospital NHS Foundation Trust; UCL Institute of Ophthalmology; London School of Hygiene and Tropical Medicine, London, United Kingdom

Philip I. Burgess
Department of Eye and Vision Science, University of Liverpool; St Paul's Eye Unit, Royal Liverpool University Hospital, Liverpool, United Kingdom

Philippe Burlina
The Johns Hopkins University Applied Physics Lab, Laurel ; Johns Hopkins School of Medicine, Baltimore, MD, United States

Francesco Calivá
Department of Radiology and Biomedical Imaging, Musculoskeletal Quantitative Imaging Research Group, University of California, San Francisco, San Francisco, CA, United States

Aurélio Campilho
INESC TEC—Institute for Systems and Computer Engineering, Technology and Science; Faculty of Engineering, University of Porto, Porto, Portugal

Guillem Carles
School of Physics and Astronomy, University of Glasgow, Glasgow, United Kingdom

Jun Cheng
Chinese Academy of Sciences, Cixi Institute of Biomedical Engineering, Ningbo, Zhejiang, China

Li Cheng
A*STAR, Bioinformatics Institute, Singapore, Singapore; ECE, University of Alberta, Edmonton, AB, Canada

Carol Yim-lui Cheung
Department of Ophthalmology and Visual Sciences, The Chinese University of Hong Kong, Shatin, Hong Kong

Piotr Chudzik
School of Computer Science, University of Lincoln, Lincoln, United Kingdom

Carlos Ciller
RetinAI Medical AG, Bern, Switzerland

Adam Cohen
The Johns Hopkins University Applied Physics Lab, Laurel; Johns Hopkins School of Medicine, Baltimore, MD, United States

Pedro Costa
INESC TEC—Institute for Systems and Computer Engineering, Technology and Science, Porto, Portugal

Gabriela Czanner
Department of Applied Mathematics, Liverpool John Moores University; Clinical Eye Research Centre, Royal Liverpool University Hospital; Department of Eye and Vision Science, University of Liverpool, Liverpool, United Kingdom

Behdad Dashtbozorg
Department of Surgery, Netherlands Cancer Institute, Amsterdam, The Netherlands

Alexander Doney
Division of Population Health and Genomics, University of Dundee, Ninewells Hospital and Medical School, Dundee, United Kingdom

Huazhu Fu
A*STAR, Institute for Infocomm Research, Singapore, Singapore; Inception Institute of Artificial Intelligence, Abu Dhabi, United Arab Emirates

Adrian Galdran
INESC TEC—Institute for Systems and Computer Engineering, Technology and Science, Porto, Portugal

Jakob Grauslund
Department of Ophthalmology and Department of Clinical Research, Odense University Hospital and University of Southern Denmark, Odense, Denmark

Zaiwang Gu
Chinese Academy of Sciences, Cixi Institute of Biomedical Engineering, Ningbo, Zhejiang, China

Pedro Guimarães
Chair for Clinical Bioinformatics, Saarland University, Saarbrücken, Germany

Maged Habib
Sunderland Eye Infirmary, South Shields and Sunderland City Hospitals NHS Foundation Trust, Sunderland, United Kingdom

Andrew R. Harvey
School of Physics and Astronomy, University of Glasgow, Glasgow, United Kingdom

Carlos Hernandez-Matas
Institute of Computer Science, Foundation for Research and Technology— Hellas (FORTH), Heraklion, Greece

Stephen Hogg
VAMPIRE Project, Computing (SSEN), University of Dundee, Dundee, United Kingdom

Wynne Hsu
School of Computing, National University of Singapore, Singapore, Singapore

Zhihong Jewel Hu
Doheny Eye Institute, Los Angeles, CA, United States

Fan Huang
Department of Biomedical Engineering, Eindhoven University of Technology, Eindhoven, The Netherlands

Yan Huang
Artificial Intelligence Innovation Business (AIIB), Baidu, Beijing, China

Emily R. Jefferson
Health Informatics Centre, University of Dundee, Dundee, United Kingdom

Ryo Kawasaki
Department of Vision Informatics, Osaka University Graduate School of Medicine, Suita, Japan

Le Van La
Baidu Research Institute (BRI), Baidu, Sunnyvale, CA, United States

Mong Li Lee
School of Computing, National University of Singapore, Singapore, Singapore

Huiqi Li
Beijing Institute of Technology, Beijing, China

Xing Li
Baidu Research Institute (BRI), Baidu, Sunnyvale, CA, United States

Zhengguo Li
Agency for Science, Technology and Research, Institute for Infocomm Research, Singapore

Gilbert Lim
School of Computing, National University of Singapore, Singapore, Singapore

Jiang Liu
Chinese Academy of Sciences, Cixi Institute of Biomedical Engineering, Ningbo, Zhejiang, China

Xuan Liu
Artificial Intelligence Group, Baidu, Beijing, China

Xingzheng Lyu
Zhejiang University, Hangzhou, China

Tom MacGillivray
VAMPIRE Project, Centre for Clinical Brain Sciences, University of Edinburgh, Edinburgh, United Kingdom

Sarah McGrory
Centre for Cognitive Ageing and Cognitive Epidemiology, University of Edinburgh, Edinburgh, United Kingdom

Andrew McNeil
VAMPIRE Project, Computing (SSEN), University of Dundee, Dundee, United Kingdom

Muthu Rama Krishnan Mookiah
VAMPIRE Project, Computing (SSEN), University of Dundee, Dundee, United Kingdom

Giovanni Ometto
Optometry and Visual Science, School of Health Sciences, University of London, London, United Kingdom

Christopher G. Owen
Population Health Research Institute, St. George's University of London, London, United Kingdom

Adrian Podoleanu
School of Physical Sciences, University of Kent, Canterbury, United Kingdom

Alicja R. Rudnicka
Population Health Research Institute, St. George's University of London, London, United Kingdom

Alfredo Ruggeri
Department of Information Engineering, University of Padua, Padua, Italy

Srinivas Reddy Sadda
Doheny Eye Institute; Department of Ophthalmology, University of California—
Los Angeles, Los Angeles, CA, United States

Ursula Schmidt-Erfurth
Christian Doppler Laboratory for Ophthalmic Image Analysis, Department of
Ophthalmology, Medical University of Vienna, Vienna, Austria

Raphael Sznitman
ARTORG Center, University of Bern, Bern, Switzerland

Bart M. ter Haar Romeny
Department of Biomedical Engineering, Eindhoven University of Technology,
Eindhoven, The Netherlands

Daniel Shu Wei Ting
Singapore Eye Research Institute, Singapore National Eye Centre, Singapore,
Singapore

Emanuele Trucco
VAMPIRE Project, Computing (SSEN), University of Dundee, Dundee, United
Kingdom

Wolf-Dieter Vogl
Christian Doppler Laboratory for Ophthalmic Image Analysis, Department of
Ophthalmology, Medical University of Vienna, Vienna, Austria

Sebastian M. Waldstein
Christian Doppler Laboratory for Ophthalmic Image Analysis, Department of
Ophthalmology, Medical University of Vienna, Vienna, Austria

Lei Wang
Artificial Intelligence Innovation Business (AIIB), Baidu, Beijing, China

Roshan A. Welikala
School of Computer Science and Mathematics, Kingston University, Kingston
upon Thames, United Kingdom

Jeffrey Wigdahl
VisonQuest Biomedical LLC, Albuquerque, NM, United States

Bryan M. Williams
Department of Eye and Vision Science, University of Liverpool; St Paul's Eye
Unit, Royal Liverpool University Hospital, Liverpool, United Kingdom

Sebastian Wolf
Department of Ophthalmology, Inselspital, University Hospital, University of
Bern, Bern, Switzerland

Damon Wing Kee Wong
Nanyang Technological University, Singapore

Posey Po-yin Wong
Department of Ophthalmology and Visual Sciences, The Chinese University of
Hong Kong, Shatin, Hong Kong

Tien Yin Wong
Singapore Eye Research Institute, Singapore National Eye Centre, Singapore, Singapore

Yanwu Xu
AI Innovation Business Department, Baidu Online Network Technology (Beijing) Co., Ltd.; Ningbo Institute of Materials Technology and Engineering, Chinese Academy of Sciences (CAS); Artificial Intelligence Innovation Business (AIIB), Baidu, Beijing, China

Dalu Yang
Artificial Intelligence Innovation Business (AIIB), Baidu, Beijing, China

Yehui Yang
Artificial Intelligence Innovation Business (AIIB), Baidu, Beijing, China

Xenophon Zabulis
Institute of Computer Science, Foundation for Research and Technology— Hellas (FORTH), Heraklion, Greece

Sandro De Zanet
RetinAI Medical AG, Bern, Switzerland

Jiong Zhang
Keck School of Medicine, University of Southern California, Los Angeles, CA, United States

He Zhao
Beijing Institute of Technology, Beijing, China

Yalin Zheng
Department of Eye and Vision Science, University of Liverpool; St Paul's Eye Unit, Royal Liverpool University Hospital, Liverpool, United Kingdom

A brief introduction and a glimpse into the past

1

Emanuele Trucco[a], Yanwu Xu[b], Tom MacGillivray[c]

[a]VAMPIRE Project, Computing (SSEN), University of Dundee, Dundee, United Kingdom
[b]AI Innovation Business Department, Baidu Online Network Technology (Beijing) Co., Ltd.,
Beijing, China
[c]VAMPIRE Project, Centre for Clinical Brain Sciences, University of Edinburgh,
Edinburgh, United Kingdom

1 Why this book?

This book offers an overview of the main aspects of contemporary retinal image analysis (RIA) in the context of clinical applications, healthcare informatics and artificial intelligence. The book aims to be not just another collection of papers on technical advancements; these are reported more timely by conferences papers, online journal pre-prints and repositories like arXiv or bioRxiv. Instead, the book aspires to be a comprehensive introduction to the field. A logical progression of chapters takes the reader through an overview of RIA, its clinical motivations, technical foundations (image acquisition modalities, instruments), computational techniques for essential operations (e.g., anatomical landmarks location, blood vessel segmentation), lesion detection (e.g., optic disc in glaucoma, microaneurysms in diabetes) and the important topic of validation, all the way to a showcase of current investigations drawing from artificial intelligence and big data (retinal biomarkers for risk of systemic conditions) and the future, e.g., large-scale screening programs, precision medicine, computer-assisted personalized eye care and the challenges of creating, maintaining and making available to research inceasingly large collections of clinical data.

2 Casting an eye into the distant past: The history of eye research in the West

Zusammengestohlen aus verschiedenem diesem und jenem[a]
Ludwig van Beethoven, comment on his String Quartet no. 14

For an overview of retinal imaging including a brief history of modern techniques we refer the reader to Keane and Sadda's review [1]. Chapter 3 of this book offers

---

[a] "Put together from bits stolen from here and there."

Computational Retinal Image Analysis. https://doi.org/10.1016/B978-0-08-102816-2.00001-0

a contemporary view on retinal imaging. We add here a brief summary of the origin of eye-related research in the West, which we hope may interest the reader; the present cannot be understood completely but in the context of the past. Beyond the western world, a concise history of ancient vision and eye-related theory in India and some comparisons with western theories is given by Deshpande [2]. Our short account follows loosely Pierantoni's detailed book [3], with elements from the history of ophthalmology (anatomy and physiology) available on the UK Royal College of Ophthalmologists website [4]. Bynum [5] is a concise, non-technical but informative account of the history of medicine, including of course ophthalmology.

The curiosity of man for the eye goes back a long way. It may seem therefore extraordinary that the first anatomically accurate drawing of the ocular bulb did not appear before the early 17th century, in *Rosa Ursina* by the German Jesuit priest and scientist Christoph Scheiner (1575–1650). Before then, all drawings of the eye put religious or philosophical beliefs before anatomical observation. This fascinating story starts, in the West, with the oldest known drawing of the ocular bulb and its main component, due to the medieval arab scholar Hunain ibn Ishak, who lived in the 9th century BC, in his *"Ten essays on the structure of the eye, its diseases and cures."* The drawing was first reproduced by the neurologist Stephen Polyak during WWII [6] and is itself a copy of an older drawing which did not reach us, perhaps a Greek manuscript from many centuries before. Ibn Ishak's eye looks very inaccurate to us: it is almond-shaped; the lens is in the center; the optic nerve, the pupil and the lens are aligned along the middle axis of the ocular bulb; the optic nerve is hollow. Vision is explained through the flow of a "vital spirit" *emitted* by the eye (an idea already found in Pythagoras and Euclid), which required the hollow optical nerve to flow out of the eye and back. As Pierantoni observes, the drawing is best interpreted as a *functional* diagram, as all functional elements are in place, but not anatomically accurate. Yet dissecting an eye does not require particularly sophisticated instruments. But the influence of the philosophical giants of the antiquity, in addition to the aversion to cadaver dissection of religion and state, was obviously immense—and would last for many centuries to come.[b] Hence dissection was often practiced on animals, assuming that their anatomy was similar or the same to the human one.

The first drawing showing a connection between the eye and the brain is due to another arab scholar, Abu Ja'far Ahmad ibn Muhammad (906–963), again most likely a copy of a previous Greek document. This drawing is also the first diagram giving an account of binocular vision: it shows two ocular bulbs, now round but still equipped with hollow channels carrying the "visual spirit" responsible for vision. A relation of Ja'far, the scholar Ibn al-Haitam (also known as Alheizen, c.965–1040), proposed however in his *Book of Optics* that vision was made possible by the rays of light *entering* the eye. Precursors of this idea were already present in the work of the highly regarded Greek physician and surgeon, Galen (129–c.200 AD), who thought that the light entering the eye interacted with a "visual spirit" (*pneuma*) generated in

---

[b] Interestingly, some of the ideas from ancient Greece still permeate parts of contemporary western medicine [5].

the brain. The *pneuma* would carry the shapes carried by the light to the brain, in a bi-directional flow. In contrast, early functional theories of vision, including those by Pythagoras and Euclid, who lived between the mid-5th and the mid-3rd century BC, stated that the *pneuma* was emitted into the world and would bounce off objects carrying back their shapes into the eye. Democritus (4th–3rd century BC) had raised a dissenting voice, postulating that objects emitted continuously images of themselves (*éidola*, or "figures," "representations"), that entered the eye (*intromission* theory) making perception possible.

The eye model undergoes an idealization in the Middle Ages, seemingly to reflect more the geometry of the divinely perfect, symmetric universe, in which the circle represented the supreme geometric perfection. The anatomy of the eye was therefore inspired by the orbits of the known planets, that had to be rigorously circular. Such models are found in the work by Roger Bacon (1214–92) and John Pecham (1230–92), Archbishop of Canterbury. An eye model based on tradition, not anatomy, is found even in Leonardo da Vinci's well-known section of a man's head in his *Anatomical Studies*, folio 32r. Here the eye is depicted as a spherical bulb containing a central, spherical lens. Leonard's eye is connected to the brain by a channel that he believed was composed by many smaller ones, to keep separate the images of the different things perceived simultaneously. Leonardo never took a definite position in the controversy between emission and intromission theories.

Dissection and direct observations re-start in earnest with Andreas Vesalius, the Flemish physician regarded as the father of modern anatomy. Vesalius's drawing of the eye in his *De humani corporis fabrica* (on the structure of the human body, 1543) suggests direct observation (e.g., the bulb is spherical, the anterior chamber is present) but still reflects the burden of the tradition: the lens is central, the optic nerve is hollow and aligned with the central axis of the bulb through the center of the pupil.

In the work by Johann Kepler (1571–1630), the German astronomer and physicist, optics plays a crucial role and allows Kepler to propose an explanation for the paradox of the inverted image, which had puzzled Leonardo himself: if the pupil, as a small aperture, makes the image appear inverted on a screen, why don't we perceive the world upside down? Kepler understands that an "opposite inversion" must happen in the brain. Finally, shortly after Kepler, Scheiner publishes the first anatomical drawing of the eye which we can accept completely. A correct understanding of the anatomy was finally achieved. Centuries would still be needed to attain accurate *physiological* models, but this goes beyond the scope of this short historical note.

3 Book structure

The book is organized in five parts following logically from each other and taking the reader from an introductory presentation of computational techniques for RIA to cutting-edge topics, including of course the promises and challenges of artificial intelligence for eye-related healthcare.

Part 1. Three introductory chapters offering a short presentation of, respectively, this book together with a short historical note (this chapter), of the contemporary clinical motivations and needs for RIA in healthcare, and of the modalities for imaging the retina.

Part 2. Six chapters reviewing an essential set of computational techniques for retinal image analysis, focusing on processing fundus cameras and optical coherence tomography (OCT) images. These chapters cover landmark detection, segmentation, quality assessment and algorithm validation.

Part 3. Seven chapters dedicated to algorithms for the detection of the main lesions of interest in fundus camera and OCT images, covering among others optic disc diseases, diabetic retinopathy (DR), and neurodegeneration and fluid segmentation in OCT scans.

Part 4. Three chapters offering a healthcare perspective, discussing the growing field of retinal biomarkers for systemic diseases, screening for DR, and eye-oriented diagnosis.

Part 5. Three chapters dedicated to artificial intelligence for retina-related research, including discussions of deep learning and big-data techniques, and the practical challenges of creating, maintaining and making available to research very large collections of clinical data under data governance rules.

Acknowledgments

Our sincere thanks go to the Elsevier team for their assistance with the production of this book from an idea to publication, especially Tim Pitts and Mariana Kuhl, including for unshakeable patience with our multiple infringements of deadlines.

We thank the many colleagues who have authored the chapters forming this book. We hope that they, and indeed all readers, will find it useful and worth recommending for many years to come.

Finally, thank you to you, the reader, for buying this book. We hope you will find it a valuable resource for teaching and research alike. We welcome your feedback.

References

[1] P. Keane, S. Sadda, Retinal imaging in the 21st century: state of the art and future directions, Ophthalmology 121 (12) (2014) 2489–2500.

[2] V. Deshpande, Ophthalmic ideas in ancient India, Indian J. Hist. Sci. 48 (2) (2013) 175–205.

[3] R. Pierantoni, L'Occhio e l'Idea, second ed., Boringhieri, Italy, 1982.

[4] Royal College of Ophthalmologists. http://www.mrcophth.com/Historyofophthalmology/anatomy.htm, (Accessed 31 July 2019).

[5] W. Bynum, A Short History of Medicine. A Very Short Introduction, Oxford University Press, 2008.

[6] S.L. Polyak, The Retina, Chicago University Press, Chicago, IL, 1941.

Clinical motivation and the needs for RIA in healthcare

2

Ryo Kawasaki[a], Jakob Grauslund[b]

[a]Department of Vision Informatics, Osaka University Graduate School of Medicine, Suita, Japan,
*[b]Department of Ophthalmology and Department of Clinical Research, Odense University Hospital
and University of Southern Denmark, Odense, Denmark*

1 Introduction

The retina provides a unique window to observe blood vessels and neural tissue in vivo. The intervention of the ophthalmoscope by Hermann von Helmholtz in 1851 has uncovered the retina behind the pupil of the eye [1]. Observing the retina and the optic disc has formed the foundation of modern ophthalmology by describing ocular diseases in detail.

Ophthalmologists diagnose retinal diseases by identifying specific signs on the retina. In the clinical setting, the primarily method to examine the retina is through direct or indirect ophthalmoscopy. Expanding use of retinal photographs contributed to retinal image analysis tremendously. Not long since the invention of photography, Jackman and Webster reported the first fundus photography in 1886 [2]. Carl Zeiss produced the first commercial fundus camera in 1926. Since then, fundus photography has been used as the main imaging modality in clinical settings. In the 1970s, the non-mydriatic fundus camera was introduced to the market and it contributed to expanding the field of fundus photography use to health screening programs or epidemiological studies. In the early days, retinal image analysis was done by literally applying scales or a Vernier caliper on the films or projected images on a large screen (e.g. measuring vessel caliber, optic disc diameter, and standard circles for signs of age-related macular degeneration). At that time, as one can imagine, retinal image analyses were limited because of its workload and so mainly used for research purposes.

Landmark expansion of retinal imaging was achieved by a transition from film to digital image. Digital fundus camera was introduced by Eastman Kodak in 1975. It took several decades to fully shift from analog film to digital imaging by persuading clinicians to accept color replication and high resolution to capture subtle changes on the retinal images (and maybe cost of the equipment). Digital fundus photography is now the standard imaging modality in both ophthalmic clinics and screening facilities. Since the inclusion of a digital camera along with matching computing power

Subjective impression + Objective measurement
Qualitative assessment + Quantitative assessment
Apparently visible changes + Subtle subclinical changes
On-site diagnosis + Off-site diagnosis
Repetitive work + Automation

FIG. 1

What values does RIA add to the current medical assessment?

and storage capacity, computer aided diagnosis (CAD) has been expected to assist diagnosing eye diseases by adding quantitative information, automated detection, and decision making for treatment choice.

Now, what value does RIA add to the current ophthalmological or medical management? (Fig. 1) There are huge potentials and expectations in RIA to make retinal assessment more precise, reliable, and quantifiable. It is also expected to discover unseen information in the images with computer assessed image processing techniques. Also, repetitive but simple tasks such as filtering fundus images in the screening setting could be automated within a diagnostic system. With this capability, off-site diagnosis, known as a tele-ophthalmology or tele-medicine, has a potential to spread a quality of medical standard throughout geographic areas where ophthalmological medical resource is scarce. This chapter will discuss how RIA has and can be applied in ophthalmology and broader healthcare (Fig. 2) in order to understand the motivation and needs.

1.1 Assisting diagnosis of clinical eye diseases

To date, there has been an accumulated expert knowledge to detect and diagnose clinical eye diseases on the retina. RIA has been utilized to assist diagnosis of eye diseases both in research and in clinical practice. One example is diabetic retinopathy. In the mid 19th century, Eduard Jëger had himself improved the ophthalmoscope, and described yellowish round spots in the macular area, the first description of diabetic retinopathy. Signs of diabetic retinopathy at early stage are relatively easy to recognize and defined by rules. Basically, they are "red lesions," i.e., microaneurysms and hemorrhages, and hard "yellow lesions," i.e., hard and soft exudates. To date, diabetic retinopathy is one eye disease studied for CAD and automated detection intensively.

There are two reasons why CAD and automated detection of diabetic retinopathy have been studied extensively. First, there is a clear medical need. The prevalence of diabetes has quadrupled since 1980, and it is estimated that at present the disease affects 422 million adults world-wide [3]. Diabetic retinopathy is the most common complication in diabetes and almost universal in patients with long-term diabetes [4, 5]. Even though the risk of blindness is estimated to decrease, long-term data have demonstrated a 25-year incidence of blindness of 9.5% in patients with type 1 diabetes [6]. Screening for diabetic retinopathy among patients with diabetes is considered an important strategy to prevent blindness or severe visual impairment. Indeed, diabetic retinopathy is a good candidate to be screened at the clinically asymptomatic

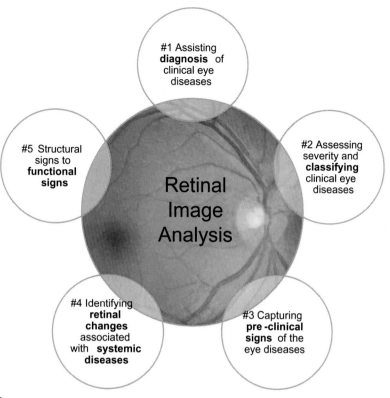

FIG. 2

Retinal image analysis and key five areas for application.

stage so that timely treatment can be provided. Given that there has been a great advance in the management and treatment of diabetic retinopathy, early diagnosis and timely treatment has potential to minimize burden of this blinding disease. However, the number of ophthalmologists for screening is lacking. Therefore, optometrists, nurses, or trained image graders have been reading retinal images for screening purposes. The United Kingdom, for example, has a nation-wide screening program for diabetic retinopathy, and many other countries are to establish such screening programs as well. Thus, there is already an environment expecting an automated retinal image diagnosis to replace ophthalmologists or experienced graders for diabetic retinopathy in a screening setting. The aim of screening for diabetic retinopathy is to detect sight-threatening diabetic retinopathy (proliferative diabetic retinopathy [PDR] and diabetic macular edema) prior to irreversible loss of vision. This is well-aligned with the World Health Organization that has recommended screening should be performed for diseases with a given number of criteria [7]. These include:

(1) *the condition should be an important health problem,*
(2) *there should be an accepted treatment for patients with recognized disease,*

(3) *facilities for diagnosis and treatment should be available,*
(4) *there should be a recognizable latent or early symptomatic stage,*
(5) *there should be a suitable test or examination,*
(6) *the test should be acceptable to the population,*
(7) *the natural history of the condition, including development from latent to declared disease, should be adequately understood,*
(8) *there should be an agreed policy on whom to treat as patients, and*
(9) *the cost of case-finding should be economically balanced in relation to possible expenditure on medical care.*

These criteria are all met in diabetic retinopathy, and it has been confirmed that eye screening in diabetes is cost-effective [8]. Likewise, the introduction of the national UK diabetic retinopathy screening program led to data demonstrating that DR for the first time in half a century is no longer the leading cause of blindness in the working-age population [9]. Understanding the above conditions for successful screening is quite important when automated image grading system is to be introduced to the real world setting. Because even when high sensitivity and specificity is achieved with RIA technically, some diseases are not suitable for screening by their nature.

Second, classification and definitions of retinal signs of diabetic retinopathy have been clearly standardized through clinical trials and epidemiological studies. The classification of diabetic retinopathy has been standardized according to the Early Treatment Diabetic Retinopathy Study (ETDRS) scale based on the modified Airlie House classification [10]. The scale has stood the test of time, and it has now been commonly accepted as the gold standard classification. However, even though the ETDRS scale is well suited for research settings, its practical use is limited by the high complexity of the scale with a high number of specific and sophisticated steps. A potential solution for this was presented by the American Academy of Ophthalmology in 2003, when Wilkinson et al. proposed the International Clinical Diabetic Retinopathy Disease Severity (IC-DR-DS) scale [11]. This was a five step scale with two major advantages. Firstly, the numbers of steps are limited and easy to learn. Secondly, the scale is well-suited to stratify patients according to risk of diabetic retinopathy progression. Specifically, patients with severe non-proliferative diabetic retinopathy (NPDR) are important to identify given a high risk of progression to PDR, which approximates 50% and 71% in 1 and 3 years, respectively. In most countries, this level of diabetic retinopathy is considered as "referable diabetic retinopathy" in screening meaning that patients with this level of diabetic retinopathy should be referred to ophthalmologists for further management. Hence, classification according to the IC-DR-DS scale would be important in health care programs that rely on DR-screening with flexible and individualized time intervals.

Even though the introduction of DR-screening has been successful in many countries, other issues have arisen. The repetitive screening of DR is costly and strenuous, and specialized health care providers are burdened by the task. These issues may all be addressed by automated retinal image analysis (ARIA) based on algorithms with the capability to detect diabetic retinal lesions. However, such programs often introduce a generalization problem, when the algorithms are set out to classify images not equivalent to those used for training. Consequently, the performances of most ARIA models have been limited by moderate specificities despite very high sensitivities [12, 13]. Deep-learning models may provide a solution to this with results approaching human performance with high levels of sensitivity as well as specificity [14, 15]. Now with an advanced boost with deep learning technology, the FDA approved the first fully automated diagnostic system to screen people with diabetes—if the individual has a certain level of diabetic retinopathy they are seen by an ophthalmologist otherwise they continue annual screening by the system if it is in a milder stage.

1.2 Assessing severity and classifying clinical eye diseases

Ophthalmologists inspect retinal images to capture signs of clinical disease, and then signs to determine the severity of the disease. Although retinal images provide both qualitative and quantitative information, ophthalmologists or image graders mainly focus on the qualitative aspects to determine the severity of the diseases. Traditionally, qualitative information such as presence, shapes or location of the signs specific to each eye disease are used as evidence for decision making in a clinical or screening setting. CAD can enhance this process by adding quantitative retinal imaging analysis and providing more precise, reproducible, measurable, and comparable assessment for clinical eye diseases.

Glaucoma is one of the leading blinding eye diseases in developed countries reflecting an aging society [16]. Imaging diagnosis and severity assessment of glaucoma is based on optic disc appearance such as an enlarged cup-to-disc ratio, optic disc rim thinning, and retinal nerve fiber layer defect. These signs shape the characteristics of glaucomatous retinal changes. However, the very initial pathological changes of glaucoma develop far before those signs are clinically visible. In fact, optic disc changes are detectable after ganglion cells are lost at a certain level. Optical coherence tomography (OCT) can capture the early changes of ganglion cell layer complex thinning and following thinning of the retinal nerve fiber layer. Quantification of the specific retinal layer contributes to assessing severity, progression and treatment response of eyes with glaucoma, and provides invaluable information to manage the disease.

Another good example of RIA in clinical eye disease classification and management is the assessment of macular edema. OCT also provides a quantitative assessment to the macular edema caused by diabetic retinopathy. Classification of diabetic macular edema has traditionally been performed according to the clinically significant diabetic macular edema (CSME) in the ETDRS [17]. However, the scale was developed at a time where OCT had not been introduced and at present an evidence-based update on the scale is needed to account for the different abilities to measure macular edema by OCT as compared to stereo fundus evaluation. In terms of this, a considerable inconsistency in detection of diabetic macular edema and CSME exhibits when fundus photography and OCT were compared [18]. In fact, differences went both ways, but in general there was a higher prevalence of diabetic macular edema and CSME by fundus photography (61.4% and 48.5%) as compared to OCT (21.1% and 21.3%). Thus it is now standard to use OCT for the evaluation of diabetic macular edema. In addition to qualitative assessment such as presence of cysts in the retina or sub/intra-retinal fluids, direct measurements of the macular thickness have been utilized as a parameter to represent disease severity of diabetic macular edema. Along with a wide spread use of intra-vitreal injection of anti-vascular endothelial growth factor to treat macular edema, quantitative retinal thickness assessment is quite informative to decide initiating or continuing the treatment in addition to the patients' visual acuity. It should also be noted that active research has been done investigating whether RIA provides qualitative classification by adopting deep neural network to filter images with intra-retinal edema, sub-retinal fluids, epiretinal membranes, or other anatomical signs. Coupled with quantitative and qualitative feature classification using OCT, there is a huge expectation that the management of macular edema can be optimized by automated decision support [19].

1.3 Capturing pre-clinical signs of the eye diseases

Even before clinical eye diseases become detectable, there is an expectation that RIA can provide predictive information by detecting subtle changes in the retina before developing clinical diseases.

Retinal arteriolar narrowing, for example, is linked to an increased risk of developing glaucoma. Background hypothesis includes a decreased blood supply or dysregulation of blood flow in the retina before glaucoma is clinically detectable. RIA can measure retinal vessel caliber size as an indicator of blood supply, and narrowing of the retinal arteriolar vessel caliber seems to precede the clinical development of glaucoma [20].

Difference in vessel widths between eyes have been also linked to the risk of developing retinal vein occlusion. Although retinal vein occlusion is considered to be associated with cardiovascular risks, it develops in one eye at a time, not involving both eyes at the same time (eventually, there are some patients who develops retinal vein occlusion in both eyes over time, usually years). Here, un-balanced ratio of the retina arteriolar and venular vessel widths, known as the arterio-venous ratio, between right and left eye in the same individual indicates a risk of retinal vein occlusion [21].

1.4 Identifying retinal changes associated with systemic diseases

Retinal signs can be an indicator to some systemic diseases. The retina is a rare organ in that it allows physicians to observe microvasculature in vivo. Therefore, a fundus examination provides a window to visualize microvascular changes caused by systemic disease.

Cardiovascular risks and retinal vascular changes have been studied since retinal examinations became available. The classic example of retinal vascular change associated with systemic disease is its association with hypertension and cardiovascular diseases. In the late 19th century, Marcus Gunn reported signs in the retina observed in a series of patients with renal disease with hypertension [22]. Since then, retinal

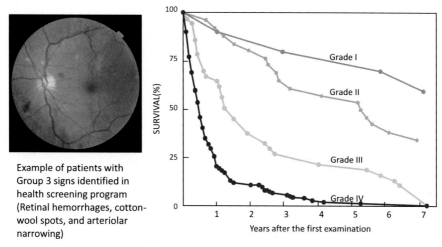

Example of patients with Group 3 signs identified in health screening program (Retinal hemorrhages, cotton-wool spots, and arteriolar narrowing)

FIG. 3

Keith Wegener Barker classification and mortality prediction.

Graph recreated with permission based on N.M. Keith, H.P. Wagener, N.W. Barker, Some different types of essential hypertension: their course and prognosis. Am. J. Med. Sci. 197 (1939) 332–43.

vascular signs associated with hypertension have been well described in evaluating individuals with high risk of developing cardiovascular diseases. Keith-Wegener-Barker (KWB) classification has been a reference for the assessment of hypertensive retinal changes (Fig. 3) [23]. Its concept is to identify individuals with high risk of mortality based on the retinal vascular changes. Here, these milder retinal changes of group 1 or group 2 are not clinically relevant from an ophthalmological viewpoint. However, these changes can assist decision making into whether an individual should consider treatment for hypertension to avoid cardiovascular risks.

Retinal vessel caliber measurements by CAD contributed to updating the classic KWB classification by quantifying the narrowing of the retinal arterioles. The Atherosclerosis Risks in Communities study (ARIC study) has developed a method to estimate the central retinal artery and vein diameter as the central retinal artery equivalent (CRAE) and central retinal vein equivalent (CRVE) [24, 25]. With this method, it is now understood that diffuse arteriolar narrowing assessed as decreased CRAE or venular widening assessed as increased CRVE (Fig. 4).

Now, quantification of the retinal vascular size expanded its potential association to other cardiovascular risks when arteriolar size and venular size are analyzed separately. Widening of venular vessel width is linked with increased inflammatory markers [26], obesity [27], pregnancy [28, 29] and smoking [30]. Potentially, retinal vascular size can capture response to intervention to hypertension with anti-hypertensive medication [31], smoking cessation [30] and dyslipidemia with statin use [32].

It is also promising that some retinal features precede some development of systemic diseases. Retinal vessel widths have shown to be associated with future

Retinal vessel appearance of healthy individual

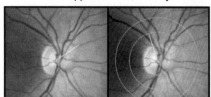

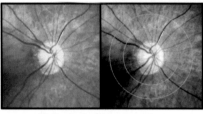
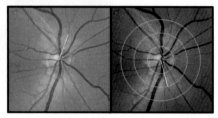

| Retinal arteriolar narrowing | Retinal venular widening |

FIG. 4

Retinal vessel appearance of healthy individual, with retinal arteriolar narrowing *(left bottom)* and retinal venular widening *(right bottom)*.

development of stroke [33], coronary heart disease [34], hypertension [35] and other cardiovascular related risk factors.

In addition to clinical retinal diseases or retinal vessel widths, various objective and quantitative changes in the retinal vasculature were sought to be used as markers of systemic diseases [36]. The rationale for exploring this field is based on the concept that the retinal vasculature is dynamically changing in its morphological properties to optimize the blood flow. Murray's law, for example, is one of the principal theories to simulate or speculate hypothetical optimal circulations in human body. There have been research tools to quantify the morphological features such as vessel widths (caliber and length-to-diameter ratio) and the arterio-venous ratio, optimality parameters at vascular junctions (junctional exponent and optimality parameter), vascular bifurcation or branching angles, vascular tortuosity, and the fractal dimensions. Image analysis software such as SIVA [37] and VAMPIRE tools [38] are available for research purpose.

RIA is also investigated to be linked with neurological diseases. This is based on a hypothesis that retina, as a part of neural organ directly connected with brain, can be involved in the early manifestation of neurological diseases such as Alzheimer's disease and Parkinson's disease. Indeed, there has been an accumulation of evidence that persons with neurological diseases have retinal changes. In regards to Alzheimer's disease, one of the most challenging tasks in aging countries, early non-invasive detection of high risk of developing the disease is an emerging issue. In the retina, there is a study that successfully visualized amyloid beta protein deposit around the retinal vasculature [39]. There are studies reporting that patients with Alzheimer's disease have narrowing of the retinal vessels [40], and the thinning of the retina and choroid [41]. There is a newer finding that retinal vessel density is decreased both in the retina and choroid [42]. Current challenges include whether there is a specific change or combination of changes that can be used to stratify risk specific to different diseases [43].

1.5 Structural signs to functional signs

Although it is often the case that a single retinal image is used for assessment, this is only capturing a static state. Expectations to RIA include an assessment of dynamically changing features based on real-time monitoring or changes over stimulations.

Dynamic vessel analyzer is a fundus camera equipped with light stimulation and real-time monitoring system introduced by IMEDOS. The response of retinal vessels to flickering light can be measured non-invasively (Fig. 5) [44]. With a flickering light stimulation, there is a quick response of vasodilation reflecting endothelial function of the retinal circulation via nitric oxide. A study showed that individuals with diabetes and diabetic retinopathy have reduced flicker-induced retinal vasodilation response, i.e., individuals with reduced flicker light-induced vasodilation were 20 times more likely to have diabetes and among participants with diabetes, those with reduced flicker induced

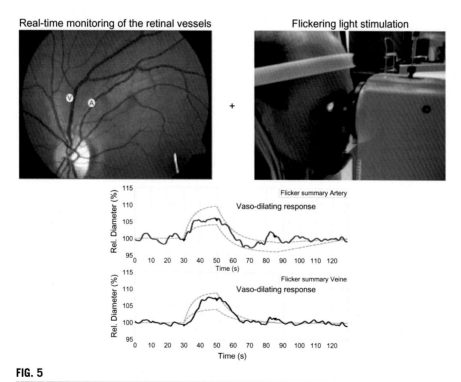

FIG. 5

Capturing functional response (vasodilation) to the flickering light stimulation using Dynamic Vessel Analyzer (IMEDOS, Germany).

vasodilation were 2 times more likely to have diabetic retinopathy [45].These findings further support the concept that dynamic changes or functional changes could capture earlier alteration even before morphological change is visible in the retinal vasculature.

There have been a variety of methods challenged to visualize and quantify retinal blood flow. However, it has been a challenging task to be incorporated in clinical practice. Attempts include fluorescein angiography, laser Doppler flowmetry and velocimetry, ultrasound, and more recently, with Doppler OCT [46]. Recent advances in OCT, especially its capability to capture multiple images in a very short time, have made the Doppler OCT technique the most promising modality to quantify retinal blood flow and other parameters non-invasively. Static visualization of the retinal and choroidal vasculature has been achieved and equipped in current OCT machines on the market as OCT angiography. Post processing the images acquired for OCT angiography has a potential to produce volumetric or velocimetric parameters. Retinal blood flow is considered to be quite important in retinal vascular diseases such as diabetic retinopathy, retinal vein occlusion and age-related macular degeneration, and also glaucoma. In addition to the static morphological features, assessment of dynamic blood flow would expand the window to detect early clinical manifestations and to monitor disease activity including treatment response.

2 Perspectives—Precise diagnosis, replacing repetitive work, and exploring novel signs

This chapter overviewed five key areas that have been enhanced with RIA in both ophthalmological and systemic disease diagnosis, and prediction. RIA can enrich clinicians to understand the pathophysiology of the disease by identifying features in retinal images. RIA provides a non-invasive tool to probe the role of the microvasculature in the development of clinical eye diseases and systemic diseases. RIA provides additional information to stratify risks of developing diseases in the future. By visualizing subtle changes with quantification, RIA enable clinicians to use imaging markers as surrogate outcomes to monitor and evaluate response to the treatment.

There is an emerging application of imaging techniques and automated classification or processing in RIA. There is an expectation that repetitive screening grading can be replaced with automated grading systems without compromising high accuracy. Also deep learning classification might provide a new insight into what clinicians do not see in the image so far. One example might be predicting gender based on retinal images by a deep learning model [47]. Coupled with advanced imaging modalities, RIA is a key element to boost improved healthcare for both ophthalmology and overall healthcare.

References

[1] C.R. Keeler, The ophthalmoscope in the lifetime of Hermann von Helmholtz. Arch. Ophthalmol. 120 (2) (2002) 194–201, https://doi.org/10.1001/archopht.120.2.194.
[2] T. Jackman, J.D. Webster, On photographing the eye of the living human retina, Phila. Photogr. (June 5) (1886).

[3] L. Guariguata, D.R. Whiting, I. Hambleton, J. Beagley, U. Linnenkamp, J.E. Shaw, Global estimates of diabetes prevalence for 2013 and projections for 2035, Diabetes Res. Clin. Pract. 103 (2) (2014) 137–149.

[4] J. Grauslund, A. Green, A.K. Sjolie, Prevalence and 25 year incidence of proliferative retinopathy among Danish type 1 diabetic patients, Diabetologia 52 (9) (2009) 1829–1835.

[5] R. Klein, M.D. Knudtson, K.E. Lee, R. Gangnon, B.E. Klein, The Wisconsin Epidemiologic Study of Diabetic Retinopathy: XXII the twenty-five-year progression of retinopathy in persons with type 1 diabetes, Ophthalmology 115 (11) (2008) 1859–1868.

[6] J. Grauslund, A. Green, A.K. Sjolie, Blindness in a 25-year follow-up of a population-based cohort of Danish type 1 diabetic patients, Ophthalmology 116 (11) (2009) 2170–2174.

[7] J.M.G. Wilson, G. Jungner, Principles and Practice of Screening for Disease, World Health Organization, Geneva, 1968.

[8] E. Stefansson, T. Bek, M. Porta, N. Larsen, J.K. Kristinsson, E. Agardh, Screening and prevention of diabetic blindness, Acta Ophthalmol. Scand. 78 (4) (2000) 374–385.

[9] G. Liew, M. Michaelides, C. Bunce, A comparison of the causes of blindness certifications in England and Wales in working age adults (16–64 years), 1999–2000 with 2009–2010, BMJ Open 4 (2) (2014). e004015.

[10] Early Treatment Diabetic Retinopathy Study Research Group, Grading diabetic retinopathy from stereoscopic color fundus photographs—an extension of the modified Airlie House classification. ETDRS report number 10, Ophthalmology 98 (5 Suppl) (1991) 786–806.

[11] C.P. Wilkinson, F.L. Ferris, R.E. Klein, et al., Proposed international clinical diabetic retinopathy and diabetic macular edema disease severity scales, Ophthalmology 110 (9) (2003) 1677–1682.

[12] A. Tufail, V.V. Kapetanakis, S. Salas-Vega, et al., An observational study to assess if automated diabetic retinopathy image assessment software can replace one or more steps of manual imaging grading and to determine their cost-effectiveness, Health Technol. Assess. 20 (92) (2016) 1–72.

[13] M.F. Norgaard, J. Grauslund, Automated screening for diabetic retinopathy—a systematic review, Ophthalmic Res. 60 (1) (2018) 9–17. https://www.doi.org/10.1159/000486284.

[14] V. Gulshan, L. Peng, M. Coram, et al., Development and validation of a deep learning algorithm for detection of diabetic retinopathy in retinal fundus photographs, JAMA 316 (22) (2016) 2402–2410.

[15] M.D. Abramoff, Y. Lou, A. Erginay, et al., Improved automated detection of diabetic retinopathy on a publicly available dataset through integration of deep learning, Invest. Ophthalmol. Vis. Sci. 57 (13) (2016) 5200–5206.

[16] Y. Morizane, N. Morimoto, A. Fujiwara, R. Kawasaki, H. Yamashita, Y. Ogura, F. Shiraga, Incidence and causes of visual impairment in Japan: the first nation-wide complete enumeration survey of newly certified visually impaired individuals. Jpn. J. Ophthalmol. (2018). https://doi.org/10.1007/s10384-018-0623-4.

[17] ETDRS, Early treatment diabetic retinopathy study research group. Photocoagulation for diabetic macular edema. Early treatment diabetic retinopathy study report number 1, Arch. Ophthalmol. 103 (12) (1985) 1796–1806.

[18] Y.T. Wang, M. Tadarati, Y. Wolfson, S.B. Bressler, N.M. Bressler, Comparison of prevalence of diabetic macular edema based on monocular fundus photography vs optical coherence tomography, JAMA Ophthalmol. 134 (2) (2016) 222–228.

[19] J. De Fauw, J.R. Ledsam, B. Romera-Paredes, S. Nikolov, N. Tomasev, S. Blackwell, H. Askham, X. Glorot, B. O'Donoghue, D. Visentin, G. van den Driessche, B. Lakshminarayanan, C. Meyer,

F. Mackinder, S. Bouton, K. Ayoub, R. Chopra, D. King, A. Karthikesalingam, C.O. Hughes, R. Raine, J. Hughes, D.A. Sim, C. Egan, A. Tufail, H. Montgomery, D. Hassabis, G. Rees, T. Back, P.T. Khaw, M. Suleyman, J. Cornebise, P.A. Keane, O. Ronneberger, Clinically applicable deep learning for diagnosis and referralin retinal disease, Nat. Med. 24 (9) (2018) 1342–1350.

[20] R. Kawasaki, J.J. Wang, E. Rochtchina, A.J. Lee, T.Y. Wong, P. Mitchell, Retinal vessel caliber is associated with the 10-year incidence of glaucoma: the Blue Mountains Eye Study, Ophthalmology 120 (1) (2013) 84–90.

[21] R. Kawasaki, E. Nagano, M. Uno, M. Okada, Y. Kawasaki, A. Kitamura, Retinal vascular features associated with risk of branch retinal vein occlusion, Curr. Eye Res. 38 (9) (2013) 989–993.

[22] R.M. Gunn, Ophthalmoscopic evidence of (1) arterial changes associated with chronic renal diseases and (2) of increased arterial tension, Trans. Am. Ophthalmol. Soc. 12 (1892) 124–125.

[23] N.M. Keith, H.P. Wagener, N.W. Barker, Some different types of essential hypertension: their course and prognosis, Am J Med Sci 197 (1939) 332–343.

[24] L.D. Hubbard, R.J. Brothers, W.N. King, L.X. Clegg, R. Klein, L.S. Cooper, A.R. Sharrett, M.D. Davis, J. Cai, Methods for evaluation of retinal microvascular abnormalities associated with hypertension/sclerosis in the Atherosclerosis Risk in Communities Study, Ophthalmology 106 (12) (1999) 2269–2280.

[25] M.D. Knudtson, K.E. Lee, L.D. Hubbard, T.Y. Wong, R. Klein, B.E. Klein, Revised formulas for summarizing retinal vessel diameters, Curr. Eye Res. 27 (3) (2003) 143–149.

[26] V. Daien, I. Carriere, R. Kawasaki, J.P. Cristol, M. Villain, P. Fesler, K. Ritchie, C. Delcourt, Retinal vascular caliber is associated with cardiovascular biomarkers of oxidative stress and inflammation: the POLA study, PLoS ONE 8 (7) (2013). e71089.

[27] K. Saito, Y. Tanabe, R. Kawasaki, M. Daimon, T. Oizumi, T. Kato, S. Kawata, T. Kayama, H. Yamashita, Is retinal vasculature change associated with risk of obesity? Longitudinal cohort study in Japanese adults: the Funagata study, J. Diabetes Investig. 2 (3) (2011) 225–232.

[28] S.J. Lupton, C.L. Chiu, L.A. Hodgson, J. Tooher, S. Lujic, R. Ogle, T.Y. Wong, A. Hennessy, J.M. Lind, Temporal changes in retinal microvascular caliber and blood pressure during pregnancy, Hypertension 61 (4) (2013) 880–885.

[29] S.J. Lupton, C.L. Chiu, L.A. Hodgson, J. Tooher, R. Ogle, T.Y. Wong, A. Hennessy, J.M. Lind, Changes in retinal microvascular caliber precede the clinical onset of preeclampsia, Hypertension 62 (5) (2013) 899–904.

[30] M. Yanagi, M. Misumi, R. Kawasaki, I. Takahashi, K. Itakura, S. Fujiwara, M. Akahoshi, K. Neriishi, T.Y. Wong, Y. Kiuchi, Is the association between smoking and the retinal venular diameter reversible following smoking cessation? Invest. Ophthalmol. Vis. Sci. 55 (1) (2014) 405–411.

[31] A.D. Hughes, A.V. Stanton, A.S. Jabbar, N. Chapman, M.E. Martinez-Perez, S.A. McG Thom, Effect of antihypertensive treatment on retinal microvascular changes in hypertension, J. Hypertens. 26 (8) (2008) 1703–1707.

[32] M. Sasaki, W.L. Gan, R. Kawasaki, L. Hodgson, K.Y. Lee, T.Y. Wong, E. Lamoureux, L. Robman, R. Guymer, Effect of simvastatin on retinal vascular caliber: the Age-Related Maculopathy Statin Study, Acta Ophthalmol. 91 (5) (2013) e418–e419.

[33] K. McGeechan, G. Liew, P. Macaskill, L. Irwig, R. Klein, B.E. Klein, J.J. Wang, P. Mitchell, J.R. Vingerling, P.T. de Jong, J.C. Witteman, M.M. Breteler, J. Shaw, P. Zimmet, T.Y. Wong, Prediction of incident stroke events based on retinal vessel

caliber: a systematic review and individual-participant meta-analysis, Am. J. Epidemiol. 170 (11) (2009) 1323–1332.

[34] K. McGeechan, G. Liew, P. Macaskill, L. Irwig, R. Klein, B.E. Klein, J.J. Wang, P. Mitchell, J.R. Vingerling, P.T. Dejong, J.C. Witteman, M.M. Breteler, J. Shaw, P. Zimmet, T.Y. Wong, Meta-analysis: retinal vessel caliber and risk for coronary heart disease, Ann. Intern. Med. 151 (6) (2009) 404–413.

[35] J. Ding, K.L. Wai, K. McGeechan, M.K. Ikram, R. Kawasaki, J. Xie, R. Klein, B.B. Klein, M.F. Cotch, J.J. Wang, P. Mitchell, J.E. Shaw, K. Takamasa, A.R. Sharrett, T.Y. Wong, Meta-Eye Study Group, Retinal vascular caliber and the development ofhypertension: a meta-analysis of individual participant data, J. Hypertens. 32 (2) (2014) 207–215.

[36] N. Patton, T.M. Aslam, T. MacGillivray, I.J. Deary, B. Dhillon, R.H. Eikelboom, K. Yogesan, I.J. Constable, Retinal image analysis: concepts, applications and potential, Prog. Retin. Eye Res. 25 (1) (2006) 99–127.

[37] www.accelerate.tech/innovation-offerings/ready-to-sign-licenses/siva-overview-n-specifications.

[38] vampire.computing.dundee.ac.uk/tools.html.

[39] Y. Koronyo, D. Biggs, E. Barron, D.S. Boyer, J.A. Pearlman, W.J. Au, S.J. Kile, A. Blanco, D.T. Fuchs, A. Ashfaq, S. Frautschy, G.M. Cole, C.A. Miller, D.R. Hinton, S.R. Verdooner, K.L. Black, M. Koronyo-Hamaoui, Retinal amyloid pathology and proof-of-concept imaging trial in Alzheimer's disease, JCI Insight 2 (16) (2017) (pii: 93621).

[40] F. Berisha, G.T. Feke, C.L. Trempe, J.W. McMeel, C.L. Schepens, Retinal abnormalities in early Alzheimer's disease, Invest. Ophthalmol. Vis. Sci. 48 (5) (2007) 2285–2289.

[41] L.P. Cunha, A.L. Almeida, L.V. Costa-Cunha, C.F. Costa, M.L. Monteiro, The role of optical coherence tomography in Alzheimer's disease, Int. J. Retina Vitreous 2 (2016) 24.

[42] M. Bulut, F. Kurtuluş, O. Gözkaya, M.K. Erol, A. Cengiz, M. Akıdan, A. Yaman, Evaluation of optical coherence tomography angiographic findings in Alzheimer's type dementia, Br. J. Ophthalmol. 102 (2) (2018) 233–237.

[43] A.I. Ramirez, R. de Hoz, E. Salobrar-Garcia, J.J. Salazar, B. Rojas, D. Ajoy, I. López-Cuenca, P. Rojas, A. Triviño, J.M. Ramírez, The role of microglia in retinal neurodegeneration: Alzheimer's disease, Parkinson, and Glaucoma. Front. Aging Neurosci. 9 (2017) 214. https://doi.org/10.3389/fnagi.2017.00214.

[44] www.imedos.de/.

[45] T.T. Nguyen, R. Kawasaki, J.J. Wang, A.J. Kreis, J. Shaw, W. Vilser, T.Y. Wong, Flicker light-induced retinal vasodilation in diabetes and diabetic retinopathy, Diabetes Care 32 (11) (2009) 2075–2080.

[46] R.A. Leitgeb, R.M. Werkmeister, C. Blatter, L. Schmetterer, Doppler optical coherence tomography, Prog. Retin. Eye Res. 41 (2014) 26–43.

[47] R. Poplin, A.V. Varadarajan, K. Blumer, Y. Liu, M.V. McConnell, G.S. Corrado, L. Peng, D.R. Webster, Nat. Biomed. Eng. 2 (2018) 158–164.

The physics, instruments and modalities of retinal imaging

3

Andrew R. Harvey[a], Guillem Carles[a], Adrian Bradu[b], Adrian Podoleanu[b]

[a]School of Physics and Astronomy, University of Glasgow, Glasgow, United Kingdom
[b]School of Physical Sciences, University of Kent, Canterbury, United Kingdom

1 Introduction

The vital importance of the human eye has stimulated an enormous effort into imaging the retina and other parts of the eye to provide clinical diagnostic information on disease and for fundamental research. In this chapter we discuss how the physics underpinning the formation of images of the retina impacts the salient features important for analysis of retinal images.

The fascination of the physicist with the eye dates back, at least, to the first gruesome insertion by Newton, in 1665, of a 'bodkin' (needle) behind his eye ball [1]. Over the succeeding three-and-a-half centuries we have developed a deep understanding of image formation and vision in the eye. This has included the development of increasingly elaborate imaging systems, originating with the first ophthalmoscopes at the time of von Helmhotz [2] in 1851 and progressing through modern scanning-laser ophthalmoscopes (SLO) for improved contrast and depth sectioning; optical-coherence tomography for imaging the three-dimensional structure of the retina [3]; to emerging techniques such as adaptive optics that enables the imaging of individual photoreceptors [4]. A vast range of imaging techniques are used in ophthalmic research and clinical application. Over the past two decades the digital recording of retinal images has become pervasive—and with it the possibility of automated analysis of images for screening and providing objective metrics to aid diagnosis. The aim of this chapter is to highlight how the physics of image formation within the eye leads to specific characteristics of retinal images. For example: why is it that images recorded with a SLO appear different from those recorded with a fundus camera? Why is it difficult to record images of individual blood cells and the smallest capillaries? Why do arteries and veins appear so different?

The eye has more than a passing resemblance to a camera in terms of function and shares many similar components. Like a modern camera, there is a lens for forming an image, which can be varied for optimal focus at a range of distances (referred to as accommodation by clinicians), an iris for adjusting the amount of transmitted light, and an array of opto-electronic photoreceptors transduce the optical image into an electronic signal for transmission and processing. Importantly, when we record

Computational Retinal Image Analysis. https://doi.org/10.1016/B978-0-08-102816-2.00003-4

an image of the retina we are using the camera in reverse: in this way, it has the characteristics of a microscope in which the cornea and lens focus the light like a microscope objective and the retina sits in the object plane like a biological sample.

A key distinction between the eye and a camera or microscope however is that the eye is integrated within the human visual system and the brain, and has evolved to provide a necessary-and-sufficient performance for the tasks we need to accomplish. The eye actually has a relatively poor optical performance, but the brain is able to compensate for many of the shortcomings to provide a perceived wide-field image quality that exceeds the objective quality of the eye. For example even a low-cost camera system, such as is found in a modern mobile phone, is able to record a 10-Megapixel image with a uniformly high angular resolution of 0.015° across a field of 60°. Conversely the human eye is able to form images over a field of view of almost 200°, but a comparable angular acuity to the low-cost camera can be achieved for only a central field of view of 0.3° or about 0.001% of the total visible solid angle. The limitations on the acuity of vision are determined by a combination of the optical aberrations of the eye and also the variation in concentrations of photoreceptors (the rods and cones). For imaging the retina, where we use the optical system of the eye as a microscope, it is fundamental physics and the quality of the eye optics that determines our ability to record high-resolution images of small retinal features.

To get the best performance out of any electronic imaging system it is common to compensate for systematic effects such as fixed pattern noise (using *flat fielding*) or interpolation to correct for malfunctioning pixels. The human visual system demonstrates similar capabilities: an image of the retina recorded with an ophthalmoscope shows a network of blood vessels and an optic disc (corresponding to the 'blind spot'), yet the image perceived by the eye's owner is normally devoid of such patterning. Indeed retinal disease can lead to extended areas of the retina not functioning before the effects become overtly apparent—and this highlights the importance of the early detection of disease using retinal imaging. Quantitative computer analysis of retinal images is therefore important for both fundamental understanding of retinal processes and for screening for disease. The aim of this chapter is to explain the main physics that underpins the observable characteristics of retinal images that are important for quantitative computer analysis. We use the established concepts of optics and image formation as the basis for our discussion and the interested reader is invited to consult one of the many excellent text books on optics, such as the accessible *Optics* by Hecht [5] and the more advanced *Principles of Optics* by Born and Wolf [6], for explanation on the underpinning physics.

In Section 2 we discuss the important principles for imaging the retina, where the eye acts as a microscope, including the effects of aberrations, diffraction and reflections. In Section 3 we review the main optical instruments or imaging modalities used for retinal imaging, including an in-depth review of Optical Coherence Tomography for its increasing importance. We discuss how differing imaging modalities affect the characteristics of retinal images in Sections 2.4 and 2.5. In Section 4 we provide a brief summary of the importance of polarization and birefringence in retinal imaging.

2 Optics of the eye

The eyeball is approximately spherical with a typical diameter in adulthood of 24 mm. The main components are the cornea and lens separated by the aqueous chamber at the front (anterior), and the retina (comprising several layers) at the back (anterior), filled with the jelly substance called the vitreous humor [7]. Like a camera, the eye focuses light from objects in the outside world onto the retina, where the photoreceptor cells lie. Notably, as depicted in Fig. 1, the photoreceptors within the retina are arranged in a spherical geometry, unlike the planar detector found in a camera.

The focusing power of the eye is accomplished through the fixed optical power of the cornea, combined the variable optical power of the lens, which provides accommodation for focusing at different distances. About two-thirds of the optical power is in the cornea and one third in the lens. The stronger focusing power of the cornea is because the refractive index discontinuity between the air and the cornea is much greater than between the lens and surrounding media and so, in accordance with Snell's law, provides more refraction and focusing of transmitted light.

2.1 Using the eye to record images of the retina

When imaging the retina, the optics of the eye are used in reverse: the retina is illuminated via the pupil and a small fraction of the reflected light (more accurately the light is 'scattered') is transmitted back through the pupil. For an emmetropic eye the retina is at the focal distance of the eye and so an image of the eye is focused at infinity by the lens and cornea. Ophthalmoscopes therefore require optical power to focus the light passing back through the pupil to form a retinal image onto a detector. An ophthalmoscope that is appropriately focused to image the retina will therefore also be able to form a well-focused image of distant objects.

Both the illumination and imaging of the retina are performed through the pupil of the eye. The diameter of the pupil varies between about 2 mm in bright conditions to up to 8 mm for a dark-adjusted eye or with mydriasis. This 16-fold variation in area has an important impact on the techniques used within various ophthalmoscopes to illuminate the retina and also to acquire images through the retina. A particular

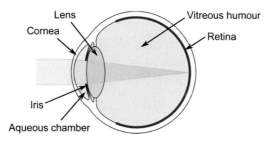

FIG. 1

The human eye as an optical system.

challenge is to prevent reflections of illumination at the cornea and lens surfaces (the Purkinje reflections) since these can greatly reduce contrast of images or introduce strong reflection artifacts. The strategies used vary between the main modalities: fundus cameras, laser scanning ophthalmoscopes, indirect ophthalmoscopes and slit-lamp scopes (see Section 3). A common approach employs a high-power objective lens to form an aerial image of the retina at its back focal plane as shown in Fig. 2. Additional imaging optics are used for a double purpose: to re-image this aerial image onto a detector for image acquisition and also to enable illumination to be coupled through the pupil via a beam-split arrangement. There are various planes in the ophthalmoscope where the reflections from the cornea and eye lens are mutually displaced or somehow distinct and spatial filtering at these planes enables attenuation of ocular reflections. For example, an image of the corneal reflection is normally formed at a location between the aerial image of the retina and the detector and so a small obscuration placed there (e.g., a black spot on a plate of glass) blocks this light while introducing minimal attenuation of the retinal image. This technique may be also used to block reflections from the ophthalmoscope lens surfaces. Similarly, it is possible to illuminate through one area of the pupil and image through a distinct non-illuminated and consequently dark area of the pupil. Desktop fundus cameras normally employ this approach: the illumination system within the camera focuses the illumination to an annulus of light that fits just inside the pupil and a reflex-free retinal image is recorded through the dark center of the annulus.

2.2 Spatial resolution of retinal images

Features of interest in the retina range in size from the rods and cones at about 2-μm diameter, through blood cells and capillaries in the 7–10 μm range through to the major blood vessels with calibers of 100–130 μm and the optic disc with a diameter of about 1.8 mm. In this section we discuss our ability to image these varying structures using the eye optics.

The imaging performance of the eye inevitably introduces some blurring in the recorded images: that is the eye acts as a spatially-variant low-pass filter of spatial frequencies. The resolution of the eye, like any imaging system, is limited by both aberrations of the eye ocular media and, when the pupil is small, by diffraction. The

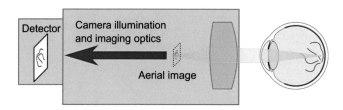

FIG. 2

An objective lens is used to produce an aerial image of the illuminated (illumination not shown) retina at an intermediate plane, which is re-imaged onto a detector to record an image.

blurring during the image formation is described by the point-spread function (PSF). The PSF serves a similar purpose in describing image formation as the concept of the 'impulse response' in the analysis of signals and systems—in fact the PSF is the square of the modulus of the two-dimensional spatial impulse response. The PSF of the ocular media varies significantly across the eye and can be accurately modeled using optical ray-tracing programs and various *schematic eye models* [8–10], but over small areas of the retina, the blurring of the retinal image can be considered as the convolution of an ideal retinal image with the local eye PSF.

The concept of the 'ideal retinal image' requires some comment: whereas opaque objects such as, optical test targets, do not change appearance substantially with changes in illumination, light propagates diffusely through the complex structure of the retina and this imprints a further signature on image quality. Although the concept of a *tissue PSF* can help in the appreciation of the reduction of image contrast in biomedical imaging [11] the complex heterogeneity of the retina limits the usefulness of this concept for retinal imaging. Nevertheless retinal images exhibit a contrast that varies strongly with the size of an approximate tissue PSF, between for example blue light, where the tissue PSF is typically a few tens of microns and red or near infrared light where it can be a few millimeters. This is discussed further in Section 2.5 and highlighted by the images in Fig. 5.

The low-pass filter function for the spatial frequencies in a retinal image is determined by the modulation-transfer-function (MTF) of the eye, which is determined both by the physics of diffraction and also by the optical aberrations of the eye. Additional optical aberrations introduced by the ophthalmoscope can further reduce resolution, particularly at large field angles or with unintentional defocus. As for any imaging system, when the pupil is small (corresponding to a large f/#, or a small numerical aperture, henceforth NA), the wave nature of light means that diffraction limits the full-width, half-maximum (FWHM) angular resolution to

$$\delta\theta = 1.22\frac{\lambda}{nD} \tag{1}$$

where λ is the wavelength of light, n is refractive index (about 1.3 for the ocular media) and D is the diameter of the imaging aperture. The corresponding feature size that can be imaged at the retina is given simply by $d = f \times \delta\theta$ where f is the focal length of the eye (assumed equal to the internal diameter of the eye ball). If the resolution of the eye is limited only by diffraction then for green light and a dilated pupil with $D = 8$ mm, the limiting angular resolution of 60 µradians would enable imaging of retinal features as small as 1.4 µm—that is the rods and cones could easily be resolved. However, the optical aberrations of the eye, like any imaging system, tend to limit the angular resolution above a certain pupil diameter: for the human eye the limiting angular resolution corresponds to the diffraction limit of a 2-mm pupil [13]: that is about 250 µradians enabling features down to a width of about 6 µm to be imaged. It should be noted however, that the use of adaptive optics can enable correction of optical aberrations to enable imaging with a resolution close to the diffraction limit, which enables individual photoreceptors to be imaged [14]. It should further be noted, that the eye, like any imaging system, acts as a low-pass filter of spatial frequencies such that the contrast of smaller features in the image is reduced in relation to their spatial frequency content and above the optical cutoff frequency, $v_c = \dfrac{Dn}{\lambda f}$, where D is pupil diameter, the contrast is reduced to zero. This is in addition to contrast reduction by scattering in the ocular media [15], which in many cases dominates, particularly in the eyes of older subjects, and is a major issue in image analysis based on measurement of image contrast.

A practical limit on spatial resolution is associated with simple blurring due to incorrect focusing of the ophthalmoscope including correction for refractive error of the eye—an error greater than about 0.5 Dioptcrs can produce a significant reduction in contrast of the smaller features. Furthermore, as for any optical instrument the eye has a small depth of field over which sharp focus is achieved and this decreases with increasing pupil diameter according to the laws of diffraction and the aberrations of the eye [16]. Typically the depth of field is about 50 μm; that is, less than the thickness of the retina, but the lack of sharp features in the retina means that variations in focus within retinal images is not generally obvious, except around the optic disc (particularly when it is distorted by high intra-ocular pressure) or as a result of severe distortions of diseased retinas. Recording multiple images with a small range of focuses can be useful so that post hoc assessment can select the best-focused image. This is particularly important where accurate quantification of contrast of, for example, blood vessels, is important.

2.3 Glare, contrast and image quality

The reflectivity of the eye fundus is rather low and typically below 1% in the blue to about 10% at red and infrared wavelengths [17] (see Section 2.5). This means that reflections from the surfaces of the cornea and eye lens may be significantly stronger than the light received from the retina, and may appear as localized reflections as well as glare. Thus, mitigation of reflections is a major issue for retinal imaging. Four so-called Purkinje reflections, depicted in Fig. 3, originate at the outer and inner surfaces of the cornea and the anterior and posterior surfaces of the eye lens. The refractive index change is the greatest for the first Purkinje reflection from front surface of the cornea and so, according to the Fresnel relations, the intensity of this reflection is much greater than the other three Purkinje reflections.

Cross-polarized illumination and imaging provides a simple mechanism to attenuate these reflections. Laser light is normally polarized, but light from LEDs, flash lamps and incandescent filaments, such as are used in fundus cameras and indirect ophthalmoscopes is naturally unpolarized and can be simply polarized using polarizers. Transmission of light through biological media and scattering tend to depolarize light however and so this rejection of reflected or scattered light through cross-polarized imaging is imperfect. See Section 4 for more details.

When polarized light is reflected at a surface or undergoes a single or a small number of scattering events (from blood cells for example) it tends to retain its polarization. Conversely, light that is scattered multiple times is effectively depolarized. This is the case for light diffused and backscattered within the retinal volume,

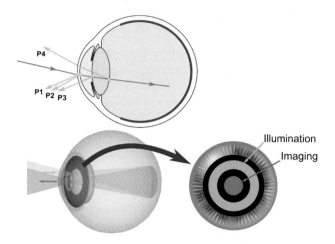

FIG. 3

Left, the four main surfaces that produce the four Purkinje reflections/images. Right, illustration of the traditional illumination annulus used to separate the illumination and imaging light paths.

whereas polarization is partially retained at the reflections at surfaces such as the cornea. These reflections are therefore highly attenuated by polarization in the imaging path (for example with a linear polarizer orthogonal to the illumination, i.e., at cross polarization), and this is normally implemented in ophthalmic instrumentation. However, except for narrow fields of view, this is not sufficient to suppress reflections and glare in practice due to the acute angles at the reflection interfaces and the birefringence of some tissues, which alter polarization. Another mechanism normally used to block reflections (either from the cornea or from the surfaces of the objective lens) is the placement of a corneal reflex blocker: implemented as an obscuration dot placed at a plane where an image of the cornea is formed.

However, the main mechanism to suppress reflections is to employ independent paths for the illumination and imaging, at planes close to the cornea and pupil of the eye. This is known as the Gullstrand principle [18], and is illustrated in Fig. 3. In fact, it has been the standard strategy used to illuminate and image the retina for over a century. It is based on projecting an annular illumination that propagates through the pupil of the eye, without illuminating the central part. Light forming this annular illumination, is focused at or near the pupil, and propagates to uniformly illuminate the eye fundus. Upon diffusion and backscattering at the retina, some light propagates back towards the pupil and the portion that passes through the pupil is captured by the ophthalmoscope imaging optics to form an image of the retina at the detector plane.

To work well, the Gullstrand principle states that not only the light paths need to be different but must also be separated at the pupil. That is, it requires a separation between the inner radius of the annulus and the outer radius of the imaging pupil, to allow for light scattering at the anterior segment of the eye. This separation is more important for instruments that image a wide field of view. For this reason fundus cameras with wider fields of view are more difficult to operate on eyes with small pupils. To facilitate this separation, mydriasis, is routinely used on eye examinations. Some cameras are designed to operate with a mydriatic pupil whereas non-mydriatic cameras are designed for a smaller pupil, but often should be operated in a dark room and use (invisible) infrared light for the inspection illumination (before triggering the flash of the camera) so as to benefit from the natural pupil dilation.

2.4 How the physics of light propagation affects retinal image quality

In a conventional imaging system, such as in photography, light reflected from the objects is captured through the camera aperture to form an image, which then becomes a measure of the reflectance of points across the (angularly two-dimensional) scene. The retina is not a simple reflecting surface but rather a complex and multi-layered volume with which light interacts by scattering and absorption through its 3D structures as shown in Fig. 4. An understanding of this process enables an appreciation of the characteristics of retinal images.

The multi-layered volume structure of the retina comprises a complex structure of about 10 distinct layers accommodating different cell types, which perform the photoreception, retinal processing and transmission of the visual signals through the retinal-nerve-fiber layer and optic nerve to the brain. The fovea, at

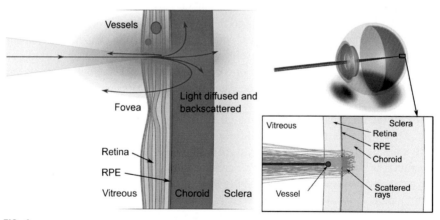

FIG. 4

Left, illustration of the light diffusion through the multi-layered structure of the retina, scattering and diffusing light. Right, Monte-Carlo simulation of light scattering using ray-tracing. A schematic model eye is used to model illumination (top) and Monte-Carlo ray-tracing computes the different light paths involved in image formation (bottom). Note that scattered rays are plotted in *light red* but absorption is not illustrated and only rays that backscatter toward the pupil of the eye are plotted.

the center of the retina and slightly displaced from the optical axis of the eye ball, contains the highest concentration of photoreceptor cones. There are widely varying optical characteristics for each component of the retina. With regard to the effect of the paths that light travels, the following simplification of layers may be considered: the retina, the retinal pigment epithelium (RPE), the choroid, and the outer sclera. The retina is in turn multi-layered, is highly transparent and has retinal blood vessels embedded within it. It is about 200 μm to 300 μm thick with a depression at the fovea. The retinal pigment epithelium is a single layer of cells, highly absorbing (depending on retinal pigmentation) of about 10 μm. The choroid is a vascular layer of about 250 μm thick containing highly oxygenated blood and also melanin. The sclera (the white of the eye) is the outer and opaque shell that protects the eye.

Light incident upon the retina is scattered and absorbed, and eventually diffused through the volume. To model such diffusion it is convenient, if not necessary, to employ a Monte-Carlo approach in which light rays are traced, using a stochastic model, according to scattering and absorption models at the retinal structures [19–21]. These models are defined by a mean-free path and a scattering phase function, which define stochastically the distance a light ray will travel before it is scattered (i.e., it changes direction of propagation) and the angular probability density function of scattering towards a new direction, respectively. Effectively, light rays enter the tissue, propagate, scatter (change direction), propagate, and so on. On propagation, the intensity associated with each light ray is absorbed according to the Lambert-Beer law [11].

After tracing sufficient rays, the macroscopic light transport, both in the ballistic and diffuse regimes (few and many scattering events respectively) are reproduced as illustrated in Fig. 4. Defining mean-free paths, phase functions, absorption coefficients, and refractive indices for all involved tissues, and noting that many of these parameters are wavelength-dependent, enables numeric but accurate modeling of light diffusion within the retina. The power of Monte-Carlo modeling is that, given these parameters are known, it enables the computation of light diffusion under conditions of arbitrary geometrical complexity. Importantly, it is possible to track the polarization of each individual light ray. An alternative use of Monte-Carlo simulation becomes useful if the optical properties of the tissue are not known but experimental data is available: Monte-Carlo simulations may then be used to actually compute what optical parameters explain experiments, in what is called inverse Monte-Carlo approach.

As discussed in the next section the optical properties of the retina vary greatly with wavelength: in particular red light is less absorbed than blue light. This results in a higher fundus reflectance but also a lower contrast in red light and so it is common to employ red-free filters in fundus cameras to increase the contrast of the retinal vasculature. More generally spectral imaging of the retina can be used to detect vascular oxygenation to aid classification of arteries and veins [22–27].

2.5 Spectral characteristics of the eye

The characteristics of retinal images vary strongly with wavelength and imaging modality as can be appreciated by the multispectral retinal images shown in Fig. 5 (recorded with a hyperspectral fundus camera [12]) and the two-wavelength images in Fig. 6 (recorded with a two-wavelength SLO operating in non-confocal and hybrid-confocal modes [30]). The differing recording principles of the fundus camera and the SLO are discussed in Sections 3.3 and 3.5. We discuss here the reasons for the variation of the appearance of these images with wavelength and imaging modality. It should be noted that the intensity of retinal images varies greatly

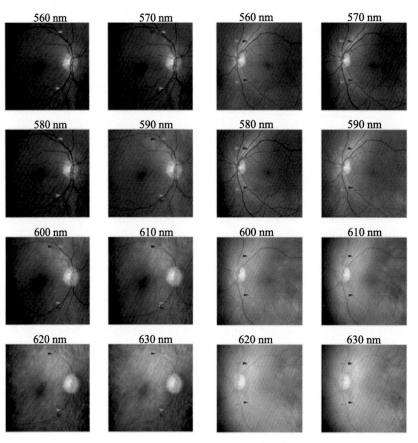

FIG. 5

Two sets of narrowband images of normal retina recorded with a hyperspectral fundus camera [12]. Arterioles and venules are highlighted by *red* and *blue arrows* respectively. The arterioles exhibit much lower contrast at the longer wavelengths due to the lower extinction coefficient of oxygenated blood. The lighter retinal pigmentation for the left images results in increased visibility of the choriocapillaris at red wavelengths.

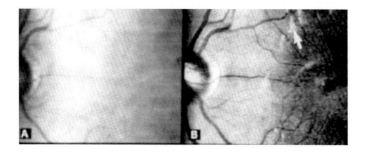

FIG. 6

Images recorded (A) in direct mode using a large (1000 μm) aperture and (B) using a small (100 μm) confocal aperture [28]. The confocal aperture increases the contrast of vasculature due to increased absorption by the double-pass of light through the vessel.

with wavelength. This is partly because the intensity of light sources and maximum safe light intensities for illuminating the retina (see Section 3.2) are higher at longer wavelengths, leading to brighter images with higher signal-to-noise ratios for red and infrared wavelengths. In addition retinal reflectivity (also known, with caveats, as *albedo*) is much greater at longer wavelengths—varying from about 0.1% at 420 nm to about 10% at 700 nm [17].

This variation in reflectivity is predominantly due to the spectral absorption characteristics of hemoglobin in blood as shown in Fig. 8. Absorption is high in the blue and low in the red, which explains the obvious observation that retinal images are red. The retina is quite transparent and the dominant contribution to the color of the retina is due to light transmission and scattering within the choroid. The presence of melanin in the choroid and in the retinal pigment epithelium introduces additional attenuation, particularly at bluer wavelengths, and reduces the overall transmission of light through the choroid leading to a reduced reflectivity at all wavelengths. The concentration of melanin correlates strongly with skin pigmentation and eye color. Lower levels of melanin, as is typical for Nordic complexions, enable the transmission of light with relatively little scattering so that the structure of the choriocapillaris is sufficiently visible for quantitative assessment within the choroid [29], while for higher levels of pigmentation the choroid forms a more uniform, less reflective brown-red background to the retinal structures. This distinction is apparent for the images recorded at longer wavelengths in the left-most image of Fig. 5 (or a low-pigmentation retina).

The optic disc has the highest reflectivity within the retina, (typically >12%) and is slightly pink. While the capillaries within the optic nerve contribute to the pink color so does the spectrum of the incident light scattered from the choroid and retina—in fact a hemoglobin spectrum can also be measured for light scattered from a white optical calibration tile located close to the retina [31].

A rigorous understanding of light propagation in blood is complex and accurate models tend to rely on Monte-Carlo methods for light propagation in scattering media [19, 20] as discussed in the previous section. Useful approximations and heuristic understanding can also be obtained however from simplified models based on the Beer-Lambert law for light propagation in absorbing media [11, 32] or the more accurate and complex modified Beer-Lambert law [22] for light propagation in scattering and absorbing media. The Beer-Lambert law states that the intensity of light transmitted through a medium of thickness l, extinction coefficient ε and concentration c is given by

$$I_t = I_o e^{-\varepsilon cl} \tag{2}$$

where I_o is the incident light intensity. For wavelengths between about 600 nm and 800 nm, ε is much higher for deoxyhemoglobin than for oxyhemoglobin (see Fig. 8) and so oxygenated blood is more transparent than deoxygenated blood. The retina is relatively transparent so light absorption by the highly oxygenated blood in the choroid dominates the main spectral characteristics of the retina and explains the very high reflectivity of the retina in red and infrared light.

For light transmission through the blood vessels, the Beer-Lambert law provides a reasonable approximation to both the absolute absorption and also for calculation of the spatial intensity profile across the width of the vessel [23, 24]. For the venules, which contain blood with oxygen saturations of 50–70% [25], and with a maximum diameter of about 130 μm the product εcl is such that attenuation is typically sufficient to yield good contrast. For the deoxygenated blood in arteries, ε is several times smaller and l also tends to be a little smaller (maximum caliber is about 100 μm). Consequently the product εcl is sufficiently small for arteries that arteries have very low contrast, often almost transparent, in this wavelength regime. Between the wavelengths of 500 nm and 600 nm the product εcl is relatively close to unity so that contrast is moderately high and varies sufficiently strongly that it can be used as to provide accurate measurement of blood oxygenation [23–27].

A lower value of extinction coefficient, ε, leads to a higher optical transmission in both the axial direction (as described above) and also for scattering in the transverse direction to yield a more extended so-called tissue point-spread function, which extends in three dimensions. At red and near infrared wavelengths this tissue point-spread function is quite large (several mm) and leads to a smoothing of a retinal image compared to in the green and blue where the tissue point-spread function is more compact (10s of microns). A consequence of this is the smoothing of the retinal images in Fig. 5 at the redder wavelengths. An additional consequence is that, as shown in Fig. 4, blood vessels tend to be back illuminated by light that has diffused through the choroid so that the most accurate value for l to be used within the Beer-Lambert law corresponds to a single pass transmission through the blood vessel, although there is a also contribution from light that has been transmitted twice through the vessel [20, 32]. The ratio of single pass light to double-pass light can be derived by calibration [33], fitting of multi-spectral data [26, 27] or Monte-Carlo modeling [20, 21].

When a confocal SLO is employed, the dominant light path corresponds almost exclusively to a double-pass through the vasculature increasing the contrast as can be seen in Fig. 6. A so-called indirect SLO is also possible, which images only single-pass, multiply-scattered light can be useful for enhancing the contrast of opaque objects such as drusen, since they are effectively back illuminated [32]. A notable quid pro quo for the enhanced contrast of confocal imaging is the reduced image intensity, but some optimization is possible by employing a hybrid between direct and indirect detection as shown in Fig. 7 for a two-wavelength SLO image [30]. For both

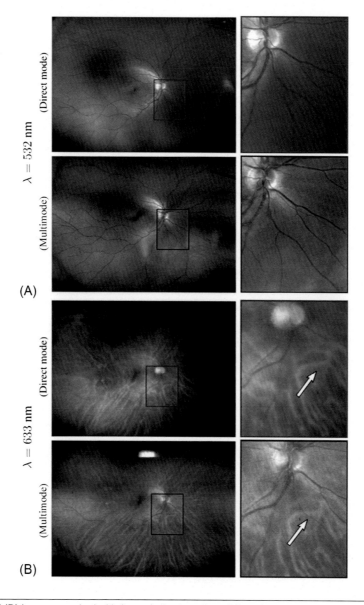

FIG. 7

(A) and (B) Images acquired with (upper) direct mode and (lower) multimode. Right images are a closed-up of the rectangle. Illumination wavelength is 532 nm in (A) and 633 nm in (B) [30].

the green (532 nm) and red (633 nm) wavelengths it is notable that the hybrid multi-mode images, which employ an agile combination of confocal and direct imaging, yield images of the vasculature with increased contrast. This is particularly true for the arterioles, which are not visible in the direct-mode images at the red wavelengths. Also notable is that the choriocapillaris is visible in the red images, due to the higher transparency, but not in the green images (Fig. 8).

2.6 The use of eye phantoms to simulate retinal imaging

Eye phantoms are commonly used to perform experimental, simulation tests and validation. To model the optics of the eye as an imaging system, several simulation models have been proposed, called *schematic eye* models [8, 9]. They take into account the geometric shapes and index of refraction of each ocular component: the cornea, lens, vitreous humor and aqueous humor, with varying degree of rigor. These models enable optical simulation based on ray-tracing, and thus they can be inserted in the design of ophthalmic instruments to model and optimize their performance, and to account for the effects of the eye such as aberrations, optical scatter by the ocular media and diffraction. These models range from simple approximations, based on simpler geometrical shapes and models of refractive index, to more complete descriptions that may include accurate chromatic dispersion, aspheric surfaces and graded-index (GRIN) models, birefringence, and other properties [7], and may describe better the optical performance on a wider range of angles (e.g., for a wide field-of-view). For experimental assessment and validation, phantom eyes can be built to mimic the eye such as are shown in Fig. 9. These range from simple models based on a single lens and a flat target resembling the retina, to more complex and accurate models based on a lens pair mimicking the cornea and crystalline lens, enclosed in a case filled with water and a curved and layered target to mimic volumetric scattering at the retina [35, 36].

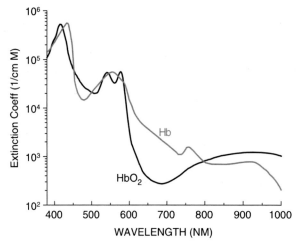

FIG. 8

Absorption coefficients for oxyhemoglobin and deoxyhemoglobin.

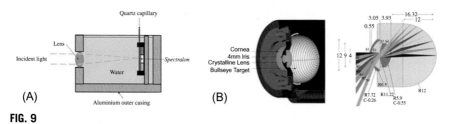

FIG. 9

(A) A simple phantom eye used to assess retinal oximetry using quartz capillaries filled with blood of controlled oxygenation [36] and (B) a realistic phantom based on a schematic eye model [34].

3 Ophthalmic instruments

3.1 Brief history

The fundamental principles used for observing the eye fundus were established at the time of van Helmholtz, when the ophthalmoscope was invented [2, 37]. These are mainly the concept of indirect ophthalmoscopy [11] and the Gullstrand principle [18] (to enable the simultaneous illumination and imaging of the fundus through the pupil of the eye) as depicted in Fig. 3. These principles remain the basis of modern fundus photography, despite dating back more than a century and a half ago. In the early days, ophthalmic artists specialized in drawing retinal atlases. Achieving wider fields of view through improved designs, and image quality, through the use of electronic flash lamps, were significant milestones. The digital revolution is a key advance in fundus photography, enabling the recording and analysis of digital images of the retina. This has enabled the recording and monitoring of progression of retinal disease, the objective assessment of retinal features to aid diagnosis, and their automated analysis using image processing techniques. The invention of the Scanning Laser Ophthalmoscope [38–40] is certainly a key advance in the field, by providing higher contrasted images, and the confocal configuration provided greater insight into the retinal structure.

3.2 Safety exposure limits

All modern optical instruments must be regulated and approved for clinical use, in particular the intensity (*radiance* and *irradiance* of the illumination at the retina and cornea) must be at safe levels to avoid thermal damage and the effects of phototoxicity. *The International Commission on Non-Ionizing Radiation Protection*, publishes a series of recommendations for the maximum permissible exposure limits [40a], and Sliney et al. reported a conservative adaptation of the most relevant exposure limits for ophthalmic imaging [41]. We reproduce here a summary of recommendations for the exposure limits that apply to ophthalmic instruments classified in three groups: thermal damage of anterior segment (including cornea, iris, crystalline lens), thermal damage of the retina, and photochemical damage of the retina (also referred as blue-light hazard).

Thermal damage is most important at longer wavelengths (>500nm). The sensitivity of the eye to damage depends on the intensity of the radiation and on the ability of the tissue to diffuse the localized heat, and therefore it has different exposure limits based on whether the illumination is a point-light or extended source and whether it is pulsed or continuous. That is not the case for photochemical damage, which dominates for shorter (blue, UV) wavelengths and longer exposures, as it depends only on the dose of exposure. That is, the same damage can occur from intense radiation on short duration than from less intense radiation but on longer durations (called the reciprocal principle). Exposure hazards at cornea and lens are thermal and apply mainly to infrared wavelengths. The relevant recommendations of maximum exposure limits for ophthalmic instruments can be: thermal or blue-light hazards, for continuous or pulsed sources, and the limits vary with duration, extension and spectrum of the light source.

3.3 The fundus camera

The imaging principle of the fundus camera is similar to the indirect ophthalmoscope and is essentially a low-magnification microscope, where the eye fulfills a similar function to a microscope objective for imaging the retina. The short-focal length objective of the fundus camera forms an aerial image of the retina in its back focal plane. Additional optics then re-image the aerial image onto a digital camera. The traditional design invariably implements the Gullstrand principle to suppress reflections (separation of the illumination and imaging light paths near the cornea and pupil of the eye as shown in Fig. 3 and also in Fig. 10). It includes an illumination system that projects an annulus of light onto the eye pupil. The angular subtense of the cone of the illumination light at each point of the annulus corresponds to the field of the retina that is illuminated and this is adjusted to ensure even illumination across the imaged field of view. For cameras with an adjustable field of view (zoom) the illumination also adjusts in synchronism with the zoom. This variable illumination has clear implications if flat fielding is used to compensate for variations in retinal illumination.

The coaxial illumination annulus and imaging is typically achieved using an annular mirror for combining illumination and imaging beams as shown in Fig. 10. A low-intensity inspection lamp is combined with high-intensity flash illumination using some beam-splitting arrangement. The flash illumination has a duration of between about 1 and a few 10s of ms, depending on energy setting, enabling the freezing of eye motion that is desirable for a high-quality image to be recorded. Filters are incorporated into the fundus camera to prevent harmful ultraviolet and infrared light from illuminating the eye.

Fundus cameras that are designed for use with mydriasis enable an annulus with a larger diameter in the region of 6–8 mm to be used, whereas a non-mydriatic fundus camera requires that the annulus must fit within a smaller pupil of typically 4 mm diameter. In consequence the central dark region is about twice the diameter for a mydriatic camera allowing four-times greater light transmission to the camera. Some non-mydriatic cameras employ infrared illumination for inspection and require a dark room to enable natural dilation of the pupil.

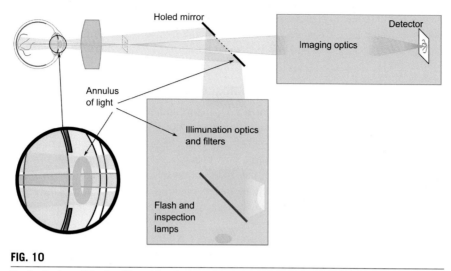

FIG. 10

Basic design of the traditional fundus camera.

Very wide fields of view require wide-angle illumination which compromises the separation of illumination and imaging paths through the ocular media, and in practice fundus cameras cannot provide ultrawide glare-free field-of-view due to reflections and glare reducing image quality. See Fig. 3 and associated text for a discussion. The considered "normal" field of view has traditionally been 30°, although standard fundus cameras provide excellent quality images of 45° and even higher [42].

The fundus camera can operate with different imaging modalities: in color, to record an image with similar color characteristics to the images that are observed with the naked eye using an indirect ophthalmoscope; red-free, where the illumination is filtered to remove red light and improve contrast of the vessels and other retinal structures; and angiographic, where optical excitation of a fluorescent dye combined with imaging of the fluorescence at a longer wavelength enables high-contrast imaging of the retinal vasculature and sequential recording enables the dynamics of vessel filling to be recorded.

3.4 Indirect ophthalmoscopes

To use an indirect ophthalmoscope a high-power condensing lens is held a few cm from the eye to form an aerial image of the retina in its back focal plane. The aerial image of the retina is viewed with a head mounted indirect ophthalmoscope, which also provides illumination of the retina through the condensing lens. The field of view is typically only a few degrees requiring the viewer to navigate around the retina to view the whole retina in time sequence. A particular challenge is to view the retina while reducing the impact of the reflections from the cornea. Choosing a lens with a higher optical power will: decrease the magnification, decrease the working distance, and (generally) increase the field of view, although the latter depends on the diameter of the lens. Because the observed image is inverted, use of the device for navigation is not intuitive and requires some training (Fig. 11).

3.5 The scanning laser ophthalmoscopes

The Scanning Laser Ophthalmoscope (SLO) is a fundamentally different approach to recording retinal images involving the scanning of a laser spot across the retina. An image is formed by the detection of light that is backscattered through the pupil, through the SLO optics to a detector. This provides a measurement of the fundus reflectance at the particular point of the illumination spot. In contrast to the snapshot image acquisition by the fundus camera, raster scanning of the laser across the retina to record a 2D image can take as long as a second, which can lead to image artifacts if the eye moves during recording.

Interestingly, the SLO illumination concept reverses the Gullstrand principle of illumination: a narrow laser beam (typically <1 mm) is transmitted through the center of the pupil and the rest of the pupil is used to collect backscattered light [39, 40]. This inversion of the illumination-imaging light paths enables a larger area of the pupil to be dedicated to the collection of light, increasing optical efficiency. Fundamentally, it is possible to reduce the illumination area only because of the higher intensity of lasers compared to thermal light sources. A penalty for the use of the smaller beam is that it yields a smaller angular and spatial resolution: according to Eq. (1), this yields a spatial resolution of about 10 μm at the retina, which is insufficient to resolve individual blood cells and the smaller capillaries.

As can be seen from a comparison of the images in Fig. 12, images recorded with a SLO can look strikingly different from those recorded with a broadband light

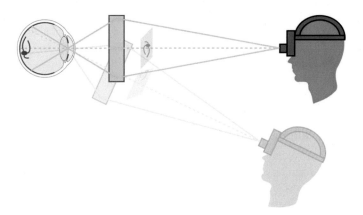

FIG. 11

Illustration of the operation of an indirect opthalmoscope, the ophthalmologist wears a head-mounted illumination and holds an ophthalmic lens with the hand to observe the retina.

source such as a LED, flashlamp or tungsten lamp. The color rendition is inevitably different. SLOs may use a single wavelength or may use multiple lasers of different wavelengths to simulate color imaging [43]. As shown in Fig. 12b, even images recorded with just two lasers (green, 532 nm and red, 633 nm) give a useful color effect, largely because the reflectivity (*albedo*) of the retina is much higher in the red and green and so color images of the retina contain very little blue light.

The two images of an optic disc shown in Fig. 12c, recorded with a fundus camera and a three-wavelength SLO are however significantly different and an understanding of these differences can be important for analysis of the images. The RGB intensities in a color image are due to a the multiplication of the source spectrum, chromophore absorption spectrum and the system spectral response. For conventional color imaging each band is a weighted integral of the absorption spectrum, whereas for imaging using a narrowband source such as a laser (or LED), the spectrum is sampled at only the narrow laser wavelength. A small change in this wavelength can make a very significant difference: for example as can be appreciated by the difference between the images recorded at 590 nm and 600 nm in Fig. 5. In particular, note that the arteries have much greater contrast at 590 nm. Differences in the color of other retinal features, such as drusen and neural structures can also be significant [27].

The diffusion of light away from the laser spot in the retina is also important. That is to say, the retina exhibits an extended 'tissue point-spread function' [11] that tends to smooth the image in a similar way to a convolution process, although the heterogeneity of the retina means the effect is strongly spatially variant and differs substantially from a convolution process. The effect also depends on the size of the detector in the SLO as described below. A detailed quantitative understanding can be obtained using Monte-Carlo modeling, but a heuristic understanding can be quite useful as we discuss below and in Section 2.5. As discussed above, the width of this tissue point-spread function varies greatly between the red and near-infrared where it can be several mm to the blue where it is a few 10s of microns. This variation can be readily appreciated by observing the differing amounts of diffusion of a red, green or blue laser light shone onto a human hand— light from a green or blue laser pointer diffuses only a very short distance from the laser spot, whereas the light from a red laser will diffuse through the whole width of a thumb.

In contrast to a fundus camera, the SLO illuminates only a single point (more precisely a diffraction-limited spot about 10 μm wide) and records scattered light from only a restricted volume of the retina close to the illumination spot. A small pinhole located in front of the detector, as used in a confocal SLO, restricts detected light to the illumination 'point', while a larger pinhole enables detection of light from an extended volume of retina around the illumination. In terms of a simplified model [32] images of the vasculature (for example) recorded with a confocal SLO are due to light that has passed twice through a blood vessel whereas for a large pinhole, light is transmitted only once through the vessel. A small pinhole thus yields an image with a higher contrast, but the rejection of scattered light reduces the optical intensity and so an optimum trade of contrast against signal-to-noise ratio may be obtained by careful empirical and modeling-based optimization of pinhole size [30]. One clear consequence of this double-pass phenomena is that at red and infrared wavelengths

(600–800 nm) the low absorption coefficient of oxygenated blood means that arterioles exhibit low contrast in fundus images (Fig. 5, Fig. 12c(A)) and in non-confocal SLOs (Fig. 12c), but contrast is quite high in confocal-SLO images (Fig. 12a and c(A)). It should be noted that a small pinhole also restricts the axial range (depth of field) for detection of light to provide sectioning and profiling of the retina.

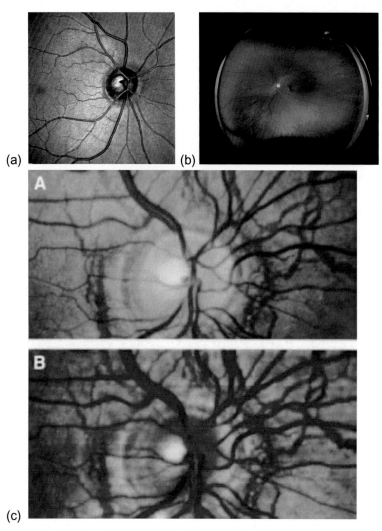

(a)   (b)

(c)

FIG. 12

(a) Infrared (820 nm) reflectance image recorded with Heidelberg Spectralis [33]. (b) Widefield two-wavelength ultra-widefield image recorded with ultrawidefield Optos SLO. (c) (A) Fundus-camera photograph and (B) color SLO image [43]. Notable features are the 'silver wiring' in image (a) and the different color and renditions and spatial resolutions of the two images in (c).

3.6 Handheld retinal cameras

In the recent years there has been an increased interest in low-cost, handheld retinal cameras. Some of these devices result from an emphasis on portability while providing useful imaging quality, while some are focused on very low cost, and some are even based on attaching an adaptor to smartphones. In general, the compromises involved in the optical design of such devices mean it is difficult to yield consistent and good image quality, especially for moderate to high fields of view. Common problems are low contrast and strong reflection artifacts. Although there are no rigorous comparisons on performance, some of these devices are not capable of producing images with sufficient quality to enable their use in clinical settings.

3.7 Ultrawide field imaging

Imaging with an ultrawide field of view is important for a complete exploration of the retina, in particular for the detection of diseases that occur in the retinal periphery. Achieving ultrawide field of view however compromises the widely adopted Gullstrand principle, and normally it is not possible to acquire reflex-free images with a fundus camera. The *Retcam* achieves widefield, artifact free imaging by use of optical contact between the optical head and the cornea to prevent corneal reflections, but is targeted at imaging of the retinas of neonates, for which the eye contact can be acceptable. For non-contact eye imaging, the freedom provided by the design of the Laser Scanning Ophthalmoscope, such as the *Optos* SLO (which produced the *Optomap* image in Fig. 12b) can provide high-quality ultrawide field imaging. A common approach to extend the field of view is by acquiring a navigated sequence of narrow-field images, which are stitched with post-detection image processing to yield a single wide-field image. This requires however some expertise in operation of the camera and increases significantly the time required to obtain an appropriate set of images.

3.8 Optical coherence tomography

Optical coherence tomography (OCT) is a non-invasive high-resolution optical imaging technology based on constructive interference between light back-reflected by the sample under investigation and some "reference" light. OCT has the potential to generate, in real-time, cross-section images of the sample, i.e., two-dimensional images in the XZ or YZ space (X,Y: transversal (lateral) coordinate, Z: longitudinal (axial) coordinate). Confocal microscopy, as described in Section 3.5 can also be used to image the retina of the human eye, however due to the limited numerical aperture of the eye and its optical aberrations, the axial resolution of a confocal microscope is inferior to that provided by OCT. In confocal microscopy, both lateral and axial resolutions are determined by the numerical aperture of the eye lens, whereas in OCT, the axial resolution is decoupled from the optical characteristics of the eye being exclusively determined by the spectral range of the optical source employed. Consequently, the retina of the human eye can be imaged with an axial resolution of at least 100 times better than that provided by a confocal microscope [44]. An example of an in vivo high axial-resolution cross-section image of the human retina is presented in Fig. 13. This image was produced using a Time-Domain (TD) OCT instrument employing a broadband optical source emitting light over a spectral range of 150 nm and central wavelength 890 nm. The axial resolution of the instrument, in the retina, of 3 μm allows for identifying a multitude of layers along the axial coordinate.

In this section, a short explanation behind the operation of the OCT imaging systems is provided. We are going to look at the two methods of implementing OCT, time domain (TD)-OCT and spectral domain (SD)-OCT. A presentation of the procedure to generate images as well as of the advantages and disadvantages of various types of OCT instruments when used for imaging the human eye is also illustrated. Special attention is paid to issues arising from the high acquisition speed of the modern SD-OCT instruments. In the last decade, the increase in data acquisition speed has enabled the OCT community to contemplate in vivo real-time volumetric display of the biological tissues. To reach this goal, several, software and hardware techniques were developed.

3.8.1 Time domain optical coherence tomography. The beauty of the en-face view

A sketch of a TD-OCT experimental setup is presented in Fig. 14. The instrument includes a broadband optical source (typically a super luminescent diode (SLD)) and an interferometer. Light from the SLD is conveyed towards the sample via a beamsplitter (BS), a scanning head (GXY) incorporating two orthogonal galvo-mirrors and two achromatic lenses (L_1 and L_2) and towards a reference arm. Light backreflected by the sample, conveyed into one of the single-mode fiber inputs of a directional coupler (DC, 50/50) using a microscope objective L_S and from the reference arm, conveyed into the other input of DC via the microscope objective L_R, interferes in DC, then is detected using a balance photo-detector (BPD). Finally, the electronic signal is processed using the processing unit PU and an axial reflectivity profile (A-scan) is generated.

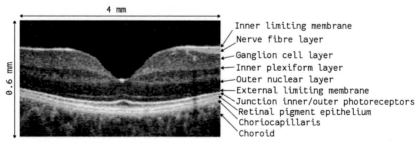

FIG. 13

In vivo cross-section image of the retina using an TD-OCT system.

Adapted with permission from R. Cucu, A. Podoleanu, J. Rogers, J. Pedro, R. Rosen, Combined confocal scanning ophthalmoscopy/en face T-scan based ultrahigh resolution OCT of the human retina in vivo, Opt. Lett. 31 (2006) 1684–1687.

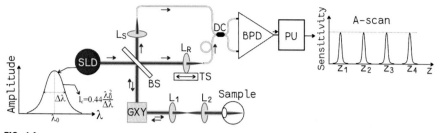

FIG. 14

Schematic diagram of a TD-OCT instrument. The device uses a super-luminescent diode (SLD), a pair of orthogonal galvo-scanners (SXY), achromatic lenses (L_1 and L_2), a 50/50 beam-splitter (BS), directional coupler (DC) and a balance photo-detector (BPD). L_S and L_R are microscope objectives whereas data processing is achieved in the processing unit (PU).

For constructive interference to happen the difference between the optical paths of the two arms of the interferometer (optical path difference—OPD) must be less than the coherence length of the optical source, which for a Gaussian shape of the source spectrum is mathematically expressed as $l_c = 0.44\lambda_0^2/\Delta\lambda$. Therefore l_c, which only depends on the spectral bandwidth ($\Delta\lambda$) and the central wavelength (λ_0) of the spectrum, is a measure of the axial resolution in OCT. An SLD providing a spectral bandwidth of 150 nm around a central wavelength of 850 nm should in theory be able to deliver an axial resolution of 2.1 μm in air.

In the sketch presented in Fig. 14, constructive interference takes place for waves back-scattered by each location within the sample along the depth, which satisfies the condition OPD < l_c. Hence, by adjusting the values of the OPD (by actuating on the position of the translation stage TS), a TD-OCT device outputs an axial reflectivity profile, termed as an A-scan.

The beauty of this approach is that there is no limitation with regards the axial size of the A-scans whereas there is no need to use a fast digitizer. Another advantage of the technology is represented by the fact that there is practically no need for data processing, hence A-scans can be generated in real-time (points are generated along the A-scan in synchronism with the change in the position of the TS).

By collecting a succession of A-scans, as the optical beam laterally scans the sample, a cross-section (B-scan) image is produced (as illustrated in Fig. 15). For each lateral position x_i, reflectivity information is collected for $q = 1..Q$ positions of TS. Thus, a number of P A-scans are ensembled together to produce, in real-time, a B-scan TD-OCT image of size $P \times Q$. This type of cross-section image is often referred to as A-scan based B-scan, and the technology referred to as axial or longitudinal TD-OCT. This was the method used by Huang et al. [45] to demonstrate the first OCT image of a human retina, in vitro, back in 1991.

To generate a C-scan image (XY plane), a 3D volume must first be generated, followed by rendering the XY plane at the desired axial position. As the axial TD-OCT relies on mechanical movement of parts of the system, inevitably, the speed at which the TS is moved is limited. In principle, to ensure a decent signal-to-noise ratio in the image, a B-scan image constructed of for example 500 A-scans is produced in 5 s, and a 3D volume in which the size of the C-scans is 500×500 pixels in 2500 s, making the axial TD-OCT unusable for in vivo imaging of the human eye. Another way of producing images in TD-OCT is, for a given position of TS, to produce a lateral reflectivity profile by transversally scanning the beam over the sample. These profiles (T-scans) can be used to generate cross-sections by producing them for various values of the OPD (T-scan based B-scans). If, for a given axial position z_i, T-scans for various y_j positions are assembled, a C-scan or *en-face* image is produced. The advantage of this procedure is that an *en-face* image, at a constant depth can be produced directly, much faster, as there is no need to build the whole 3D volume. This technique has the advantage that the quality of the image is not affected by repeated movements of the translation stage. Thus, good quality *en-face* TD-OCT images can be produced in real-time in as fast as 0.5 Hz.

Another advantage of the *en-face* TD-OCT is that it can be complemented by other imaging techniques. Thus, multimodality imaging instruments were reported. In Fig. 16A, examples of Scanning Laser Ophthalmoscopy (SLO) of the human retina and two *en-face* OCT images, collected from two axial positions are presented [46]. There is pixel to pixel correspondence between the three images. The SLO image has a poorer axial resolution, but it can serve for guidance purposes. Further progress in the development of the multimodality imaging of human retina allowed for sequential [47] and/or simultaneous [48] display of the *en-face* SLO and TD-OCT images. Efforts were also made to increase the number of en-face images simultaneously displayed [49] as illustrated in Fig. 17.

In addition, the multichannel potential of the OCT/SLO system was demonstrated by the addition of a third hardware channel which acquires and generates indocyanine green (ICG) fluorescence images. Thus, three *en-face* images, SLO, OCT and ICG fluorescence images were simultaneously presented and the synergy between the simultaneously provided perspectives demonstrated. With information

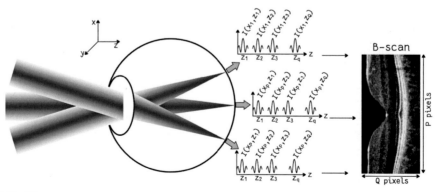

FIG. 15

Procedure for producing a B-scan image in TD-OCT. For each lateral position x_p, $p=1..P$, the signal $I(x_p,z_q)$ (q = 1..Q) is collected for each position z_q of the translation stage TS.

now available from three channels, an enhanced diagnostic tool was created facilitating internal correction of movement artifacts within *en-face* and B-scan OCT images using information provided by the SLO channel [50]. The efficiency of a multimodal, multi-depth imaging tools was successfully demonstrated in various clinical studies, an example showing simultaneously OCT, SLO and ICG images of a patient with a well-defined classic choroidal neovascular membrane in the post-injection phase is demonstrated in Fig. 18 [50a].

3.8.2 Spectral domain optical coherence tomography

The key value of spectral (Fourier) domain OCT is its ability to encode spatial or temporal data into the spectrum at the interferometer output. Currently, there are two modalities on transducing this information from the optical domain into electrical: camera based (CB)-OCT where, as in TD-OCT, a broadband optical source is employed together with a spectrometer and swept source (*SS*)-OCT, where a tuneable (swept) laser is used and signal is delivered by a photo-detector. When producing B-scans, SD-OCT is clearly superior to conventional TD-OCT, in terms of both sensitivity and acquisition speed. However, *en-face* imaging is still of high interest in ophthalmology as it can often offer enhanced visualization and additional information on sample microstructures, due to additional information conveyed that enhances the physician's understanding of the underlying pathology [51]. Also, *en-face* imaging can be used for absolute position registration of the individual B-scan image [52]. When implemented with TD-OCT systems, *en-face* OCT imaging does not allow reasonably high-speed data acquisition to mitigate motion artifacts [53] as they require a quite fast phase modulation procedure in the reference arm which can be

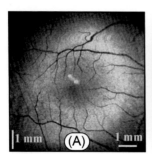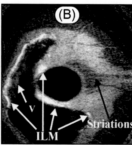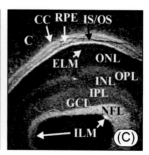

FIG. 16

En-face images of the macular region of the human retina in vivo: (A) SLO image (B) and (C) TD-OCT images from two axial positions. *ILM*, inner limiting membrane; *V*, the vitreous; *NFL*, nerve fiber layer; *GCL*, ganglion cell layer; *IPL*, inner plexiform layer; *INL*, inner nuclear layer; *OPL*, outer plexiform layer; *ELM*, external limiting membrane; *IS/OS*, junction between inner and outer photoreceptors; *RPE*, retinal pigment epithelium; *CC*, choriocapillaris; *C*, choroid.

Adapted with permission from R. Cucu, A. Podoleanu, J. Rogers, J. Pedro, R. Rosen, Combined confocal scanning ophthalmoscopy/en face T-scan based ultrahigh resolution OCT of the human retina in vivo, Opt. Lett. 31 (2006) 1684–1687.

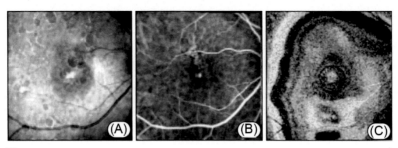

FIG. 17

Example of simultaneously displayed en-face images (A) SLO, (B) ICG and (C) OCT showing age-related macular degeneration with occult choroidal neovascular membrane [49]. Image size 12°×12°.

implemented at the expense of complicated optical designs and can potentially trigger some other issues such as galvo-scanner synchronization and dispersion compensation problems that need to be addressed.

3.8.3 Camera based optical coherence tomography and exceptional spatial resolutions

A typical schematic diagram of a CB-OCT system is depicted in Fig. 19. Here, instead of a photo-detector, a spectrometer, is employed. Light from the sample and from the reference mirror MR interferes at DC. The beam is then dispersed into its wave-number components by a diffraction grating TG. Finally, the spectrum obtained is digitized by a fast, linear camera (1 DC).

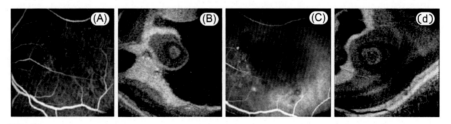

FIG. 18

Example of en-face ICG fluorescence of the right fundus of a patient with a well-defined classic choroidal neovascular membrane in the post-injection phase at a 10s (A) and 15s (C) and en-face OCT images are 10s (B) and 15s (D) after injection. The ICG images highlight the vascular component of the membrane, while the accompanying OCT images reveal the surrounding serous retinal elevation. Image sizes: 4×4mm.

Adapted with permission from A.G. Podoleanu, G.M. Dobre, R. Cernat, J.A. Rogers, P. Justin, R.B. Rosen, P. Garcia, Investigations of the eye fundus using a simultaneous optical coherence tomography/indocyanine green fluorescence imaging system, J. Biomed. Opt. 12 (1) (2007) 014019.

To process the signal, the processing unit PU performs an apparent simple mathematical operation to generate an A-scan: a Fast Fourier Transform (FFT) of the electrical signal, proportional to the photo-detected spectrum. However, due to the nonlinearities in the spectrometer, an irregular modulation (chirp) of the electrical signal read out by the spectrometer occurs. An unbalanced dispersion in the interferometer and the sample itself [54] can also contribute to the chirp. Unless this chirp is compensated for, after sophisticated linearization procedures, an FFT applied to the electrical signal leads to a wider and at the same time, reduced amplitude of the reflectivity profile peaks. Imperfections in these procedures become more obvious at larger OPD values in the interferometer and more pronounced as the spectral bandwidth is increased.

By collecting a succession of A-scans as the optical beam laterally scans the sample, a cross-section image is produced (as illustrated in Fig. 20). For each lateral position x_i, A-scans are obtained with no need of any mechanical movements. Thus, a number of P A-scans are ensembled together to produce, a B-scan CB-OCT image of size $P \times Q$. Here, Q is typically half the number of points used to digitize the spectrum (i.e., the number of pixels in the linear camera employed).

Generating real-time A-scans in CB-OCT is quite challenging. The frequency at which spectra are acquired is typically over 100 kHz. This mean that to ensure a real-time operation, the FFT operation must not take longer than 10 µs. This is possible using a modern multicore PC however the electric signal must be corrected for chirping before FFT via time consuming sequential interpolation procedures. As CB-OCT and TD-OCT instruments are using the same optical sources, they will deliver images with similar axial resolutions.

In terms of sensitivity, CB-OCT has a 20–30 dB advantage over TD-OCT [55], however a limited axial imaging range due to the finite size of camera's pixels. The production of *en-face* CB-OCT images is done in a manner similar to axial TD-OCT, i.e., by rendering the *en-face* view from the 3D volume. The acquisition time of the

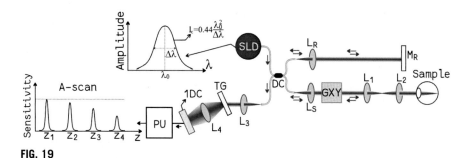

FIG. 19

Schematic diagram of a CB-OCT instrument. The device uses a super-luminescent diode (SLD), a pair of orthogonal galvo-scanners (GXY), achromatic lenses (L_1–L_4), a directional coupler (DC). LS and LR are microscope objectives whereas data processing is achieved in the processing unit (PU). TG, transmission diffraction grating; 1DC, linear camera (CCD or InGaAs).

3D dataset needed to build a volume is in the order of 2.5 s (for 500×500 pixels^2 in the *en-face* plane), hence even if produced in real-time, a single *en-face* image is produced 5 times slower than in *en-face* TD-OCT.

3.8.4 Swept source optical coherence tomography. Going faster and deeper into the tissue

Any TD-OCT instrument can be converted into a SS-OCT one simply by replacing the broadband source by a swept-source laser, and by using faster detectors and digitizers. The processing of data is done in a similar way to CB-OCT, i.e., to produce an A-scan an FFT of the digitized signal is required. This signal is still chirped now due to sweeping non-linearities of the laser and unbalanced dispersion. A schematic diagram of a typical SS-OCT instrument is depicted in Fig. 21.

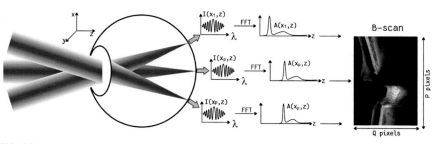

FIG. 20

Procedure of producing a B-scan image in SD-OCT. For each lateral position x_p, $p=1..P$, the signal $I(xp,z)$ is collected then a FFT of the spectrum is performed to produce an A-scan. By assembling P A-scans a B-scan of $Q \times P$ pixels^2 is obtained.

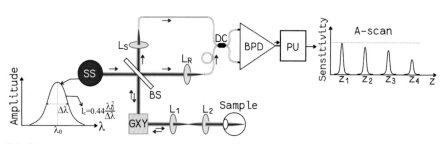

FIG. 21

Schematic diagram of a SS-OCT instrument. The device uses a swept laser (SS), a pair of orthogonal galvo-scanners (GXY), achromatic lenses (L_1–L_2), a directional coupler (DC). LS and LR are microscope objectives whereas data processing is achieved in the processing unit (PU). BPD is a fast balanced photo-detector.

The axial size of the images is restricted now by the instantaneous coherence length of the source, however this is not limited to a couple of mm as in the case of CB-OCT. Typically MEMS based SSs can provide axial ranges from 3 to 4 mm to 1 cm depending on the speed data is sampled. In terms of axial resolutions, SSs have a more limited spectral range, of maximum 100 nm. As current technology only allows for fast (>100 kHz), stable SSs for wavelengths superior to 1060 nm, SS-OCT instruments can only deliver image with axial resolutions of 4.8 μm in air. However, SS-OCT instruments provide better sensitivity than CB-OCT and a better depth penetration in the choroid as the scattering is reduced at longer wavelength. The use of CB-OCT at longer wavelengths is restricted due to the unavailability of the fast cameras.

3.8.5 Methods of generating images in SD-OCT

To produce an A-scan in SD-OCT, the integral of the product between an experimentally acquired spectrum, obtained by interfering light from the sample and reference arm of the interferometer and a kernel function is calculated. To eliminate the chirping due to nonlinear wavelength mapping and due to unbalanced dispersion, two methods can be used: a wide spread method is based on FFT that operates on the experimental spectra, or a novel method (Master/Slave) that operates on the kernel function.

When using the FFT based method, each experimental spectrum is re-sampled then multiplied by a function that cancel the effect of the unbalanced dispersion. A relationship between the phase of the modified spectrum and a new wavenumber distribution is obtained, then an A-scan compensated for broadening is produced by calculating the FFT of the product between the re-sampled spectrum and an apodization function. The process of calibration (computing the new wavenumber distribution) is performed at each spectral acquisition, before imaging is carried out. To produce accurate information on the reflectivity from within the sample, each acquired experimental spectrum is resampled according, typically via a cubic B-spline interpolation, then correct for the unbalanced dispersion. All these operations limit the capability of the FFT based instruments to operate in real-time as they are executed sequentially. In addition, the resampling operation is time consuming and must be applied to each acquired experimental spectrum. In contrast to the FFT method, the process of obtaining an axial reflectivity profile utilizing the MS method consists in modifying the kernel function [56]. Thus, a transversal reflectivity profile (T-scan), for a given axial position z_i can be reduced to a simple matrix multiplication [57]. The advantage of this mathematical representation of a T-scan is that it can be generated in real-time. Collections of T-scans can be produced in real-time as now all operations are parallelizable. Furthermore, an entire *en-face* MS based SD-OCT image can be produced in real-time, multiple *en-face* images from different axial positions along depth can also be generated without producing entire large 3D volumes. This allows for defining axial regions of interest where B-scans can be generated without producing redundant data, hence shorter axial range B-scan images can be produced in real-time [58]. As illustrated in Table 1, the MS is the only spectral domain technique that truly allows for real-time operation.

In Fig. 22A a B-scan image of the anterior chamber of the eye, produced in real-time (50 Hz) using a MS SS-OCT instrument is demonstrated. The real-time operation is achievable as the MS technique allows to limit the mathematical calculations to a specific region of interest. This would not be possible with the same CPU if FFT based technique is employed.

The sensitivity advantage of SD-OCT over conventional TD-OCT was not only demonstrated theoretically [55] but also proven in clinical studies. It has been for example shown that when used to evaluate macular morphology alterations, SD-OCT performs better as these alterations are typically related to choroidal neovascularization [59], of which SD-OCT is able to provide better images. This is obvious if we compare the TD base B-scan image from Fig. 1 to the SS based B-scan from Fig. 23. Fig. 23 was produced in real-time, at 50 Hz using a swept-source of 100 nm spectral bandwidth and central wavelength 1060 nm.

TD-OCT still has the advantage of producing *en-face* views in real-time, however of lower sensitivity than the SD-OCT methods. The MS approach can nevertheless deliver *en-face* images in real-time whilst taking advantage of the greater sensitivity of the SD methods. Such an example is presented in Fig. 24B, where real-time *en-face* images from 36 axial positions are displayed simultaneously, together with one (or more) B-scan views (Fig. 24A) and a confocal image allowing for guidance.

3.8.6 Modern topics in optical coherence tomography for eye imaging

In the recent years, several functional extensions of optical coherence tomography have emerged to broaden the potential clinical applications of OCT by providing novel ways to understand tissue activity.

Optical Coherence Tomography—Angiography (OCTA). OCTA can be used to measure or monitor the motion and flows of biologic fluids. This method provides a depth resolved profile of the flow velocity in the blood vessel, with the resolution determined by the coherence length of the source employed. OCT- microangiography can provide enhanced visualization of retinal and choroidal vasculature. The beauty of this technology is that it does not require any dye injection as initially demonstrated in combined *en-face* fluorescence/TD-OCT instruments [60].

Spectroscopic OCT (SOCT) allows simultaneous OCT measurements in multiple spectral windows. SOCT can provide information on the oxygenation or on the concentration of specific constituents of the tissue by exploiting their spectral absorption behavior. The larger the number of interrogating wavelengths the better the quantitative analysis. The availability now of large bandwidth sources, such as supercontinuum ones allows novel implementation of SOCT to provide depth resolved distribution of chromophores in tissue, not technologically possible using combinations of discrete sources as well as the development of *ultra-high resolution OCT (UHR-OCT)* instruments.

Table 1 Typical capabilities of various OCT instruments employed to image the human eye.

Typical values (capability)	En-face TD-OCT	Axial TD-OCT	CB-OCT		SS-OCT	
			FFT	MS	FFT	MS
Axial resolution	2–10μm	2–10μm	2–10μm		5–10μm	
Axial imaging range	Unlimited	Unlimited	2–3mm		3–5mm	
Sensitivity vs. depth	Constant	Constant	Fast drop from OPD=0		Slow drop from OPD=0	
Line rate	2Hz	100Hz	>50kHz		>100kHz	
Time to produce an en-face image[a]	0.5s	2500s	12.5s		6.25s	
Real-time en-face imaging	Yes	Yes	Possible	Yes	Possible	Yes
Time to produce a 3D volume[b]	250s	2500s	12.5s		6.25s	
Real-time 3D volume	Yes	Yes	Possible	Yes	Possible	Yes
Penetration in retina	RPE/choroid	RPE/choroid	Better for RPE		Better for choroid	

[a] Size en-face image 500×500 pixels.
[b] Size 3D volume 500×500×500 pixels.

Visible Optical Coherence Tomography (V-OCT). V-OCT is an emerging imaging modality [61], providing novel capabilities of the current OCT instruments in both anatomical and functional imaging of the eye. In contrast with most commercial and research OCT devices, where near-infrared light is used for illumination, it relies on visible light. Although V-OCT requires distinctive considerations in devising the instrument and is mainly suitable for imaging superficial tissue due to the limited depth penetration of visible light in tissue, it provides a much better

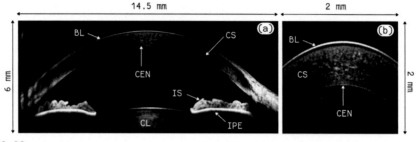

FIG. 22

(A) Wide, real-time, in vivo cross-section image of the ocular anterior segment of a healthy volunteer. The image consists of 1000 pixels laterally and 1048 pixels axially. BL, Bowman's layer; CS, corneal stroma; CEN, corneal endothelium; IS, iris stroma; IPE, iris pigment epithelium; CL, crystalline lens. (B) Inset, only showing the tip of the cornea.

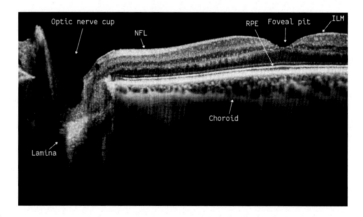

FIG. 23

In vivo real-time cross-section image of the retina using an MS-OCT system. Image size: 7.5 mm (lateral)×3.7 mm (axial), measured in the retina. Visible layers: ILM, inner limiting membrane; NFL, nerve fiber layer; GCL, ganglion cell layer; IPL, inner plexiform layer; INL, inner nuclear layer; OPL, outer plexiform layer; ONL, outer nuclear layer; ELM, external limiting membrane; IS/OS, junction between the inner and outer photoreceptors; RPE, retinal pigment epithelium; CC, choriocapillaris; C, choroid.

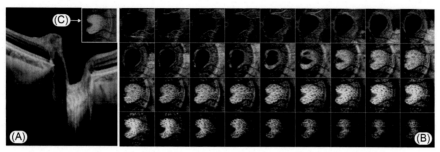

FIG. 24

(A) In vivo B-scan image of the human optic nerve showing lamina cribrosa. Size of the image: 4.2×3.7 mm. (B) 36 images of human lamina produced simultaneously and in real-time using a MS OCT instrument. (C) Confocal en-face image produced at the same time as the OCT images. The size of each en-face image is 2×2 mm. The en-face images are separated by 15 μm. Here only 36 images are presented, however the technology allows more images to be displayed in real-time. All distances are measured in air.

resolution than the near-infrared instruments, as well as different spectroscopic contrast hence unique benefits to both fundamental research and clinical care of several eye diseases [62].

Optical Coherence Elastography (OCE). Unlike OCT, which uses endogenous contrast mechanisms within a sample, OCE adds an externally induced mechanical stimulus alongside OCT to obtain structural information about the biomechanical properties of the sample. Although not demonstrated yet for real-time in vivo investigations of the human eye, the technique has a huge clinical potential as OCE relies on the fact that the elastic properties of tissues depend on whether they are diseased or not.

Real-time OCT (RT-OCT). Speed on data acquisition and processing is crucial when imaging moving organs and for instruments equipped with hand-held probes. Although in the last years, in terms of data acquisition, a huge progress has been made with the development of MHz line-rate swept lasers, the processing of data is still not sufficiently fast to allow for true real-time display of images. To alleviate the problem of data processing and display, parallel approaches involving graphics processing unit (GPU) cards on CUDA parallel computing platforms or field programmable gate arrays (FPGAs) are used but they add to the cost of the instrument. Even if the processing time is drastically reduced, such methods are not genuinely real-time, as the brightness of each pixel in the transversal section is not established simultaneously with the beam being incident on that pixel. To allow for real-time display, methods such as the Master/Slave, which do not add complexity to the instrument is probably a trend that many researchers in the field will follow.

4 Polarization and birefringence

The polarization state of light used to image the retina, and the way in which polarization can be modified by ophthalmic instruments and by the eye can have a profound impact on the appearance of retinal images. The polarization of light refers to the direction of the electric field vector of light. In linear polarization, the electric field oscillates in only one plane: for example, the vertical or horizontal plane, while circular polarization can be produced by combining two orthogonally polarized light beams with a 90° phase difference (or quarter wavelength path difference). Elliptically polarized light is produced by combining linearly polarized light with a phase difference other than 90°. Natural light such as is produced by broadband sources, such as the LEDs, tungsten lamp sources and flash lamps suited in direct and indirect ophthalmoscopes and fundus cameras, produce unpolarized light. Unpolarized light can be polarized, however, by transmission through a polarizer—most commonly a linear or circular polarizer. Similarly light that is linearly polarized will be absorbed by a film polarizer aligned with the transmission axis orthogonal to the polarization direction. Importantly a linear polarizer aligned with narrowband sources, such as lasers or super-luminescent LEDs, such as are used in scanning laser ophthalmoscopes or OCT systems respectively normally generate polarized light.

When light is reflected, such as from a glass surface, or from the cornea, or the eye lens, the reflected light has the same polarization state as the incident light. If then, the light that is transmitted through the pupil to illuminate the retina is linearly polarized then the reflection from the cornea will have the same polarization state. A linear polarizer, oriented to transmit only the orthogonal polarization, placed between the detector and the light reflected from the cornea, will then not transmit the linearly polarized corneal light. As explained below, the linearly polarized illumination transmitted to the retina will tend to be depolarized by *multiple scattering* in the retina and will be transmitted with an efficiency of 50% (for an ideal polarizer). In consequence the use of this so-called crossed-polarizer technique can yield an image with a strongly suppressed corneal reflection, albeit with a four-fold reduction in intensity. Additional reflections deeper into the eye also exist, for example the Purkinje images from the back of the cornea and from the two lens surfaces (see Section 2.3), although these are much weaker than the front corneal reflection. Retinal images are also commonly characterized by strong specular reflections, from, for example, blood vessels and from the retinal nerve fiber layers and these can also be suppressed by use of cross-polarized imaging. The suppression of the Purkinje reflections and the retinal specular reflections is not very efficient: indeed the spatial characteristics of the retinal specular reflections can vary significantly with orientation of the imaging linear polarizer. As discussed below, this is due to the birefringence of the ocular media.

In a uniaxial birefringent material, the refractive index experienced by light depends on the orientation of the polarization of light with respect to a so-called optic axis of the material. In general, linearly polarized light incident upon a birefringent material will be converted to elliptically polarized light with a polarization state defined by the magnitude of the birefringence, the relative orientation of light direction and the optic axis and the thickness of the material traversed by the light. Non-isotropic crystals, such as quartz and calcite, have very well defined birefringence that is commonly exploited in optical instruments to control polarization. But *form birefringence* exists in biological materials where anisotropy is due to aligned cells; such as are found in the cornea, the lens and the retinal nerve fiber layer [63]. In consequence, linearly polarized light incident upon the cornea will be converted into elliptically polarized light transmitted through the lens and cornea. Furthermore this change in polarization state varies across the aperture of the pupil with the variation in the orientation of the cells and the thickness of the layers of cells that compose the cornea and lens. In consequence polarization modification by the lens and cornea varies both across the pupil of the eye and across the retina and also between eyes. In consequence polarization cannot be reliably used to remove specular reflections, but with care it can be used to provide some suppression of reflections and to extract additional information the retina [64]: for example polarimetric imaging of the retinal nerve-fiber layer exploits the form birefringence arising from the co-alignment of nerve fibers to provide an estimate of the thickness of the RNFL [65] although this requires a careful calibration of the effects of birefringence of the cornea and lens and OCT is now the most commonly used technique for this measurement.

We have so far described the importance of polarization on specular reflections, but most of the light used to form an image of the retina is unpolarized, even when the illumination is polarized. This is because light incident upon the complex structure of the retina tends to undergo many random reflections (scattering events) from an extended volume of the many biological components of the retina, such as the blood cells, nerve fibers, connective tissue etc. and these many reflections tend to randomize the light-ray polarization orientation such that for many light rays the resultant effect is to produce depolarization of light. In consequence, images of the retina are characterized typically by unpolarized light due to multiple scattering combined with strong polarization effects due to the cornea, lens, retinal nerve fiber layer and specular reflections from blood vessels, the optic nerve head and nerves. Also particularly notable is the central reflex within images of blood vessels which varies between images. The origin of this reflex may be associated with specular reflections from the vessels, overlying tissue of from the alignment of blood cells that is associated with laminar flow of blood [66]. The reflex can be partially attenuated using cross polarized light—although with erratic efficiency.

5 Conclusions

In this chapter we have reviewed the main retinal imaging instruments and the how their imaging modalities interact with the physics of light in the eye. The optics and geometry impose limits on the transverse and axial achievable resolution and introduce difficulties in achieving reflex-free illumination and imaging of the retina. We discussed how they produce the specific characteristics of recorded images in particular the variations in image characteristics with wavelength and between fundus cameras, various types of SLO and OCT systems.

Owing to its importance in retinal imaging, and also the anterior segment of the eye, we have given a particular emphasis to OCT, and have detailed the principles of operation and the implications from for image analysis and clinical application. In particular, it is difficult to exaggerate importance of the depth profiling ability of OCT: this is a striking exemplar of translation of research from the physics lab to clinical application.

Looking to the future, there is an increasing trend to combine multiple imaging modalities within a single device, to increase the field of view for the detection of pathologies that affect or originate at the retinal periphery and to implement devices that are portable and more convenient to use in primary care. Lastly there is strong motivation for telemedicine and cost reduction in devices that provide a necessary and sufficient performance at a price that is affordable to the majority of the world's population living in low-to-middle societies. This will involve a clear increase in the role of computational imaging to reduce the cost of these Systems [67] and automated computer analysis.

References

[1] Footprints of the Lion—Isaac Newton at Work. http://www.lib.cam.ac.uk/exhibitions/Footprints_of_the_Lion/private_scholar.html. (Accessed January 20, 2019).

[2] H. von Helmholtz, Beschreibung eines Augenspiegels zur Untersuchung der Netzhaut im lebenden Auge, Arch. Ophthalmol. 46 (1851) 565.

[3] D. Thomas, G. Duguid, Optical coherence tomography—a review of the principles and contemporary uses in retinal investigation, Eye 18 (2004) 561–570.

[4] M. Pircher, R.J. Zawadzki, Review of adaptive optics OCT (AO-OCT): principles and applications for retinal imaging [Invited], Biomed. Opt. Express 8 (2017) 2536–2562.

[5] E. Hecht, Optics, Addison-Wesley, 2002.

[6] M. Born, E. Wolf, Principles of Optics, Cambridge University Press, 1999.

[7] D.A. Atchison, G. Smith, Optics of the Human Eye, Butterworth-Heinemann, Elsevier, 2000.

[8] R. Navarro, J. Santamaria, J. Bescos, Accommodation-dependent model of the human eye with aspherics, J. Opt. Soc. Am. A 2 (1985) 1273–1281.

[9] A.V. Goncharov, C. Dainty, Wide-field schematic eye models with gradient-index lens, J. Opt. Soc. Am. A 24 (2007) 2157–2174.

[10] A. Corcoran, G. Muyo, J. van Hemert, A. Gorman, A.R. Harvey, Application of a wide-field phantom eye for optical coherence tomography and reflectance imaging, J. Mod. Opt. 62 (2015) 1828–1838.

[11] V.V. Tuchin, Tissue Optics: Light Scattering Methods and Instruments for Medical Diagnosis, second ed., SPIE, 2008.

[12] D.J. Mordant, Human retinal oximetry using multispectral imaging (PhD thesis), Institute of Ophthalmology, University College London, 2010.

[13] D.G. Curry, G.L. Martinsen, D.G. Hopper, Capability of the human visual system, SPIE 5080 (2003) 58–69.

[14] T. Chui, H.X. Song, S.A. Burns, Adaptive-optics imaging of human cone photoreceptor distribution, J. Opt. Soc. Am. 25 (12) (2008) 3021–3029.

[15] R. Navarro, Incorporation of intraocular scattering in schematic eye models, J. Opt. Soc. Am. A 2 (1985) 1891–1894.

[16] S. Marcos, E. Moreno, R. Navarro, The depth-of-field of the human eye from objective and subjective measurements, Vis. Res. 39 (1999) 2039–2049.

[17] F.C. Delori, K.P. Pflibsen, Spectral reflectance of the human ocular fundus, Appl. Opt. 28 (6) (1989) 1061–1077.

[18] A. Gullstrand, Neue Methoden der reflexlosen Ophthalmoskopie, Ber. Dtsch. Ophthalmol. Gesellsch. 36 (1910) 75.

[19] S.J. Preece, E. Claridge, Monte Carlo modelling of the spectral reflectance of the human eye, Phys. Med. Biol. 47 (2002) 2863–2877.

[20] P.I. Rodmell, J.A. Crowe, A. Gorman, A.R. Harvey, G. Muyo, D.J. Mordant, A.I. McNaught, S.P. Morgan, Light path-length distributions within the retina, J. Biomed. Opt. 19 (2014) 36008.

[21] G. Carles, P. Zammit, A.R. Harvey, Holistic Monte-Carlo optical modelling of biological imaging, Sci. Rep. 9 (2019) 15832.

[22] L. Kocsis, P. Herman, A. Eke, The modified Beer–Lambert law revisited, Phys. Med. Biol. 51 (2006) N91–N98.

[23] L.E. MacKenzie, A.R. Harvey, A.I. McNaught, Spectroscopic oximetry in the eye: a review. Exp. Rev. Ophthalmol. 12 (4) (2017) 345–356, https://doi.org/10.1080/174698 99.2017.1318067.

[24] L.E. MacKenzie, A.R. Harvey, Oximetry using multispectral imaging: theory and application, J. Opt. 20 (2018) 063501–063525.

[25] S.H. Hardarson, A. Harris, R.A. Karlsson, G.H. Halldorsson, L. Kagemann, E. Rechtman, G.M. Zoega, T. Eysteinsson, J.A. Benediktsson, A. Thorsteinsson, P.K. Jensen, J. Beach, E. Stefansson, Automatic retinal oximetry, Invest. Ophthalmol. Vis. Sci. 47 (2006) 5011–5016.

[26] M.A. van der Putten, J.M. Brewer, A.R. Harvey, Multispectral oximetry of murine tendon microvasculature with inflammation, Biomed. Opt. Express 8 (2017) 2896–2905.

[27] L.E. MacKenzie, T.R. Choudhary, A.I. McNaught, A.R. Harvey, In vivo oximetry of human bulbar conjunctival and episcleral microvasculature using snapshot multispectral imaging, Exp. Eye Res. 149 (2016) 48–58.

[28] P.F. Sharp, A. Manivannan, The scanning laser ophthalmoscope. Phys. Med. Biol. 42 (1997) 951–966, https://doi.org/10.1088/0031-9155/42/5/014.

[29] J.V. Kristjansdottir, S.H. Hardarson, A.R. Harvey, O.B. Olafsdottir, T.S. Eliasdottir, E. Stefansson, Choroidal oximetry with a noninvasive spectrophotometric oximeter, Invest. Ophthalmol. Vis. Sci. 54 (2013) 3234–3239.

[30] G. Carles, G. Muyo, J. van Hemert, A.R. Harvey, Combined high contrast and wide field of view in the scanning laser ophthalmoscope through dual detection of light paths, J. Biomed. Opt. 22 (2017) 1–11.

[31] D. Salyer, K. Denninghoff, N. Beaudry, S. Basavanthappa, R. Park, R. Chipman, Diffuse spectral fundus reflectance measured using subretinally placed spectralon, J. Biomed. Opt. 13 (2008) 044004.

[32] M.H. Smith, K.R. Denninghoff, A. Lompado, L.W. Hillman, Effect of multiple light paths on retinal vessel oximetry, Appl. Opt. 39 (2000) 1183–1193.

[33] J. Cameron, T. MacGillivray, B. Dhillon, S. Chandran, Right Eye Retinal SLO Image. University of Edinburgh, 2016, https://doi.org/10.7488/ds/1468.

[34] A.T. Corcoran, Ultra-widefield optical coherence tomography of the human retina (PhD Thesis), University of Glasgow, UK, 2015.

[35] D.J. Mordant, Human retinal oximetry using spectral imaging (PhD thesis), Institute of Ophthalmology, University College London, 2011.

[36] D.J. Mordant, I. Al-Abboud, G. Muyo, A. Gorman, A. Sallam, P. Rodmell, J. Crowe, S. Morgan, P. Ritchie, A.R. Harvey, A.I. McNaught, Validation of human whole blood oximetry, using a hyperspectral fundus camera with a model eye, Invest. Ophthalmol. Vis. Sci. 52 (2011) 2851.

[37] C.R. Keeler, A brief history of the ophthalmoscope, Optom. Pract. 4 (2) (2003) 137–145.

[38] R.H. Webb, G.W. Hughes, O. Pomerantzeff, Flying spot TV ophthalmoscope, Appl. Opt. 19 (17) (1980) 2991–2997.

[39] R.H. Webb, G.W. Hughes, F.C. Delori, Confocal scanning laser ophthalmoscope, Appl. Opt. 26 (8) (1987) 1492–1499.

[40] F.J. Van de Velde, The relaxed confocal scanning laser ophthalmoscope, Bull. Soc. Belge Ophtalmol. 302 (2006) 25–35.

[40a] International Commission on Non-Ionizing Radiation Protection, ICNIRP Guidelines on limits of exposure to incoherent visible and infrared radiation, Health Phys 105 (2013) 74–96.

[41] D. Sliney, et al., Adjustment of guidelines for exposure of the eye to optical radiation from ocular instruments: statement from a task group of the International Commission on Non-Ionizing Radiation Protection (ICNIRP), Appl. Opt. 44 (2005) 2162–2176.

[42] M.E. Tyler, P.J. Saine, T.J. Bennet, Practical Retinal Photography and Digital Imaging Techniques, Butterworth-Heinemann, Elsevier, 2003.

[43] A. Manivannan, J.N.P. Kirkpatrick, P.F. Sharp, J.V. Forrester, Novel approach towards colour imaging using a scanning laser ophthalmoscope, Br. J. Ophthalmol. 82 (1998) 342–345.

[44] W. Drexler, J. Fujimoto (Eds.), Optical Coherence Tomography Technology and Applications, Series: Biological and Medical Physics, Biomedical Engineering, XXVIII, Springer, Berlin/Heidelberg, 2008.

[45] D. Huang, E.A. Swanson, C.P. Lin, et al., Optical coherence tomography, Science 254 (1991) 1178–1181.

[46] R. Cucu, A. Podoleanu, J. Rogers, J. Pedro, R. Rosen, Combined confocal scanning ophthalmoscopy/en face T-scan based ultrahigh resolution OCT of the human retina in vivo, Opt. Lett. 31 (2006) 1684–1687.

[47] A. Podoleanu, G. Dobre, R. Cucu, R. Rosen, Sequential optical coherence tomography and confocal imaging, Opt. Lett. 29 (2004) 364–366.

[48] A. Podoleanu, G. Dobre, D. Webb, D. Jackson, Simultaneous en-face imaging of two layers in the human retina by low-coherence reflectometry, Opt. Lett. 22 (1997) 1039–1041.

[49] R. Rosen, M. Hathaway, J. Rogers, J. Pedro, P. Garcia, G. Dobre, A. Podoleanu, Simultaneous OCT/SLO/ICG imaging, Invest. Ophthalmol. Vis. Sci. 50 (2009) 851–860.

[50] R. Rosen, M. Hathaway, J. Rogers, J. Pedro, P. Garcia, P. Laissue, G. Dobre, A. Podoleanu, Multidimensional en-Face OCT imaging of the retina, Opt. Express 17 (2009) 4112–4133.

[50a] A.G. Podoleanu, G.M. Dobre, R. Cernat, J.A. Rogers, P. Justin, R.B. Rosen, P. Garcia, Investigations of the eye fundus using a simultaneous optical coherence tomography/indocyanine green fluorescence imaging system, J. Biomed. Opt. 12 (1) (2007) 014019.

[51] V. Srinivasan, D. Adler, Y. Chen, I. Gorczynska, R. Huber, J. Duker, J. Schuman, J. Fujimoto, Ultrahigh-speed optical coherence tomography for three-dimensional and en face imaging of the retina and optic nerve head, Invest. Ophthalmol. Vis. Sci. 49 (2008) 5103–5110.

[52] S. Jiao, C. Wu, R.W. Knighton, G. Gregori, C.A. Puliafito, Registration of high-density cross sectional images to the fundus image in spectral-domain ophthalmic optical coherence tomography, Opt. Express 14 (2006) 3368–3376.

[53] M. Pircher, B. Baumann, E. Götzinger, C.K. Hitzenberger, Imaging the human retina and cone mosaic in vivo with PS-OCT, Proc. SPIE 6429 (2007) 64290T.

[54] M. Wojtkowski, V. Srinivasan, T. Ko, A.K.J. Fujimoto, J. Duker, Ultrahigh resolution, high-speed, FD-OCT and methods for dispersion compensation, Opt. Express 12 (2004) 2404–2422.

[55] M. Choma, M. Sarunic, C. Yang, J. Izatt, Sensitivity advantage of swept source and Fourier domain optical coherence tomography, Opt. Express 11 (2003) 2183–2189.

[56] S. Rivet, M. Maria, A. Bradu, T. Feuchter, L. Leick, A. Podoleanu, Complex master slave interferometry, Opt. Express 24 (2016) 2885–2904.

[57] A. Bradu, N. Israelsen, M. Maria, M. Marques, S. Rivet, T. Feuchter, O. Bang, A. Podoleanu, Recovering distance information in spectral domain interferometry, Sci. Rep. 8 (2018) 15445.

[58] A. Bradu, S. Rivet, A. Podoleanu, Master/slave interferometry—ideal tool for coherence revival swept source optical coherence tomography, Biomed. Opt. Express 7 (2016) 2453–2468.

[59] L. Pierro, E. Zampedri, P. Milani, M. Gagliardi, V. Isola, A. Pece, Spectral domain OCT versus time domain OCT in the evaluation of macular features related to wet age-related macular degeneration, Clin. Ophthalmol. 6 (2012) 219–223.

[60] G. Dobre, A. Podoleanu, R. Rosen, Simultaneous optical coherence tomography–indocyanine green dye fluorescence imaging system for investigations of the eye's fundus, Opt. Lett. 30 (2005) 58–60.

[61] J. Yi, W. Liu, S. Chen, V. Backman, N. Sheibani, C. Sorenson, A. Fawzi, R. Linsenmeier, H. Zhang, Visible light optical coherence tomography measures retinal oxygen metabolic response to systemic oxygenation, Light Sci. Appl. 4 (2015) e334.

[62] X. Shu, L. Beckmann, H. Zhang, Visible-light optical coherence tomography: a review, J. Biomed. Opt. 22 (2017) 121707.

[63] X.R. Huang, Polarization properties of the retinal nerve fiber layer, Bull. Soc. Belge Ophtalmol. (302) (2006) 71–88.

[64] K.M. Twietmeyer, R.A. Chipman, A.E. Elsner, Y. Zhao, D. VanNasdale, Mueller matrix retinal imager with optimized polarization conditions, Opt. Express 16 (2008) 21339–21354.

[65] X.-R. Huang, R.W. Knighton, Linear birefringence of the retinal nerve fiber layer measured in vitro with a multispectral imaging micropolarimeter, J. Biomed. Opt. 7 (2002) 199–204.

[66] P. Cimalla, J. Walther, M. Mittasch, E. Koch, Shear flow-induced optical inhomogeneity of blood assessed in vivo and in vitro by spectral domain optical coherence tomography in the 1.3 μm wavelength range, J. Biomed. Opt. 16 (2011) 116020.

[67] X.-M. Hu, J.-M. Wu, J.-L. Suo, Q.-H. Dai, Emerging theories and technologies on computational imaging, Front. Inf. Technol. Electron. Eng. 18 (2017) 1207–1221.

Retinal image preprocessing, enhancement, and registration

4

Carlos Hernandez-Matas[a], Antonis A. Argyros[a,b], Xenophon Zabulis[a]

[a]Institute of Computer Science, Foundation for Research and Technology—Hellas (FORTH), Heraklion, Greece
[b]Computer Science Department, University of Crete, Heraklion, Greece

1 Introduction

The first fundus images were acquired after the invention of the ophthalmoscope. The concept of storing and analyzing retinal images for diagnostic purposes exists ever since. The first work on retinal image processing was based on analog images and regarded the detection of vessels in fundus images with fluorescein [1]. The fluorescent agent enhances the appearance of vessels in the image, facilitating their detection and measurement by the medical professional or the computer. However, fluorescein angiography is an invasive and time-consuming procedure and is associated with the cost of the fluorescent agent and its administration.

Digital imaging and digital image processing have proliferated the use of retinal image analysis in screening and diagnosis. The ability to accurately analyze fundus images has promoted the use of noninvasive, fundus imaging in these domains. Moreover, the invention of new imaging modalities, such as optical coherence tomography (OCT) and scanning laser ophthalmoscopy (SLO), has broadened the scope and applications of retinal image processing. This review regards both fundus imaging, as implemented by fundus photography and SLO and OCT imaging.

Retinal image analysis supports pertinent diagnostic procedures. A number of symptoms and diseases are diagnosed through observation of the human retina. Retinal image analysis is useful not only in the diagnosis of ophthalmic diseases, but also in that of systemic chronic diseases. Hypertension and diabetes are two important examples of such diseases that affect small vessels and microcirculation and which are noninvasively screened and assessed through the contribution of retinal image analysis [2, 3]. In this context, two widely employed tasks are the detection and measurement of anatomical features and properties, such as lesion detection and measurement of vessel diameters. Achieving these tasks typically includes a preprocessing stage, tuned according to the measured features and the method of image analysis. This preprocessing stage usually regards the normalization of image

Computational Retinal Image Analysis. https://doi.org/10.1016/B978-0-08-102816-2.00004-6

intensities after image formation, as well as the enhancement of the image through noise reduction and contrast enhancement.

Image analysis methods capable of matching and aligning retinal images of the same eye have enabled the task of retinal image registration (RIR), which also plays a significant role in the diagnosis and the monitoring of diseases. By registering images acquired during the same examination, higher resolution and definition images of the retina can be obtained and enable high-precision measurements. Moreover, the registering images into mosaics facilitates mapping wider retinal regions than a single image does. Registration of images from different examinations facilitates follow-up examinations and assessment of treatment through the speed of symptom reversal.

2 Intensity normalization

Intensity normalization is the form of preprocessing closest to image acquisition, as it deals with the interpretation of pixel values for image formation. Digital sensors have built-in intensity normalization algorithms that subsequent image processing methods account for. Intensity normalization is also employed in the compensation of artifacts, due to uneven illumination of retinal tissue by the imaging modality.

2.1 Fundus imaging

The interplay between optics, light source, and eye shape casts illumination of the retina to be spatially uneven. This complicates feature detection and segmentation, often requiring local adaptation of processing.

Contrast normalization is usually applied to the "green" channel [4–7], as it is less sensitive to noise. Contrast enhancement in all three channels was proposed through 3D histogram equalization [8], or independent normalization of each channel [9]. In Ref. [10], intensity is adjusted based on information from the histograms of both red and green channels, in an attempt to reap benefits from information in both channels.

Generic, global approaches to intensity normalization have not fully solved this problem. Zero-mean normalization and unit variance normalization compensate only partially for lighting variation, as they introduce artifacts due to noise amplification [11–13]. A polynomial remapping of intensities [7] exhibits similar issues.

Generic, local approaches, based on the statistics of image neighborhoods, have been more effective and more widely adopted. To this end, Zhao et al. [14] employ a color-constancy method. Locally adaptive histogram equalization (CLAHE) [15] is one of the most widely used contrast normalization steps [16–23] including also adaptations of the initial method [24–26].

Retinal imaging-specific approaches estimate a model of illumination and rectify intensities according to the luminance it predicts [27–30]. This model is a mask image, where pixel values are estimates of tissue reflectivity. As the illumination source is usually unknown, this estimate is obtained assuming that local illumination variation is smaller than across the entire image.

2.2 Tomographic imaging

In OCT imaging, the need for intensity rectification stems from the automatic intensity rescaling and averaging of the sensor, which may differ in each scan. Generic intensity normalization has been applied to individual scans [31]. However, prominent noise reduction methods utilize multiple scans that image the same area and average measurements corresponding to the same tissue points [32–34]. The central step in such approaches is the registration of scans (see Section 4.2).

3 Noise reduction and contrast enhancement

Noise reduction and contrast enhancement are typical preprocessing steps in multiple domains of image analysis. Their goal is to improve image definition and fidelity, by accenting image structure and reducing image noise. Generic approaches to these tasks have been employed for all retinal image types. Nonetheless, approaches targeted to the particular modality and the subsequent analysis have been more widely adopted. Notably, in OCT imaging, noise reduction methods address an imaging artifact pertinent only to this modality, besides conventional image noise.

3.1 Fundus imaging

Generic approaches to local contrast and structural adjustment have been proposed [6, 7, 35–37], but are culpable in amplifying noise or noninteresting structures. Single-scale [38] and multi-scale [13, 39–41] linear filterings have also been tools of similar approaches but conversely they filter out useful fine image structure at fine scales. Morphological transformations have also been proposed, such as the contourlet [42] and the top-hat transformations [43], and were combined with histogram equalization [44] and matched filters [45]. Nonlinear filtering approaches have also been proposed. A diffusion-based "shock" filter was employed in Ref. [46]. In Ref. [47], inverse diffusion provided feature-preserving noise reduction. In Ref. [48], sparse coding and a representation dictionary were utilized to represent vessels and reconstruct the original image without noise.

Target-oriented contrast enhancement methods have also been tailored. Image sharpness was amplified by compensating for the blur of the eye's point spread function, through the modeling of the former [49]. Multi-orientation filtering kernels that mimic and highly correlate with vessel intensity profiles were used in Refs. [50–52] to enhance vessels. By modeling vessel appearance as ridge structures, the "vesselness," or Frangi filter in Ref. [53] has been widely utilized to accent vessels over the rest of the image.

Combination of multiple images has also been based on the information redundancy that is provided when imaging the same tissue multiple times, using averaging [54], or blind deconvolution [55]. The central step in these approaches is image registration (see Section 4.2).

3.2 Tomographic imaging

In OCT imaging, noise reduction addresses an additional source of noise, besides conventional noise due to electronics. "Speckle noise" is an OCT artifact [56], due to the reflective nature of the retina. So-called "speckles" are due to the interference of the illumination with back-scattered light.

Generic, single-image noise reduction has been based on linear filtering [57], adaptive transforms [58], wavelets [59–63], and wave atom transformations [64]. Nonlinear filtering has also been proposed, using conventional [65] or multiscale anisotropic diffusion [66]. Other approaches include regularization [67], PCA [68], Bayesian inference [69], and stochastic methods [70]. Compressive sensing and sparse representations were proposed in Refs. [71–73]. A comparative evaluation of such approaches can be found in Ref. [74].

Nevertheless, the main focus of noise reduction approaches is on speckle noise reduction, as speckles significantly obscure retinal structure in the acquired images. The majority of noise reduction approaches averages multiple, uncorrelated scans of the same section. In this way, image structure due to transient speckle noise is attenuated over structure due to actual tissue. Some techniques include adaptations upon the conventional OCT apparatus, leading to more complex image acquisition. In these cases, acquisition of uncorrelated scans is based on modulation of the incidence angle of illumination [75–77], detection angle of back-scattered light [77], laser illumination frequency [78–80], and illumination polarization [81–83]. On the other hand, spatial compounding techniques [32–34, 84] do not require modification of the OCT scanner, as they use the purposeful motion of the scanner to acquire overlapping and adjacent scans. Motion is a priori known minus the uncertainty of mechanical motion and, thus, only minor alignment is required. As the aforementioned techniques image the same tissue multiple times, they are limited by eye motion (i.e., saccadic). Thereby, the brevity of acquisition time is required to reduce the probability of corresponding motion artifacts.

Accidental and purposeful motions call for scan alignment, through image registration (see Section 4.2). Once scans are registered, postprocessing further enhances the volumetric signal. In Refs. [32, 85], 3D wavelet filters are applied to volumetrically registered scans. In Ref. [86], volumetric neighborhoods are matched and averaged. In Ref. [87], a physical model of speckle formation is employed and estimated as a convex optimization problem upon the volumetric data.

4 Retinal image registration

The problem of image registration regards a test and a reference image. The goal is the estimation of the aligning transformation that warps the test image, so that retinal points in the warped image occur at the same pixel locations as in the reference image. RIR is challenging due to optical differences across modalities or devices, optical distortions due to the eye lens and vitreous humor, anatomical changes due to lesions or disease, as well as acquisition artifacts. Viewpoint differences (i.e., due to eye motion) complicate image registration further, due to projective distortion of the curved surface of the eye.

Applications of RIR can be classified according to whether images are acquired in the same or different examinations. Images from the same examination are devoid of anatomic changes. If their overlap is significant, they can be combined into images of higher resolution and definition [88–90], enabling more accurate measurements. Images with small overlap are utilized to create image mosaics that broaden the sensor's field of view [91–93] (see Fig. 1).

Longitudinal studies of the retina [97, 98] are facilitated by the registration of images acquired at different examinations (i.e., initial and follow-up). Pertinent studies enable disease monitoring and treatment evaluation, through tracking of symptom reversal. In this context, accurate registration of images of the same retinal region proves valuable in the detection of minute but critical changes, such as local hemorrhages or differences in vasculature width (see Fig. 2).

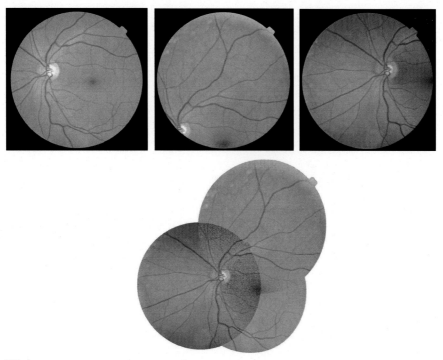

FIG. 1

Registration of retinal images into a mosaic. *Top*: Original images, from the public dataset in Refs. [94, 95]. *Bottom*: Registration result, using Hernandez-Matas [96].

From C. Hernandez-Matas, Retinal Image Registration Through 3D Eye Modelling and Pose Estimation (Ph.D. thesis), University of Crete, 2017.

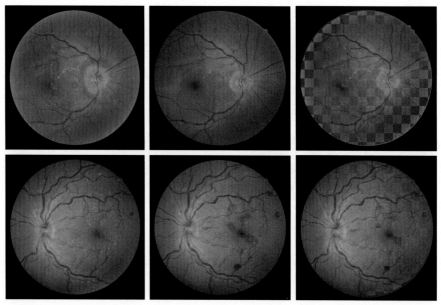

FIG. 2

Registration of fundus images from the same retinal region that exhibit differences, for longitudinal studies. *Left*: Original images from the public dataset in Refs. [99, 100]. *Right*: Registration results using Hernandez-Matas [96].

From C. Hernandez-Matas, Retinal Image Registration Through 3D Eye Modelling and Pose Estimation (Ph.D. thesis), University of Crete, 2017.

4.1 Fundus imaging

Initial approaches to RIR attempted similarity matching of the entire test and reference image as encoded in the spatial [101–106] or frequency [107] domains. A central assumption in global methods is that intensities in the test and reference image are consistent. However, this does not always hold due to uneven illumination, eye curvature, and anatomical changes that may occur between the acquisition of the test and reference images.

Instead of matching all image pixels, local approaches rely on matching well-localized features or keypoints [90, 92, 98, 103, 108–131] (see Fig. 3). The approaches in Refs. [117, 123] match feature points, based only on their topology. General purpose features associated with local descriptors have been more widely utilized for RIR. SIFT [132] features are the ones that have provided the greatest accuracy [109, 130], with SURF [133] features comprising a close second [126, 128]. Harris corners associated with a descriptor of their neighborhood have also been proposed [120, 126]. Features tuned to retinal structures include vessels, bifurcations, and crossovers [92, 114, 115]. As these features are not associated with descriptors, SIFT or SURF descriptors have been computed at their locations to

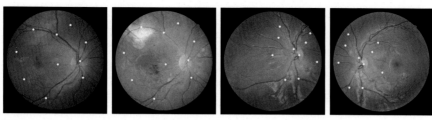

FIG. 3

Corresponding features in two pairs of retinal images, from the public dataset in Ref. [99, 100]. *White dots* show matched features.

From C. Hernandez-Matas, Retinal Image Registration Through 3D Eye Modelling and Pose Estimation (Ph.D. thesis), University of Crete, 2017.

facilitate matching [134]. In general, local methods have been more widely utilized, particularly for images with small overlap, due to the increased specificity that point matches provide. Moreover, local methods are more suitable for the registration of images with anatomical changes, as they are robust to partial image differences. In addition, they require less processing power, leading to faster registration.

At the heart of local approaches is the establishment of point correspondences, or matches, across the test and reference images. Pertinent methods utilize these correspondences to estimate a transform that, optimally, brings the matched points into coincidence. As some correspondences are spurious, robust estimation of the transform is utilized to relieve the result from their influence [90].

A range of 2D and 3D transforms has been utilized. Similarity transforms include rotation, scaling, translation, and modulation of aspect ratio [102–107, 110, 113, 114, 117, 119, 120, 124, 126, 127], while the affine transform is utilized to approximate projective distortion [92, 98, 101, 104, 110, 112–117, 117–120, 123–127, 131]. Projective transformations treat more appropriately perspective distortion at the cost of more degrees of freedom that imply higher computational cost and potential instability in optimization [90, 109, 110, 112, 128–130]. Quadratic transformations [92, 92, 104, 110, 111, 113, 114, 117, 119–122, 125, 125–127] allow further compensation for eye curvature. However, these transformations do not necessarily include consideration of the shape of the eye. Conversely, utilizing an eye model safeguards for unreasonable parameter model estimates and provides more accurate registration. In Refs. [96, 128–130], the RIR problem is formulated as a 3D pose estimation problem, solved by estimating the rigid transformation that relates the views from which the two images were acquired. Considering the problem in 3D enables 3D measurements, devoid of perspective distortion. Though 3D models account for perspective, they require knowledge of the shape of the imaged surface, either via modeling or via reconstruction. Even simple eye shape models have shown to improve registration accuracy of retinal images [128].

4.2 Tomographic imaging

Approaches to the registration of OCT images differ to fundus image registration approaches, due to their tomographic content. In some cases, OCT image registration is guided by the use of an additional fundus as a reference, which does not contain motion artifacts as it is instantaneously acquired.

Noise reduction in OCT images is based on averaging registered scans. In Ref. [32], the known translational motion of the scanner is assumed as accurate enough to juxtapose individual scans as volumetric data. In Ref. [33], an initial manual registration is refined through cross-correlation alignment. In Ref. [85], detecting the retinal pigment epithelium and requiring its continuity in adjacent scans provide a cue to registration. The work in Ref. [34] utilizes correlation maps of adjacent images. In Ref. [135], hierarchical affine-motion estimation approach is proposed. Low-rank and sparse image decomposition alignment has been employed in Ref. [136].

Eye motion estimation through OCT image registration has also been used to compensate for eye motion. In Ref. [137], an SLO-based eye tracker measured eye motion during image acquisition and images were registered according to these motion estimates. In Ref. [138], individual scans are registered to an SLO image. In Ref. [139], scans are registered without the use of a reference image; a particle filtering optimization is utilized to align scans in 3D as a dynamic system, which is optimized when adjacent scans are in consensus. In Ref. [140], registration is also optimization-based, but further exploits the temporal ordering of the scans and external information on their spatial arrangement. In Ref. [141], a semiautomatic approach is proposed to register and compare OCT scans, in order to study retinal changes in the corresponding data.

Mosaics of OCT volumes have been formed, using a fundus image as a reference. In Ref. [142], volumes are registered using vessel ridges and cross-correlation as a registration cue and based on the Iterative Closest Point algorithm. In Ref. [143], a reference image is not required, but adjacent volumes are registered based on a B-spline free-deformation method. In Ref. [144], a six-degree-of-freedom registration scheme for OCT volumes is proposed, which includes bundle adjustment corrections. In Refs. [145, 146], OCT volumes are registered in 3D without any prior knowledge of sensor or eye motion, based on correspondence of feature points.

4.3 Intramodal vs. cross-modal image registration

The combination of imaging modalities results in improved understanding of the retinal tissue and its pathologies. Cross-modal registration enables analysis and comparison of images that may emphasize complementary retinal features. In tomographic imaging, registration of axial scans to a frontal, fundus image enables registration of OCT scans, despite eye motion (see Section 4.2).

Methods in Refs. [112, 115, 116, 131] register fundus images and fluoroangiographies, by performing vessel segmentation and matching common vessel structures across the two cross-modal images. Vessel segmentation, detection, and matching of bifurcation points have been utilized to establish point correspondences across cross-modal images [113, 121]. Keypoint features, such as SIFT and SURF, and their descriptors have also been employed for the same purpose [92, 109, 114, 116, 117, 119, 120]. In addition, novel descriptors associated with conventional keypoints have been proposed [125, 125, 131].

In Refs. [101, 102], mutual information was proposed as a cue to the registration of fundus and SLO images. The methods in Refs. [138, 142] register frontal OCT scans with SLO images, in a similar fashion. As frontal images are visually similar across modalities, registration is achieved by conventional matching of vessels or vessel features.

More challenging is the registration of axial OCT scans with frontal fundus images. This registration facilitates the acquisition of a volumetric reconstruction of retinal tissue, below the retinal surface. The works in Refs. [147–149] utilize retinal vessels as the cue to the registration of frontal fundus images and axial OCT scans, requiring vessel segmentation as an initial step. However, as retinal vessel segmentation is still an open problem, vessel segmentation errors are propagated in the registration phase. In Ref. [150], a feature-based approach is proposed, which capitalizes on corner features as control points and utilizes histograms of oriented gradients to better match the neighborhoods of these points. A robust approach is also included to remove correspondence outliers and estimate the transform that better registers the OCT scans to the fundus image.

5 Conclusions

A wide range of methods exists for the preprocessing, enhancement, and registration of retinal images acquired by conventional and emerging imaging modalities.

The preprocessing and enhancement tasks are required in a broad variety of uses. The most straightforward is the inspection of the image by the medical professional, where preprocessing and enhancement are required to preserve the fidelity of the acquired image while clarifying or accenting its structure and anatomical features. Preprocessing and enhancement are also utilized as initial steps in algorithmic image analysis, to facilitate and increase the accuracy of detection, recognition, and measurement of anatomical features. For these cases, generic image preprocessing methods have been applied, though more recently, approaches carefully select and tailor image preprocessing according to the subsequent image analysis goals. Due to the aforementioned variety of uses, benchmarking of image preprocessing tasks has been difficult and scarce. In addition, as preprocessing is typically only part of an image analysis method, when evaluation is available it regards the entire method and not the image preprocessing part in isolation.

RIR is also the basis for a wide spectrum of tasks. First, registration of multiple images allows to combine them into improved or wider retinal images. Moreover, RIR has been employed the comparison of retinal images, which is essential for monitoring a disease and the assessment of its treatment. As image registration is a well-defined task, attempts to provide pertinent benchmarks are starting to appear, as in Ref. [99] where existing datasets for RIR are compared and a benchmark methodology is also proposed. Still, there is a clear need for new approaches to benchmarking that will allow for more direct comparisons of methods and will account for optical phenomena, such as optical distortions due to the eye lens, vitreous humor, and chromatic aberrations.

Acknowledgment

The authors thank Polykarpos Karamaounas for technical assistance in the preparation of the manuscript.

References

[1] M. Matsui, T. Tashiro, K. Matsumoto, S. Yamamoto, A study on automatic and quantitative diagnosis of fundus photographs (Transl. from Japanese), Nippon Ganka Gakkai Zasshi 77 (8) (1973) 907–918.

[2] A. Grosso, F. Veglio, M. Porta, F.M. Grignolo, T.Y. Wong, Hypertensive retinopathy revisited: some answers, more questions, Br. J. Ophthalmol. 89 (12) (2005) 1646–1654, https://doi.org/10.1136/bjo.2005.072546.

[3] R.P. Danis, M.D. Davis, Proliferative diabetic retinopathy, Diabetic Retinopathy, Humana Press, Totowa, NJ, 2008, pp. 29–65.

[4] A. Chernomorets, A. Krylov, Blur detection in fundus images, International Conference on BioMedical Engineering and Informatics, 2012, pp. 243–246.

[5] S. Mohammad, D. Morris, N. Thacker, Segmentation of optic disc in retina images using texture, International Conference on Computer Vision Theory and Applications, 2014, pp. 293–300.

[6] A. Fleming, S. Philip, K. Goatman, J. Olson, P. Sharp, Automated microaneurysm detection using local contrast normalization and local vessel detection, IEEE Trans. Med. Imaging 25 (9) (2006) 1223–1232.

[7] T. Walter, P. Massin, A. Erginay, R. Ordonez, C. Jeulin, J. Klein, Automatic detection of microaneurysms in color fundus images, Med. Image Anal. 11 (6) (2007) 555–566.

[8] A. Pujitha, G. Jahnavi, J. Sivaswamy, Detection of neovascularization in retinal images using semi-supervised learning, IEEE International Symposium on Biomedical Imaging, 2017, pp. 688–691.

[9] A. Deshmukh, T. Patil, S. Patankar, J. Kulkarni, Features based classification of hard exudates in retinal images, International Conference on Advances in Computing, Communications and Informatics, 2015, pp. 1652–1655.

[10] N. Salem, A. Nandi, Novel and adaptive contribution of the red channel in pre-processing of colour fundus images, J. Frankl. Inst. 344 (3) (2007) 243–256.

[11] C. Liu, M. Chang, Y. Chaung, S. Yu, A novel retinal image color texture enhancement method based on multi-regression analysis, International Symposium on Computer, Consumer and Control, 2016, pp. 793–796.

[12] J. Zhang, B. Dashtbozorg, E. Bekkers, J. Pluim, R. Duits, B.M. ter Haar Romeny, Robust retinal vessel segmentation via locally adaptive derivative frames in orientation scores, IEEE Trans. Med. Imaging 35 (12) (2016) 2631–2644.

[13] J. Sivaswamy, A. Agarwal, M. Chawla, A. Rani, T. Das, Extraction of capillary non-perfusion from fundus fluorescein angiogram, A. Fred, J. Filipe, H. Gamboa (Eds.), Biomedical Engineering Systems and Technologies, Springer, Berlin, Heidelberg, 2009, pp. 176–188.

[14] Y. Zhao, Y. Liu, X. Wu, S. Harding, Y. Zheng, Retinal vessel segmentation: an efficient graph cut approach with Retinex and local phase, PLoS ONE 10 (4) (2015) 1–22.

[15] K. Zuiderveld, Contrast limited adaptive histogram equalization, Graphics Gems IV, Academic Press, San Diego, CA, 1994, pp. 474–485.

[16] G. Manikis, V. Sakkalis, X. Zabulis, P. Karamaounas, A. Triantafyllou, S. Douma, C. Zamboulis, K. Marias, An image analysis framework for the early assessment of hypertensive retinopathy signs, IEEE E-Health and Bioengineering Conference, 2011, pp. 1–6.

[17] U. Acharya, E. Ng, J. Tan, V. Sree, K. Ng, An integrated index for the identification of diabetic retinopathy stages using texture parameters, J. Med. Syst. 36 (3) (2012) 2011–2020.

[18] M. Zhou, K. Jin, S. Wang, J. Ye, D. Qian, Color retinal image enhancement based on luminosity and contrast adjustment, IEEE Trans. Biomed. Eng. 65 (3) (2018) 521–527.

[19] Sonali, S. Sahu, A. Singh, S. Ghrera, M. Elhoseny, An approach for de-noising and contrast enhancement of retinal fundus image using CLAHE, Opt. Laser Technol. 110 (2019) 87–98.

[20] A. Ajaz, B. Aliahmad, D. Kumar, A novel method for segmentation of infrared scanning laser ophthalmoscope (IR-SLO) images of retina, IEEE Engineering in Medicine and Biology Society, 2017, pp. 356–359.

[21] M. Esmaeili, H. Rabbani, A.M. Dehnavi, Automatic optic disk boundary extraction by the use of curvelet transform and deformable variational level set model, Pattern Recogn. 45 (7) (2012) 2832–2842, https://doi.org/10.1016/j.patcog.2012.01.002.

[22] A. Sopharak, B. Uyyanonvara, S. Barman, T. Williamson, Automatic detection of diabetic retinopathy exudates from non-dilated retinal images using mathematical morphology methods, Comput. Med. Imaging Graph. 32 (2008) 720–727.

[23] S.M. Shankaranarayana, K. Ram, A. Vinekar, K. Mitra, M. Sivaprakasam, Restoration of neonatal retinal images, Proceedings of the Ophthalmic Medical Image Analysis Third International Workshop, OMIA, 2016, pp. 49–56.

[24] A. Aibinu, M. Iqbal, M. Nilsson, M. Salami, A new method of correcting uneven illumination problem in fundus images, International Conference on Robotics, Vision, Information, and Signal Processing, 2007, pp. 445–449.

[25] K. Huang, M. Yan, A local adaptive algorithm for microaneurysms detection in digital fundus images, Computer Vision for Biomedical Image Applications, 2005, pp. 103–113.

[26] R. GeethaRamani, L. Balasubramanian, Retinal blood vessel segmentation employing image processing and data mining techniques for computerized retinal image analysis. Retinal blood vessel segmentation in fundus images, Biocybern. Biomed. Eng. 36 (1) (2016) 102–118.

[27] M. Foracchia, E. Grisan, A. Ruggeri, Luminosity and contrast normalization in retinal images, Med. Image Anal. 9 (3) (2005) 179–190.

[28] H. Narasimha-Iyer, A. Can, B. Roysam, V. Stewart, H.L. Tanenbaum, A. Majerovics, H. Singh, Robust detection and classification of longitudinal changes in color retinal fundus images for monitoring diabetic retinopathy, IEEE Trans. Biomed. Eng. 53 (6) (2006) 1084–1098.

[29] E. Grisan, A. Giani, E. Ceseracciu, A. Ruggeri, Model-based illumination correction in retinal images, IEEE International Symposium on Biomedical Imaging: Nano to Macro, 2006, pp. 984–987.

[30] R. Kolar, J. Odstrcilik, J. Jan, V. Harabis, Illumination correction and contrast equalization in colour fundus images, European Signal Processing Conference, 2011, pp. 298–302.

[31] A. Lang, A. Carass, M. Hauser, E. Sotirchos, P. Calabresi, H. Ying, J. Prince, Retinal layer segmentation of macular OCT images using boundary classification, Biomed. Opt. Express 4 (7) (2013) 1133–1152.

[32] M. Avanaki, R. Cernat, P. Tadrous, T. Tatla, A. Podoleanu, S. Hojjatoleslami, Spatial compounding algorithm for speckle reduction of dynamic focus OCT images, IEEE Photon. Technol. Lett. 25 (2013) 1439–1442.

[33] M. Mayer, A. Borsdorf, M. Wagner, J. Hornegger, C. Mardin, R. Tornow, Wavelet denoising of multiframe optical coherence tomography data, Biomed. Opt. Express 3 (3) (2012) 572–589.

[34] M. Jorgensen, J. Thomadsen, U. Christensen, W. Soliman, B. Sander, Enhancing the signal-to-noise ratio in ophthalmic optical coherence tomography by image registration method and clinical examples, J. Biomed. Opt. 12 (4) (2007) 041208.

[35] R. Phillips, J. Forrester, P. Sharp, Automated detection and quantification of retinal exudates, Graefe's Arch. Clin. Exp. Ophthalmol. 231 (2) (1993) 90–94.

[36] N. Patton, T. Aslam, T. MacGillivray, I. Deary, B. Dhillon, R. Eikelboom, K. Yogesan, I. Constable, Retinal image analysis: concepts, applications and potential, Prog. Retin. Eye Res. 25 (1) (2006) 99–127.

[37] E. Peli, T. Peli, Restoration of retinal images obtained through cataracts, IEEE Trans. Med. Imaging 8 (4) (1989) 401–406.

[38] U. Qidwai, U. Qidwai, Blind deconvolution for retinal image enhancement, IEEE EMBS Conference on Biomedical Engineering and Sciences, 2010, pp. 20–25.

[39] P. Dai, H. Sheng, J. Zhang, L. Li, J. Wu, M. Fan, Retinal fundus image enhancement using the normalized convolution and noise removing, J. Biomed. Imaging 2016 (2016) 1–12.

[40] J. Soares, J. Leandro, R. Cesar, H. Jelinek, M. Cree, Retinal vessel segmentation using the 2-D Gabor wavelet and supervised classification, IEEE Trans. Med. Imaging 25 (9) (2006) 1214–1222.

[41] T.R. Mengko, A. Handayani, V.V. Valindria, S. Hadi, I. Sovani, Image processing in retinal angiography: extracting angiographical features without the requirement of contrast agents, Proceedings of the IAPR Conference on Machine Vision Applications (IAPR MVA 2009), Keio University, Yokohama, Japan, May 20–22, 2009, pp. 451–454.

[42] P. Feng, Y. Pan, B. Wei, W. Jin, D. Mi, Enhancing retinal image by the Contourlet transform, Pattern Recogn. Lett. 28 (4) (2007) 516–522.

[43] X. Bai, F. Zhou, B. Xue, Image enhancement using multi scale image features extracted by top-hat transform, Opt. Laser Technol. 44 (2) (2012) 328–336.

[44] R. Kromer, R. Shafin, S. Boelefahr, M. Klemm, An automated approach for localizing retinal blood vessels in confocal scanning laser ophthalmoscopy fundus images, J. Med. Biol. Eng. 36 (4) (2016) 485–494.

[45] J. Xu, H. Ishikawa, G. Wollstein, J. Schuman, Retinal vessel segmentation on SLO image, IEEE Eng. Med. Biol. Soc. 2008 (2008) 2258–2261.

[46] H. Rampal, R. Kumar, B. Ramanathan, T. Das, Complex shock filtering applied to retinal image enhancement, World Congress on Medical Physics and Biomedical Engineering, 2013, pp. 900–903.

[47] L. Wang, G. Liu, S. Fu, L. Xu, K. Zhao, C. Zhang, Retinal image enhancement using robust inverse diffusion equation and self-similarity filtering, PLoS ONE 11 (7) (2016) 1–13.

[48] B. Chen, Y. Chen, Z. Shao, T. Tong, L. Luo, Blood vessel enhancement via multi-dictionary and sparse coding: Application to retinal vessel enhancing, Neurocomputing 200 (2016) 110–117.

[49] A. Marrugo, M. Millán, M. Sorel, J. Kotera, F. Sroubek, Improving the blind restoration of retinal images by means of point-spread-function estimation assessment, International Symposium on Medical Information Processing and Analysis, vol. 9287, 2015, p. 92871D.

[50] A. Hoover, V. Kouznetsova, M. Goldbaum, Locating blood vessels in retinal images by piecewise threshold probing of a matched filter response, IEEE Trans. Med. Imaging 19 (3) (2000) 203–210.

[51] T. Lin, M. Du, J. Xu, The preprocessing of subtraction and the enhancement for biomedical image of retinal blood vessels, J. Biomed. Eng. 1 (20) (2003) 56–59.

[52] S. Chaudhuri, S. Chatterjee, N. Katz, M. Nelson, M. Goldbaum, Detection of blood vessels in retinal images using two-dimensional matched filters, IEEE Trans. Med. Imaging 8 (3) (1989) 263–269.

[53] A.F. Frangi, W.J. Niessen, K.L. Vincken, M.A. Viergever, Multiscale vessel enhancement filtering, Medical Image Computing and Computer-Assisted Intervention—MICCAI'98: First International Conference Cambridge, MA, USA, October 11–13, 1998 Proceedings, Springer, Berlin, Heidelberg, 1998, pp. 130–137, https://doi.org/10.1007/BFb0056195.

[54] S. Crespo-Garcia, N. Reichhart, C. Hernandez-Matas, X. Zabulis, N. Kociok, C. Brockmann, A. Joussen, O. Strauss, In-vivo analysis of the time and spatial activation pattern of microglia in the retina following laser-induced choroidal neovascularization, Exp. Eye Res. 139 (2015) 13–21.

[55] A. Marrugo, M. Millan, M. Sorel, F. Sroubek, Retinal image restoration by means of blind deconvolution, J. Biomed. Opt. 16 (11) (2011) 1–16.

[56] J. Schmitt, A. Knüttel, Model of optical coherence tomography of heterogeneous tissue, J. Opt. Soc. Am. A 14 (6) (1997) 1231–1242.

[57] M. Pircher, E. Götzinger, R. Leitgeb, A. Fercher, C. Hitzenberger, Measurement and imaging of water concentration in human cornea with differential absorption optical coherence tomography, Opt. Express 11 (18) (2003) 2190–2197.

[58] J. Rogowska, M. Brezinski, Evaluation of the adaptive speckle suppression filter for coronary optical coherence tomography imaging, IEEE Trans. Med. Imaging 19 (12) (2000) 1261–1266.

[59] Z. Jian, Z. Yu, L. Yu, B. Rao, Z. Chen, B. Tromberg, Speckle attenuation in optical coherence tomography by curvelet shrinkage, Opt. Lett. 34 (10) (2009) 1516–1518.

[60] S. Chitchian, M.A. Mayer, A.R. Boretsky, F.J. van Kuijk, M. Motamedi, Retinal optical coherence tomography image enhancement via shrinkage denoising using double-density dual-tree complex wavelet transform, J. Biomed. Opt. 17 (11) (2012) 116009.

[61] Q. Guo, F. Dong, S. Sun, B. Lei, B. Gao, Image denoising algorithm based on contourlet transform for optical coherence tomography heart tube image, IET Image Process. 7 (5) (2013) 442–450.

[62] D.C. Adler, T.H. Ko, J.G. Fujimoto, Speckle reduction in optical coherence tomography images by use of a spatially adaptive wavelet filter, Opt. Lett. 29 (24) (2004) 2878–2880, https://doi.org/10.1364/OL.29.002878.

[63] P. Puvanathasan, K. Bizheva, Speckle noise reduction algorithm for optical coherence tomography based on interval type II fuzzy set. Opt. Express 15 (24) (2007) 15747–15758, https://doi.org/10.1364/OE.15.015747.

[64] Y. Du, G. Liu, G. Feng, Z. Chen, Speckle reduction in optical coherence tomography images based on wave atoms, J. Biomed. Opt. 19 (5) (2014) 1–7.

[65] H. Salinas, D. Fernandez, Comparison of PDE-based nonlinear diffusion approaches for image enhancement and denoising in optical coherence tomography, IEEE Trans. Med. Imaging 26 (6) (2007) 761–771.

[66] F. Zhang, Y. Yoo, L. Koh, Y. Kim, Nonlinear diffusion in Laplacian pyramid domain for ultrasonic speckle reduction, IEEE Trans. Med. Imaging 26 (2007) 200–211.

[67] D. Marks, T. Ralston, S. Boppart, Speckle reduction by I-divergence regularization in optical coherence tomography, J. Opt. Soc. Am. 22 (11) (2005) 2366–2371.

[68] H. Lv, S. Fu, C. Zhang, L. Zhai, Speckle noise reduction of multi-frame optical coherence tomography data using multi-linear principal component analysis, Opt. Express 26 (9) (2018) 11804–11818.

[69] A. Wong, A. Mishra, K. Bizheva, D. Clausi, General Bayesian estimation for speckle noise reduction in optical coherence tomography retinal imagery, Opt. Express 18 (8) (2010) 8338–8352.

[70] A. Cameron, D. Lui, A. Boroomand, J. Glaister, A. Wong, K. Bizheva, Stochastic speckle noise compensation in optical coherence tomography using non-stationary spline-based speckle noise modelling, Biomed. Opt. Express 4 (9) (2013) 1769–1785.

[71] L. Fang, S. Li, Q. Nie, J. Izatt, C. Toth, S. Farsiu, Sparsity based denoising of spectral domain optical coherence tomography images, Biomed. Opt. Express 3 (5) (2012) 927–942.

[72] L. Fang, S. Li, R. McNabb, Q. Nie, A. Kuo, C. Toth, J. Izatt, S. Farsiu, Fast acquisition and reconstruction of optical coherence tomography images via sparse representation, IEEE Trans. Med. Imaging 32 (2013) 2034–2049.

[73] D. Thapa, K. Raahemifar, V. Lakshminarayanan, A new efficient dictionary and its implementation on retinal images, International Conference on Digital Signal Processing, 2014, pp. 841–846.

[74] A. Ozcan, A. Bilenca, A. Desjardins, B. Bouma, G. Tearney, Speckle reduction in optical coherence tomography images using digital filtering, J. Opt. Soc. Am. 24 (7) (2007) 1901–1910.

[75] N. Iftimia, B. Bouma, G. Tearney, Speckle reduction in optical coherence tomography by "path length encoded" angular compounding, J. Biomed. Opt. 8 (2003) 260–263.

[76] H. Wang, A.M. Rollins, OCT speckle reduction with angular compounding by B-scan Doppler-shift encoding, Proc. SPIE, 7168, 2009, https://doi.org/10.1117/12.809852.

[77] A. Desjardins, B. Vakoc, W. Oh, S. Motaghiannezam, G. Tearney, B. Bouma, Angle-resolved optical coherence tomography with sequential angular selectivity for speckle reduction, Opt. Express 15 (10) (2007) 6200–6209.

[78] M. Pircher, E. Götzinger, R. Leitgeb, A. Fercher, C. Hitzenberger, Speckle reduction in optical coherence tomography by frequency compounding, J. Biomed. Opt. 8 (3) (2003) 565–569.

[79] J. Kim, D.T. Miller, E.K. Kim, S. Oh, J.H. Oh, T.E. Milner, Optical coherence tomography speckle reduction by a partially spatially coherent source, J. Biomed. Opt. 10 (2005) 064034, https://doi.org/10.1117/1.2138031.

[80] B. Karamata, P. Lambelet, M. Laubscher, R.P. Salathé, T. Lasser, Spatially incoherent illumination as a mechanism for cross-talk suppression in wide-field optical coherence tomography, Opt. Lett. 29 (7) (2004) 736–738, https://doi.org/10.1364/OL.29.000736.

[81] H. Ren, Z. Ding, Y. Zhao, J. Miao, J.S. Nelson, Z. Chen, Phase-resolved functional optical coherence tomography: simultaneous imaging of in situ tissue structure, blood flow velocity, standard deviation, birefringence, and Stokes vectors in human skin, Opt. Lett. 27 (19) (2002) 1702–1704, https://doi.org/10.1364/OL.27.001702.

[82] M. Kobayashi, H. Hanafusa, K. Takada, J. Noda, Polarization-independent interferometric optical-time-domain reflectometer, J. Lightwave Technol. 9 (5) (1991) 623–628.

[83] J. Schmitt, Array detection for speckle reduction in optical coherence microscopy, Phys. Med. Biol. 42 (7) (1997) 1427.

[84] R.J. Zawadzki, B. Cense, Y. Zhang, S.S. Choi, D.T. Miller, J.S. Werner, Ultrahigh-resolution optical coherence tomography with monochromatic and chromatic aberration correction, Opt. Express 16 (11) (2008) 8126–8143, https://doi.org/10.1364/OE.16.008126.

[85] Z. Jian, L. Yu, B. Rao, B. Tromberg, Z. Chen, Three-dimensional speckle suppression in optical coherence tomography based on the curvelet transform, Opt. Express 18 (2) (2010) 1024–1032.

[86] C. Gyger, R. Cattin, P. Hasler, P. Maloca, Three-dimensional speckle reduction in optical coherence tomography through structural guided filtering, Opt. Eng. 53 (7) (2014) 1024–1032.

[87] L. Bian, J. Suo, F. Chen, Q. Dai, Multiframe denoising of high-speed optical coherence tomography data using interframe and intraframe priors, J. Biomed. Opt. 20 (2015) 36006.

[88] N. Meitav, E.N. Ribak, Improving retinal image resolution with iterative weighted shift-and-add, J. Opt. Soc. Am. A 28 (7) (2011) 1395–1402, https://doi.org/10.1364/JOSAA.28.001395.

[89] G. Molodij, E.N. Ribak, M. Glanc, G. Chenegros, Enhancing retinal images by extracting structural information, Opt. Commun. 313 (2014) 321–328, https://doi.org/10.1016/j.optcom.2013.10.011.

[90] C. Hernandez-Matas, X. Zabulis, Super resolution for fundoscopy based on 3D image registration, 36th Annual International Conference of the IEEE Engineering in Medicine and Biology Society, 2014, pp. 6332–6338, https://doi.org/10.1109/EMBC.2014.6945077.

[91] A. Can, C.V. Stewart, B. Roysam, H.L. Tanenbaum, A feature-based technique for joint, linear estimation of high-order image-to-mosaic transformations: mosaicing the curved human retina, IEEE Trans. Pattern Anal. Mach. Intell. 24 (3) (2002) 412–419, https://doi.org/10.1109/34.990145.

[92] N. Ryan, C. Heneghan, P. de Chazal, Registration of digital retinal images using landmark correspondence by expectation maximization, Image Vis. Comput. 22 (11) (2004) 883–898, https://doi.org/10.1016/j.imavis.2004.04.004.

[93] P.C. Cattin, H. Bay, L. Van Gool, G. Székely, Retina mosaicing using local features, Medical Image Computing and Computer-Assisted Intervention—MICCAI 2006: 9th International Conference, Copenhagen, Denmark, October 1–6, 2006. Proceedings, Part II, Springer, Berlin, Heidelberg, 2006, pp. 185–192.

[94] K.M. Adal, P.G. van Etten, J.P. Martinez, L.J. van Vliet, K.A. Vermeer, Accuracy assessment of intra- and intervisit fundus image registration for diabetic retinopathy screening. Invest. Ophthalmol. Vis. Sci. 56 (3) (2015) 1805–1812, https://doi.org/10.1167/iovs.14-15949.

[95] RODREP: Rotterdam ophthalmic data repository longitudinal diabetic retinopathy screening data, Available from: http://www.rodrep.com/longitudinal-diabetic-retinopathy-screening--description.html (Accessed 25 May 2017).

[96] C. Hernandez-Matas, Retinal Image Registration Through 3D Eye Modelling and Pose Estimation (Ph.D. thesis), University of Crete, 2017.

[97] H. Narasimha-Iyer, A. Can, B. Roysam, H.L. Tanenbaum, A. Majerovics, Integrated analysis of vascular and nonvascular changes from color retinal fundus image sequences, IEEE Trans. Biomed. Eng. 54 (8) (2007) 1436–1445, https://doi.org/10.1109/TBME.2007.900807.

[98] G. Troglio, J.A. Benediktsson, G. Moser, S.B. Serpico, E. Stefansson, Unsupervised change detection in multitemporal images of the human retina, Multi Modality State-of-the-Art Medical Image Segmentation and Registration Methodologies, vol. 1, Springer US, Boston, MA, 2011, pp. 309–337.

[99] C. Hernandez-Matas, X. Zabulis, A. Triantafyllou, P. Anyfanti, S. Douma, A.A. Argyros, FIRE: fundus image registration dataset, J. Model. Ophthalmol. 1 (4) (2017) 16–28.

[100] FIRE: fundus image registration dataset, Available from: http://www.ics.forth.gr/cvrl/fire (Accessed 18 May 2019).

[101] P.S. Reel, L.S. Dooley, K.C.P. Wong, A. Börner, Robust retinal image registration using expectation maximisation with mutual information, IEEE International Conference on Acoustics, Speech and Signal Processing, 2013, pp. 1118–1122, https://doi.org/10.1109/ICASSP.2013.6637824.

[102] P.A. Legg, P.L. Rosin, D. Marshall, J.E. Morgan, Improving accuracy and efficiency of mutual information for multi-modal retinal image registration using adaptive probability density estimation, Comput. Med. Imaging Graph. 37 (7–8) (2013) 597–606, https://doi.org/10.1016/j.compmedimag.2013.08.004.

[103] E. Peli, R.A. Augliere, G.T. Timberlake, Feature-based registration of retinal images, IEEE Trans. Med. Imaging 6 (3) (1987) 272–278, https://doi.org/10.1109/TMI.1987.4307837.

[104] K.M. Adal, R.M. Ensing, R. Couvert, P. van Etten, J.P. Martinez, K.A. Vermeer, L.J. van Vliet, A hierarchical coarse-to-fine approach for fundus image registration, Biomedical Image Registration. WBIR 2014. Lecture Notes in Computer Science, 8545, 2014, pp. 93–102.

[105] J. Noack, D. Sutton, An algorithm for the fast registration of image sequences obtained with a scanning laser ophthalmoscope, Phys. Med. Biol. 39 (5) (1994) 907.

[106] A. Wade, F. Fitzke, A fast, robust pattern recognition system for low light level image registration and its application to retinal imaging, Opt. Express 3 (5) (1998) 190–197.

[107] A.V. Cideciyan, S.G. Jacobson, C.M. Kemp, R.W. Knighton, J.H. Nagel, Registration of high resolution images of the retina, SPIE Med. Imaging 1652 (1992) 310–322, https://doi.org/10.1117/12.59439.

[108] Z. Li, F. Huang, J. Zhang, B. Dashtbozorg, S. Abbasi-Sureshjani, Y. Sun, X. Long, Q. Yu, B. ter Haar Romeny, T. Tan, Multi-modal and multi-vendor retina image registration, Biomed. Opt. Express 9 (2) (2018) 410–422.

[109] Y. Lin, G. Medioni, Retinal image registration from 2D to 3D, IEEE Conference on Computer Vision and Pattern Recognition, 2008, pp. 1–8, https://doi.org/10.1109/CVPR.2008.4587705.

[110] J. Zheng, J. Tian, K. Deng, X. Dai, X. Zhang, M. Xu, Salient feature region: a new method for retinal image registration, IEEE Trans. Inf. Technol. Biomed. 15 (2) (2011) 221–232, https://doi.org/10.1109/TITB.2010.2091145.

[111] S.K. Saha, D. Xiao, S. Frost, Y. Kanagasingam, A two-step approach for longitudinal registration of retinal images, J. Med. Syst. 40 (12) (2016) 277, https://doi.org/10.1007/s10916-016-0640-0.

[112] G.K. Matsopoulos, N.A. Mouravliansky, K.K. Delibasis, K.S. Nikita, Automatic retinal image registration scheme using global optimization techniques, IEEE Trans. Inf. Technol. Biomed. 3 (1) (1999) 47–60, https://doi.org/10.1109/4233.748975.

[113] F. Laliberte, L. Gagnon, Y. Sheng, Registration and fusion of retinal images—an evaluation study, IEEE Trans. Med. Imaging 22 (5) (2003) 661–673, https://doi.org/10.1109/TMI.2003.812263.

[114] C.V. Stewart, C.-L. Tsai, B. Roysam, The dual-bootstrap iterative closest point algorithm with application to retinal image registration, IEEE Trans. Med. Imaging 22 (11) (2003) 1379–1394, https://doi.org/10.1109/TMI.2003.819276.

[115] G.K. Matsopoulos, P.A. Asvestas, N.A. Mouravliansky, K.K. Delibasis, Multimodal registration of retinal images using self organizing maps, IEEE Trans. Med. Imaging 23 (12) (2004) 1557–1563, https://doi.org/10.1109/TMI.2004.836547.

[116] T.E. Choe, G. Medioni, I. Cohen, A.C. Walsh, S.R. Sadda, 2-D registration and 3-D shape inference of the retinal fundus from fluorescein images. Med. Image Anal. 12 (2) (2008) 174–190, https://doi.org/10.1016/j.media.2007.10.002.

[117] G. Yang, C.V. Stewart, M. Sofka, C.L. Tsai, Registration of challenging image pairs: initialization, estimation, and decision, IEEE Trans. Pattern Anal. Mach. Intell. 29 (11) (2007) 1973–1989, https://doi.org/10.1109/TPAMI.2007.1116.

[118] A.R. Chaudhry, J.C. Klein, Ophthalmologic image registration based on shape-context: application to Fundus Autofluorescence (FAF) images, Visualization, Imaging, and Image Processing (VIIP), September, Palma de Mallorca, Spain. Medical Imaging, track 630-055, 2008.

[119] C.L. Tsai, C.Y. Li, G. Yang, K.S. Lin, The edge-driven dual-bootstrap iterative closest point algorithm for registration of multimodal fluorescein angiogram sequence, IEEE Trans. Med. Imaging 29 (3) (2010) 636–649, https://doi.org/10.1109/TMI.2009.2030324.

[120] J. Chen, J. Tian, N. Lee, J. Zheng, R.T. Smith, A.F. Laine, A partial intensity invariant feature descriptor for multimodal retinal image registration, IEEE Trans. Biomed. Eng. 57 (7) (2010) 1707–1718, https://doi.org/10.1109/TBME.2010.2042169.

[121] K. Deng, J. Tian, J. Zheng, X. Zhang, X. Dai, M. Xu, Retinal fundus image registration via vascular structure graph matching, J. Biomed. Imaging 2010 (2010) 14:1–14:13, https://doi.org/10.1155/2010/906067.

[122] A. Perez-Rovira, R. Cabido, E. Trucco, S.J. McKenna, J.P. Hubschman, RERBEE: robust efficient registration via bifurcations and elongated elements applied to retinal fluorescein angiogram sequences, IEEE Trans. Med. Imaging 31 (1) (2012) 140–150, https://doi.org/10.1109/TMI.2011.2167517.

[123] S. Gharabaghi, S. Daneshvar, M.H. Sedaaghi, Retinal image registration using geometrical features, J. Dig. Imaging 26 (2) (2013) 248–258, https://doi.org/10.1007/s10278-012-9501-7.

[124] L. Chen, X. Huang, J. Tian, Retinal image registration using topological vascular tree segmentation and bifurcation structures, Biomed. Signal Process. Control 16 (2015) 22–31, https://doi.org/10.1016/j.bspc.2014.10.009.

[125] J.A. Lee, J. Cheng, B.H. Lee, E.P. Ong, G. Xu, D.W.K. Wong, J. Liu, A. Laude, T.H. Lim, A low-dimensional step pattern analysis algorithm with application to multimodal retinal image registration, IEEE Conference on Computer Vision and Pattern Recognition (CVPR), 2015, pp. 1046–1053, https://doi.org/10.1109/CVPR.2015.7298707.

[126] G. Wang, Z. Wang, Y. Chen, W. Zhao, Robust point matching method for multimodal retinal image registration, Biomed. Signal Process. Control 19 (2015) 68–76, https://doi.org/10.1016/j.bspc.2015.03.004.

[127] Z. Ghassabi, J. Shanbehzadeh, A. Mohammadzadeh, A structure-based region detector for high-resolution retinal fundus image registration, Biomed. Signal Process. Control 23 (2016) 52–61, https://doi.org/10.1016/j.bspc.2015.08.005.

[128] C. Hernandez-Matas, X. Zabulis, A.A. Argyros, Retinal image registration based on keypoint correspondences, spherical eye modeling and camera pose estimation, 37th Annual International Conference of the IEEE Engineering in Medicine and Biology Society (EMBC), 2015, pp. 5650–5654, https://doi.org/10.1109/EMBC.2015.7319674.

[129] C. Hernandez-Matas, X. Zabulis, A. Triantafyllou, P. Anyfanti, A.A. Argyros, Retinal image registration under the assumption of a spherical eye, Comput. Med. Imaging Graph. 55 (2017) 95–105, https://doi.org/10.1016/j.compmedimag.2016.06.006.

[130] C. Hernandez-Matas, X. Zabulis, A.A. Argyros, Retinal image registration through simultaneous camera pose and eye shape estimation, 38th Annual International Conference of the IEEE Engineering in Medicine and Biology Society (EMBC), 2016, pp. 3247–3251, https://doi.org/10.1109/EMBC.2016.7591421.

[131] C. Liu, J. Ma, Y. Ma, J. Huang, Retinal image registration via feature-guided Gaussian mixture model, J. Opt. Soc. Am. A 33 (7) (2016) 1267–1276, https://doi.org/10.1364/JOSAA.33.001267.

[132] D.G. Lowe, Distinctive image features from scale-invariant keypoints, Int. J. Comput. Vis. 60 (2) (2004) 91–110, https://doi.org/10.1023/B:VISI.0000029664.99615.94.

[133] H. Bay, A. Ess, T. Tuytelaars, L.V. Gool, Speeded-up robust features (SURF), Comput. Vis. Image Underst. 110 (3) (2008) 346–359, https://doi.org/10.1016/j.cviu.2007.09.014.

[134] C. Hernandez-Matas, X. Zabulis, A.A. Argyros, An experimental evaluation of the accuracy of keypoints-based retinal image registration, 39th Annual International Conference of the IEEE Engineering in Medicine and Biology Society (EMBC), 2017, pp. 377–381.

[135] D. Alonso-Caneiro, S. Read, M. Collins, Speckle reduction in optical coherence tomography imaging by affine-motion image registration, J. Biomed. Opt. 16 (11) (2011) 116027.

[136] A. Baghaie, R. D'Souza, Z. Yu, Sparse and low rank decomposition based batch image alignment for speckle reduction of retinal OCT images, International Symposium on Biomedical Imaging, 2015, pp. 226–230.

[137] M. Pircher, B. Baumann, E. Götzinger, H. Sattmann, C. Hitzenberger, Simultaneous SLO/OCT imaging of the human retina with axial eye motion correction, Opt. Express 15 (25) (2007) 16922–16932.

[138] S. Ricco, M. Chen, H. Ishikawa, G. Wollstein, J. Schuman, Correcting motion artifacts in retinal spectral domain optical coherence tomography via image registration, Med. Image Comput. Comput. Assist. Interv. 12 (1) (2009) 100–107.

[139] J. Xu, H. Ishikawa, G. Wollstein, L. Kagemann, J. Schuman, Alignment of 3-D optical coherence tomography scans to correct eye movement using a particle filtering, IEEE Trans. Med. Imaging 31 (2012) 1337–1345.

[140] M. Kraus, J. Liu, J. Schottenhamml, C. Chen, A. Budai, L. Branchini, T. Ko, H. Ishikawa, G. Wollstein, J. Schuman, J. Duker, J. Fujimoto, J. Hornegger, Quantitative 3D-OCT motion correction with tilt and illumination correction, robust similarity measure and regularization, Biomed. Opt. Express 5 (8) (2014) 2591–2613.

[141] M. Röhlig, C. Schmidt, R.K. Prakasam, P. Rosenthal, H. Schumann, O. Stachs, Visual analysis of retinal changes with optical coherence tomography, Vis. Comput. 34 (9) (2018) 1209–1224, https://doi.org/10.1007/s00371-018-1486-x.

[142] Y. Li, G. Gregori, R. Knighton, B. Lujan, P. Rosenfeld, Registration of OCT fundus images with color fundus photographs based on blood vessel ridges, Opt. Express 19 (1) (2011) 7–16.

[143] H. Hendargo, R. Estrada, S. Chiu, C. Tomasi, S. Farsiu, J. Izatt, Automated non-rigid registration and mosaicing for robust imaging of distinct retinal capillary beds using speckle variance optical coherence tomography, Biomed. Opt. Express 4 (6) (2013) 803–821.

[144] K. Lurie, R. Angst, A. Ellerbee, Automated mosaicing of feature-poor optical coherence tomography volumes with an integrated white light imaging system, IEEE Trans. Biomed. Eng. 61 (7) (2014) 2141–2153.

[145] M. Niemeijer, M.K. Garvin, K. Lee, B. van Ginneken, M.D. Abràmoff, M. Sonka, Registration of 3D spectral OCT volumes using 3D SIFT feature point matching, Proc. SPIE, 7259, 2009, https://doi.org/10.1117/12.811906.

[146] M. Niemeijer, K. Lee, M.K. Garvin, M.D. Abràmoff, M. Sonka, Registration of 3D spectral OCT volumes combining ICP with a graph-based approach, Proc. SPIE, 8314, 2012, https://doi.org/10.1117/12.911104.

[147] M.S. Miri, M.D. Abramoff, K. Lee, M. Niemeijer, J. Wang, Y.H. Kwon, M.K. Garvin, Multimodal segmentation of optic disc and cup from SD-OCT and color fundus photographs using a machine-learning graph-based approach, IEEE Trans. Med. Imaging 34 (9) (2015) 1854–1866, https://doi.org/10.1109/TMI.2015.2412881.

[148] R. Kolar, P. Tasevsky, Registration of 3D retinal optical coherence tomography data and 2D fundus images, Biomedical Image Registration, 2010, pp. 72–82.

[149] M. Golabbakhsh, H. Rabbani, Vessel-based registration of fundus and optical coherence tomography projection images of retina using a quadratic registration model, IET Image Process. 7 (8) (2013) 768–776.

[150] M.S. Miri, M.D. Abràmoff, Y.H. Kwon, M.K. Garvin, Multimodal registration of SD-OCT volumes and fundus photographs using histograms of oriented gradients, Biomed. Opt. Express 7 (12) (2016) 5252–5267, https://doi.org/10.1364/BOE.7.005252.

Automatic landmark detection in fundus photography

5

Jeffrey Wigdahl[a], Pedro Guimarães[b], Alfredo Ruggeri[c]

[a]VisonQuest Biomedical LLC, Albuquerque, NM, United States,
[b]Chair for Clinical Bioinformatics, Saarland University, Saarbrücken, Germany,
[c]Department of Information Engineering, University of Padua, Padua, Italy

1 Background

This section provides background anatomical information for the retinal landmarks of interest, the optic disc and the macula lutea (including the fovea centralis). Researchers have been using this information to help them extract the pertinent features that become the basis for their automatic detection algorithms. It is recognized that the main vessel arcades also serve as retinal landmarks, but the amount of information and developed techniques for vessel segmentation require a separate chapter to properly cover.

1.1 Optic disc

The optic nerve head (optic disc (OD)) is the most distinguishing feature of the retina. It does not have the same layers as the rest of the retina, containing only the nerve fiber layer and the internal limiting membrane. This accounts for the pale, yellowish appearance (Fig. 1), as there is no retinal pigment epithelial layer with the dark melanin to absorb light. There are no photoreceptors in this region which makes it our natural blind spot. This is also the region where all of the ganglion cell axons converge and exit the eye through the optic nerve to the brain. The OD also contains the optic cup, which presents in fundus photography as a bright central region, and whose inner and outer layers become the retinal neural and pigmented layers respectively.

The average optic disc is an oval with a major axis of approximately 1.8 mm and minor axis of 1.5 mm [1]. It shares a geometric relation with the fovea, generally being located 3–4 mm to its nasal side and 3° above. The optic disc is also the entry point for the main retinal vessels, the central retinal artery and vein. The vessel arcades leave vertically from the optic disc before curving into a parabolic shape around the macula.

Computational Retinal Image Analysis. https://doi.org/10.1016/B978-0-08-102816-2.00005-8

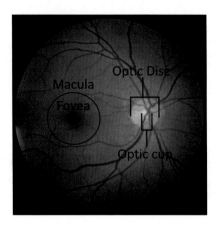

FIG. 1

Typical retinal image taken using a Canon CR2. Overlays highlight the optic disc, optic cup, macula and fovea regions.

1.2 Macula lutea

The macula or macula lutea is located near the center of the retina of the human eye. It appears as a darkened oval region with a yellow tint. The tonality of the macula derives from lutein and zeaxanthin, two xanthophyll pigments present throughout the entire retina but with higher concentration in this region. These pigments are gradually accumulated from the diet, and are nearly non-existent at birth. The macula's color acts as a filter, reducing UV radiation damage and chromatic aberration.

The macula is approximately 5.5 mm in diameter and is subdivided into perifovea, parafovea, fovea, and foveola [2]. These areas are not easily differentiated. The parafovea and perifovea are the inner and outer surrounding peripheric areas to the fovea, respectively. The fovea is the shallow pit depression in the center of the macula about 1.5 mm in diameter. Within it, retinal layers are displaced, which leaves only photoreceptors at its center, the foveola. These center regions also lack blood vessels. With no other cells and no blood vessels, light passes unobstructed to the photoreceptors. Within the fovea the highest concentration of cones can be found, and at its center no rods exist. Thus, the fovea and foveola play a major part in vision enabling color and detail discrimination.

Curiously, clinical and anatomical definitions of macula and fovea differ considerably. Macula is typically a clinical term that describes the darker coloration seen in fundus photography at the anatomical fovea. The clinical fovea is then the center of this area, and what anatomically is described as the foveola.

2 Fovea and disc detection/segmentation—Utility

The following section lists the different use cases for detecting the OD as part of a pipeline of image understanding and/or disease detection.

- **OD detection to aid in the detection of other landmarks**—As previously mentioned, the OD and fovea share a geometric relationship that can be utilized to limit the fovea search area once the OD has been found. The OD is also the entrance point of the main retinal vessels onto the retina. Starting a search around the found OD can help to initialize the detection of these vessels [3].

- **OD detection/segmentation for disease detection**—To determine a glaucoma suspect from fundus photography, features in and around the OD are used as biomarkers. These include disc elongation, vascular nasal shift, cup-to-disc ratio, disc damage likelihood scale and damage to the neuro-retinal rim [4]. In diabetic retinopathy (DR), neovascularization at the disc is important sign of proliferation of the disease [5]. Also, analysis of the OD boundary can aid in the detection of OD swelling in papilledema [6].

- **OD and Fovea detection/segmentation to delineate areas of interest**— One OD diameter is a commonly used measurement to determines areas of interest for finding disease or making measurements. In DR, hard exudates within one disc diameter of the fovea center are used as markers for clinically significant macular edema [7]. In hypertensive retinopathy, arteriovenous ratio measurements are usually taken between one to two disc radii from the boundary of the OD [8].

- **OD detection for preprocessing**—Masking the OD out of the image can be helpful to future processing steps as it removes a bright region with sharp contrast that could be falsely detected as part of the vasculature or as pathology. The OD region may also be completely saturated which can affect other processing steps, such as image normalization or background correction.

3 Retinal imaging databases

Over the years, multiple databases have been put together and made available to researchers to enable them to test their developed algorithms. These databases also allow different methods to be tested against one another to objectively measure performance. Each database has a different focus that is not necessarily landmark detection, but generally provide OD location ground truth and real-world images with different amounts of disease and levels of image quality. The databases listed below are those that are generally accepted and tested against in the literature:

DRIVE: Digital Retinal Images for Vessel Extraction—Although the DRIVE dataset (2004) was created to compare vessel segmentation algorithms, it has been used to benchmark OD detection algorithms for a long time and is included for this reason. The dataset consists 40 images with little or no DR. Images were acquired on a Canon CR5 non-mydriatic camera at 45° field of view and 768×584 pixel resolution [9]. https://www.isi.uu.nl/Research/Databases/DRIVE/

Messidor—The Messidor database (2008) was made publicly available in 2008 and consists of 1200 retinal images (800 with dilation, 400 without). All images were captured using a Topcon TRC NW6 non-mydriatic camera at 45° field of view at pixel resolutions of 1440×960, 2240×1488 or 2304×1536 [10]. http://www.adcis.net/en/Download-Third-Party/Messidor.html

STARE: Structured Analysis of the Retina—The STARE database (2000) consists of ~400 images taken on a TopCon TRV-50 at 35° field of view. The film was digitized at 605×700 pixels per color plane. The database contains ground truth marking for the optic disc center if present and boasts a wide variety of disease and image quality levels to contend with [11]. http://cecas.clemson.edu/~ahoover/stare/

Other databases in use include the DRIONS-DB: Digital Retinal Images for Optic Nerve Segmentation Database which contains 110 images and multiple ground truth segmentations of the optic nerve head (http://www.ia.uned.es/~ejcarmona/DRIONS-DB.html) [12]. The DIARETDB0 and DIARETDB1 contain 130 and 89 images respectively and contain mostly images with at least mild DR (http://www.it.lut.fi/project/imageret/diaretdb0/) [13, 14]. The e-ophtha database contains 463 images with DR lesions and ground truth segmentations for each lesion (http://www.adcis.net/en/Download-Third-Party/E-Ophtha.html) [15]. The Kaggle DR database was made available for a DR labeling competition in 2015. The large dataset from EyePACs contains images from multiple cameras at multiple pixel resolutions. Over 80,000 retinal images with DR grades were made available to train and validate deep learning models [16] (https://www.kaggle.com/c/diabetic-retinopathy-detection/data).

4 Algorithm accuracy

In order to test an algorithm's accuracy, there must be some level of ground truth available for the image. For OD and fovea detection, an ophthalmologist or experienced image grader generally marks the center point pixels for both. These values are recorded and used to compare against. In this case, results for an algorithm may be stated as the distance from the ground truth pixel. Average and standard deviations can then be measured for a dataset. For binary accuracy, an acceptable distance from the ground truth pixel is used as a threshold. Usually 1 disc radius is used as an acceptable value. In other cases, the boundary of the OD may be delineated or an OD mask will be available. If the detected OD is within the ground truth boundary, it is considered correctly found.

When researchers compare their algorithm against others, they usually do so by including results on one or more of the open datasets. Processing time is also considered along with the detection accuracy. There has generally been a tradeoff between these two factors, but more recent methods have shown that both can be achieved [17]. Also, older methods that self-report running time would be sped up by the processing power of today's computers.

5 Optic disc and fovea detection

There have been many algorithms developed over the last 30 years for automatically detecting the optic disc and fovea in retinal fundus photography. The reasons for doing so have been stated above and this is generally a first image processing step in a pipeline of algorithms, whether they be for automatic or semiautomatic systems. In semiautomatic systems, where a human can intervene after certain processing steps and make changes, the consequences of incorrectly identifying the OD and fovea are minor. It would simply take a little extra time for the user to make the correction and continue. In automatic systems, the wrongly detected OD or fovea can affect the accuracy of future algorithms, possibly impacting disease diagnosis.

Algorithms for the detection of the optic disc vary widely, but the approaches can generally be narrowed into subsets based on the type of information they use to make their OD prediction. These subsets include (1) detecting the OD as the brightest region in the image, (2) Detecting the OD as the convergence of the retinal vasculature, (3) Detecting the OD through template matching and (4) Detecting the OD through supervised methods. The next section will give examples of methods developed using information from these subsets and show the ways researchers have combined this information to make robust algorithms that can detect the OD in the presence of disease, low image quality or even when the OD is not present in the image. The methods highlighted in this chapter were chosen to cover a large period of time (20 years) and show how popular early methods were built upon to address inherent shortcomings. To find in-depth literature reviews on this topic, please see [18, 19]. There are fewer methods available for fovea detection. A priori knowledge, such as eye side and field of view, can constrain the problem and make detection much easier. When available in the following OD methods, fovea detection is also highlighted.

5.1 Automated localization of the optic disc, fovea, and retinal blood vessels from digital color fundus images (Sinthanayothin et al., 1999 [20])

This method was chosen as the starting point for this review because it is one of the earliest papers in this area and is subsequently very highly cited. The authors developed methods to detect all the retinal landmarks and shows how fairly simple methods were able to detect both the OD and fovea with high accuracy. First, the images were preprocessed to enhance local contrast. The images were converted from the RGB color space to the intensity hue saturation space. This separates the intensity and color information so that the contrast can be adjusted without affecting perceived color. A variance image is then created by calculating the mean variance within 81×81 pixels ROI's within the main image, with the maximum value being the found OD. The reasoning being that the bright OD combined with the dark vessels and OD border will provide the maximum variance within a sub-image roughly

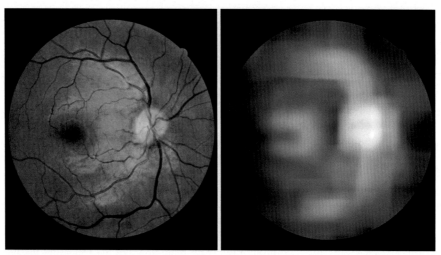

FIG. 2

(Left) Retinal image cropped and resized. (Right) Variance image used in the voting process to detect the optic disc. Mean variance calculated in 81×81 neighborhood, roughly the size of the optic disc in the image.

the size of the OD. A variance image is shown in Fig. 2, with the maximum being in and around the OD.

Skipping ahead, the method for detecting the fovea is based on template matching and distance from the OD. The assumption is that the fovea is the darkest region of the image and can be modeled by a Gaussian function:

$$g(x,y) = 128 \left[1 - \frac{1}{2} \exp \frac{-\left(x^2 + y^2\right)}{2\sigma^2} \right] \tag{1}$$

The template used in this paper was 40×40 pixels with a standard deviation of 22 pixels. This template was correlated throughout the retinal image, and the pixel with the maximum correlation value becomes the fovea candidate. For this candidate to be accepted, the correlation coefficient had to be greater than 0.5 and be the proper distance 2.5 disc-diameters) away from the found center of the OD.

This paper predates the standard databases used to benchmark retinal landmark algorithms. They used a set of 112 images from a Topcon TRC-NW5S, 570×550 pixels at a 40° field of view. The OD detection algorithm was able to detect the OD correctly in all but one image. The fovea detection algorithm not only had to detect the correct position, but also determine if the fovea was present in the image. For these tasks, the algorithm had a sensitivity and specificity of 80.4% and 99.1%.

5.2 Locating the optic nerve in a retinal image using the fuzzy convergence of the blood vessels (Hoover and Goldbaum, 2003 [11])

Another highly cited paper, this method was chosen because of its focus on diseased retinas. Detecting the OD in a normal retina is often a straight forward task where the simplest methods can achieve very high accuracy. This method performs well on diseased retinas with sacrificing performance on normals. As the convergent point of all the retinal vasculature, this method finds the OD as the densest area of vessel endpoints based on fuzzy line geometry. The first step in this method is to perform an arbitrary vessel segmentation. This segmentation is then skeletonized so that each vessel is one pixel thick. Next, all branch and bifurcation pixels are removed from the skeleton. This leaves vessel segments, each with its own unique start and end point. From this point, the fuzzy segment model is employed on each vessel segment. A fuzzy segment **F**, is defined as the family of line segments:

$$x(t) = x_1 + r\cos(\alpha + \theta) + (x_2 - x_1 - 2r\cos\theta\cos\alpha)t \qquad (2)$$

$$y(t) = y + r\sin(\alpha + \theta) + (y_2 - y_1 - 2r\cos\theta\sin\alpha)t$$

Where (x_1, y_1) and (x_2, y_2) denote the start and end points of the line respectively and r represents a radius around the endpoints for which the line is rotated and α is the starting orientation of the line. As the line is rotated around the endpoints, all pixels that contact this path become part of the set that defines **F**. The fuzzy segment ends up being thicker on the ends compared to the central region of the segment. The key is to determine a suitable radius, which essentially adds to the length of the segment and discretization's of θ and t to properly cover the pixels of interest for each segment. Each "on" pixel in the fuzzy segment casts a single vote. Once this has been done for each segment in the image, the votes are tallied, the vote map is blurred and a region of interest is determined through a set of rules based on pixel intensities and region sizes. Key steps to the process are seen in Fig. 3, showing the original image, vessel segmentation and vote-tallied image.

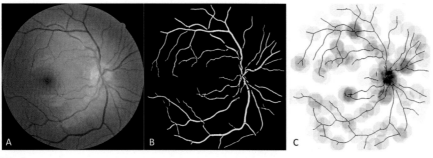

FIG. 3

(A) Cropped fundus image. (B) Vessel segmentation before thinning and removal of branch points. (C) Vote-tallied image with vessel skeleton overlaid.

The best results for this method occur when the fuzzy model is calculated on the illumination corrected image using a multiscale approach to vessel segmentation (vessel segmentations that target different widths of vessels in the image). The method is run on six different scales of vessel segmentations. If there is no consensus on the vessel voting, the largest bright region from a predetermined number of pixels in the illumination corrected image is used as the found OD. The method was tested on the STARE database (81 images) and achieved 89% accuracy (100% accuracy on the 31 healthy retinas).

5.3 Detection of optic disc in retinal images by means of a geometrical model of vessel structure (Foracchia et al., 2004 [21])

This method is noted both for being state-of-the-art at its time of publication and beyond, but also for its ability to detect the OD even when it was not present in the image. This method is similar to the method developed by Hoover and Goldbaum (2003) by which they both are looking for the convergence of vessels at the OD. This method, however, creates a geometric model that is fit to the directional information of all the blood vessels in the image. This model, which is essentially two parabolic arches, finds the OD center as the convergence of these two parabolas, symbolizing the convergence of the retinal vasculature.

To develop the model, an arbitrary vessel tracking algorithm can be used to provide vessel centerline position and direction. The two parabolas, which come together at the OD and represent the main vessel paths across the retina can be describe by the following locus of points:

$$\Gamma = \left\{ (x,y) : ay^2 = |x| \right\} \tag{3}$$

Where a controls the aperture of the parabola. This only describes the course of the main vessels in the image. To capture the fact that the vessels branch and bifurcate, with vessels inside the parabola bending toward the center of the image and vessels outside the parabola bending toward the periphery. To account for this, the complete model for vessel direction in the image is:

$$\theta^{mod}(x,y,\mathbf{p}) = arctan\left\{ sgn(x)sgn(y)\frac{1}{2\sqrt{a|x|}} + d(x,y,\mathbf{p}) \right\} \tag{4}$$

Where

$$d(x,y,\mathbf{p}) = \frac{y - sgn(y)\sqrt{\frac{|x|}{a}}}{\frac{c_1}{1+e^{-x}} + \frac{c_2}{1+e^{x}}} \tag{5}$$

$\mathbf{p}$ contains the model parameters a and the optic disc center points. In a cartesian coordinate system, the x and y values in these formulas should be shifted by values of

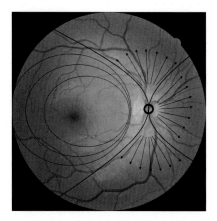

FIG. 4

Model of the general vessel gradient directions shown at intervals across the image.
Best fit parabola is superimposed on the image.

x_{OD} and y_{OD} to accurately represent the meeting of the parabolas as a point on the OD.
To choose model parameters, minimization was done using the weighted residual
sum of squares using simulated annealing optimization procedure. This is performed
multiple times to make sure the minimization does not fall into a local minimum, but
find the global minima as the detected OD. Fig. 4 shows an example of the gradient
information extracted from the vasculature and the best fit parabolic model overlaid
on the image.

    This method was tested on STARE dataset. 81 images full of pathology and
varying levels of image quality. Two different techniques to extract the vascular
information were tested and able to detect the OD in 79 each time (failed images
were different for each method). They also showed on non-STARE images that if
enough vasculature is present, the model is able to localize an OD that is not present
in the image.

5.4 Fast localization and segmentation of the optic disc in retinal images using directional matched filtering and level sets (Yu et al., 2012 [22])

This method was chosen to highlight that algorithm speed and accuracy do not need
to be a trade-off. At publication, this was one of the fastest and most accurate methods on the Messidor database. This method performs a two-step process to detect
the optic disc and fits into three of the previously stated subcategories (OD as the
brightest region, template matching, vessel convergence). The first step is to create a
bright template that mimics the appearance of the OD. The OD is bright and circular
in appearance with darker vessel running vertically through the OD center or pushed
slightly to the nasal side. Using these features, several different templates were created, including a binary bright circle on a black background, the same circle with a

vertical dark bar and different width X patterns running through the middle of the circle. While the dark bar and X patterns make sense in trying to represent the darker vasculature, the bright circle on black background provided the best results through empirical means. This method also adapts the template to the pixel size of the OD based on the field of view (FOV) of the image, pixel footprint and known average values for retinal area and OD size in millimeters. The formulas to calculate the OD size in pixels then become:

$$f_{img} = \frac{A_{FOV}}{N_{FOV}} \tag{6}$$

where the image foot print, f_{img}, is equal to A_{FOV}, a known area that a certain FOV covers, over N_{FOV}, the pixel footprint of the image. For instance, a 45° FOV has an average area of 124.8 mm². The radius of the OD in pixels, r_{OD_img}, then becomes:

$$r_{OD\_img} = \sqrt{\frac{(D_{OD}/2)^2}{f_{img}}} \tag{7}$$

Where D_{OD} is a known average value for the disc diameter, in this case 1.85 mm. Using these formulas, the template can be adjusted based on the pixel footprint and FOV to help ensure accurate template matching.

The actual template matching is performed on an illumination corrected version of the image. To speed up the matching, the template is correlated (using the Pearson correlation coefficient, c_{ij}) to the image on a grid, as opposed to each pixel in the image.

$$c_{ij} = \frac{\sum_{x,y}\left(f(x,y)-f_m\right)\left(t(x-i,y-j)-t_m\right)}{\sqrt{\left(\sum_{x,y}\left(f(x,y)-f_m\right)^2\right)\left(\sum_{x,y}\left(t(x-i,y-j)-t_m\right)^2\right)}} \tag{8}$$

where t_m and f_m are the mean intensities of the template and the sub-image overlapping the template. This speeds up the processing, recognizing that this is the first of a two-step process that will be refined. To avoid being stuck in a local maximum that may or may not be the OD (due to bright lesions or camera artifacts), a small percentage of candidates are chosen for the second step of processing.

Once the candidates have been found, the final OD is localized through vertical matched filtering. The main vessel arcades leave the OD vertically before curving to a parabolic shape around the retina. A Gaussian kernel is used to match the intensity profile across the vessels in the green channel image through convolution.

$$G(x,y) = -ae^{\frac{-x^2}{2\sigma^2}}, for\,|y| \leq \frac{L}{2} \tag{9}$$

The length, L, is the length for which the vessel has fixed orientation. The size of the Gaussian kernel should be fixed to the width of the main retinal vessels. The candidate

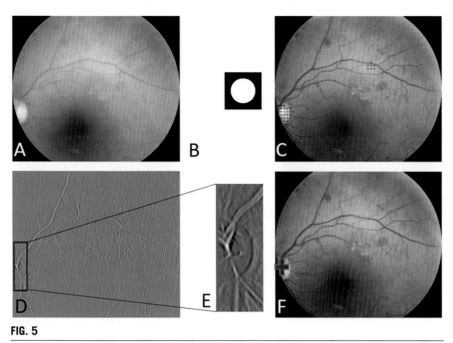

FIG. 5

(A) Example of a gray scale image that is correlated with a (B) bright template that mimics the OD. (C) The found OD candidates are marked as red plus signs. (D) The maximum value of the vertical vessel information is highlighted in (E). The final OD location from the two-step process is marked in (F).

showing the maximum response (maximum standard deviation) in the region of interest is then found as the final OD location.

This method was tested on the Messidor dataset consisting of 1200 image, 400 each at different resolutions. The method was able to find the OD in 99.1% of the images, based on ground truth boundary measurements. A correctly found OD was considered anything inside the OD boundary area. Fig. 5 shows an example of the processing steps involved, including the template matching to first find candidate OD locations and then the analysis of vertical vessel information to determine the final location.

5.5 Multiscale sequential convolutional neural networks for simultaneous detection of the fovea and optic disc (Al-Bander et al., 2018 [23])

The authors of this paper propose to use a deep convolutional neural network (CNN) to detect both the OD and fovea. Over the past few years, deep learning has revolutionized the field of machine learning, where deep networks have outperformed tradition machine learning techniques across a wide range of fields. Traditional machine learning requires a set of handcrafted features that are "learned" with the aid of ground truth (supervised learning), clustered based on intrinsic properties (unsupervised learning), or some area in between. Given enough training examples, deep networks learn their own set of features from internal convolutions with a set of filters, generally performed at different scales and abstractions of the input data. If large amounts of labeled data are available along with sufficient computing power for training, one is likely to see performance gains over traditional methods on the same data.

Deep CNNs are best known for their classification abilities. Given an input image, predict a level of disease such as for diabetic retinopathy. They can also be used for regression tasks. In this case, the training labels are the OD and fovea center points marked by two graders on the Messidor and Kaggle datasets. The first step is to preprocess the data. Remarkably, the only preprocessing done on the images is to convert the image to grayscale, resize to 256×256 and perform contrast limited adaptive histogram equalization [24]. The deep CNN is built from a combination of standard layers:

Convolutional layer—sets of filters convolved with the input to produce feature maps.
Pooling layer—form of subsampling of the convolutional layers. In this case max-pooling is used, where a window slides over a feature map and the max value in that window is selected.
Dropout layer—with a certain probability, drops the output (ignores) of certain hidden units to prevent overfitting in the training phase.
Fully connected layer—each node in this layer is connected to every node in the previous layer. This is usually the final layer of a deep CNN.

All layers except the output layer use a Rectified Linear Unit [25] as an activation function, define as:

$$\varphi : x \rightarrow \max(0,x) \qquad (10)$$

So that the output of any particular node is 0 if the output is less than 0 and x otherwise. The output layer uses a linear function to combine the output layer activations. The layers used in this architecture can be visualized in Fig. 6. There are two steps to detection the fovea and OD. The first step runs the preprocessed image through the network and the found areas become areas of interest. These areas of interest are then run through other networks to fine tune the found locations (Fig. 6).

10,000 images from the Kaggle dataset were used for training and testing (7000 for training and validation, 3000 for testing) and 1200 images from the Messidor dataset were also used for testing. Results were presented as percent of images with OD and fovea found within 1 disc radius, 0.5 disc radii and 0.25 disc radii. Results using the 1 disc radius criteria were 97/96.6% for OD and fovea respectively in the Messidor dataset and 96.7/95.6% in the Kaggle dataset. Further, with all the overhead timewise in the training of the model, this method is able to run almost instantaneously (0.007 s).

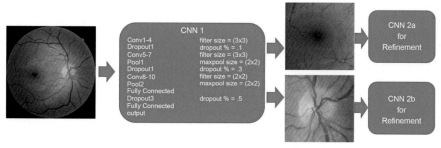

FIG. 6

Visualization of the deep architecture used in this method. There are 10 convolution layers, 3 dropout, 2 pooling and 2 fully connected layers. The input image is run through the network to first produce areas of interest. These areas of interest are run through another network to refine the results.

The OD location accuracy for this algorithm, at least for the Messidor dataset, would not be considered among the best performing, as one might expect. Deep Learning methods have consistently outperformed traditional methods on an array of medical imaging tasks. It is not to say that deep learning methods do not perform as well for this task. There may be small tweaks to the preprocessing or the network that would boost the performance 1–2% to match the best performing algorithms. Traditional image processing and machine learning techniques also do well when problems are constrained as in the OD and fovea detection problem. Traditional methods boast accuracies upward of 99%, leaving little room for improvement. The great advantage of this method is the simultaneous detection of both landmarks in less than a 100th of a second, making it useful in real-time applications.

Summary

The methods highlighted in this chapter are just a fraction of those developed and are meant to show the diverse approaches and advancements over time. These efforts have also led to an abundance of freely available retinal imaging datasets and ground truth to help train and test future algorithm development. It is important to remember that landmark detection is a first processing step and should be done quickly and accurately to ensure future processing steps do not suffer from past mistakes. In an ideal dataset, devoid of image quality issues or disease, OD and fovea detection are trivial tasks. One could simply find the brightest and darkest regions in the image and be right more than 90% of the time. It is the difficult cases, where accurate detection can mean catching and quantifying sight-threatening disease, that have spurred the continued interest in this field as shown by the 20 years time gap between highlighted methods. The future will likely see more deep learning methods trained on even larger datasets that push the limits of accuracy in this field.

References

[1] H. Quigley, A. Brown, J. Morrison, S. Drance, The size and shape of the optic disc in normal human eyes, Arch. Ophthalmol. 108 (1) (1990) 51–57.

[2] M. Yanoff, J. Sassani, Ocular Pathology, Mosby/Elsevier, Edinburgh, 2009.

[3] Y. Tolias, S.M. Panas, A fuzzy vessel tracking algorithm for retinal images based on fuzzy clustering, IEEE Trans. Med. Imaging 17 (1998) 263–273. ieeexplore.ieee.org.

[4] G. Joshi, J. Sivaswamy, S.R. Krishnadas, Optic disk and cup segmentation from monocular color retinal images for glaucoma assessment, IEEE Trans. Med. Imaging 30 (2011) 1192–1205. ieeexplore.ieee.org.

[5] K. Goatman, A. Fleming, S. Philip, G.J. Williams, J.A. Olson, P.F. Sharp, Detection of new vessels on the optic disc using retinal photographs, IEEE Trans. Med. Imaging 30 (2011) 972–979. ieeexplore.ieee.org.

[6] S. Echegaray, G. Zamora, H. Yu, W. Luo, P. Soliz, R. Kardon, Automated analysis of optic nerve images for detection and staging of papilledema, Investig. Ophthalmol. Vis. Sci. 52 (10) (2011) 7470–7478.

[7] H.F. Jelinek, M.J. Cree (Eds.), Automated Detection of Retinal Pathology, CRC Press, Boca Raton, FL, 2009.

[8] L. Hubbard, R. Brothers, W. King, L. Clegg, R. Klein, Methods for evaluation of retinal microvascular abnormalities associated with hypertension/sclerosis in the Atherosclerosis Risk in Communities Study, Ophthalmology (1999) 2269–2280.

[9] J.J. Staal, M.D. Abramoff, M. Niemeijer, M. a Viergever, B. Van Ginneken, Ridge based vessel segmentation in color images of the retina, IEEE Trans. Med. Imaging 23 (4) (2005) 501–509.

[10] E. Decencière, et al., Feedback on a publicly distributed image database: the Messidor database, Image Anal. Stereol. 33 (3) (2014) 231–234.

[11] A. Hoover, M. Goldbaum, Locating the optic nerve in a retinal image using the fuzzy convergence of the blood vessels, IEEE Trans. Med. Imaging 22 (8) (2003) 951–958.

[12] E. Carmona, M. Rincón, J. García-Feijoó, J.M. Martínez-de-la-Casa, Identification of the optic nerve head with genetic algorithms, Artif. Intell. Med. 43 (3) (2008) 243–259. Elsevier.

[13] T. Kauppi, V. Kalesnykiene, J.-K. Kamarainen, et al., DIARETDB0: Evaluation Database and Methodology for Diabetic Retinopathy Algorithms, www.it.lut.fi, 2006.

[14] T. Kauppi, et al., DIARETDB1 diabetic retinopathy database and evaluation protocol, in: Medical Image Understanding and Analysis 2007 University of Wales Aberystwyth, 17–18th July, 2007, p. 61.

[15] E. Decencière, G. Cazuguel, X. Zhang, G. Thibault, et al., TeleOphta: machine learning and image processing methods for teleophthalmology, IRBM 34 (2013) 196–203. Elsevier.

[16] Kaggle n.d. Diabetic Retinopathy Detection Competition.

[17] B. Harangi, A. Hajdu, Detection of the optic disc in fundus images by combining probability models, Comput. Biol. Med. 65 (2015) 10–24. Elsevier.

[18] A.A.H.A.R. Youssif, A.Z. Ghalwash, A.A.S.A.R. Ghoneim, Optic disc detection from normalized digital fundus images by means of a vessels' direction matched filter, IEEE Trans. Med. Imaging 27 (1) (2008) 11–18.

[19] M. Haleem, L. Han, J. van Hemert, B. Li, Automatic extraction of retinal features from colour retinal images for glaucoma diagnosis: a review, Comput. Med. Imaging Graph. 37 (7–8) (2013) 581–596.

[20] C. Sinthanayothin, J.F. Boyce, H.L. Cook, T.H. Williamson, Automated localisation of the optic disc, fovea and retinal blood vessels from digital color fundus images, Br. J. Ophthalmol. 4 (83) (1999) 902–910.

[21] M. Foracchia, E. Grisan, A. Ruggeri, Detection of optic disc in retinal images by means of a geometrical model of vessel structure, IEEE Trans. Med. Imaging 23 (10) (2004) 1189–1195.

[22] H. Yu, et al., Fast localization and segmentation of optic disc in retinal images using directional matched filtering and level sets, IEEE Trans. Inf. Technol. Biomed. 16 (4) (2012) 644–657.

[23] B. Al-Bander, W. Al-Nuaimy, B.M. Williams, Y. Zheng, Multiscale sequential convolutional neural networks for simultaneous detection of fovea and optic disc, Biomed. Signal Process. Control 40 (2018) 91–101. Elsevier.

[24] K. Zuiderveld, Contrast Limited Adaptive Histogram Equalization, Academic Press Professional, Inc, 1994.

[25] V. Nair, G.E. Hinton, Rectified linear units improve restricted boltzmann machines, in: Proceedings of the 27th international conferenceon Machine Learning, 2010. cs.toronto.edu.

CHAPTER

Retinal vascular analysis: Segmentation, tracing, and beyond

6

Li Cheng[a,b], Xingzheng Lyu[c], He Zhao[d], Huazhu Fu[e], Huiqi Li[d]

[a]A*STAR, Bioinformatics Institute, Singapore, Singapore
[b]ECE, University of Alberta, Edmonton, AB, Canada
[c]Zhejiang University, Hangzhou, China
[d]Beijing Institute of Technology, Beijing, China
[e]A*STAR, Institute for Infocomm Research, Singapore, Singapore

1 Introduction

As the proverb goes, the eye is a window to your soul. In fact, the eye is also a window to your health, as many diseases such as eye diseases, diabetes, cardiovascular, and systemic diseases manifest themselves via different structures, especially the blood vessels, in an eye. For example, it is of clinical interest to examine the width of artery or vein vessels, the branching ratio, the vessel length between junction points, etc. As illustrated in, for example, Ref. [1], stemmed from the ophthalmic artery, the arterial inflow to the eye is further branched. In particular, the central retinal artery travels along the optic nerve and spreads out in branches to cover the retina. Being parallel and countercurrent to the central retinal artery, the venous outflow exits the eye through the central retinal vein, again along the optic nerve. Together, the retinal vasculature is responsible for supplying oxygen and nutrients and removing metabolic waste from the retina. Impaired oxygen supply can as well damage the health of the retina.

Readouts from vessel structure or vasculature have been linked to various diseases. Subtle vessel changes may also occur during the early stage of disease cycle. The departure of vasculature geometry from normal state may also underlie the development of other signs such as retinal lesions. For example, it is known that the vasculature geometry including vessel diameter and tortuosity provide predictive information for hypertension, diabetes, Alzheimer disease, and cardiovascular disease [2–8]. It is thus used frequently in reliable and automated procedures in analyzing the vasculature and its associated properties. This chapter will focus on analyzing vessel structure in retinal images. Note that there also exist artery and vein branches that serve the rest part of the eye including cornea and iris, which are not the main theme of this chapter.

Retinal imaging has been around for over a hundred years, with the first instrument being invented in 1851 [9] and the first practical fundus camera developed in 1921 by Gullstrand who was later awarded Nobel Prize for this contribution. Recently, color fundus (CF) photography and optical coherence tomography (OCT) are among the noninvasive and popular clinical choices.

Vasculature analysis in retinal images has, therefore, a longstanding history. Arguably the first research effort was by Matsui et al. [10], 45 years ago, where a mathematical morphology approach is construed toward the problem of vessel segmentation. Overall, there has been relatively sporadic research efforts in the 1970s and 1980s. In particular, the work of Akita and Kuga [11] considers building up a holistic approach for understanding retinal fundus images, including segmenting retinal blood vessels and recognizing individual artery and vein trees, and detecting vessel structural changes such as arteriovenous nicking (AVN). Their efforts were ambitious even by current standards, since each of the tasks is typically pursued by a separate research paper today. The review paper by Gilchrist [12] summarizes these early research activities. Since the 1990s, the research activities in retinal vasculature image analysis start to proliferate, mostly owing to the change of clinical practice in wide-spread adoption of digital retinal imaging. Over the years, it has resulted in an enormous amount of literature on wide-spread-related topics. In this chapter, we strive to provide an up-to-date account, focusing more on the recent progresses and challenges in retinal vessel analysis perspective, especially about the problems of vessel segmentation, tracing, and classification, as, for example, shown in Fig. 1 on CF images. Regarding the related topics, such as retinal image quality assessment, registration and stitching of overlapping retinal images, segmentation of fovea/macular and optic disk (OD), lesion detection and segmentation, and OCT-based segmentation and analysis, they are covered by other chapters of this book. There are also review articles: in Ref. [13], Abramoff and coworkers provide an excellent overview of the history up to 2010, current status, and future perspective in both retinal imaging and image analyses. While the survey of Kirbas and Quek [14] is from the general perspective of segmenting and tracing vessels, the review articles of Fraz et al. [15] and Almotiri et al. [16] focus specifically on retinal vessel segmentation. Miri et al. [17] conduct a comprehensive study of retinal vessel classification. Meanwhile, the reviews by Faust et al. [18] and Mookiah et al. [19] are dedicated to image-based detecting and diagnosing of diabetic retinopathy disease, respectively. The knowledge of retinal scans and vasculature analysis could also be helpful in robot-assisted eye surgery [20,21]. In addition to medical applications, retinal vasculature analysis has also been used for biometrics and authentication purposes, see, for example, Refs. [22,23].

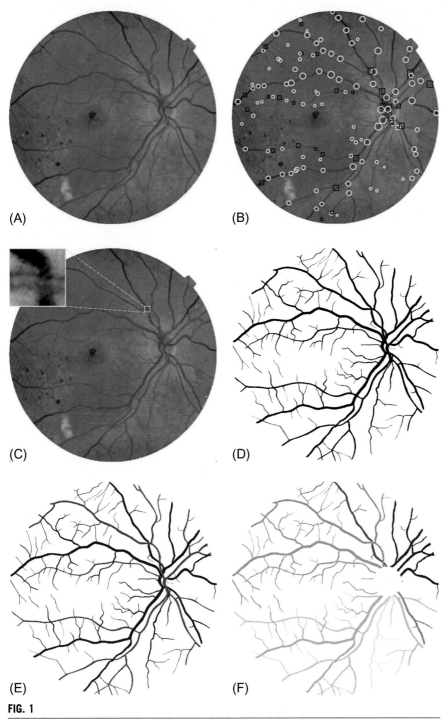

(A)

(B)

(C)

(D)

(E)

(F)

FIG. 1

Typical retinal vascular annotations of a color fundus image. Panel (A) is an original retinal fundus image. Panel (B) marks out the bifurcation and crossing points by *yellow circles* and *blue rectangles*, respectively. Panel (C) highlights the AVN signature in panel (A), with a *zoomed-in inlet* showing an enhanced image patch by subtracting local mean image from the raw image. Panel (D) presents an annotation of blood vessel segmentation, which is classified into artery and vein vessels in panel (E). Panel (F) displays the individual vascular trees, each with a unique color.

2 Benchmark datasets and evaluation metrics

2.1 Datasets

Table 1 provides a summary of 12 representative retinal imaging benchmark datasets. As some URLs of these published datasets are relocated over the years, we strived to identify the current web addresses.

DRIVE[1] [24] and STARE[2] [25] are two popular benchmarks for vessel segmentation. DRIVE contains 40 fundus images of size 768×584, obtained using Canon CR5 nonmydriatic 3CCD camera with field of view (FOV) of 45 degrees. STARE involves 20 fundus images of size 605×700 taken from a TopCon TRV-50 fundus camera at 35-degree FOV. Apart from segmented vessel masks, the artery/vein vessel annotations are further labeled by RITE[3] [26, 27] for DRIVE dataset. Azzopardi and Petkov [28] provided vessel junction annotations, including vascular bifurcations and crossovers.

HRF[4] [29] consists of 45 images, of which one-third are images from healthy patients, one-third are patients with diabetic retinopathy (DR), and the rest are images of glaucomatous patients. Binary gold standard vessel segmentation images, generated by a group of experts, are available for each image. The size of fundus images is 3504×2336.

CHASEDB1[5] [30] includes 28 retinal fundus scans from 14 children. Images were recorded using a Nidek NM-200-D fundus camera with a 30-degree FOV, with a resolution of 999×960 pixels. Two experts' segmentations are available for each images as ground truth.

ARIA[6] [31] consists of 143 images taken from either healthy subjects, diabetics, or patients with age-related macular degeneration (AMD). Obtained with a Zeiss FF450+ fundus camera with a 50-degree FOV. In addition to vessel segmentation, annotations of the OD and fovea are also provided.

The DR HAGIS[7] [32] dataset is composed of 40 fundus images, which were acquired in different screening centers in the United Kingdom for DR screening purpose, using a Topcon TRC-NW6s, a Topcon TRC-NW8, or a Canon CR DGi fundus camera with a horizontal 45-degree FOV. The resulting images are of different sizes, being either 4752×3168, 3456×2304, 3126×2136, 2896×1944, or 2816×1880 pixels. The dataset is divided into four comorbidity subgroups, that is, DR, hypertension, AMD, and glaucoma. Each subgroup comprises 10 images, with the image of only one patient being duplicated into two subgroups. Vessel segmentation annotation is also provided for each image.

---

[1] See http://www.isi.uu.nl/Research/Databases/DRIVE/.
[2] See http://www.ces.clemson.edu/~ahoover/stare/.
[3] See https://medicine.uiowa.edu/eye/rite-dataset.
[4] See https://www5.cs.fau.de/research/data/fundus-images/.
[5] See https://blogs.kingston.ac.uk/retinal/chasedb1/.
[6] See https://eyecharity.weebly.com/aria_online.html.
[7] See https://personalpages.manchester.ac.uk/staff/niall.p.mcloughlin/.

Table 1 A summary of representative retinal image datasets and benchmarks.

Database	IT	No. of images	Vessel masks	Vessel trees[a]	A/V	Junctions	Tortuosity	AVR
DRIVE [24]	CF	40	✓	✓	✓	✓		
STARE [25]	CF	20	✓					
HRF [29]	CF	45	✓					
CHASEDB1 [30]	CF	28	✓					
ARIA [31]	CF	143	✓					
DR HAGIS [32]	CF	40	✓					
VICAVR	CF	58	✓	✓	✓			
INSPIRE-AVR [33]	CF	40		✓	✓			✓
RVTD [34]	CF	60	✓		✓			
IOSTAR [35]	SLO	24		✓	✓			
AV-WIDE [36]	UWFI	30		✓	✓		✓	
VAMPIRE [37]	FA	8	✓					

Notes: For retinal imaging technique (IT), CF refers to color fundus photography, SLO is for scanning laser ophthalmoscopy, FA is for fluorescein angiogram, and UWFI is for ultra-wide fundus imaging. "Vessel masks" denotes vessel segmentation annotation, while "Vessel trees" is for annotation of individual vessel trees, and "A/V" stands for artery and vein vessel annotations. "Junctions" is bifurcation and crossing labeling. "Tortuosity" and "AVR" are two clinical relevant vessel readouts (see Section 4.4 for details).
[a]For DRIVE, IOSTAR, VICAVR, and INSPIRE-AVR, individual vessel trees out of the OD are manually annotated and make available online (http://imed.nimte. ac.cn/vetovessel-topology-groundtruth.html).

The dataset of VICAVR[8] includes 58 images, acquired by a TopCon NW-100 nonmydriatic camera with a resolution of 768 × 584. Annotated vascular patterns include the caliber of the vessels measured at different radii from the optic disc as well as the vessel type (artery/vein) labeled by three experts.

INSPIRE-AVR[9] [33] has 40 images of 2392 × 2048 pixels and corresponding arteriolar-to-venular diameter ratio (AVR) values observed by two ophthalmologists. The artery/vein vessel centerlines and the vessel types are further labeled by Dashtbozorg et al. [27].

RVTD[10] [34] is for vascular tortuosity evaluation. It contains 60 zoomed images with 30 arteries and 30 veins that are ranked by vessel tortuosity. These image patches are extracted from 60 retinal images with 50-degree FOV and 1300 × 1100 pixels.

In addition to the typical CF photography, there are also benchmarks on different retinal imaging devices, including scanning laser ophthalmoscopy (SLO), ultra-wide fundus imaging (UWFI), and fluorescein angiogram (FA).

- IOSTAR[11] [35] includes 24 images, vessel segmentation, artery/vein, and OD annotations. Images are acquired with an EasyScan SLO camera with a 45-degree FOV.
- AV-WIDE[12] [36] has 30 ultra-wide FOV images, includes both healthy eyes as well as eyes with AMD. Each image is from a different individual, was obtained using obtained using an Optos 200Tx UWFI camera, and is of around 900 × 1400 in size. Annotations of the vessel segmentation and the artery-vein labels are provided.
- VAMPIRE[13] [37] contains eight ultra-wide FOV FA images, obtained from OPTOS SLO ultra-wide FOV device which may achieve up to 200-degree FOV with scanning SLO technique. These images were taken from two different FA image sequences, with vessel segmentation annotation being provided.

Fig. 1 shows a CF image and various vessel annotations, including vascular junctions, vessel segmented, artery/vein, and tree masks. Meanwhile, there are also efforts in applying multispectral imaging to retinal studies. For example, CMIF[14] [38] is a dedicated multispectral fundus image dataset of 35 sets of images from 35 healthy young individuals of diverse ethnicities. The multispectral images are acquired by implementing a filter wheel into fundus camera, which gives rise to a set of 17 narrow band-pass filters for designated wavelengths in the range of 480–705 nm.

---

[8] See http://www.varpa.es/research/ophtalmology.html.
[9] See https://medicine.uiowa.edu/eye/inspire-datasets.
[10] See http://bioimlab.dei.unipd.it/RetinalVesselTortuosity.htm.
[11] See http://www.retinacheck.org/datasets.
[12] See http://people.duke.edu/~sf59/Estrada_TMI_2015_dataset.htm.
[13] See https://vampire.computing.dundee.ac.uk/vesselseg.html.
[14] See http://www.cs.bham.ac.uk/research/projects/fundus-multispectral/.

This development is yet to be ready for clinical translation, nevertheless it offers novel insights into retinopathy.

As shown in Table 1, the number of images in each dataset ranges from 8 to 143. The typical dataset size is often several order-of-magnitude smaller when comparing to the popular image detection/segmentation benchmarks used in the broader computer vision community, such as ImageNet [39] and COCO [40] that typical have 20–200 K images or more in the training and validation sets. In a sense, this dataset characteristic makes the practical situation less appealing. The situation is especially pronounced when deep learning methods such as convolutional neural networks (CNN) are engaged, as CNN models often require access to large and well-annotated training set. The CNN models trained in the retinal datasets thus tend to be less robust, and tend to be more vulnerable to small perturbation of input images or adversarial attacks at test run.

2.2 Evaluation metrics

With the increasing amount of activities toward vessel segmentation and tracing, there is naturally a demand for proper evaluation metrics, where different methods can be compared quantitatively and objectively on the same ground. The typical metrics are usually individual pixel-based, which including, for example, the precision-recall curve, and the F1 score as a single-value performance indicator. The sensitivity and specificity pair could be another popular choice. It is worth noting that the commonly used metric of receiver operating characteristic curve or ROC curve may not be suitable in our situation here, since the positive vessel and negative background pixels or examples are severely imbalanced. As a well-established mean to globally quantify pixel-based deviations, a major drawback of this type of metrics is that the vasculature geometric information is not well preserved in evaluation. This motives the construction of structural type of metrics [41–43] to best account for the differences from vasculature geometry perspective. The metric considered in Ref. [41] places more emphasis toward the aspects of both detection rate and detection accuracy, where the vascular structures between the predicted and the reference are optimally matched as a solution to the induced maximum-cardinality minimum-cost graph matching problem. Meanwhile, the structural metric proposed by Gegundez-Arias et al. [42] involves the comparison of three aspects between the predicted vessel segmentation and the corresponding reference annotation, namely number, overlap, and length. Number refers to comparing the number of connected segments presented in prediction as well as in the annotation images. Overlap is to assess the amount of overlaps between the predicted segmentation and the reference annotation. Length is to examine the length similarity between the predicted and the annotated vessel skeletons. In a more recent attempt [43], a structural similarity score is designed to incorporate both location and thickness differences that the segmentation is departed from the reference vessel trees. A very detailed discussion on validation of retinal image analysis can be found in Ref. [44]. See also Chapter 9 in this book for a discussion on validation techniques.

In addition to the aforementioned situation where there exists full annotations in the dataset for performance evaluation, there are often practical vessel segmentation scenarios when no reference is available. This is tackled by, for example, the paper of Galdran et al. [45], where a similarity metric is presented to quantify the segmentation performance in the absence of reference annotation. A web-based client-server system is described in Ref. [46], which consists of a component for vessel tracing, an interactive editing interface for refining parameters and fixing prediction errors, and a component responsible for outputting the clinical indexes.

3 Vessel segmentation

It is often of foremost interest to segment the retinal blood vessels pixel by pixel in a retinal image, corresponding to the blood column within the vessels. An example of vessel segmentation on CF images is shown in Fig. 1D.

Existing methods can be roughly divided into two categories based on whether an annotated training set is required: unsupervised and supervised methods. While supervised methods learn their models based on a set of training examples, unsupervised methods do not require a training set.

3.1 Unsupervised segmentation

As mentioned, arguably the first research effort of retinal segmentation is by Matsui et al. [10], 45 years ago, where a mathematical morphology approach is taken toward the problem of vessel segmentation.

Matched filtering and mathematical morphology-based techniques were popular choices in the early days. In Ref. [47], Chaudhuri et al. approximate the vessel segment profiles by a set of 1D Gaussian shaped filters over various spatial directions. As part of an initiative at the Vienna Eye Clinic for diagnosis and treatment of AMD, a dedicated pipeline is presented [48] to analyze retinal images based on SLO. In addition to separate modules for detecting the optic disk, fovea, and scotoma locations, its vessel segmentation module operates by matching the prototype zero-crossing of the gradient profiles and applying grouping. Hoover et al. [25] discuss the application of 12 Gaussian shape-matched filters in 2D, which produces a response image recording the highest response at each pixel. This is followed by a sequence of carefully designed threshold probing steps to produce the predicted segmentation. The STARE dataset is introduced in this paper. A second-order Gaussian matched filtering approach is considered by Gang et al. [49] to detect vessels. The work of Staal et al. [24] focuses on extracting the centerlines or ridges of the 2D vessels, which is achieved by means of a k-nearest neighbor classifier and sequential forward feature selection-based method. Importantly, it contributes the widely used DRIVE dataset. A set of three vessel detection variants are studied in Ref. [50] to account for noisy input images. The methods are derived from the likelihood ratio test in making local decisions, and model selection for choosing the optimal intrinsic parameters.

A supervised likelihood ratio test is developed in Ref. [51] that combines matched-filter responses, and customized measures of confidence and vessel boundary-ness. A systematic approach is conducted in Ref. [52], where vessel structure is segmented using morphological operators, based on which the OD and macular are then localized by likelihood ratio tests. Mendonca et al. [53] use four directional differential operators to detect the vessel centerlines, which then facilitate the morphological reconstruction of vessels. The work of Miri and Mahloojifar [54] proposes to use curvelet transform and morphology operators for edge enhancement, then apply a simple threshold along with connected components analysis for delivering the final segmentation. Martinez-Perez et al. [55] conduct segmentation by a combination of multiscale analysis of gradient and Hessian information and region-growing approach. A multiresolution 2D Hermite model is investigated in Ref. [56], where a quad-tree is used to organize the spatial configuration, an expectation-maximization type optimization procedure is developed to estimate the model parameters. Moreover, Bankhead et al. [57] utilize isotropic undecimated wavelet transform for unsupervised segmentation. In segmenting UWFI Fundus FA images, Perez-Rovira et al. [37] employ steerable filters and adaptive thresholding. An iterative approach is devised in Ref. [58] to include new vessel structures by local adaptive thresholds. A similar strategy is also considered by Xu et al. [59], where a tree-structured shape space is considered and for retinal vessel segmentation, local threshold is applied recursively. The work of Kovacs and Hajdu [60] advocates a two-step process. First, generalized Garbor filter-based template matching is used to extract the centerlines. Second, iterative contour reconstruction is carried out based on the intensity characteristics of the vessel contours.

Variational methods have been another popular line of techniques in retinal vascular segmentation. A deformable contour model is adopted by Espona et al. [61], by incorporating the snake method with domain-specific knowledge such as the topological properties of blood vessels. In Ref. [62], a dedicated active contour model is developed that uses two pairs of contours to capture each side of the vessel edges. To address the challenging pathological images, Lam and Yan [63] investigate the application of divergence operator in the gradient vector field. Moreover, to deal with the issue of multiconcavity in the intensity profile of especially pathological fundus images, a variational approach is taken in Ref. [64] based on perceptual transform and regularization-based techniques. An active contour model with local morphology fitting is discussed in Ref. [65] to segment vessels in 2D angiogram. The combined use of regional information and active contour techniques is further considered in Refs. [66, 67]. In Ref. [35], new filters are proposed based on lifting a 2D image is lifted by Lie-group into a 3D orientation score, and by applying multiscale second-order Gaussian derivatives, and follow-up eigensystem analysis of the left-invariant Hessian matrix. After projecting back from 3D space to 2D image plane, the segmentation result is obtained by applying a global threshold. Recently, a minimal path approach is reported in Ref. [68], where a dynamic Riemannian metric is updated during the course of a single-pass fast marching method. It is sometimes advantageous to perform interactive image analysis. This is addressed by Poon et al. [69], where a multiscale filtering approach is designed to simultaneously compute center-lines and boundaries of the retinal vessels.

Other techniques also exist. For example, by establishing an analogy between quantum mechanics and image processing, it is proposed in Ref. [70] to transform image pixels to quantum systems such that they can be evolved from an initial state to a final state governed by the Schrodinger equation.

3.2 Supervised segmentation

The alternative to the unsupervised paradigms are learning-based methods, in which a set of training examples is provided to learn a model that is expected to segment input retinal images at test time as well as the performance it has gained during training. One early work is that of Akita and Kuga [11], where neural networks are used in segmenting retinal vasculature. A system is developed in Ref. [71], where a patch-based neural network model is learned by backpropagation to classify each pixel as being vessel or not, then OD and fovea regions are obtained via template matching.

A typical supervised approach is to first construct or develop a set of dedicated features or filters, then to build a statistical model based on the features as sufficient statistics, with model parameters being estimated (i.e., learned) from a set of training examples. For example, a local patch-based approach is considered in Ref. [72], where an AdaBoost classifier is in place to work with 41 features extracted from the local image patch of the current pixel, where the pixel is to be predicted as being either vessel or not. Martin et al. [73] devise gray-level and moment invariants-based features for segmenting the retinal vessels using neural networks. Ricci et al. [74] work with orthogonal line operators and support vector machine to perform pixel-wise segmentation. Becker et al. [75] present a discriminative method to learn convolutional features using gradient boosting regression technology. In Ref. [76], a pool of difference-of-Gaussian (DoG) filters is used that after training, filters are adaptively selected to best fit the current vessel of interest. A learning-based DoGs filtering approach is proposed in Ref. [77], with one application focus being about the detection of vascular junction points, where orientation is achieved via shifting operations. Empirically it is shown robust to contrast variations and the presence of noises. Furthermore, many learning-based methods [78–81] also advocate the automation of the feature learning process. For example, Soares et al. [78] elaborate upon 18-dimensional Gabor response features to train two Gaussian mixture models (GMMs), which are further employed to produce a binary probability map for a test image. The method of Becker et al. [81] employs a gradient boosting framework to optimize filters and often produces impressive performance.

Several learning paradigms, including graphical models and ensemble learning, are presented with very promising results. A discriminatively trained, fully connected CRF approach is developed by Orlando and Blaschko [82]. This is followed by Orlando [83] with more expressive features in their fully connected CRF model. Besides, the work of Fraz et al. [30] showcases an ensemble classification approach consisting of bagged and boosted decision trees, with features from a variety of aspects including orientations of local gradients, morphological transformations, and Gabor filter responses.

Instead of segmenting vessel pixels directly, a radial projection method is utilized in Ref. [84] to locate centerlines, based on steerable wavelet filtered output of a fundus image. Meanwhile, a semisupervised learning step extracts the remaining vessel structures. Similarly, an iterative algorithm is introduced by Gu and Cheng [85], where starting from the main vessel trunk, small and thin vessel branches and difficult regions around the boundaries are iteratively refined by retrieving and executing a proper local gradient Boosting classifiers, which is stored in a latent classification tree model constructed by Chow-Liu method.

3.3 Deep learning

As a particular supervised segmentation paradigm, a number of end-to-end deep learning approaches have been developed in our problem scenario with notable performance improvements. The N4-field [86], as an example, combines the CNN with nearest neighbor search to detect local patches of natural edges as well as thin and long objects. A CNN model is also trained in Ref. [87] based on 400,000 preprocessed image patches obtained from the training sets of DRIVE, STARE, or CHASEDB1 datasets, which are essential for ensuring reliable test performance. Similarly, a deep neural network is used by Li et al. [88] to model the cross-modality data transform for vessel segmentation in retinal images. Fu et al. [89] propose to incorporate both CNN and CRF models for segmenting the full input fundus image. The deep learning approach of Yan et al. [90] incorporates both conventional pixel-wise loss and segment-level loss terms to achieve a globally plausible solution. In addition, as demonstrated with the impressive performance in Ref. [91], it is possible to address multiple tasks jointly, including vessel segmentation and, for example, optic disk detection.

There exists, however, one major issue with the current segmentation task. DRIVE (40 annotated images) and STARE (20 annotated images) datasets have been the de facto benchmark in empirical examination of retinal image segmentation techniques. Meanwhile, annotations from, DRIVE and STARE are from multiple medical experts, which result in different reference ("gold") standards. The disagreement from multiple experts may be attributed to the inevitable subjectiveness and variability of expert judgment. It also reflects the difficulty level of the task and the reliability of the gold standard in the context. As our algorithms are approaching human-level performance, it becomes increasingly difficult to quantitatively validate new algorithms, as the vessels produced by these methods on test images are more agreeable to the particular reference standard they are trained with, when comparing with the other reference standards. This suggests an overall performance saturation of the current benchmark, most possibly due to the small dataset size, and stresses the need for larger benchmark datasets. Some steps have been taken toward addressing this concern. Among them, it is shown in Ref. [92] that the retinal segmentation performance can be improved by incorporated (potentially infinitely many) synthesized images into the typically small training set. An even more challenging problem is performing fundus image segmentation on a new and distinct fundus image dataset in the absence of manual annotations. To address this problem, Zhao et al. [93] present a supervised learning pipeline. The key is the construction of a synthetic retinal image dataset capable of bridging the gap between an existing reference dataset (where annotated vessel structures are available) and the new query dataset (where no annotation is available). Then existing supervised learning segmentation methods are to be engaged to learn a model dedicated to the set of query images.

Due to the visual similarity between retinal vessels from, for example, fundus imaging and neurons from, for example, confocal microscope, there are also many efforts in devising algorithms to address the more general problem of segmenting such tubular structured objects [85, 94–100], with retinal blood vessel being a special case. For example, the well-known local Hessian-based vessel enhancement method developed by Frangi et al. [94] has been widely used for segmenting both 2D and 3D vessels. A mathematical morphology and curvature evaluation-based method was developed by Zana and Klein [95] to segment the vessel-like structures from background. Minimal path techniques are considered in a series of closely related efforts [101–103] to connect vessel segments in 2D or 3D. The work of Benmansour and Cohen [96] also addresses generic 2D and 3D segmentation of tubular structured objects in images, with an interactive method using minimal path and anisotropic enhancement. A multiscale centerline detection method is presented in Ref. [98] based on learned filters and GradientBoost regression technique. The method of Gu et al. [100] attempts to capture structural and contextual features from fundus images through their proposed data-driven feature learning procedure.

4 Vessel tracing

The topological and geometrical properties of retinal vessel trees are vital in screening for and diagnosing diseases, which call for proper tracing of the individual vessel trees from fundus images. The problem of vessel tracing is more than segmentation where vessel pixels are separated from the backgrounds, in that we would like to first separate artery and vein vessels, as shown in Fig. 1E. An equivalent problem is to detect junctions and decide as being either branching or crossing. Individual vessel trees usually could be distinguished from the rim of the optic disk, as shown in Fig. 1F, thus we answer the question of which pixel belongs to which of the vessel trees.

4.1 Vascular junction identification

Detecting and categorizing the junction points into either bifurcation or crossing is useful in vessel tree extraction and classification. Fig. 1B illustrates an exemplar annotation of such bifurcation and crossing points. In one of the early efforts, a morphological-type edge detection algorithm is used in Ref. [104] to automate the recognition of arteriovenous intersections. An image processing-based approach is considered in Ref. [105] that first extracts the vessels by preprocessing filtering and k-means, then utilizes a combined cross-point number method for thinning, and pattern-matching classification of the junction points as either branching or crossover. Calvo et al. [106] consider the detection and classification of key points pertaining to bifurcations and crossovers in the retinal vessel trees. A two-step method is proposed, which uses filters and morphologic operations for detection, and the extracted key point-based features for classification into either bifurcations or crossovers. Started with a segmented retinal image, Azzopardi and Petkov [28] deploy a set of blurred and shifted Gabor filters that are trained from a set of predefined bifurcation prototypes, and demonstrate satisfactory detection performance on DRIVE and STARE datasets. In addition to their initial work [107] where self-organizing feature maps are used to perceptually group the retinal segments around the junction points, Qureshi et al. [108] develop a probabilistic model of various junction points such as terminals, bridges, and bifurcations, and their configurations.

4.2 Vascular tree separation

The work of Tamura et al. [109] is among the early efforts, where the blood vessels are traced by a second-order derivative Gaussian filter from an initial point, while the width of the blood vessel is obtained as the zero-crossing interval of the filter output. Similarly, starting from a set of initial points, the work of Can et al. [110] tracks vessels by recursively applying a set of directional low-pass filters to the proper directions along the vessel centerlines detected so far from the input retinal angiogram images. It also extracts the branching and crossover points as a by-product. A three-step approach is proposed in Ref. [111] to reliably detect vascular bifurcations and crossovers, which involves initialization of junction locations, iterative estimation, and backtrace-based refinement.

One important observation is that both local and global contexts are helpful in resolving the bifurcation and crossover issue. For example, at a junction, it is valuable to examine the angular, morphological, and textural properties of all segments at the junction. In fact, the inclusion of information from nearby junctions could also facilitate a better local decision at current junction. This line of thoughts inspires the graph-based formulation where each vessel segment becomes a node, and a contact between two adjacent segments is represented by an edge between the two nodes. This naturally leads to an undirected graph representation. The tracing problem has been thus formulated as an inference problem in a Markov random field [114], a label propagation problem on undirected graphs [115], or directed graphs [116–118]. Similar graph-based methods are also adopted in Refs. [119, 120].

Variational approaches have also been considered in this context. Inspired biologically by the cortical orientation columns in primary visual cortex, Bekkers et al.

[121] advocate a special Euclidean group, SE(2), on which to base their retinal vessel tracking system. Bekkers and co-workers subsequently introduce an interesting differential geometry approach [122], where vessel tracing is formulated as sub-Riemannian geodesics on a projective line bundle. This is further investigated in Ref. [123] as a nilpotent approximations of sub-Riemannian distances for fast perceptual grouping of blood vessels in 2D and 3D. Abbasi-Sureshjani et al. [124] consider a 5D kernel approach obtained as the fundamental solution of the Fokker-Planck equation to deal with the presence of interrupted lines or highly curved blood vessels in retinal images. A mathematical contour completion scheme is proposed by Zhang et al. [125] based on the rotational-translational group SE(2). The original 2D disconnected vessel segments are lifted to a 3D space of 2D location and an orientation, where crossing and bifurcations can be separated by their distinct orientations. The contour completion problem can then be characterized by left-invariant PDE solutions of the convection-diffusion process on SE(2).

The tracing problem has indeed attracted research attentions from diverse perspectives that go beyond the paradigms mentioned so far. In terms of deep learning, the work of Ventura et al. [126] extracts the retinal artery and vein vessel networks by iteratively predicting the local connectivity from image patches using deep CNN. Uslu and Bharath [127] consider a multitask neural network approach to detect junctions in retinal vasculature, which is empirically examined in DRIVE and IOSTAR benchmarks with satisfactory results. A fluid dynamic approach is introduced in Ref. [128] to determine the connectivity of overlapping venous and arterial vessels in fundus images. Moreover, aiming to balance the trade-off between performance and real-time computation budget, Shen et al. design and analyze in Ref. [129] the optimal scheduling principle in achieving early yield of tracing the vasculature and extracting crossing and branching junctions. It is also worth mentioning that similar problem has also been encountered by the neuronal image analysis community with numerous studies of datasets and methods [130–132]. There are also efforts in addressing the more general problem of tracing tubular structured objects that include retinal vessel tracing as a special case [117,118,126].

4.3 Arterial/venous vessel classification

The classification of blood vessels into arterioles and venules is a fundamental step in retinal vasculature analysis, and is a basis of clinical measurement calculation, such as AVR. This requires not only identifying individual vessel trees, but also assigning each vessel tree as being formed by either arteries or veins. Interested readers may consult Miri et al. [17] for a detailed review of this subject.

As an early research effort, Akita and Kuga [11] consider the propagation of artery/vein labeling by a structure-based relaxation scheme on the underlying vascular graph. A vessel tracking method is presented in Ref. [111] to resolve the connectivity issues of bifurcations and crossings. A semiautomatic system is described in Ref. [133], consisting of segmenting the vessel pixels, thinning to obtain vessel skeletons, and tracking individual vessel trees. As a result, a number of geometric and topological properties are subsequently quantified, which include vessel segment lengths, diameters, branching ratios, and angles. In Ref. [134], the problem of artery versus vein separation from a vascular graph is cast as a SAT-problem, where a heuristic AC-3 algorithm is utilized to address a double-layered constrained search problem. Instead of working with fundus image of a single wavelength, it is considered in Ref. [135] to work with a specific fundus imaging set-up that acquires two images simultaneously, at different wavelengths of 570 and 600 nm, respectively. By exploiting the difference between artery and vein vessels that have distinct central reflex patterns, an SVM classification-based method is proposed to identify the vessel types. A multistep pipeline is considered in Ref. [136]. First, a vesselness value is computed for each pixel, which forms a vessel score image. Then points are sampled from local maxima points of the score image, and these points are linked into spanning trees by solving the induced k-cardinality arborescence problem with ant colony optimization-based algorithm. Based on 27 hand-crafted features, a linear discriminant classifier is used in the work of Niemeijer et al. [33] to classify vessel segments into arteries and veins. In Ref. [26], Hu et al. use a graph-based metaheuristic algorithm to segment and separate a fundus image into multiple anatomical trees, while the RITE dataset is also constructed. In Ref. [27], the classification of artery versus vein vessel segments is carried out based on the analysis of a graph extracted from the retinal vasculature, where the annotation of annotate artery and vein vessels is also provided for both DRIVE and INSPIRE-AVR datasets. For ultra-wide field SLO, Pellegrini et al. [137] also consider a graph-cut-based approach, where the node and edge-related features are manually designed features based on local vessel intensity and vascular morphology. A system is developed in Ref. [138] to segment vessels by Otsu binary thresholding, and obtain skeleton by applying mathematical morphology. This is followed by localization of branch points, crossing points, and end points. As a result, a graph structure is formed, and the Dijkstra algorithm is used to search vessel subtrees by minimizing the accumulative edge costs. Finally, a k-means clustering algorithm is executed to separate artery and vein subtrees.

Targeting at wide-FOV images, a planar graph-based method is considered by Estrada et al. [36] in constructing a likelihood model to take into account the prior knowledge regarding color, overlap, and local growth aspects of vessel segments at junctions. A heuristic search is thus carried out for optimal separation of the artery and vein vessel trees.

4.4 Clinical relevant vessel readouts

Retinal vascular abnormalities, for example widening or narrowing of retina blood vessels and increased vascular tortuosity, provide significant hints on various diseases, such as diabetes, hypertension, and coronary heart disease. Measurements to quantify retinal vascular changes are as follow:

> *Diameter changes.* AVR, AVN, and FAN are three quantification measurements of diameter changes. AVR calculation is restricted to an area of 0.5–1.0 disc

diameters from the OD. An automated pipeline is presented in Ref. [139], which segments and skeletonizes the vessels, and classifies arterial/venous vessel segments that are separated at the junction points. The six widest artery and vein segments are selected for AVR calculation, which is measured by an iterative algorithm. AVN is a phenomenon where venular caliber decreases as an arteriole crosses over a venule. A four-level grading approach of AVN is proposed in Ref. [140]. FAN refers to arterial vascular segment whose diameter ≥ 50 μm narrows. Severity degree of FAN is evaluated by the length of narrowing vessels compared with the diameter of OD.

Tortuosity alteration. This is an early indicator of a number of vascular diseases. Some of tortuosity quantification of arteries and veins approaches are (1) tortuous or nontortuous classification; (2) tortuosity ranking of vessel segments [34]; and (3) tortuosity grading of individual vascular trees [141].

5 Summary and outlook

A significant amount of effor has been devoted to vasculature analysis from retinal images, which have led to noticeable progress in clinical quantifications to improve diagnosis and prognosis of related diseases. There are also a number of promising research directions, some of them discussed in the following sections.

5.1 Vasculature analysis in emerging imaging techniques

We highlight here the emerging retinal imaging techniques referred to as 3D, multi-modal, and mobile imaging.

3D vessel analysis. To date, the majority of existing benchmark datasets and research efforts are devoted to segmentation in 2D retinal fundus images. Being a 2D projection of the 3D retinal vasculature, the retinal fundus images contains necessarily only a partial observation of the underlying 3D vessels. Meanwhile, with emerging 3D imaging techniques such as spectral-domain OCT (SD OCT or 3D OCT) and plenoptic ophthalmoscopy [142], we are now capable of imaging the 3D vasculature volume of the retina. It is thus possible to directly extract the 3D retinal vasculature volumes.

The endeavors of Haeker et al. [143] and Garvin et al. [144] are among the first in devising dedicated 3D segmentation techniques for time-domain macular scans. In terms of spectral-domain OCT volumes, the work of Niemeijer et al. [145] considers a k-NN pixel classification approach where Gaussian filter banks are used to produce good features. The results are evaluated on the macular centered scans as well as the optical nerve head centered scans. An interactive 3D segmentation approach is developed by Fuller et al. [146]. Moreover, Guimaraes et al. [147] report segmentation and reconstruction of 3D retinal vasculature. With the further advancement of 3D imaging techniques, this exciting direction of 3D vessel analysis possesses excellent research potential. It is also well connected to existing 3D blood vessel analysis efforts of other organs and via different instruments such as magnetic resonance imaging. *Multimodal vessel analysis.* One prominent example of multimodal retinal image analysis could be the combined usage of 2D fundus and 3D OCT images in vessel segmentation and tracing. Here, Hu et al. [148] investigate the integration of 2D fundus image and corresponding 3D OCT images in retinal vessel segmentation. SLO fundus image and corresponding macular OCT slices are jointly considered in Ref. [149] in two steps. The first step involves 2D vessel segmentation of fundus images in curvelet domain, with the side information from multiple OCT slices. The second step focuses on 3D reconstruction of the blood vessels from the OCT data. In addition to images, patient-related information such as electronic medical records and genetic data could also be taken into account for better disease diagnosis, and patient prognosis and treatment.

Analyzing mobile retinal images. As stated in Ref. [150], the recent development of portable fundus cameras [151] and smartphone-based fundus imaging systems have led to considerable opportunities as well as new challenges to retinal image analysis, such as the demand for more affordable imaging devices with perhaps lower computation cost [152]. To address the need of the emerging mobile retinal diagnostic devices that calls for segmentation techniques with low memory and computation cost, Hajabdollahi et al. [152] propose to train a simple CNN model-based pruning and quantization of the original full-sized model, that is capable of retaining the performance with much reduced computation and size. Looking forward, we expect further and considerable progresses along this direction.

5.2 Benchmarks and metrics

Benchmark datasets, such as ImageNet [39] and COCO [40], have played a vital role in fueling the recent computer vision breakthroughs. It has been observed that these successful datasets are both of large scale, and richly annotated. For example, over the years, COCO has introduced and aggregated various annotations on categories and shapes of individual objects and stuffs (backgrounds). Currently, it is capable of hosting a broad variety of closely related tasks including instance segmentation, stuff segmentation, object detection, person keypoint localization, as well as image captioning, visual dialog, image attributes, text detection and recognition, among others. By contrast, existing retinal vasculature image datasets, as shown in Table 1, are of small size, and often not richly annotated. While most state-of-the-art results are still reported based on the well-known benchmarks of DRIVE and STARE, the low-resolution images considered in these datasets are considerably lagging behind nowadays widely available high-resolution retinal imaging in eye clinics. These practical limitation and discrepancy indeed call for the curation of better benchmark sets of large scale, richly annotated, and aligned well with the current retinal imaging practice. One major issue with empirical evaluation lies in the quantification of how much the predicted vessel trees deviate from the reference annotation. A number of structural metrics [41–43] are suggested, yet a consensus from the community is still to be reached.

References

[1] J.W. Kiel, The Ocular Circulation, Morgan & Claypool Life Sciences, San Rafael, CA, 2010.

[2] T. Wong, R. Klein, D. Couper, L. Cooper, E. Shahar, L. Hubbard, M. Wofford, A. Sharrett, Retinal microvascular abnormalities and incident stroke: the atherosclerosis risk in communities study, Lancet 358 (9288) (2001) 1134–1140.

[3] M. Sasongko, T. Wong, T. Nguyen, C. Cheung, J. Shaw, J. Wang, Retinal vascular tortuosity in persons with diabetes and diabetic retinopathy, Diabetologia 54 (9) (2011) 2409–2416.

[4] C. Cheung, E. Lamoureux, M. Ikram, M. Sasongko, J. Ding, Y. Zheng, P. Mitchell, J. Wang, T. Wong, Retinal vascular geometry in Asian persons with diabetes and retinopathy, J. Diabetes Sci. Technol. 6 (3) (2012) 595–605.

[5] N. Witt, T. Wong, A. Hughes, N. Chaturvedi, B. Klein, R. Evans, M. McNamara, S. Thom, R. Klein, Abnormalities of retinal microvascular structure and risk of mortality from ischemic heart disease and stroke, Hypertension 47 (5) (2006) 975–982.

[6] R. Wu, C. Cheung, S. Saw, P. Mitchell, T. Aung, T. Wong, Retinal vascular geometry and glaucoma: the Singapore Malay eye study, Ophthalmology 120 (1) (2013) 77–83.

[7] P. Zhu, F. Huang, F. Lin, Q. Li, Y. Yuan, Z. Gao, F. Chen, The relationship of retinal vessel diameters and fractal dimensions with blood pressure and cardiovascular risk factors, PLoS ONE 9 (9) (2014) 1–10.

[8] C. Cheung, Y. Ong, M. Ikram, S. Ong, X. Li, S. Hilal, J. Catindig, N. Venketasubramanian, P. Yap, D. Seow, C. Chen, T. Wong, Microvascular network alterations in the retina of patients with Alzheimer's disease, Alzheimers Dement 10 (2) (2014) 135–142.

[9] C. Keeler, 150 Years since Babbage's ophthalmoscope, Arch. Ophthalmol. 115 (11) (1997) 1456–1457.

[10] M. Matsui, T. Tashiro, K. Matsumoto, S. Yamamoto, A study on automatic and quantitative diagnosis of fundus photographs. I. Detection of contour line of retinal blood vessel images on color fundus photographs, Nippon Ganka Gakkai Zasshi 77 (8) (1973) 907–918.

[11] K. Akita, H. Kuga, A computer method of understanding ocular fundus images, Pattern Recogn. 15 (6) (1982) 431–443.

[12] J. Gilchrist, Computer processing of ocular photographs—a review, Ophthalmic Physiol. Opt. 7 (4) (1987) 379–386.

[13] M. Abramoff, M. Garvin, M. Sonka, Retinal imaging and image analysis, IEEE Rev. Biomed. Eng. 1 (3) (2010) 169–208.

[14] C. Kirbas, F. Quek, A review of vessel extraction techniques and algorithms, ACM Comput. Surv. 36 (2000) 81–121.

[15] M. Fraz, P. Remagnino, A. Hoppe, B. Uyyanonvara, A. Rudnicka, C. Owen, S. Barman, Blood vessel segmentation methodologies in retinal images—a survey, Comput. Methods Programs Biomed. 108 (1) (2012) 407–433.

[16] J. Almotiri, K. Elleithy, A. Elleithy, Retinal vessels segmentation techniques and algorithms: a survey, Appl. Sci. 8 (2) (2018) 1–31.

[17] M. Miri, Z. Amini, H. Rabbani, R. Kafieh, A comprehensive study of retinal vessel classification methods in fundus images, J. Med. Signals Sens. 7 (2) (2017) 59–70.

[18] O. Faust, U. Acharya, E. Ng, K. Ng, J. Suri, Algorithms for the automated detection of diabetic retinopathy using digital fundus images: a review, J. Med. Syst. 36 (1) (2012) 145–157.

[19] M. Mookiah, U. Acharya, C. Chua, C. Lim, E. Ng, A. Laude, Computer-aided diagnosis of diabetic retinopathy: a review, Comput. Biol. Med. 43 (12) (2013) 2136–2155.

[20] Y. Douven, Retina Tracking for Robot-Assisted Vitreoretinal Surgery (Master's thesis), Eindhoven University of Technology, 2015.

[21] D. Braun, S. Yang, J. Martel, C. Riviere, B. Becker, EyeSLAM: real-time simultaneous localization and mapping of retinal vessels during intraocular microsurgery, Int. J. Med. Robot. 14 (1) (2018) 1–10.

[22] S. Lajevardi, A. Arakala, S. Davis, K. Horadam, Retina verification system based on biometric graph matching, IEEE Trans. Image Process. 22 (9) (2013) 3625–3635.

[23] Z. Waheed, U. Akram, A. Waheed, M. Khan, A. Shaukat, Person identification using vascular and non-vascular retinal features, Comput. Electr. Eng. 53 (2016) 359–371.

[24] J. Staal, M. Abramoff, M. Niemeijer, M. Viergever, B. van Ginneken, Ridge-based vessel segmentation in color images of the retina, IEEE Trans. Med. Imaging 23 (4) (2004) 501–509.

[25] A. Hoover, V. Kouznetsova, M. Goldbaum, Locating blood vessels in retinal images by piecewise threshold probing of a matched filter response, IEEE Trans. Med. Imaging 19 (3) (2000) 203–210.

[26] Q. Hu, M. Abramoff, M. Garvin, Automated separation of binary overlapping trees in low-contrast color retinal images, in: MICCAI, 2013.

[27] B. Dashtbozorg, A. Mendonca, A. Campilho, An automatic graph-based approach for artery/vein classification in retinal images, IEEE Trans. Image Process. 23 (3) (2014) 1073–1083.

[28] G. Azzopardi, N. Petkov, Automatic detection of vascular bifurcations in segmented retinal images using trainable COSFIRE filters, Pattern Recogn. Lett. 34 (8) (2013) 922–933.

[29] T. Kohler, A. Budai, M. Kraus, J. Odstrcilik, G. Michelson, J. Hornegger, Automatic no-reference quality assessment for retinal fundus images using vessel segmentation, in: IEEE Int. Symp. on Computer-Based Medical Systems, 2013, pp. 95–100.

[30] M. Fraz, P. Remagnino, A. Hoppe, B. Uyyanonvara, A. Rudnicka, C. Owen, S. Barman, An ensemble classification-based approach applied to retinal blood vessel segmentation, IEEE Trans. Biomed. Eng. 59 (9) (2012) 2538–2548.

[31] D. Farnell, F. Hatfield, P. Knox, M. Reakes, S. Spencer, D. Parry, S. Harding, Enhancement of blood vessels in digital fundus photographs via the application of multiscale line operators, J. Frankl. Inst. 345 (7) (2008) 748–765.

[32] S. Holm, G. Russell, V. Nourrit, N. McLoughlin, DR HAGIS—a novel fundus image database for the automatic extraction of retinal surface vessels, SPIE J. Med. Imaging 4 (1) (2017) 1–11.

[33] M. Niemeijer, X. Xu, A. Dumitrescu, P. Gupta, B. Ginneken, J. Folk, M. Abramoff, Automated measurement of the arteriolar-to-venular width ratio in digital color fundus photographs, IEEE Trans. Med. Imaging 30 (11) (2011) 1941–1950.

[34] E. Grisan, M. Foracchia, A. Ruggeri, A novel method for the automatic grading of retinal vessel tortuosity, IEEE Trans. Med. Imaging 27 (3) (2008) 310–319.

[35] J. Zhang, B. Dashtbozorg, E. Bekkers, J. Pluim, R. Duits, B. Romeny, Robust retinal vessel segmentation via locally adaptive derivative frames in orientation scores, IEEE Trans. Med. Imaging 35 (12) (2016) 2631–2644.

[36] R. Estrada, M. Allingham, P. Mettu, S. Cousins, C. Tomasi, S. Farsiu, Retinal artery-vein classification via topology estimation, IEEE Trans. Med. Imaging 34 (12) (2015) 2518–2534.

[37] A. Perez-Rovira, R. Cabido, E. Trucco, S. McKenna, J. Hubschman, RERBEE: robust efficient registration via bifurcations and elongated elements applied to retinal fluorescein angiogram sequences, IEEE Trans. Med. Imaging 30 (1) (2012) 140–150.

[38] I. Styles, A. Calcagni, E. Claridge, F. Espina, J. Gibson, Quantitative analysis of multispectral fundus images, Med. Image Anal. 10 (4) (2016) 578–597.

[39] O. Russakovsky, J. Deng, H. Su, J. Krause, S. Satheesh, S. Ma, Z. Huang, A. Karpathy, A. Khosla, M. Bernstein, A. Berg, L. Fei-Fei, ImageNet large scale visual recognition challenge, Int. J. Comput. Vis. 115 (3) (2015) 211–252.

[40] T.-Y. Lin, M. Maire, S. Belongie, J. Hays, P. Perona, D. Ramanan, P. Dollar, C.L. Zitnick, Microsoft COCO: common objects in context, in: European Conf. Computer Vision (ECCV), 2014.

[41] X. Jiang, M. Lambers, H. Bunke, Structural performance evaluation of curvilinear structure detection algorithms with application to retinal vessel segmentation, Pattern Recogn. Lett. 33 (2012) 2048–2056.

[42] M. Gegundez-Arias, A. Aquino, J. Bravo, D. Marin, A function for quality evaluation of retinal vessel segmentations, IEEE Trans. Med. Imaging 31 (2) (2012) 231–239.

[43] Z. Yan, X. Yang, K. Cheng, A skeletal similarity metric for quality evaluation of retinal vessel segmentation, IEEE Trans. Med. Imaging 37 (4) (2018) 1045–1057.

[44] E. Trucco, A. Ruggeri, T. Karnowski, L. Giancardo, E. Chaum, J. Hubschman, B. Al-Diri, C. Cheung, D. Wong, M. Abramoff, G. Lim, D. Kumar, P. Burlina, N. Bressler, H. Jelinek, F. Meriaudeau, G. Quellec, T. MacGillivray, B. Dhillon, Validating retinal fundus image analysis algorithms: issues and a proposal, Invest. Ophthalmol. Vis. Sci. 54 (2013) 3546–3559.

[45] A. Galdran, P. Costa, A. Bria, T. Araujo, A. Mendonca, A. Campilho, A no-reference quality metric for retinal vessel tree segmentation, in: MICCAI, 2008.

[46] L. Tramontan, E. Poletti, D. Fiorin, A. Ruggeri, A web-based system for the quantitative and reproducible assessment of clinical indexes from the retinal vasculature, IEEE Trans. Biomed. Eng. 38 (3) (2011) 818–821.

[47] S. Chaudhuri, S. Chatterjee, N. Katz, M. Nelson, M. Goldbaum, Detection of blood vessels in retinal images using two-dimensional matched filters, IEEE Trans. Med. Imaging 8 (3) (1989) 263–269.

[48] A. Pinz, S. Bernogger, P. Datlinger, A. Kruger, Mapping the human retina, IEEE Trans. Med. Imaging 17 (4) (1998) 606–619.

[49] L. Gang, O. Chutatape, S. Krishnan, Detection and measurement of retinal vessels in fundus images using amplitude modified second-order Gaussian filter, IEEE Trans. Med. Imaging 49 (2) (2002) 168–172.

[50] V. Mahadevan, H. Narasimha-Iyer, B. Roysam, H. Tanenbaum, Robust model-based vasculature detection in noisy biomedical images, IEEE Trans. Inf. Technol. Biomed. 8 (3) (2004) 360–376.

[51] M. Sofka, C. Stewart, Retinal vessel centerline extraction using multiscale matched filters, confidence and edge measures, IEEE Trans. Med. Imaging 25 (12) (2006) 1531–1546.

[52] K. Tobin, E. Chaum, P. Govindasamy, T. Karnowski, Detection of anatomic structures in human retinal imagery, IEEE Trans. Med. Imaging 26 (12) (2007) 1729–1739.

[53] A. Mendonca, A. Campilho, Segmentation of retinal blood vessels by combining the detection of centerlines and morphological reconstruction, IEEE Trans. Med. Imaging 25 (9) (2006) 1200–1213.

[54] M. Miri, A. Mahloojifar, Retinal image analysis using curvelet transform and multi-structure elements morphology by reconstruction, IEEE Trans. Biomed. Eng. 58 (5) (2011) 1183–1192.

[55] M. Martinez-Perez, A. Hughes, S. Thom, A. Bharath, K. Parker, Segmentation of blood vessels from red-free and fluorescein retinal images, Med. Image Anal. 11 (2007) 47–61.

[56] L. Wang, A. Bhalerao, R. Wilson, Analysis of retinal vasculature using a multiresolution Hermite model, IEEE. Trans. Med. Imaging 26 (2) (2007) 137–152.

[57] P. Bankhead, C. Scholfield, J. McGeown, T. Curtis, Fast retinal vessel detection and measurement using wavelets and edge location refinement, PLoS ONE 7 (3) (2012) e32435.

[58] S. Roychowdhury, D. Koozekanani, K. Parhi, Iterative vessel segmentation of fundus images, IEEE Trans. Biomed. Eng. 62 (7) (2015) 1738–1749.

[59] Y. Xu, T. Geraud, L. Najman, Connected filtering on tree-based shape-spaces, IEEE Trans. Pattern Anal. Mach. Intell. 38 (6) (2016) 1126–1140.

[60] G. Kovacs, A. Hajdu, A self-calibrating approach for the segmentation of retinal vessels by template matching and contour reconstruction, Med. Image Anal. 29 (2016) 24–46.

[61] L. Espona, M. Carreira, M. Penedo, M. Ortega, Retinal vessel tree segmentation using a deformable contour model, in: ICPR, 2008.

[62] B. Al-Diri, A. Hunter, D. Steel, An active contour model for segmenting and measuring retinal vessels, IEEE Trans. Med. Imaging 28 (9) (2009) 1488–1497.

[63] B. Lam, H. Yan, A novel vessel segmentation algorithm for pathological retina images based on the divergence of vector fields, IEEE Trans. Med. Imaging 27 (2) (2008) 237–246.

[64] B. Lam, Y. Gao, A. Liew, General retinal vessel segmentation using regularization-based multiconcavity modeling, IEEE Trans. Med. Imaging 29 (7) (2010) 1369–1381.

[65] K. Sun, Z. Chen, S. Jiang, Local morphology fitting active contour for automatic vascular segmentation, IEEE Trans. Biomed. Eng. 59 (2) (2012) 464–473.

[66] Y. Zhao, X. Wang, X. Wang, F. Shih, Retinal vessels segmentation based on level set and region growing, Pattern Recogn. 47 (7) (2014) 2437–2446.

[67] Y. Zhao, L. Rada, K. Chen, S. Harding, Y. Zheng, Automated vessel segmentation using infinite perimeter active contour model with hybrid region information with application to retinal images, IEEE Trans. Med. Imaging 34 (9) (2015) 1797–1807.

[68] D. Chen, J. Zhang, L. Cohen, Minimal paths for tubular structure segmentation with coherence penalty and adaptive anisotropy, IEEE Trans. Image Process. 28 (2019) 1271–1284.

[69] M. Poon, G. Hamarneh, R. Abugharbieh, Live-vessel: extending livewire for simultaneous extraction of optimal medial and boundary paths in vascular images, in: MICCAI, 2007.

[70] A. Youssry, A. El-Rafei, S. Elramly, A quantum mechanics-based algorithm for vessel segmentation in retinal images, Quantum Inf. Process. 15 (6) (2016) 2303–2323.

[71] C. Sinthanayothin, J. Boyce, H. Cook, T. Williamson, Automated localisation of the optic disc, fovea, and retinal blood vessels from digital colour fundus images, Br. J. Opthalmol. 83 (8) (1999) 902–910.

[72] C. Lupascu, D. Tegolo, E. Trucco, FABC: retinal vessel segmentation using AdaBoost, IEEE Trans. Inf. Technol. Biomed. 14 (5) (2010) 1267–1274.

[73] D. Marin, A. Aquino, M. Gegundez-Arias, J. Bravo, A new supervised method for blood vessel segmentation in retinal images by using gray-level and moment invariants-based features, IEEE Trans. Med. Imaging 30 (1) (2011) 146–158.

[74] E. Ricci, R. Perfetti, Retinal blood vessel segmentation using line operators and support vector classification, IEEE. Trans. Med. Imaging 26 (10) (2007) 1357–1365.

[75] C. Becker, R. Rigamonti, V. Lepetit, P. Fua, Supervised feature learning for curvilinear structure segmentation, in: Medical Image Computing and Computer-Assisted Intervention (MICCAI), 2013.

[76] G. Azzopardi, N. Strisciuglio, M. Vento, N. Petkov, Trainable COSFIRE filters for vessel delineation with application to retinal images, Med. Image Anal. 19 (1) (2015) 46–57.

[77] G. Azzopardi, N. Petkov, Trainable COSFIRE filters for keypoint detection and pattern recognition, IEEE Trans. Pattern Anal. Mach. Intell. 35 (2) (2013) 490–503.

[78] J. Soares, J. Leandro, R. Cesar, H. Jelinek, M. Cree, Retinal vessel segmentation using the 2-D Gabor wavelet and supervised classification, IEEE Trans. Med. Imaging 25 (9) (2006) 1214–1222.

[79] R. Rigamonti, V. Lepetit, Accurate and efficient linear structure segmentation by leveraging ad hoc features, in: MICCAI, 2012.

[80] E. Turetken, F. Benmansour, B. Andres, H. Pfister, P. Fua, Reconstructing loopy curvilinear structures using integer programming, in: CVPR, 2014.

[81] C. Becker, R. Rigamonti, V. Lepetit, P. Fua, Supervised feature learning for curvilinear structure segmentation, in: MICCAI, 2013.

[82] J. Orlando, M. Blaschko, Learning fully-connected CRFs for blood vessel segmentation in retinal images, in: MICCAI, 2014.

[83] J. Orlando, E. Prokofyeva, M. Blaschko, A discriminatively trained fully connected conditional random field model for blood vessel segmentation in fundus images, IEEE Trans. Biomed. Eng. 64 (1) (2017) 16–27.

[84] X. You, Q. Peng, Y. Yuan, Y. Cheung, J. Lei, Segmentation of retinal blood vessels using the radial projection and semi-supervised approach, Pattern Recogn. 44 (10–11) (2011) 2314–2324.

[85] L. Gu, L. Cheng, Learning to boost filamentary structure segmentation, in: ICCV, 2015.

[86] Y. Ganin, V. Lempitsky, N4-Fields: neural network nearest neighbor fields for image transforms, in: Asian Conference on Computer Vision, 2014, pp. 536–551.

[87] P. Liskowski, K. Krawiec, Segmenting retinal blood vessels with deep neural networks, IEEE Trans. Med. Imaging 35 (11) (2016) 2369–2380.

[88] Q. Li, B. Feng, L. Xie, P. Liang, H. Zhang, T. Wang, A cross-modality learning approach for vessel segmentation in retinal images, IEEE Trans. Med. Imaging 35 (1) (2016) 109–118.

[89] H. Fu, Y. Xu, S. Lin, D. Wong, J. Liu, DeepVessel: retinal vessel segmentation via deep learning and conditional random field, in: MICCAI, 2016.

[90] Z. Yan, X. Yang, K. Cheng, Joint segment-level and pixel-wise losses for deep learning based retinal vessel segmentation, IEEE Trans. Biomed. Eng. 65 (9) (2018) 1912–1923.

[91] K. Maninis, J. Pont-Tuset, P. Arbelaez, L. Gool, Deep retinal image understanding, in: MICCAI, 2016.

[92] H. Zhao, H. Li, S. Maurer-Stroh, L. Cheng, Synthesizing retinal and neuronal images with generative adversarial nets, Med. Image Anal. 49 (2018) 14–26.

[93] H. Zhao, H. Li, S. Maurer-Stroh, Y. Guo, Q. Deng, L. Cheng, Supervised segmentation of un-annotated retinal fundus images by synthesis, IEEE Trans. Med. Imaging 38 (1) (2018) 46–56.

[94] R. Frangi, W. Niessen, K. Vincken, M. Viergever, Multiscale vessel enhancement filtering, in: Medical Image Computing and Computer-Assisted Interventation (MICCAI), 1998, pp. 130–137.

[95] F. Zana, J. Klein, Segmentation of vessel-like patterns using mathematical morphology and curvature evaluation, IEEE Trans. Image Proc. 10 (7) (2001) 1010–1019.

[96] F. Benmansour, L. Cohen, Tubular structure segmentation based on minimal path method and anisotropic enhancement, Int. J. Comput. Vis. 92 (2) (2011) 192–210.

[97] A. Sironi, V. Lepetit, P. Fua, Segmentation of the surfaces of the retinal layer from OCT images, in: ICCV, 2015.

[98] A. Sironi, E. Turetken, V. Lepetit, P. Fua, Multiscale centerline detection, IEEE Trans. Pattern Anal. Mach. Intell. 38 (7) (2016) 1327–1341.

[99] R. Annunziata, E. Trucco, Accelerating convolutional sparse coding for curvilinear structures segmentation by refining SCIRD-TS filter banks, IEEE Trans. Med. Imaging 35 (11) (2016) 2381–2392.

[100] L. Gu, X. Zhang, H. Zhao, H. Li, L. Cheng, Segment 2D and 3D filaments by learning structured and contextual features, IEEE Trans. Med. Imaging 36 (2) (2017) 569–606.

[101] L. Cohen, T. Deschamps, Grouping connected components using minimal path techniques. Application to reconstruction of vessels in 2D and 3D images, in: IEEE Conference on Computer Vision and Pattern Recognition (CVPR), 2001.

[102] M. Pechaud, R. Keriven, G. Peyre, Extraction of tubular structures over an orientation domain, in: IEEE Conference on Computer Vision and Pattern Recognition (CVPR), 2009.

[103] W. Liao, S. Worz, C. Kang, Z. Cho, K. Rohr, Progressive minimal path method for segmentation of 2D and 3D line structures, IEEE Trans. Pattern Anal. Mach. Intell. 40 (3) (2018) 696–709.

[104] S. Yamamoto, H. Yokouchi, Automatic recognition of color fundus photographs, in: K. Preston, M. Onoe (Eds.), Digital Processing of Biomedical Images, Springer, Berlin, 1976.

[105] D. Calvo, M. Ortega, M. Penedo, J. Rouco, Vascular intersection detection in retina fundus images using a new hybrid approach, Comput. Biol. Med. 40 (1) (2010) 81–89.

[106] S. Yamamoto, H. Yokouchi, Automatic recognition of color fundus photographs, Dig. Process. Biomed. Images 103 (1) (2011) 28–38.

[107] B. Al-Diri, A. Hunter, D. Steel, M. Habib, Automated analysis of retinal vascular network connectivity, Comput. Med. Imaging Graph. 34 (6) (2010) 462–470.

[108] T. Qureshi, A. Hunter, B. Al-Diri, A Bayesian framework for the local configuration of retinal junctions, in: CVPR, 2014.

[109] S. Tamura, Y. Okamoto, K. Yanashima, Zero-crossing interval correction in tracing eye-fundus blood vessels, Pattern Recogn. 21 (3) (1988) 227–233.

[110] A. Can, H. Shen, J. Taylor, H. Tanenbaum, B. Roysam, Rapid automated tracing and feature extraction from retinal fundus images using direct exploratory algorithm, IEEE Trans. Inf. Tech. Biomed. 3 (2) (1999) 125–138.

[111] C. Tsai, C. Stewart, H. Tanenbaum, B. Roysam, Model-based method for improving the accuracy and repeatability of estimating vascular bifurcations and crossovers from retinal fundus images, IEEE Trans. Inf. Technol. Biomed. 8 (2) (2004) 122–130.

[112] T. Yedidya, R. Hartley, Tracking of blood vessels in retinal images using Kalman filter, in: DICTA, 2008.

[113] K.S. Lin, C.L. Tsai, C.H. Tsai, M. Sofka, S.J. Chen, W.Y. Lin, Retinal vascular tree reconstruction with anatomical realism, IEEE Trans. Biomed. Eng. 59 (12) (2012) 3337–3347.

[114] J. De, T. Ma, H. Li, M. Dash, L. Cheng, Automated tracing of retinal blood vessels using graphical models, in: Scandinavian Conference on Image Analysis, 2013.

[115] J. De, H. Li, L. Cheng, Tracing retinal vessel trees by transductive inference, BMC Bioinformatics 15 (20) (2014) 1–20.

[116] L. Cheng, J. De, X. Zhang, F. Lin, H. Li, Tracing retinal blood vessels by matrix-forest theorem of directed graphs, in: MICCAI, 2014.

[117] J. De, L. Cheng, X. Zhang, F. Lin, H. Li, K. Ong, W. Yu, Y. Yu, S. Ahmed, A graph-theoretical approach for tracing filamentary structures in neuronal and retinal images, IEEE Trans. Med. Imaging 35 (1) (2016) 257–272.

[118] J. De, X. Zhang, F. Lin, L. Cheng, Transduction on directed graphs via absorbing random walks, IEEE Trans. Pattern Anal. Mach. Intell. 40 (7) (2018) 1770–1784.

[119] Q. Lau, M. Lee, W. Hsu, T. Wong, Simultaneously identifying all true vessels from segmented retinal images, IEEE Trans. Biomed. Eng. 60 (7) (2013) 1851–1858.

[120] X. Lyu, Q. Yang, S. Xia, S. Zhang, Construction of retinal vascular trees via curvature orientation prior, in: IEEE International Conference on Bioinformatics and Biomedicine, 2016.

[121] E. Bekkers, R. Duits, T. Berendschot, B.M. ter Haar Romeny, A multi-orientation analysis approach to retinal vessel tracking, J. Math. Imaging Vis. 49 (3) (2014) 583–610.

[122] E. Bekkers, R. Duits, A. Mashtakov, Y. Sachkov, Vessel tracking via sub-Riemannian geodesics on the projective line bundle, in: International Conference on Geometric Science of Information, 2017.

[123] E. Bekkers, D. Chen, J. Portegies, Nilpotent approximations of sub-Riemannian distances for fast perceptual grouping of blood vessels in 2D and 3D, J. Math. Imaging Vis. 60 (2018) 882–899.

[124] S. Abbasi-Sureshjani, M. Favali, G. Citti, A. Sarti, B.M. ter Haar Romeny, Curvature integration in a 5D kernel for extracting vessel connections in retinal images, IEEE Trans. Image Process. 27 (2) (2018) 606–621.

[125] J. Zhang, E. Bekkers, D. Chen, T. Berendschot, J. Schouten, J. Pluim, Y. Shi, B. Dashtbozorg, B.M. ter Haar Romeny, Reconnection of interrupted curvilinear structures via cortically inspired completion for ophthalmologic images, IEEE Trans. Biomed. Eng. 65 (5) (2018) 1151–1165.

[126] C. Ventura, J. Pont-Tuset, S. Caelles, K. Maninis, L.V. Gool, Iterative deep retinal topology extraction, in: International Workshop on Patch-Based Techniques in Medical Imaging, 2018.

[127] F. Uslu, A. Bharath, A multi-task network to detect junctions in retinal vasculature, in: MICCAI, 2018.

[128] F. Caliva, A. Hunter, P. Chudzik, G. Ometto, L. Antiga, B. Al-Diri, A fluid-dynamic based approach to reconnect the retinal vessels in fundus photography, in: International Conference of the IEEE Engineering in Medicine and Biology Society, 2017.

[129] H. Shen, B. Roysam, C. Stewart, J. Turner, H. Tanenbaum, Optimal scheduling of tracing computations for real-time vascular landmark extraction from retinal fundus images, IEEE Trans. Inf. Technol. Biomed. 5 (1) (2001) 77–91.

[130] K. Al-Kofahi, S. Lasek, D. Szarowski, C. Pace, G. Nagy, J. Turner, B. Roysam, Rapid automated three-dimensional tracing of neurons from confocal image stacks, IEEE Trans. Inf. Tech. Biomed. 6 (2) (2002) 171–187.

[131] K. Brown, G. Barrionuevo, A. Canty, V.D. Paola, J. Hirsch, G. Jefferis, J. Lu, M. Snippe, I. Sugihara, G. Ascoli, The DIADEM data sets: representative light microscopy images of neuronal morphology to advance automation of digital reconstructions, Neuroinformatics 9 (2011) 143–157.

[132] M. Radojevic, E. Meijering, Automated neuron tracing using probability hypothesis density filtering, Bioinformatics 33 (7) (2017) 1073–1080.

[133] M. Martinez-Perez, A. Hughes, A. Stanton, S. Thom, N. Chapman, A. Bharath, K. Parker, Retinal vascular tree morphology: a semi-automatic quantification, IEEE Trans. Biomed. Eng. 49 (8) (2002) 912–917.

[134] K. Rothaus, X. Jiang, P. Rhiem, Separation of the retinal vascular graph in arteries and veins based upon structural knowledge, Image Vis. Comput. 27 (7) (2009) 864–875.

[135] H. Narasimha-Iyer, J. Beach, B. Khoobehi, B. Roysam, Automatic identification of retinal arteries and veins from dual-wavelength images using structural and functional features, IEEE Trans. Biomed Eng. 54 (8) (2007) 1427–1435.

[136] E. Turetken, C. Blum, G. Gonzalez, P. Fua, Reconstructing geometrically consistent tree structures from noisy images, in: Medical Image Computing and Computer-Assisted Intervention (MICCAI), 2010.

[137] E. Pellegrini, G. Robertson, T. MacGillivray, J. van Hemert, G. Houston, E. Trucco, A graph cut approach to artery/vein classification in ultra-widefield scanning laser ophthalmoscopy, IEEE Trans. Med. Imaging 37 (2) (2018) 516–526.

[138] V. Joshi, J. Reinhardt, M. Garvin, M. Abramoff, Automated method for identification and artery-venous classification of vessel trees in retinal vessel networks, PLoS ONE 9 (2) (2014) 1–12.

[139] M. Niemeijer, X. Xu, A. Dumitrescu, P. Gupta, B.V. Ginneken, J. Folk, M. Abramoff, Automated measurement of the arteriolar-to-venular width ratio in digital color fundus photographs, IEEE Trans. Med. Imaging 30 (11) (2011) 1941–1950.

[140] U. Nguyen, A. Bhuiyan, L. Park, R. Kawasaki, T. Wong, J. Wang, P. Mitchell, K. Ramamohanarao, An automated method for retinal arteriovenous nicking quantification from color fundus images, IEEE Trans. Biomed. Eng. 60 (11) (2013) 3194–3203.

[141] M. Aghamohamadian-Sharbaf, H. Pourreza, T. Banaee, A novel curvature-based algorithm for automatic grading of retinal blood vessel tortuosity, IEEE J. Biomed. Health Inform. 20 (2) (2016) 586–595.

[142] M. Adam, W. Aenchbacher, T. Kurzweg, J. Hsu, Plenoptic ophthalmoscopy: a novel imaging technique, Ophthalmic Surg. Lasers Imaging Retina 9 (7) (2018) 3178–3192.

[143] M. Haeker, M. Abramoff, R. Kardon, M. Sonka, Segmentation of the surfaces of the retinal layer from OCT images, in: MICCAI, 2006.

[144] M. Garvin, M. Abramoff, R. Kardon, S. Russell, X. Wu, M. Sonka, Intraretinal layer segmentation of macular optical coherence tomography images using optimal 3-D graph search, IEEE Trans. Med. Imaging 27 (10) (2008) 1495–1505.

[145] M. Niemeijer, M. Garvin, B. van Ginneken, M. Sonka, M. Abramoff, Vessel segmentation in 3D spectral OCT scans of the retina, in: SPIE Medical Imaging: Image Processing, 2008.

[146] A. Fuller, R. Zawadzki, S. Choi, D. Wiley, J. Werner, B. Hamann, Segmentation of three-dimensional retinal image data, IEEE Trans. Vis. Comput. Graph. 13 (6) (2007) 1719–1726.

[147] P. Guimaraes, P. Rodrigues, D. Celorico, P. Serranho, R. Bernardes, Three-dimensional segmentation and reconstruction of the retinal vasculature from spectral-domain optical coherence tomography, J. Biomed. Opt. 20 (1) (2015) 1–11.

[148] Z. Hu, M. Niemeijer, M. Abramoff, M. Garvin, Multimodal retinal vessel segmentation from spectral-domain optical coherence tomography and fundus photography, IEEE Trans. Med. Imaging 31 (10) (2012) 1900–1911.

[149] R. Kafieh, H. Rabbani, F. Hajizadeh, M. Ommani, An accurate multimodal 3-D vessel segmentation method based on brightness variations on OCT layers and curvelet domain fundus image analysis, IEEE Trans. Biomed. Eng. 60 (10) (2013) 2815–2823.

[150] N. Panwar, P. Huang, J. Lee, P. Keane, T. Chuan, A. Richhariya, S. Teoh, T. Lim, R. Agrawal, Fundus photography in the 21st century—a review of recent technological advances and their implications for worldwide healthcare, Telemed. e-Health 22 (3) (2016) 198–208.

[151] D. Palmer, T. Coppin, K. Rana, D. Dansereau, M. Suheimat, M. Maynard, D. Atchison, J. Roberts, R. Crawford, A. Jaiprakash, Glare-free retinal imaging using a portable light field fundus camera, Biomed. Opt. Express 47 (11) (2016) 1038–1043.

[152] M. Hajabdollahi, R. Esfandiarpoor, S. Soroushmehr, N. Karimi, S. Samavi, K. Najarian, Low complexity convolutional neural network for vessel segmentation in portable retinal diagnostic devices, in: International Conference on Image Processing, 2018.

OCT layer segmentation

7

Sandro De Zanet[a], Carlos Ciller[a], Stefanos Apostolopoulos[a], Sebastian Wolf[b], Raphael Sznitman[c]

[a]*RetinAI Medical AG, Bern, Switzerland*
[b]*Department of Ophthalmology, Inselspital, University Hospital, University of Bern, Bern, Switzerland* [c]*ARTORG Center, University of Bern, Bern, Switzerland*

Retinal layer segmentation methods in OCT images has been one of the most researched areas of ophthalmic medical image analysis of the last decade. Largely driven by improved image quality and the need to quantify retinal thickness and perturbations, a variety of different automated methods have been proposed and have been validated across patients with different retinal diseases. In this chapter we explore the task of OCT layer segmentation and some of the key methods of the past decade, highlighting some of the challenges that remain.

1 Anatomical description and clinical relevance

Volumetric OCT imaging provides remarkable capabilities in visualizing retinal tissue. With OCT, normal retinal tissue exhibits multiple retinal layers that sit on top of each other to form the core elements of the retina. These cover the vast majority of the posterior part of the eye and have the important role of transforming light energy into neural signals to be interpreted by the brain. Briefly, light that interacts with light-sensitive cells known as rods and cones, convert photons into action potentials that are then transmitted by bipolar and ganglion cells. The axons of ganglion cells ultimately exit the eye toward the brain by way of the eye's optic nerve. Using OCT imaging, several important retinal layers are visible in healthy retinas and are summarized in Table 1.

These interconnected layers form the neural retinal tissue that lies above the choroid and choriocapillaris. In most cases, OCT volumes centered on the macula image these layers with high resolution, contrast and intensity (see Fig. 1).

OCTs of pathological retinas, however, can additionally depict a variety of different biomarkers such a subretinal fluid (SRF), intraretinal fluid (IRF), intraretinal cysts (IRC), fibrovascular pigment epithelium detachments (PED), reticular pseudodrusen

Computational Retinal Image Analysis. https://doi.org/10.1016/B978-0-08-102816-2.00007-1

Table 1 Description of major retinal layers and their functioning.

Layer name	Function
Nerve fiber layer (NFL)	Axons of ganglion cells
Ganglion cell layer (GCL)	Ganglion cell bodies
Inner plexiform layer (IPL)	Synapses connecting bipolar cells and ganglion cells
Inner nuclear layer (INL)	Nuclei of bipolar cells
Outer plexiform layer (OPL)	Synapses between rod and cone projections
Outer nuclear layer (ONL)	Rod and cone cell bodies
External limiting membrane (ELM)	Separation junction between cell nucleus and photoreceptors
Photoreceptive layer	Rods and cones
Retinal pigment epithelium (RPE)	Layer of pigmented cells

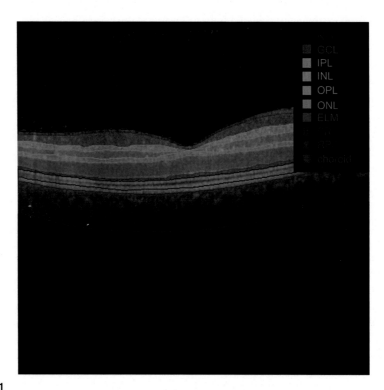

FIG. 1

OCT cross-section of a normal retina with highlighted layers.

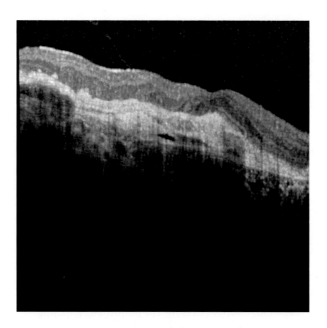

FIG. 2

OCT cross-section of a retina from an AMD patient. Notice the severe change in retinal layer shape due to the subretinal fluid and intraretinal fluid highlighted.

(RPD), drusen or atrophy. Critically, these pathological biomarkers impact the integrity of retinal layers and can severely modify the shape of the retina as a whole, depending on their quantity and severity (see Fig. 2), which usually directly affects the visual acuity of the patient.

2 Algorithmic evaluation and benchmarking

A critical aspect of layer segmentation algorithm development is the ability to evaluate how well a method can perform. To do this, both a gold standard and a measure to measure how well a given solution is similar to the gold standard are necessary. The former involves defining what a correct delineation of retinal boundaries means on a given OCT image, while the latter corresponds to how deviations from the gold standard solution are considered. In the case of retinal layer segmentation methods, it turns out that defining both has been challenging in the past.

By and large, the gold standard to validate layer segmentations in OCT volumes of the macula or other regions of the eye has hinged on provided manual delineations. While time consuming, manual delineations over large datasets of patient OCT images provides a first-order approximation to layer compositions typically witnessed in histological cuts of the retina. Manual delineations of retinal layers in OCT volumes is thus commonplace in most published works and remains so to this day. Some manual segmentation datasets such as that found in Chiu et al. [1] or Chiu et al. [2] are publically available, but remain few at this time. Critically, most papers that use manual delineations are validated on datasets, public or not, with tens or hundreds of volumes.

Yet, from their anatomical definitions, retinal layers viewed in OCT images have been subject to interpretation ever since OCT devices were introduced in ophthalmology. This is mainly due to obfuscations engendered by poor signal-to-noise and image artifacts. Beyond this, the ability of consistently define each retinal layer is extremely challenging when considering pathological cases (e.g., diabetic and especially macula degeneration patients). For instance, when retinal layers atrophy and retinal layer structures dissipate, spatial definitions of where layers begin and end are broadly ill-defined. In addition, inter-observer variability plays an important role in the definition of such gold standards. The work of Chiu et al. [1] was one of the first to explore how inter-grader variability could impact performance of automated methods and the work of Dubose et al. [3] explores a theoretical framework to bound the accuracy of any such derived gold standard. Hence the notion of consistent standards for retinal layer segmentation in OCT images remains a challenge and an open problem.

Given a gold standard, or *ground truth*, layer segmentation and an automatically generated segmentation, a variety of different performance measures have been used in recent years to validate the quality of produced layers. One of the most common measures of performance involves the per-pixel differences between layer surface produced and its corresponding ground truth. From this, the mean unsigned or signed errors can be computed for each layer [4–6]. Others have also computed the pixelwise mean absolute difference (MAD) and root mean squared error (RMSE) between layer boundaries [7]. Alternatively, the Dice score and Chamfer distance between predicted and reference layers have also been used [7a, 8].

3 Intensity based methods

In its infancy, research focused on retinal layer segmentation methods primarily dealt with significant noise levels in OCT images and at its core with finding the boundaries or edges of the layers taking into account different constraints and anatomical properties. For most methods prior to 2010, this involved developing methods that could segment layers while overcoming signal-to-noise challenges that appeared in individual OCT cross sections, or B-scans. Such methods heavily relied on model based approaches, as opposed to more recent data-driven methods that have become common today.

Simple approaches that attempted to segment layers by finding layer boundaries in individual columns, or A-scans, of OCT images using pixel thresholds, hand-crafted filtering and correlation exploitation techniques [9–11] were perhaps the first of their kind conceptually to segment layers. A number of different works then built on top of this, by providing more anatomically specific methods for the macula [12, 13] or the optic nerve [14].

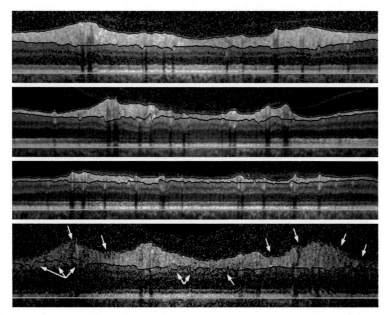

FIG. 3

Examples of segmentations produced by the method in Mayer et al. [16]. From top to bottom: Normal eye, Glaucomatous eye, Glaucomatous eye and Normal eye. *White arrows* denote segmentation errors. Notice the effect of increase image noise on the segmentation quality (bottom example).

From M.A. Mayer, J. Hornegger, C.Y. Mardin, R.P. Tornow, Retinal nerve fiber layer segmentation on FD-OCT scans of normal subjects and glaucoma patients, Biomed. Opt. Express, 1 (5) (2010) 1358–1383.

Mayer et al. [16] also proposed the use of edge filters banks and denoising steps to extract layers in OCT cross-sections. An extensive review of such methods can also be found in Kafieh et al. [15] (Fig. 3).

While preliminary, these methods showed great potential even though they failed to generalize to a wide number of clinical cases. Yet, many of the techniques developed in the earlier works laid the groundwork as pre-processing steps for the generation of algorithms that followed, namely graph-based methods which we discuss in the following subsection.

4 Graph based methods

In the early 2010s, the influence of machine learning had fully propagated in the domain of OCT layer segmentation and an entire family of new methods was introduced. These operated on both B-scans and C-scans to leverage as much information as possible, and relied on datasets of training data to optimize intrinsic model parameters in automatic and semi-automatic ways. The outcome of this wave were automated methods that strongly outperformed earlier approaches, and in particular, showed a much better capability to generalize to more complex pathological cases.

Based on discrete optimization methods of energy functions in image domains, the core of these methods involved reformulating the OCT layer segmentation problem as a graph-based optimization problem. In practice, this involved defining an energy function that contained a unary term that modeled pixel wise evidence of boundaries, as well as a pairwise term that enforced spatial regularization. Based on the seminal work of Boykov et al. [17] and with some conditions, such functions could be solved optimally extremely efficiently.

Using these results and building on them, the work of Garvin et al. [18] introduced the "Iowa Reference Algorithms" as one of the earlier graph-based methods. Available online for free, this method used unary terms derived from filter responses and multiple constraints from the different retinal layers to segment seven different layers. Similarly Lang et al. [18a] also used a graph-cut based solution to infer nine segmentation layers, but augmented the complexity of the method by using a Random Forest classifier to compute the unary terms of the energy function. At the same time, Dufour et al. [19] had a similar approach but leveraged soft constraints in the pairwise terms of the optimization based on patient-statistical knowledge to allow more challenging layer shape perturbations (Fig. 4).

Overall, the advantage of the above methods is that the inference of layers in OCT volumes, be it B-scans or C-scans, provide far greater robustness to typical variations encountered in the clinical routine. Additionally, while these require training data to estimate the model parameters, the number of training examples remains low (i.e., less than 30). A major challenge of these methods remained the parameter tuning between the data and different regularization terms.

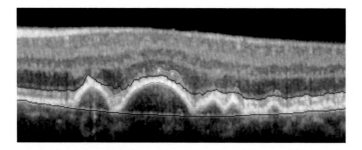

FIG. 4

Segmentation of OCT with visible drusen from Dufour et al. [19]. The *red line* shows a smooth the methods segmentation with soft constraints. Comparison is shown in *green* when hard constraint are used.

From P.A. Dufour, L. Ceklic, H. Abdillahi, S. Schröder, S. De Zanet, U. Wolf-Schnurrbusch, J. Kowal, Graph-based multi-surface segmentation of OCT data using trained hard and soft constraints, IEEE Trans. Med. Imaging (2013).

5 **Deep learning based methods**

Since 2017 a number of methods have been described for retinal cell layer prediction in OCT using deep learning methods. Two major approaches have been identified to approach this task. The first treats all locations in the OCT as a prediction task, where pixels are associated to a retinal layer class directly. This is the canonical segmentation task. The second approach identifies boundaries between layers without identifying the classes. These methods need an additional step to, on the one hand, extract the real boundary from a probability map and, on the other hand, to identify the classes of the separated layers.

The number and types of segmented retinal layers vary significantly between published work (see Fig. 1 for an overview of possible layers). While the definitions of the layers remain the same, various works bundle layers together, commonly NFL to BM as total retinal thickness or RPE and PR.

5.1 **Preprocessing and augmentation**

To reduce variability in OCT data, some methods apply image preprocessing. A common preprocessing is flattening of the B-scan, by identifying the Bruch's membrane and rolling each A-scan to a predetermined vertical position [20–23].

As is common in medical data, images with an annotated ground truth are scarce. Authors propose to augment the images to make the trained networks more robust to variability: rolling using a parabola, rotation around the center, changes in illumination, vertical and horizontal translation, scale changes, horizontal flip, mild shearing, additive noise and Gaussian blur. Augmentations are kept realistic in terms of how an OCT device might deteriorate or change an acquired image (Fig. 5).

5.2 **Pixelwise semantic segmentation methods**

Pixelwise semantic image segmentation methods assign each pixel/voxel of an OCT images a layer class. Most proposed deep learning methods make use of a U-Net [24] or variations of it, with different kinds of convolutions, up- and downsampling, depth, dropout, residuals and/or batch normalization. In the following we present recent advancements.

The ReLayNet by Roy et al. [25] modifies the U-Net by replacing the deconvolution decoder-branch with an unpooling layer. It uses the indices from the encoder max pool layer to upscale the image in these positions, while filling the remaining gaps with zeros. Instead of training on full B-scan, the authors propose vertical slices of a constant width (bands), to be able to train in larger mini-batch sizes at the cost of losing context. A weighted multi-class logistic loss in addition with a smooth dice loss is used to optimize the network. Layer boundaries receive a higher weight, to focus training on hard-to-identify tissue transitions/borders. As a preprocessing step, the RPE is extracted using traditional methods, to vertically align all A-scans (flattening). ReLayNet segments seven retinal layers and fluids. Ben-Cohen et al. [20]

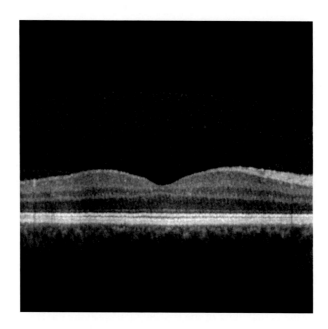

FIG. 5

OCT B-scan flattened on the RPE to reduce variability of the scans.

use a U-Net to segment 4 retinal layers—RNFL, GCL+IPL, INL, OPL—from a dataset of 24 patients (ERM, DME). Another variation of the U-Net, the U2-Net by Orlando et al. [26], introduces dropout layers after every convolution block. The addition of dropout allows for epistemic uncertainty estimation, by applying the network multiple times and measuring class prediction variance. While an interesting approach, this work focuses only on the segmentation of photoreceptor layers. Using a 3D version of the U-Net, Kiaee et al. [27] segment six retinal layers on an entire OCT. They show superior segmentation (Dice similarity coefficient) compared to its 2D variant, at the cost of performance (Fig. 6).

In addition to direct segmentation, authors propose to either soft or hard constraint retinal anatomy. He et al. [22] propose a two-step segmentation of eight retinal layers, which enforces and later guarantees the topological constraint of retinal layer ordering. A first rough segmentation is performed using a U-Net. In their preliminary work they use a layer ordering heuristic to check anatomically validity. A second network transforms the output toward a correct layer ordering until convergence. In their later work, instead of the correction network, a regression network is used to extract the layer thickness per A-scan directly, which enforces anatomically correct layer ordering. Based on a variation of DenseNet, Pekala et al. [29] segment four retinal layers. In a post-processing step they ensure continuous surfaces, eliminating outliers using Gaussian processes. Results are compared to state of the art algorithms (graph- and U-Net based), showing an improvement in terms of pixel-wise differences. Liu et al. [30] propose a variation of the U-Net based on ReLayNet, adding

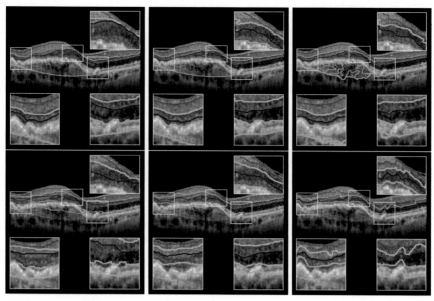

FIG. 6

Qualitative comparison of different segmentation approaches. *Top row, left to right*: ground truth, Apostolopoulos et al. [7a], Ronneberger et al. [24]; *bottom row, left-to-right*: Dufour et al. [19], Chen et al. [28], Mayer et al. [16].

From S. Apostolopoulos, R. Sznitman, Efficient OCT volume reconstruction from slitlamp microscopes, IEEE Trans. Biomed. Eng. 64 (10) (2017) 2403–2410.

a boundary refinement layer based on Peng et al. [31]. They segment nine retinal layers and fluid. The network is trained on vertical bands extracted from B-scans. To make the network more stable, it is learned with a combined loss of smooth dice and multiclass cross-entropy. The loss is weighted to counter class imbalance within a B-scan. Unlabeled images are added to the training process to fool a discriminator network based on the predicted segmentation. This adversarial loss akin to how GANs are trained, and improves the segmentation further. To provide image information at each scale, BRUnet [7a], a U-Net variant, uses an image pyramid on each level (branches) and residual connections to allow deeper network training. In contrast to the segmentation being viewed as a pixel-wise classification, this method performs a regression to the indexed segmentation, adding a soft constraint on anatomical retinal layer order. This shows improvement in highly pathological scans with AMD compared to graphical methods and the U-Net. Finally, Shah et al. [6] propose an AlexNet-architecture [32] tailored as a regression network that outputs a layer thickness for each of the two considered retinal areas (BM to RPE and RPE to RNFL). This also preserves layer ordering explicitly.

5.3 Boundary detection methods

The second large set of methods predicts cell layer boundaries first, instead of direct semantics segmentation. Boundaries are usually optimized with graph-based methods and in some cases transformed to pixel-wise segmentations.

An example of this approach was conducted by Gopinath et al. [21], who use a Fully-Connected—CNN to predict the pixel-wise class for nine retinal layers. They use an additional FCNN to identify edges, cut it into eight vertical bands and refine the segmentation with a BLSTM to reproduce a final consistent segmentation. In their work Fang et al. [33] find boundaries of nine retinal layers. A CNN is trained on patches to infer a boundary probability map. Applying Dijkstra's algorithm on the map they create a partition for each boundary layer. The results are evaluated on 117 OCT from 39 participants with non-exudative AMD.

Similarly, Liu et al. [34] propose a method that considers accurate boundary probabilities in order to perform the task of seven retinal layer segmentation at multiple scales and multi-dimensional features. The boundaries are then provided to a graph segmentation algorithm that refines the final result with Dijkstra's algorithm (see also Fang et al. [33]).

Hamwood et al. [35] evaluate whether patch size affects the quality of boundary segmentation in a significant way, or not. Patch size indeed affects the outcome, but also architecture and number of target classes. This suggests that even for boundary-based methods, specific results for the segmentation improve with more classes. Enough classes guide the learning process to make a better distinction, reducing the number of false positives.

Over the last few years segmentation of retinal layers has also served as the precursor for segmentation of other regions in retinal OCT, such as the region of the choroid, critical in the development of diseases such as diabetic macular edema (DME). In this area we would find methods such as developed by Masood et al. [36], where the efforts went in the direction of providing a segmentation of the Bruch's membrane (BM) using baseline thresholding and choroid using a combination of deep learning based neural network for patchwise classification. These approaches together with traditional medical image processing techniques and standard pre-processing techniques facilitate the task of segmentation. The inhomogeneity of the choroid in some cases makes the problem of segmentation of choroid a real challenge.

Sui et al. [37] focused on tackling the same problem using a graph-search segmentation technique focused on identifying edges combined with deep learning. In this work the authors learn the optimal graph weight via a data-driven strategy which is reached by using a new multi-scale end-to-end CNN architecture. Alonso-Caneiro et al. [38] used a CNN (ReLayNet) providing a probability map that marked the predicted location of the boundaries. The map was subsequently refined and adjusted using a graph-search approach to extract the boundaries from the probability maps. In this case the authors highlighted that the graph-search algorithm used to extract boundaries would often decrease the quality of the results.

Kugelman et al. [39] use a recurrent neural network to classify layer boundaries, trained on image patches. They segment three layer (NFL, RPE, BM) in Healthy and AMD cases. A CRF postprocessing is applied to create smooth layer boundaries.

6 Discussion and conclusion

The abundance of publications in OCT layer segmentation of the retina in the last years shows a big interest in furthering this field. With the advent of deep learning big improvements have been achieved in terms of performance, especially in pathological cases (AMD, DME, etc.), replacing the state of the art of graph-based methods. The latter cannot deal with highly degenerate retinal layers, where boundaries do not follow mostly horizontal paths or are even completely absent due to atrophy and fluids. Instead, data-driven methods cover a broader spectrum of pathologies and do not need a model-based approach.

While there is a large progress in the field, there are still very few of standard public datasets to be able to compare the results of published methods. This makes it hard to rank algorithms against each other, as they usually test against their own private datasets. In addition, there is disagreement of the assessment on visible anatomy and boundaries thereof in OCT in clinical application. This effect is amplified especially in pathological cases and the lack of reliable metrics, as no single value such as Dice similarity or chamfer distance present a complete picture. A reliable comparison of the performance of published methods becomes thus hard or even impossible. It is therefore of importance to thrive toward extensive, multi-observer and public retinal layer segmentation datasets in OCT.

References

[1] S.J. Chiu, J.A. Izatt, R.V. O'Connell, K.P. Winter, C.A. Toth, S. Farsiu, Validated automatic segmentation of AMD pathology including drusen and geographic atrophy in SDOCT images, Invest. Ophthalmol. Vis. Sci. 53 (1) (2012) 53–61.

[2] S.J. Chiu, M.J. Allingham, P.S. Mettu, S.W. Cousins, J.A. Izatt, S. Farsiu, Kernel regression based segmentation of optical coherence tomography images with diabetic macular edema, Biomed. Opt. Express 6 (2015) 1172–1194.

[3] B. Dubose, D. Cunefare, E. Cole, P. Milanfar, J.A. Izatt, S. Farsiu, Statistical models of signal and noise and fundamental limits of segmentation accuracy in retinal optical coherence tomography, IEEE Trans. Med. Imaging 37 (9) (2018) 1978–1988.

[4] J. Tian, B. Varga, G.M. Somfai, W. Lee, W.E. Smiddy, D.C. DeBuc, Real-time automatic segmentation of optical coherence tomography volume data of the macular, PLoS ONE 10 (8) (2015) e0133908.

[5] J. Tian, B. Varga, E. Tatrai, P. Fanni, G.M. Somfai, W.E. Smiddy, D.C.C. DeBuc, Performance evaluation of automated segmentation software on optical coherence tomography volume data, J. Biophotonics 9 (5) (2016) 478–489.

[6] A. Shah, L. Zhou, M.D. Abramoff, X. Wu, Multiple surface segmentation using convolution neural nets: application to retinal layer segmentation in OCT images, Biomed. Opt. Express 9 (9) (2018) 4509–4526.

[7] B. Dodo, Y. Li, K. Eltayef, X. Liu, Graph-cut segmentation of retinal layers from OCT images, in: Proceedings of the 11th International Joint Conference on Biomedical Engineering Systems and Technologies, 2018.

[7a] S. Apostolopoulos, R. Sznitman, Efficient OCT volume reconstruction from slitlamp microscopes, IEEE Trans. Biomed. Eng. 64 (10) (2017) 2403–2410.

[8] Y. He, A. Carass, Y. Yun, C. Zhao, B. Jedynak, S.D. Solomon, S. Saidha, P.A. Calabresi, J.L. Prince, Towards topological correct segmentation of a macular OCT from cascaded FCNs, in: International Conference of Medical Image Computing and Computer Assisted Intervention, Workshop on Ophthalmic Medical Image Analysis, 2017.

[9] M.R. Hee, J.A. Izatt, E.A. Swanson, D. Huang, J.S. Schuman, C.P. Lin, et al., Optical coherence tomography of the human retina, Arch. Ophthalmol. 113 (1995) 325–332.

[10] A. George, J.A. Dillenseger, A. Weber, A. Pechereau, Optical coherence tomography image processing, Invest. Ophthalmol. Vis. Sci. 41 (2000) 165–173.

[11] A.M. Bagci, M. Shahidi, R. Ansari, M. Blair, N.P. Blair, R. Zelkha, Thickness profile of retinal layers by optical coherence tomography image segmentation, Am J. Ophthalmol. 146 (2008) 679–687.

[12] T. Fabritius, S. Makita, M. Miura, R. Myllyla, Y. Yasuno, Automated segmentation of the macula by optical coherence tomography, Opt. Express 17 (2009) 15659–15669.

[13] M. Baroni, J.G. Fortunato, A.L. Torre, Towards quantitative analysis of retinal features in optical coherence tomography, Med. Eng. Phys. 29 (2007) 432–441.

[14] K.L. Boyer, A. Herzog, C. Roberts, Automatic recovery of the optic nerve head geometry in optical coherence tomography, IEEE Trans. Med. Imaging 25 (2006) 553–570.

[15] R. Kafieh, H. Rabbani, S. Kermani, A review of algorithms for segmentation of optical coherence tomography from retina, J. Med. Signals Sens. 3 (2013) 45–60.

[16] M.A. Mayer, J. Hornegger, C.Y. Mardin, R.P. Tornow, Retinal nerve fiber layer segmentation on FD-OCT scans of normal subjects and glaucoma patients, Biomed. Opt. Express 1 (5) (2010) 1358–1383.

[17] Y. Boykov, O. Veksler, R. Zabih, Fast approximate energy minimization via graph cuts, in: International Conference on Computer Vision (ICCV), vol. I, 1999, pp. 377–384.

[18] M.K. Garvin, M.D. Abràmoff, X. Wu, S.R. Russell, T.L. Burns, M. Sonka, Automated 3-D intraretinal layer segmentation of macular spectral-domain optical coherence tomography images, IEEE Trans. Med. Imaging 28 (9) (2009) 1436–1447, https://doi.org/10.1109/TMI.2009.2016958.

[18a] A. Lang, A. Carass, M. Hauser, E.S. Sotirchos, P.A. Calabresi, H.S. Ying, J.L. Prince, Retinal layer segmentation of macular OCT images using boundary classification, Biomed. Opt. Express 4 (7) (2013) 1133–1152.

[19] P.A. Dufour, L. Ceklic, H. Abdillahi, S. Schröder, S. De Zanet, U. Wolf-Schnurrbusch, J. Kowal, Graph-based multi-surface segmentation of OCT data using trained hard and soft constraints, IEEE Trans. Med. Imaging 32 (2013) 531–543.

[20] A. Ben-Cohen, D. Mark, I. Kovler, D. Zur, A. Barak, M. Iglicki, R. Soferman, Retinal Layers Segmentation Using Fully Convolutional Network in OCT Images, 2017.

[21] K. Gopinath, S.B. Rangrej, J. Sivaswamy, A deep learning framework for segmentation of retinal layers from OCT images, in: Proceedings—4th Asian Conference on Pattern Recognition, ACPR 2017, 2018.

[22] Y. He, A. Carass, B.M. Jedynak, S.D. Solomon, S. Saidha, P.A. Calabresi, J.L. Prince, Topology guaranteed segmentation of the human retina from OCT using convolutional neural networks, arXiv (2018) 1–9. preprint arXiv:1803.05120.

[23] B. Chen, Y. He, A. Carass, Y. Yun, C. Zhao, B.M. Jedynak, S.D. Solomon, J.L. Prince, Fetal, Infant and Ophthalmic Medical Image Analysis, vol. 10554, 2017, pp. 202–209.

[24] O. Ronneberger, P. Fischer, T. Brox, U-Net: convolutional networks for biomedical image segmentation, in: N. Navab, J. Hornegger, W.M. Wells, A.F. Frangi (Eds.), Medical Image Computing and Computer-Assisted Intervention—MICCAI 2015: 18th International Conference, Munich, Germany, October 5–9, 2015, Proceedings, Part III, 2015, pp. 234–241.

[25] A.G. Roy, S. Conjeti, S.P.K. Karri, D. Sheet, A. Katouzian, C. Wachinger, N. Navab, ReLayNet: retinal layer and fluid segmentation of macular optical coherence tomography using fully convolutional networks, Biomed. Opt. Express 8 (8) (2017) 3627–3642.

[26] J.I. Orlando, P. Seeböck, H. Bogunović, S. Klimscha, C. Grechenig, S. Waldstein, U. Schmidt-Erfurth, U2-Net: A Bayesian U-Net Model with Epistemic Uncertainty Feedback for Photoreceptor Layer Segmentation in Pathological OCT Scans, 2019, pp. 2–7.

[27] F. Kiaee, H. Fahimi, R. Kafieh, A. Brandt, H. Rabbani, Three Dimensional Fully Convolutional Networks for Segmentation of Optical Coherence Tomography Images in Neurodegenerative Disease (1), 2018, pp. 2–4.

[28] X. Chen, M. Niemeijer, L. Zhang, K. Lee, M.D. Abramoff, M. Sonka, Three- dimensional segmentation of fluid-associated abnormalities in retinal OCT: probability constrained graph-search-graph-cut, IEEE Trans. Med. Imaging 31 (8) (2012) 1521–1531.

[29] M. Pekala, N. Joshi, D.E. Freund, N.M. Bressler, D.C. DeBuc, P.M. Burlina, Deep learning based retinal OCT segmentation, arXiv (2018). preprint arXiv:1801.09749.

[30] X. Liu, J. Cao, T. Fu, Z. Pan, W. Hu, K. Zhang, J. Liu, Semi-supervised automatic segmentation of layer and fluid region in retinal optical coherence tomography images using adversarial learning, IEEE Access 7 (2019) 3046–3061.

[31] C. Peng, X. Zhang, G. Yu, G. Luo, J. Sun, Large kernel matters—improve semantic segmentation by global convolutional network, in: Proc. IEEE Conference on Computer Vision and Pattern Recognition, July, 2017, pp. 1743–1751.

[32] A. Krizhevsky, I. Sutskever, G.E. Hinton, ImageNet classification with deep convolutional neural networks, in: Advances in Neural Information Processing Systems, 2012.

[33] L. Fang, D. Cunefare, C. Wang, R.H. Guymer, S. Li, S. Farsiu, Automatic segmentation of nine retinal layer boundaries in OCT images of non-exudative AMD patients using deep learning and graph search, Biomed. Opt. Express 8 (5) (2017) 2732.

[34] Y. Liu, G. Ren, G. Yang, X. Xi, X. Chen, Y. Yin, Fully convolutional network and graph-based method for co-segmentation of retinal layer on macular OCT images, in: Proceedings—International Conference on Pattern Recognition, 2018-August, 2018, pp. 3081–3085.

[35] J. Hamwood, D. Alonso-Caneiro, S.A. Read, S.J. Vincent, M.J. Collins, Effect of patch size and network architecture on a convolutional neural network approach for automatic segmentation of OCT retinal layers, Biomed. Opt. Express 9 (7) (2018) 3049.

[36] S. Masood, R. Fang, P. Li, H. Li, B. Sheng, A. Mathavan, W. Jia, Automatic choroid layer segmentation from optical coherence tomography images using deep learning, Sci. Rep. 9 (1) (2019) 1–18.

[37] X. Sui, Y. Zheng, B. Wei, H. Bi, J. Wu, X. Pan, … S. Zhang, Choroid segmentation from optical coherence tomography with graph-edge weights learned from deep convolutional neural networks, Neurocomputing 237 (2017) 332–341 (August 2016).

[38] D. Alonso-Caneiro, S.A. Read, J. Hamwood, S.J. Vincent, M.J. Collins, Use of convolutional neural networks for the automatic segmentation of total retinal and choroidal thickness in OCT images, in: Midl conference, 2018, pp. 1–7.

[39] J. Kugelman, D. Alonso-Caneiro, S.A. Read, S.J. Vincent, M.J. Collins, Automatic segmentation of OCT retinal boundaries using recurrent neural networks and graph search, Biomed. Opt. Express 9 (11) (2018) 5759.

Image quality assessment

**Sarah A. Barman[a], Roshan A. Welikala[a], Alicja R. Rudnicka[b],
Christopher G. Owen[b]**

[a]*School of Computer Science and Mathematics, Kingston University,
Kingston upon Thames, United Kingdom,*
[b]*Population Health Research Institute, St. George's University of London, London,
United Kingdom*

1 Introduction

The application of automated analysis techniques to large numbers of ophthalmic images to retrieve useful clinical information is becoming more widespread due to increasing use of routine fundus imaging, availability of datasets and the emergence of increasingly sophisticated analysis techniques. Applications range from population screening for ophthalmic disease detection to epidemiological studies which seek to link retinal morphometric measurements to disease risk and processes. The performance of automated image analysis systems on large sets of images is often dependent on the quality of the image being assessed and this important aspect is reflected in a growing scientific literature which focuses on image quality assessment (IQA) algorithms and their use.

The scope of the main sections of this chapter will be based on IQA algorithms applied to retinal fundus camera images. The applications covered are limited to clinical examples, and biometric applications are not included. The first section will describe how retinal fundus images can vary in quality. Example applications will also be summarized to give an overview of the main challenges. An overview of different algorithms that have been employed to assess image quality and the datasets and metrics used for evaluation will be given in the second section. Summaries of selected algorithms to highlight particular methods and applications follow. The final concluding section includes comment on IQA techniques related to other imaging modalities such as optical coherence tomography.

1.1 Image quality of ophthalmic images

The quality of an image is an important factor that affects image and video analysis systems across a range of different applications including image capture, compression, transmission, segmentation and registration [1]. The reliability of automated algorithms applied to images are linked very closely to the range of image quality that they operate upon. Ophthalmic images can vary in quality for a variety of reasons. These are sometimes related to the ocular health of the patient. For example, in the case of retinal imaging, poor image quality can be caused by media opacity such as cataract, vitreous hemorrhages, asteroid hyalosis, etc. Variation in pupil size (either as a consequence of dilation or natural variation) can affect image quality [2]. Changes in the quality of an image can also be caused by differences in operator behaviour at the time of image capture where differences in camera exposure and focal plane error can all lead to differences in quality. Artifacts relating to the lens of the image capture system (such as debris on the lens) can also lead to changes in image quality. The subject may blink, therefore leading to eye-lashes being inadvertently included in the image. Also, the subject may move their head or eyes, leading to blurring of the image. Image compression techniques can also affect the quality of an image. The factors described above affect the appearance of an image in terms of low contrast, poor focus (e.g. blurring), dark areas on the image and artifacts on the image. Some examples of different retinal fundus images showing how image quality is affected in different ways are shown in Fig. 1.

Algorithms that correct features of poor image quality, such as correcting for uneven illumination and increasing contrast [4, 5], can improve image quality in cases where specific image capture problems arise. Algorithms that evaluate image quality have the potential to alert operators to image clarity problems very soon after the original image has been captured and the subject is still in-situ. A further image can be captured to improve the clarity of the image with minimum inconvenience to the operator or subject. The judgment of the quality of an image relates to how the image will be used in the context of different clinical purposes. IQA algorithms reflect the requirement of a range of different applications; examples of these are discussed in the following section.

1.2 Applications of image quality assessment algorithms

The judgment of whether an image is high quality or low quality is highly dependent on the application that the image is intended for. For example, some images are required for inclusion in ophthalmic screening systems while others may contribute to an epidemiological study requiring morphometric measurements of retinal vessels. Both applications require different aspects of image quality to be evaluated. For screening systems, clarity of the entire image is required to ensure signs of pathology are not missed. In order to obtain reliable vessel morphometric measurements however, image clarity should be adequate to allow accurate vessel segmentation for at least a portion of the image [6]. Human observers judge the quality of images in different ways depending on the application, and automated IQA algorithms reflect these different judgements of image quality, given that automated algorithms are normally evaluated against subjective human evaluation [1]. Non-clinical applications of retinal fundus imaging include analysis for biometric identification, but this is beyond the scope of the applications described in this chapter.

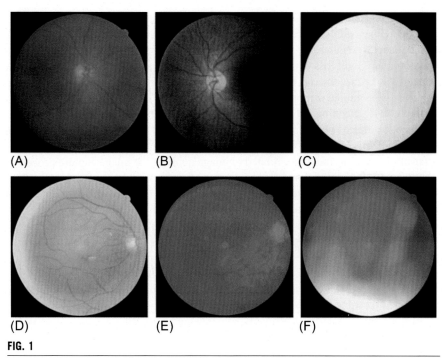

FIG. 1

Examples of impaired/ungradable images. (A) Poor focus and clarity due to overall haze. (B) Poor macula visibility due to uneven illumination. (C) Poor optic disc visibility due to total blink. (D) Edge haze due to pupillary restriction. (E) Dust and dirt artifacts on the lens image capture system (near the center). (F) Lash artifact.

From J.M. Pires Dias, C.M. Oliveira, L.A. da Silva Cruz, Retinal image quality assessment using generic image quality indicators, Inf. Fusion 19 (2014) 73–90.

1.2.1 Screening for diabetic retinopathy

Diagnostic image quality is important in scenarios where individual clinicians judge images to ascertain the ophthalmic health of the patient. For example, a clinician may examine a fundus image to ascertain if a patient has glaucoma, paying close attention to the optic disc area. Optical coherence tomography images may be examined to diagnose diabetic macular oedema. To make a clinical diagnosis which includes the use of information from images, it is important for the image to be of high quality over areas of interest where abnormalities may be expected. In addition to clinical diagnosis on individual patients in a clinic setting, a major requirement for assessment of image quality in a diagnostic application is related to screening programs. Screening for diabetic retinopathy (DR) is the most well-known and established screening system, but automated diagnostic systems are emerging to address screening requirements for diseases such as glaucoma [7]. DR screening programs are covered more fully elsewhere in the book, hence the following summary provides an image quality assessment perspective.

One in ten adults were estimated to have diabetes in 2014 [8], and numbers are increasing. Given sight-loss caused by diabetic retinopathy is a common consequence of the diabetes, regular eye screening among the diabetic population is an effective way to reduce sight loss caused by diabetic retinopathy. Screening for diabetic retinopathy can reduce the risk of blindness by less than half compared with unscreened controls [9]. National screening programs, such as the UK National Health Service Diabetic Eye Screening Programme (NHS DESP) [10] generally rely upon the assessment of images performed remotely from the point of capture. Currently in the NHS DESP, this is performed by human graders at reading centers. Screening programs face specific challenges related to image quality. The image capture process is tightly controlled with defined camera types and image capture protocols. However, because the images are often taken at different sites, the trained ophthalmic photographers may have various degrees of experience, which can affect the quality of image capture. Moreover, subjects may have differing degrees of lenticular/media opacities or subjects may move while the image is being taken, which can lead to images of inferior quality being collected from screening programs. It has been reported that in some cases 12% of total images in a screening program are low-quality and ungradable [11]. One of the aims of a diabetic retinopathy screening system is to detect the first signs of diabetic retinopathy. A pathognomonic sign of early diabetes is the presence of microaneurysms, which are small and difficult to see. If an image is low quality these subtle signs can be missed causing the patient to be incorrectly diagnosed as disease free, i.e., a false negative. A crucial opportunity will therefore be missed to prescribe treatment or lifestyle changes that could slow down or halt the progression of diabetic retinopathy.

In the NHS DESP, images are graded in terms of severity of retinopathy if the image is of adequate quality. In general, image clarity across the entire image is important to ensure subtle abnormalities are detected. If an image is low quality or "inadequate" this is also recorded in a systematic manner. An image is graded as adequate if "the area of interest is positioned within the defined limits and has enough clarity for a reliable decision on the patient's status" [12]. Within the English NHS DESP, one optic disc centered image and one fovea centered image, both with field of view 45°, are captured for each eye of the subject. The correct position of the image is defined in terms of correct centration of the area of interest. For example, the optic disc centered image is classified as adequate if a complete optic disc can be seen in the image which should be more than two optic disc diameters from the edge of the image. In addition, fine vessels should be visible on the surface of the disc. An image is graded as inadequate if the area of interest is not correctly positioned and/or the clarity of the image is not sufficient for a reliable decision on retinopathy grade to be made [12].

Because screening programs have to collect and store large numbers of images, compression techniques are selected that reduce the image size from over 20 MB down to 1–2 MB without loss of image quality and any clinically significant information [13]. The uncompressed images taken in the screening programs often rely on pharmacologically dilated pupils (mydriasis) to maximize image quality. The impact of mydriasis on accuracy in assessment of images was reported by Hansen et al. [14]. The use of mydriasis in screening programs is not universal. Routine mydriasis is implemented for UK NHS DESP, however screening programs elsewhere may operate without routine mydriasis.

Algorithms that are aimed at automating the diabetic retinopathy grading process are emerging [8, 15–18], which will enable grading to be performed with automated software. Image quality assessments are increasingly being used as part of this automation process. With respect to mydriasis, this is often undertaken in diabetic screening systems and can affect image quality. However, Gulshan et al. [16], reports that the performance of their algorithm does not drop significantly when analyzing images captured with and without pharmacological pupil dilation. Further to the diabetic screening programs, progress is also being made to produce automated methods to assist with other disease-screening programs such as glaucoma, macular degeneration and retinopathy of prematurity [7]. Retinopathy of prematurity is a condition that affects pre-term infants and algorithms have focused on retinal vasculometry assessment [19].

1.2.2 Teleophthalmology and clinical decision making

A further example of where image quality relating to diagnostic criteria requires consideration relates to teleophthalmology where the use of portable imaging systems can often lead to wide variations in image quality during routine clinical use. With the arrival of smaller and more portable retinal imaging systems, ranging from portable cameras (e.g. EpiCam M by Epipole Ltd.) to lens attachments for use with mobile phones (e.g. Peek Retina by Peek Vision Ltd.), telemedicine in the form of teleophthalmology can be realized by sending ophthalmic images to specialist centers, to obtain expert opinion on a range of conditions. This technique offers an efficient and cost-effective use of medical resource in communities that may not have any access to expert opinion [20]. Teleophthalmology can also contribute to screening programs such as diabetic retinopathy [21] by expanding the availability of the service from existing established screening centers, to populations with less access to health services.

In addition to diabetic retinopathy, teleophthalmology systems have been explored in relation to retinopathy of prematurity (ROP) [22] where images acquired by a neonatal nurse have been compared to those acquired by an experienced ophthalmologist. Giancardo et al. [23] describes a telemedicine network that performed teleophthalmology in the US, which provided screening for diabetic retinopathy and other diseases of the retina.

Image quality is a vital aspect to be considered in any teleophthalmology system due to the remoteness of image capture and the asynchronous nature of image capture and image analysis (either human or automated). Teleophthalmology systems rely on capturing the image at a remote location and then transmitting the image to an expert some geographical distance away. On most occasions, the expert opinion of the diagnosis is made some time after the original image was captured. Therefore, image quality is an issue that should be addressed at the point of capture for these systems, allowing the opportunity for repeat image capture. Automated analysis techniques are not common in telemedicine systems given the varying quality of the images taken from portable devices and the relatively low-resolution of images captured from portable devices that are suitable for transmission. However, the combination of real-time IQA algorithms combined with advances in analysis techniques and transmission technology is likely to lead to further developments in this area.

1.2.3 Epidemiology study requirements

In addition to large scale screening programs, population based datasets, such as UK Biobank [24], containing tens of thousands of retinal fundus and optical coherence tomography (OCT) images have recently become available. In addition to imaging data, UK Biobank includes general health status (including self-reported health), and information from routine secondary data sources (such as primary care records and Hospital Episode Statistics), data from physical examination (including anthropometry, measures of body composition and blood pressure) and biological samples (including blood, urine and saliva samples) for each participant, providing a valuable resource for the prediction and prevention of both ophthalmic and systemic disease. Progress in linking retinal images with a range of disease biomarkers using this large dataset have been reported [25–28]. The image quality requirements of these systems are very different to those required for diagnostic purposes. For epidemiological studies, the criteria are that the image clarity must be sufficient to allow for the accurate recognition of features on the image (for example vessel segmentation) for a sufficient portion of the image. This holds because useful information can still be extracted from images where a portion of the image is clear, and this can contribute towards analyses relating retinal morphometry to disease risk and outcomes. This approach reduces wastage of images and allows maximum information to be extracted for epidemiological analysis, since for many large population based datasets image quality is often compromised due to avoidance of pharmacological mydriasis to maximize participation [6].

2 Automated image quality assessment algorithms
2.1 An overview of techniques

The majority of automated image quality assessment algorithms have been developed to determine the suitability of an image for diagnostic purposes. However, automated IQA algorithms applied to epidemiological studies have emerged more recently. The following brief overview will summarize IQA algorithms firstly, according to those that are based on generic image quality parameters such as illumination, contrast and sharpness. Second, algorithms will be grouped according to those that are based on structuring image quality parameters such as field definitions (e.g. the position of the main anatomical features within the image) and vascular structure. Finally, algorithms that combine both types of information, in addition to algorithms based on deep learning techniques that have been described recently will be summarized.

The automated IQA algorithms that are based on generic image quality parameters examine characteristics of the image that include the representation of illumination and contrast information. Lee et al. [29] compared the histogram of an image with a template intensity histogram that was obtained from a set of retinal images judged as being of sufficient quality to produce a similarity measure to aid both evaluation of image enhancement methods and clinical diagnosis. Lalonde et al. [30] extended this technique by including a histogram of the edge magnitude distribution in the image in addition to the local intensity histogram templates. Bartling et al. [31] utilized a measurement of illumination quality and image sharpness to produce a pooled quality indicator from non-overlapping image regions. Davis et al. [32] combined 17 features to evaluate the quality of the image in terms of color, luminance and contrast. Pires Dias et al. [3] used the fusion of generic image quality indicators (including color, focus, contrast and illumination) for image quality assessment relating to diagnostic applications. Structural parameters of the image have been considered by Usher et al. [2] which incorporated the area of the vessel segmentation map as an image quality metric. Fleming et al. [33] included both the area of segmented vasculature with the macula and the field definition of the image in order to determine image quality. Hunter et al. [34], with an application aimed at diabetic retinopathy screening, calculated the contrast and quality of segmented vessels within the macular region and combined this with the contrast of the foveal region compared against the retinal background. Lowell et al. [35] proposed an algorithm based on blood vessel structure within an automatically identified circular area around the macular. Niemeijer et al. [36] used image structure clustering on a set of response filter vectors to characterize a set of normal images against which other image structures were compared. Giancardo et al. [37] used an elliptical local vessel density technique that extracted local measures of vessel density in a method aimed to assist diabetic retinopathy screening. Welikala [6] utilized a three dimensional feature vector related to a segmented vessel map to match to epidemiological study requirements.

Paulus et al. [38] used a combination of generic and structural image quality parameters to provide image quality information relating to diagnosis of ophthalmic disease. The method combined texture metrics and image structure clustering to cluster pixels into anatomical structures. Abdel-Hamid et al. [39] tested four different retinal image quality assessments. The analysis investigated how a change in image resolution can affect different image quality assessment algorithms. Algorithms that make use of convolutional neural networks to assess image quality have recently been described. Mahapatra et al. [40] utilized a combination of convolutional neural network approaches with saliency values across different scales to evaluate images in the context of diabetic retinopathy. Sun et al. [41] also used a convolutional neural network approach and explored fine tuning of pre-trained networks. Gulshan et al. [16] applied a convolutional neural network to automatically grade diabetic retinopathy and diabetic macular oedema in retinal fundus images. The algorithm was also assessed in terms of its performance in judging image quality.

All the algorithms described in this section aim to provide an indication of image quality in relation to various applications. Images are either divided into distinct classes (e.g. excellent, good etc.) or quantify image quality (usually on a scale from 0 to 1). The processing speeds of the algorithms described above is variable. Methods that use generic image quality often have low computational requirements, while methods that use structural parameters have higher requirements. Image quality assessment related to epidemiological studies usually take place off-line once the entire dataset has been captured. In applications where image quality assessments are required at the point of capture, such as in diabetic retinopathy screening systems, real-time operation could enhance the accuracy of automated analysis algorithms such as the automated recognition of microaneurysms.

2.2 Datasets and metrics used to evaluate image quality

A number of datasets have been used to evaluate IQA algorithms, which have been described in the literature. In this section, we describe some of the main datasets used along with an indication of their size. Pires Dias et al. [3] used the public datasets of DRIVE [42], Messidor [17], ROC [43] and STARE [44] and two proprietary datasets (it is reported that access is available on request) from DR screening initiatives in the central region of Portugal and Channai, India. The images from Portugal were graded by a human grader from the Association for Innovation and Biomedical Research on Light (AIBILI). An evaluation of the method was performed on a total of 2032 retinal images. Fleming et al. [33] used a private dataset of 1039 retinal images from 489 patients attending a diabetic retinopathy screening program. The images were graded by a clinician for image clarity and field of view. Hunter et al. [34], used a private dataset of two hundred retinal fundus images randomly drawn from a diabetic retinopathy screening dataset which were accompanied by a 1–5 scale of image quality graded by an ophthalmologist, where low scores were associated with poorer quality. Niemeijer et al. [36] used a total of 2000 images from a dataset obtained from a diabetic retinopathy screening program in the Netherlands. Each image was classified by an ophthalmologist to give an image quality category on a scale from one to four. Giancardo et al. [37] used a dataset of 84 macula centered fundus images. They were divided into four classes: "Good", "Fair", "Poor" and "Outliers". The first 3 classes were composed of a subset of a fundus images [11, 45]. Welikala et al. [6] utilized the UK Biobank dataset, which is a large scale population based dataset, with access via an application process. The dataset included 68,151 participants. For evaluation of image quality 800 images were used from 400 random participants. Images were defined by an experienced retinal grader as adequate or inadequate. Paulus et al. [38] used a private dataset of 301 retinal images. Three human observers, including one eye expert, decided on the quality of each image according to set criteria and they judged the image quality to be adequate for a reliable diagnosis to be made, otherwise the images were judged as inadequate. Mahapatra et al. [40] used a dataset acquired from a DR screening initiative. All images were assessed by human graders to confirm if they were suitable for grading. The dataset (D1) consisted of 9653 ungradable retinal images and 11,347 gradable images. Sun et al. [41] used an open source dataset to evaluate the method from the Kaggle coding website [46]. 2894 images and 2170 images as the training set and test set respectively were randomly selected from the 80,000 images available. All the images were tagged by experts regarding the quality of the image in terms of being gradable or not. Abdel-Hamid et al. [39] applied four different retinal image quality assessment algorithms to images originating from four different public datasets: HRF [47], DRIMDB [48], DR2 [49], Messidor [17]. Giancardo et al. [23] made use of datasets that included 10,862 images from a Netherlands study [50]. Access to public image datasets and their accompanying clinical grades are increasing year-on-year. With on-line competitions, such as Kaggle [46], where researchers can compare algorithm performance using access to public training sets, the importance of IQA algorithms is key to enabling reliable and consistent retinal image analysis systems to be developed.

As we have seen, IQA algorithm development is dependent upon the clinical application being used. In order to evaluate an automated algorithm, it must be judged against a ground truth. The ground truth is a classification of an image that has been made by a human observer, who is usually an expert within the field. When IQA algorithms are evaluated, each image contained within a test set is normally classified by experts into two classes that reflect the quality of an image as either "adequate" or "inadequate". If an image is labeled as inadequate, then the image quality is too poor for the clinical objectives for which the image has been taken to be achieved. Given two ground truth classifications of adequate or inadequate, four outcomes are possible with respect to the outcome of the IQA algorithm. Table 1 shows the outcomes if the algorithm is aiming to detect images of inadequate quality [6]. The outcomes can be combined to represent the standard image analysis performance metrics to assess the quality of a binary classification of sensitivity (SN) and specificity (SP) (shown in Table 2). In addition, a receiver operating characteristic (ROC) curve can provide useful insight into the performance of a system to summarize the relative change in sensitivity and specificity at various operating points of the IQA algorithm. The ROC curve plots the true positive rate (SN) against the false positive rate (1-SP) across different operating points of the algorithm. The area under the ROC curve (AUC) is also used by most systems in the literature to summarize the performance of an IQA algorithm. The balance required between optimizing both sensitivity and specificity is highly dependent on the requirements of the clinical application.

Table 1 Four outcomes of classification relating to image quality where the algorithm is detecting inadequate quality images.

	Inadequate original image	Adequate original image
Inadequate image detected by IQA algorithm	True positive (TP)	False positive (FP)
Inadequate image **not** detected by IQA algorithm	False negative (FN)	True negative (TN)

Table 2 Metrics for assessment of image quality classification.

Metric	Description
Sensitivity	TP/(TP+FN)
Specificity	TN/(TN+FP)

Alternatively, some IQA algorithms described in the literature focus on producing a machine quality score. Instead of dividing into categories, a numerical scale is used to define image quality for each image. Systems that use this approach include Lee et al. [29] Giancardo et al. [37] and in this case evaluation methods will differ from the technique applied to the majority of systems described above.

2.3 Examples of retinal image quality assessment systems

A sample of image quality assessment systems are described in more detail in this section. A variety of techniques which have been applied to different applications and use different methodologies are summarized. A brief overview of the methodology is given for each system, in addition to an outline of the application area and method of evaluation.

2.3.1 Algorithms based on generic image quality parameters

Information fusion

Generic image quality parameters relate to focus, clarity and absence of artifacts (e.g. eyelashes or dust) in the image. Image quality assessment methods based on these generic image quality parameters generally have reduced computational complexity, making them appealing for generating real-time results in mobile systems. However, these types of algorithms do not yield information that identifies image quality with location on the retina, which may be important if these are key areas of interest for the diagnosis of a particular condition.

Generic image quality parameters formed the basis of the system described by Pires Dias et al. [3] which aimed to provide an image quality assessment that is relevant to the application of screening and diagnosis of diabetic retinopathy and age related macular degeneration. The algorithm consisted of a number of different stages. In the first stage, pre-processing to remove any non-retinal information was applied. The second stage consisted of image feature evaluation and classification of four image attributes: color, focus, contrast and illumination. The third stage fused the information from the four features and the final classification determined the image to be either "gradable" or "ungradable".

Three of the assessment algorithms (color, contrast and illumination) utilized the approach of histogram backprojection [51], which assessed how pixels in an image were similar to the distribution of pixels in a histogram model. With respect to the assessment of color, for each image class of "bright" or "dark" or "normal" a specific colourmap was constructed from training images. Each colourmap was used to perform color indexing of the retinal image to be assessed for quality, resulting in three color measures which were combined to form a feature vector. Classification techniques were applied to determine the image class of "bright", "dark" or "normal".

The assessment of contrast was also related to the indexing approach and applied a histogram backpropagation to derive an indexed image, which was used to achieve a contrast quality score. The assessment of illumination assessed homogeneity in illumination across the retinal image and a histogram backprojection of the retinal image using an illumination colourmap. The assessment of focus used a combination of a Sobel operator and multi-focus-level analysis. The final classification into an image quality assessment binary decision integrated the previous measures computed from the image that represented image color, focus, contrast and illumination quality. An overview of the method can be seen in Fig. 2.

The final classifier was evaluated with a dataset composed of 848 "ungradable" and 1184 "gradable" retinal images taken from a proprietary dataset and the Messidor dataset respectively. The best overall results were obtained by a Feed-Forward Backpropagation Neural Network with 14 neurons in the hidden layer. The performance of the classifier was plotted on an ROC curve with an AUC=0.9987. The assessment of four generic image quality parameters in the algorithm of color, focus, contrast and illumination combined with the speed of the algorithm could provide useful information for a fundus camera operator with the aim of correction of low quality images at the point of image capture.

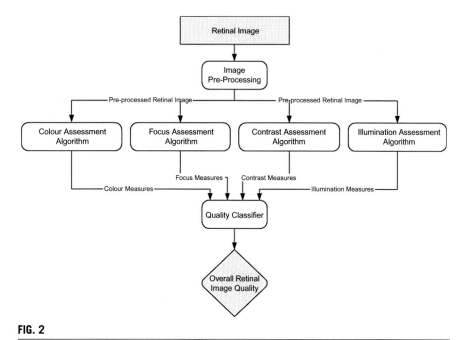

FIG. 2

Retinal image quality assessment algorithm flowchart.

From J.M. Pires Dias, C.M. Oliveira, L.A. da Silva Cruz, Retinal image quality assessment using generic image quality indicators, Inf. Fusion 19 (2014) 73–90.

2.3.2 Algorithms based on structural image quality parameters

The following algorithms show how techniques which rely on structural image quality parameters have been applied to different applications (diabetic retinopathy screening and population based studies).

Image structure clustering

Techniques that rely upon structural image parameters are particularly suited where an image capture protocol is in place, such as is the case for diabetic screening systems. The image structuring technique described by Niemeijer et al. [36] utilized the consistency of structures within a retinal image and their relative ratios. If an image is of low quality this image structure will be disturbed. Niemeijer et al. [36] utilized Image Structure Clustering (ISC) to represent the structures of a retinal image. ISC is a supervised method that enables image structure and their relative ratios to be learnt from a set of images. The method determined the main structures present in a set of normal quality images by the application of a number of filters to generate a set of response vectors. The response vectors were then clustered and the clusters corresponded broadly to anatomical features in the image such as the optic disc. Image structures from unseen images were then compared to those found in the training set.

The response vectors were generated by a filterbank which included various filters at multiple scales. Given the vasculature in retinal images can have different orientations and be located at different points in the retinal image, the filters included in the filterbank were selected to be first and second order filters that were rotation and translation invariant. The filters were applied with different scales to cover the range of image structures found in retinal images. Initially, the image structures from the training set were generated by applying the filterbank to each pixel. Because the structures in retinal images are limited, a random sample of pixels is adequate to produce a representative set of response vectors. K-means clustering was applied, and five clusters were determined as optimum to give the best classification performance [36].

The approach described in[36] involved generating the features from a set of 1000 training images. The features consisted of a histogram of the ISC clustered pixels, in addition to raw RGB histograms. A classifier was trained using selected features and then the classifier was applied to the test set of 1000 images. A support vector machine classifier was shown to achieve optimal performance when compared to other classifiers. The AUC was 0.9968. Misclassifications sometimes occurred where local image quality problems existed, since global histograms were used as features in the system. The training and test set images were derived from a DR screening program in the Netherlands. The images were graded as either low quality or normal by ophthalmologists. An image was graded as low quality if the ophthalmologist felt a "reliable judgement about the absence or presence of DR in the image" was not possible. To compare the performance of the automatic method with a second observer, an ophthalmologist divided the images into four categories of normal quality (definitely or possibly) and low quality (definitely or possibly). The image structuring method above used image structure parameters similar to [33] and [35]. However, the method did not require the segmentation of the vasculature and other anatomical features. This makes the method generalizable and may be useful therefore to extend to other medical imaging applications.

Segmentation map feature analysis

An approach utilizing support vector machines to classify information from segmentation maps was employed by Welikala et al. [6] to ensure retinal image quality assessment for epidemiological study requirements. The requirements for inclusion of retinal images into epidemiological studies are different to those required by DR screening programs. For epidemiological studies, maximizing the amount of data for analysis is key to maximizing statistical power to examine morphometric associations with disease risk and outcome. In Welikala et al. [6] retinal vessel morphometric measurements were analyzed from the UK Biobank [24] fundus image dataset with the aim of understanding the link between retinal vessel morphology and cardiovascular disease risk. Within the UK Biobank dataset, image quality varies significantly across the dataset and therefore a method for assessing the image quality automatically for each image was important to allow for in the analyses. The IQA algorithm developed examined the segmentation map as an indicator of image quality. Criteria for a reliable segmentation in terms of the epidemiological study requirements was defined in terms of three different factors: (i) more than half the vasculature should be segmented (ii) segmentation should not be considerably fragmented/unconnected, and (iii) non-vessel objects should not be segmented (e.g. choroidal vessels, hemorrhages, light reflexes, etc.). Fig. 3 shows the effect of poor image quality (poor illumination in this case) on segmentation quality.

Features were selected to reflect these criteria which summarized the vessel maps in terms of quantitative measures of area, fragmentation and complexity. An SVM was used to divide the retinal images into two classes of "adequate" or "inadequate" quality.

The algorithm was developed to ensure the accurate processing of UK Biobank images and is included in a software system to measure vessel morphometry [52]. The UK Biobank image dataset currently contains images from near 70,000 adults who underwent retinal imaging. A subset of 800 images drawn randomly from this large prospective study was used to train and test the algorithm. An ophthalmic grader graded the quality of the images with respect to the criteria listed above. The performance of the algorithm was reported as achieving a sensitivity of 95.33% and a specificity of 91.13% for the detection of inadequate images. The AUC was 0.9828. Application of the algorithm to the UK Biobank dataset [53] of 135,867 retinal images (68,549 participants) resulted in 71.5% being of adequate quality, equating to 81% participants with at least one image of adequate quality. If images were detected as inadequate they were removed from the analysis. The algorithm correctly detected low quality images that contained incorrect segmentations due to a range of causes including segmentation of choroidal vessels, retinal scars, light reflexes, etc.

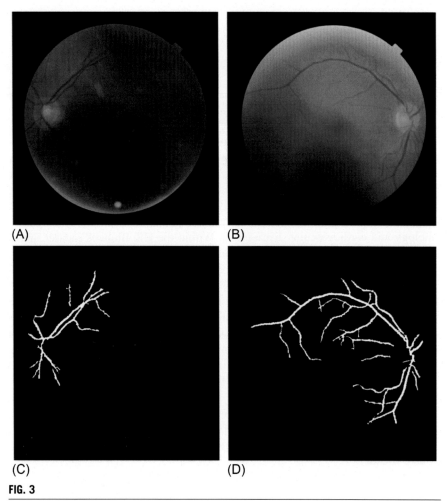

FIG. 3

(A) and (B) show poorly illuminated retinal images, (C) and (D) segmentation of (A) and (B). The human grader has labeled (C) inadequate and (D) adequate.

© UK Biobank.

2.4 Algorithms based on deep learning

Deep learning is emerging as a leading method in the automated assessment of retinal images with respect to diabetic retinopathy detection [16] and cardiovascular risk [28]. Deep learning methods have emerged recently in the area of retinal image quality assessment.

2.4.1 Convolutional neural networks

Gulshan et al. [16] applied a deep learning method to automatically detect diabetic retinopathy (DR) and diabetic macular oedema (DMO) in retinal fundus images. The algorithm was evaluated for its performance in detecting these two diseases and in addition, the algorithm's performance was also evaluated for predicting gradable and ungradable images.

Previous traditional machine learning methods discussed in earlier methods require features to be selected as input to various classifiers such as SVM, ensemble etc. Deep learning algorithms require a neural network classifier with many (deep) layers to be trained, but they do not require features to be selected before training. The neural network takes the intensities of pixels from a large set of fundus images as its training data input and gradually adjusts parameters during the training process until a complex mathematical function is optimized so that the neural network prediction matches the expert grader assessment as closely as possible. Once the training phase is complete, the trained algorithm can be applied to assess diabetic retinopathy severity on unseen images.

The method utilized a convolutional neural network (CNN) that was trained for image classification relating to detection of diabetic retinopathy and diabetic macular oedema in retinal fundus images. The algorithm was trained on a dataset of 128,175 pre-processed retinal images. The training and test set of images were graded for the presence of DR and DMO in addition to image quality by ophthalmic experts.

The CNN architecture used was based on work by Szegedy et al. [54] who used inception-v3 architecture. It was reported that distributed stochastic gradient descent was used to train the network. Batch normalization was also utilized. The network was trained on a variety of images that included mydriatic and non-mydriatic images. The network was trained to make multiple binary predictions that included severity of DR and DMO. Training on 80% of the data was used to optimize the network weights and 20% was used to optimize hyperparameters. An ensemble of 10 networks with the same training data was combined to produce a final prediction.

The evaluation of the algorithm with respect to detection of DR and DMO was reported on two datasets consisting of 9963 images (EyePACS) and 1748 images (Messidor). At an operating point selected for high sensitivity for detecting diabetic retinopathy or macular oedema, sensitivities of 97.5% and 96.1%, and specificities of 93.4% and 93.9% were reported in the 2 validation sets, respectively.

The evaluation of the algorithm with respect to gradable and ungradable images was reported. The algorithm was evaluated for accuracy in assessing image quality for a subset of the data of the main study. The Messidor data set was not included as the number of ungradable images were low. Analysis was reported for the EyePACS-1 dataset. Eight ophthalmologists were involved in grading the 9963 EyePACS-1 images using a grading tool that recorded overall image quality. The image quality was assessed according to criteria relating to focus, illumination, image field definition and artifacts. For fully gradable images the sensitivity and specificity were reported as 93.9% and 90.9%, respectively. AUC was reported as 0.978.

Additionally, the algorithm performance in detecting diabetic retinopathy was also assessed in terms of its performance in handling mydriatic and non-mydriatic images in the EyePACS-1 dataset, which may affect image quality. The authors report similar performance for mydriatic images compared to non-mydriatic images and these findings could impact screening protocols with respect to routine use of mydriasis.

2.4.2 Human visual system information combined with convolutional neural networks

A further implementation of deep learning was reported by Mahapatra et al. [40] that was aimed specifically at providing retinal image quality assessment and taking into account the role of the human visual system (HVS) by the inclusion of saliency map information. Saliency maps aim to define where a particular region is different (or noticeable) from its neighbors with respect to image features. Itti et al. [55] previously developed a visual attention system to select conspicuous locations of a scene. The saliency model proposed combines multiscale feature maps to form a local saliency map which takes both local and global features into account that are relevant for image quality assessment and the identification of gradable and ungradable images.

In addition to information from the saliency maps, information from a trained convolutional neural network (CNN) was included in the final image quality assessment system. The CNN included five convolution layers and five max pooling layers. Rectified Linear Units were used to facilitate faster training and to reduce sensitivity to the scale of the input. During training negative log-likelihood was used as the loss function and stochastic gradient descent using dropout was implemented to reduce overfitting. Data augmentation was applied to expand the training set by image translation and horizontal reflections to expand the dataset size by 50 times. The training data comprised 80% of the total dataset size.

To produce the image quality classification, feature vectors derived from the saliency maps were used to train one random forest (RF) classifier. A second feature vector derived from the last fully connected layer of the CNN was used to train a second RF classifier. Both classifiers used the same image labels. A combination of the probability outputs from the two RF classifiers was used to give a final classification of "gradable" or "ungradable", therefore combining both supervised and unsupervised image features.

The algorithm was evaluated against three other techniques and the data set was acquired from a DR screening program and included 9653 ungradable images and 11,347 gradable images. All images were non-mydriatic and were graded by human graders. The sensitivity was reported as 98.2%, with a specificity of 97.8%. The system was reported to have low computation time and therefore could contribute towards rapid assessment of image quality to inform whether further images are needed while the patient is still in situ.

3 Conclusion

This chapter has focused on IQA of retinal fundus camera images, given that this method of imaging is currently most widespread in clinical applications. Retinal fundus camera imaging provides a two-dimensional image of the eye and white light combined with a specialized microscope attached to a camera is used to acquire the image. Different angles of view of the retina can be taken with varying magnification. The resolution of the retina in fundus images lies in the region of 7–20 μm [27]. Other methods of imaging the retina also require assessment of image quality. Optical Coherence Tomography (OCT) is an important and increasingly widespread retinal imaging method. Near infra-red light combined with interferometry are used to generate a three-dimensional view of the layers of the retina with a resolution in the region of 4 microns [27]. Consensus criteria related to image quality assessment of OCT images has been explored [56] in relation to the application of identification of imaging biomarkers for neurodegeneration in multiple sclerosis. Scanning Laser Ophthalmoscopy (SLO) is a further principal method for imaging the retina and uses a scanning focused laser beam to generate two-dimensional views of the retina at one or two wavelengths by collecting the light through a confocal pinhole. Various fields of view are available (including wide-field). Typical resolutions are in the region of 10–15 microns [27]. Image quality is reported as affecting landmark detection in the analysis of SLO images [57].

The work described in this chapter has focused on image quality assessment algorithms applied to retinal images taken from adult participants. Variations in image quality resulting from prominent arteriole light reflexes in retinal fundus camera images taken from school-age children has been reported with respect to vascular morphometric analysis [58]. Pre-term infants require regular retinal images to be taken to screen for ROP. Swanson reported assessment of quality [59] and IQA was reported for ROP images [60].

In this chapter, we have demonstrated how retinal fundus images can vary in quality according to a number of issues relating to image capture protocol and the condition of the subject. We have shown how the assessment of image quality is dependent upon the application, and how automated IQA algorithms can be evaluated in terms of human judgment of quality relating to how the image will be used for different clinical/epidemiological purposes. Applications covering screening, teleophthalmology and epidemiology studies demonstrate the range of IQA requirements necessary for different applications. A review of different IQA algorithms is given. Following an overview of the field, the main public and private datasets used are summarized together with an account of the metrics used to evaluate IQA algorithms. Finally, to demonstrate the main methodologies that have been applied to different applications, selected examples of IQA assessment algorithms are discussed in further detail. Algorithms based on information fusion, structural image parameter analysis, and machine learning (including deep learning) were included.

Image quality assessment algorithms will play a large part in the future development of analysis systems. Given the emergence of opportunities for the application of deep learning to generate highly automated analysis systems, achieving consistent and high image quality ensures maximum performance of these systems. Real-time feedback of image quality assessment embedded in image capture protocols is likely to become an integral feature of future automated retinal image analysis systems.

References

[1] H.R. Sheikh, M.F. Sabir, A.C. Bovik, A statistical evaluation of recent full reference image quality assessment algorithms, IEEE Trans. Image Process. 15 (2006) 3440–3451.

[2] D.B. Usher, M. Himaga, M.J. Dumskyj, J.F. Boyce, Automated assessment of digital fundus image quality using detected vessel area, in: Proceedings of Medical Image Understanding and Analysis, Citeseer, 2003, pp. 81–84.

[3] J.M. Pires Dias, C.M. Oliveira, L.A. da Silva Cruz, Retinal image quality assessment using generic image quality indicators, Inf. Fusion 19 (2014) 73–90.

[4] M. Foracchia, E. Grisan, A. Ruggeri, Luminosity and contrast normalization in retinal images, Med. Image Anal. 9 (2005) 179–190.

[5] E. Grisan, A. Giani, E. Ceseracciu, A. Ruggeri, Model-based illumination correction in retinal images, in: 3rd IEEE International Symposium on Biomedical Imaging: Nano to Macro, 2006, 2006, pp. 984–987.

[6] R.A. Welikala, M.M. Fraz, P.J. Foster, P.H. Whincup, A.R. Rudnicka, C.G. Owen, et al., Automated retinal image quality assessment on the UK biobank dataset for epidemiological studies, Comput. Biol. Med. 71 (2016) 67–76.

[7] N. Patton, T.M. Aslam, T. MacGillivray, I.J. Deary, B. Dhillon, R.H. Eikelboom, et al., Retinal image analysis: concepts, applications and potential, Prog. Retin. Eye Res. 25 (2006) 99–127.

[8] A. Tufail, C. Rudisill, C. Egan, V.V. Kapetanakis, S. Salas-Vega, C.G. Owen, et al., Automated diabetic retinopathy image assessment software: diagnostic accuracy and cost-effectiveness compared with human graders, Ophthalmology 124 (2017) 343–351.

[9] J. Mason, National screening for diabetic retinopathy: clear vision needed, Diabet. Med. 20 (2003) 959–961.

[10] Diabetic Eye Screening: Programme Overview, https://www.gov.uk/guidance/diabetic-eye-screening-programme-overview, (Accessed August 13, 2018).

[11] M.D. Abràmoff, M. Niemeijer, M.S.A. Suttorp-Schulten, M.A. Viergever, S.R. Russell, B. van Ginneken, Evaluation of a system for automatic detection of diabetic retinopathy from color fundus photographs in a large population of patients with diabetes, Diabetes Care 31 (2008) 193–198.

[12] Pathway for Adequate/Inadequate Images and Where Images can not be taken, https://assets.publishing.service.gov.uk/government/uploads/system/uploads/attachment_data/file/403107/Pathway_for_adequate_inadequate_images_and_where_images_cannot_be_taken_v1_4_10Apr13.pdf (Accessed August 14, 2018).

[13] P.H. Scanlon, The English National Screening Programme for diabetic retinopathy 2003–2016, Acta Diabetol. 54 (2017) 515–525.

[14] A.B. Hansen, N.V. Hartvig, M.S. Jensen, K. Borch-Johnsen, H. Lund-Andersen, M. Larsen, Diabetic retinopathy screening using digital non-mydriatic fundus photography and automated image analysis, Acta Ophthalmol. Scand. 82 (2004) 666–672.

[15] M.D. Abràmoff, J.C. Folk, D.P. Han, J.D. Walker, D.F. Williams, S.R. Russell, et al., Automated analysis of retinal images for detection of referable diabetic retinopathy, JAMA Ophthalmol. 131 (2013) 351–357.

[16] V. Gulshan, L. Peng, M. Coram, M.C. Stumpe, D. Wu, A. Narayanaswamy, et al., Development and validation of a deep learning algorithm for detection of diabetic retinopathy in retinal fundus photographs, JAMA 316 (2016) 2402–2410.

[17] E. Decencière, X. Zhang, G. Cazuguel, B. Lay, B. Cochener, C. Trone, et al., Feedback on a publicly distributed image database: the Messidor database, Image Anal. Stereol. 33 (2014) 231–234.

[18] Diabetic Retinopathy Detection, https://www.kaggle.com/c/diabetic-retinopathy-detection, 2018 (Accessed August 6, 2018).

[19] C. Swanson, K.D. Cocker, K.H. Parker, M.J. Moseley, A.R. Fielder, Semiautomated computer analysis of vessel growth in preterm infants without and with ROP, Br. J. Ophthalmol. 87 (2003) 1474–1477.

[20] K. Johnston, C. Kennedy, I. Murdoch, P. Taylor, C. Cook, The cost-effectiveness of technology transfer using telemedicine, Health Policy Plan. 19 (2004) 302–309.

[21] J. Choremis, D.R. Chow, Use of telemedicine in screening for diabetic retinopathy, Can. J. Ophthalmol. 38 (2003) 575–579.

[22] K.G. Yen, D. Hess, B. Burke, R.A. Johnson, W.J. Feuer, J.T. Flynn, Telephotoscreening to detect retinopathy of prematurity: preliminary study of the optimum time to employ digital fundus camera imaging to detect ROP, J. Am. Assoc. Pediatr. Ophthalmol. Strabismus 6 (2002) 64–70.

[23] L. Giancardo, F. Meriaudeau, T.P. Karnowski, E. Chaum, K. Tobin, Quality assessment of retinal fundus images using elliptical local vessel density, in: New Developments in Biomedical Engineering, InTech, 2010.

[24] Home | UK Biobank Eye and Vision Consortium, http://www.ukbiobankeyeconsortium.org.uk/, 2018 (Accessed August 15, 2018).

[25] C.G. Owen, A.R. Rudnicka, R.A. Welikala, M.M. Fraz, S.A. Barman, R. Luben, et al., Retinal vasculometry associations with cardiometabolic risk factors in the European prospective investigation of Cancer Norfolk study, Ophthalmology (2018), https://doi.org/10.1016/j.ophtha.2018.07.022.

[26] T.J. MacGillivray, J.R. Cameron, Q. Zhang, A. El-Medany, C. Mulholland, Z. Sheng, et al., Suitability of UK biobank retinal images for automatic analysis of morphometric properties of the vasculature, PLoS One 10 (2015) e0127914.

[27] T.J. MacGillivray, E. Trucco, J.R. Cameron, B. Dhillon, J.G. Houston, E.J.R. van Beek, Retinal imaging as a source of biomarkers for diagnosis, characterization and prognosis of chronic illness or long-term conditions, Br. J. Radiol. 87 (2014) 20130832.

[28] R. Poplin, A.V. Varadarajan, K. Blumer, Y. Liu, M.V. McConnell, G.S. Corrado, et al., Prediction of cardiovascular risk factors from retinal fundus photographs via deep learning, Nat. Biomed. Eng. 2 (2018) 158–164.

[29] S.C. Lee, Y. Wang, Automatic retinal image quality assessment and enhancement, in: Medical Imaging 1999: Image Processing, International Society for Optics and Photonics, 1999, pp. 1581–1591.

[30] M. Lalonde, L. Gagnon, M.-C. Boucher, Automatic visual quality assessment in optical fundus images, Proc Vis Interface 32 (2001).

[31] H. Bartling, P. Wanger, L. Martin, Automated quality evaluation of digital fundus photographs, Acta Ophthalmol. 87 (2009) 643–647.

[32] H. Davis, S. Russell, E. Barriga, M. Abramoff, P. Soliz, Vision-based, real-time retinal image quality assessment, in: 2009 22nd IEEE International Symposium on Computer-Based Medical Systems, 2009, pp. 1–6.

[33] A.D. Fleming, S. Philip, K.A. Goatman, J.A. Olson, P.F. Sharp, Automated assessment of diabetic retinal image quality based on clarity and field definition, Invest. Ophthalmol. Vis. Sci. 47 (2006) 1120–1125.

[34] A. Hunter, J.A. Lowell, M. Habib, B. Ryder, A. Basu, D. Steel, An automated retinal image quality grading algorithm, in: 2011 Annual International Conference of the IEEE Engineering in Medicine and Biology Society, 2011, pp. 5955–5958.

[35] J. Lowell, A. Hunter, M. Habib, D. Steel, Automated quantification of fundus image quality, in: Proceedings of the 3rd European Medical and Biological Engineering Conference, 2005, p. 1618.

[36] M. Niemeijer, M. Abramoff, B. Vanginneken, Image structure clustering for image quality verification of color retina images in diabetic retinopathy screening, Med. Image Anal. 10 (2006) 888–898.

[37] L. Giancardo, M.D. Abramoff, E. Chaum, T.P. Karnowski, F. Meriaudeau, K.W. Tobin, Elliptical local vessel density: a fast and robust quality metric for retinal images, in: 2008 30th Annual International Conference of the IEEE Engineering in Medicine and Biology Society, 2008, pp. 3534–3537.

[38] J. Paulus, J. Meier, R. Bock, J. Hornegger, G. Michelson, Automated quality assessment of retinal fundus photos, Int. J. Comput. Assist. Radiol. Surg. 5 (2010) 557–564.

[39] L. Abdel-Hamid, A. El-Rafei, S. El-Ramly, G. Michelson, Performance dependency of retinal image quality assessment algorithms on image resolution: analyses and solutions, Signal Image Video Process. 12 (2018) 9–16.

[40] D. Mahapatra, P.K. Roy, S. Sedai, R. Garnavi, Retinal image quality classification using saliency maps and CNNs, in: International Workshop on Machine Learning in Medical Imaging, Springer, 2016, pp. 172–179.

[41] J. Sun, C. Wan, J. Cheng, F. Yu, J. Liu, Retinal image quality classification using fine-tuned CNN, in: Fetal, Infant and Ophthalmic Medical Image Analysis, Springer, 2017, pp. 126–133.

[42] DRIVE: Digital Retinal Images for Vessel Extraction, http://www.isi.uu.nl/Research/Databases/DRIVE/, 2018 (Accessed August 15, 2018).

[43] Retinopathy Online Challenge, http://webeye.ophth.uiowa.edu/ROC/, 2018 (Accessed August 15, 2018).

[44] The STARE Project, http://cecas.clemson.edu/~ahoover/stare/ (Accessed August 15, 2018).

[45] M.D. Abramoff, M.S. Suttorp-Schulten, Web-based screening for diabetic retinopathy in a primary care population: the EyeCheck project, Telemed. J. E Health 11 (2005) 668–674.

[46] Kaggle: Your Home for Data Science, https://www.kaggle.com/, 2018 (Accessed August 7, 2018).

[47] T. Kohler, A. Budai, M.F. Kraus, J. Odstrcilik, G. Michelson, J. Hornegger, Automatic no-reference quality assessment for retinal fundus images using vessel segmentation, in: Proceedings of the 26th IEEE International Symposium on Computer-Based Medical Systems, IEEE, Porto, Portugal, 2013, pp. 95–100.

[48] U. Şevik, C. Köse, T. Berber, H. Erdöl, Identification of suitable fundus images using automated quality assessment methods, J. Biomed. Opt. 19 (2014) 046006.

[49] R. Pires, H.F. Jelinek, J. Wainer, A. Rocha, Retinal image quality analysis for automatic diabetic retinopathy detection, in: 2012 25th SIBGRAPI Conference on Graphics, Patterns and Images, IEEE, Ouro Preto, Brazil, 2012, pp. 229–236.

[50] M. Niemeijer, M.D. Abramoff, B. van Ginneken, Segmentation of the optic disc, macula and vascular arch in fundus photographs, IEEE Trans. Med. Imaging 26 (2007) 116–127.

[51] M.J. Swain, D.H. Ballard, Color indexing, Int. J. Comput. Vis. 7 (1991) 11–32.

[52] M.M. Fraz, R.A. Welikala, A.R. Rudnicka, C.G. Owen, D.P. Strachan, S.A. Barman, QUARTZ: quantitative analysis of retinal vessel topology and size—an automated system for quantification of retinal vessels morphology, Expert Syst. Appl. 42 (2015) 7221–7234.

[53] R.A. Welikala, M.M. Fraz, M.M. Habib, S. Daniel-Tong, M. Yates, P.J. Foster, et al., Automated quantification of retinal vessel morphometry in the UK biobank cohort, in: 2017 Seventh International Conference on Image Processing Theory, Tools and Applications (IPTA), 2017, pp. 1–6.

[54] C. Szegedy, V. Vanhoucke, S. Ioffe, J. Shlens, Z. Wojna, Rethinking the Inception Architecture for Computer Vision, ArXiv151200567 Cs, http://arxiv.org/abs/1512.00567, 2015 (Accessed August 15, 2018).

[55] L. Itti, C. Koch, E. Niebur, A model of saliency-based visual attention for rapid scene analysis, IEEE Trans. Pattern Anal. Mach. Intell. 20 (1998) 1254–1259.

[56] P. Tewarie, L. Balk, F. Costello, A. Green, R. Martin, S. Schippling, et al., The OSCAR-IB consensus criteria for retinal OCT quality assessment, PLoS One 7 (2012) e34823.

[57] A. Perez-Rovira, T. MacGillivray, E. Trucco, K.S. Chin, K. Zutis, C. Lupascu, et al., VAMPIRE: vessel assessment and measurement platform for images of the REtina, in: 2011 Annual International Conference of the IEEE Engineering in Medicine and Biology Society, IEEE, Boston, MA, 2011, pp. 3391–3394.

[58] C.G. Owen, A.R. Rudnicka, C.M. Nightingale, R. Mullen, S.A. Barman, N. Sattar, et al., Retinal arteriolar tortuosity and cardiovascular risk factors in a multi-ethnic population study of 10-year-old children; the child heart and health study in England (CHASE), Arterioscler. Thromb. Vasc. Biol. 31 (2011) 1933–1938.

[59] C. Swanson, K.D. Cocker, K.H. Parker, M.J. Moseley, A.R. Fielder, Semiautomated computer analysis of vessel growth in preterm infants without and with ROP, Br. J. Ophthalmol. 87 (2003) 1474–1477.

[60] A. Toniappa, S.A. Barman, E. Corvee, M.J. Moseley, K. Cocker, A.R. Fielder, Image quality assessment in retinal images of premature infants taken with RetCam 120 digital fundus camera, Imaging Sci. J. 53 (2005) 51–59.

Validation

Emanuele Trucco[a], Andrew McNeil[a], Sarah McGrory[b], Lucia Ballerini[c], Muthu Rama Krishnan Mookiah[a], Stephen Hogg[a], Alexander Doney[d], Tom MacGillivray[c]

[a]*VAMPIRE Project, Computing (SSEN), University of Dundee, Dundee, United Kingdom*
[b]*Centre for Cognitive Ageing and Cognitive Epidemiology, University of Edinburgh, Edinburgh, United Kingdom*
[c]*VAMPIRE Project, Centre for Clinical Brain Sciences, University of Edinburgh, Edinburgh, United Kingdom*
[d]*Division of Population Health and Genomics, University of Dundee, Ninewells Hospital and Medical School, Dundee, United Kingdom*

1 Introduction: Why is validation difficult?

Our observation of nature must be diligent, our reflection profound, and our experiments exact

Denis Diderot

The truth is rarely pure and never simple

Oscar Wilde, The Importance of Being Earnest

We start from the conventional definition of validation adopted in nearly all MIA papers [1–5]: *the experimental procedure aimed to show that the output of an algorithm is sufficiently close to a reference standard given a specific image analysis task.* Examples of "specific tasks" are detecting image regions of interest, e.g., microaneurysms or blood vessels in fundus camera images, or macular holes in OCT scans; or grading fundus camera images for diabetic retinopathy. "Sufficiently close to a reference standard" means that quantitative test criteria, e.g., sensitivity and specificity, achieve or exceed some desired levels. The reference standard is provided in the form of *annotations*, i.e., any information added to an image or video by experts. Examples include labels (e.g., a binary flag for the presence or not of a specific lesion, or the name of a lesion from a dictionary of possibilities), grades (e.g., diabetic retinopathy for a whole fundus image, or the tortuosity level of a vessel), and contours traced manually on images (e.g., the contour of the optic disc in a fundus image, or of a layer in an OCT image).

Mission accomplished then? Hardly. Expanding the definition of "validation" above even just a little more [6], we realize that, for a well-specified image analysis problem (see above), one must:

(i) procure clinically relevant, well-characterized data sets (of sufficient size);

(ii) procure a sufficient quantity of annotations from well-characterized experts;

(iii) compute automatic measurements;

(iv) compare statistically the annotations from experts with the automatic results.

Even this limited expansion exposes some nontrivial questions. For instance, when exactly is a data set *clinically relevant*? What do we need to know to declare experts and data sets *well characterized*? *How do we reconcile* different annotations for the same images? What should we do, if anything, when different annotators disagree (the usual situation) *before* we compare their annotations with automatic results? What does *sufficient quantity* mean in practice?

If we think a little broader, further challenges appear. For example, the answers to the questions above change if considering a proof-of-concept validation for a novel algorithm, say suitable for publication in research journals, or the actual translation of the technology into healthcare: the latter requires, among others, much larger, more carefully selected (from a clinical point of view) patient cohorts, replications in multiple, independent cohorts, and conformity with rules from regulatory bodies like the FDA in the United States or the EMA in Europe.

This chapter opens with a concise discussion of the issues making validation a serious challenge (Section 2). It then reviews tools and techniques that we regard as good practice, including data selection and evaluation criteria (Section 3). Further discussion is devoted to the important point of the design of annotation protocols for annotators (Section 4). The chapter closes with a summary and ideas for spreading good practice internationally (Section 5).

2 Challenges

The gross national product measures everything, except what makes life worthwhile.

Robert Kennedy

2.1 Annotations are expensive

Validating and training contemporary computational systems like deep learning systems requires larger and larger volumes of annotations [7–9], but annotating images is time consuming, hence expensive in terms of time and money. The time of clinical practitioners is normally at a premium. The cost of an annotation task depends on what and how much must be annotated: for example, assigning a grade to a fundus image for diabetic retinopathy is quicker than tracing blood vessels with a software tool in the same image.

2.2 Annotation tasks are often unfamiliar to clinicians

Some annotations required to validate image analysis algorithms, especially tracing the detailed contours of regions of interest, are not part of normal clinical practice, or not in the form ideally needed to validate retinal image analysis (RIA) algorithms. This forces specialists to find extra time in their busy schedule, and, in the worst case, images are annotated without sufficient time and concentration.

2.3 Consistency is hard to achieve

The factors just mentioned, added to the different experience of the annotators, are likely to introduce inconsistency in the annotations: some annotators may trace contours in great details, others trace approximate ones; some may be more conservative than others in scoring disease or highlighting lesions; the same specialist may change his/her decisions while going through an image set. For annotations to be useful they must be consistent over different annotators (*inter-observer variability*), and also over the set created by a single annotator (*intra-observer variability*). To mitigate the effects of variations and capture a representative set of opinions one should have access, ideally, to teams of experts, each annotating the same sets multiple times, to characterize statistically both *inter-* and *intra-operator variability*. However, one does not want to impose too strict constraints on annotators, as the inter-observer variability contains useful information; importantly, *the range of variation among expert annotations defines the best performance that an automatic system can achieve meaningfully.*

2.4 Collecting annotations may be limited by data governance

Clinical images and data sets, especially large ones, may not be allowed outside their hospital of origin, be it abroad or within the same country. In some cases, images and data can be made available only within a certified safe haven (SH), which requires strict information governance protocols to be adhered to. This forces one to install and run annotation and processing software within the safe haven, which may introduce restrictions. Similar observations apply to cloud processing for clinical data, a field which is evolving apace.

2.5 Image quality may vary across images and data sets

This is caused by a plethora of factors, including differences in instruments, operators, patients, and local image acquisition protocols and practices. Differences in quality may introduce unwanted noise and lead to significantly different results.

2.6 Absence of unambiguous ground truth

Famously, medical image analysis does not have the benefit of highly accurate ground truth measured objectively. Ground truth consists of gold-standard judgements from experts (see Section 2.3), the *real* accuracy of which cannot be established easily, or not at all. This is not the case in image analysis fields; in metrology, for instance, the accuracy of an optical instrument measuring lengths within a target accuracy of, say,

±10 μm can be tested by comparisons with interferometric measurements accurate to a much higher level (nanometers). In MIA, expert annotations are always different, depending, among others, on annotator's experience and background, image quality, completeness and possible interpretations of the annotation protocol [2, 4, 5].

2.7 Time-varying quantities are not well represented by a single measurement

Medical objects of interest naturally vary in time, adding further complexity to validation. For instance, changes in the width of the larger arterioles in the retina within the heart cycle can be observed near the OD in small-field-of-view fundus camera videos [10]. Hence, accurate arteriolar width would really be best described by a range of values; a single measurement taken at a random time is just a random sample from that range. Incidentally, estimating the effect of this approximation on calculations and statistical analysis using such approximate measurements is another open (and currently underresearched) challenge.

2.8 Test criteria and data sets are not uniform in the literature

RIA and MIA algorithms addressing the same problem (e.g., in retinal image analysis, optic disc contour detection, or drusen localization, or blood vessel segmentation and classification) are often tested with different data sets and criteria (e.g., sensitivity, specificity, accuracy, area under the curve, others) or combinations thereof. This makes objective comparisons very difficult. A revealing (and somewhat concerning) analysis of the effect of changing performance criteria on the ranking of algorithms in international challenges is given in Maier-Hein et al. [4].

2.9 Dependency on application/task

As noted in Trucco et al. [5], annotations of the same quantity or of an image can vary depending on the task a clinician has in mind. For instance, the width of retinal vessels in fundus images may be systematically overestimated by doctors thinking surgically, hence trying to keep at a distance from the vessel. In such cases, it seems advisable to group reference annotations also by clinical task and to specify annotation protocols accordingly.

2.10 Human in the loop

Some RIA systems are semi-automatic, i.e., require intervention of a trained operator to generate results. Well-known examples are SIVA [11], VAMPIRE (including fundus and SLO tools) [12–14], and IVAN [15], all used internationally by many clinical groups. Such systems generate rich quantitative characterizations of the morphometry of the retinal vasculature in fundus images, computing measurements defined a priori. Manual intervention by trained operators limits errors and inaccuracies, hence rejection rates and wrong data passed to statistical analysis, but complicates the evaluation of the overall system and limits processing speed. Notice that the measurements generated by the systems mentioned above do not always agree; this is being investigated by various groups [13, 16, 17].

---

3 Tools and techniques

If your only tool is a hammer, make all your problems look like nails.
Variant of the Law of the Instrument

In practice, comparing the results of an algorithms with the ground truth (annotations) available means studying the statistical agreement or disagreement between two sets of data [5, 18]. Statistics offers well-known instruments (see, e.g., Chapter 10), but no standard protocol has ever been agreed explicitly by the RIA/MIA international communities. In this section we review concisely the techniques available and their rationale, starting from a few considerations on how to choose images sets.

3.1 Choosing images: Aligning data set with clinical criteria

The criteria for choosing test image sets are technical *and* clinical; awareness of both is essential to promote effective interdisciplinarity and translation.

3.1.1 Technical criteria

These address *how difficult it is for the algorithm being tested to produce the correct answer for a given image*. Hence technical criteria help to choose a set of images spanning all levels of difficulty. Such levels must reflect what the software application is *likely to encounter when deployed in the target environment*. For example, low contrast makes detection and segmentation difficult, hence different levels of contrast should be present in the test set; similarly, a single lesion may appear differently, so representative variations must be included. While it is impossible to account for all possible factors and their variations in a test set, an effort should be made to cover at least the major (most common) ones for the target environment. *The choices and rationale applied for building a data set should be reported in publications using the set.*

3.1.2 Clinical criteria

These address *how representative the set of patients is for the clinical question* to which the software system refers, or in the clinical context of which the system will be used. The characterization of the patient cohorts used in a study is a mandatory and detailed part of clinical papers, typically in a section called "Materials." To image processing specialists, such a characterization may look unnecessary for testing novel image processing algorithms; it may seem that a large set of images satisfying the technical criteria is enough. This may be true to achieve publication in medical image processing journals, but not for translation and clinical relevance: clinicians will be interested in testing with images chosen by clinical criteria too, to decide whether an algorithm can actually work with real patients in the real world.

In an effective interdisciplinary collaboration on RIA/MIA, it is important for computer scientists to realize that clinicians will find it difficult to see the value of an application tested only on technical criteria. It is similarly important for clinicians to realize that computer scientists will aim to achieve high performance first (Section 3.2), but are likely to have to learn how to create a *clinically* interesting data set.

3.2 Direct techniques: Focus on the image processing task

We review briefly the performance assessment techniques that we consider an essential toolkit for RIA/MIA. We do not aim to provide a complete tutorial, only to list the techniques that we regard as essential.

The purpose of direct techniques is to *compare quantitatively the output of a program* (e.g., contours of regions, labels for images or parts thereof) *with annotations given in the same format as the program output*. Notice that the latter excludes, at this stage, validation on outcome (Section 3.3).

3.2.1 Receiver operating characteristic (ROC) curves

A receiver operating characteristic curve, or ROC curve [19], is a plot that demonstrates the performance of a test to discriminate between two classes compared to a gold standard (e.g., a computer generated segmentation vs a hand-drawn segmentation by an expert human grader) or cases (e.g., separating disease cases from normal ones). It is created by plotting the true positive rate (TPR), or Sensitivity, against the false positive rate (FPR), i.e., 1-Specificity, for different threshold settings of a parameter. For every possible parameter value selected to discriminate between two classes or cases, some data will be correctly classified as positive (TP = True Positive) and some incorrectly classified as negative (FN = False Negative fraction). Conversely, some data will be correctly classified as negative (TN = True Negative), but some incorrectly classified as positive (FP = False Positive). Plotting TPR against FPR generates a curve in which each point represents a sensitivity/specificity pair corresponding to a particular threshold. The area under the ROC curve (AUC) is a measure of accuracy, in the sense of the ability of an algorithm to distinguish between two classes or groups.

3.2.2 Accuracy and related measures

In the context of segmentation, for example, comparing the output of a computer algorithm to the ground truth generated by an expert human grader, accuracy (Acc) is often assessed by summing the number of correctly identified image pixels—those belonging to a region (i.e., TP) and those external to the region (i.e., TN) and expressing as a fraction of the total number of pixels, P, in the image, $Acc = (TP + TN)/P$. However, this can sometimes be misleading if there are a disproportionate number of pixels belonging to the region. For instance, when segmenting pixels as depicting blood vessels in a retinal image, there may be more than 10 times vessel pixels than non-vessel pixels. As long as the majority of non-vessel pixels are correctly identified the accuracy will always be high, even if the identification of vessel pixels is poor. The Jaccard Coefficient (JC) offers an alternative and is expressed as $JC = TP/(TP + FP + FN)$. If the vessel segmentation by an algorithm matches exactly with the ground truth then JC is one; if there is no overlap JC is 0.

3.2.3 Confusion matrices

For our purposes, a confusion matrix captures the performance of a classifier by showing the number of times the program and an annotator, or two annotators, make any possible pair of joint decisions. The annotator list is the same on both rows and columns. As a simple example, consider two annotators asked to grade the tortuosity of a set of, say, 30 vessels on a 3-point scale, in order to validate a program assessing vessel tortuosity. The data set contains 10 vessels per tortuosity level. The following confusion matrices might result from experiments, where O1, O2 indicate the observers, P the program, and Lk the tortuosity level. The entries can of course be expressed also as percentages, e.g., in our case, 10 (0.33%), 8 (27%), 3 (10%), and so on.

O1	**O2**			
		L1	*L2*	*L3*
	L1	8	2	1
	L2	2	7	1
	L3	0	0	9
O1	**P**			
		L1	*L2*	*L3*
	L1	6	2	3
	L2	2	6	1
	L3	1	2	7
O2	**P**			
		L1	*L2*	*L3*
	L1	10	1	0
	L2	1	9	0
	L3	0	0	9

We can see that the program agrees very well with observer O2, but less well with observer O1. We can also see that the observers do not agree perfectly with each other on the classification of level 1 and 2 (two vessels are labeled L1 by O1 but L2 by O2, and vice versa). Notice that this disagreement defines the best performance we can hope to achieve meaningfully by the program, *given our annotators and data set*. See Gwet [18] for a discussion on confusion matrices, Kappa coefficient and related measures.

3.2.4 Bland-Altman graphs

Bland-Altman graphs [20, 21] are a much-used way in the medical literature to visualize the agreement between two sets of paired numerical measurements, for instance the true and estimated values of, say, diameter of the optic disc, or systolic blood pressure and fractal dimension of the retinal vasculature [22]. They plot the differences d_k, $k = 1, \ldots, N$, of N paired values against their mean, and indeed you can think of them as scattergrams of the pairs' differences against the pairs' means. A Bland-Altman graph also plots two horizontal lines defining limits of agreement, e.g., at $d = d_m \pm \sigma$, where d_m and σ are, respectively, the mean and standard deviation of the differences, or within an interval of confidence (e.g., 95%). Hence, if the measurements in all pairs are very close to each other, all differences are very small, and the plot follows closely the horizontal line at $d_k = 0$. A bias is immediately visualized by plotting the line $d = d_m$.

The motivation behind Bland-Altman graphs, introduced by the authors in 1986 [21], was that the much-used correlation does not indicate the *agreement* of two sets of paired measures, but their *degree of linear dependence* (a particular relation between the variables). The authors give a cogent example of the difference between agreement and correlation: the correlation between a set of caliper measurements and their respective halves is 1 (perfect linear dependence), but the two sets do not agree. An example is given in Fig. 1 [23]. The agreement zone is given by the two dashed lines at the 95% limits of agreement (LOA), defined as the two lines $d_m \pm 1.96\sigma$. The plot shows reasonable agreement, with only one point outside the LOA zone, and very few close to its borders. What level of agreement is acceptable depends on the specific application. Notice the negative bias in the graph (-0.58).

3.2.5 Cohen's kappa and related measures

Cohen's kappa [24] estimates the agreement between two sets of paired *categorical* decisions, accounting for the possibility that the agreement may occur by chance. Its definition is

$$K = \frac{p_0 - p_e}{1 - p_e},$$

where p_o is the observed agreement and p_e the probability of random agreement, estimated from the data (contingency tables). There are no ultimate guidelines on what values constitute good or bad agreement; indicatively, values of K above ~0.7 indicate very good to excellent agreement, between ~0.4 and ~0.7 good agreement, and below ~0.4 poor agreement. Such definitions must be used with care.

If there are more than two sets, *Fleiss's kappa* is used [25]. The *weighted kappa* [26] allows one to weigh measurements differently.

3.2.6 Error histograms

It is often useful to visualize error histograms for each variable measured, to have a feeling for the underlying error distribution. To create a meaningful histogram, attention must be given to two factors: *eliminating outliers* and *choosing an appropriate number of bins*.

Eliminating outliers

What constitutes an outlier in a data sample is a well-investigated topic in the literature, which must be considered carefully in the light of one's knowledge about the data at hand. Much work exists on this topic in statistics and we refer the reader to Ref. [27] for a comprehensive introduction. Well-known methods in computer vision are the Least Median of Squares [28], RANSAC and its many variants [29, 30], and X84 [31].

Choosing an appropriate number of bins

Various rules compute the number of bins most likely, in some statistical sense, to *make the histogram of the sample at hand representative of the underlying distribution*. Getting the number of bin wrong may make the histogram significantly different from the underlying distribution (e.g., more bins than sample generates a flat histogram). A commonly used rule is the one due to Freedman-Diaconis [32]. Briefly, given a sample of numerical measurements $S = \{s_1, \ldots, s_N\}$ *not containing outliers*, the Freedman-Diaconis bin width, w, is

$$w = 2\frac{IRQ(S)}{\sqrt[3]{N}},$$

where $IRQ(S)$ is the interquartile range of S and N is the total number of measurements.

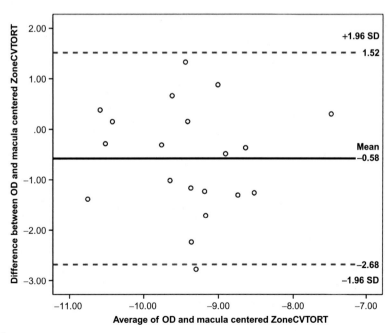

FIG. 1

A Bland-Altman graph visualizing the agreement of venular tortuosity in Zone C for images centered on the OD and on the macula; for details see Ref. [23].

3.3 Validation on outcome: Focus on the clinical task

Validation on outcome aims to validate an algorithm or software tool within the system of which it is a part. Consider for instance an algorithm detecting microaneurysms in retinal fundus images, meant as a component of an automatic refer/do not refer system [33]. Direct validation requires annotations of individual microaneurysms. Validation on outcome requires only the referral decision. *At a parity of other conditions during testing,* the microaneurysms detection module is validated successfully when automatic referral decisions achieve the accuracy desired.

An important advantage of this approach is that it avoids creating additional tasks for doctors providing annotations. In our example, referral decisions are generated in normal practice, but detailed annotations of lesions on images are not. A challenge is that deciding what constitutes the "outcome" may not always be obvious [5].

4 Annotations and data, annotations as data

In God we trust; others must provide data

Edwin R. Fisher

Further, important elements involved in validation emerge if we stand back from the discussion so far, and attempt to look at validation in all its aspects. We discuss concisely a few in this section.

4.1 Annotation protocols and their importance

The collection of ground truth to validate RIA and MIA systems requires the development of a protocol for annotating images or videos, in itself a complex task. Various tasks are involved; we summarize the main ones below.

- *Protocol design.* The protocol must be designed jointly by the clinical and technical (MIA) team. Multiple clinicians ought to be involved [2, 3, 34]. A pilot study can, in our experience, help to identify key parameters of the protocol: for instance, if an ordinal grading scale is involved (e.g., scoring tortuosity, or the severity of a lesion), the optimal number of levels may be identified not only on the basis of current clinical practice, but also of pilot experiments suggesting the number yielding the most accurate results with an automatic system. Hence the final number is obtained by discussion as a compromise between the original one (clinical practice) and the result of the pilot study.
- *Ground truth type.* Once a protocol is agreed, the designers may simply decide to output a set of measurements for each annotator, or also define summative ones capturing some form of consensus among annotators to reconcile differences in measurements. Note that we use "consensus" in a general sense: generating a single value from a set of differing ones (e.g., the tortuosity level of an artery given the different estimates of, say, three annotators).

The difference between deciding the consensus type during protocol design and leaving it to the MIA team (i.e., after annotations are provided) is that the former encapsulates consensus-achieving procedures in the protocol design stage, in which all decisions regarding the generation of the ground truth take place, promoting consistency and awareness to the whole interdisciplinary team. Consensus measurements are best obtained by discussion among the annotators, typically in cases where the disagreement is above a level defined as acceptable (a problem-specific decision). Other, simple consensus measurements include the average (for numerical values) and majority (for categorical or ordinal labels, given at least three annotators). Descriptive statistics characterizing the disagreement among annotators may also be provided, in the form of basic statistics (mean and standard deviation of the signed and absolute differences), histograms or others.

- *Software tool*. An appropriate software tool must be provided to the annotators, selected or designed and developed to make the annotation task as efficient and unambiguous as possible. It is again important to involve clinicians in the choice or design of the software annotation tool.

- *Training sessions*. Once a protocol has been agreed and a software tool identified or created, the technical team should run training sessions to ensure that the annotators follow the protocol consistently. Experience indicates that such training sessions are valuable to avoid inconsistencies in the data which may weaken the subsequent validation of the MIA algorithm.

- *How much detail?* An annotation protocol must support the *consistent* generation of a set of measurements by different annotators. We stress that it is the *procedure* that must be consistent, not the *measurements*: there is important information in the variability among annotators, *assuming that they followed the same procedure*. If annotators make independent decisions or depart from the protocol in various ways, random variations *not related to the target measurements* are introduced in their annotations, weakening the validation of MIA algorithms. It is critical to discuss these aspects with the clinical team.

4.2 Reducing the need for manual annotations

An important trend of contemporary research addresses techniques for limiting the volume of annotations needed for validating a medical image analysis system *maintaining its accuracy* and related performance parameters. Research aimed to reduce the number of annotations needed is particularly important to achieve all-round automation on a large scale, given the unabating proliferation of deep learning systems (artificial intelligence) where a typical network must train millions of parameters. We refer the reader to recent papers [35–38] and to the related literature on automatic annotations in computer vision [39, 40].

We note that *validation on outcome* (Section 3.3) can be regarded as a paradigm for limiting the burden and so to some extent the volume of annotations, as it aims to use information recorded anyway when seeing patients, instead of asking clinicians for additional work like tracing contours on images.

5 Conclusion

Unless somebody like you / Cares a whole awful lot / Nothing is going to get better; / It's not.

Dr. Seuss, The Lomax

The definition and practice of validation of medical image analysis algorithms and software must adapt to the transformations brought about by deep learning and supporting hardware, enabling analysis of larger and larger volumes of data. This challenges the conventional paradigm of specialists annotating images in detail, triggering the need for effective techniques limiting the amount of annotations required to train a model. At the same time, research has exposed the pitfalls of the conventional wisdom of comparing annotations with the output of programs. The quantitative effect of uncertainty on measurements from image analysis on the results of statistical studies aimed at biomarker discovery, among others, remains unclear. We feel that these issues, taken together, are at the very core of the difference between reliable and unreliable science.

How can validation practice be improved to facilitate the translation of novel, reliable technology into healthcare? Part of the answer are visible international consortia promoting good practice in technical challenges with large, public data sets; establishing, as much as possible, agreement on validation definition, criteria, practice and protocols across different challenges and groups in different domains (e.g., automatic analysis of images from radiology or ophthalmology, from surgery-related instruments, etc.); the consequent generation of recommendations approved by international, high-quality consortia of visible groups from both the image/data processing and medical disciplines; ideally, and ultimately, the generation of international standards approved by relevant regulatory bodies.

Acknowledgments

A. Doney, S. Hogg, M.R.K. Mookiah and E. Trucco acknowledge funding from the National Institute for Health Research (INSPIRED: India-Scotland grant on precision medicine for diabetes). A. McNeil acknowledges funding from Medical Research Scotland. L. Ballerini, A. Doney, T. MacGillivray, S. McGrory and E. Trucco acknowledge funding from the Engineering and Physical Science Research Council (EP/M005976/1). L. Ballerini acknowledges funding from LBC1936 Age UK, the Medical Research Council (MR/M01311/1), the Fondation Leducq (Network for the Study of Perivascular Spaces in Small Vessel Disease, 16 CVD 05) and the UK Dementia Research Centre at the University of Edinburgh. T. MacGillivray acknowledges funding from the Edinburgh Clinical Research Facility at the University of Edinburgh.

References

[1] P. Jannin, C. Grova, C.R. Maurer, Model for defining and reporting reference-based validation protocols in medical image processing, Int. J. Comput. Assist. Radiol. Surg. 1 (2006) 63–73.

[2] L. Joskowicz, D. Cohen, N. Caplan, J. Sosna, Automatic segmentation variability estimation with segmentation priors, Med. Image Anal. 50 (2018) 54–64.

[3] L. Maier-Hein, A. Groch, A. Bartoli, et al., Comparative validation of single-shot optical techniques for laparoscopic 3-D surface reconstruction, IEEE Trans. Med. Imaging 33 (10) (2014) 1913–1930.

[4] L. Maier-Hein, M. Eisenmann, A. Reinke, et al., Why rankings of biomedical image analysis competitions should be interpreted with care, Nat. Commun. 9 (2018) 5217.

[5] E. Trucco, A. Ruggeri, T. Karnowski, et al., Validating retinal fundus image analysis algorithms: issues and a proposal, Investig. Ophthalmol. Vis. Sci. 54 (2013) 3546–3559.

[6] C.P. Friedman, J.C. Wyatt, Evaluation Methods in Biomedical Informatics, second ed., Springer-Publishing, New York, 2006.

[7] J. De Fauw, J.R. Ledsam, B. Romera-Paredes, et al., Clinically applicable deep learning for diagnosis and referral in retinal disease, Nat. Med. 24 (2018) 1342–1350.

[8] R. Poplin, A.V. Varadarajan, K. Blumer, et al., Prediction of cardiovascular risk factors from retinal fundus photographs via deep learning, Nat. Biomed. Eng. 2 (2018) 158–164.

[9] D.S.W. Ting, L.R. Pasquale, L. Peng, et al., Artificial intelligence and deep learning in ophthalmology, Br. J. Ophthalmol. 103 (2019) 167–175.

[10] D.W. Palmer, T. Coppin, K. Rana, et al., Glare-free retinal imaging using a portable light field fundus camera, Biomed. Opt. Express 9 (7) (2018) 3178–3192.

[11] Q.P. Lau, M.L. Lee, W. Hsu, T.Y. Wong, The Singapore eye vessel assessment system, in: E.Y.K. Ng, U.R. Acharya, A. Campilo, J.S. Suri (Eds.), Image Analysis and Modeling in Ophthalmology, CRC Press, Boca Raton, FL, 2014, pp. 143–160.

[12] S. McGrory, A.M. Taylor, J. Corley, et al., Retinal microvascular network geometry and cognitive abilities in community-dwelling older people: the Lothian Birth Cohort 1936 Study, Br. J. Ophthalmol. 101 (7) (2017) 993–998.

[13] S. McGrory, A.M. Taylor, E. Pellegrini, et al., Towards standardization of quantitative retinal vascular parameters: comparison of SIVA and VAMPIRE measurements in the Lothian Birth Cohort 1936, Transl. Vis. Sci. Technol. 7 (2) (2018) 12.

[14] E. Pellegrini, G. Robertson, E. Trucco, Blood vessel segmentation and width estimation in ultra-wide field scanning laser ophthalmoscopy, Biomed. Opt. Express 5 (2014) 4329–4337.

[15] T.Y. Wong, M.D. Knudtson, R. Klein, B.E. Klein, et al., Computer-assisted measurement of retinal vessel diameters in the Beaver Dam Eye Study: methodology, correlation between eyes, and effect of refractive errors, Ophthalmology 111 (2004) 1183–1190.

[16] F.F. Wei, Z.Y. Zhang, T. Petit, et al., Retinal microvascular diameter, a hypertension-related trait, in ECG-gated vs. non-gated images analyzed by IVAN and SIVA, Hypertens. Res. 39 (2016) 886–892.

[17] W. Yip, Y.C. Tham, W. Hsu, et al., Comparison of common retinal vessel caliber measurement software and a conversion algorithm, Transl. Vis. Sci. Technol. 5 (2016) 11.

[18] K.L. Gwet, Handbook of Inter-Rater Reliability: The Definitive Guide to Measuring the Extent of Agreement Among Raters, 2014.

[19] J.A. Hanley, Receiver operating characteristic (ROC) curves, in: Wiley StatsRef: Statistics Reference Online, 2014.

[20] J.M. Bland, D.G. Altman, Comparing methods of measurement: why plotting difference against standard method is misleading, Lancet 346 (1995) 1085–1087.

[21] J.M. Bland, D.G. Altman, Statistical methods for assessing agreement between two methods of clinical measurement, Lancet 1 (1986) 307–310.

[22] T. Stosic, B.D. Stosic, Multifractal analysis of human retinal vessels, IEEE Trans. Med. Imaging 25 (8) (2006) 1101–1107.

[23] M.R.K. Mookiah, S. McGrory, S. Hogg, et al., Towards standardization of retinal vascular measurements: on the effect of image centering, in: Computational Pathology and Ophthalmic Medical Image Analysis, Proc MICCAI OMIA-5 Intern. Workshop, Granada, Spain, Sep 2018, Lecture Notes in Computer Science, vol. 11039, Springer, 2018.

[24] J. Cohen, A coefficient of agreement for nominal scales, Educ. Psychol. Meas. 20 (1) (1960).

[25] J.L. Fleiss, Measuring nominal scale agreement among many raters, Psychol. Bull. 76 (5) (1971) 378–382.

[26] J. Cohen, Weighted kappa: nominal scale agreement with provision for scaled disagreement or partial credit, Psychol. Bull. 70 (4) (1968).

[27] S. Hawkins, Identification of Outliers, Monographs in Statistics an Applied Probability, Springer, 1980.

[28] Y.-H. Kim, A.C. Kak, Error analysis of robust optical flow estimation by least median of squares methods for the varying illumination model, IEEE Trans. Pattern Anal. Mach. Intell. 28 (9) (2006) 1418–1435.

[29] M.A. Fischler, R.C. Bolles, Random sample consensus: a paradigm for model fitting with applications to image analysis and automated cartography, Commun. ACM 24 (6) (1981) 381–395.

[30] R. Raguram, M. Frahm, M. Pollefeys, A comparative analysis of RANSAC techniques leading to random sample consensus, in: Proc. Europ. Conf. on Computer Vision (ECCV), Part II, Lecture Notes in Computer Science, vol. 5303, Springer, 2008.

[31] T. Tommasini, A. Fusiello, E. Trucco, V. Roberto, Making good features track better, in: Proc. IEEE Int. Conf. on Computer Vision and Pattern Recognition (CVPR), 1998.

[32] D. Freedman, P. Diaconis, On the histogram as a density estimator: L2 theory, Probab. Theory Relat. Fields 57 (4) (1981) 453–476.

[33] S. Philip, A.D. Fleming, K.A. Goatman, et al., The efficacy of automated "disease/no disease" grading for diabetic retinopathy in a systematic screening programme, Br. J. Ophthalmol. 91 (2007) 1512–1517.

[34] B.H. Menze, A. Jakab, S. Bauer, et al., The multimodal brain tumor image segmentation benchmark (BRATS), IEEE Trans. Med. Imaging 34 (10) (2015) 1993–2024.

[35] Y. Huo, Z. Xu, H. Moon, et al., SynSeg-Net: synthetic segmentation without target modality ground truth, IEEE Trans. Med. Imaging 38 (4) (2019) 1016–1025.

[36] T. Joyce, A. Chartsias, S.A. Tsaftaris, Deep multi-class segmentation without ground-truth labels, in: Proc. Int. Conf. Medical Imaging with Deep Learning, Amsterdam, 2018.

[37] T. Kohlberger, V. Singh, C. Alvino, et al., Evaluating segmentation error without ground truth, in: Proc. Int. Conf. on Medical Image Computing and Computer-Assisted Intervention (MICCAI), Springer, 2012.

[38] V.V. Valindria, I. Lavdas, W. Bai, et al., Reverse classification accuracy: predicting segmentation performance in the absence of ground truth, IEEE Trans. Med. Imaging 36 (8) (2017) 1597–1606.

[39] D.P. Papadopoulos, J.R.R. Uijlings, F. Keller, et al., Extreme clicking for efficient object annotations, in: Proc. IEEE Int. Conf. on Computer Vision (ICCV), 2017.

[40] X. Wang, Y. Peng, L. Lu, et al., TieNet: text-image embedding network for common thorax disease classification and reporting in chest X-rays, in: Proc. IEEE/CVF Conference on Computer Vision and Pattern Recognition, 2018.

Statistical analysis and design in ophthalmology: Toward optimizing your data

10

Gabriela Czanner[a,b,c], **Catey Bunce**[d,e,f,g]

[a]*Department of Applied Mathematics, Liverpool John Moores University, Liverpool, United Kingdom*
[b]*Clinical Eye Research Centre, Royal Liverpool University Hospital, Liverpool, United Kingdom*
[c]*Department of Eye and Vision Science, University of Liverpool, Liverpool, United Kingdom*
[d]*Faculty of Life Sciences and Medicine, King's College London, London, United Kingdom*
[e]*Moorfields Eye Hospital NHS Foundation Trust, London, United Kingdom*
[f]*UCL Institute of Ophthalmology, London, United Kingdom*
[g]*London School of Hygiene and Tropical Medicine, London, United Kingdom*

1 Introduction

1.1 Data analysis in ophthalmic and vision research

Statistics is the science of learning from data, and of measuring, controlling and communicating uncertainty.

(Marie Davidian and Thomas A. Louis)

Research in ophthalmology and vision seeks to discover the mechanism by which pathology manifests, to find ways for efficient diagnosis and monitoring of diseases, to compare treatments for pathology and make recommendations on preventative measures. Typical questions might be: What pathological lesions in the retina are predictive of losing sight in 2 years from now? Why do some eyes respond well to a therapy and others not? Can we use the functional properties of the eye such as electroretinography to diagnose stages of diabetic retinopathy? Answering such questions is the grand ambition of this broad enterprise. While much is already known forming the basis for our current knowledge, the methods that produce this knowledge, the scientific method, involves both observations and running clinical studies producing the data, are evolving, offering real potential to extend our knowledge. We rely upon data to answer questions but as new techniques are discovered these data are becoming increasingly complex—while previous research was conducting using perhaps simple measurements such

Computational Retinal Image Analysis. https://doi.org/10.1016/B978-0-08-102816-2.00010-1

as intraocular pressure, nowadays we have the opportunity to go so much further with much richer and more complex data sets such as retinal images. The explosion of data (which perhaps exceeds the limits of traditional statistical methods) has led to increasing analyses being conducted by those without formal training in statistical methodology. Good statistical principles still apply, however, and for these reasons for a modern researcher in ophthalmology a working knowledge of traditional and more modern statistical methods is indispensable. Statistical errors in medical research can harm the very people that researchers seek to help. Computational analysis has this same potential, which is why the learnings from traditional statistical methodology must be handed over.

Our primary goal in this chapter is to give a comprehensive review of the current most important design paradigms and data analysis methods used in ophthalmology and show briefly how all the concepts link together within the discipline of the statistical science. We have a second goal. This comes from our experience of reading numerous published reports that are analyzed by people who lack training in statistics. Many researchers have excellent quantitative skills and intuitions, and most times they apply statistics correctly. Yet, there are situations when statistics or design is not done properly, or the data are not used to the full potential which may be due to a simple lack of statistical training. Some statistical concepts are challenging and if introduced too early or without warning that the methods they use might take time to sink in leave people hating the very word statistics. This is a huge shame. Clinical researchers have the clinical expertise to translate findings from complex statistics to have meaning. Computer scientists have the skills to program methods that are more complex than traditional statistical techniques needed. Different disciplines need to engage with each other in order to best use the innovative data explosion that we face. Different disciplines develop their own terminology but it is not new science if in reality the same discovery is simply being made within a different academic discipline with a new name. It is a wasted opportunity. If instead of re-inventing the wheel we hand over learning by speaking with each other, we will go further with our discovery. With increasing use of data science and machine learning (ML) methods to analyze imaging data and to illustrate data, we aim to try to establish a link between statistical science and retinal image analysis and machine learning: for instance, what are the differences and commonalities between statistics and ML? Is it worth discussing ML techniques for retinal data analysis, from the point of view of statisticians?

1.2 The contribution of statistics in ophthalmic and vision research

Some researchers believe that statistics is a collection of methods for design of studies and for analysis of data such as *t*-test, analysis of variance, linear regression etc. This is true in part. Statistics is also a scientific discipline where statisticians strive for something deeper, for the development of statistical methods of study designs, data collection, data analysis and communication of results. They build this on principles of combinatorics and probability and by doing so they bring quantification of knowledge and rationalizing the learning and decision-making process.

There are two main tenets of the statistics [1]:

- Statistical models are used to express knowledge and uncertainty about a signal in the presence of noise, via inductive reasoning.
- Statistical methods may be analyzed to determine how well they are likely to perform. These methods include: exploratory data analysis, statistical inference, predictive or prognostic modeling, and methods of discrimination or classification. The performance of the methods depends on data collection and management and study designs.

Here we elaborate on these principles and mention ways in which statistics has contributed in ophthalmology. The first tenet says that the statistical models serve to describe regularity and variations of data in terms of probability distributions. When data are collected, repeatedly, under conditions that are as nearly identical as an investigator can make them, the measured responses exhibit variation. For example, the corneal curvature measured via the maximum keratometric reading (Kmax) exhibits variation between measurements done on the same day with a short break between the measurements [2]. Therefore, the most fundamental principle of the statistics and its starting point is to describe this variability via probability distributions. What do we mean? Probability distributions will allow to describe the curvature to be equal to the mean curvature, hence the regular component, and to the random variation due random change in light conditions or random change in the direction of the camera, hence the noise component. For example, when the underlying mathematical expression of the signal is $y = f(x)$, which is then replaced by a statistical model having the form, $Y = f(x) + \varepsilon$, where the capital letter Y denotes a random variable that we aim to measure, the letter ε is the noise and hence the expression above becomes *signal plus noise*. The simplest form is when $f(x)$ is a constant, such as mean μ, or a linear regression line, such as $\beta_0 + \beta_1 x$, where the coefficients μ, β_0, β_1 are unknown *parameters*, denoted by Greek letter to follow statistical convention. Then the parameters are estimated together with some measure of uncertainty about them (e.g. P-value or confidence interval) and this is then used to infer about the values of the parameters, μ, β_0, β_1.

The second tenet says that each statistical method is a tool whose properties can be analyzed. This is important statement. It means that each statistical method (such as two-sample independent t-test) is a method and as such it works well only in certain scenarios. The two-sample t-test works well if assumptions on which the test was built are satisfied. Those assumptions are normality of the measured data and the design is that two independent random samples were obtained (such as two unrelated groups of patients). However, statistical theory can be used to study how well would a two-sample t-test work if some of the assumptions are not satisfied, i.e. if is it *robust* to some violations [3].

2 Data classification, data capture and data management
2.1 Data classification

Measurements are everywhere in ophthalmology and vision science. As machinery develops, we are able to capture things that previously were not possible. In past times there was no topography and so ophthalmologists could not explore Kmax measurements and how they change over time. While glaucoma researchers have for many years looked at measurements of Intraocular Pressure (IOP) there are now new methods for measuring this and they may now need to capture corneal thickness. Measurements may be intuitively understood by many to be data but what about information such as whether or not a patient has improved following a treatment, how the patient feels about a particular condition. This also has value and serves as data. In order to understand how to use statistical methods to convert data into meaningful information that can answer questions of interest in ophthalmology research it is important to be able to classify data. Classification is needed as a step toward understanding which statistical method can be employed.

There are several ways that data can be classified. One approach that is found within many statistical textbooks is to first consider data as being either categorical or numerical data. Categorical data is viewed by some as perhaps the simplest type of data. A categorical variable may have two categories (dichotomous) such as whether or not a patient has a diagnosis of glaucoma (yes or no) or may have several categories such as the quality of an image measured as excellent, good, fair, or poor. In the second example, we can see that there is a natural ordering to the data—an excellent image quality is readily understood by a researcher as being *better* than a good quality image and a fair image quality might be readily understood to be *better* than a poor image quality. Such quality data can be termed ordinal. For other categorical data with several categories however there may be no intuitive way of ordering data—for example, eye color. Such data may be termed nominal. Measurement data may be continuous or discrete—discrete data occur when the observation in question can take only on discrete values, such as the number of events (e.g. number of lesions in retinal image). The numerical continuous data are usually obtained by some form of measurement. Typical examples are weight, height, blood pressure, cup-to-disc ratio, curvature of vessels, size of a lesion or the central foveal thickness or an average thickness of retinal layers across whole macula, corneal topography. These numerical continuous measurements can take on any value from a continuous scale range, except they may be limited by the precision of the instrument or precision of the recording (e.g. we may decide to store the weight to the closest 100 g). The type of data can be critically important in determining which statistical method of analysis will be appropriate and valid [4]. In many ophthalmic studies many types of variables are collected, so that several different analytical methods may be needed.

Another important way of classifying data is into whether it is independent or paired. This information is also needed in order to best select the appropriate form of analysis. If observations come from different individuals they may be regarded as independent. If however there is a relationship between observations—for example the intraocular pressure in a glaucomatous eye pre- and post-delivery of eye drops, or indeed the intraocular pressure of the right and left eyes of the individual, the data are not independent. Within imaging data there may be several thousand different values measured on a single eye yielding data that are not independent. It is therefore important that the statistical technique used to explore such data addresses such potential nonindependence as well as addresses the unit of analysis [12].

A further issue to consider is whether or not a value being analyzed is an actual measurement or whether it is actually a summary score that represents some pre-processing of data. If the later has occurred it is necessary to know how the pre-processing has been done. Failure to do this may result in spurious associations between variables being seen (see e.g. ocular perfusion and intraocular pressure in Refs. [5, 6]). Measuring devices often pre-process the data. This is a point that is often forgotten.

2.2 Data collection and management

Many statistical textbooks and courses on statistics begin with a clean data set. Unfortunately in the real word researchers are often faced with something that is very different to a clean dataset. They are presented with data sets that may have missing values for some patients, there may be values recorded which are not feasible, dates may be captured in varying forms (day/month/year) (month/day/year) and variables might be captured as *text fields*. Below are two tables from spreadsheets (both fictitious). One would require considerable modification prior to data analysis (Table 1) while the other would not (Table 2). An example of the modification that would be needed would be to convert all weights captured so that they are in the same units—not alternating between kg and stones and pounds. If weights of differing units were to be read as a single variable then a summarizing such data would be meaningless. In the *dirty spreadsheet* Ethnicity has been captured as free text. A variety of entries have been made for this variable but if we consider the category *White* there are three terms (White, W and w) that have been used within this column to indicate that the subject was *white*. Prior to data analysis these need to be converted into the same term so that when the categories are summed, the correct totals are provided rather than having to tally several sub-totals. The example (Tables 1 and 2) illustrate a very small data set, but consider this amplified by several tens, hundreds or thousands. While code can be written to facilitate the data conversion, writing such code can be time consuming and may introduce error. This can be avoided by carefully considering how to capture data correctly in the first place. Time spent planning data capture—avoiding free text, use of standard coding systems where possible (such as the ICD coding for capturing disease) mean that data analysis can be conducted efficiently and results delivered in a timely fashion.

Table 1 A spreadsheet requiring a lot of cleaning

	Age of patient	Patient gender	Height (in.)	Weight (pound)	24 h hct	Blood pressure	Tumor stage	Ethnicity	Date enrolled	Complications
Comparison of drug A and drug B										
Drug A										
1	25	Male	61"	>350	38%	120/80	2–3	Hipanic	1/15/9?	No
2	65+	Female	5'8"	161	32	140/90	II	White	02/05/1999	Yes
3	?	Male	120 cm		12	>160/110	IV	Black	Jan-98	Yes, pneumonia
4	31	m	5'6"	obse	40	140 sys 105 dias	?	African-Am	?	
5	42	f	>6ft	Normal	39	Missing	≥2	W	Feb-99	
6	45	f	5.7	160	29	80/120	NA	B	Last fall	n
7	Unknown	?	6	145	35	Normal	1	W	2/30/99	n
8	55	m	72	161.45	12/39	120/95	4	African-Am	6/15/00	y
9	6 months	f	66	174	38	160/110	3	Asian	14/12/0C	y
10	21	f	5'							
Drug B										
1	55	m	61	145	Normal	120/80 120/90	IV	Native Am	6/20/	3
2	45	f	4"11	166	?	135/95	2b	None	7/14/99	n
3	32	Male	5'13"	171	38	140/80	Not staged	NA	8/30/99	n
4	44	na	65	?	40	120/80	2	?	09/01/00	n
5	66	fem	71	0	41	140/90	4	w	Sep 14	y, sepsis
6	71	Unknown	172	199	38	>160/110	3	b	Unknown	y, died
7	45	m	?	204	32	140 sys 105 dias	1	b	12/25/00	n
8	34	m	NA	145	36	130	3	w	Jul-97	n
9	13	m	66	161	39	166/115	2a	w	06/06/99	n
10	66	m	68	176	41	1120/80	3	w	01/21/58	n

Table 2 A spreadsheet not requiring a lot of cleaning

Case	Group	Age	Sex	Ht	Wt	HCT	BPSYS	BPDIAS	Stage	Ethnicity	Date	Complic
1	1	25	1	61	350	38	120	80	3	3.0	1/15/1999	0
2	1	65	2	68	161	32	140	90	2	1.0	2/5/1999	1
3	1	25	1	47	150	38	160	110	4	2.0	1/15/1998	1
4	1	31	1	66	161	40	140	105	2	2.0	4/1/1999	0
5	1	42	2	72	177	39	130	70	2	1.0	2/15/1999	0
6	1	45	2	67	160	29	120	80	1	2.0	3/6/1999	0
7	1	44	1	72	145	35	120	80	1	1.0	2/28/1999	0
8	1	55	1	72	161	39	120	95	4	2.0	6/15/2000	1
9	1	0.5	2	66	174	38	160	110	3	4.0	12/14/2000	1
10	1	21	2	60	155	40	190	120	2	2.0	11/14/2000	0
11	2	55	1	61	145	41	120	80	4	5.0	6/20/1999	1
12	2	45	2	59	166	39	135	95	2	1.0	7/14/1999	0
13	2	32	1	73	171	38	140	80	1	1.0	8/30/1999	0
14	2	44	2	65	155	40	120	80	2	2.0	9/1/2000	0
15	2	66	2	71	145	41	140	90	4	1.0	9/14/1999	1
16	2	71	1	68	199	38	160	110	3	2.0	1/14/1999	1
17	2	45	1	69	204	32	140	105	1	2.0	12/25/2000	0
18	2	34	1	66	145	36	130	75	3	1.0	7/15/1997	0
19	2	13	1	66	161	39	166	115	2	1.0	6/6/1999	0
20	2	66	1	68	176	41	120	80	3	1.0	1/21/1998	0

The use of new technology clearly means that many measurements are now captured and exported automatically. Such automation should reduce error but it is important to acknowledge that sometimes it can introduce new error if an algorithm within a computer has not been correctly programmed for example. Even if the data are captured robustly there will still be a need for careful indexing of such exports so that the correct export is assigned to the correct patient. Within big data a new term is evolving called provenance. The term *data provenance* refers to a record trail that accounts for the origin of a piece of data (in a database, document or repository) together with an explanation of how and why it got to the present place. It should be noted that many statisticians would simply describe this as good statistical practice! Formalizing the process however may well reduce errors that are arising because of a lack of involvement with the statistical community.

2.3 Words of caution about data collection in the current era of big data

Big data may mean that researchers have little control over data collection since they are combining datasets, which have been compiled by others. It is nevertheless important for all involved in research to understand the need for rigor in data collection and management.

When data are first imported into a statistical program a statistician conducts a descriptive analysis of the data. For continuous data this typically involves construction of histograms and scatter plots. These allow detection of values that are inconsistent with other data—so called *outliers*. Different statistical packages may identify different values as outliers because they used different definitions. This can cause confusion to those new to statistical analysis but in reality, the idea is to assess whether there are values that are atypical. If these are found, it is important to go back to the laboratory to assess whether or not they are errors. Most statisticians would not routinely advise dropping outliers. They may, however, advise that an analysis is conducted with and without the unusual observations to assess whether or not their inclusion impacts upon results.

In the past, the scientific community typically analyzed the data that they had. If there were missing observations on a few subjects then it became challenging to know what to use as denominator for percentages (the total number of subjects or the number of subjects reporting that value) but beyond this, missing data was not really considered. In 1987, however a *revolution* took place in relation to thinking about missing data. This came about following two highly influential books and the development of powerful personal computing [7, 8]. Researchers started to acknowledge that data that were missing might systematically differ to data that were not missing and that analyzing only available data had the potential to distort results and mislead. New concepts were introduced—missing at random, missing completely at random, missing not at random and researchers were strongly advised to document the degree of missing data and how this might impact upon results (see more about data missingness in Section 5).

3 Uncertainty and estimation
3.1 Uncertainty

In ophthalmology we face many uncertainties and they can be of many types. For example, we may not know if a treatment will work for a specific patient i.e. an uncertainty for one particular patient. Another example can be that we do not know the true corneal thickness due the precision of the measurement i.e. we face uncertainty in the measurement caused by a measurement error, which can be either due to the device, the slight change in the light conditions, the training of the technician taking the measurement, or patient's fatigue. A third example can be that we are not certain how a treatment affects visual acuity in diabetic patients i.e. we are uncertain how patients with treatment compare to patients with standard care and we may not be certain if there are other factors to take into account like age or life style.

What do we humans do when we face uncertainty? We rationalize by listing all possible outcomes and assign probabilities of how likely each outcome is. Some of us may be better at this, some of us may panic, but usually our estimation of uncertainty and our decisions get better as we get older. For example, in rolling a fair six-sided dice with numbers 1–6, we may be interested in the outcome of having an odd number. Such an outcome is uncertain and we can estimate the uncertainty easily realizing that there is a probability of exactly ½ of observing the odd number in any of the dice rolls. Throwing a fair dice and estimating the probability is simple. A more challenging can be estimating the chance of a rain. Some of us may not like taking a walk in the rain so we estimate the probability of the rain and if the probability is sufficiently small we go for a walk. An even more challenging scenario is to estimate the uncertainty of a person dying in a car accident. We may decide to estimate the probability ourselves or we can let someone else to estimate it. If we let someone else to estimate the probability of dying in a car crash, then we need to decide if we trust such an estimate, as there is an also an uncertainty on how good is his/her estimation. In other words we need to judge the credibility of the estimation, and to do so we may want to consider factors of how credible is this statistician judging by the quality of his/her publications in the area of car crashes and the risk estimation.

In ophthalmology, we typically have complex scenarios of uncertainty and they follow three main types (as in most of the medical fields). Firstly, we face uncertainty in the values of patients' outcomes. For example, we may be clear about the plausible range of visual acuity in patients with diabetes, but we maybe uncertain about which visual acuity value will be measured and recorded for the right eye of a randomly chosen patient. Visual acuity can take on many values (on e.g. Early Treatment Diabetic Retinopathy Study (ETDRS) scale) and each value has a different probability of occurring. In statistical terms this means that we quantify the uncertainty in VA via a probability distribution. We usually do not know this probability distribution so we can estimate this uncertainty via e.g. a histogram. Secondly, we may be clear that age affects the visual acuity but we may be uncertain about other factors affecting the visual acuity, such as treatment, diet of the patient and life style.

A solution would be to quantify the uncertainty in VA in the presence of factors such as age, treatment, diet etc. and see which of them are relevant. This brings us to the third uncertainty. We may be uncertain about the data analysis itself. The uncertainty in the data analytical process involves numerical data obtained on patients or eyes, it can involve expert judgment (e.g. in Bayesian analysis), it involves assumptions (e.g. normality) that can be verified but seldom known exactly (more in Section 3.2).

To quantify uncertainties the statistics relies on ***theory of probability***. Probability is a rich and beautiful subject, a scientific discipline unto itself. Here, however, we assume that the reader is knowledgeable in the main concepts of probability and how they are used in statistics, as this is taught in most of statistical, data science and machine learning courses. One excellent reference is [3] which is suitable for graduate students of computer science and honors undergraduates in math, statistics, and computer science as well as graduate students of statistics who need to learn mathematical statistics. The book teaches probability, the formal language of uncertainty, as well as showing how they are used in the process of learning from data, about statistics.

3.2 The problem of estimation, *P*-values and confidence intervals

As we mentioned above in the statistics we aim to quantify the uncertainty. We assume that we have a ***population*** of patients that we are studying, we choose a ***sample*** from the population (often as a ***random sample*** of several patients or eyes), collect measurements on the patients or eyes to build the ***data***. Then using the data we do estimation, and from this estimation, we do ***inference*** about the whole population. This process is called the concept of ***statistical inference*** and it follows the essence of ***inductive reasoning***, see e.g. Ref. [3].

In quantifying the uncertainty, most of the time we use methods that involve free ***parameters***. For example linear regression model has the form

$$Y_i = \beta_0 + \beta_1 X_i + \varepsilon_i \, .$$

The parameters β_0, β_1 need to be estimated, in other words the model is fitted to the data. Following a convention in the statistical literature, we use θ to denote a generic parameter vector. In our discussion we focus on the case of a single, scalar parameter, but in most real-world problems θ becomes a vector, e.g. $\theta = (\beta_0, \beta_1)$. The problem of parameter estimation is to determine a method of estimating θ from the data. To constitute a well-defined estimation method we must have an explicit procedure, that is, a formula or a rule by which a set of data values $x_1, x_2, \ldots, x_n$ produces an estimate of θ. We consider an ***estimator*** of θ to have the form $T = T(X_1, X_2, \ldots, X_n)$, i.e., the estimator is a random variable derived from the random sample, $X_1, X_2, \ldots, X_n$. The properties of an estimator may be described in terms of its probabilistic behavior.

It is important to make two comments on statistical notation for estimation. First, when we write $T = T(X_1, X_2, \ldots, X_n)$ we are using capital letters to indicate clearly that we are considering the estimator, T, to be a random variable, and the terminology distinguishes the random *estimator* from an *estimate* the latter being a value the estimator takes, $T(x_1, x_2, ..., x_n)$. Nonetheless, neither we nor others in the literature are systematically careful in making this distinction; it is important conceptually, but some sloppiness is OK as long as the reader understands what is being talked about. Second, we often write $est(\theta)$ or $\widehat{\theta}$ for the value of an estimator, so we would have, say, $T = \widehat{\theta}$. The latter notation, using $\widehat{\theta}$ to denote an estimate, or an estimator, is very common in the statistical literature. Sometimes, however, $\widehat{\theta}$ refers specifically to the maximum likelihood estimator (MLE).

The most common methods of parameter estimation are:

- The method of moments uses the sample mean and variance to estimate the theoretical mean and variance.
- The method of maximum likelihood maximizes the likelihood function, which is defined up to a multiplicative constant. A related method is method of restricted likelihood.
- The method of least squares finds the parameter estimate so that it minimizes the sum of residual squares.
- Markov Chain Monte Carlo Methods (MCMC) are computationally intensive methods that give an estimate of the parameter vector as well as of its multivariate distribution.

For the scientific inference, the parameter estimates are useless without some notion of *precision* of the estimate i.e. the *certainty* of the estimate. One of the simplest illustrations of the precision is in estimation of a normal mean. A statistical theorem states that if $X_1, X_2, ..., X_n$ is a random sample from a $N(\mu, \sigma^2)$ distribution, with the value of σ known, then the interval

$$\left(\overline{X} - 1.96 \cdot SE\left(\overline{X}\right), \overline{X} + 1.96 \cdot SE\left(\overline{X}\right)\right)$$

is a 95% confidence interval (CI) for μ, where $SE\left(\overline{X}\right)$ is given by $SE\left(\overline{X}\right) = \sigma / \sqrt{n}$. The beauty of this confidence interval lies in the simple manipulations, that allow us to reason the form of the confidence interval. We take the description of variation given above and convert it to a quantitative inference about the value of the unknown parameter μ. For more explanation of confidence intervals and how they relate to hypothesis testing see e.g. Refs. [3, 4]. For example of statistical inference in retinal imaging see e.g. Refs. [9, 10].

3.3 Words of caution on statistical and clinical significance and multiple tests

When the *P*-value of a statistical test is lower than a predefined level of significance, i.e. when $P < \alpha$, we have *statistical significance* or we say that the result is statistically significant. Here we elaborate on two main issues or misconceptions of statistical significance: clinical significance and multiple testing problem.

Statistical significance alone is not a sufficient basis to interpret the findings of a statistical analysis for the knowledge generation about clinical phenomena [11].

In ophthalmic research (as well as other medical areas) very often the researchers declare that there is statistical difference (or significance) but they do not provide a discussion on the size of the difference; or they find no statistically significant difference between treatments when in reality the study may simply lacked the power to detect a difference [13]. Clinical trials today typically are powered at over 85% (ideally 90%)—they cost a lot to run and are very time consuming and the last thing that anyone wants is an inconclusive trial—there is no difference but it is possibly that there was insufficient power to detect a difference that was of real clinical impact. If ever a study declares non-significance, identify the research question, identify the null hypothesis, compute the *effect size* with a 95% confidence interval—then consider the implications of changing practice if in reality the truth is the upper or lower bound of the confidence interval.

An example of this might be a trial exploring whether or not posturing is needed for patients undergoing vitrectomy surgery. The null hypothesis here would be that there is no difference between the risk of failure in patients posturing face down after surgery and the risk of failure in patients not posturing after surgery. Suppose a clinical trial is then conducted with 200 patients in each arm of the study. In the face-down group one patient requires additional surgery because their macular hole re-opens. In the non-posturing group, two patients require repeat surgery. The odds ratio for this would be 2.02 with a confidence interval of (0.18–22.3). The P-value would be 0.999. This is a statistically nonsignificant result but does that mean that there is no requirement for patients to posture after surgery? There were twice as many patients in the non-posturing group who required repeat surgery and if we look at the confidence interval we see that although the data are consistent with there being no difference in risk between trial arms, there is much uncertainty attached to the estimate as presented by a very wide confidence interval.

Another important issue is *multiple hypothesis testing*. When we conduct a test of significance at the conventional 5% significance level we have a 1 in 20 chance (or 0.05 probability) of concluding that there is significance when there is no real difference and we have a 1–0.05 or 0.95 chance of concluding that there is no difference. If we conduct two tests of statistical significance the probability that neither are statistically significant is $0.95 \times 0.95 = 0.90$. If we were to test 5 independent tests of significance the probability that none are statistically significant would be 0.95^5 and the probability that at least one is significant is 0.226. This means that if many tests of significance are conducted it is highly likely that there will be a spurious statistically significant result. This is called the multiplicity issue or the problem of multiple comparisons or the problem of multiple testing. To deal with this problem there are statistical adjustments that can be applied. The one perhaps most widely known is the Bonferroni adjustment which simply divides the P value of the significance test by the number of tests conducted [14]. This adjustment has disadvantages in that it over-corrects i.e. is very conservative if there are a large number of tests or if the tests (more precisely, the test statistics) are positively correlated. This is because the Bonferroni adjustment assumes that each test is independent of all other tests. In MRI imaging research the random field theory is being used to correct for the millions of comparisons. However, there are scenarios where we do not need to adjust for multiple testing. If the study is clearly stated as exploratory and an acknowledgment made that the research is being conducted in order to generate hypothesis for further testing, corrections for multiple testing may not be needed. It is best however to avoid multiple testing.

4 On choosing the right statistical analysis method
4.1 The most common statistical methods

Here we aim to give a quick glimpse into the most commonly used methods in ophthalmology. This list is not exhaustive, by any means, and it is based on our research practice. Our introduction is very short, however, a keen medical reader, who is new to statistics, is welcome to read a gentle intuitive introduction to the statistical methods by Altman [4]. Those would like a more mathematical overview and understanding of statistics are advised to consult a monograph by Wasserman [3] which was written as a textbook for statisticians or computer scientists. For a good ophthalmic introduction to diagnostic studies, sensitivity and specificity we recommend [15]. A discussion of multivariate versus multivariable statistical methods is in [22].

It is important to note that statistics is an evolving scientific discipline with new methods being developed to better analyze real world data of increasing complexity. It is impossible to give a guide to all the statistical methods. Instead, we attempt to give a guide to simpler statistical methods used in ophthalmology.

We created a table (Table 3) of the most used methods and in doing so we divided them by their goal, specific objective, design of data collection, and type of data. Some more complex modern methods that we do not list in the table are: longitudinal modeling, joint-modeling and predictive modeling.

4.2 How to decide what method to use?

"What statistical method should I use?" This is a question that statisticians are often asked when approached by researchers. The answer is often not straightforward. It depends on several factors, some factors are common to all studies some are specific to a type of study (see Table 3). It is fair to say that the answer to this question is only found after a thorough discussion between the statistician and the researcher.

The main factors that determine the data analysis method are:

- Goal of the analysis together with specific objectives e.g. Is the goal to describe the sample?, Is the goal to test a hypothesis?, Is the goal to derive and evaluate a diagnostic method?
- Type of data being collected e.g. Are the collected data continuous skewed or normally distributed, are they categorical?
- Design of the study e.g. Is the study a prospective study or randomized study? Are there repeated measurements taken on eyes? Is it a longitudinal study?

Table 3 A summary of the most used statistical analysis methods used in ophthalmology and vision research

Goal of the analysis	Specific objective	Design	Type of data or type of dependent variable		
			Categorical	Continuous normal	Continuous skewed
Describe the data i.e. descriptive methods	Numerical summary of one variable	Random sample	Frequency tables	Mean, standard deviation	Median and interquartile range
	Graphical summary of one variable	Random sample	Barcharts	Histogram, boxplots	Histogram, boxplots
Infer from data about the population i.e. confirmatory or exploratory methods	Inference about one variable in one group	Random sample	Binomial test if binary data	One-sample t-test	One-sample median test
	Relationship of one DV with one EV where EV has two levels, e.g. two groups	Random sample, two *independent* groups	Chi-squared test, Fisher's exact test, logistic regression if DV binary	Independent two sample t-test	Mann-Whitney U test
		Random sample, *related* groups	McNemar's test	Paired t-test	Wilcoxon test
	Relationship of one DV with one EV has three or more levels, e.g. three or more groups	Random sample, *independent* groups	Chi-squared test, Fisher's exact test, logistic regression if DV binary	One-way ANOVA[a]	Kruskal-Wallis test
		Random sample, *related* groups	Repeated measures logistic regression, conditional logistic, if EV is binary	One-way repeated measures ANOVA[a]	Friedman test
	Relationship of one DV with two or more EV	Random sample	A suitable type of logistic regression if DV binary	ANCOVA[a], Linear regression[a]	Poisson regression, survival regression if DV is time to event
Derive, evaluate a diagnostic test and methods of measurement i.e. diagnostic methods and methods of measurement	Derive a diagnostic test, prognosis, prediction, screening test	Random sample	Discriminant analysis, cluster analysis, predictive modeling using generalized linear or nonlinear models, empirical Bayes, etc.		
	Reliability (consistency) of the test, method comparison	Random sample	Kappa[a] or weighted Kappa for ordered categories	Bland-Altman plot (intra-rater and inter-rater reliability)	Apply transformations to make data normally distributed, then use Bland-Altman plot
	Validity (accuracy) of the diagnostic test	Random sample	Validation techniques[a] (AUROC, sensitivity, specificity, negative predictive value etc.)		

[a] Always check that the assumptions of the statistical method are satisfied; and be aware that if the assumptions are violated, then the results cannot be trusted.
Note that, for the brevity, we did not include here all the assumptions of the methods. The listed methods are just an example of the simple statistical methods that can be used.
DV, dependent variable; EV, explanatory variables.

What is the response of the statistician to the question of choosing the right statistical method? A good statistician will respond with clarifying questions: "Can you give me some clinical background? What is the goal of your research study and do you have a hypothesis?" Here the statistician will aim to find out if your study is exploratory (i.e. hypothesis generating), confirmatory (i.e. inferential or hypothesis testing), diagnostic (including prognostic or predictive). Then the statistician will follow with questions on how you designed the study and how you collected the data. Ideally, however, a statistician would be part of the study already and would have been involved in the decision making process when the study design was being developed, and hence the statistician would not have to ask all these questions.

4.3 Words of caution in the data analysis method selection

Visualizing data is very important and underrated. In his famous Exploratory Data Analysis, Tukey [16] wrote: "The greatest value of a picture is when it forces us to notice what we never expected to see." A misconception is that we do not need the exploratory analysis if we are doing a confirmatory (inference) study. Exploratory analysis (such as examining means and medians, histograms, piecharts) are crucial for research. They are often termed as descriptive data analysis methods (see Table 3). There are several reasons why we need them. They help us to understand data, check for outliers, any expected or unexpected patterns. They help us to create the demographics tables and summaries for the reports. They help to verify the distribution of the data so that we can make informed decision about the data analysis selection (Section 4). Furthermore, when using a complex data analysis methods (e.g. adjusted logistic regression), it is essential to understand the way the results agree, or disagree, with those from simpler methods (e.g. unadjusted logistic regression). Therefore, when we write a research report, we are obliged to include both: the results from the simple data analysis methods as well as the complex methods, so that reviewers can judge the consistency between the results.

Sophisticated statistical analytic techniques are rarely able to compensate for deficiencies in data collection. A common misconception is that a flaw in the data collection, in study design can be adjusted for via a complex fancy statistical data analysis method. It is indeed true that an alternative data analysis technique may be able to help avoid some difficulty, such as by adjusting for confounders when analyzing data from observational study rather than controlling for confounders via randomization or careful selection of subjects. However, there are many scenarios where a complex statistical method will not help to rectify the flaws. For example in a study of association between intraocular pressure and diabetes a potential confounder is systolic blood pressure. If we collect this confounder as a dichotomous data (or if we do not collect it at all) then the estimated association between diabetes and intraocular pressure will be underpowered and/or biased [17].

Often *case control* studies involve matching at the study design stage so as to make comparator groups more similar to each other. It is important to note that if this is captured within the design the analysis must reflect the design by use of conditional logistic regression or another analysis which allows for the preservation of matching.

A special caution needs to be given to parametric and non-parametric methods. As we said before the statistical methods use probabilistic models to express the way regularity and variation in the data are to be understood. The variation can be expressed in two ways: we can use a methods that assumes a particular distribution of data (e.g. normal) with a finite number of parameters (two parameters in case of univariate normal distribution) which would be a **parametric method**. The second possibility to express the variation in data is by not imposing any assumptions on the distribution of the data, hence there are no parameters involved, hence a **non-parametric method**. For example if we compare means using an independent two sample *t*-test, then such approach is a parametric approach as it assumes that the data are normally distributed i.e. that the noise is normally distributed with two parameters (mean zero and unknown variance). An alternative, nonparametric method would be to use Mann-Whitney test (Table 3). When to use parametric methods and when non-parametric methods? There are two principles to remember. Firstly, where assumptions of parametric methods are plausible, possibly after a transformation of data, parametric methods are preferable providing extra power and allowing adjustment for other factors [19]. For example for a comparison of two samples, if data are normal, or normal after a log or square root transformation, we can use two-sample *t*-test, otherwise Mann-Whitney test may be more appropriate [20]. An alternative to non-parametric methods is given by bootstrapping or resampling, but such methods should not be considered without reference to a statistician [21]. Secondly, it is important to remember that the parametric methods are often not robust to outliers while the non-parametric methods are in general robust. Outliers may be more often identified in smaller samples, small samples are hard or impossible to check for normality, which leads to a misconception that non-parametric methods are for small samples. This is indeed wrong.

There are several other important concepts that are often misunderstood. For completeness, we will briefly list them here and we will also give references for further reading. One concept that is often misunderstood is the distinction between multivariable vs multivariate methods [22]. Next, in the data design with data at baseline and follow-up we need to be careful to incorporate the baseline values [23]. Next, a caution is needed for adjusting for the confounders. We need to be careful about the criteria for control or confounding [24]. Another area of misunderstanding relates to the choice of the statistical model. In the choice of the model, we need to be careful what the goal of the analysis is. Often a goal is either to do the inference (e.g. explain) or to estimate the future values of the outcome (e.g. predict). These two goals may seem similar, but there are several differences that translates to how a model should be chosen [25]. Another commonly misunderstood area is in using the correlation coefficient for evaluation of the agreement [2, 26]. Final caution is for all of us to remember, "All models are wrong but some are useful" by George Box. His point was that we should focus more on finding a model that is useful to answer a particular real life question; rather than focusing on finding a model that will be correct in all scenarios and that will answer all the questions.

5 Missingness of data

5.1 Main mechanisms of data missingness

With the increase in the number of randomized clinical trials and cohort studies analyzing imaging data, even the most robustly designed study can have missing data [27]. Missing data, or missing values or images, occur when no data value is collected and stored for the variable in an observation e.g. eye or patient. Missing data are a common problem in research and can have a negative impact on the conclusions of the analysis. Here, we first discuss types of missingness and then the strategies for dealing with missing data but what we hope emerges is a very clear message that there is no ideal solution to missing data and prevention is the best strategy [18].

It is important to identify why data are missing. Missing data can occur because of a nonresponse for the patient (e.g. the patient drops out of the study early), or for some variables of a patient (e.g. patient is in the study but is not able to have fluorescein angiography taken, or data are lost). There may be various reasons for the missingness, sometimes missing values are caused by the researcher (e.g. when the data collection is done improperly or mistakes are made in data entry) or by patient (e.g. patient refuses to report or have a measurement done, or patient leaves the study). These reasons of missingness can have a different impact on the validity of conclusions from research.

There are three main types of data missingness. Suppose we are studying visual acuity (Y) as a function of diabetes (X). Some patients wouldn't have their visual acuity recorded, so you are missing some values for Y. There are three possible mechanisms for the missingness:

- There may be no particular reason why some patients have Y recorded and others didn't. That is, the probability that Y is missing has no relationship to X or Y. Pattern of missingness is independent of missing values and the values of any measured variables. In this case our data is missing completely at random (MCAR).
- Those without diabetes may be less likely to have their visual acuity recorded. That is, the probability that Y is missing depends only on the value of X. Such data are missing at random (MAR).
- Those with good sight may be less likely to their visual acuity recorded. That is, the probability that Y is missing depends on the unobserved value of Y itself. Such data are not missing at random (MNAR).

5.2 Main strategies to tackle missing data

There are several strategies to analyze the dataset if missingness is present. Here we highlight the main points:

- The most common approach to deal with missing data is to simply analyze everyone with complete data only—an *available case* or *complete case* (CC) analysis (see scenario 1 in Ref. [18]) where cases or subjects with missing data are simply omitted from the analysis.

- An alternative to complete case analysis is to impute the missing data. Imputation replaces the missing data with some plausible value predicted from that subject's (or another subject's) data. One method of imputation, which is commonplace in ophthalmic literature, is that of *last observation carried forward* (LOCF), where any missing data is replaced with the last observed value for that patient. Such method assumes that there was no change in the variable over time since the last observation was obtained and recorded.
- There are *multiple imputation* (MI) methods that draw plausible values multiple times from the observed distributions of relevant variables and aggregates the results incorporating the differences between them in the estimates of uncertainty. A multiple imputation method is a superior method to simple imputation methods or to LOCF, but is only appropriate when the assumption of MAR can be made [28].
- There are model based approaches, that that do not impute data but rather fit the model to all the data available hence they do not omit any cases or patients with missing data, i.e. all cases and patients data are utilized. Those methods are, for example, generalized estimating equations (GEE), multivariate normal linear models (MNLM) also referred to as mixed-model repeated measures (MMRM). Such methods are only valid for MAR.
- Finally, there are model based approaches that do not impute data, they model the data available as well as they model the drop-out (i.e. the missingness mechanism). Some of the methods are selection models (SM), pattern-mixture models (PMM) and joint modeling.

Appropriateness of the statistical analysis methods depends on the reason of data missingness. The main points to remember are the following:

- In MCAR scenario, complete case analysis is valid, though there is a loss of information. In a longitudinal study LOCF is valid if there are not trends with time. While this method may be appropriate when there is little missing data, it can lead to incorrect conclusions. If an available case analysis is conducted, it is essential to examine reasons for data being missing. If there are not many missing data, an available case analysis with a valid assumption of data being MCAR may be unbiased (i.e. it does not overestimate or underestimate a treatment difference or evidence of association), but it will have lower power to detect a difference or association than if all data were present [29].
- In MAR scenarios, CC, LOCF and GEE are invalid, as they can yield biased estimates of associations. The methods MI, MNLM and weighted GEE may be appropriate to use [30].
- In MNAR scenarios, CC, LOCF, GEE, MI and MNLM are not recommended to use because they can lead to biased inference. SM, PMM or joint modeling may be appropriate in this scenario.

5.3 **Words of caution for dealing with missing data**

Clearly there are situations where there is no information about those who are missing. In such cases, we would recommend drawing attention to the presence of missing data and the fact that it was not possible to investigate further. By doing this, readers are aware of the potential for bias. Best and worst-case scenarios could be considered to show how conclusions might have differed under such circumstances. E.g, in a study comparing drugs A and B, and where the primary outcome is treatment success, a best case scenario might be that all those lost to follow-up on treatment A were successes while all those on treatment B were failures. A worst-case scenario would reverse these assumptions.

The consequence of missingness clearly increase with larger number of missing data. If the numbers lost are smaller this clearly limits their likely impact on study conclusions, yet even small numbers can alter study conclusions [18].

It is important to note that different missing data analytical approaches can yield different conclusions. For example, in a detailed study Fielding et al. [31] describes the REFLUX trial which randomized 357 participants with gastro-oesophageal reflux disease to surgery or medicine and had an overall high response rate of 89%, i.e. 11% of patients did not have a record of the primary outcome. The authors examined the impact of missing data on a quality of life outcome measure, the EuroQuol EQ-5D which is the primary outcome of a large clinical trial currently being conducted on patients with glaucoma. Fielding et al. explored eight different approaches to missing data and show that while two approaches gave statistically significant results, six did not; and that for the statistically significant models, one estimated an effect that was of clinical significance, the other did not. Choice of analysis method for missing data can thus impact on conclusions. A word of caution on complexity of advanced statistical methods is provided by Streiner, however: "the easy methods are not good and the good ones … are not easy" [32].

In summary, it is the best to take preventive measures to avoid missing data. This can be done by closely following the study protocol and taking preventative measures to avoid mistakes, this also includes the recording of the reasons for the missingness. If missing data occur then it is essential to visualize summaries or plots for the pattern of the missingness. It is important to remember that if the assumptions made in relation to missingness are incorrect, then the analyses may lead to misleading results and conclusions. Therefore, it is crucial to report the amount and the pattern of the missingness and to report the methods used to handle the missing data in the analyses. For cohort studies it is advisable to follow the reporting guidelines of Strengthening the Reporting of Observational studies in Epidemiology (STROBE) STROBE [33–35]. For randomized clinical trials it is advisable to follow the guidelines of CONsolidated Standard of Reporting Trials (CONSORT) [36] and for diagnostic studies to follow the STARD publication standard [37]. This will ensure that missing data are reported with enough detail to allow readers to assess the validity of the results. It is important to remember, that incomplete data and the statistical methods used to deal with the missing data can lead to bias, or can be inefficient.

Another possibility is that the authors are encouraged to use online supplements (if necessary) as a way of publishing both the details of the missing data in their study and the details of the methods used to deal with the missing data. A cohesive summary of this approach to the missing data is the flowchart in Ref. [18] which was designed with a clinical trial in mind, but applied to observational studies too.

6 Designing an ophthalmic study

6.1 Study designs, sample size calculation and power analysis

There is a large amount of literature written on designs and the pyramid of the evidence, for example: Refs. [4, 38]. In what follows, we will focus on a related challenging question: on how to do sample size calculations.

Why do we do sample size calculations, or in other words, why do we know how many patients we need to recruit? If we recruit too small number of patients, then our data will not allow us to make conclusions, which is not a good use of resources and patients and hence not ethical. If we recruit too many patients, then we use too many patients and hence do not use resources economically and may unnecessarily expose patients to harmful medication (e.g. in a safety study), which is not ethical either [39].

To determine the sample size means to find a minimum number of patients so that the data collected will provide enough evidence to support our investigation in the presence of the uncertainty that surrounds our investigation. This complex statement consist from several points. It explicitly states that the sample size depends on what we believe would be the sufficient level of evidence i.e. the *level of significance*, often denoted as α. Secondly, the sample size depends on the research question (i.e. the null and alternative hypothesis or whether we doing a diagnostic study etc.). Thirdly, the sample size depends on the amount of uncertainty affecting our investigation (e.g. often quantified via standard deviation). Fourthly, the null and alternative hypotheses need to be testable and they will be tested against each other, using an appropriate statistical test. Since each statistical tests has its own statistical properties this consequently means that, each statistical test has its own sample size calculation procedure. Some calculations can be done explicitly (such as for a t-test [40]) some need to be done via simulations.

The simplest sample size calculation is for a t-test which is the simplest of the group comparisons test. There are differences in the strategy to calculate the sample size for hypothesis testing (e.g. group comparison, descriptive modeling) vs prediction (e.g. the disease detection for an individual eye, diagnosis, discrimination, classification into disease groups).

Main points to consider in the sample size calculations:

- First, it is important to consider the study design and the analytical method to analyze the data. They are the main determinants for the sample size calculation. Then further determinants can be (if relevant): uncertainty, correlations, distribution of the data.
- Second, it is crucial to know that the sample size is the number of units of analysis (e.g. patients, or eyes, or tissues) that we need to recruit for our study.

- If we believe that there may be a loss to follow up of the patients (e.g. because the patient decides not to participate, or patient dies) the sample size needs to be increased to allow for the expected loss during the follow-up. Such an increase in the sample size must be done at the planning stage of the study.
- Some useful references to understand the topic further and to do the simpler calculations by hand can be found in [4, 40]. For more complex sample size calculations, a dedicated sample size software is needed. For even more complex scenarios, a skilled statistician or mathematician may be able to do computer simulations.

While we strongly recommend to work with statistician on sample size (or power) calculations, some recommended software for simpler sample size calculations are:

- Commercial software available e.g. nQuery Advisor or GPower
- Most of statistical packages (such as SPSS, SAS, Minitab, STATA) do offer some functionality for sample size calculations.
- There are also several online sample size calculators such as PS Power and Sample Size, http://biostat.mc.vanderbilt.edu/wiki/Main/PowerSampleSize (free Windows program).

6.2 Words of caution for two eyes: What to do and what not to do?

In clinical studies the focus of interest is very often on the patient e.g. we want to know if the quality of life of the patient has improved. On the contrary, in ophthalmic studies very often the focus is on the eye of the patient e.g. we want to know if the vision improved in a treated eye rather than in patient. If an ophthalmologist wants to evaluate an effectivity of a treatment of AMD, it may be tempting to use both eyes of a patient, whenever possible, with an illusion that this will allow to test the treatment on less number of patients, but this is not so obvious. The issue is that the eyes may be correlated in the primary outcome that is being used for the treatment evaluation (e.g. visual acuity) because they come from the same patient. Many statistical methods (such as *t*-test or regression analysis) assume that the units of analysis are independent (i.e. unrelated) of each other (Table 3).

The fact that patients have two eyes presents challenges in the design, analysis and interpretation of ophthalmic research [12]. This problem is also known as ***unit of analysis*** issue [41] i.e. the unit of analysis can be the patient or the eye. This issue still frequently gives rise to statistical errors and it is not uncommon for studies that are brilliant in terms of methodology and clinical trial design to ignore this issue.

What to do when designing an ophthalmic study and deciding on unit of analysis? First of all, one needs to be clear what the unit of analysis is, and write this into the data analysis section of the report or published paper. Then one needs to decide how the data will be analyzed and write this in the data analysis section of the report. Bunce et al. (see Fig. 2 in Refs. [12, 41]) provides a brief overview of when ocular unit of analysis issues may arise and illustrates ways that these can be dealt with.

7 Biomarkers

A term that has become very common within ophthalmic and vision research is *biomarker*. This is quite a broad term however as is true of disease it means different things to different people. While there are precise definitions within the literature, they overlap considerably and it is probable that many who use the term have not applied its strict definition. Perhaps the most commonly adopted definition is "any substance or biological structure that can be measured in the human body and may influence, explain or predict the incidence of outcome of a disease" [42]. Other definitions require that a biomarker must be able to be measured with certain accuracy and reproducibility but that measurement may be made using molecular, biochemical and cytogenic techniques but also by modern imaging methods such as corneal topography and optical coherence [43]. One of the reasons that biomarkers have become so prevalent in medical research is the potential they offer to accelerate the research process from bench to bedside and back to the bench.

Historically clinical trials have relied upon *clinical endpoints*—endpoints that capture the patient's clinical state. Initially these were largely determined by the clinician—for example, intraocular pressure measurement in glaucoma studies but over time the importance of relating the outcome to the patient was emphasized so that outcomes which truly reflected a patient experience (for example loss of sight) were used. Conditions may take a long time however to lead to such outcomes and if trials have to rely upon these they may be very costly and time consuming. Technology and biomarkers offer the potential to reduce this considerably. An example in ophthalmology is seen with the UKGTS study—repeat measurement of visual field led to more precision in estimates and statistical significance was observed with fewer patients [44]. Biomarkers used in this fashion are termed *surrogate endpoints*, however, there are strict criteria which must be considered if a biomarker is being considered for this purpose. To be used as a surrogate endpoint there must be solid scientific evidence that a biomarker consistently and accurately predicts a clinical outcome. Obtaining such evidence is, however, itself time consuming. If such evidence is obtained it is still important not to take this beyond what has been shown—for example by assuming that other measures of pathology in a particular condition will show the same relationship with the surrogate as that between surrogate and clinical endpoint [45].

8 Ophthalmic imaging data challenges on intersection of statistics and machine learning

In the above text, we focussed on the statistical analysis of data as well as designs in ophthalmology. Here we try and indicate a link between statistics, retinal image analysis and machine learning (ML): for instance, is it worth discussing ML techniques for retinal data analysis, from the point of view of statisticians? What is the difference between ML and statistics especially in relation to retinal imaging and where does data science fit?

Both statistics and ML are scientific disciplines to extract knowledge from data. They are evolving disciplines so their remit is changing over time [46]. We would define these disciplines as follows: ***Statistics*** is a scientific discipline that provides framework to learn from data, via statistical algorithms and statistical inference. The statistical algorithms, in a broad sense, do parameter estimation, they include the exploratory analyses (e.g. averages, histograms), predictive and prognostic modeling (predict future observation, discrimination methods, classification). The statistical inference is focused upon the accuracy of the algorithms and inferring about the population (explanatory modeling). It includes P-values, confidence intervals, and uncertainty measures. ***Machine learning*** is a scientific discipline that focuses primarily on the predictive and prognostic algorithms (deep neural network, Support Vector Machine, etc.) and brings strength in improving the computational power and speed in highly dimensional data such as images. ***Data science*** is a scientific discipline that mainly focuses on the exploratory and explanatory (i.e. inference) goals [46]. It investigates the data generating mechanisms and it generates new hypotheses.

Statisticians and computer scientists often use different language for the same thing, which may create the illusion that they are speaking about different phenomena. This may lead to confusion among students and users of computer science, statistics as well as among clinicians. Here we created a table of terms with our explanation of the meaning (see Table 4), which extends on the table in Ref. [3]. There are many similarities between statistics and machine learning—as they both aim to learn from the data and many of their methods are based on probability. There are also differences (see Table 4) in the methods that they use.

Is it worth discussing ML techniques for retinal data analysis, from the point of view of statisticians? Yes, it is. The statistics can provide the framework for methods of measurement, validation of diagnostic tests and provides the framework for calculation of the uncertainty estimation and reporting in ML algorithms (e.g. Monte Carlo dropout method in deep learning algorithms). Furthermore, a collaboration of ML and statistic researchers is needed in developing the validation and interpretation of ML techniques as well as in provision of reproducible research.

What is the difference between ML and statistics especially in relation to retinal imaging? The ML approach is predominantly pixel-wise oriented. The statistical approaches to retinal imaging require maximization of a likelihood, which is tractable only after a suitable data reduction such as downsampling or division of the image in a smaller number of sectors. The statistical methods for ophthalmic images are less common and are now an intensive area of research e.g. Refs. [9, 10, 47].

Statistical science and probability can provide the theoretical framework for the complex data analysis and machine learning algorithms. Efron and Hastie say, "It is the job of statistical inference to connect dangling algorithms to the central core of well-understood methodology. The connection process is already underway." As an example they illustrate how Adaboost, the original machine learning algorithm, could be restated as a close cousin of logistic regression. They envisage an optimistic scenario of "the big-data/data-science prediction world rejoining the mainstream of statistical inference, to the benefit of both branches" [46].

Table 4 The summary of the most frequently used terms and some differences between disciplines

	Statistics and data science	Machine learning	Explanation
Terminology used	Data	Training sample	Values of X and Y
	Estimation, model fitting	Learning	Using data to estimate an unknown quantity
	Model	Network, graphs	Multivariate distribution with assumed relations
	Covariates and parameters	Features and weights	The X_i's and Beta's
	Hypothesis and inference	– (ML is not focusing on hypothesis testing)	An inductive process to learn about a parameter
	Classification, discrimination	Supervised learning	Predicting the value of Y of a single patient (or eye) from X, groups are known *apriory*
	Cluster analysis, density estimation	Unsupervised learning	Putting data into groups that are not known *apriory*
	Generalization or test set performance	Generalization or test set performance	Evaluating if the results can be generalized to whole population
	Linear and nonlinear models for prognosis or classification	Probabilistic generative models	Model is fit to data and then it is used to derive a posterior probability for Y
Differences	Large grant=£200,000	Large grant=£1,000,000	There is a difference in what is considered a large grant.
	Publishing new statistical methods in journals, taking 3 years to publish	Publishing new methods in proceedings, taking <1 year to publish	There is a different culture of publishing.
	Objectives are mainly in the study design, computation, inference and prediction	Objectives are mainly in the prediction and large scale computation	There is a difference in objectives of the two disciplines.
	Approaches not used in ML: e.g. regression diagnostics, significance testing.	Development of new methods not related to statistics: e.g. Max-margin methods, support vector machines.	There are some methods *not* shared across the two disciplines.

9 Discussion

Here we highlight several main points and give some further thoughts or references to statistics in ophthalmology and vision research.

The design of study and data collection are crucial to any clinical study. This determines the data quality. Sophisticated statistical methods will not make up for a bad quality data. This is true also of machine learning and computational methods. There is a term that is familiar to many statisticians but needs to be more widely used in big data—the term being **garbage in garbage out**. Statisticians and computer scientists are not alchemists. They cannot turn base metal into gold. So to avoid this problem the clinical study should be carefully designed with a thoughtful consideration of the unit of analysis, sample size, randomization, methods of measurement, consideration of confounders and missing data possibilities. It is highly recommended, for the success of the study, to have a statistician on board as a partner to contribute to the decision about the study design, database construction, and coding of categorical variables.

The appropriate analytical strategies to data analysis depend crucially on the purpose of the study as well as on the way the data are collected. We have seen that a wrong choice of a data analysis method may lead to biased estimates of the studied associations. Another crucial point is that the decision of the data analysis method should ideally be done at the point of designing the study. Indeed, in randomized clinical trials, which are near the top of the pyramid of the evidence, the standard is to write a statistical analysis plan before the data is locked for the analysis [39].

The reporting of the results of the ophthalmic study is critical. Some funders and journals impose that authors follow relevant reporting guidelines; in some journals, the use of guidelines is not mandatory. Each report should lead to a reproducible work. We listed some of the guidelines in the Section 5. A full up-to-date list of all the guidelines is being created by the EQUATOR team (https://www.equator-network.org/).

There is a steady rise of advanced complex analytical methods for imaging data: statistical, machine learning and data science. While statistical modeling methods may be simpler in the number of parameters (than machine leaning methods) and they are inherently interpretable; the drawback is that they commonly require a thoughtful process to build the model and may be less accurate due the lower number of parameters (though depending on research question they may be sufficiently accurate). On the other hand computationally complex machine learning methods require less time and less clinical expertise to be built and may be more accurate in e.g. diagnosis or prognosis, but they involve a very large number of parameters (hundreds of thousand or millions) and larger number of patients data such as large number of annotated images for training. These are the pros and cons to be weighted for each study separately.

Alongside major investments in strengthening the measurements via imaging, genotyping, and biomarker assessments, there is clearly a need for methodological advances in statistics, machine learning and data science; and especially a need for these disciplines to collaborate. Only then the great promise to accelerate progress toward successful prevention and treatment of ophthalmic diseases will be delivered.

References

[1] E.N. Brown, R.E. Kass, What is statistics? Am. Stat. 63 (2009) 105–123.

[2] M. Brunner, et al., Improving precision for detecting change in the shape of the cornea in patients with keratoconus, Sci. Rep. 8 (2018) 12345.

[3] L.A. Wasserman, All of Statistics: A Concise Course in Statistical Inference, Springer Science+Business Media, Inc, New York, 2004.

[4] D.G. Altman, Practical Statistics for Medical Research, Chapman and Hall, London, 1991.

[5] A. Khawaja, D. Crabb, N. Jansonious, Time to abandon over-simplified surrogates of ocular perfusion pressure in glaucoma research, Acta Ophthalmol. 93 (1) (2015) e85.

[6] A. Khawaja, D. Crabb, N. Jansonius, The role of ocular perfusion pressure in glaucoma cannot be studied with multivariable regression analysis applied to surrogates, Invest. Ophthalmol. Vis. Sci. 54 (7) (2013) 4619–4620.

[7] R.J. Little, D.B. Rubin, Statistical Analysis With Missing Data, second ed., John Wiley & Sons, Inc, New Jersey, 2014.

[8] D.B. Rubin, Multiple Imputation for Nonresponse in Surveys, John Wiley & Sons, New York, 1987.

[9] S.G. Gadde, et al., Quantification of vessel density in retinal optical coherence tomography angiography images using local fractal dimension, Invest. Ophthalmol. Vis. Sci. 57 (2016) 246–252.

[10] I.J. MacCormick, et al., Spatial statistical modelling of capillary non-perfusion in the retina, Sci. Rep. 7 (2017) 16792.

[11] J. Cook, C. Bunce, C. Doré, N. Freemantle, Ophthalmic statistics note 6: effect sizes matter, Br. J. Ophthalmol. 99 (2015) 580–581.

[12] C. Bunce, et al., Ophthalmic statistics note 1: unit of analysis, Br. J. Ophthalmol. 98 (2014) 408–412.

[13] C. Bunce, et al., Ophthalmic statistics note 2: absence of evidence is not evidence of absence, Br. J. Ophthalmol. 98 (2014) 703–705.

[14] V. Ciprinani, et al., Ophthalmic statistics note 7: multiple hypothesis testing—to adjust or not to adjust, Br. J. Ophthalmol. 99 (2015) 1155–1157.

[15] L. Saunders, et al., Ophthalmic statistics note 5: diagnostic tests—sensitivity and specificit, Br. J. Ophthalmol. 99 (2015) 1168–1170.

[16] J.W. Tukey, Exploratory Data Analysis, Addison-Wesley Pub., Reading, MA, 1977.

[17] P. Cumberland, et al., Ophthalmic statistics note: the perils of dichotomising continuous variables, Br. J. Ophthalmol. 98 (2014) 841–843.

[18] C. Bunce, A. Quartilho, N. Freemantle, C. Doré, Ophthalmic statistics note 8: missing data—exploring the unknown, Br. J. Ophthalmol. 100 (2016) 291–294.

[19] C. Bunce, J. Stephenson, C. Doré, N. Freemantle, Ophthalmic statistics note 10: data transformations, Br. J. Ophthalmol. 100 (2016) 1591–1593.

[20] S. Skene, C. Bunce, N. Freemantle, C. Doré, Ophthalmic statistics note 9: parametric versus non-parametric methods for data analysis, Br. J. Ophthalmol. 100 (2016) 877–878.

[21] P. Armitage, G. Berry, J. Matthews, Statistical Methods in Medical Research, fourth ed., Wiley-Blackwell, London, 2001.

[22] C. Bunce, et al., Ophthalmic statistics note 12: multivariable or multivariate: what's in a name? Br. J. Ophthalmol. 101 (2017) 1303–1305.

[23] R. Nash, et al., Ophthalmic Statistics Note 4: analysing data from randomised controlled trials with baseline and follow-up measurement, Br. J. Ophthalmol. 98 (2014) 1467–1469.

[24] S. Greenland, J. Pearl, J.M. Robins, Causal diagrams for epidemiologic research, Epidemiology 10 (1) (1999) 37–49.

[25] G. Shmueli, To explain or to predict? Stat. Sci. 25 (3) (2010) 289–310.

[26] C. Bunce, Correlation, agreement, and Bland–Altman analysis: statistical analysis of method comparison studies, Am J. Ophthalmol. 148 (1) (2009) 4–6.

[27] D. Altman, J. Bland, Missing data, BMJ 334 (2007) 424.

[28] P. Li, E.A. Stuart, D.B. Allison, Multiple imputation: a flexible tool for handling missing data, JAMA 314 (2015) 1966–1967.

[29] M.L. Bell, D.L. Fairclough, Practical and statistical issues in missing data for longitudinal patient-reported outcomes. Stat. Methods Med. Res. 23 (2014) 440–459, https://doi.org/10.1177/0962280213476378.

[30] J.J. Horton, J. Carpenter, et al., Strategy for intention to treat analysis in randomised trials with missing outcome data, BMJ 342 (2011) d40.

[31] S. Fielding, P. Fayers, C. Ramsay, Analysing randomised controlled trials with missing data: choice of approach affects conclusions, Contemp. Clin. Trials 33 (3) (2012) 461–469.

[32] D.J. Streiner, Statistics commentary series: commentary #3—last observation carried forward, J. Clin. Psychopharmacol. 34 (2014) 423–425.

[33] J.A. Sterne, et al., Multiple imputation for missing data in epidemiological and clinical research: potential and pitfalls, BMJ 338 (2009) b2393.

[34] J.P. Vandenbroucke, et al., Strengthening the reporting of observational studies (STROBE): explanation and elaboration, PLoS Med. 4 (10) (2007) 1628–1654.

[35] E. von Elm, et al., The strenghtening the reporting of observational studies in epidemiology (STROBE) statement: guidelines for reporting observational studies, Lancet 370 (2007) 1453–1457.

[36] D.G. Altman, et al., The revised CONSORT statement for reporting randomized trials: explanation and elaboration, Ann. Intern. Med. 134 (2001) 663–694.

[37] P.M. Bossuyt, J.B. Reitsma, D.E. Bruns, C.A. Gatsonis, P.P. Glasziou, L. Irwig, et al., STARD 2015: an updated list of essential items for reporting diagnostic accuracy studies, BMJ 351 (2015) h5527.

[38] K.J. Rothman, T.L. Lash, S. Greenland, Modern Epidemiology, third ed., Lippincott Williams & Wilkins, Philadelphia, 2008.

[39] The Institute of Clinical Research, ICH Guideline for good clinical practice, in: International Conference on Harmonisation of Technical Requirements for Registration of Pharmaceuticals for Human Use, 1996.

[40] D. Machin, M.J. Campbell, P. Fayers, A. Pinol, Statistical Tables for the Design of Clinical Studies, second ed., Blackwell, Oxford, 1998.

[41] D.G. Altman, J.M. Bland, Statistics notes. Units of analysis, BMJ 314 (1997) 1874.

[42] M. Porta, A Dictionary of Epidemiology, fifth ed., New York Oxford University Press, New York and Oxford, 2008.

[43] V. Gallo, et al., STrengthening the reporting of OBservational studies in Epidemiology-Molecular Epidemiology (STROBE-ME): an extension of the STROBE statement, Eur. J. Clin. Investig. 42 (1) (2012) 1–16.

[44] D.F. Garway-Heath, et al., Latanoprost for open-angle glaucoma (UKGTS): a randomised, multicentre, placebo-controlled trial, Lancet 385 (9975) (2015) 1295–1304.

[45] K. Strimbu, J.A. Tavel, What are biomarkers? Curr. Opin. HIV AIDS 5 (6) (2010) 463–466.

[46] B. Efron, T. Hastie, Computer Age Statistical Inference: Algorithms, Evidence, and Data Science, Cambridge University Press, Cambridge, 2016.

[47] I.J. MacCormick, et al., Accurate, fast, data efficient and interpretable glaucoma diagnosis with automated spatial analysis of the whole cup to disc profile, PLoS ONE 14 (1) (2019) e0209409.

Structure-preserving guided retinal image filtering for optic disc analysis

11

Jun Cheng[a], Zhengguo Li[b], Zaiwang Gu[a], Huazhu Fu[c], Damon Wing Kee Wong[d], Jiang Liu[a]

[a]*Chinese Academy of Sciences, Cixi Institute of Biomedical Engineering, Ningbo, Zhejiang, China*
[b]*Agency for Science, Technology and Research, Institute for Infocomm Research, Singapore*
[c]*Inception Institute of Artificial Intelligence, Abu Dhabi, United Arab Emirates*
[d]*Nanyang Technological University, Singapore*

1 Introduction

Glaucoma is a chronic eye disease where the optic nerve is progressively damaged. It is the second-leading cause of blindness predicted to affect around 80 million people by 2020 [1]. It leads to loss of vision, which often occurs gradually over a long period of time. As the symptoms of the disease only occur when it is quite advanced, glaucoma is called the silent thief of sight. Glaucoma cannot be cured, but its progression can be slowed down by treatment. Therefore, detecting glaucoma in time is critical. However, more than 50–90% of people are unaware of the disease until it has reached an advanced stage [2, 3]. Since glaucoma progresses silently, screening of people at high risk for the disease is vital. Three types of methods to detect glaucoma exist and are based on the following: (1) raised intraocular pressure (IOP), (2) abnormal visual field, and (3) damaged optic nerve head. Since glaucoma can be present with or without increased IOP, the IOP measurement is not accurate enough to be an effective screening tool. A functional test for vision loss requires special equipments only present in territory hospitals and therefore unsuitable for screening. Assessment of the damaged optic nerve head is superior to IOP measurement or visual field testing for glaucoma screening. Optic nerve head assessment can be done by a trained professional. However, manual assessment is subjective, time consuming, and expensive. Therefore, automatic optic nerve head assessment would be very beneficial.

The optic nerve head or the optic disc (in short, disc) is the location where ganglion cell axons exit the eye to form the optic nerve, through which visual information of the photo-receptors is transmitted to the brain. In 2D images, the disc can be divided into two distinct zones: a central bright zone called the optic cup (in short,

Computational Retinal Image Analysis. https://doi.org/10.1016/B978-0-08-102816-2.00011-3

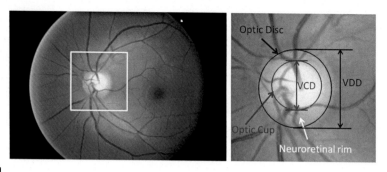

FIG. 1

Major structures of the optic disc: The region enclosed by the *blue line* is the optic disc; the central bright zone enclosed by the *red line* is the optic cup; and the region between the *red and blue lines* is the neuroretinal rim.

cup) and a peripheral region called the neuroretinal rim. Fig. 1 shows the major structures of the disc. The cup-to-disc ratio (CDR) is computed as the ratio of the vertical cup diameter to vertical disc diameter clinically. Accurate segmentations of disc and cup are essential for CDR measurement.

In recent years, many computer-aided diagnosis methods [4] have been developed for automatic optic disc segmentation [5–8], optic cup segmentation, CDR computation [9–12], and glaucoma detection [13, 14]. Besides the optic disc analysis, vessel detection [15, 16], diabetic retinopathy detection [4, 17], age-related macular degeneration detection [18, 19], and pathological myopia detection [20] have received much attention as well. In this chapter, we focus on glaucoma and the related optic disc analysis.

Optic disc segmentation

Optic disc segmentation is an important step in retinal image analysis. Many methods have been proposed for optic disc segmentation, which can be classified as template-based methods [6, 8, 21], deformable model-based methods [22–25], and pixel classification-based methods [9]. In [6, 21], the circular Hough transform is used to model the disc boundary because of its computational efficiency. However, clinical studies have shown that a disc has a slightly oval shape with the vertical diameter being about 7–10% larger than the horizontal one [26]. Circular fitting might lead to an under-estimated disc and an over-estimated CDR, so ellipse fitting is often adopted for glaucoma detection [8]. In [22], Lowell et al. employed the active contour model, which consists in finding optimal points based on the image gradient and the smoothness of the contour. In [23], Xu et al. employed the deformable model technique through minimization of the energy function defined by image intensity, image gradient, and boundary smoothness. In [24], a level set is used to estimate the disc followed by ellipse fitting to smooth the boundary. In [25], the authors proposed a modified Chan-Vese model using texture features. In [27], edge detection and the circular Hough transform are combined with an active shape model to extract the disc. To overcome the limitations of pixel classification-based methods and deformable model-based methods, we propose a superpixel classification-based method [10] and combine it with the deformable model-based methods. With the rapid development of convolutional neural network (CNN) in image and video processing [28], automatic feature learning algorithms using deep learning have emerged as feasible approaches for retinal image analysis. Recently, some OD segmentation algorithms [12, 29, 30] based on deep learning, especially fully convolution network structure [31], have been proposed. Sevastopolsky [30] adopted a modified U-Net to directly segment the OD and optic cup for further CDR calculation and glaucoma diagnosis. In a further extension of the U-Net, Fu [12] proposed a novel architecture called M-Net to jointly segment OD and OC as well as a disc-aware method [29] for direct glaucoma detection, where the OD segmentation is the of a series of operations. These methods can greatly improve the performance of OD segmentation, based on the strong learning capacity of deep learning.

Optic cup segmentation

Optic cup segmentation is another important task in retinal image analysis. Detecting the cup boundary from 2D fundus images without depth information is a challenging task as depth is the primary indicator for the cup boundary. In 2D fundus images, one landmark to determine the cup region is the pallor, defined as the area of maximum color contrast inside the disc [23]. Another landmark is the vessel bends at the boundary of the cup [26, 32]. Compared with disc segmentation, fewer methods have been proposed for cup segmentation from 2D fundus images. Thresholding is used to determine the cup in [33–35], relying on intensity difference between cup and neuroretinal rim. A level set-based approach is used in [36]. It relies on the edges between cup and neuroretinal rim. This method and thresholding-based methods are essentially based on pallor information. However, in many subjects from screening data, there is no obvious pallor or edge within the disc to mark the cup boundary. In [37], small vessel bends ("kinks") near the initially estimated cup have been used to aid the cup segmentation. The challenge is to exclude vessel bends from a boundary not belonging to the cup, especially when the initial estimation is inaccurate. A similar concept is used in [25] to locate relevant-vessel bends ("r-bend") near a pallor region determined by bright pixels. This method, again, requires the pallor information to determine a good initial estimation of the cup boundary. Moreover, it requires at least a few bends in the nasal, inferior and superior angular regions of the disc for the cup boundary fitting, which is not necessarily true for many images in our experience. Xu et al. [38] proposed a sliding window and regression-based method. Although this performs better than earlier methods, the sliding window strategy imposes a heavy computational cost. Yin et al. [39] developed a deformable model-based method for cup segmentation, where the initialization of the cup boundary is based on pallor combined with prior knowledge of the cup. Previously, superpixel classification was also proposed in [10] for optic cup segmentation.

In recent years, deep learning approaches have been applied for optic cup segmentation as well. In the M-Net introduced above [12], the cup is segmented jointly with the optic disc. In [29], the joint disc and cup segmentation is combined with image-level features for direct glaucoma detection. In [40], fast R-CNN is adopted to segment the optic cup. Besides the deep learning approaches, we have also proposed a direct approach to compute the cup diameters using sparse learning and its variations [11, 41, 42].

Joint optic disc and optic cup segmentation

Because of the relative location constraint between the optic disc and optic cup, the optic disc boundary could provide some useful prior information for optic cup segmentation, for example, shape constraint and structure constraint [43]. The work in [10, 25] deals with disc and cup in two separate stages with different features, where the cup is segmented from the disc region. Zheng et al. [44] integrated the disc and cup segmentation within a graph-cut framework. However, they consider the disc and cup as two mutually exclusive labels, which means that any pixel can only be assigned to one label (i.e., background, disc, or cup). Moreover, the method only employs color features within a Gaussian mixture model to decide a posterior probability of the pixel, which makes it unsuitable for fundus images with low contrast. In [30], a modified U-Net deep network is introduced to segment the disc and cup. However, it still separates disc and cup segmentation in a sequential way. In [45], an ensemble learning method is proposed to extract disc and cup based on the CNN architecture. An entropy sampling technique is used to select informative points, and then a graph-cut algorithm is employed to obtain the final segmentation result. However, this multiple-step deep system limits effectiveness in the training phase. We proposed a M-Net [12] to segment the optic disc and cup simultaneously. Instead of segmenting the cup from the disc region or segmenting the cup from the full image, the M-Net adopts a multilabel loss function to achieve the joint segmentation of the optic disc and cup. Fig. 2 illustrates the M-Net framework. M-Net is an end-to-end multilabel deep network which consists of four main parts. The first is a multiscale layer used to construct an image pyramid input and achieve multilevel receptive field fusion. The second is a U-shape convolutional network, which is employed as the main body structure to learn a rich hierarchical representation. The third part is a side-output layer that works on the output of early convolutional layers to support deep layer supervision. Finally, a multilabel loss function is proposed to achieve simultaneous segmentation of OD and OC.

Image quality

A common challenge in analysis is the image quality [46], which has been neglected in most earlier algorithms. Very often, low-quality images lead to poor performance. There are many factors that might affect the image quality, including the cooperation of the patient, the experience of the operator, the imaging device, the image processing algorithms, etc. One factor that has been overlooked by most researchers

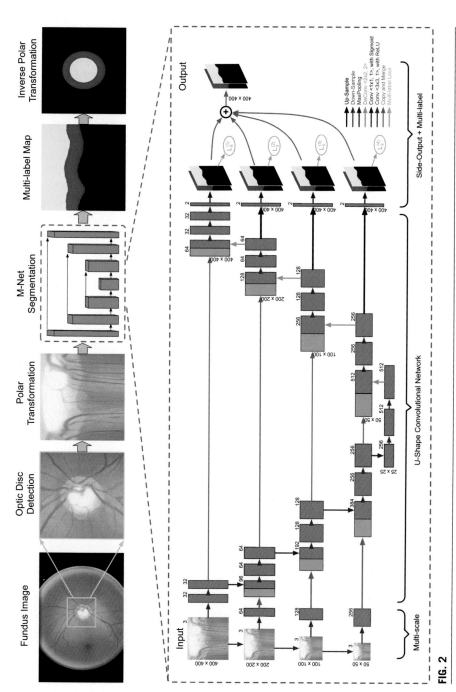

FIG. 2

Illustration of the M-Net framework.

is the presence of disease. Our experience shows that some diseases might affect the imaging of the retina. In fundus imaging, the illumination light passes through the lens of the human eye before reaching the retina, where it is reflected back to the camera to form the image. However, the human lens is not a perfect optical system and it often attenuates the light passing along the path. The attenuation can be serious when the lens is affected by diseases such as cataracts. Cataract leads to the clouding of the lens, which implies attenuation and scattering of the light travelling through it. This is similar to the case of a cloudy camera lens reducing the quality of a picture. We refer to this as clouding and to the processing to remove the effect as declouding. Studies show that cataract accounts for 33% of blindness worldwide [47] and its global prevalence in adults over 50 years of age was about 47.8% in 2002 [48]. The high prevalence of the disease makes it an important factor that cannot be neglected. The retinal images are often degraded at different levels of severity, depending on the locations and the severity of the clouding in the lens. Fig. 3 shows two retinal images, where the first one is from an eye with cataract and the second one is from an eye without cataract. As these images show, the dynamic range of the images from cataractous human lens is greatly reduced. Since the degradation is caused by light scattering, we call the scattered light lens light. The poor image quality due to the clouding lens often makes it difficult to learn a good representation of the images for analysis tasks such as structure segmentation, lesion detection, and other analysis. Specifically, it may affect the boundary between the optic cup and neuroretinal rim, which is important in optic cup segmentation. It may also obscure the intensity changes identifying the blood vessels. Therefore, it is important to remove the clouding effect and increase the contrast of the retinal images for more accurate analysis of the images.

The degradation due to cataracts is modeled as follows [49]:

$$I_c(p) = \alpha L_c r_c(p) t(p) + L_c(1 - t(p)),$$ (1)

where α denotes the attenuation due to the cataract; $c \in \{r, g, b\}$ denotes the red, green, or blue channel of the image; $r_c(p)$ denotes the reflectance function of the

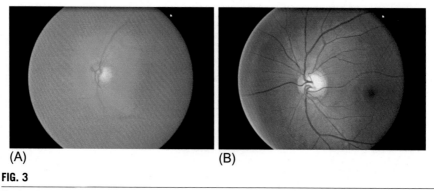

(A)   (B)

FIG. 3

Retinal images: (A) from eye with cataract and (B) from eye without cataract.

retina; L_c is the illumination of the camera; and $t(p)$ describes the portion of the light that does not reach the camera.

This model uses a precataract clear image as a reference to estimate α. However, such image is seldom available and the illumination light can be different if the precataract image is captured under different conditions. Therefore, it is not likely to have an accurate estimation of α. Meanwhile, the value of α only affects the scale of the final image. Given this, the following simplified model is proposed:

$$I_c(p) = D_c(p)t(p) + L_c(1 - t(p)),$$

(2)

where $D_c(p) = L_c r_c(p)$ denotes the image captured under ideal condition. The model in Eq. (2) is similar to the dehaze model in computer vision, where the attenuation by haze or fog is modeled by air attenuation and scattering [50]. The model is a special case of Eq. (1) by letting $\alpha = 1$. By applying the model on the retinal image, the task of removing the clouding effect due to cataracts is converted to a common dehaze task in computer vision.

In computer vision, many methods [50–55] have been proposed to solve the dehaze problem in Eq. (2). Tan et al. [50] used Markov random field to enhance the local contrast. However, this often produces over-saturated images. Fattal [51] proposed to account for both surface shading and scene transmission, but this solution does not perform well with heavy haze. He et al. [52] proposed a novel dark channel prior assumption. However, the assumption is not always true for retinal images without much shadows or complex structures. Recently, guided image filtering (GIF) [53] was proposed recently for single image dehaze. This has a limitation, that it does not preserve the fine structures which might be important in retinal image analysis tasks. To overcome this limitation, we propose a new method to preserve the structure in the original images. Motivated by GIF, we propose a structure-preserving guided retinal image filtering (SGRIF), which is composed of a global structure transfer filtering and a global edge-preserving smoothing. Different from most work reported, that ends with image quality evaluation, we also explore how the process affects the subsequent automatic analysis tasks. Two different applications including deep learning-based optic disc segmentation and sparse learning-based CDR computation are conducted to show the advantages of the method.

Contributions

The main contributions are summarized as follows.

1. We give a review of existing optic disc and optic cup segmentation algorithms.
2. We introduce an SGRIF for declouding the retinal images.
3. The experimental results show that the SGRIF algorithm improves the contrast of the image and maintains the edges for further analysis.
4. The method benefits subsequent analysis as well. It improves both accuracies in the deep learning-based optic disc segmentation and sparse learning-based CDR computation.

The remaining sections of this chapter are organized as follows. Section 2 introduces the method to remove the clouding effect, which includes a step of global structure transferring and a step of global edge-preserving smoothing. Section 3 shows the effectiveness of the method to improve the contrast of the retinal images as well as its application in optic cup segmentation and CDR computation. Conclusions are drawn in the last section.

2 Structure-preserving guided retinal image filtering

In GIF [53], a guidance image G is used to guide the process. G could be identical to the input image I. The output image O is computed by a linear transformation of G in a window W_p centered at the pixel p, that is,

$$O_i = a_p G_i + b_p, \quad \forall i \in W_p, \tag{3}$$

where i indicates pixel index.

The linear transform coefficients a_p, b_p are determined by minimizing the following objective function:

$$E = (O_i - I_i)^2 + \epsilon a_p^2, \tag{4}$$

where ϵ is a regularization parameter.

The solution is given as:

$$a_p = \frac{\frac{1}{|W_p|} \sum_{i \in W_p} G_i I_i - \mu_p \bar{I}_p}{\sigma_p^2 + \epsilon}, \tag{5}$$

$$b_p = \bar{I}_p - a_p \mu_p, \tag{6}$$

where $\bar{I}_p$ denotes the mean of I in W_p; $|W_p|$ denotes the cardinality of W_p; and μ_P and σ_p^2 denote the mean and variance of G in W_p, respectively.

Each pixel i is included in many overlapping window W_p, and the outputs of Eq. (5) from different windows are not identical. GIF [53] adopts an averaging strategy, that is,

$$O_i = \bar{a}_p G_i + \bar{b}_p, \tag{7}$$

where $\bar{a}_p$ and $\bar{b}_p$ denote the mean values of $a_{p'}$ and $b_{p'}$ in W_p:

$$\bar{a}_p = \frac{1}{|W_p|} \sum_{p' \in W_p} a_{p'}, \tag{8}$$

$$\bar{b}_p = \frac{1}{|W_p|} \sum_{p' \in W_p} b_{p'}. \tag{9}$$

It has been pointed out that a pixel from a high-variance area will retain its value while the intensity of a pixel from a flat-contrast area will be smoothed by its nearby pixels. The averaging in the above process often smooths away the fine structure in regions close to flat-costrast ones, which is not optimal for retinal images: for example, the boundaries between the optic cup and the neuroretinal rim can be weak in some cases. The averaging in such regions might smooth away the weak boundaries and make the segmentation of optic cup more challenging.

To address this problem, we propose a novel structure-preserving guided retinal image filter (SGRIF). Inspired by GIF [53], we aim to transfer the structure of G to I to preserve the edges and smooth the transferred image. The proposed SGRIF is composed of a global structure transfer filter to transfer the structure in the retinal image and a global edge-preserving smoothing filter to smooth the transferred retinal image. To achieve that, we need to compute a guidance vector field $V = (V^h, V^v)$. The inputs of the proposed SGRIF are a retinal image and the vector V. A term computing the difference of the gradients of the output image O and the vector V is computed to penalize the transfer:

$$\sum_i \| \nabla O_i - V_i \|^2, \tag{10}$$

where ∇ denotes gradient. Combining this with the first item in Eq. (4), we obtain the objective function of the global structure transfer filter:

$$\lambda \sum_i (O_i - I_i)^2 + \| \nabla O_i - V_i \|^2, \tag{11}$$

where λ controls the trade-off between the two terms. The above cost function can be rewritten as:

$$\lambda (O-I)^T (O-I) + (D_x O - V^h)^T (D_x O - V^h) \\ + (D_y O - V^v)^T (D_y O - V^v), \tag{12}$$

where D_x and D_y denote discrete partial differentiation operators. The output O is then obtained by solving the following equation:

$$(\lambda A + D_x^T D_x + D_y^T D_y) O = \lambda I + D_x^T V^h + D_y^T V^v, \tag{13}$$

where A is the identity matrix.

The problem in Eq. (13) is solved using the fast separating method [56]. Although the solution of the previous equation can lead already to a good result, the output O^* based on Eq. (13) often needs to be smoothed. Fig. 4 shows an example where the output image O^* contains visible artifacts. To overcome the problem, we decompose the output image into two layers via an edge-preserving smoothing filter [57–59], which is formulated as

$$\min_\phi \sum_i \left[(\phi_i - O_i^*)^2 + \gamma \left(\frac{\left(\frac{\partial \phi_i}{\partial x} \right)^2}{|V_i^h|^\theta + \epsilon} + \frac{\left(\frac{\partial \phi_i}{\partial y} \right)^2}{|V_i^v|^\theta + \epsilon} \right) \right], \tag{14}$$

where γ, θ, and ϵ are empirically set as 2048, 13/8, and 1/64, respectively. The thresholds are determined by searching from a reasonable range based on physical meaning and experience. For example, γ is large to make sure that the first term in Eq. (14) will not dominate the results. Then, we conducted tests using different γ values and determined an optimal value. Note that our experience shows that small changes of the parameters do not affect much the results.

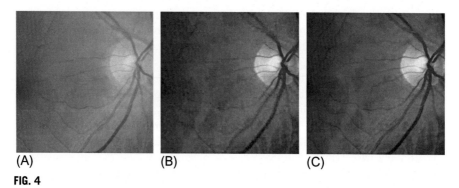

(A)   **(B)**   **(C)**

FIG. 4

Effect of the global edge-preserving smoothing filter. (A) Original image. (B) Output image O^* without edge-preserving smoothing filter. (C) Output image after edge-preserving smoothing filter.

Eq. (14) is rewritten as

$$(\phi - O^*)^T(\phi - O^*) + \gamma(\phi^T D_x^T B_x D_x \phi + \phi^T D_y^T B_y D_y \phi), \tag{15}$$

where $B_x = \text{diag}\left\{\dfrac{1}{|V_i^h|^\theta + \epsilon}\right\}$, $B_y = \text{diag}\left\{\dfrac{1}{|V_i^v|^\theta + \epsilon}\right\}$.

Setting the derivative of Eq. (15) to zero, the vector ϕ minimizing the previous cost function is computed as follows:

$$(A + \gamma(D_x^T B_x D_x + D_y^T B_y D_y))\phi = O^*. \tag{16}$$

Similar to that in Eq. (13), the problem in Eq. (16) is solved by the fast separate method in Ref. [56] as well.

To apply the above models to retinal images, we first need to estimate L_c, $c \in \{r, g, b\}$. In this chapter, we estimate L_c, $c \in \{r, g, b\}$, using the idea of minimal color channel and simplified dark channel [60]. The simplified dark channel is decomposed into a base layer and a detail layer to determine the transmission map. The simplified dark channels of the normalized degraded and ideal images are computed as I_c/L_c and D_c/L_c. Define $\tilde{I}_{\min}(p)$ and $\tilde{D}_{\min}(p)$ as

$$\tilde{I}_{\min}(p) = \min\left\{\frac{I_r(p)}{L_r}, \frac{I_g(p)}{L_g}, \frac{I_b(p)}{L_b}\right\}, \tag{17}$$

$$\tilde{D}_{\min}(p) = \min\left\{\frac{D_r(p)}{L_r}, \frac{D_g(p)}{L_g}, \frac{D_b(p)}{L_b}\right\}. \tag{18}$$

Note that we do not consider the difference among the RGB channels in this chapter, though some earlier work [61] shows that the blue channel may contain more noise than other channels. Since the transmission map t is independent to the color channels, we have

$$\tilde{I}_{\min}(p) = (1 - t(p)) + \tilde{D}_{\min}(p)t(p). \tag{19}$$

Let $W\kappa(p)$ be a $\kappa \times \kappa$ window centered at pixel p. The simplified dark channels of the normalized images are given as:

$$J_d^{\tilde{D}}(p) \ = \min_{p' \in W_\kappa(p)} \{\tilde{D}_{min}(p')\}, \tag{20}$$

$$J_d^{\tilde{I}}(p) \ = \min_{p' \in W_\kappa(p)} \{\tilde{I}_{min}(p')\}. \tag{21}$$

We approximate $t(p)$ within $W(p)$ as a constant, therefore

$$J_d^{\tilde{I}}(p) = (1-t(p)) + J_d^{\tilde{D}}(p)t(p). \tag{22}$$

The guidance vector field $V = (V^h, V^v)$ is calculated as

$$V^h(m,n) \ = \tilde{I}_{min}(m, n+1) - \tilde{I}_{min}(m,n), \tag{23}$$

$$V^v(m,n) \ = \tilde{I}_{min}(m+1,n) - \tilde{I}_{min}(m,n). \tag{24}$$

Combining the gradient vector field with Eq. (11), we obtain the output O^*.

We further smooth the first item $\phi(p) = 1 - t(p)$ using the edge-preserving smoothing filter in Eq. (14) and obtain $\phi^*(p)$.

The transmission map $t(p)$ is then computed as:

$$t^*(p) = 1 - \phi^*(p). \tag{25}$$

The underlying (dehazed) image is computed as:

$$D_c(p) = \frac{I_c(p) - L_c}{t^*(p)} + L_c. \tag{26}$$

Recalled that we ignore α in our model, however, in the cases where the attenuation α cannot be ignored, we can still solve the problem by estimating α using a precataract image and computing the final output image as $\frac{1}{\alpha} D_c(p)$. In this chapter, we simply restore the image based on Eq. (26).

3 Experimental results

3.1 Dataset

We conduct experiments using the images in the ORIGA dataset [41, 62]. The ORIGA dataset contains 650 images, including 203 images from eyes with cataracts and 447 images from eyes without any cataract. We mainly apply SGRIF on the optic disc area and evaluate how it affects subsequent analysis on the optic disc. To prevent error propagation from optic disc segmentation to optic cup segmentation, we use the disc from the original image and the disc boundaries are kept the same.

3.2 Evaluation metrics

To evaluate the performance of SGRIF, we first compute how it affects the image contrast in the area of the optic disc. Two evaluation metrics, namely the histogram flatness measure (HFM) and the histogram spread (HS) are used to evaluate performance [63]:

$$HFM = \frac{\left(\prod_{i=1}^{n} x_i\right)^{1/n}}{\frac{1}{n}\sum_{i=1}^{n} x_i}, \qquad (27)$$

where x_i is the histogram count for the ith histogram bin and n is the total number of histogram bins.

$$HS = \frac{(3\text{rd quartile-1st quartile) of histogram}}{(\text{Maximum-minimum) of the pixel value range}}. \qquad (28)$$

Another measurement is the mean variability of the local luminosity (VLL) [64] throughout the optic disc. Given an image I, divided into $N \times N$ blocks $B_{i,j}$, $i, j = 1$, ..., N with equal sizes. VLL is computed as

$$VLL = \frac{1}{N}\sqrt{\frac{1}{\bar{I}^2}\sum_{N}^{i=1}\sum_{N}^{j=1}(\mu(i,j) - \bar{I})^2}, \qquad (29)$$

where $\bar{I}$ stands for the mean intensity of the entire image and $\mu(i,j)$ for the mean of block $B_{i,j}$. For all the above metrics, a high value indicates a better result.

3.3 Results

Table 1 summarizes the results observe that the proposed method improves the HFM, HS, and VLL by 5.9%, 4.3%, and 134.8%, respectively, compared with original images. GIF improves VLL, but does not increase HFM and HS. This is because GIF oversmooths some regions close to flat-contrast ones, and reduces the dynamic range of the histograms. Fig. 5 shows results from five sample images of optic disc. As we can see, the proposed SGRIF enhances the contrast between the optic cup and the neuroretinal rim while the improvement by GIF is less clear. Visually, it is difficult to tell if GIF has oversmoothed some regions but we will show the differences from subsequent analysis in the next section.

3.4 Application

To evaluate how the declouding benefits the retinal analysis tasks, we conduct the following experiments: (1) deep learning-based optic cup segmentation; (2) sparse learning-based CDR measurement.

3.4.1 Deep learning-based optic cup segmentation

In the first application, we evaluate how the declouding affects optic cup segmentation. Since deep learning [65] has shown to be promising in segmentation, we use deep learning as the baseline approach and the U-Net architecture [66] is adopted in this chapter. U-Net is a fully convolutional neural network suitable for biomedical image segmentation. In our implementation, we use a simplified U-Net as it requires

Table 1 Performance by various methods.

	Histogram flatness measure			Histogram spread			Variability of local luminosity		
	All	Cataract	No cataract	All	Cataract	No cataract	All	Cataract	No cataract
Original	0.5786	0.5295	0.6009	0.2856	0.2692	0.2930	0.0517	0.0363	0.0537
GIF	0.4779	0.4324	0.4986	0.2505	0.2329	0.2584	0.1014	0.0999	0.1021
Proposed	0.6129	0.5817	0.6271	0.2980	0.2806	0.3059	0.1214	0.1076	0.1277

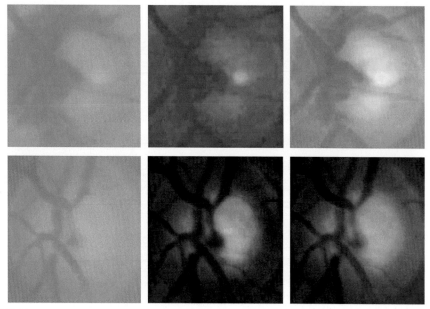

FIG. 5

Retinal images of optic disc: from the left to right are the original disc images, the images processed by GIF, and the images processed by proposed filter.

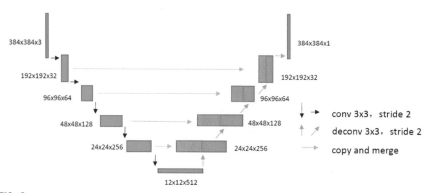

FIG. 6

Simple U-Net architecture.

fewer parameters to be trained compared with the original U-Net. As shown in Fig. 6, our network contains an encoder and a decoder similar to the original U-Net. For each layer in the encoder, it just adopts a convolution layer with stride 2, replacing the original two convolution layers and one pooling layer. For each layer in the decoder, it takes two inputs: (i) the output of last layer in the encoder; (ii) the corresponding layer in the encoder with the same size. Then, two middle-layer feature maps are concatenated and transferred to the next deconvolution layer as its input. Finally, our simplified U-Net outputs a prediction grayscale map, which ranges from 0 to 255. We calculate the mean square error between prediction map and ground truth as loss function. In our simple U-Net, we use a mini-batch stochastic gradient decent (SGD) algorithm to optimize the loss function, specifically, Adagrad-based SGD [67]. The adopted learning rate is 0.001 and the batch size is 32 under the Tensorflow framework based on Ubuntu 16.04 system. We use a momentum of 0.9. All images are resized to 384 × 384 for training and testing. The obtained probability map is resized back to original size to obtain the segmentation results.

In our experiments, the 650 images have been divided randomly into set A of 325 training images and set B of 325 testing images. To evaluate the performance of the algorithm in the presence of cataracts, the 325 images in set B are further divided into a subset of 113 images with cataracts and 212 images without cataract. We then compare the results in the following three different scenarios: (1) Original: the original training and testing images are used for training and testing the U-Net model; (2) GIF: all images are first processed by GIF before U-Net model training and testing; (3) SGRIF: all images are first filtered by SGRIF before U-Net model training and testing.

The commonly used overlapping error E is computed as the evaluation metric.

$$E = 1 - \frac{Area(S \cap G)}{Area(S \cup G)}, \tag{30}$$

where S and G denote the segmented and the manual "ground truth" optic cup, respectively. Table 2 summarizes the results. As we can see, the proposed SGRIF reduces the overlapping error by 7.9% relatively from 25.3% without filtering image to 23.3% with SGRIF. The statistical t-test indicates that the reduction is significant with $P < .001$. However, GIF reduces the accuracy in optic cup segmentation. To visualize the segmentation results, we also draw the boundaries of segmented optic cup by the deep learning models. Fig. 7 shows two examples, from an eye without cataract (first row) and one with cataract (second row), respectively. Results show that SGRIF improves the optic cup segmentation in both scenarios. SGRIF reduces the segmentation error as it improves the boundary at the temporal side of the disc. GIF does not appear effective as it often smooths away the boundaries in areas close to flat-contrast regions. This often happens on the temporal side of the retinal image where the gradient change is low. The previous observation is in line with our discussion in Section 2 on the fact that GIF might smooth away the weak boundaries and make the segmentation task more challenging.

Table 2 Overlap error in optic cup segmentation.

	All	Cataract	No cataract
Original	25.3	24.4	25.8
GIF	25.6	24.8	26.0
Proposed	23.3	22.8	23.5

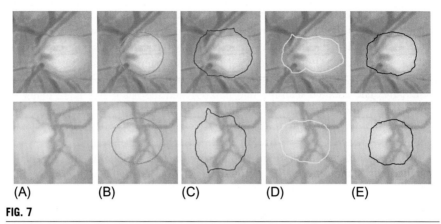

(A)   (B)   (C)   (D)   (E)

FIG. 7

Effect of filtering on optic cup segmentation: (A) original disc; (B) manual ground truth cup boundary; (C) segmentation based on original disc image; (D) segmentation based on GIF processed disc image; (E) segmentation based on proposed SGRIF processed disc image.

To visualize how the processing affects the image, Fig. 8 shows the intensity profiles of horizontal lines (in white) from two images. From the results, we observe that both GIF and SGRIF improve the contrast near the vessels and SGRIF performs slightly better. In the third row, it is more difficult to judge the location of optic cup boundary from the profiles in the red and the blue than in the green channel, as highlighted by the arrow. Such small difference in the profiles can be critical for subsequent analysis tasks such as optic cup boundary detection.

3.4.2 Sparse learning-based CDR computation

In the second application, we explore how the declouding affects a direct vertical CDR computation. We use the previously proposed sparse dissimilarity-constrained coding (SDC) [11] algorithm as an example in our test. The method reconstructs each testing disc image y using n reference disc images $X = [x_1, x_2, ..., x_n]$ with known CDRs $r = [r_1, r_2, ..., r_n]$. SDC finds a solution w to approximate y by Xw by solving the following objective function:

$$\arg\min_{w} \| y - Xw \|^2 + \lambda_1 \cdot \| d \circ w \|^2 + \lambda_2 \cdot \| w \|_1, \tag{31}$$

where $d = [d_1, d_2, ..., d_n]$ denotes the similarity cost between y and X, $\circ$ denotes dot product. The CDR of testing image y is then computed as

$$\hat{r} = \frac{1}{1_w^T w} r^T w, \tag{32}$$

where $\mathbf{1}$ is a vector of 1s with length n.

To justify the benefits of SGRIF for CDR computation, we conduct the latter based on Eq. (31). Similarly, the following three scenarios are tested and compared: (1) original reference and testing images; (2) all images are processed by GIF; and (3) all images are processed by SGRIF. Table 3 shows the CDR error between the

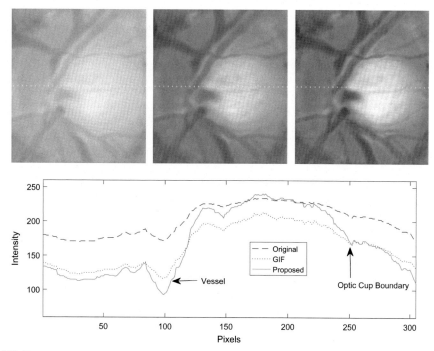

FIG. 8

Intensity profiles across the dash lines of the first sample in Fig. 7. The intensity profiles from the original images, the images processed by GIF, and the images processed by the proposed method are shown in *red-dashed*, *blue-dotted*, and *solid-green lines*, respectively. From left to right are the original images, images processed by GIF, and images processed by the proposed method.

Table 3 Accuracy of CDR computation.

	All	Cataract	No cataract
Original	0.0657	0.0626	0.0674
GIF	0.0665	0.0625	0.0686
Proposed	0.0639	0.0603	0.0658
Interobserver error	0.0767	0.0761	0.0771

automatically computed and the manually measured CDRs. The errors for retinal images from eyes with and without cataract are computed separately. We achieve a relative reduction of 3.7% for retinal images from eyes with cataract and a reduction of 2.4% for retinal images from those without. Besides the above comparison, we have also included interobserver error computed from measurements by an ophthalmologist [11] in Table 3.

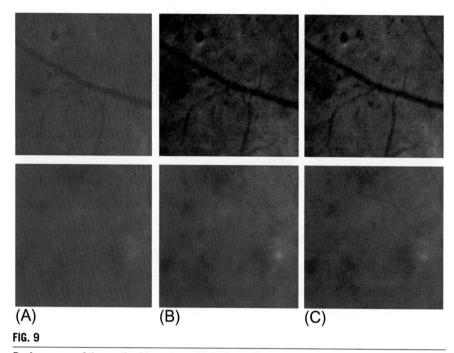

(A)   (B)   (C)

FIG. 9

Performance of the method in region with lesions: (A) original; (B) image processed by GIF; and (C) image processed by SGRIF (best viewed on a computer screen).

3.5 Performance on regions with lesions

Besides the optic disc area, we have also applied the method to regions with lesions. As shown in Fig. 9, both GIF and SGRIF enhance the image contrast. However, a quantitative measurement on how GIF or SGRIF improves lesion detection is challenging.

4 Conclusions

Optic disc and optic cup segmentation are important steps for glaucoma detection. In the past, many methods have been proposed to segment the optic disc and optic cup for glaucoma detection. Many deep learning-based methods have been proposed as well recently. However, most of these methods neglect image quality, an important factor that affects the performance of retinal image analysis. In this chapter, we introduced a novel SGRIF technique to remove artifacts caused by cataractous lens, a frequent cause of limited image quality. Experimental results show that the method enhances the contrast of retinal images, as measured by HFM, HS, and VLL. The technique is further validated with retinal image analysis tasks including optic cup segmentation and CDR measurement. Both experiments show that the method improves the accuracy of the tasks results. In this chapter, we mainly apply the algorithm in the optic disc region and not for optic disc segmentation as the optic disc boundary is usually much stronger and will not be smoothed away in GIF. Therefore, the benefit from our method is less obvious. Since our method improves the image quality in the optic disc area, it could be used to improve automatic analysis for disc-related disease detection. Our results also suggest, qualitatively, that the method enhances the blood vessel. In future work, we will also explore how it affects other analysis tasks such as vessel detection and lesion detection quantitatively.

References

[1] H.A. Quigley, A.T. Broman, The number of people with glaucoma worldwide in 2010 and 2020, Br. J. Ophthalmol. 90 (3) (2006) 262–267.

[2] S.Y. Shen, T.Y. Wong, P.J. Foster, J.L. Loo, M. Rosman, S.C. Loon, W.L. Wong, S.M. Saw, T. Aung, The prevalence and types of glaucoma in Malay people: the Singapore Malay eye study, Invest. Ophthalmol. Vis. Sci. 49 (9) (2008) 3846–3851.

[3] P.J. Foster, F.T. Oen, D. Machin, T.P. Ng, J.G. Devereux, G.J. Johnson, P.T. Khaw, S.K. Seah, The prevalence of glaucoma in Chinese residents of Singapore: a cross-sectional population survey of the Tanjong Pagar district, Arch. Ophthalmol. 118 (8) (2000) 1105–1111.

[4] M.D. Abràmoff, M.K. Garvin, M. Sonka, Retinal imaging and image analysis, IEEE Trans. Med. Imaging 3 (2010) 169–208.

[5] H. Li, O. Chutatape, Boundary detection of optic disc by a modified ASM method, Pattern Recogn. 36 (2003) 2093–2104.

[6] A. Aquino, M. Gegundez-Arias, D. Marin, Detecting the optic disc boundary in digital fundus images using morphological, edge detection, and feature extraction techniques, IEEE Trans. Med. Imaging 29 (2010) 1860–1869.

[7] C. Muramatsu, T. Nakagawa, A. Sawada, Y. Hatanaka, T. Hara, T. Yamamoto, H. Fujita, Automated segmentation of optic disc region on retinal fundus photographs: comparison of contour modeling and pixel classification methods, Comput. Methods Prog. Biomed. 101 (2011) 23–32.

[8] J. Cheng, J. Liu, D.W.K. Wong, F. Yin, C. Cheung, M. Baskaran, T. Aung, T.Y. Wong, Automatic optic disc segmentation with peripapillary atrophy elimination, in: International Conference of IEEE Engineering in Medicine and Biology Society, 2011, pp. 6624–6627.

[9] M.D. Abràmoff, W.L.M. Alward, E.C. Greenlee, L. Shuba, C.Y. Kim, J.H. Fingert, Y.H. Kwon, Automated segmentation of the optic disc from stereo color photographs using physiologically plausible features, Invest. Ophthalmol. Vis. Sci. 48 (2007) 1665–1673.

[10] J. Cheng, J. Liu, Y. Xu, F. Yin, D.W.K. Wong, N.-M. Tan, D. Tao, C.-Y. Cheng, T. Aung, T.Y. Wong, Superpixel classification based optic disc and optic cup segmentation for glaucoma screening, IEEE Trans. Med. Imaging 32 (6) (2013) 1019–1032.

[11] J. Cheng, F. Yin, D.W.K. Wong, D. Tao, J. Liu, Sparse dissimilarity-constrained coding for glaucoma screening, IEEE Trans. Biomed. Eng. 62 (5) (2015) 1395–1403.

[12] H. Fu, J. Cheng, Y. Xu, D.W.K. Wong, J. Liu, X. Cao, Joint optic disc and cup segmentation based on multi-label deep network and polar transformation. IEEE Trans. Med. Imaging 37 (7) (2018) 1597–1605, https://doi.org/10.1109/TMI.2018.2791488.

[13] A. Li, J. Cheng, D.W.K. Wong, J. Liu, Integrating holistic and local deep features for glaucoma classification. in: 2016 38th Annual International Conference of the IEEE Engineering in Medicine and Biology Society (EMBC), 2016, pp. 1328–1331, https://doi.org/10.1109/EMBC.2016.7590952.

[14] M. Mishra, M.K. Nath, S. Dandapat, Glaucoma detection from color fundus images, Int. J. Comput. Commun. Technol. 2 (2011) 7–10.

[15] J. Staal, M.D. Abramoff, M. Niemeijer, M.A. Viergever, B. Ginneken, Ridge-based vessel segmentation in color images of the retina, IEEE Trans. Med. Imaging 23 (4) (2004) 501–509.

[16] Y. Zhao, Y. Zheng, Y. Liu, Y. Zhao, L. Luo, S. Yang, T. Na, Y. Wang, J. Liu, Automatic 2D/3D vessel enhancement in multiple modality images using a weighted symmetry filter, IEEE Trans. Med. Imaging 37 (2) (2017) 438–450.

[17] V. Gulshan, L. Peng, M. Coram, et al., Development and validation of a deep learning algorithm for detection of diabetic retinopathy in retinal fundus photographs, JAMA 316 (22) (2016) 2402–2410.

[18] Z. Liang, D.W.K. Wong, J. Liu, K.L. Chan, T.Y. Wong, Towards automatic detection of age-related macular degeneration in retinal fundus images, in: International Conference of the IEEE Engineering in Medicine and Biology, 2010, pp. 4100–4103.

[19] C. Agurto, E.S. Barriga, V. Murray, S. Nemeth, R. Crammer, W. Bauman, G. Zamora, M.S. Pattichis, P. Soliz, Automatic detection of diabetic retinopathy and age-related macular degeneration in digital fundus images, Investig. Ophthalmol. Vis. Sci. 52 (8) (2011) 5862–5871.

[20] J. Liu, D.W.K. Wong, J.H. Lim, N.M. Tan, Z. Zhang, H. Li, F. Yin, B.H. Lee, S.M. Saw, L. Tong, T.Y. Wong, Detection of pathological myopia by PAMELA with texture-based features through an SVM approach, J. Healthcare Eng. 1 (2010) 1–11.

[21] X. Zhu, R.M. Rangayyan, Detection of the optic disc in images of the retina using the Hough transform, in: International Conference of IEEE Engineering in Medicine and Biology Society, 2008, pp. 3546–3549.

[22] J. Lowell, A. Hunter, D. Steel, A. Basu, R. Ryder, E. Fletcher, L. Kennedy, Optic nerve head segmentation, IEEE Trans. Med. Imaging 23 (2) (2004) 256–264.

[23] J. Xu, O. Chutatape, E. Sung, C. Zheng, P.C.T. Kuan, Optic disk feature extraction via modified deformable model technique for glaucoma analysis, Pattern Recogn. 40 (2007) 2063–2076.

[24] Z. Zhang, J. Liu, N.S. Cherian, Y. Sun, J.H. Lim, W.K. Wong, N.M. Tan, S. Lu, H. Li, T.Y. Wong, Convex hull based neuro-retinal optic cup ellipse optimization in glaucoma diagnosis, in: International Conference of IEEE Engineering in Medicine and Biology Society, 2009, pp. 1441–1444.

[25] G.D. Joshi, J. Sivaswamy, S.R. Krishnadas, Optic disk and cup segmentation from monocular color retinal images for glaucoma assessment, IEEE Trans. Med. Imaging 30 (2011) 1192–1205.

[26] J.B. Jonas, W.M. Budde, S. Panda-Jonas, Ophthalmoscopic evaluation of the optic nerve head, Surv. Ophthalmol. 43 (4) (1999) 293–320.

[27] F. Yin, J. Liu, S.H. Ong, Y. Sun, D.W.K. Wong, N.M. Tan, C. Cheung, M. Baskaran, T. Aung, T.Y. Wong, Model-based optic nerve head segmentation on retinal fundus images, in: International Conference of the IEEE Engineering in Medicine and Biology Society, 2011, pp. 2626–2629.

[28] A. Krizhevsky, I. Sutskever, G.E. Hinton, Imagenet classification with deep convolutional neural networks, in: Advances in Neural Information Processing Systems, 2012, pp. 1097–1105.

[29] H. Fu, J. Cheng, Y. Xu, C. Zhang, D.W.K. Wong, J. Liu, X. Cao, Disc-aware ensemble network for glaucoma screening from fundus image, IEEE Trans. Med. Imaging 37 (11) (2018) 2493–2501.

[30] A. Sevastopolsky, Optic disc and cup segmentation methods for glaucoma detection with modification of U-Net convolutional neural network, Pattern Recogn. Image Anal. 27 (3) (2017) 618–624.

[31] J. Long, E. Shelhamer, T. Darrell, Fully convolutional networks for semantic segmentation, in: Proceedings of the IEEE Conference on Computer Vision and Pattern Recognition, 2015, pp. 3431–3440.

[32] R.R. Allingham, K.F. Damji, S. Freedman, S.E. Moroi, G. Shafranov, Shields' Textbook of Glaucoma, fifth ed., Lippincott Williams & Wilkins, Philadelphia, PA, 2005.

[33] K. Stapor, A. Świtonski, R. Chrastek, G. Michelson, Segmentation of fundus eye images using methods of mathematical morphology for glaucoma diagnosis, in: Proc. Int. Conf. Computer Science, 2004, pp. 41–48.

[34] N. Inoue, K. Yanashima, K. Magatani, T. Kurihara, Development of a simple diagnostic method for the glaucoma using ocular fundus pictures, in: International Conference of the IEEE Engineering in Medicine and Biology Society, 2005, pp. 3355–3358.

[35] G.D. Joshi, J. Sivaswamy, K. Karan, R. Krishnadas, Optic disk and cup boundary detection using regional information, in: Proc. IEEE Int. Symp. Biomed. Imaging, 2010, pp. 948–951.

[36] D.W.K. Wong, J. Liu, J.H. Lim, X. Jia, F. Yin, H. Li, T.Y. Wong, Level-set based automatic cup-to-disc ratio determination using retinal fundus images in ARGALI, in: International Conference of the IEEE Engineering in Medicine and Biology Society, 2008, pp. 2266–2269.

[37] D.W.K. Wong, J. Liu, J.H. Lim, H. Li, T.Y. Wong, Automated detection of kinks from blood vessels for optic cup segmentation in retinal images, in: Proc. SPIE 7260, 2009, p. 72601J.

[38] Y. Xu, D. Xu, S. Lin, J. Liu, J. Cheng, C.Y. Cheung, T. Aung, T.Y. Wong, Sliding window and regression based cup detection in digital fundus images for glaucoma diagnosis, in: MICCAI 2011, Part III, LNCS, 2011, pp. 1–8.

[39] F. Yin, J. Liu, D.W.K. Wong, N.M. Tan, C. Cheung, M. Baskaran, T. Aung, T.Y. Wong, Automated segmentation of optic disc and optic cup in fundus images for glaucoma diagnosis, in: IEEE Int. Symp. on Computer-Based Medical Systems, 2012, pp. 1–6.

[40] Y. Jiang, H. Xia, Y. Xu, J. Cheng, H. Fu, L. Duan, Z. Meng, J. Liu, Optic disc and cup segmentation with blood vessel removal from fundus images for glaucoma detection, in: 40th Annual International Conference of the IEEE Engineering in Medicine and Biology Society (EMBC), 2018, pp. 862–865.

[41] J. Cheng, Z. Zhang, D. Tao, D.W.K. Wong, J. Liu, M. Baskaran, T. Aung, T.Y. Wong, Similarity regularized sparse group lasso for cup to disc ratio computation, Biomed. Opt. Express 8 (8) (2017) 3763–3777.

[42] J. Cheng, Sparse range-constrained learning and its application for medical image grading, IEEE Trans. Med. Imaging 37 (12) (2018) 2729–2738.

[43] Y. Xu, J. Liu, S. Lin, D. Xu, C.Y. Cheung, T. Aung, T.Y. Wong, Efficient optic cup detection from intra-image learning with retinal structure priors, in: Proc. MICCAI, vol. 15, 2012, pp. 58–65.

[44] Y. Zheng, D. Stambolian, J. O'Brien, J.C. Gee, Optic disc and cup segmentation from color fundus photograph using graph cut with priors, in: Proc. MICCAI, 2013, pp. 75–82.

[45] J. Zilly, J.M. Buhmann, D. Mahapatra, Glaucoma detection using entropy sampling and ensemble learning for automatic optic cup and disc segmentation, Comput. Med. Imaging Graph. 55 (2017) 28–41.

[46] E. Trucco, A. Ruggeri, T. Karnowski, L. Giancardo, E. Chaum, J.P. Hubschman, B. Al-Diri, C.Y. Cheung, D. Wong, M. Abramoff, G. Lim, D. Kumar, P. Burlina, N.M. Bressler, H.F. Jelinek, F. Meriaudeau, G. Quellec, T. Macgillivray, B. Dhillon, Validating retinal fundus image analysis algorithms: issues and a proposal, Invest. Ophthalmol. Vis. Sci. 54 (5) (2013) 3546–3559.

[47] D. Pascolini, S.P. Mariotti, Global estimates of visual impairment: 2010, Br. J. Ophthalmol. 96 (5) (2012) 614–618, https://doi.org/10.1136/bjophthalmol-2011-300539.

[48] S. Resnikoff, D. Pascolini, D. Etya'ale, I. Kocur, R. Pararajasegaram, G.P. Pokharel, S. Mariotti, Global data on visual impairment in the year 2002, Bull. World Health Org. 82 (2004) 844–851.

[49] E. Peli, T. Peli, Restoration of retinal images obtained through cataracts, IEEE Trans. Med. Imaging 8 (4) (1989) 401–406.

[50] R.T. Tan, Visibility in bad weather from a single image, in: IEEE Conference on Computer Vision and Pattern Recognition, 2008, pp. 1–8.

[51] R. Fattal, Single image dehazing, ACM Trans. Graph. 27 (3) (2008) 1–9.

[52] K. He, J. Sun, X. Tang, Single image haze removal using dark channel prior, IEEE Trans. Pattern Anal. Mach. Intell. 33 (12) (2011) 2341–2353.

[53] K. He, J. Sun, X. Tang, Guided image filtering, IEEE Trans. Pattern Anal. Mach. Intell. 35 (6) (2013) 1397–1409.

[54] Z. Li, J. Zheng, Z. Zhu, W. Yao, S. Wu, Weighted guided image filtering, IEEE Trans. Image Process. 24 (1) (2015) 120–129.

[55] Z. Li, J. Zheng, Edge-preserving decomposition-based single image haze removal, IEEE Trans. Image Process. 24 (12) (2015) 5432–5441.

[56] D. Min, S. Choi, J. Lu, B. Ham, K. Sohn, M. Do, Fast global image smoothing based on weighted least squares, IEEE Trans. Image Process. 23 (2014) 5638–5653.

[57] Z.G. Li, J.H. Zheng, S. Rahardja, Detail-enhanced exposure fusion, IEEE Trans. Image Process. 21 (11) (2012) 4672–4676.

[58] Z. Farbman, R. Fattal, D. Lischinski, R. Szeliski, Edge-preserving Decompositions for multi-scale tone and detail manipulation, ACM Trans. Graph. 27 (3) (2008) 67:1–67:10.

[59] Z. Li, J. Zheng, Single image de-hazing using globally guided image filtering, IEEE Trans. Image Process. 27 (1) (2018) 442–450.

[60] J.-H. Kim, W.-D. Jang, J.-Y. Sim, C.-S. Kim, Optimized contrast enhancement for real-time image and video dehazing, J. Vis. Commun. Image Represent. 24 (3) (2013) 410–425.

[61] A.G. Marrugo, M.S. Millan, M. Sorel, F. Sroubek, Retinal image restoration by means of blind deconvolution, J. Biomed. Opt. 16 (11) (2011) 116016.

[62] Z. Zhang, F. Yin, J. Liu, W.K. Wong, N.M. Tan, B.H. Lee, J. Cheng, T.Y. Wong, ORIGA-light: an online retinal fundus image database for glaucoma analysis and research, in: International Conference of the IEEE Engineering in Medicine and Biology Society, 2010, pp. 3065–3068.

[63] A.K. Tripathi, S. Mukhopadhyay, A.K. Dhara, Performance metrics for image contrast, in: Int. Conf. Image Inf. Process., 2011, pp. 1–4.

[64] M. Foracchia, E. Grisan, A. Ruggeri, Luminosity and contrast normalization in retinal images, Med. Image Anal. 9 (3) (2005) 179–190.

[65] Y. LeCun, Y. Bengio, G. Hinton, Deep learning, Nature 521 (7553) (2015) 436–444.

[66] O. Ronneberger, P. Fischer, T. Brox, U-Net: convolutional networks for biomedical image segmentation, in: Medical Image Computing and Computer-Assisted Intervention: Part III, Springer International Publishing, 2015, pp. 234–241.

[67] J. Duch, E. Hazan, Y. Singer, Adaptive subgradient methods for online learning and stochastic optimization, J. Mach. Learn. Res. 12 (2011) 2121–2159.

Diabetic retinopathy and maculopathy lesions

12

Bashir Al-Diri[a], Francesco Calivá[b], Piotr Chudzik[a], Giovanni Ometto[c], Maged Habib[d]

[a]*School of Computer Science, University of Lincoln, Lincoln, United Kingdom*
[b]*Department of Radiology and Biomedical Imaging, Musculoskeletal Quantitative Imaging Research Group, University of California, San Francisco, San Francisco, CA, United States*
[c]*Optometry and Visual Science, School of Health Sciences, University of London, London, United Kingdom*
[d]*Sunderland Eye Infirmary, South Shields and Sunderland City Hospitals NHS Foundation Trust, Sunderland, United Kingdom*

1 Introduction

Diabetic retinopathy (DR) is a chronic progressive sight-threatening disease of the retinal microvasculature associated with prolonged high elevated blood sugar levels (hyperglycemia) as well as other linked conditions such as hypertension. DR can be asymptomatic for long periods and as the disease progresses, patients can experience mild sight impairments. However, late stages of the disease can lead to severe sight-threatening conditions and potential blindness, if untreated. Vision loss can occur secondary to either leak in the center of the retina (macula)—leading to diabetic macular edema—or due to the development of new vessels that can bleed inside the eye. DR can manifest in forms of blurred and/or fluctuating vision, dark spots fluctuating during saccades, empty vision areas, and reduced vision. From a clinical perspective, DR can be classified as a nonproliferative stage (NPDR) or as a more advanced proliferative stage (PDR). In NPDR, damages occur in the inner retinal blood vessels, which leak of fluids onto the retina, resulting in edema and swelling [1]. In this scenario, Frank [2] defines lesions as the major sign of retinopathy, and clusters them as microaneurysms (MAs), hemorrhages (HMs), hard and soft exudates (EXs), intraretinal microvascular abnormalities (IRMA), and venous beading (VB). NPDR can be graded as mild, moderate, or severe. Mild NPDR occurs with at least one MA. Moderate NPDR occurs with scattered retinal deep dot and blot HMs, and/or cotton wool spots CWS (soft exudates) and IRMAs but not as extensive as severe NPDR. The diagnosis of severe NPDR is based on the 4:2:1 rule of the ETDRS [2a]. Furthermore, IRMA can be present in each quadrant. With respect to PDR, abnormal development and angiogenesis of new vessels are the main representative characteristics of the disease: new blood vessels can grow in different areas of retinal surface or at the surface of the optic disc. The former are defined as New Vessels Elsewhere (NVE), the latter as New Vessels on Disc (NVD). These abnormal new vessels can easily bleed and are considered as the major leading cause of DR-related blindness.

2 The clinical impact of DR and maculopathy lesions

DR should be detected in the early stages so that treatment can be initiated before the development of vision-threatening retinopathy (ETDRS report number 9 1991). Regular retinal screening is appropriate because DR constitutes a major health problem, which is frequent among diabetic patients, can be detected and treated, and also because screening is cost-effective [3–10]. Screening for DR includes the measurement of best-corrected visual acuity and fundus photography. The photographic procedure has been standardized, and generally includes seven-field photography with 30-degree images in the United States, and two 60-degree fundus photographs (FPs) in Europe, one centered on the foveal area and another centered on the optic disc [11, 12]. The grading of DR in these FPs is performed by trained graders, and the degree of retinopathy is compared with a set of standard images representing the range of severity of the disease. This results in a semiquantitative grading of retinopathy. After each screening examination, the recommended interval to the following examination is assessed on the basis of rules designed so that progression to a vision-threatening condition is detected even in patients with the fastest disease progression [13, 14]. The screening interval is mainly defined on the basis of retinopathy grade, but diabetes type and diabetes duration are also included in the recommendation. Therefore, there is a lot of interest in the identification of early signs of the disease. MAs are the most frequent type of lesions to appear on the retina and the first symptom of DR [15]. It has been found that MAs are so important for the diagnosis that the presence of even one or two in an eye should be considered seriously [16]. Small solitary MAs can be potentially missed or overlooked by DR graders and screeners who are involved in reviewing thousands of screening images on regular basis, hence automated detection of DR lesions can help reduce human error and alleviate work burden of the retinopathy graders.

3 Type of lesions/clinical features

As alluded to earlier, DR has no early warning signs, nevertheless initial changes of DR manifest as a direct consequence of retinal capillary damage. In order, abnormal changes of the large arterioles and venules may be seen. Morphological alterations, which are shown in Fig. 1, may reflect an ongoing series of pathological changes, including previous retinal damage.

Donnellyand Horton [17] and Van Bijsterveld [18] explain that while DR progresses, there are mainly two type of clinical features, which display at different

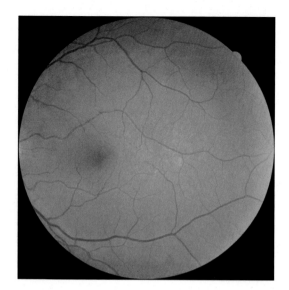

FIG. 1

Diabetic parafoveal MAs.

stages of DR: lesions and vascular anomalies. The former include MAs and HMs, cotton wool spots and exudates. The latter refer to VB, IRMAs, neovascularization, loop and fibrous proliferation.

–   MA refers to red, small, circular-shaped leakage of small vessels [19]. They emerge predominant in the posterior pole of the eye, and multiply with the increasing severity of retinopathy. From a geometrical perspective, MAs' diameter appears smaller than that of widest veins visible in an FP. Furthermore, Van Bijsterveld [18] showed that MAs often appear in clusters (see Fig. 1).
–   HMs are a consequence of an MAs' wall failure. Two types of HMs are known: dot and blot HMs. These differentiate based on their size and color. Dot HMs are bright red small dots, whereas blot HMs are darker in color and larger in size. Both MAs and HMs are referred to as "dark lesions." In addition, Donnelly and Horton [17] describe the existence of flame-shaped HMs, generally visible within the superficial layer of the nerve fiber layer (see Fig. 2).
–   Cotton wool spots are grayish-white patches of discoloration in the nerve fiber layer, which have ill-defined edges. They are the result of local ischemia, so multiple cotton wool spots indicate generalized retinal ischemia and this is a feature of preproliferative retinopathy [17].
–   VB is a localized increase in venous diameter. Due to the continuous alternating of narrowing and widening of a long vessel course, when captured on an FP, vessels appear like "sausages on a string." Donnelly and Horton [17] and Van Bijsterveld [18] define the degree of VB as a useful predictor of PDR and diffuse retinal ischemia.

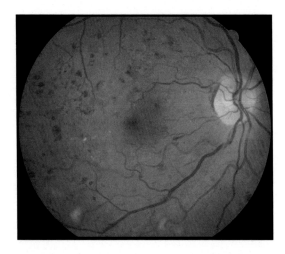

FIG. 2

Scattered dot and blot HMs.

- Interretinal microvascular abnormalities usually appear as irregular loops of vessels within the retina, which may straddle normal vessels [17]. Loops cause deviation of vein curvature from its normal course. Such deviations can be minor gentle curvatures as well as resemble omega-shaped (see Fig. 3).
- Neovascularization is a process of abnormally growing new vessels. These new vessels stem from large veins or major arcade vessels. They appear initially as fine tufts on the surface of the retina. These new vessels are fragile and bleed easily [17] (see Figs. 4 and 5).

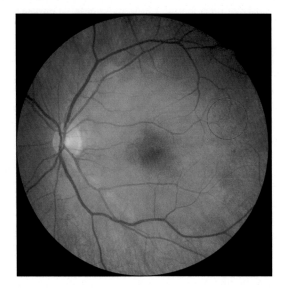

FIG. 3

Intraretinal microvascular abnormalities (annotated).

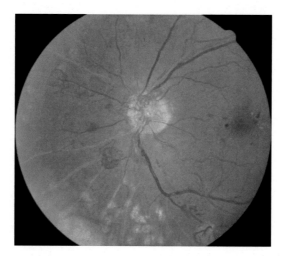

FIG. 4

New vessels at the disc (NVD) in PDR.

– Vitreous HMs refer to the bleeding happening within the vitreous cavity. If extensive, they can bar a clear view of the retina. According to Donnelly and Horton [17], the appearance of HMs on the macula has high incidence on sharp vision loss.
– Preretinal or subhyaloid HMs involve the presence of blood in the area just anterior to the retina and under the posterior vitreous face. These type of HMs often appear as capsized boat-shaped (see Fig. 6).
– Retinal detachment is an outcome of neovascular traction. It usually occurs slowly and may remain stable for years, assuming laser treatment has been applied to control the neovascular process [17].

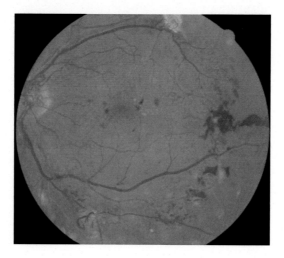

FIG. 5

New vessels at the disc and elsewhere (NVD and NVE) in PDR.

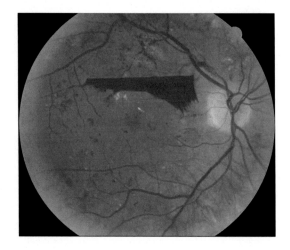

FIG. 6

Subhyaloid HM secondary to PDR.

- Hard exudates are mainly formed by leaked cellular lipid from abnormal intraretinal capillaries, appearing as shiny yellow-white deposits with sharp margins, varying from small spots to larger patches, which may evolve into rings known as circinate. If the leaked lipids coalesce and enlarge into the fovea, then vision can be severely compromised [17] (see Figs. 7 and 8).
- Fibrous proliferation is structurally supportive fibrotic tissue sufficiently opaque to be seen on the surface of, or in front of, the retina associated with new vessels.

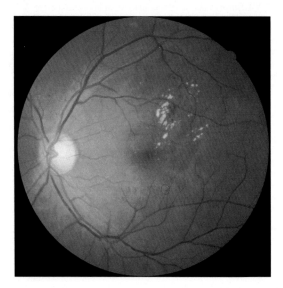

FIG. 7

Cluster of hard exudates in diabetic maculopathy.

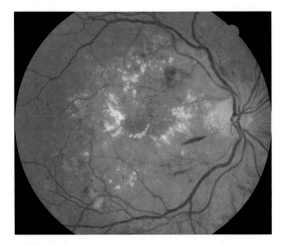

FIG. 8

Diabetic maculopathy with circinate hard exudates and diffuse maculopathy (mixed diabetic maculopathy.

4 Lesion detection and segmentation

Detection and segmentation of lesions is performed by ophthalmologists and trained graders through visual inspection of FPs. Unfortunately, the annotation process is tedious, time-consuming, and error-prone with high interobserver variability [20]. Furthermore, retinal lesions are complex structures with irregular shapes, which makes it challenging to manually measure and monitor their development. Therefore, research groups across the world have been working for decades to create a fully automated system for lesions detection and segmentation. Initially researchers used fluorescein angiograms to detect and segment DR lesions in retina. Fluorescein angiography uses an intravenous contrast agent to improve the contrast between lesions and background. Unfortunately the image acquisition process requires highly trained personnel and can have negative effect on patient's health [21]. As such research efforts moved toward color fundus photography. DR lesions can be divided into two main groups: red lesions (RLs: MAs and HMs) and bright lesions (BLs: exudates and cotton wool spots). The vast majority of lesion detection and segmentation algorithms consist of five consecutive processing stages:

1 *Preprocessing* involves the removal of noise, uneven illumination, and improving contrast between foreground objects and background.
2 *Vessel removal.* Lesions appear close to vessels, which makes their detection more challenging. Thus, removing vessels can make the detection process more straightforward.
3 *Candidate identification.* Identifying possible lesion candidates reduces the amount of data analyzed by subsequent algorithms.
4 *Candidate feature extraction.* Representing candidates in terms of features reduces the data dimensionality and improves the classification performance.
5 *Classification.* Each object/pixel is assigned to a probability value of being a lesion.

Furthermore, depending on methodology, these techniques can be divided into following six categories: morphology, machine learning, region growing, thresholding, deep learning, or miscellaneous.

4.1 Morphology

These methods use morphological operations to find lesions. They are sensitive to changes in shape and size of structuring elements which can negatively affect detection accuracy. Baudoin et al. [22] are one the first researchers that worked on MA detection in 1983 using fluorescein angiogram images. They employed a mathematical morphology-based approach to remove vessels and applied a top-hat transformation with linear structuring elements. Several methods followed this approach; however, since intravenous use of fluorescein can cause death in 1 in 222,000 cases [21], these methods were abandoned. Walter et al. [23] also used a top-hat-based method and automated thresholding to extract MA candidates. They extracted 15 features and applied kernel density estimation with variable bandwidth for MA classification. Similarly, Streeter and Cree [24] combined top-hat transform with matched filtering to find lesion candidates. Subsequently, linear discriminant analysis was used to produce final segmentation. Harangi et al. [25] used morphological operators to identify exudate candidates. Next, an active contour model was employed to find lesions' edges. Similarly Xiaohui and Chutatape [26] combined morphological transformations for candidate extraction with contextual features to segment BLs.

4.2 Machine learning

Machine learning-based methods include both supervised (e.g., neural networks) and unsupervised (e.g., clustering) learning algorithms. Niemeijer et al. [27] combined k-nearest neighbor and linear discriminant classifiers to label each pixel as either BL or background. Rocha et al. [28] introduced a method based on a dictionary of visual words constructed using SIFT and SURF features. Each image was treated as a bag of features and used as input to support vector machines (SVMs) for final classification. Veiga et al. [29] presented an algorithm using law texture features. SVMs were used in a cascading manner: the first SVM was used to extract MA candidates whereas the second SVM performed final MA classification. Srivastava et al. [30] used Frangi-based filters that were manually fine-tuned to distinguish vessels from RLs. Filters were applied to multiple-sized image patches to extract features. Finally, these features were classified using an SVM. Osareh et al. [31] combined fuzzy c-means clustering and a genetic algorithm for candidate extraction with shallow neural network for exudates (EX) classification. Grisan and Ruggeri [32] presented a two-stage classifier for BL and RL detection. A Bayesian classifier was used for pixel classification and followed by linear discriminative analysis that performed lesion classification. Massey and Hunter [33] combined spatial clustering of objects with multilayered neural networks and SVMs to detect BL and RL.

4.3 Region growing

Region growing methods examine neighborhoods of seed points and determine whether they should be part of a specific region. Spencer et al. [34] proposed matched filtering and bilinear top-hat transformation to find initial MAs. Subsequently, they used a region growing algorithm to produce final segmentation results. Cree et al. [35] extended [34] with more intensity-based features and novel region growing algorithm. Frame et al. [36] combined region growing approach with three different classifiers: shallow neural network, linear discriminant analysis, and rule-based system. They concluded that manually created rule-based system provides best results; however, their experimental dataset consisted of only 20 images. Fleming et al. [37] emphasized the importance of contrast normalization and proposed a "Watershed Retinal Region Growing" algorithm to segment lesions. Li and Chutatape [38] proposed a fusion of edge detection and region growing algorithm for exudate detection. Sinthanayothin et al. [39] introduced the "moat operator" that was used to sharpen lesions' edges. They combined it with the recursive region growing algorithm to segment both BL and RL.

4.4 Thresholding

Threshold-based methods exploit differences in color intensity between various image regions. Zhang et al. [40] proposed a method based on dynamic thresholding and correlation coefficients of a multiscale Gaussian template to detect MAs. They used 31 manually designed features based on intensity, shape, and response of a Gaussian filter. Pereira et al. [41] combined a thresholding approach with the ant colony optimizer to segment EXs. EX candidates were identified using a thresholding method, whereas the unsupervised ant colony optimizer was used to enhance EXs' edges. García et al. [42] suggested a combination of adaptive and global thresholding approaches to find EX candidates. Next, a radial basis function classifier was designed to classify lesions based on features mainly derived from lesions' shape and color. Saleh and Eswaran [43] developed a decision support system to find RLs. They combined H-maxima transform for candidate selection with multilevel thresholding to create final segmentation. Phillips et al. [44] used a combination of global, local, and adaptive thresholding algorithms to find lesions. To tackle uneven illumination of FPs, Sánchez et al. [45] combined dynamic thresholding based on mixture models with edge detection.

4.5 Deep learning

Deep learning (DL) algorithms use hierarchical models with multiple levels of transformations to learn highly abstract representations of data. They revolutionized the world of machine learning and were becoming increasingly popular in medical image analysis. Unfortunately, publicly available retinal imaging datasets are scarce, small, and lack necessary annotations, which severely limit DL applicability to this domain. Nevertheless, authors believe that this will change in the forthcoming future, and we will see more DL method used for lesion detection. As such we decided to create a separate category for DL algorithms, even though they are machine learning-based methods.

Convolutional neural networks (CNNs) are the main DL algorithm to deal with image data because they are able to learn the multidimensional relationships between data points (pixels/voxels). van Grinsven et al. [46] presented a selective data sampling technique to improve the CNN training time. They combined it with a vanilla-type CNN to find HMs in color fundus images. Orlando et al. [47] used CNN as a feature extractor and combined it with the random forest classifier to find MAs. Chudzik et al. [48] created a novel CNN architecture with inception modules to segment exudates. They showed that transfer knowledge between even small retinal datasets of different modalities results in better performance. Next, they proposed a novel fine-tuning scheme called "interleaved freezing" that optimizes the transfer learning process [49]. They combined it with a U-Net type CNN to find MAs. Subsequently, they improved their results by combining their dedicated CNN with an auxiliary codebook built from the network's intermediate layers output [50]. The auxiliary codebook allowed to identify the most difficult data samples and improved their segmentation results. Finally, they proposed a fully CNN with batch normalization layers and DICE loss function to segment MAs [20]. Fig. 9 depicts an example of MA detection in FPs. Compared to other methods that require the aforementioned five stages of image analysis, the proposed algorithm required only two: preprocessing and classification. Dai et al. [51] proposed a clinical report guided multisieving CNN which combined multimodal information from text reports with image data. Clinical reports are used to bridge the semantic gap between low-level image features and high-level diagnostic information.

4.6 Miscellaneous

Miscellaneous techniques are all remaining works that do not fit in previous categories. Agurto et al. [52] proposed a multiscale amplitude-modulation-frequency-modulation (AM-FM) method to find both BL and RL. The cumulative distribution functions of instantaneous value of frequency, relative instantaneous value of frequency angle, and instantaneous value of amplitude were used for feature analysis. Javidi et al. [53] proposed a technique which is used 2D Morlet wavelet to find MA candidates. At the next stage, a discriminative dictionary learning approach was employed to distinguish MAs from other structures. Quellec et al. [54] detected lesions by locally matching a lesion template in subbands of wavelet transformed images. A genetic algorithm was used to find the optimal wavelet. Köse et al. [55] combined inverse segmentation method with Naive Bayes classifier to detect both BL and RL. Figueiredo et al. [56] extracted a number of multiscale features based on Hessian analysis and wavelet transform. Subsequently, they devised a number of lesion-specialized binary classifiers to find all DR lesions.

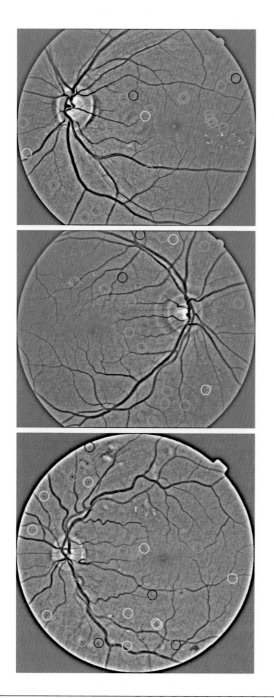

FIG. 9

Examples of MA detections from Chudzik et al. [20]. True positives are *green circled*, false positives are *yellow circled*, and false negatives are *red circled*.

4.7 Performance comparison

Table 1 presents a comparison of representative RL and BL detection methods. It is important to note that the fair performance comparison of the aforementioned methods is impossible because they were validated using different datasets and metrics. As such, we only report their performance against specific datasets. It can be observed that there is no single superior approach across all available methodologies.

Table 1 Performance comparison of lesion detection methods.

Method	Method type	Task	Dataset	Performance metric
Chudzik et al. [20]	Deep learning	MA detection	E-Ophtha [57]	FROC: 0.562
van Grinsven et al. [46]	Deep learning	HM detection	Messidor [58]	SN: 0.94, SP: 0.87
Orlando et al. [47]	Deep learning	RL detection	DIARETDB1 [59]	FROC: 0.4874
Walter et al. [23]	Morphology	MA detection	Private	SN: 0.89
Harangi and Hajdu [60]	Morphology	EX detection	DIARETDB1	SN: 0.75
Xiaohui and Chutatape [26]	Morphology	BL detection	Private	SN: 0.97, SP: 0.96
Niemeijer et al. [27]	Machine learning	BL detection	Private	SN: 0.96, SP: 0.86
Niemeijer et al. [27]	Machine learning	BL detection	Private	AUC: 0.953
Veiga et al. [29]	Machine learning	MA detection	E-Ophtha	FROC: 0.328
Frame et al. [36]	Region growing	MA detection	Private	SN: 0.84, SP:0.85
Li and Chutatape [38]	Region growing	BL detection	Private	SN: 1.00, SP:0.71
Sinthanayothin et al. [39]	Region growing	RL detection	Private	SN: 0.78, SP:0.89
Sánchez et al. [45]	Thresholding	RL detection	HEI-MED [61]	MA SN: 0.84, HM SN: 0.88
Pereira et al. [41]	Thresholding	EX detection	HEI-MED	SN: 0.81, SN:0.99
Zhang et al. [40]	Thresholding	MA detection	ROC [62]	FROC: 0.20
Figueiredo et al. [56]	Miscellaneous	BL detection	Private	SN: 0.90, SP: 0.97
Javidi et al. [53]	Miscellaneous	MA detection	ROC	FROC: 0.27
Köse et al. [55]	Miscellaneous	HM detection	Private	SN: 0.93, SP: 0.98

Notes: FROC, free-response receiver operatic characteristic; SN, sensitivity; SP, specificity; AUC, area under the receiver operatic characteristic curve.

From the clinical point of view, finding a DR lesion is more important than segmenting it, especially for screening, diagnosis, and monitoring purposes. Thus, the table provides a comparison of detection methods only. The reader is referred to Chudzik et al. [20, 50] for the in-depth discussion of evaluation metrics.

5 Lesion localization

Screening programs are common in western countries for the detection of early DR. The rule-based assessment of intervals must be conservative to reduce the risk of vision-threatening conditions occurring between examinations. Consequently, the frequency of screening visits can be overestimated. Superfluous examinations could be avoided if the frequency could be reduced in patients without progression. A number of known risk factors for the development and progression of DR are not included in currently employed rule-based decision models: metabolic regulation of blood glucose (HbA1c), arterial hypertension, and gender. In recent years, several models have been presented for individualized determination of the screening interval in DR [65–67]. The model presented by Mehlsen et al. included the number of MAs and HMs, HbA1c, blood pressure, gender, diabetes duration, and diabetes type, and with this information the screening interval could on average be prolonged with a factor of 2.88 in type 1 diabetic (T1D) patients and with a factor of 1.24 in type 2 diabetic (T2D) patients. However, since the screening interval defined by the grader was itself a risk factor it was concluded that the recommendation by the grader had depended on observations during grading of the FP that were not described by the number of MA/HM. This was supported by findings that early progression of DR lesions temporal in the macular area and peripheral from the larger temporal vascular arcades can predict the development of retinopathy to a vision-threatening stage [64]. Recently, a study by Ometto et al. [68] investigated the role of regional distribution of the earliest retinopathy lesions showing in FPs. This work identified the need for a spatial system that is repeatable to compare the distribution of lesions showing across photographs from different eyes. A coordinate system based on the main retinal landmarks, fovea, optic disc, and main vascular arcades, and suitable for automatic identification was proposed as in reference [63]. The x-axis of a retinal coordinate system was identified by the line connecting the fovea and optic disc centers, and their distance was used to define one unit of length. The unit of length in the normal y-axis was defined by the average of the distances between the fovea and the main vascular temporal arcades. Using these definitions, a coordinate system with the origin at the fovea and dividing the photographs into four quadrants was identified for each retina (Fig. 10). This retinal system made it possible the analysis of the location of the first MA/HM in a dataset of two groups of 30 patients. The first selected group included all patients in whom no signs of DR were present in the first screening examination, who were screened regularly for at least 9 years, and who developed either PDR or diabetic maculopathy (DM) during

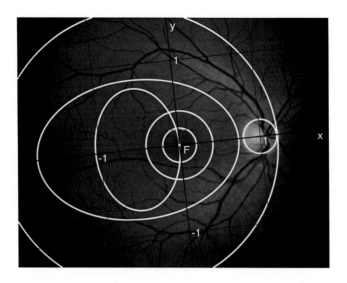

FIG. 10

The landmark-based coordinate system (*black lines*) centered on the fovea (F) of an FP from the dataset used in Ometto et al. [63]. The circular and elliptical regions described by Hove et al. [64] are delimited by *white lines*.

this period. The second group included patients pair-wise matched with those in the first group. The match was based on the diabetes type, age at onset, and duration of diabetes mellitus and was obtained from all patients in the database of the Aarhus University Hospital who had been followed for a similar period as the other group but without developing vision-threatening DR. The MA/HM showing in the FPs of the dataset were identified and their coordinates were adjusted to the proposed coordinate retinal system. The adjusted coordinates were analyzed to look for statistical evidence that the location of early MA/HM is not independent to the risk of progression to vision-threatening DR. For each patient, the coordinates of the early MAs/HMs were used to obtain the probability distribution in each point of the map using the kernel density estimation technique (Fig. 11). The maps generated by using all early lesions within the patients of the two groups were averaged to obtain the final probability density functions. The probability of the location of the first observed MA/HM given progression to vision-threatening retinopathy was used to obtain the probability of progression to vision-threatening retinopathy given the location of the first observed lesion using Bayes formula. The average probability of progression was estimated from the number of patients referred for either PDR or DM in the screening program of the Aarhus University Hospital and was 0.0386. A 99% confidence interval was provided from a derivation of the bias-corrected and accelerated bootstrap confidence interval [69, 70] and was used in a hypothesis testing. The null hypothesis was that the probability of progression to vision-threatening DR was

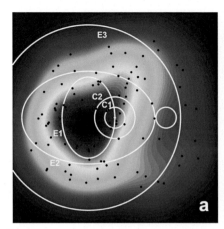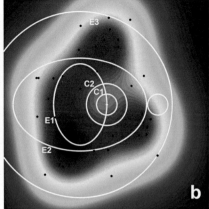

FIG. 11

Probability density functions obtained with kernel density estimation for the locations of early MA/HM from the patients with (A) and without (B) progression. The color scale ranging from *blue* (lowest values) to *dark red* (highest values) represents the surface under which the area totals to 1 in each diagram. The *black dots* represent the locations of the observed MA/HM in the retina-based coordinate system, with the observation from the left eyes flipped around the vertical axis to be represented in the coordinate system of the right eye. The circular and elliptical regions described by Hove et al. [64] are delimited by *white lines.*

independent of the location of the first RL. If the average probability of progression (3.86%) was within the lower and upper boundaries of the 99% confidence interval at every location of the map, the hypothesis was not rejected. In the test, rejection supported the alternative hypothesis that the location of the first RL was a risk factor for progression.

Fig. 12 shows the area in the map where the information in the dataset supported the hypothesis that early MA/HM were not independent of the development of vision-threatening DR within the 99% confidence limit. This area mainly appeared around and temporal to the fovea. The maximum value (5.39%) represented a risk of progression 39.5% higher than the average. The study confirmed the results from previous investigations [71, 72] that the earliest DR lesions appeared in the macular area temporal from the fovea, and that the occurrence of lesions in this area was correlated to the development of DM [73]. The study also improves the definition of the area where the occurrence MA/HM is a risk factor for the development of vision-threatening DR. These findings prepare for the introduction of automated image processing during screening for DR and suggest that the information about the location of early retinopathy lesions should be introduced as individual risk factors in decision models used to recommend examination intervals in screening programs for DR.

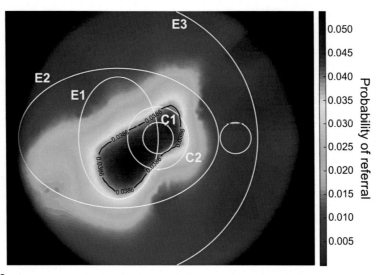

FIG. 12

The risk of progression to vision-threatening DR obtained with the 99% confidence interval. The *black line* represents the average risk of progression and identifies the area of increased risk.

6 Conclusions

DR and maculopathy lesions play a big role in developing progressive sight impairment as a consequence of a continuous exposition to hyperglycemia and/or hypertension. Although DR is asymptomatic, the appearance of lesions and especially their localization can be informative of the harm that can cause to the eye. For instance, Ometto et al. [68] showed that by analyzing the regional differences in the distribution of retinal blood flow, it is possible to predict how likely it is that the appearance of HMs and/or MAs in specific regions causes the development of vision-threatening DR. Based on clinical data, Ometto et al. [68] asserted that the occurrence of RLs within a region located temporal to the fovea, slightly below the horizontal meridian can predict with 99% certainty that the development of DR will lead to sight impairment. Therefore, it is important to detect DR in the early stages and initiate treatments before the development of substantial sight-threatening retinopathy. Currently, lesion detection and segmentation are manually performed by ophthalmologists and retinopathy graders and screeners upon visual inspection of the ocular fundus by means of digital fundus photography. Like in other domains, manual annotations are prone to human ingenuous errors. This makes it desirable to be at disposal automated systems deployable in clinical scenarios. Compared to traditional hand-engineered systems, modern deep learning-based architectures are capable of taking advantage of the vast amount of data available and achieving excellent performance, comparable to humans [20]. Moreover, the long-term complications of diabetes might affect different vascular systems of the body. An assessment of the presence and severity of retinal microvascular abnormalities may provide a deeper understanding of other concurrent systemic vascular disease associated with diabetes. The retinal pathological changes may have valuable future use as a marker of various other cerebrovascular and systemic disorders.

References

[1] R.P. Crick, P.T. Khaw, A Textbook of Clinical Ophthalmology: A Practical Guide to Disorders of the Eyes and Their Management, World Scientific, Singapore, 2003.

[2] R.N. Frank, On the pathogenesis of diabetic retinopathy: a 1990 update, Ophthalmology 98 (5) (1991) 586–593.

[2a] R.P. Murphy, Management of diabetic retinopathy, Am. Fam. Physician 51 (4) (1995) 785–796.

[3] T.E. Rohan, C.D. Frost, N.J. Wald, Prevention of blindness by screening for diabetic retinopathy: a quantitative assessment, Bmj 299 (6709) (1989) 1198–1201.

[4] M.O. Bachmann, S.J. Nelson, Impact of diabetic retinopathy screening on a British district population: case detection and blindness prevention in an evidence-based model, J. Epidemiol. Community Health 52 (1) (1998) 45–52.

[5] J.C. Javitt, L.P. Aiello, Cost-effectiveness of detecting and treating diabetic retinopathy, Ann. Intern. Med. 124 (1 Pt 2) (1996) 164–169.

[6] E. Stefánsson, T. Bek, M. Porta, N. Larsen, J.K. Kristinsson, E. Agardh, Screening and prevention of diabetic blindness, Acta Ophthalmol. Scand. 78 (4) (2000) 374–385.

[7] K. Facey, E. Cummins, K. Macpherson, A. Morris, L. Reay, J. Slattery, Health Technology Assessment Report 1: Organisations of Services for Diabetic Retinopathy Screening, Health Technology Board for Scotland, Glasgow, Scotland, 2002.

[8] B.S. Sutton, A Cost-Effectiveness and Probabilistic Sensitivity Analysis of Opportunistic Screening Versus Systematic Screening for Sight-Threatening Diabetic Eye Disease (Thesis). Saint Louis University, USA, 2003.

[9] P. Jeppesen, T. Bek, The occurrence and causes of registered blindness in diabetes patients in Århus County, Denmark, Acta Ophthalmol. Scand. 82 (5) (2004) 526–530.

[10] E. Olafsdottir, E. Stefansson, Biennial eye screening in patients with diabetes without retinopathy: 10-year experience, Br. J. Ophthalmol. 91 (12) (2007) 1599–1601.

[11] S.J. Aldington, E.M. Kohner, S. Meuer, R. Klein, A.K. Sjølie, Methodology for retinal photography and assessment of diabetic retinopathy: the EURODIAB IDDM complications study, Diabetologia 38 (4) (1995) 437–444.

[12] Early Treatment Diabetic Retinopathy Study Research Group, Grading diabetic retinopathy from stereoscopic color fundus photographs—an extension of the modified Airlie House classification: ETDRS report number 10, Ophthalmology 98 (5) (1991) 786–806.

[13] D.E. Singer, D.M. Nathan, H.A. Fogel, A.P. Schachat, Screening for diabetic retinopathy, Ann. Intern. Med. 116 (8) (1992) 660–671.

[14] J. Mehlsen, M. Erlandsen, P.L. Poulsen, T. Bek, Identification of independent risk factors for the development of diabetic retinopathy requiring treatment, Acta Ophthalmol. 89 (6) (2011) 515–521.

[15] Early Treatment Diabetic Retinopathy Study Research Group, Early photocoagulation for diabetic retinopathy: ETDRS report number 9, Ophthalmology 98 (5) (1991) 766–785.

[16] E.M. Kohner, I.M. Stratton, S.J. Aldington, R.C. Turner, D.R. Matthews, UK Prospective Diabetes Study (UKPDS) Group, Microaneurysms in the development of diabetic retinopathy (UKPDS 42), Diabetologia 42 (9) (1999) 1107–1112.

[17] R. Donnelly, E. Horton, Vascular Complications of Diabetes: Current Issues in Pathogenesis and Treatment, second ed., Wiley-Blackwell, 2005. Available from: https://www.amazon.com/Vascular-Complications-Diabetes-Pathogenesis-Treatment/dp/1405127856.

[18] O.P. Van Bijsterveld, Diabetic Retinopathy, Martin Dunitz, London, 2000.

[19] A.K. Sjølie, R. Klein, M. Porta, T. Orchard, J. Fuller, H.H. Parving, R. Bilous, S. Aldington, N. Chaturvedi, Retinal microaneurysm count predicts progression and regression of diabetic retinopathy. Post-hoc results from the DIRECT Programme, Diabet. Med. 28 (3) (2011) 345–351.

[20] P. Chudzik, S. Majumdar, F. Caliva, B. Al-Diri, A. Hunter, Microaneurysm detection using fully convolutional neural networks, Comput. Methods Programs Biomed. 158 (2018) 185–192.

[21] L.A. Yannuzzi, K.T. Rohrer, L.J. Tindel, R.S. Sobel, M.A. Costanza, W. Shields, E. Zang, Fluorescein angiography complication survey, Ophthalmology 93 (5) (1986) 611–617.

[22] C.E. Baudoin, B.J. Lay, J.C. Klein, Automatic detection of microaneurysms in diabetic fluorescein angiography, Rev Epidemiol. Sante Publique 32 (3–4) (1983) 254–261.

[23] T. Walter, P. Massin, A. Erginay, R. Ordonez, C. Jeulin, J.-C. Klein, Automatic detection of microaneurysms in color fundus images, Med. Image Anal. 11 (6) (2007) 555–566.

[24] L. Streeter, M.J. Cree, Microaneurysm detection in colour fundus images, Image and Vision Computing, 2003, pp. 280–284.

[25] B. Harangi, I. Lazar, A. Hajdu, Automatic exudate detection using active contour model and regionwise classification, Engineering in Medicine and Biology Society (EMBC), 2012 Annual International Conference of the IEEE, IEEE, 2012, pp. 5951–5954.

[26] Z. Xiaohui, A. Chutatape, Detection and classification of bright lesions in color fundus images, International Conference on Image Processing, 2004, ICIP'04, vol. 1, IEEE, 2004, pp. 139–142.

[27] M. Niemeijer, B. van Ginneken, S.R. Russell, M.S.A. Suttorp-Schulten, M.D. Abramoff, Automated detection and differentiation of drusen, exudates, and cotton-wool spots in digital color fundus photographs for diabetic retinopathy diagnosis, Invest. Ophthalmol. Vis. Sci. 48 (5) (2007) 2260–2267.

[28] A. Rocha, T. Carvalho, H.F. Jelinek, S. Goldenstein, J. Wainer, Points of interest and visual dictionaries for automatic retinal lesion detection, IEEE Trans. Biomed. Eng. 59 (8) (2012) 2244–2253.

[29] D. Veiga, N. Martins, M. Ferreira, J. Monteiro, Automatic microaneurysm detection using laws texture masks and support vector machines, Comput. Methods Biomech. Biomed. Eng. Imaging Vis. 6 (4) (2018) 405–416.

[30] R. Srivastava, L. Duan, D.W.K. Wong, J. Liu, T.Y. Wong, Detecting retinal microaneurysms and hemorrhages with robustness to the presence of blood vessels, Comput. Methods Programs Biomed. 138 (2017) 83–91.

[31] A. Osareh, B. Shadgar, R. Markham, A computational-intelligence-based approach for detection of exudates in diabetic retinopathy images, IEEE Trans. Inf. Technol. Biomed. 13 (4) (2009) 535–545.

[32] E. Grisan, A. Ruggeri, A hierarchical Bayesian classification for non-vascular lesions detection in fundus images, IFMBE Proc, 11, 2005, pp. 1727–1983. vol.

[33] E.M. Massey, A. Hunter, Augmenting the classification of retinal lesions using spatial distribution, Engineering in Medicine and Biology Society, EMBC, 2011 Annual International Conference of the IEEE, 2011, pp. 3967–3970.

[34] T. Spencer, J.A. Olson, K.C. McHardy, P.F. Sharp, J.V. Forrester, An image-processing strategy for the segmentation and quantification of microaneurysms in fluorescein angiograms of the ocular fundus, Comput. Biomed. Res. 29 (4) (1996) 284–302.

[35] M.J. Cree, J.A. Olson, K.C. McHardy, P.F. Sharp, J.V. Forrester, A fully automated comparative microaneurysm digital detection system, Eye 11 (5) (1997) 622.

[36] A.J. Frame, P.E. Undrill, M.J. Cree, J.A. Olson, K.C. McHardy, P.F. Sharp, J.V. Forrester, A comparison of computer based classification methods applied to the detection of microaneurysms in ophthalmic fluorescein angiograms, Comput. Biol. Med. 28 (3) (1998) 225–238.

[37] A.D. Fleming, S. Philip, K.A. Goatman, J.A. Olson, P.F. Sharp, Automated microaneurysm detection using local contrast normalization and local vessel detection, IEEE Trans. Med. Imaging 25 (9) (2006) 1223–1232.

[38] H. Li, O. Chutatape, Automated feature extraction in color retinal images by a model based approach, IEEE Trans. Biomed. Eng. 51 (2) (2004) 246–254.

[39] C. Sinthanayothin, J.F. Boyce, T.H. Williamson, H.L. Cook, E. Mensah, S. Lal, D. Usher, Automated detection of diabetic retinopathy on digital fundus images, Diabet. Med. 19 (2) (2002) 105–112.

[40] B. Zhang, X. Wu, J. You, Q. Li, F. Karray, Detection of microaneurysms using multiscale correlation coefficients, Pattern Recogn. 43 (6) (2010) 2237–2248.

[41] C. Pereira, L. Gonçalves, M. Ferreira, Exudate segmentation in fundus images using an ant colony optimization approach, Inf. Sci. 296 (2015) 14–24.

[42] M. García, C.I. Sánchez, J. Poza, M.I. López, R. Hornero, Detection of hard exudates in retinal images using a radial basis function classifier, Ann. Biomed. Eng. 37 (7) (2009) 1448–1463.

[43] M.D. Saleh, C. Eswaran, An automated decision-support system for non-proliferative diabetic retinopathy disease based on MAs and HAs detection, Comput. Methods Programs Biomed. 108 (1) (2012) 186–196.

[44] R. Phillips, J. Forrester, P. Sharp, Automated detection and quantification of retinal exudates, Graefe's Arch. Clin. Exp. Ophthalmol. 231 (2) (1993) 90–94.

[45] C.I. Sánchez, M. García, A. Mayo, M.I. López, R. Hornero, Retinal image analysis based on mixture models to detect hard exudates, Med. Image Anal. 13 (4) (2009) 650–658.

[46] M.J.J.P. van Grinsven, B. van Ginneken, C.B. Hoyng, T. Theelen, C.I. Sánchez, Fast convolutional neural network training using selective data sampling: application to hemorrhage detection in color fundus images, IEEE Trans. Med. Imaging 35 (5) (2016) 1273–1284.

[47] J.I. Orlando, E. Prokofyeva, M. del Fresno, M.B. Blaschko, An ensemble deep learning based approach for red lesion detection in fundus images, Comput. Methods Programs Biomed. 153 (2018) 115–127.

[48] P. Chudzik, S. Majumdar, F. Caliva, B. Al-Diri, A. Hunter, Exudate segmentation using fully convolutional neural networks and inception modules, Medical Imaging 2018: Image Processing, vol. 10574, 2018, p. 1057430.

[49] P. Chudzik, S. Majumdar, F. Caliva, B. Al-Diri, A. Hunter, Microaneurysm detection using deep learning and interleaved freezing, Medical Imaging 2018: Image Processing, vol. 10574, 2018, p. 105741I.

[50] P. Chudzik, B. Al-Diri, F. Calivá, G. Ometto, A. Hunter, Exudates segmentation using fully convolutional neural network and auxiliary codebook, 40th Annual International Conference of the IEEE Engineering in Medicine and Biology Society (EMBC), IEEE, 2018, pp. 770–773.

[51] L. Dai, R. Fang, H. Li, X. Hou, B. Sheng, Q. Wu, W. Jia, Clinical report guided retinal microaneurysm detection with multi-sieving deep learning, IEEE Trans. Med. Imaging 37 (5) (2018) 1149–1161.

[52] C. Agurto, V. Murray, F. Barriga, S. Murillo, M. Pattichis, H. Davis, S. Russell, M. Abràmoff, P. Soliz, Multiscale AM-FM methods for diabetic retinopathy lesion detection, IEEE Trans. Med. Imaging 29 (2) (2010) 502–512.

[53] M. Javidi, H.-R. Pourreza, A. Harati, Vessel segmentation and microaneurysm detection using discriminative dictionary learning and sparse representation, Comput. Methods Programs Biomed. 139 (2017) 93–108.

[54] G. Quellec, S.R. Russell, M.D. Abràmoff, Optimal filter framework for automated, instantaneous detection of lesions in retinal images, IEEE Trans. Med. Imaging 30 (2) (2011) 523–533.

[55] C. Köse, U. Şevik, C. İkibaş, H. Erdöl, Simple methods for segmentation and measurement of diabetic retinopathy lesions in retinal fundus images, Comput. Methods Prog. Biomed. 107 (2) (2012) 274–293.

[56] I.N. Figueiredo, S. Kumar, C.M. Oliveira, J.D. Ramos, B. Engquist, Automated lesion detectors in retinal fundus images, Comput. Biol. Med. 66 (2015) 47–65.

[57] E. Decencière, G. Cazuguel, X. Zhang, G. Thibault, J.-C. Klein, F. Meyer, B. Marcotegui, G. Quellec, M. Lamard, R. Danno, D. Elie, P. Massin, Z. Viktor, A. Erginay, B. Laÿ, A. Chabouis, TeleOphta: machine learning and image processing methods for teleophthalmology, IRBM 34 (2) (2013) 196–203.

[58] E. Decencière, X. Zhang, G. Cazuguel, B. Lay, B. Cochener, C. Trone, P. Gain, R. Ordonez, P. Massin, A. Erginay, B. Charton, J.-C. Klein, Feedback on a publicly distributed image database: the Messidor database, Image Anal. Stereol. 33 (3) (2014) 231–234.

[59] T. Kauppi, V. Kalesnykiene, J.-K. Kamarainen, L. Lensu, I. Sorri, A. Raninen, R. Voutilainen, H. Uusitalo, H. Kälviäinen, J. Pietilä, The DIARETDB1 diabetic retinopathy database and evaluation protocol, BMVC, 2007, pp. 1–10.

[60] B. Harangi, I. Lazar, A. Hajdu, Automatic exudate detection using active contour model and regionwise classification, Annual International Conference of the IEEE Engineering in Medicine and Biology Society, IEEE, 2012, pp. 5951–5954.

[61] L. Giancardo, F. Meriaudeau, T.P. Karnowski, Y. Li, S. Garg, K.W. Tobin Jr, E. Chaum, Exudate-based diabetic macular edema detection in fundus images using publicly available datasets, Med. Image Anal. 16 (1) (2012) 216–226.

[62] M. Niemeijer, B. Van Ginneken, M.J. Cree, A. Mizutani, G. Quellec, C.I. Sánchez, B. Zhang, R. Hornero, M. Lamard, C. Muramatsu, X. Wu, G. Cazuguel, J. You, A. Mayo, Q. Li, Y. Hatanaka, B. Cochener, C. Roux, F. Karray, M. Garcia, H. Fujita, M.D. Abramoff, Retinopathy online challenge: automatic detection of microaneurysms in digital color fundus photographs, IEEE Trans. Med. Imaging 29 (1) (2010) 185–195.

[63] G. Ometto, F. Calivá, B. Al-Diri, T. Bek, A. Hunter, Automated detection of retinal landmarks for the identification of clinically relevant regions in fundus photography, Medical Imaging 2016: Image Processing, vol. 9784, International Society for Optics and Photonics, 2016, p. 978429.

[64] M.N. Hove, J.K. Kristensen, T. Lauritzen, T. Bek, Quantitative analysis of retinopathy in type 2 diabetes: identification of prognostic parameters for developing visual loss secondary to diabetic maculopathy, Acta Ophthalmol. Scand. 82 (6) (2004) 679–685.

[65] T. Aspelund, Ó. Thórisdóttir, E. Olafsdottir, A. Gudmundsdottir, A.B. Einarsdóttir, J. Mehlsen, S. Einarsson, O. Pálsson, G. Einarsson, T. Bek, Individual risk assessment and information technology to optimise screening frequency for diabetic retinopathy, Diabetologia 54 (10) (2011) 2525–2532.

[66] J. Mehlsen, M. Erlandsen, P.L. Poulsen, T. Bek, Individualized optimization of the screening interval for diabetic retinopathy: a new model, Acta Ophthalmol. 90 (2) (2012) 109–114.

[67] I.M. Stratton, S.J. Aldington, D.J. Taylor, A.I. Adler, P.H. Scanlon, A simple risk stratification for time to development of sight-threatening diabetic retinopathy, Diabet. Care 36 (3) (2013) 580–585.

[68] G. Ometto, P. Assheton, F. Calivá, P. Chudzik, B. Al-Diri, A. Hunter, T. Bek, Spatial distribution of early red lesions is a risk factor for development of vision-threatening diabetic retinopathy, Diabetologia 60 (12) (2017) 2361–2367.

[69] B. Efron, Bootstrap methods: another look at the jackknife annals of statistics, Ann. Statist. 7 (1979) 1–26.

[70] B. Efron, Better bootstrap confidence intervals, J. Am. Stat. Assoc. 82 (397) (1987) 171–185.

[71] E. Taylor, J.H. Dobree, Proliferative diabetic retinopathy. Site and size of initial lesions, Br. J. Ophthalmol. 54 (1) (1970) 11.

[72] T. Bek, Regional morphology and pathophysiology of retinal vascular disease, Prog. Retin. Eye Res. 36 (2013) 247–259.

[73] M.N. Hove, J.K. Kristensen, T. Lauritzen, T. Bek, The relationships between risk factors and the distribution of retinopathy lesions in type 2 diabetes, Acta Ophthalmol. Scand. 84 (5) (2006) 619–623.

Drusen and macular degeneration

13

Bryan M. Williams[a,b], Philip I. Burgess[a,b], Yalin Zheng[a,b]

[a]Department of Eye and Vision Science, University of Liverpool, Liverpool, United Kingdom
[b]St Paul's Eye Unit, Royal Liverpool University Hospital, Liverpool, United Kingdom

1 Introduction

Age-related macular degeneration (AMD) is a spectrum of related diseases that have in common the progressive decline of vision as a consequence of dysfunction of the central retina and its underlying supporting elements in older adults [1]. The spectrum of disease encompasses non-neovascular components (drusen and RPE abnormalities) and neovascular lesions (choroidal neovascular membrane formation and other choroidal abnormalities). Advanced AMD refers to two entities: "dry" geographic atrophy (GA) and "wet" neovascular changes. The histopathological and clinical characteristics of these lesions are described below. AMD is estimated to affect more than 196 million people worldwide by 2020. The advanced forms of the disease adversely affect quality of life, causing loss of independence in later years. Despite new therapies for the prevention and treatment of AMD, the prevalence is expected to rise to 288 million by 2040, in part due to rapidly aging populations [2].

AMD is a complex disease with multiple genetic and environmental associations. Advanced AMD is more common in Caucasians than people of African origin or Latinos [3, 4]. Rates of late AMD reported in Asian populations are comparable to Caucasians; approximately half of Asian patients have the polypoidal variant of the disease [5] which is much less common in other racial groups. Strong associations exist between development of AMD and genetic variants of the complement factor H gene as well as other genes in the alternative complement pathway [6, 7]. Modifiable risk factors include smoking [8] and obesity [9]. Diets high in antioxidant-rich vegetables and fruits are associated with a lower risk of AMD [10]; the Age Related Eye Disease Study (AREDS) demonstrated that antioxidant and zinc supplementation can reduce the risk of progression to advanced AMD and of vision loss [11].

The principle treatment for neovascular AMD is repeated intravitreal injections of monoclonal antibody therapies. Results of treatment are strongly influenced by rapid commencement of therapy. The increasing availability of cross-sectional imaging to community optometrists in high-resource settings is driving demand for automated image analysis to detect neovascular lesions. While there are currently

Computational Retinal Image Analysis. https://doi.org/10.1016/B978-0-08-102816-2.00013-7

no treatments that can halt or reverse the progression of advanced non-neovascular AMD, a number of candidate therapies are in development. When treatment becomes available, detection and monitoring of disease progression will be important in routine clinically practice.

2 Histopathological lesions and clinical classification

A spectrum of degenerative diseases (including both inherited and acquired pathologies) affects the macula. This chapter focuses on image analysis in AMD: the most common of these entities. Many of the pathological features of AMD are common to other disease states, for example choroidal neovascularization. However, the appearance on imaging of individual lesions is characteristic of particular disease states, in part due to associated pathology in neighboring tissues such as the retinal pigment epithelium (RPE).

2.1 Normal aging of the macula

AMD must be differentiated from normal aging of the macula. This distinction causes difficulties in the classification of AMD. The retina (and central nervous system) are comprised of cell types that do not undergo renewal with mitotic division; these tissues are particularly prone to age-related changes. The choriocapillaris, Bruch's membrane and RPE provide anatomical and metabolic support for the photoreceptors. With age, rod and cone photoreceptor outer segments become disrupted [12]. Outer segment material accumulates adjacent to the RPE apical surface and lipofuscin is deposited in cone inner segments [13].

Cumulative damage to the RPE with age leads to impairment of phagocytosis and molecular degradation of photoreceptor outer segments. Progressive accumulation of lipofuscin causes the RPE cells to enlarge [14]; there is patchy deposition of material termed basal laminar deposits between the RPE and its basement membrane [15, 16]. Bruch's membrane thickens with age due to deposition of membrane-bound bodies, collagen and mineralized deposits [16]. Even with normal aging, the presence of a small number of drusen is evident histologically. The density and diameter of the choriocapillaris decreases with age resulting in a reduction in choroidal thickness [17].

2.2 Lesions of non-neovascular AMD

The principle histopathologic features of AMD are degeneration of the RPE and presence of membranous debris and extensive basal laminar deposits [18]. Enlarged RPE cells with increased pigmentation and deposited lipofuscin are visible clinically as focal areas of hyper- or hypopigmentation. Progressive disorder of the RPE is accompanied by loss of photoreceptors and reduction of nuclei in the outer nuclear layer (ONL); necrotic, hyperpigmented portions of cells containing membrane-bound granules are released into the sub-RPE and sub-retinal space. Generalized thickening of Bruch's membrane is accompanied by focal areas of thinning and small breaks [19].

Drusen are the characteristic clinical feature of AMD. They consist of extracellular hyalinized material deposited between the basement membrane of RPE cells and Bruch's membrane. Drusen can be described in terms of size, color, morphology and extent. The size of a druse is estimated by comparing its shortest diameter to the width of a major retinal vein as it crosses the edge of the optic disc (approximately 125 μm). Small drusen are <63 μm (less than half the width of a vein); medium 63 to 125 μm and large ≥125 μm [20]. More precise measurements are possible with digital software. Drusen vary in color from bright yellow to white. Drusen morphology can be divided into hard and soft groups (differing in their relative proportions of component material). Soft drusen are usually medium size or larger, have an amorphous appearance and may converge. Hard (nodular) drusen are generally small and exist separately from one another. The extent or severity of macular involvement may be assessed by counting drusen or estimating the total macular area occupied [21]. Drusen may grow larger in diameter and height and may coalesce. Alternatively, they may spontaneously regress which may be accompanied by neighboring RPE and photoreceptor atrophy.

The principle clinical characteristic of AMD is the presence of at least one medium-sized druse or extensive small drusen [22]. On FA small, hard drusen fluoresce brightly in the mid-venous phase (demonstrating distinct edges) and fade soon after. Coalescent small drusen remain fluorescent through the mid-phase followed by late fading [23]. Soft drusen are not usually hyperfluorescent in the early phases of FA but become so in the later stages. Small, hard drusen are not evident on indocyanine green (ICG) imaging; soft drusen are hypofluorescent and show a hyperfluorescent margin in the late phase [24]. Unless there are changes in the overlying RPE, small drusen are not seen on autofluorescence (AF) imaging (see Fig. 1(ii)). Soft drusen may demonstrate mild hyperautofluorescence. On optical coherence tomography (OCT) imaging, small drusen appear as slight elevations of the RPE (see Fig. 1(iii)). Soft drusen are seen as 63–1000 μm deposits posterior to the RPE of low, high or, most commonly, intermediate reflectivity [25]. Changes to the neurosensory retina are common anterior to drusen including thinning of the photoreceptor layer, variable alterations in the ellipsoid zone and hyperreflective foci [26].

Other patterns of drusen are seen in non-neovascular AMD. Subretinal drusenoid deposits (SDD, reticular drusen, reticular pseudodrusen) are seen as pale yellow deposits approximately 250 μm in diameter forming a network at the macula but sparing the fovea (see Fig. 2). On color photography, SDD are best seen with blue light. On AF imaging, the lesions exhibit hypoautofluorescence. OCT imaging demonstrates cone shaped deposits anterior to the RPE some of which breach the ellipsoid layer [27]. Basal laminar or cuticular drusen are round, uniform sub-RPE deposits 50–75 μm in size [28]. These lesions exhibit a "saw-toothed" pattern on OCT and are not part of the AMD spectrum.

Deposits in the subretinal space of extracellular photoreceptor material ranging between 350 and 1760 μm in diameter are referred to as vitelliform lesions (see Fig. 3). These deposits are part of a spectrum of changes described as pattern dystrophy. They are not common in AMD and may indeed represent a separate disease

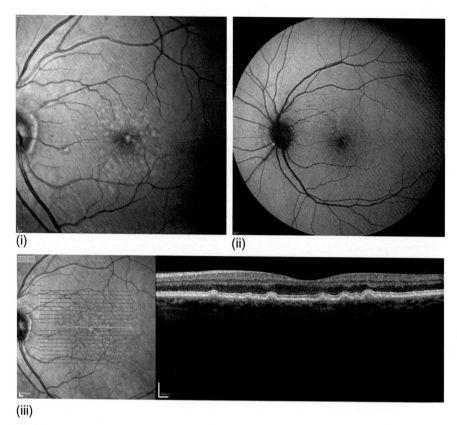

(i)

(ii)

(iii)

FIG. 1

Macular drusen in a single patient (i) scanning laser ophthalmoscopy (SLO) color
(ii) blue autofluorescence, (iii) optical coherence tomography (OCT) with an infra-red
image on the left.

Credit: David Parry, St Paul's Eye Unit, Royal Liverpool University Hospital.

process. Vitelliform lesions are seen clinically as yellowish deposits with indistinct
borders usually evident as a single lesion at the fovea. Their hallmark on imaging is
hyperautofluorescence which correlates with the amount of deposited material [29].
FA shows hypofluorescence (blocked fluorescence) during the early phase and late
hyperfluorescence due to staining. OCT shows uniform hyperreflective deposits in
the subretinal space that may lie anterior to drusen or PED. Subretinal fluid may occur in the absence of neovascularization [30].

Other characteristic features of AMD are RPE abnormalities that include a range
of features from focal hyper- and hypopigmentation to geographic atrophy (GA). A
continuum of pigment abnormalities that may culminate in GA have been described
clinically. Focal hyperpigmentation is commonly located at the border of a druse or
anterior to drusen or drusenoid pigment epithelial detachments (PEDs). On spectral

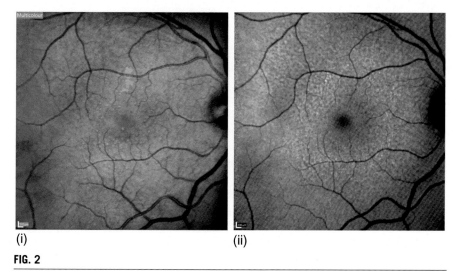

(i)   (ii)

FIG. 2

Reticular drusen (i) Scanning laser ophthalmoscopy (SLO) color (ii) blue autofluorescence.

Credit: David Parry, St Paul's Eye Unit, Royal Liverpool University Hospital.

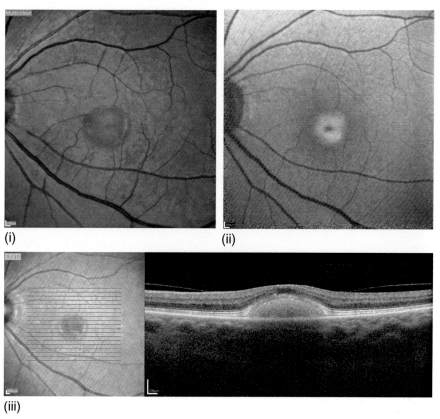

(i)   (ii)

(iii)

FIG. 3

Vitelliform lesions viewed in (i) SLO color, (ii) autofluorescence, and (iii) OCT.

Credit: David Parry, St Paul's Eye Unit, Royal Liverpool University Hospital.

domain optical coherence tomography (SD-OCT) imaging, moderate to intense hyperreflective foci within various layers of the retina correspond to foci of hyperpigmentation [31]. Nongeographic atrophy may immediately precede GA. Detachments of the RPE may accompany the changes of AMD. Soft drusen (usually those larger than 500 μm) accompanied by serous fluid are termed drusenoid PEDs. Drusenoid PEDs have variable elevation but tend to be shallower than serous PEDs and have less variable topography than fibrovascular PEDs (see below).

GA is characterized histologically by well-demarcated regions of attenuated or absent RPE with associated loss of the overlying photoreceptors and underlying choriocapillaris [32]. Clinically, GA appears as sharply circumscribed areas of RPE loss through which the choroidal vessels are visible (see Fig. 4). Color fundus photography has been used to grade and quantify soft drusen and GA. GA lesions appear as sharply defined and homogeneous areas of hypoautofluorescence on fundus autofluorescence (FAF) imaging due to RPE loss with corresponding loss of lipofuscin.

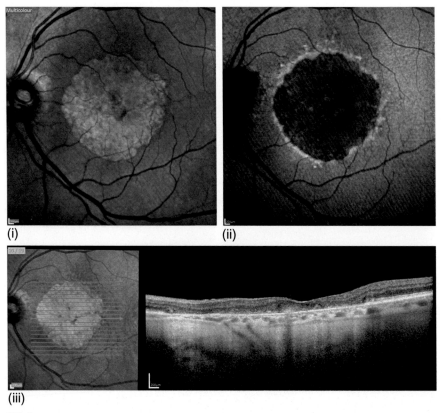

(i) (ii)

(iii)

FIG. 4

Geographic atrophy viewed in (i) SLO color, (ii) autofluorescence, and (iii) OCT.

Credit: David Parry, St Paul's Eye Unit, Royal Liverpool University Hospital.

SD-OCT images show the absence of the ONL, ELM, and the ellipsoid layer, and either absence or marked attenuation of the RPE and Bruch's membrane complex. Due to the absence of these layers there is enhanced choroidal reflectivity [33]. On fluorescein angiography, GA appears as well demarcated areas of hyperfluorescence that appear during the transit phase of the angiogram, sometimes with visualization of the choroidal vessels. A rim of blocked fluorescence from pigment may surround the edge. In late-phase, the hyperfluorescence decreases in intensity; some staining may persist.

2.3 Lesions of neovascular AMD

Neovascular AMD refers to the proliferation of new vessels either under the RPE, breaking through the RPE, or within the retina layers. Exudation of fluid, lipids and blood leads to the death of photoreceptors and subsequently fibrosis. Untreated progression may be rapid resulting in permanent legal blindness. Choroidal neovascular membrane (CNV) may appear as a gray-green elevation of tissue deep to the retina with overlying detachment of the neurosensory retina. Other signs visible on biomicroscopy and color photography are lipid exudates and blood (which may be subretinal, intraretinal or pre-retinal). CNV can be classified by anatomical location. Type 1 membranes are beneath the RPE (usually proliferating within the inner aspect of an abnormally thickened Bruch's membrane). Type 2 membranes are located between the RPE and the photoreceptors. Retinal angiomatous proliferation (RAP or type 3 membranes) are characterized by intraretinal neovascularization. RPE tears (rip or dehiscence) are a recognized complication associated with CNV, particularly when fibrovascular PED. Tears occur at the junction of attached and detached RPE. The free edge of the RPE retracts and rolls toward the fibrovascular tissue.

CNV may also be classified on the basis of stereoscopic fluorescein angiography (FA) imaging (see Fig. 5). FA can determine the pattern of fluorescence (classic or occult and the proportions of each), boundaries (well defined or poorly defined) and location of the neovascular lesions with respect to the center of the foveal avascular zone (FAZ). The fluorescein angiographic appearance of classic CNV is an area of hyperfluorescence identified in the early phase of the angiogram that progressively intensifies throughout the transit phase, with leakage of dye obscuring the boundaries of this area by the late phases of the angiogram [34]. Two types of occult CNV are described. Fibrovascular PED is characterized by irregular elevation (best seen with stereoscopic view) of the RPE with stippled or granular irregular fluorescence first seen early in the angiogram, usually by 1–2 min (see Fig. 6). There is progressive leakage from these regions, with a stippled hyperfluorescent pattern. Late leakage of undetermined origin is characterized by regions of fluorescence at the level of the RPE that are best appreciated in the late phases of an angiogram; they do not correspond to classic CNV or to areas of irregular elevation of the RPE during the early or mid-phases of the angiogram [34]. Angiographic features of RAP lesions include a retinal vessel directed into the lesion and retinal-retinal anastomosis. ICG imaging is essential for identifying polypoidal choroidopathy. Video ICG may demonstrate pulsatile choroidal polyps.

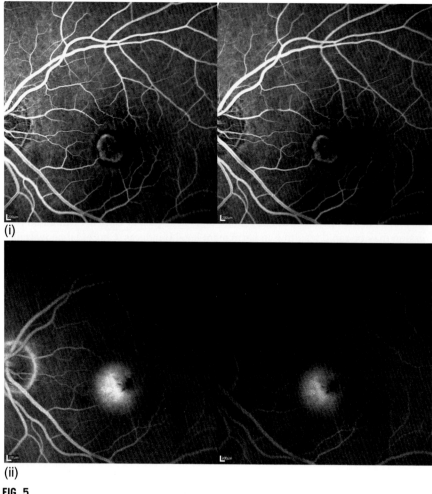

FIG. 5

Classic CNV visualized by stereoscopic fluorescein angiography (FA) (i) peak phase, (ii) late phase.

Credit: David Parry, St Paul's Eye Unit, Royal Liverpool University Hospital.

OCT imaging provides additional diagnostic information in neovascular AMD and is the imaging modality of choice for monitoring response to treatment. Sub-retinal and intraretinal fluid is simple to identify. Retinal thickness can also be measured. Sub-retinal hyperreflective material (SHRM) is thought to represent the neovascular complex. Fibrosis as a result of CNV is seen on OCT imaging as highly reflective tissue that shows characteristic lamination. OCT angiography (OCTA) is able to image the chorioretinal microcirculation without contrast medium. Type 1 CNV is seen on OCTA imaging as a branching neovascular complex with afferent vessel which originates in the choroid. Type 2 CNV is evident as a neovascular

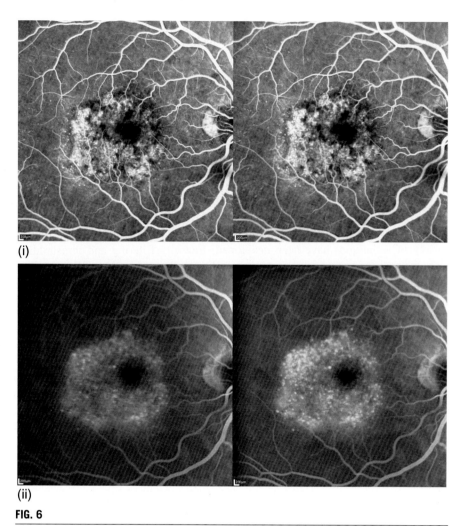

(i)

(ii)

FIG. 6

Fibrovascular PED visualized by stereoscopic FA (i) peak phase (ii) late phase.

Credit: David Parry, St Paul's Eye Unit, Royal Liverpool University Hospital.

network that traverses the RPE-Bruch's membrane complex to involve the subretinal space. Type 3 membranes (RAP) are identified by intra- and subretinal blood with intraretinal anastomosis originating in the deep capillary plexus of the retina [35].

3 Automatic analysis of drusen and AMD-related pathologies

The range of clinically relevant pathologies associated with AMD across multiple imaging modalities gives rise to many challenges in automated image analysis.

Much of the work in this area to date has been in the detection and assessment of drusen, which appear as yellow deposits in the retina when viewed via fundus photography. Drusen vary in size, number and confluence degree, and are a dominant characteristic of AMD. The early detection of drusen is useful in diagnosing AMD, and fundamental to many potential systems for automatically providing a diagnosis of AMD. There are several common, related aims in the computer assisted analysis of drusen: (i) identification of the presence of drusen in fundus photography and localization, (ii) quantification/counting of drusen, (iii) segmentation and measurement of drusen, and (iv) attempting to link such measurements to a diagnosis of AMD.

3.1 Drusen detection in retinal fundus photography

Given its prevalence in ophthalmology for visualizing drusen, fundus photography has been the focus for the majority of work in detecting drusen and a huge variety of techniques have been developed. Intensity filtering and thresholding were the basis of many techniques in the earlier work, such as that of Rapantzikos et al. [36], who in 2003 presented a novel segmentation algorithm for automatically detecting and mapping drusen in retina fundus images. The authors use a multilevel histogram equalization to enhance local intensity structures and develop a novel segmentation technique called histogram-based adaptive local thresholding (HALT). This involves extracting the useful information from an image without being affected by the presence of other structures and is followed by median filtering. The algorithm was tested on 23 fundus images, including images from eight pairs of eyes, achieving an impressive overall sensitivity/specificity of 98.85%/99.32%.

In 2004, Mora et al. [37] developed a methodology for automatic unsupervised detection and modeling of Drusen spots for evaluating therapy effectiveness. A gradient-based image segmentation technique is firstly used to detect Drusen spots and facilitate estimation of their strength. For each detected spot, the authors optimize a 3D model with a Gaussian function using Levenberg-Marquardt nonlinear least-squares. The drusen is then shown using a contour of the Gaussian functions at a pre-defined amplitude percentage. The results were demonstrated on only two images. Later, in 2009, Remeseiro et al. [38] proposed a method of automatically detecting drusen from retinal images using a top-down strategy, Gaussian template matching and thresholding. They achieved sensitivity/specificity of 83%/87% calculated over four images.

It is important to note that, while these works have achieved good quality results, the algorithms were tested on only a limited number of images. In order to demonstrate robustness and real applicability, it is increasingly more important to develop and evaluate medical image analysis algorithms on larger datasets, including multiple stages of disease and types of pathologies, including healthy cases. For example, the more recent works of Quellec et al. [39] and Deepak et al. [40] have evaluated their models on multiple patients and multiple datasets, showing pathologies of different diseases and types of lesion.

3.1.1 Characterization, classification and quantification of drusen

The distinction of different types of detected lesion is an important task for disease diagnosis. Quellec et al. [39] proposed a framework for not only detecting but also characterizing target lesions. Their method relies on a feature space derived from reference image samples of target lesions. These were obtained from both expert- and data-driven approaches. The authors derived filters using Factor analysis to classify the image samples. This approach was tested for detecting microaneurysms on images from 2739 patients including 67 with referable diabetic retinopathy (DR), and for differentiating drusen from Stargardt's disease lesions on a set of 300 manually detected drusen and 300 manually detected flecks. A key benefit of this method is the speed, taking less than 1 s on a standard PC. Comparable performance was obtained for both the expert- and data-driven approaches, indicating that annotation of a limited number of lesions suffices for building a detection system for any type of lesion in retinal images. This is significant for cases where no expert-knowledge is available.

Deepak et al. [40] were interested in anomaly detection as the first step in medical image evaluation for diagnosis, followed by disease-specific anomaly evaluation. Motivated by the idea that experts primarily focus on abnormal structures during visual examination, they aimed to model this behavior in automated image analysis by visual saliency. The authors propose a framework for detecting abnormalities using visual saliency computation for sparse representation of the image data, preserving the essential features of a normal image. They evaluate their approach for bright lesion detection and classification in retinal fundus images on five publicly available datasets, achieving accuracies from 93% to 96% for lesion discrimination, demonstrating the potential of visual saliency in automated abnormality detection.

An important goal for the diagnosis of diseases such as AMD and DR is quantification of the found anomalies or pathologies. In the case of drusen detection for AMD diagnosis, counting the drusen is an aim that is achievable given successful detection. In 2004, Barakat et al. [41] developed a method for automatically quantifying drusen for clinical trials using region of interest (ROI) Selection and intensity based thresholding. Over 20 test images, they achieved a sensitivity/specificity of 86%/96%.

3.1.2 Machine learning based approaches

Beyond saliency, clustering and intensity-based thresholding approaches, machine learning has been a popular basis for designing methods of drusen detection in retinal Fundus images, due to the impressive results achieved in other fields and the speed at which results can be obtained.

In order to find anomalies in the imaging of AMD patients vs healthy controls, Freund et al. [42] proposed a two-step approach following pre-processing of the data by selecting the green channel and using intensity based equalization. In the first step, using multiscale analysis to build a feature vector of the image response to filtering at different scales. This was followed by a kernel-based anomaly detection approach based on a Support Vector Data Description [43] test statistic. As a post-processing step, the authors remove blood vessels using a Canny edge detector and morphological processing. They evaluated their approach using one image from a healthy patient and six images from six AMD-affected patients. Each was trained on 600 vectors; anomalies were found for the AMD patients while none was found for the healthy patient.

Using a larger dataset, Cheng et al. [44] aimed to detect drusen, and hence AMD, using biologically inspired features. They first detect the optic disc and macula in order to zoom in on the macula for feature extraction. These extracted features are classified using support vector machines (SVM). Tested on 350 images, the results demonstrate the effectiveness for drusen detection with a sensitivity/specificity of 86.3%/91.9%.

Following on from this, a considerable amount of work was published in 2013–14 on drusen detection using Machine Learning techniques, particularly focused on SVM. Many of these approaches followed a framework of pre-processing, using a filter bank to extract features, and classification via SVM. Akram et al. [45] presented a method for drusen detection in retinal color images. After pre-processing for contrast enhancement, they used a filter bank to extract potential drusen regions and eliminated false positives relating to similarity with the optic disc. An SVM approach was then used to classify these regions as drusen or not. The authors evaluate the system's performance on the STARE database, achieving accuracy/sensitivity/specificity of 97%/95%/98.4%. Raza et al. [46] proposed a hybrid classifier technique for drusen detection from fundus images by using a Gabor kernel based filter bank and eliminating spurious regions, which may be confused with drusen. Their system represented each region with a number of features and then applied hybrid classifier as an ensemble of Naive Bayes and SVM to classify the regions as either drusen or non-drusen. The proposed system was evaluated on the STARE database, achieving sensitivity/specificity/accuracy of 97%/99%/98%. Waseem et al. [47] presented a method for the detection of soft and hard drusen. After some pre-processing, the proposed method computed color and Gabor filter-based features for each pixel to classify and extract all possible drusen pixels. Connected component labeling was used to remove the suspicious pixels from the drusen region. Finally, the optic disk was removed to avoid false positives. Performance was evaluated on STARE, achieving 96% accuracy for drusen detection.

Zheng et al. [48] developed an automated drusen detection system, aiming to automatically assess the risk of developing AMD. The authors develop a learning-based system incorporating both optimal color descriptors and robust multiscale local image descriptors. Their multi-step system included a considerable pre-processing step involving denoising, generation of the retinal mask, correcting illumination and color transfer. This was followed by feature selection in a pixel-wise way using Adaboost [49] and in a region-based way using LS-SVM [50]. The authors evaluated their system with color fundus photographs from two AMD clinical studies [51, 52] against manually drawn segmentations. Using a leave-one-out strategy, they achieved a mean accuracy of 80% compared to a trained grader on [51] and mean accuracies of 86% and 83% on [52] compared to an ophthalmologist and trained grader respectively. Each of these outperformed the well-known STARE [53] and HALT [36] studies.

ROI identification k-means clustering was used to develop a system called THALIA [54] for the automatic detection of drusen for AMD assessment. The system first detects the macular region of interest using a seeded mode tracking approach, and then map this into a new representation using a hierarchical word transform (HWI) which generates generate structured pixels which embed local context. These structured pixels are then clustered using hierarchical k-means clustering, and these clusters are classified using a SVM-based classifier. THALIA was evaluated on a dataset of 350 images, achieving an accuracy of 95.5%.

The idea of using SVM was extended to AMD detection by Mookiah et al. [55], who proposed an automated AMD detection system using a discrete wavelet transform (DWT) and feature ranking. Many statistical measures including the first four-order statistical moments, energy, entropy, and Gini index-based features were extracted. Five feature-ranking strategies were used to identify an optimal feature set. SVM, decision tree, k-nearest neighbor (k-NN), Naive Bayes, and probabilistic neural network were used to evaluate the highest performance measure using the minimum number of features in classifying normal and dry AMD classes. The proposed framework obtained an average accuracy of 93.7%, sensitivity of 91.1%, and specificity of 96.3% using KLD ranking and SVM classifier.

Methods have also been developed toward detecting drusen for diabetic retinopathy diagnosis. Niemeijer et al. [56] presented a machine learning-based system to automatically detect exudates and cotton-wool spots in color fundus photographs and differentiate them from drusen, aiming for the early diagnosis of diabetic retinopathy. The authors used 300 retinal images from 300 diabetic patients (1 eye per patient) from a diabetic retinopathy tele-diagnosis database, 100 with lesions and 200 without. The images were annotated manually by two expert graders to reach a consensus. They developed a machine learning approach involving a k-nearest neighbor classifier to classify pixels, producing a probability map that was used to group lesion clusters. Based on these characteristics, each probably lesion cluster was assigned a probability that the cluster was in fact a lesion using a linear discriminant classifier. Finally, each cluster was distinguished as (hard) exudate, cotton-wool spot or drusen. They achieved sensitivity/specificity of 95%/88% for lesion detection, 95%/86% for exudate, 70%/93% for cotton-wool spots, and 77%/88% exudates. These results were generally lower than, but similar to, the performance of a third retinal specialists annotation results of 95%/74% for lesions, 90%/98% for exudates, 87%/98% for cotton wool spots, and 92%/79% for drusen.

3.2 Drusen segmentation and measurement

Brandon and Hoover [57] aimed to automatically detect and segment drusen in retinal fundus images in an unsupervised way. They used a multi-level approach, beginning with pixel level classification and proceeding to region, area, and finally image level. This is to allow the classification to be tuned to detect faint drusen and those that are difficult to distinguish from the background, relying upon the higher levels of classification for broader context. The method was tested on 119 images containing many types of drusen and images without drusen or other lesions. The authors achieved a correct detection rate of 87%. Smith et al. [58] aimed to segment drusen by developing an interactive semi-automated method. The authors used 12 color fundus photographs of patients with AMD and drusen, sequentially raised the gray scale values of all structures within defined elliptical boundaries until a uniform background was obtained, and segmented the drusen in the central and middle subfields (at 1 and 3 mm diameters) by uniform thresholding. They compared their results with two expert graders in terms of area achieving good results.

The authors of [59] propose a three-phase method for segmenting the drusen so that they can be quantified in terms of their sizes, area and number. The authors pre-processing the images to remove artifacts such as non-uniform illumination and noise and improve the quality of the image using homomorphic and Gaussian filtering. The authors also took the common approach of selecting only the green channel. Drusen candidate edge detection was performed by determining the gradient, suppressing pixels that were not local maxima and thresholding. Hysteresis was used to track the edges to remove breaks caused by weak points. Boundaries of the drusen were then extracted using iterative edge thinning and end-point recovery and labeling, and edge linking. The method was tested on images containing drusen with 37 selected from the Structured Analysis of Retina (STARE) dataset [60, 61] and 11 from the Automated Retinal Image Analysis (ARIA) [62, 63] dataset. The reported results for drusen detection demonstrated good accuracy/sensitivity/specificity of 96.2%/89.8%/99.0% on STARE and ARIA. The authors further quantified the size of detected drusen as small, intermediate and large with an accuracy of 88.5%, 98.6%, and 88.37%, respectively.

Mora et al. [64] also aimed to measure drusen with illumination correction and gradient-based path labeling. Testing on 22 images, they achieved sensitivity/specificity of 68%/96%. Kumari and Mittal [65] used Otsu thresholding, morphological operations and pixel-wise feature extraction to find the boundaries of drusen and measure the area, achieving sensitivity/specificity/accuracy of 95%/97%/96.3%. Köse et al. [66] proposed an inverse segmentation method to identify healthy and unhealthy areas in the AMD fundus image. Initially, the optic disc and macula are located using the Sobel filter and relative locations of these two structures. Further, region-growing algorithm is initialized around macula to segment out healthy and unhealthy regions. Next, the inverse of segmented image is taken to generate the unhealthy segmentation result. Their method achieved a segmentation accuracy of more than 90%.

3.3 Quantifying drusen area and distinguishing drusen type

Distinguishing the type of drusen present is an important task in early and intermediate AMD detection. Van Grinsven et al. [67] aimed to develop a method of detecting drusen and quantifying their location, area, and size to assist the computer aided diagnosis of non-advanced AMD. The authors developed a machine learning system was developed to automatically detect and quantify drusen on 407 randomly selected a European multi-center database of fundus photographs which either had no AMD or moderate AMD. The results were evaluated by comparison with two expert graders. The system was demonstrated to approach the performance of the human observers in detecting drusen and the estimated area showed excellent agreement, achieving sensitivity/specificity of 85/96. The authors also computed an automatic AMD risk assessment, achieving area under the receiver operating characteristic curves (AUROCs) of 94.8% and 95.4%.

Bhuiyan et al. [68] aimed to quantify drusen area and classify them as intermediate or soft drusen using a region growing technique. The authors used local intensity distribution, adaptive intensity thresholding and edge information to detect potential drusen areas. 50 images with various types of drusen were used to test detection and 12 of these were selected to evaluate the segmentation. The images were annotated by an expert grader. The method achieved 100% accuracy for detection and accuracies of 79.6% and 82.1% for classifying intermediate and soft drusen respectively.

3.3.1 Texture-based methods

Texture has commonly been used for distinguishing drusen from the background. Parvathi and Devi [69] presented two methods for detection and counting of drusen, exploiting their morphological characteristics such as texture and their 3D profiles. In the first method, the authors attempt to characterize the drusen by texture and use a multi-channel filtering technique; in the second, they characterize drusen by its topographic profile and use a curvature-based detection method. The authors of [70] developed a spatially adaptive algorithm for drusen detection based on GLCM based textural features. The accuracy of the classifier was improved using OD localization and blood vessels with morphological operators. The authors evaluated performance against a hand-labeled ground truth, achieving an accuracy of 98.05% on 120 samples. Lee et al. [71] presented a method for learning non-homogenous textures, mimicking the idea of selective learning, performing probabilistic boosting and structural similarity clustering for fast selective learning. They applied their idea to drusen segmentation.

Garnier et al. [72] presented a preliminary study for AMD detection from color fundus photographs using a multiresolution texture analysis and wavelet decomposition. To avoid dimensionality problems, the authors use Linear Discriminant Analysis for feature dimension reduction, followed by image classification. They tested their method using a dataset of 45 images (23 healthy, 22 diseased). Significantly, they used images from different cameras and of varying quality, achieving a recognition rate of 93.3%, with sensitivity/specificity of 91.3%/95.5%.

3.4 Other imaging modalities

3.4.1 Angiography

While color fundus has been the dominant modality for investigating drusen, other technologies have also been explored. The authors of [73] presented a 3-stage approach to segmenting drusen in retinal angiographic images taken in 1983 and 1988 respectively in order to track changes. Their method involved an optimal partitioning of the gray-level image intensity values followed by a parametric transformation to improve the homogeneity of the classification. A fuzzy logic approach was taken to classifying the uncertain pixels based on local mean intensity values. Given the coarse segmentation that this achieves, the authors aimed to quantify changes in drusen over time. Patients were followed up over time across two visits 5 years apart, and the study confirmed clinical qualitative observations that drusen change in number and size.

3.4.2 Scanning laser ophthalmoscopy

It has been observed in several studies that scanning laser ophthalmoscopy (SLO) is also an effective imaging modality for viewing drusen. As early as 1995, Kirkpatrick et al. [74] noted that drusen also appear as characteristic structures in indirect mode infrared scanning laser ophthalmoscope (SLO) images, with manual counting of drusen in SLO showing no significant difference from that in standard fundus photographs for 6 out of 5 patients tested. In 2011, Acton et al. [75] observed similar findings with a commercial SLO device. They aimed to assess drusen quantification using retro-mode imaging with the Nidek F-10 scanning laser ophthalmoscope. The authors captured both stereoscopic fundus photographs and retro-mode images in 31 eyes of 20 patients at varying stages of AMD. The images were independently assessed by two experienced graders for the number and size of drusen. Drusen were further assessed in eight of these patients using OCT. Significantly fewer drusen were observed in fundus photography than in retro-mode, and the predominant deposit diameter was on average smaller in retro-mode than in fundus. Agreement between graders for both types of imaging was substantial for number of deposits and moderate for size while retro-mode drusen corresponded to OCT in all cases.

A further comparison was made by Diniz et al. [76] aimed to evaluate the efficiency of drusen detection by scanning laser ophthalmoscopy (SLO) using several infrared confocal apertures and differential contrast strategies. The authors imaged 11 eyes with non-neovascular AMD using infrared imaging with a Nidek F-10 with the central, ring, right side (AR) and left side (AL) apertures, both with and without differential contrast. They also obtained a conventional color fundus photograph for comparison. In each image, the drusen were manually outlined by two graders. The number of drusen and total drusen area were calculated and the measures averaged. Inter-grader reliability was evaluated, with agreement between graders being high. In terms of manual grading, the addition of differential contrast did not seem to improve drusen detection. The authors found that drusen number and area grades were significantly higher using right and left apertures. Use of the lateral confocal aperture may highlight subclinical drusen.

3.4.3 Drusen detection in OCT

Drusen have been found to be visible in OCT as small elevations in the RPE, suggesting potential for this modality in drusen detection and diagnosis. The performance of the integrated automated analysis algorithms in three SD-OCT devices was evaluated by Schlanitz et al. [77] for their potential to identify drusen in eyes with early-stage

AMD. The authors analyzed 12 eyes of 12 AMD patients with three clinical SD-OCT devices: the Zeiss Cirrus (Carl Zeiss Meditec, Dublin CA), Topcon 3DOCT-1000 (Topcon, Tokyo, Japan), and Heidelberg Spectralis (Heidelberg Engineering, GmbH, Heidelberg, Germany) and five different scan patterns. It was concluded that, while SD-OCT demonstrated excellent performance for visualizing drusen-related RPE disease the automated segmentation showed distinct limitations. The authors further investigated the potential of polarization-sensitive optical coherence tomography (PS-OCT) for assessing drusen in AMD patients [78]. They examined 15 eyes from 13 patients presenting with drusen with ophthalmoscope, fundus photography, autofluorescence, and PS-OCT. They developed a segmentation algorithm based on the polarization scrambling characteristics of the RPE to evaluate the drusen location, area, and volume. Two independent graders identified the drusen in each B-scan were identified by two independent expert graders. 91.4% of the drusen were detected manually by both expert graders whereas the automated segmentation identified 96.5%. It was concluded that PS-OCT segmentation was superior to fundus photography.

3.5 Analysis of other AMD lesions

The automated analysis of other features that are characteristic of AMD is understudied compared to the analysis of drusen. We provide a brief overview here for completeness. There have been efforts to detect and segment areas of geographic atrophy in fundus auto-fluorescence (FA) images and SD-OCT. Deckert et al. proposed a region-growing technique for the segmentation of GA in AF images [79] while Chen et al. proposed a semi-automatic method for the detection of GA in SD-OCT images. A restricted summed-voxel projection (RSVP) image is first produced, to which a geometric active contour model is applied to segment the GA. The authors demonstrated good performance on 111 SD-OCT images when compared with the proprietary method currently implemented in the Cirrus software (Carl Zeiss Meditec, Jena, Germany) [80]. Schütze et al. proposed an automated lesion size detection method based on Stokes vector analysis in patients with GA using PS-OCT [81]. Results on 29 eyes of 22 patients showed significant correlation with established fundus imaging techniques such as infrared imaging, AF, and SD-OCT fundus. It is in general challenging to analyze retinal layers in OCT images, however, Chiu S et al. recently propose a segmentation framework based on graph theory and dynamic programming for the segmentation of retinal layers in SD-OCT images with drusen and GA [82]. It is imperative for us to highlight some new progress in the analysis of CNV in a new imaging technique called OCT angiography (OCTA). Zhang Q et al. proposed a technique based on morphology analysis to segment CNV from OCTA images and showed promising results on 27 eyes [83]. This may highlight the value of OCTA in the management of AMD. Techniques for the analysis of some other common pathological features of AMD, including leakage and neovascularization, have been covered in other chapters, so we will not review these here. In addition, some recent reviews on automated algorithms for the analysis of AMD have been published [84, 85].

4 Diagnosis of AMD

The development of medical image analysis tools for the diagnosis of AMD has not been as active as for diabetic retinopathy (DR), largely due to the existence of screening programs for DR, which do not exist for AMD.

However, extensive work has been done using color fundus images. Since AMD is characterized by lesions (a.k.a. image features), it would seem natural at first sight to pursue methods based on lesion segmentation. However, due to the difficulty in segmenting AMD-related lesions, this is very challenging. The diagnosis of AMD via color fundus images seem to flourish with image-based methods, which is coincident with the deep learning strategies. For instance, Zheng et al. [86] proposed a strategy using the quad-tree concept to divide fundus images reclusively until homogeneity is met: e.g. intensity-based or other metrics between parent and child regions being less than a pre-defined threshold. A graph could then be used to represent the decomposition and graph-mining techniques could be used to produce feature vectors. These derived features can then be used by classification techniques, such as SVM and Bayesian classifiers, to classify the images. Good performance has been observed using this approach.

In a follow-up study, Hijazi et al. [87] improved on the above work. The distinguishing and novel feature of the proposed approach is that the partitioning is conducted in an interleaving angular and circular manner. It achieved 100% sensitivity and specificity (see Fig. 7).

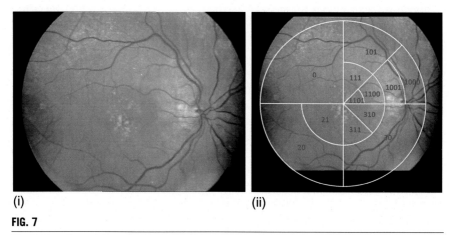

(i)   (ii)

FIG. 7

Illustration of quad-tree decomposition used in Zheng et al. [86] and Hijazi et al. [87]. The decomposition commences by splitting the entire image (the root of the quad-tree) into four equal sized quadrants. The splitting process continues recursively by further decomposing each quadrant to generate further sub-quadrants, and terminates when a desired maximum level of decomposition is reached or all sub-quadrants are homogeneous based on certain criteria. In the latter, an interleaving angular and circular manner was used.

Credit: David Parry, St Paul's Eye Unit, Royal Liverpool University Hospital.

Other data mining techniques based on spatial histogram and Dynamic Time Warping (DTW) were previously used in [88]. The authors of [89] proposed an automated dry AMD detection system using several entropies, Higher Order Spectra features, Fractal Dimension, and Gabor wavelet features, which were ranked using many ranking methods to select optimum features for classification as normal or AMD. Many classifiers were considered, including Probabilistic Neural Networks and SVMs. Performance was evaluated using a private dataset, as well as the ARIA and STARE datasets. The highest average classification accuracies of 90.19%, 95.07% and 95% were achieved using SVM for the private dataset, ARIA and STARE respectively. All these studies are quite small in terms of the number of images (patients) involved [90].

The use of FA for the diagnosis of AMD is rare, primarily because it is invasive in nature and typically used in the later stages. However, there has been some work to develop methods for the differentiable diagnosis of AMD, e.g. neovascularization.

With the advent of OCT, it has become indispensable in the management of AMD and in particular the decision-making regarding anti-VEGF treatment. Venhuizen et al. have proposed an unsupervised approach [91] and Bag of feature approach [92], where the latter was applied to a total of 3265 OCT scans from 1016 patients with either no signs of AMD or with signs of early, intermediate, or advanced AMD. The participants were randomly selected from a large European multicenter database. Different from all the other approaches, Albarrak et al. proposed an OCT-tree based method for the classification of three-dimensional OCT images directly and provided promising results [93].

Although these methods have avoided the challenge posed by segmentation, they still rely on certain features either directly (intensity, texture) or indirectly (graph patterns), which still requires the knowledge and insight of the researchers. The recent success of deep learning in computer vision has had a great impact in this field.

Recently, there have been four studies that used deep learning techniques for the diagnosis of AMD. Lee et al. selected 52,690 normal macular OCT images and 48,312 AMD macular OCT images from 2.6 million OCT images linked to clinical data points from the electronic medical records (EMRs) [94]. A modified version of the VGG16 convolutional neural network (CNN) [95] was trained to categorize images as either normal or showing AMD. At the image level, the authors achieved an AUC of 92.78% with an accuracy of 87.63%. At the patient level, an AUC of 97.45% with an accuracy of 93.45% was achieved. Peak sensitivity and specificity with optimal cut offs were 92.64% and 93.69%, respectively.

Grassman et al. reported an automated AMD classification algorithm using ensemble learning [96], evaluating on a cross-sectional population-based study. 120,656 manually graded color fundus images were used from 3654 Age-Related Eye Disease (AREDS) patients and 14 classes were defined, including 3 late AMD stages and an ungradable class. Several architectures were tried but an ensemble was found to obtain improved results. The authors also evaluated their method on a subset of the Kooperative Gesundheitsforschung in der Region Ausburg (KORA) dataset, which was not used for training. Good results were achieved, with the algorithm detecting 84% of images with definite signs of early and late AMD, and 94% of healthy images.

Kermany et al. adapted an Inception V3 architecture pre-trained on the ImageNet dataset in order to take advantage of the benefits offered by transfer learning [97]. 108,312 images out of 207,130 OCT images (37,206 with choroidal neovascularization, 11,349 with diabetic macular edema, 8617 with drusen, and 51,140 normal) from 4686 patients passed an initial image quality review and were used to train the AI system. The model was tested with 1000 images (250 from each category) from 633 patients. An accuracy of 96.6% with a sensitivity of 97.8% and specificity of 97.4% were achieved for the classification of choroidal neovascularization, diabetic macular edema, drusen, and normal images. In both studies, an occlusion test was used to highlight regions in images that contribute to the classification, which makes it easier to understand how the network has "seen" the images and made the decision.

The recent work by DeepMind has adopted a different strategy [98]. First of all, features such as layers and fluid spaces in OCT images are segmented based on U-Net [99], then a CNN is used for the diagnosis of different conditions. They used a population-based dataset from the Moorfields Hospital in London and this has demonstrated the great potential of close collaboration between academia, NHS and industry. However, the data is not publicly available.

5 Datasets

The (lack of) availability of datasets in medical research has been a considerable challenge, but the recent open access policy requirements have made a difference in this field. Below, we have listed some publicly available datasets for the research in AMD and provided a brief description of them.

1. ARIA is a publicly available dataset in Liverpool, available at https://eyecharity.weebly.com/aria_online.html. The collection includes 101 AMD images and 60 non-AMD images, which were manually pre-labeled. All images were taken using a fundus camera (FF450+, Zeiss Meditec, Inc., Dublin, CA) at a 50° field with a resolution of 576×768 pixels.

2. The STARE dataset (http://www.ces.clemson.edu/~ahoover/stare) comprises 97 images (59 AMD and 38 normal) taken using a fundus camera (TOPCON TRV-50; Topcon Corp., Tokyo, Japan) at a 35° field and with a resolution of 605×700 pixels.

3. Kermany et al. [97] have made their OCT data available in JPEG format through the public Mendeley database (https://doi.org/10.17632/rscbjbr9sj.3). The images are split into those showing CNV, DME, drusen and normal images. We initially obtained 207,130 OCT images. 108,312 images (37,206 with choroidal neovascularization, 11,349 with diabetic macular edema, 8617 with drusen, and 51,140 normal) from 4686 patients passed initial image quality review and were used to train the AI system.

4. The Age-Related Eye Disease Study (AREDS) is a long-term, multi-center, prospective study of 4757 people aged 55–80, supported by the National Eye Institute and the National Institute of Health. The study involved cataract and

AMD trials, with 128 participants on the AMD-only trial and 3512 on the AMD and Cataract Trial. Color stereoscopic fundus images were obtained from mydriatic eyes with a Zeiss FF series 30 camera (Carl Zeiss AG, Oberkochen, Germany) in field 2 (centered above the macula). A grading system for AMD was developed and participants were followed at 6-month intervals [100].

5. A dataset of 45 volumetric OCT acquisitions was developed at Duke University, Harvard University, and the University of Michigan [101]. The dataset was acquired using the Heidelberg Spectralis SD-OCT (Heidelberg Engineering Inc.) and included normal eyes, eyes showing dry AMD, and DME, with 15 subjects per class. These were used for develop a support vector machine-based classifier, which was able to correctly identify 100% of AMD and DME cases, and 86.7% of the normal cases. The set can be downloaded from http://www.duke.edu/~sf59/Srinivasan_BOE_2014_dataset.htm.

6. A dataset was developed with 148 macular OCT images along with SLO at Noor Eye Hospital in Tehran [102]. In the dataset, 50 normal eyes were included, as well as 48 showing dry AMD and 50 with DME. The dataset can be downloaded from http://www.biosigdata.com/?download=macular-oct-data-from-heidelberg-imaging-device. The authors used the dataset to develop a multi-scale convolutional mixture of expert model along with the Duke Dataset.

7. OCTID is a dataset of over 500 OCT images, classified with a variety of conditions, including normal, AMD, diabetic retinopathy, central serous chorioretinopathy, and macular holes [103]. The images were acquired using a Cirrus HD-OCT (Carl Zeiss Meditec, Inc., Dublin, CA) at Sankara Nethralaya eye hospital, Chennai, India The dataset can be downloaded at https://dataverse.scholarsportal.info/dataverse/OCTID.

8. A large dataset of 1200 retinal fundus images from non-AMD and AMD subjects was collected by Baidu Research (Sunnyvale, CA, United States) for the REFUGE challenge. The image set, which can be downloaded at https://refuge.grand-challenge.org/, includes diagnosis classifications (AMD/non-AMD), disc boundaries, fovea locations and the boundaries of lesions to allow for the training of AI models for AMD diagnosis.

9. The Kooperative Gesundheitsforschung in der Region Augsberg study has been following participants at 5-year intervals since 1984, focusing on research into old age since 2008. Images of the full macular region and optic disc of nonmydriatic eyes were acquired from participants with a 45 degrees Topcon TRC-NW5S fundus camera (Topcon Corporation, Tokyo, Japan). Researchers can register to access this dataset at https://epi.helmholtz-muenchen.de/.

10. The UK Biobank is a national and international resource, which follows the health of 500,000 volunteers, with the aim of improving the prevention, diagnosis and treatment of serious and life threatening illnesses, including eye disorders such as AMD. The collected health information can be provided to approved researchers in academia and industry, in the United Kingdom and overseas. Researchers can register at https://www.ukbiobank.ac.uk/.

6 Conclusions

The world's aging population continues to increase at an unprecedented rate, and AMD is a key global challenge posed to patients, their families, healthcare providers and society as a whole. For a long time, there have been limited options for the management of AMD. However, with advances in the understanding of the pathophysiology, new treatment options, and new imaging modalities, it seems there is a new changing point.

First, the automated diagnosis of AMD at an early stage may be useful for the prediction of the development of AMD. Deep learning techniques seem be the key enabler to transform the research in automated analysis of AMD, as with other areas in medical imaging. The availability of well-defined, large datasets is crucial for making significant improvements the field. While there has been recent effort in making data available, ethics and other regulatory requirements have to be addressed.

The engagement of ophthalmologists will be key for the development, validation and introduction of any kind of automated decisions. Clinicians are expected to perform an important role in the deep learning era. In particular, multiple experts are important in producing reference standards in order to avoid individual bias.

The challenges introduced by the invention of new imaging modalities such as OCTA need to be addressed. To use images for the classification of AMD is the current focus, but predictions of the onset and outcomes of AMD, as well as the effects of treatment will be important in the next wave. Continuing investment in research and the involvement of industry will also lead to the rapid development in terms of automated image analysis for AMD. It is our expectation that patients with AMD will soon feel the huge benefit offered by AI and automated image analysis.

References

[1] A. Bird, N. Bressler, S. Bressler, I. Chisholm, G. Coscas, M. Davis, P. De Jong, C. Klaver, B. Klein, R. Klein, An international classification and grading system for age-related maculopathy and age-related macular degeneration, Surv. Ophthalmol. 39 (1995) 367–374.

[2] W.L. Wong, X. Su, X. Li, C.M.G. Cheung, R. Klein, C.-Y. Cheng, T.Y. Wong, Global prevalence of age-related macular degeneration and disease burden projection for 2020 and 2040: a systematic review and meta-analysis, Lancet Glob. Health 2 (2014) e106–e116.

[3] K.J. Cruickshanks, R.F. Hamman, R. Klein, D.M. Nondahl, S.M. Shetterly, The prevalence of age-related maculopathy by geographic region and ethnicity: the Colorado-Wisconsin Study of Age-Related Maculopathy, Arch. Ophthalmol. 115 (1997) 242–250.

[4] R. Varma, S. Fraser-Bell, S. Tan, R. Klein, S.P. Azen, Los Angeles Latino Eye Study Group, Prevalence of age-related macular degeneration in Latinos: the Los Angeles Latino eye study, Ophthalmology 111 (2004) 1288–1297.

[5] R. Kawasaki, M. Yasuda, S.J. Song, S.-J. Chen, J.B. Jonas, J.J. Wang, P. Mitchell, T.Y. Wong, The prevalence of age-related macular degeneration in Asians: a systematic review and meta-analysis, Ophthalmology 117 (2010) 921–927.

[6] J. Maller, S. George, S. Purcell, J. Fagerness, D. Altshuler, M.J. Daly, J.M. Seddon, Common variation in three genes, including a noncoding variant in CFH, strongly influences risk of age-related macular degeneration, Nat. Genet. 38 (2006) 1055.

[7] J.B. Maller, J.A. Fagerness, R.C. Reynolds, B.M. Neale, M.J. Daly, J.M. Seddon, Variation in complement factor 3 is associated with risk of age-related macular degeneration, Nat. Genet. 39 (2007) 1200.

[8] J.M. Seddon, W.C. Willett, F.E. Speizer, S.E. Hankinson, A prospective study of cigarette smoking and age-related macular degeneration in women, JAMA 276 (1996) 1141–1146.

[9] J.M. Seddon, J. Cote, N. Davis, B. Rosner, Progression of age-related macular degeneration: association with body mass index, waist circumference, and waist-hip ratio, Arch. Ophthalmol. 121 (2003) 785–792.

[10] R.A. Bone, J.T. Landrum, L.H. Guerra, C.A. Ruiz, Lutein and zeaxanthin dietary supplements raise macular pigment density and serum concentrations of these carotenoids in humans, J. Nutr. 133 (2003) 992–998.

[11] Age-Related Eye Disease Study Research Group, A randomized, placebo-controlled, clinical trial of high-dose supplementation with vitamins C and E, beta carotene, and zinc for age-related macular degeneration and vision loss: AREDS report no. 8, Arch. Ophthalmol. 119 (2001) 1417.

[12] C. Curcio, C. Millican, K. Allen, R. Kalina, Aging of the human photoreceptor mosaic: evidence for selective vulnerability of rods in central retina, Invest. Ophthalmol. Vis. Sci. 34 (1993) 3278–3296.

[13] M. Iwasaki, H. Inomata, Lipofuscin granules in human photoreceptor cells, Invest. Ophthalmol. Vis. Sci. 29 (1988) 671–679.

[14] L. Feeney-Burns, E.R. Berman, H. Rothman, Lipofuscin of human retinal pigment epithelium, Am J. Ophthalmol. 90 (1980) 783–791.

[15] S. Sarks, Ageing and degeneration in the macular region: a clinico-pathological study, Br. J. Ophthalmol. 60 (1976) 324–341.

[16] T.L. van der Schaft, C.M. Mooy, W.C. de Bruijn, F.G. Oron, P.G. Mulder, P.T. de Jong, Histologic features of the early stages of age-related macular degeneration: a statistical analysis, Ophthalmology 99 (1992) 278–286.

[17] R.S. Ramrattan, T.L. van der Schaft, C.M. Mooy, W. De Bruijn, P. Mulder, P. De Jong, Morphometric analysis of Bruch's membrane, the choriocapillaris, and the choroid in aging, Invest. Ophthalmol. Vis. Sci. 35 (1994) 2857–2864.

[18] C.W. Spraul, G.E. Lang, H.E. Grossniklaus, Morphometric analysis of the choroid, Bruch's membrane, and retinal pigment epithelium in eyes with age-related macular degeneration, Invest. Ophthalmol. Vis. Sci. 37 (1996) 2724–2735.

[19] K. Loffler, W. Lee, Basal linear deposit in the human macula, Graefes Arch. Clin. Exp. Ophthalmol. 224 (1986) 493–501.

[20] M.L. Klein, P.J. Francis, F.L. Ferris, S.C. Hamon, T.E. Clemons, Risk assessment model for development of advanced age-related macular degeneration, Arch. Ophthalmol. 129 (2011) 1543–1550.

[21] R. Klein, M.D. Davis, Y.L. Magli, P. Segal, B.E. Klein, L. Hubbard, The Wisconsin age-related maculopathy grading system, Ophthalmology 98 (1991) 1128–1134.

[22] F.L. Ferris III, C. Wilkinson, A. Bird, U. Chakravarthy, E. Chew, K. Csaky, S.R. Sadda, Beckman Initiative for Macular Research Classification Committee, Clinical classification of age-related macular degeneration, Ophthalmology 120 (2013) 844–851.

[23] J. Sarks, S. Sarks, M. Killingsworth, Evolution of soft drusen in age-related macular degeneration, Eye 8 (1994) 269.

[24] A.A. Chang, D.R. Guyer, D.R. Orlock, L.A. Yannuzzi, Age-dependent variations in the drusen fluorescence on indocyanine green angiography, Clin. Exp. Ophthalmol. 31 (2003) 300–304.

[25] A.A. Khanifar, A.F. Koreishi, J.A. Izatt, C.A. Toth, Drusen ultrastructure imaging with spectral domain optical coherence tomography in age-related macular degeneration, Ophthalmology 115 (2008) 1883 1890. c1.

[26] J.N. Leuschen, S.G. Schuman, K.P. Winter, M.N. McCall, W.T. Wong, E.Y. Chew, T. Hwang, S. Srivastava, N. Sarin, T. Clemons, Spectral-domain optical coherence tomography characteristics of intermediate age-related macular degeneration, Ophthalmology 120 (2013) 140–150.

[27] S.A. Zweifel, R.F. Spaide, C.A. Curcio, G. Malek, Y. Imamura, Reticular pseudodrusen are subretinal drusenoid deposits, Ophthalmology 117 (2010) 303–312. e1.

[28] J.D.M. Gass, Stereoscopic Atlas of Macular Diseases: Diagnosis and Treatment (2 Volume Set), 1997.

[29] L.H. Lima, K. Laud, K.B. Freund, L.A. Yannuzzi, R.F. Spaide, Acquired vitelliform lesion associated with large drusen, Retina 32 (2012) 647–651.

[30] K.B. Freund, K. Laud, L.H. Lima, R.F. Spaide, S. Zweifel, L.A. Yannuzzi, Acquired vitelliform lesions: correlation of clinical findings and multiple imaging analyses, Retina 31 (2011) 13–25.

[31] M. Adhi, D. Ferrara, R.F. Mullins, C.R. Baumal, K.J. Mohler, M.F. Kraus, J. Liu, E. Badaro, T. Alasil, J. Hornegger, Characterization of choroidal layers in normal aging eyes using enface swept-source optical coherence tomography, PLoS ONE 10 (2015) e0133080.

[32] E.C. Zanzottera, J.D. Messinger, T. Ach, R.T. Smith, K.B. Freund, C.A. Curcio, The Project MACULA retinal pigment epithelium grading system for histology and optical coherence tomography in age-related macular degeneration, Invest. Ophthalmol. Vis. Sci. 56 (2015) 3253–3268.

[33] S. Schmitz-Valckenberg, M. Fleckenstein, A.P. Göbel, T.C. Hohman, F.G. Holz, Optical coherence tomography and autofluorescence findings in areas with geographic atrophy due to age-related macular degeneration, Invest. Ophthalmol. Vis. Sci. 52 (2011) 1–6.

[34] I. Barbazetto, A. Burdan, N. Bressler, S. Bressler, L. Haynes, A. Kapetanios, J. Lukas, K. Olsen, M. Potter, A. Reaves, Photodynamic therapy of subfoveal choroidal neovascularization with verteporfin: fluorescein angiographic guidelines for evaluation and treatment—TAP and VIP report No. 2, Arch. Ophthalmol. 121 (2003) 1253–1268.

[35] L. Kuehlewein, M. Bansal, T.L. Lenis, N.A. Iafe, S.R. Sadda, M.A. Bonini Filho, E. Talisa, N.K. Waheed, J.S. Duker, D. Sarraf, Optical coherence tomography angiography of type 1 neovascularization in age-related macular degeneration, Am J. Ophthalmol. 160 (2015) 739–748. e2.

[36] K. Rapantzikos, M. Zervakis, K. Balas, Detection and segmentation of drusen deposits on human retina: potential in the diagnosis of age-related macular degeneration, Med. Image Anal. 7 (2003) 95–108.

[37] A. Mora, P. Vieira, J. Fonseca, Drusen deposits on retina images: detection and modeling, in: International Conference on Advances in Medical Signal and Information Processing, 2004.

[38] B. Remeseiro, N. Barreira, D. Calvo, M. Ortega, M.G. Penedo, Automatic drusen detection from digital retinal images: AMD prevention, in: International Conference on Computer Aided Systems Theory, 2009, pp. 187–194.

[39] G. Quellec, S.R. Russell, M.D. Abràmoff, Optimal filter framework for automated, instanta-neous detection of lesions in retinal images, IEEE Trans. Med. Imaging 30 (2011) 523–533.

[40] K.S. Deepak, A. Chakravarty, J. Sivaswamy, Visual saliency based bright lesion detec-tion and discrimination in retinal images, in: 2013 IEEE 10th International Symposium on Biomedical Imaging (ISBI), 2013, pp. 1436–1439.

[41] M. Barakat, B. Madjarov, Automated drusen quantitaion for clinical trials, Invest. Ophthalmol. Vis. Sci. 45 (2004) 3017.

[42] D.E. Freund, N. Bressler, P. Burlina, Automated detection of drusen in the macula, in: ISBI'09. IEEE International Symposium on Biomedical Imaging: From Nano to Macro, 2009, 2009, pp. 61–64.

[43] A. Banerjee, P. Burlina, C. Diehl, A support vector method for anomaly detection in hyperspectral imagery, IEEE Trans. Geosci. Remote Sens. 44 (2006) 2282–2291.

[44] J. Cheng, D.W.K. Wong, X. Cheng, J. Liu, N.M. Tan, M. Bhargava, C.M.G. Cheung, T.Y. Wong, Early age-related macular degeneration detection by focal biologically inspired feature, in: 2012 19th IEEE International Conference on Image Processing (ICIP), 2012, pp. 2805–2808.

[45] M.U. Akram, S. Mujtaba, A. Tariq, Automated drusen segmentation in fundus images for diagnosing age related macular degeneration, in: 2013 International Conference on Electronics, Computer and Computation (ICECCO), 2013, pp. 17–20.

[46] G. Raza, M. Rafique, A. Tariq, M.U. Akram, Hybrid classifier based drusen detec-tion in colored fundus images, in: 2013 IEEE Jordan Conference on Applied Electrical Engineering and Computing Technologies (AEECT), 2013, pp. 1–5.

[47] S. Waseem, M.U. Akram, B.A. Ahmed, Drusen detection from colored fundus images for diagnosis of age related Macular degeneration, in: 2014 7th International Conference on Information and Automation for Sustainability (ICIAfS), 2014, pp. 1–5.

[48] Y. Zheng, B. Vanderbeek, E. Daniel, D. Stambolian, M. Maguire, D. Brainard, J. Gee, An automated drusen detection system for classifying age-related macular degenera-tion with color fundus photographs, in: 2013 IEEE 10th International Symposium on Biomedical Imaging (ISBI), 2013, pp. 1448–1451.

[49] Y. Freund, R.E. Schapire, A decision-theoretic generalization of on-line learning and an application to boosting, J. Comput. Syst. Sci. 55 (1997) 119–139.

[50] J. Suykens, T. Van Gestel, J. De Brabanter, B. De Moor, J. Vandewalle, Least Squares Support Vector Machines, World Scientific, Singapore, 2002.

[51] Complications of Age-Related Macular Degeneration Prevention Trial Study Group, The complications of age-related macular degeneration prevention trial (CAPT): ratio-nale, design and methodology, Clin. Trials 1 (2004) 91–107.

[52] D. Stambolian, E.B. Ciner, L.C. Reider, C. Moy, D. Dana, R. Owens, M. Schlifka, T. Holmes, G. Ibay, J.E. Bailey-Wilson, Genome-wide scan for myopia in the Old Order Amish, Am J. Ophthalmol. 140 (2005) 469–476.

[53] L. Brandon, Automated Drusen Detection in a Retinal Image Using Multi-Level Analysis, Clemson University, 2003.

[54] D.W. Wong, J. Liu, X. Cheng, J. Zhang, F. Yin, M. Bhargava, G.C. Cheung, T.Y. Wong, THALIA-An automatic hierarchical analysis system to detect drusen lesion images for amd assessment, in: 2013 IEEE 10th International Symposium on Biomedical Imaging (ISBI), 2013, pp. 884–887.

[55] M.R.K. Mookiah, U.R. Acharya, J.E. Koh, C.K. Chua, J.H. Tan, V. Chandran, C.M. Lim, K. Noronha, A. Laude, L. Tong, Decision support system for age-related macular degen-eration using discrete wavelet transform, Med. Biol. Eng. Comput. 52 (2014) 781–796.

[56] M. Niemeijer, B. van Ginneken, S.R. Russell, M.S. Suttorp-Schulten, M.D. Abramoff, Automated detection and differentiation of drusen, exudates, and cotton-wool spots in digital color fundus photographs for diabetic retinopathy diagnosis, Invest. Ophthalmol. Vis. Sci. 48 (2007) 2260–2267.

[57] L. Brandon, A. Hoover, Drusen detection in a retinal image using multi-level analysis, in: International Conference on Medical Image Computing and Computer-Assisted Intervention, 2003, pp. 618–625.

[58] R.T. Smith, T. Nagasaki, J.R. Sparrow, I. Barbazetto, C.C. Klaver, J.K. Chan, A method of drusen measurement based on the geometry of fundus reflectance, Biomed. Eng. Online 2 (2003) 10.

[59] D. Mittal, K. Kumari, Automated detection and segmentation of drusen in retinal fundus images, Comput. Electr. Eng. 47 (2015) 82–95.

[60] STARE Dataset, Available from: http://www.ces.clemson.edu/~ahoover/stare.

[61] A. Hoover, V. Kouznetsova, M. Goldbaum, Locating blood vessels in retinal images by piecewise threshold probing of a matched filter response, IEEE Trans. Med. Imaging 19 (2000) 203–210.

[62] ARIA Dataset, Available from: http://www.eyecharity.com/aria_online.

[63] P. Bankhead, C.N. Scholfield, J.G. McGeown, T.M. Curtis, Fast retinal vessel detection and measurement using wavelets and edge location refinement, PLoS ONE 7 (2012) e32435.

[64] A.D. Mora, P.M. Vieira, A. Manivannan, J.M. Fonseca, Automated drusen detection in retinal images using analytical modelling algorithms, Biomed. Eng. Online 10 (2011) 59.

[65] K. Kumari, D. Mittal, Automated drusen detection technique for age-related macular degeneration, J. Biomed. Eng. Med. Imaging 2 (2015) 18.

[66] C. Köse, U. Şevik, O. Gençalioğlu, Automatic segmentation of age-related macular degeneration in retinal fundus images, Comput. Biol. Med. 38 (2008) 611–619.

[67] M.J. van Grinsven, Y.T. Lechanteur, J.P. van de Ven, B. van Ginneken, C.B. Hoyng, T. Theelen, C.I. Sánchez, Automatic drusen quantification and risk assessment of age-related macular degeneration on color fundus images, Invest. Ophthalmol. Vis. Sci. 54 (2013) 3019–3027.

[68] A. Bhuiyan, R. Kawasaki, M. Sasaki, E. Lamoureux, K. Ramamohanarao, R. Guymer, T. Wong, Y. Kanagasingam, Drusen detection and quantification for early identification of age related macular degeneration using color fundus imaging, J. Clin. Exp. Ophthalmol. 4 (2013) 2.

[69] S.S. Parvathi, N. Devi, Automatic drusen detection from colour retinal images, in: ICCIMA, 2007, pp. 377–381.

[70] A.R. Prasath, M. Ramya, Detection of macular drusen based on texture descriptors, Res. J. Inf. Technol. 7 (2015) 70–79.

[71] N. Lee, A.F. Laine, T.R. Smith, Learning non-homogenous textures and the unlearning problem with application to drusen detection in retinal images, in: ISBI 2008. 5th IEEE International Symposium on Biomedical Imaging: From Nano to Macro, 2008, 2008, pp. 1215–1218.

[72] M. Garnier, T. Hurtut, H.B. Tahar, F. Cheriet, Automatic multiresolution age-related macular degeneration detection from fundus images, in: Medical Imaging 2014: Computer-Aided Diagnosis, 2014, p. 903532.

[73] A. Thdibaoui, A. Rajn, P. Bunel, A fuzzy logic approach to drusen detection in retinal angiographic images, in: 15th International Conference on Pattern Recognition, 2000. Proceedings, 2000, pp. 748–751.

[74] J. Kirkpatrick, T. Spencer, A. Manivannan, P. Sharp, J. Forrester, Quantitative image analysis of macular drusen from fundus photographs and scanning laser ophthalmoscope images, Eye 9 (1995) 48.

[75] J.H. Acton, R.P. Cubbidge, H. King, P. Galsworthy, J.M. Gibson, Drusen detection in retro-mode imaging by a scanning laser ophthalmoscope, Acta Ophthalmol. 89 (2011) e404–e411.

[76] B. Diniz, R.M. Ribeiro, D.C. Rodger, M. Maia, S. Sadda, Drusen detection by confocal aperture-modulated infrared scanning laser ophthalmoscopy, Br. J. Ophthalmol. 97 (2013) 285–290.

[77] F.G. Schlanitz, C. Ahlers, S. Sacu, C. Schütze, M. Rodriguez, S. Schriefl, I. Golbaz, T. Spalek, G. Stock, U. Schmidt-Erfurth, Performance of drusen detection by spectral-domain optical coherence tomography, Invest. Ophthalmol. Vis. Sci. 51 (2010) 6715–6721.

[78] F.G. Schlanitz, B. Baumann, T. Spalek, C. Schütze, C. Ahlers, M. Pircher, E. Götzinger, C.K. Hitzenberger, U. Schmidt-Erfurth, Performance of automated drusen detection by polarization-sensitive optical coherence tomography, Invest. Ophthalmol. Vis. Sci. 52 (2011) 4571–4579.

[79] A. Deckert, S. Schmitz-Valckenberg, J. Jorzik, A. Bindewald, F. Holz, U. Mansmann, Automated analysis of digital fundus autofluorescence images of geographic atrophy in advanced age-related macular degeneration using confocal scanning laser ophthalmoscopy (cSLO), BMC Ophthalmol. 5 (2005) 8.

[80] Q. Chen, L. de Sisternes, T. Leng, L.L. Zheng, L. Kutzscher, D.L. Rubin, Semi-automatic geographic atrophy segmentation for SD-OCT images, Biomed. Opt. Express 4 (2013) 2729–2750.

[81] C. Schütze, M. Bolz, R. Sayegh, B. Baumann, M. Pircher, E. Götzinger, C.K. Hitzenberger, U. Schmidt-Erfurth, Lesion size detection in geographic atrophy by polarization-sensitive optical coherence tomography and correlation to conventional imaging techniques, Invest. Ophthalmol. Vis. Sci. 54 (2013) 739–745.

[82] S.J. Chiu, J.A. Izatt, R.V. O'Connell, K.P. Winter, C.A. Toth, S. Farsiu, Validated automatic segmentation of AMD pathology including drusen and geographic atrophy in SD-OCT images, Invest. Ophthalmol. Vis. Sci. 53 (2012) 53–61.

[83] Q. Zhang, C.-L. Chen, Z. Chu, F. Zheng, A. Miller, L. Roisman, J. Rafael de Oliveira Dias, Z. Yehoshua, K.B. Schaal, W. Feuer, G. Gregori, S. Kubach, L. An, P.F. Stetson, M.K. Durbin, P.J. Rosenfeld, R.K. Wang, Automated quantitation of choroidal neovascularization: a comparison study between spectral-domain and swept-source OCT angiograms, Invest. Ophthalmol. Vis. Sci. 58 (2017) 1506–1513.

[84] M.W.M. Wintergerst, T. Schultz, J. Birtel, A.K. Schuster, N. Pfeiffer, S. Schmitz-Valckenberg, F.G. Holz, R.P. Finger, Algorithms for the automated analysis of age-related macular degeneration biomarkers on optical coherence tomography: a systematic review, Transl. Vis. Sci. Technol. 6 (2017) 10.

[85] Y. Kanagasingam, A. Bhuiyan, M.D. Abràmoff, R.T. Smith, L. Goldschmidt, T.Y. Wong, Progress on retinal image analysis for age related macular degeneration, Prog. Retin. Eye Res. 38 (2014) 20–42.

[86] Y. Zheng, M.H.A. Hijazi, F. Coenen, Automated "disease/no disease" grading of age-related macular degeneration by an image mining approach, Invest. Ophthalmol. Vis. Sci. 53 (2012) 8310–8318.

[87] M.H.A. Hijazi, F. Coenen, Y. Zheng, Data mining techniques for the screening of age-related macular degeneration, Knowl.-Based Syst. 29 (2012) 83–92.

[88] M.H.A. Hijazi, F. Coenen, Y. Zheng, A histogram approach for the screening of age-related macular degeneration, in: Medical Image Understanding and Analysis, 2009, pp. 154–158.

[89] M.R.K. Mookiah, U.R. Acharya, J.E. Koh, V. Chandran, C.K. Chua, J.H. Tan, C.M. Lim, E. Ng, K. Noronha, L. Tong, Automated diagnosis of age-related macular degeneration using greyscale features from digital fundus images, Comput. Biol. Med. 53 (2014) 55–64.

[90] M.H.A. Hijazi, F.P. Coenen, Y. Zeng, Image mining approaches for the screening of age-related macular degeneration, in: Retinopathy: New Research, Nova Science Publishers, Inc., 2012, pp. 101–142.

[91] F.G. Venhuizen, B. van Ginneken, B. Bloemen, M.J. van Grinsven, R. Philipsen, C. Hoyng, T. Theelen, C.I. Sánchez, Automated age-related macular degeneration classification in OCT using unsupervised feature learning, in: Medical Imaging 2015: Computer-Aided Diagnosis, 2015, pp. 94141I.

[92] F.G. Venhuizen, B. van Ginneken, F. van Asten, M.J. van Grinsven, S. Fauser, C.B. Hoyng, T. Theelen, C.I. Sánchez, Automated staging of age-related macular degeneration using optical coherence tomography, Invest. Ophthalmol. Vis. Sci. 58 (2017) 2318–2328.

[93] A. Albarrak, F. Coenen, Y. Zheng, Volumetric image classification using homogeneous decomposition and dictionary learning: a study using retinal optical coherence tomography for detecting age-related macular degeneration, Comput. Med. Imaging Graph. 55 (2017) 113–123.

[94] C.S. Lee, D.M. Baughman, A.Y. Lee, Deep learning is effective for classifying normal versus age-related macular degeneration OCT images, Ophthalmol. Retina 1 (2017) 322–327.

[95] K. Simonyan, A. Zisserman, Very deep convolutional networks for large-scale image recognition, in: Presented at the International Conference on Learning Representations, 2015.

[96] F. Grassmann, J. Mengelkamp, C. Brandl, S. Harsch, M.E. Zimmermann, B. Linkohr, A. Peters, I.M. Heid, C. Palm, B.H. Weber, A deep learning algorithm for prediction of age-related eye disease study severity scale for age-related macular degeneration from color fundus photography, Ophthalmology 125 (9) (2018) 1410–1420.

[97] D.S. Kermany, M. Goldbaum, W. Cai, C.C. Valentim, H. Liang, S.L. Baxter, A. McKeown, G. Yang, X. Wu, F. Yan, Identifying medical diagnoses and treatable diseases by image-based deep learning, Cell 172 (2018) 1122–1131. e9.

[98] J. De Fauw, J.R. Ledsam, B. Romera-Paredes, S. Nikolov, N. Tomasev, S. Blackwell, H. Askham, X. Glorot, B. O'Donoghue, D. Visentin, Clinically applicable deep learning for diagnosis and referral in retinal disease, Nat. Med. 24 (2018) 1342.

[99] O. Ronneberger, P. Fischer, T. Brox, U-net: convolutional networks for biomedical image segmentation, in: International Conference on Medical Image Computing and Computer-Assisted Intervention, 2015, pp. 234–241.

[100] Age-Related Eye Disease Study Research Group, The age-related eye disease study (AREDS): design implications AREDS report no. 1, Control. Clin. Trials 20 (1999) 573.

[101] P.P. Srinivasan, L.A. Kim, P.S. Mettu, S.W. Cousins, G.M. Comer, J.A. Izatt, S. Farsiu, Fully automated detection of diabetic macular edema and dry age-related macular degeneration from optical coherence tomography images, Biomed. Opt. Express 5 (2014) 3568–3577.

[102] R. Rasti, H. Rabbani, A. Mehridehnavi, F. Hajizadeh, Macular OCT classification using a multi-scale convolutional neural network ensemble, IEEE Trans. Med. Imaging 37 (2018) 1024–1034.

[103] P. Gholami, P. Roy, M.K. Parthasarathy, V. Lakshminarayanan, OCTID: Optical Coherence Tomography Image Database, arXiv preprint arXiv:1812.07056, 2018.

OCT fluid detection and quantification

14

Hrvoje Bogunović, Wolf-Dieter Vogl, Sebastian M. Waldstein, Ursula Schmidt-Erfurth

Christian Doppler Laboratory for Ophthalmic Image Analysis, Department of Ophthalmology, Medical University of Vienna, Vienna, Austria

1 Introduction

The presence of fluid in the retina is the main hallmark of several important retinal diseases, including neovascular age-related macular degeneration (nAMD), diabetic macular edema (DME), and macular edema secondary to retinal vein occlusion (RVO). The term *macular edema* refers to a fluid-induced swelling of the central retina. Fluid is generally divided into distinct types depending on its anatomical location, that is, within the retina, between the retina and the retinal pigment epithelium (RPE), and beneath the RPE. Furthermore, based on the origin of fluid, one can differentiate between exudative fluid and fluid caused by retinal degeneration. In macular diseases characterized by exudation, the presence and amount of fluid is both a diagnostic criterion and an important factor in the indication for treatment. In retinal degeneration, fluid can be measured over time to assess disease progression. A comprehensive description of the role of fluid in macular disease is provided in Ref. [1].

Optical coherence tomography (OCT) offers a fast, noninvasive 3D view of the retina by acquiring a series of cross-sectional slices (B-scans), allowing an in-depth examination of retinal tissue with cellular-level resolution [2], and has become a standard of care impacting the treatment of millions of patients every year [3]. OCT has had a profound impact on early detection of disease, and monitoring its development and the treatment response [4]. Fluid causing macular edema can be readily imaged and phenotyped using OCT (Fig. 1). The three distinct fluid types readily seen on OCT and considered relevant imaging biomarkers are introduced next.

Intraretinal cystoid fluid

Intraretinal cystoid fluid IRF (or IRC) is defined on OCT as round or ovoid spaces within the retina, with a low reflectivity content. This type of fluid is most often located in the inner and outer nuclear layers of the retina, and less frequently in the ganglion cell layer [5]. It forms confluent pools within the retinal layers that are interspaced with

Computational Retinal Image Analysis. https://doi.org/10.1016/B978-0-08-102816-2.00015-0

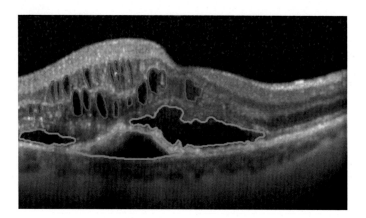

FIG. 1

The three distinct fluid types on an OCT B-scan: intraretinal fluid (*red*), subretinal fluid (*green*), and sub-RPE fluid in pigment epithelium detachment (*blue*).

retinal tissue columns. Hence, when cross-sectioned (OCT B-scan) IRF appears in a round or ovoid (cyst-like) pattern. However, when sectioned perpendicularly at equal depth (OCT C-scan), IRF shows a lobulated, honeycomb-like distribution. Exudative IRF is a consequence of intraretinal vascular leakage. It is the defining criterion of DME or RVO. In nAMD, roughly two-third of patients show IRF [6]. Among the different fluid compartments, IRF has the strongest impact on visual function. Eyes with large volumes of fluid in the foveal center show a reduced visual acuity (VA) and the resolution of IRF is linked with improvement in VA [7]. Its presence or any increase in IRF is an accepted retreatment criterion in the management of exudative macular disease.

On the one hand, IRF can also occur secondary to retinal degeneration. Retinoschisis is the separation of retinal layers by stretching. It is characterized in OCT images as large areas of elongated IRF with interspaced vertical tissue columns. On the other hand, a dysfunctional RPE can give rise to degenerative IRF, which has been described as square-shaped hyporeflective spaces overlying areas of RPE loss [8]. Outer retinal tubulation is a degenerative retinal finding that can mimic IRF [9].

Subretinal fluid

Subretinal fluid (SRF) is defined on OCT as a hyporeflective space between the RPE and the outer retinal boundary (i.e., the photoreceptor tips). SRF typically forms pools of fluid that distribute naturally in the subretinal space. For instance, in patients with DME or RVO, SRF accumulates in a central subfoveal hump. SRF is present in about 30% of patients with these diseases. In nAMD, SRF often appears around pigment epithelial detachments (PED) that are themselves topographically linked to IRF [10]. Most patients with nAMD exhibit SRF [6]. In retinal detachment, SRF defines the extent of the detached retina. Apart from retinal detachment, SRF is always a sign of exudative disease. However, in nAMD, it is not primarily linked with poorer retinal function and indeed patients with larger amounts of SRF have been shown to maintain an improved VA [11]. Although SRF is usually seen as an indication for treatment, studies have demonstrated that tolerating a small amount of SRF may be feasible in the management of these diseases [12].

Sub-RPE fluid in PED

These lesions can be subdivided into serous PED containing solely fluid and fibrovascular PED containing both fluid and fibrovascular tissue. Hence, sub-RPE fluid can either be a sub-RPE space that is homogeneously hyporeflective in serous PED or within fibrovascular PED that exhibit a more heterogeneous pattern with hyporeflective and hyperreflective areas. If a PED is purely hyperreflective without any hyporeflective elements, it is said not to contain any sub-RPE fluid. PED occur primarily in patients with nAMD. Sub-RPE fluid is a sign of active choroidal neovascularization. Any increasing sub-RPE fluid should be regarded a retreatment indication. As long as the sub-RPE fluid is covered by intact pigment epithelium, it is not associated with substantial vision loss [11].

Manual assessment of fluid with OCT is subjective and has become prohibitively time consuming due to large numbers of fluid pockets and B-scans acquired by the modern OCT that need to be visually analyzed. This calls for the development of computational retinal image analysis methods that can objectively and repeatedly detect and quantify fluid from OCT datasets. However, automated image analysis of OCT scans is hindered by OCT's anisotropic resolution, motion artifacts, and low signal-to-noise ratio (SNR) due to speckle [13]. Furthermore, there is a substantial variability in image quality and appearance between OCT devices from different vendors, as shown in Fig. 2. Thus, automated methods have to effectively overcome

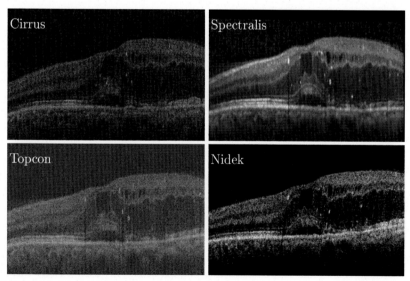

FIG. 2

Intervendor OCT image variability. An eye containing intraretinal and subretinal fluid imaged with four different OCT device vendors: Cirrus, Spectralis, Topcon, and Nidek. The B-scans were acquired at approximately the same anatomical position.

these hurdles to reach the level of clinically applicable performance. There are several scenarios where automated detection and quantification of fluid may become clinically relevant. These include, for instance, the automated screening and triage of OCT scans for the presence of macular disease, the assessment of fluid response and recurrence during a course of therapy, or the evaluation of fluid in order to provide prognostic information.

In the remainder of this chapter, we review the methods and state of the art in automated OCT fluid quantification (Section 2) and detection (Section 3), present two clinically relevant analyses that result from having fluid quantification tools available (Section 4), and, finally, summarize the main findings and conclude the chapter (Section 5).

2 OCT fluid quantification

Being able to quantitatively measure the amount of fluid present is expected to play an increasingly important clinical role in effective managements of patients with exudative macular diseases. There have already been retreatment protocols suggested that rely on knowing the fluid size, for example, Arnold et al. [12] tested a *relaxed* retinal fluid regimen that tolerated incomplete resolution of SRF ≤ 200 µm. Furthermore, the ability to quantify the three fluid types individually is an important step to enable prognostic decision support systems, as presented in Section 4.

Fluid quantification relies on having accurate OCT image segmentation methods. In addition, due to the large amount of fluid pockets typically present in a scan, the methods should be fully automated as even semiautomated approaches would be too labor intensive and consequently of very limited practical use. Nowadays, such image segmentation models are exclusively based on convolutional neural networks (CNN) due to their ability to learn without feature handcrafting, and their continual improvement with the increasing number of annotated datasets. Fast execution of the trained CNN models is also essential for their deployment in the clinic, where only limited time is available for planning between the OCT acquisition and the treatment.

2.1 Segmentation using supervised learning

As soon as CNN deep learning models were discovered to be highly successful at image recognition [14], they were redesigned to address the semantic segmentation task by making CNN learn the mapping from raw intensity images to dense pixelwise tissue class labels. A popular initial approach was based on *patch classification*, where each pixel was classified separately using an image patch surrounding it. The main reason for using patches was CNN's components made of fully connected layers that required a fixed input size image. Schlegl et al. [15] used a CNN early on with a patch-based pixel classification for the task of fluid segmentation on OCT. In this pioneering work, the multiscale CNN model was able to differentiate between IRF and SRF types and operate in a weakly supervised setting.

Fully convolutional networks (FCN) were proposed soon afterward and achieved dense predictions without the need for fully connected layers [16]. Besides being substantially faster than patch-based models, they allowed segmentations to be obtained from images of arbitrary sizes and image-to-image training. Thus, all of the subsequent segmentation works adopted the FCN paradigm. Popular and successful semantic segmentation CNN architectures consist of two processing components, an encoder and a decoder [17, 18]. The encoder gradually transforms an input image into a low-dimensional embedding, and the decoder gradually recovers this abstract image representation to an image of class labels. The mapping of the encoder from raw images to the data embedding, needed to generate the label image, and the mapping of the decoder from the embedding to a full-input resolution label image are learned simultaneously, end to end. A pixel-based cross-entropy or a smoothed Dice coefficient [19] is typically used as the network's loss function, which is optimized during training. At the end, a softmax layer estimates the probability of a pixel belonging to a class and pixel-wise class labels are obtained by computing the arg max function over the class probabilities (Fig. 3). The current state-of-the-art CNN for medical image segmentation is a U-net [20], which further includes shortcut/ skip connections across an encoder and decoder to facilitate resolution recovery by a decoder.

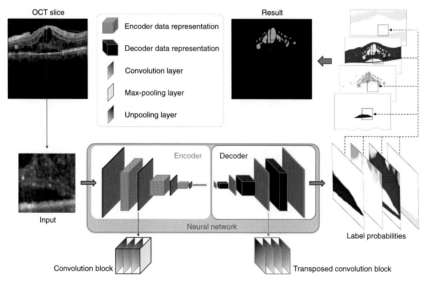

FIG. 3

Convolutional neural network with an encoder-decoder architecture to segment intraretinal fluid (*green*), subretinal fluid (*blue*), retinal tissue (*red*), and nonretinal region (*yellow*).

Reproduced from T. Schlegl, S.M. Waldstein, H. Bogunovic, F. Endstraßer, A. Sadeghipour, A.-M. Philip, D. Podkowinski, B.S. Gerendas, G. Langs, U. Schmidt-Erfurth, Fully automated detection and quantification of macular fluid in OCT using deep learning, Ophthalmology 125 (4) 2018) 549–558, 10.1016/J. OPHTHA.2017.10.031.

Lee et al. [22] used a U-net for a binary segmentation of IRF with a training and validation set composed of 1289 annotated B-scans. They achieved a Dice similarity coefficient (DSC) of 0.73, close to the interobserver variability of DSC = 0.75, on a test set of 30 B-scans, annotated by multiple experts. Roy et al. [23] used a U-net to segment seven retinal layers and IRF jointly. They solved the multiclass segmentation problem by combining Dice loss with a weighted logistic regression loss that compensated class imbalance and selectively penalized misclassification. The model was successfully trained and tested on a small publicly available dataset [24] containing 110 annotated B-scans from 10 patients acquired with Spectralis OCT.

Two large validation studies recently showed that FCN can work effectively across OCT device vendors and macular diseases. Venhuizen et al. [25] implemented a multiscale network that used a range of contextual windows to segment IRF. The method consisted of a cascade of two U-nets with two complementary tasks: the first one aimed at delimiting the retinal region [26] and the second one at segmenting IRF by integrating the output of the first U-net as both an additional input channel and a constraining weight map used in computing the loss during the training. A total of 221 OCT volumes from 151 patients (6158 B-scans) were used from which the testing and evaluation had been performed on 99 OCT volumes (2487 B-scans) from 75 patients. To obtain segmentations from scans of different OCT vendors, a small amount of vendor-specific data was used for fine tuning. They reported a DSC of 0.79 and, furthermore, demonstrated a good robustness and generalization even without the fine tuning (DSC = 0.72).

Schlegl et al. [21] developed a semantic segmentation network to segment the retina, IRF, and SRF simultaneously (Fig. 3). The method was cross-validated on a dataset of 354 fully annotated OCT volumes comprising three main exudative diseases, such as nAMD (212), DME (32), and RVO (110), and two OCT vendors, such as Cirrus (268) and Spectralis (86). Models for the two OCT vendors were trained separately as it was shown that the Cirrus model generalized well to a Spectralis dataset but not vice versa. Due to a difference in fluid distributions between diseases, the model was first trained on scans from patients with nAMD and RVO, followed by fine-tuning a second model on DME scans.

All fluid types, IRF, SRF, and PED (fibrovascular, serous, and drusenoid), within a total of 15 different semantic labels were segmented as part of a system from DeepMind for OCT diagnosis and referral [27]. Therefore, a 3D U-net [28] was developed that used nine contiguous slices as a context to segment the middle slice. In addition to identify ambiguous regions, an ensemble of five instances of the network was constructed by training with a different order over the inputs and different random weight initializations. Networks were trained on 877 (Topcon) and 152 (Spectralis) OCTs having sparse annotations, that is, three to five B-scans per volume were manually annotated, an equivalent of approximately 20 fully annotated OCT volumes. However, the segmentation performance metrics have not been reported.

2.1.1 Preprocessing and postprocessing
Denoising

OCT scans have low SNRs due to the high level of speckle noise. Standard efficient preprocessing approaches, such as Gaussian and gamma noise filtering, median and bilateral filtering [29], or total variation-based [30] denoising, are used for noise suppression. However, even without any preprocessing CNN generally showed very good robustness to noise and the degradation of image quality caused by severe retinal abnormalities attenuating the OCT signal has a stronger detrimental impact than the speckle.

Retina and layer segmentation

The retina can be effectively segmented due to the strong signal and image gradient of the inner limiting membrane (ILM) at the top of the retina and the bottom RPE interface [31, 32]. These interfaces are also often made available by built-in OCT device algorithms. Thus, a region of interest denoting the retina can be used as both a preprocessing step to limit the segmentation to this region and a postprocessing step to remove false-positive labels.

Data augmentation

Data augmentation is an effective technique to inject invariance to a desired set of geometric and intensity transformations into the deep learning models. It typically involves random cropping of a subimage from a B-scan, random rotation, mirroring and introducing multiplicative speckle noise as well as applying affine and elastic geometric transformations jointly over the image inputs and gold standard segmentations.

2.1.2 Traditional machine-learning and nonmachine-learning approaches

Before the appearance of deep learning segmentation models, traditional machine learning was applied to provide a classification of OCT voxels based on a set of hand-crafted features describing the local appearance. Such voxel classes then provided a prior for subsequent graph-based or variational-based image segmentation methods. Chen et al. [33] presented a fully 3D approach based on voxel classification followed by a graph-cut-based segmentation. Xu et al. [34] proposed a retinal voxel-classification approach stratified by presegmented layers. Wang et al. [35] proposed a combination of a fuzzy C-means for initialization followed by evolution of a level-set contour in three orthogonal OCT planes.

A simultaneous joint segmentation of retinal layers and fluid was a long-pursued goal, as it overcomes error propagation when segmenting step-wise retinal layers first and then fluid regions. Such a voxel classification approach followed by a refinement with graph-cut and dynamic programming was proposed by Chiu et al. [24]. Novosel et al. [36] developed loosely coupled-level sets to jointly segment fluid and retinal layers by modeling the fluid as an additional space-variant layer. A purely data-driven model with minimum a priori constraints was proposed by Montuoro et al. [37] based on auto-context [38] to jointly segment retinal fluid and layers by learning their mutual interaction properties.

PED segmentation was initially approached as a layer segmentation problem as it corresponds to the deformation of a space between the RPE and Bruch's membrane (BM). PED could then be easily identified from the resulting layer thickness map. Shi et al. [39] developed a multisurface segmentation using graph search by specifying different constraints on surface smoothness corresponding to the RPE and BM. Sun et al. [40] first estimated BM surface from the convex hull of the RPE, followed by a shape-constrained graph cut to obtain the final PED segmentation. Wu et al. [41, 42] proposed a 3D method to segment and differentiate between SRF and PED fluid pockets. They combined texture, intensity, and thickness scores to build a voxel-level fluid probability map and then applied a continuous max-flow to obtain the segmentations.

2.2 Segmentation using weakly supervised and unsupervised learning

A supervised learning approach for semantic segmentation requires substantial effort in producing a large-scale dataset of manual pixel-wise annotations needed for the training. As an alternative, weakly supervised techniques focus on achieving segmentation based on OCT or image region-level information of fluid presence. Finally, unsupervised learning approaches based around the concept of anomaly detection require a training set of healthy retinas only. They use a two-step process where first normal shape and appearance is learned and then anomalies such as fluid can be detected as deviations from the norm. This reflects the natural study process of medical students, who first learn what a healthy tissue looks like and subsequently gain the ability to identify pathologies deviating from this normal appearance.

An early automated approach addressed the fluid segmentation problem as a local anomaly detection based on retinal texture and thickness properties [43]. After learning normal variability from images of healthy eyes, the method was applied to determine 2D en-face footprints of fluid-filled regions, although a 3D localization was missing. Schlegl et al. [15] used the approximate spatial location of fluid in the form of its retinal layer group and centrality and reached the performance equal to ≈85% of the fully supervised approach. As a by-product of interpreting image classification results, fluid-related regions have been identified with moderate accuracy [44–46]. Seeböck et al. [47] trained a multiscale deep denoising autoencoder [48] on healthy images, and used a one-class support vector machine (SVM) that identified anomalies in new data. While Schlegl et al. [49] used generative adversarial networks [50] to embed image patches into a low-dimensional space where the deviations from the manifold of healthy patches could be measured.

2.3 Evaluation

A frequently used for evaluating segmentation performance is a DSC, corresponding to the F1 score, the harmonic average between *precision* and *recall*. It is a measure of overlap related to intersection over union between two sets X and Y, corresponding to the segmented pixels and the ground truth.

$$DSC = 2\frac{|X \cap Y|}{|X| + |Y|} = \frac{2TP}{2TP + FN + FP} = 2\frac{\text{Precision} \times \text{Recall}}{\text{Precision} + \text{Recall}}. \tag{1}$$

A downside of DSC is its high sensitivity to errors when only a small amount of fluid is present in the image. Thus, additional metrics with direct clinical interpretation are often considered, for example, fluid volume. Xu et al. [34] proposed a number of such clinically oriented measures of segmentation performance. They computed a Bland-Altman plot to measure the method's bias and the limits of agreement with the gold standard volumes. In addition to comparing volumes, they displayed scatter plots comparing properties between automated and gold standard segmentations of fluid pockets such as the average distance to BM, average distance to fovea, and their number stratified by the fluid volume quantity.

Several datasets were prepared to allow evaluation and comparison between different automated algorithms. A publicly available dataset was released by Duke containing 110 B-scans acquired with Spectralis OCT from 10 patients with DME and annotated by two experts [24]. As part of the OPTIMA Cyst Segmentation Challenge [51] organized during the MICCAI conference 2015, four teams compared their machine-learning methods in segmenting IRF using fully and double annotated OCT volumes with a training set of 15 OCT volumes and a test set of 15 OCT volumes from OCTs acquired with four different vendors: Topcon, Cirrus, Nidek, and Spectralis. In the RETOUCH challenge [52], a satellite event of the MICCAI 2017, eight teams compared their deep learning methods for IRF, SRF, and PED segmentation using 70 OCT fully annotated scans for training and 42 double annotated OCT for testing, with the scans encompassing two retinal diseases (i.e., nAMD and RVO) and three OCT vendors (i.e., Cirrus, Spectralis, and Topcon).

The datasets that have been annotated by multiple observers offer an insight into the interobserver variability and the ceiling in evaluating segmentation performance trained from manual annotations. Xu et al. [34] measured a high agreement of $R^2 = 0.98$ between extracted fluid volumes between two experts. Using a more stringent DSC metric, Lee et al. [22] reported a mean DSC for human interrater reliability of 0.75. In RETOUCH, an intercenter DSC $= 0.73$ (± 0.17) was reported on a large test dataset. This illustrates the difficulty of performing even the manual annotations of fluid on OCT.

3　OCT fluid detection

Management of exudative macular diseases is largely based on the ability to detect retinal fluid on OCT for the purpose of initial diagnosis and retreatment indications. Thus, detection of fluid on OCT has become a routine clinical task but reliable evaluation of leakage activity is difficult and subjective when performed manually, resulting in the risk of missing the fluid and subjectivity influencing the retreatment procedure.

Having an accurate fluid segmentation method available greatly facilitates the fluid detection task as detection can be achieved by either thresholding the number of segmented fluid voxels or training another classifier to learn to detect fluid from the segmented fluid maps. When fluid segmentation is not available, machine learning and deep learning are well-suited methods for such a binary image classification task, which determines whether fluid disease activity is present or not. Several methods have been proposed to differentiate retinas with macular edema from normal retinas or retinas with nonexudative diseases, indirectly detecting the fluid. However, the main downside of such image classification methods is that they only detect general fluid activity, without distinguishing the various fluid types. This limits the clinical findings of the classification as different fluid types are associated with different prognoses. In the following, we review the three fluid detection approaches as mentioned previously.

3.1 Detection using image segmentation

A fluid segmentation method proposed by Xu et al. [34] was additionally evaluated on the task of fluid detection in 30 OCT scans (Topcon) from 10 patients with nAMD undergoing anti-VEGF treatment. It achieved an area under the curve (AUC) of 0.8 and 0.92, taking two different expert annotations as the gold standard. Chakravarthy et al. [53] proposed a method using graph-based optimization and region growing to identify fluid pockets but the implementation details were scarce, as the method is part of a commercial system by Notal Vision for at-home monitoring. They reported a diagnostic accuracy of 91% compared with the majority grading by three retinal specialists on 142 OCT scans (Zeiss Cirrus) of eyes with nAMD.

The two methods mentioned previously aimed at detecting disease activity in general without the possibility to detect the presence of each fluid type individually. As part of their IRF and SRF segmentation development, direct application in the fluid detection task was demonstrated by Schlegl et al. [21]. ROC curves were computed by varying the threshold over the number of fluid pixels segmented. In the largest evaluation of individual fluid detection to date, it was evaluated against a volume-level manual grading of 1200 OCT scans of eyes with nAMD (400), RVO (400), and DME (400) with equal distribution of fluid presence and imaged with two different OCT devices, that is, Cirrus (600) and Spectralis (600). AUCs for IRF and SRF ranged from 0.91 to 0.97 and 0.87 to 0.98, respectively (Fig. 4). Detection of SRF in DME cases was the only scenario where detection AUC fell below the 0.90 level, due to SRF being a rare occurrence in patients with DME and thus harder to train and detect.

Recently, De Fauw et al. [27] developed a two-stage deep learning system for diagnosis and referral based on OCT. In the first stage, they segment multiple imaging biomarkers including IRF, SRF, and PED. The second stage uses the segmented maps to train a CNN classifier to provide a differential diagnosis. The system has been shown to be clinically applicable. Its performance indicating the need for referral was comparable to the one of retinal specialists but the detection performance of individual fluid types was not evaluated.

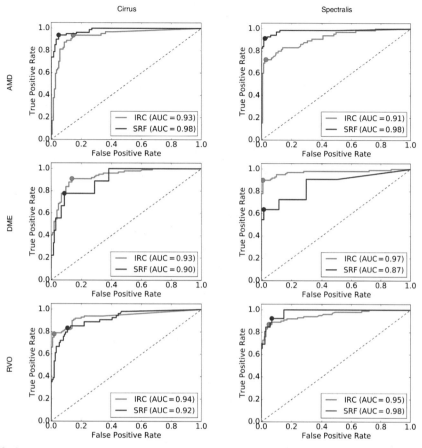

FIG. 4

Receiver operating characteristic (ROC) curves on volume-wise detection performance of intraretinal cystoid fluid (IRC) and subretinal fluid (SRF). The operating point maximizing Youden Index is indicated by the *dot*. The AUC is specified in *parentheses*.

Reproduced from T. Schlegl, S.M. Waldstein, H. Bogunovic, F. Endstraßer, A. Sadeghipour, A.-M. Philip, D. Podkowinski, B.S. Gerendas, G. Langs, U. Schmidt-Erfurth, Fully automated detection and quantification of macular fluid in OCT using deep learning, Ophthalmology 125 (4) 2018) 549–558, 10.1016/J. OPHTHA.2017.10.031.

3.2 Detection using image classification

The rise of deep learning methods brought several powerful CNN models for image classification [14]. The image classification setting has an advantage in benefiting from research efforts in the domain of a very large visual recognition challenge such as the ImageNet Large-Scale Visual Recognition Competition [54] containing millions of annotated images. This resulted in the availability of a few ready-made, pretrained image classification CNN architectures, which can be transferred to or further fine-tuned on an OCT classification task.

Kermany et al. [44] used a transfer learning approach with a pretrained Inception V3 CNN architecture [55] serving as a fixed feature extractor. They achieved a high performance ($\approx$98%) in classifying a B-scan into an nAMD, DME, early AMD, or normal retina and an almost perfect performance with an AUC = 0.999 for identifying urgent referrals (nAMD and DME). Only the final softmax layer was trained on 100,000 B-scans from 4686 patients and the model was tested with 1000 B-scans (250 from each category) from 633 patients. A similar transfer learning approach [56] successfully detected nAMD from a central OCT B-scan and was trained with 1012 B-scans. An accuracy of 0.98 was achieved on a test set of 100 B-scans equally balanced between nAMD and healthy examples. OCT-level and patient-level performances were not reported in the previous two works.

Lee et al. [45] proposed a CNN trained from scratch on more than 100,000 B-scans to distinguish nAMD B-scans from normal scans. The model relied on VGG16 [57] network architecture. A total of 80,839 B-scans (41,074 from AMD and 39,765 from normal eyes) were used for training and 20,163 B-scans (11,616 from AMD and 8547 from normal eyes) were used for validation. At a B-scan level, they achieved an AUC of 92.78% with an accuracy of 87.63%. At the macular OCT-scan level, they achieved an AUC of 93.83% with an accuracy of 88.98% [58] trained a similar deep learning architecture GoogLeNet (Inception-v1) [59], from scratch, however, with the goal of automatically determining the need for anti-VEGF retreatment rather than purely the presence of fluid. After training on 153,912 B-scans, the prediction accuracy was 95.5% with an AUC of 96.8% on a test set of 5358 B-scans. At an OCT-scan level, an AUC of 98.8% and an accuracy of 94% were reported.

With the end-to-end image classification pipeline, there is an additional need to interpret the resulting decision. Typically, an occlusion test [60] is performed, where a blank box is systematically moved across the image and the change in the output probabilities recorded. The highest drop in the probability is assumed to correspond to the region of interest with the highest importance that contributes most to the neural network's decision on the predicted diagnosis. When classifying an exudative disease, the highlighted areas should correspond to the fluid. Using such interpretability strategies, a coarse fluid segmentation can be achieved as a by-product of the image classification model. An example is shown in Fig. 5.

3.2.1 Traditional machine-learning approaches

General-purpose image descriptors were the state of the art for image recognition before the advent of deep learning. Liu et al. [61] used a local binary pattern (LBP) with PCA dimensionality reduction to obtain histograms, which are capable of encoding texture and shape information in retinal OCT images and their edge maps. The optimized model used a multiclass classifier in the form of multiple one-vs-all binary SVMs with four considered classes, macular edema, normal, macular hole, and AMD, trained on a dataset of 326 OCT central B-scans from 136 eyes. Srinivasan et al. [62] used the method based on describing the B-scan content with multiscale

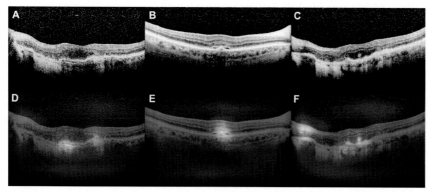

FIG. 5

Example of a fluid identification by performing an occlusion test on an image classification model. *Top row* shows three examples (A, B, C) of OCT B-scans of patients with nAMD. The *bottom row* images (D, E, F) show the corresponding pixel-level importance, where the intensity is determined by the drop in the probability of being labeled nAMD when occluded.

Reproduced from C.S. Lee, D.M. Baughman, A.Y. Lee, Deep learning is effective for classifying normal versus age-related macular degeneration OCT images, Ophthalmol. Retina 1 (4) (2017) 322–327, 10.1016/J. ORET.2016.12.009.

histograms of oriented gradient (HOG) descriptors. The image is divided into small spatial cells and a histogram of the directions of the spatial gradients, weighted by the gradient magnitudes, is calculated for each cell. For multiclass classification, three separate SVMs were trained in a one-vs-one fashion to classify 45 OCT volumes into 15 normal, 15 dry AMD, and 15 DME. Another powerful descriptor of image content is a bag of visual words model. After identifying visual words, an image can then be represented as a histogram encoding their occurrence distribution. This descriptor has been used for a random forest-based, multiclass classification of AMD stages, including nAMD, in a large dataset of ≈1000 patients [63]. Recently Vidal et al. [46] detected IRF on a dataset of 323 OCT B-scans using a set of local intensity and texture-based features, including HOG, LBP, and Gabor descriptors, supplied to a classifier trained on local image patches representative of fluid and nonfluid regions.

3.3 Evaluation

A fluid detector's performance is traditionally evaluated by measuring its ROC and calculating the associated AUC. Detection accuracy is also a commonly reported metric, in particular when the test dataset classes are balanced. There are several open datasets for evaluating OCT fluid detection and scan classification. Duke published an open dataset containing 45 OCT scans (Spectralis) from 15 normal, 15 early AMD, and 15 DME eyes [64]. Kermany et al. [44] compiled a dataset with over 100,000 B-scans distributed across normal eyes and eyes with nAMD, DME, and early AMD, and released it publicly [65].

The recently organized RETOUCH challenge [52] aimed at evaluating the state-of-the-art performance of both automated detection and segmentation of individual fluid types. After training on 70 OCT scans, the teams provided the detection results of 42 test cases for each fluid individually. The performance of the teams was within the interobserver variability. Even though detecting fluid manually can be difficult and subjective, the reported interobserver agreements were high. Chakravarthy et al. [53] compared the accuracy of four graders and found the agreement of each with the majority of the other graders was 93%. Agreement between the gradings of the two medical centers in the RETOUCH fluid detection challenge was similar with 95% across all three fluid types. Thus, the resulting gold standard gradings are considered to be of high quality, which is crucial for both training and validating supervised data-driven machine and deep learning fluid detection methods.

4 Clinical applications

A number of clinically relevant applications are enabled by having fluid detection and quantification tools available. Prediction of VA outcomes after a period of anti-VEGF treatment from a set of spatiotemporal OCT features and clinical biomarkers was proposed for all three main exudative macular diseases: nAMD [66], DME [67], and RVO [68]. The OCT biomarkers corresponding to the retinal layer thicknesses, volume, and area covered by the retinal fluid were spatially described by their mean ETDRS grid values. Similarly, Bogunovic et al. [69] proposed prediction of anti-VEGF treatment requirements in the following 2 years from a set of spatiotemporal OCT biomarkers obtained during the initiation phase and showed that the automated prediction performance was comparable to or better than that of a retina specialist. DeepMind developed a clinically applicable system for diagnosis based on OCT that relies on semantic segmentation of OCT volumes, with all three fluid types, IRF, SRF, and PED, included [27]. In this section, we describe two applications of clinical decision support that rely on fluid being accurately quantified.

4.1 Structure function

VA or with corrections (e.g., for short-sightedness) best-corrected visual acuity (BCVA) is a common measure of retinal function in terms of the resolving power of the eye. BCVA is one of the most important measures to assess disease progression and therapy response in clinical routine. It is measured by counting the total number of letters a person is capable of reading from a standardized chart with the size of letters decreasing per line. The logMar chart is an example [70].

Clinical studies have already demonstrated that the qualitative characterization of fluid types (presence/absence) affects individual VA and changes in VA during treatment are strongly affected by individual baseline levels due to a ceiling effect [6, 71]. Thus, a capability to quantify in addition to detect such fluid would enable such quantitative values to be correlated with visual function, superseding the traditional

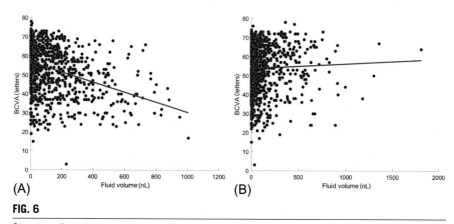

FIG. 6

Structure-function measured as Pearson correlation coefficient (r) for two different fluid types (IRF and SRF) and best-corrected visual acuity (BCVA) in a cohort of 1000 patients with neovascular AMD. (A) IRF, $r = -0.35$; (B) SRF, $r = +0.04$.

qualitative categorization. Waldstein et al. [7] did a proof-of-principle study where IRF and SRF pockets were manually annotated on each B-scan of OCT volumes. The dataset was limited to 38 OCT volumes from as many patients with nAMD due to the substantial effort in performing such dense manual annotations.

We segmented IRF and SRF in an automated way on OCT scans from a large cohort of 1000 treatment-näive patients with nAMD using the method of Schlegl et al. [21]. Two fluid types were quantified by computing their central 3-mm diameter subvolume and individually correlated to patients' BCVA. The results are shown in Fig. 6. It can be observed that IRF had a detrimental negative effect on patients' vision ($r = -0.35$, $P < .001$), while the quantity of SRF was not statistically correlated with the baseline vision.

4.2 Longitudinal analysis of VA outcomes

A main aim of treatment in macular edema is to restore and preserve *vision* by targeting fluid accumulation in the retina using anti-VEGF treatment. Thus, it is of interest to assess how vision impairment is affected by these fluid compartments in the retina and to what extent vision can be restored when fluid resolves due to treatment. Vision gain and response to treatment are monitored by repeatedly measuring a patient's VA during disease development and, furthermore, these VA trajectories can be analyzed in longitudinal studies. Fig. 7 shows such trajectories acquired from regular visits of patients. It also highlights the challenges when analyzing such longitudinal data, with a high variance in VA both at the first visit (baseline) due to different disease stages, and variance in the ongoing disease course due to differing responses to treatment. Furthermore, in this specific dataset, drops in VA can be observed due to the specific PRN treatment regime, where a patient was re-treated when a relapse of VA loss occurred. Missing observations and irregular

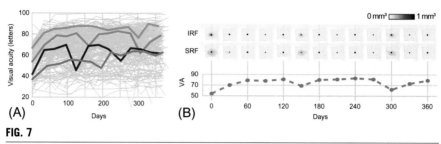

FIG. 7

(A) VA trajectories of patients receiving anti-VEGF treatment. Each *blue line* represents the development of one patient. Four cases are highlighted, illustrating the challenge in this dataset that are the high variance in the data caused by varying disease state at the first visit, different responses to treatment and drops in the VA trajectory from recurring fluid. (B) Example of a patient's disease trajectory over 1 year. The *top rows* show projections of segmented IRF and SRF volumes and the *bottom row* shows the corresponding VA measured in letters. An increase in fluid volume caused a drop in VA at months 6 and 10.

visiting intervals are a common issue in longitudinal data too and need to be considered by the model. As shown in Fig. 7B, there is an indication that vision loss corresponds with an increase of fluid.

Here, we present a summary of published work [68] and propose a longitudinal mixed effects regression model (MRM) [72] that captures the disease progression both on a population mean and on an individual level. We model the progression as a trajectory with VA measured at regular visits as the target and fluid volumes measured in OCT images as covariates. With such a model, we assess how fluid accumulations in certain retinal areas influence vision. The model particularly takes advantage of the longitudinal nature of the data, where VA measures from a patient are not treated independently, by considering the differing variances in the VA within the patients' observations and between patients. Furthermore, this MRM tackles the issue of variance introduced by various disease stages at the first visit and the differing responses to treatment. By introducing so-called subject-specific random effects into the model, individual trajectories deviating from the population mean trend can be modeled and thus variance in the disease stage at the first visit (random intercept) and speed of recovery (random slope) handled. MRMs are specifically attractive for longitudinal data analysis as they are capable of handling missing datapoints and irregular intervals.

4.2.1 Method
Obtaining fluid volumes
First, we align the follow-up OCT scans of a patient, such that the fovea position is always at the center, as described by Vogl et al. [73]. We use the semantic segmentation method of Schlegl et al. [21] to segment IRF and SRF in the OCT image. Then, we compute the total fluid volume within the central 1-mm region around the fovea, denoted as $v^{fov\text{-}irf}$ and $v^{fov\text{-}srf}$, and within the parafoveal region, which is a 1- to 3-mm radius ring around the fovea. We denote them as $v^{para\text{-}irf}$ and $v^{para\text{-}srf}$ (Fig. 8).

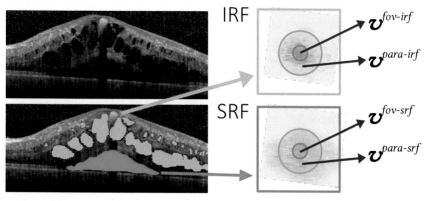

FIG. 8

Illustration of the preprocessing steps. IRF and SRF are automatically segmented and 2D projections are created. IRF and SRF volumes are computed for the central millimeter area around the fovea ($v^{fov\text{-}irf}$, $v^{fov\text{-}srf}$) and for the parafoveal ring in-between the 1- and 3-mm radius ($v^{para\text{-}irf}$, $v^{para\text{-}srf}$).

Regression model

We model the repeated measures of VA as a growth curve MRM [72], depending on a quadratic time function and fluid volumes as covariates. The repeated-measure VA value vector, y, for each subject i with n_i visits is modeled as:

$$
\begin{aligned}
y_i &= \beta_0 + \beta_1 t_i + \beta_2 t_i^2 \\
&\quad + \beta_3 v^{fov\text{-}irf} + \beta_4 v^{fov\text{-}srf} + \beta_5 v^{para\text{-}irf} + \beta_6 v^{para\text{-}srf} \\
&\quad + b_{0i} + b_{1i} t_i + \varepsilon_i,
\end{aligned}
\tag{2}
$$

where t_i contains the time of visits relative to the first visit. The β values are the *fixed effects* that weight the covariates and that are estimated over the whole set. They may be interpreted as population mean effects, similar to linear regression coefficient weights. b_{0i} and b_{1i} are *random effects* that allow for each subject i to deviate from the general mean trajectory in terms of intercept and slope. ε_i accounts for the model error. We assume a multivariate Gaussian normal distribution of the model error, $\varepsilon_i \sim \mathcal{N}(0, \sigma^2 I)$, and the subject-specific random effects, $b_i \sim \mathcal{N}(0, \Psi)$, where Ψ is a 2×2 covariance matrix of the random effects. I is an $n_i \times n_i$ similarity matrix. We assume independence of b_i and ε_i to each other.

By pooling the fixed effects and random effects into matrices X and Z, we obtain the general formulation of repeated measure MRMs as defined by [72]:

$$
y_i = X_i \beta + Z_i b_i + \varepsilon_i, \quad i = 1, \dots, N,
\tag{3}
$$

where X is the $n_i \times p$ design matrix weighted by the $p \times 1$ vector β. Z_i is an $n_i \times q$ matrix weighted by the subject-specific random effect $q \times 1$ vector b_i.

We estimate the weights, β, and the variance structures, σ and Ψ, from a dataset using restricted maximum likelihood (REML) [74]. Estimating the fixed effects, β, from the data allows us to assess the mean VA trajectory (β_0 to β_2), as well as the interpretation of the fluid coefficients (β_3 to β_6), in the sense of how much VA is lost in average by a unit increase of fluid in a retinal region. Note that the random-effect weights, b, do not need to be estimated explicitly if one is interested in the population mean effects, β, only. We obtain confidence intervals by parametric bootstrapping [75] using resampling with replacement 500 times and compute the $\alpha/2$ and $1 - \alpha/2$ quantile of the REML estimates of the resampled data. We use conditional and marginal R^2 as proposed by Nakagawa and Schielzeth [76] and Johnson [77] to determine the quality of fit.

4.2.2 Experiments and results
Dataset
We performed inference on a dataset with 13 monthly follow-up OCT scans and VA measures of patients with central RVO receiving anti-VEGF treatment using a PRN scheme ($n = 193$, 2420 scans, 89 scans removed). IRF and SRF were segmented automatically, and we computed the total fluid volumes $v^{fov\text{-}irf}$, $v^{fov\text{-}srf}$, $v^{para\text{-}irf}$, and $v^{para\text{-}srf}$.

Regression model
We fitted the model on the dataset using the package "lme4" [78] from the statistics software R. The REML estimates of the model parameters are listed in Table 1. The estimates show that an increase in IRF causes a larger drop in VA than SRF and that the impact of fluid in the fovea area is one magnitude higher than of fluid in the parafoveal area. As shown in Fig. 9, individual trajectories obtained by estimating the random effects show that the VA trajectories including the spiky deviations due to recurrent fluid are captured well by the model. The conditional R^2 of 0.887 that measures the variance explained by fixed and random effects also indicates a good model fit. However, the marginal R^2 that considers population-wide fixed effects only (fluid and general trend) is 0.109. These values show that the fluid volumes explain only a rather small part of variance observed in the BCVA trajectories (Fig. 7). The major fraction of vision loss is caused by unobserved factors, which we subsumed in the random effects covering irreversible damage as a subject-specific intercept deviation and reversible nonfluid-based damage as a subject-specific slope deviation.

Table 1 REML estimates of coefficients.

Parameters	Estimate	95% CIs	P value
Intercept	65.81	63.86–67.65	<.0001
t, Time, per day	0.049	0.041–0.058	<.0001
t^2, Time^2, per day	-9.42×10^{-5}	-1.12×10^{-4} to -7.56×10^{-5}	<.0001
$v^{fov\text{-}irf}$, per 1 mm^3	-31.17	-39.70 to -23.32	<.0001
$v^{fov\text{-}srf}$, per 1 mm^3	-17.50	-31.17 to -4.60	.008
$v^{para\text{-}irf}$, per 1 mm^3	-2.87	-4.71 to -0.44	.006
$v^{para\text{-}srf}$, per 1 mm^3	-1.24	-3.37 to 1.05	.241

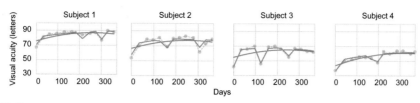

FIG. 9

Conditional model fits of four subjects, with REML estimates of fixed effects and empirical best linear unbiased predictions (BLUPs) [79] of random effect coefficients. *Blue dots* are the measured VA values. *Green line* is the growth curve estimate without fluid coefficients, the *orange* curve includes fluid volume information in the model. The nonfluid model is able to model the general trend. However, temporal drops in BCVA due to recurring fluid are modeled by the fluid model only, resulting in a more accurate model.

However, the model can be extended easily by introducing additional covariates containing further segmentations and measures obtained from OCTs.

5 Discussion and conclusions

Automated detection and quantification of fluid is becoming increasingly important as part of clinical decision support tools for early diagnosis and clinical management of exudative macular diseases. In addition, a precise quantification of *change* of in fluid is required to assess the treatment efficacy and the "stability" of retinal fluid. Finally, the ability to differentiate between the three fluid types, such as IRF, SRF, and PED, would facilitate disease phenotyping and allow finer retinal characterization for personalized prognosis.

Data-driven deep learning methods were shown to achieve the highest performance levels in a supervised setting but at the cost of requiring substantial effort in obtaining annotated datasets. Subsampling studies, which report performance for different training subset sizes, are of great value for answering the question of how many training samples are needed. Rokem et al. [80] did such a study for nAMD classification. They observed that around 20,000 balanced examples may be enough for training from scratch to reach 95% of the maximum classification accuracy. Schlegl et al. [21] did a similar study for fluid segmentation, where they showed that training with 20 densely voxel-wise annotated OCT volumes achieves 95% of the final performance trained with 60 annotated volumes. De Fauw et al. [27] showed an attractive alternative when there are plenty of OCT volumes available, where the same amount of annotation effort is spread over the scans from more patients with sparse annotations (a few B-scans) performed in each one. Another approach used by Venhuizen et al. [25] is to build annotations in a semiautomated way. In that approach, an early version of the segmentation method proposes preliminary results, which are manually corrected and used for retraining, iteratively improving the segmentation performance.

Performance in exudative disease diagnosis and fluid detection has been shown to be very high in a number of papers reviewed in this chapter. Interrater variability was also demonstrated to be small and gold standards for training OCT classification methods are generally available. This is important, as only a very high sensitivity and specificity are clinically accepted for fluid detection. False negatives and false positives bring a high risk of vision loss and an unnecessary increased treatment burden, respectively. By contrast, the segmentation performance level required and most appropriate quantification metric are currently unclear and likely depend on the particular clinical use case. Fluid segmentation methods have shown lower performance, although approaching the interrater variability. The large interrater variability reflects the difficulty of the annotation task and produces a lower quality of the pixel-wise reference standard for training. Thus, weakly supervised and unsupervised efforts are of special importance to support the segmentation methods going beyond the limit of human annotator capabilities.

OCT is a relatively young imaging modality and is still rapidly evolving. In particular, the speed of acquisition is increasing and devices already operate at over 100,000 A-scans per second [81]. Thus, the next generation of OCT is expected to have fewer artifacts and a higher SNR, facilitating the tasks of automated fluid detection and segmentation. Clinically applicable automated fluid analysis is expected to increase the set of readily available quantitative OCT biomarkers, which together will enable personalized and predictive medicine in macular disease.

Acknowledgments

This work was supported by the Christian Doppler Research Association, the Austrian Federal Ministry for Digital and Economic Affairs, and the National Foundation for Research, Technology and Development.

References

[1] U. Schmidt-Erfurth, S.M. Waldstein, A paradigm shift in imaging biomarkers in neovascular age-related macular degeneration, Prog. Retin. Eye. Res. 50 (2016) 1–24.

[2] M. Adhi, J.S. Duker, Optical coherence tomography—current and future applications, Curr. Opin. Ophthalmol. 24 (3) (2013) 213–221.

[3] E.A. Swanson, J.G. Fujimoto, The ecosystem that powered the translation of OCT from fundamental research to clinical and commercial impact, Biomed. Opt. Express 8 (3) (2017) 1638, https://doi.org/10.1364/BOE.8.001638.

[4] U. Schmidt-Erfurth, S. Klimscha, S.M. Waldstein, H. Bogunović, A view of the current and future role of optical coherence tomography in the management of age-related macular degeneration, Eye 31 (1) (2017) 26–44, https://doi.org/10.1038/eye.2016.227.

[5] B. Gerendas, C. Simader, G.G. Deak, S.G. Prager, J. Lammer, S.M. Waldstein, M. Kundi, U. Schmidt-Erfurth, Morphological parameters relevant for visual and anatomic outcomes during anti-VEGF therapy of diabetic macular edema in the RESTORE trial, ARVO, 2014.

[6] G.J. Jaffe, D.F. Martin, C.A. Toth, E. Daniel, M.G. Maguire, G.-S. Ying, J.E. Grunwald, J. Huang, Comparison of Age-Related Macular Degeneration Treatments Trials Research Group, Macular morphology and visual acuity in the comparison of age-related macular degeneration treatments trials, Ophthalmology 120 (9) (2013) 1860–1870, https://doi.org/10.1016/j.ophtha.2013.01.073.

[7] S.M. Waldstein, A.-M. Philip, R. Leitner, C. Simader, G. Langs, B.S. Gerendas, U. Schmidt-Erfurth, Correlation of 3-dimensionally quantified intraretinal and subretinal fluid with visual acuity in neovascular age-related macular degeneration, JAMA Ophthalmol. 134 (2) (2016) 182–190.

[8] G. Querques, F. Coscas, R. Forte, N. Massamba, M. Sterkers, E.H. Souied, Cystoid macular degeneration in exudative age-related macular degeneration, Am. J. Ophthalmol. 152 (1) (2011), https://doi.org/10.1016/j.ajo.2011.01.027. 100–107.e2.

[9] S.A. Zweifel, M. Engelbert, K. Laud, R. Margolis, R.F. Spaide, K.B. Freund, Outer retinal tubulation, Arch. Ophthalmol. 127 (12) (2009) 1596, https://doi.org/10.1001/archophthalmol.2009.326.

[10] S. Klimscha, S.M. Waldstein, T. Schlegl, H. Bogunović, A. Sadeghipour, A.M. Philip, D. Podkowinski, E. Pablik, L. Zhang, M.D. Abramoff, M. Sonka, B.S. Gerendas, U. Schmidt-Erfurth, Spatial correspondence between intraretinal fluid, subretinal fluid, and pigment epithelial detachment in neovascular age-related macular degeneration. Invest. Ophthalmol. Vis. Sci. 58 (10) (2017) 4039–4048, https://doi.org/10.1167/iovs.16-20201.

[11] S.M. Waldstein, C. Simader, G. Staurenghi, N.V. Chong, P. Mitchell, G.J. Jaffe, C. Lu, T.A. Katz, U. Schmidt-Erfurth, Morphology and visual acuity in Aflibercept and Ranibizumab therapy for neovascular age-related macular degeneration in the VIEW trials, Ophthalmology 123 (7) (2016) 1521–1529, https://doi.org/10.1016/j.ophtha.2016.03.037.

[12] J.J. Arnold, C.M. Markey, N.P. Kurstjens, R.H. Guymer, The role of sub-retinal fluid in determining treatment outcomes in patients with neovascular age-related macular degeneration—a phase IV randomised clinical trial with ranibizumab: the FLUID study, BMC Ophthalmol. 16 (1) (2016) 31, https://doi.org/10.1186/s12886-016-0207-3.

[13] M.D. Abramoff, M.K. Garvin, M. Sonka, Retinal imaging and image analysis, IEEE Rev. Biomed. Eng. 3 (2010) 169–208.

[14] A. Krizhevsky, I. Sutskever, G.E. Hinton, ImageNet classification with deep convolutional neural networks, Proc. Adv. Neural Inform. Process. Syst. (NIPS), 2012, pp. 1097–1105.

[15] T. Schlegl, S.M. Waldstein, W.-D. Vogl, U. Schmidt-Erfurth, G. Langs, Predicting semantic descriptions from medical images with convolutional neural networks, in: Lect. Notes Comput. Sci., Proc. Int. Conf. Inform. Process. Med. Imaging (IPMI), vol. 9123, 2015, pp. 437–448.

[16] J. Long, E. Shelhamer, T. Darrell, Fully convolutional networks for semantic segmentation, Proc. IEEE Int. Conf. Comput. Vis. Pattern Recogn. (CVPR), 2015, pp. 3431–3440, https://doi.org/10.1109/CVPR.2015.7298965.

[17] H. Noh, S. Hong, B. Han, Learning deconvolution network for semantic segmentation, in: Proc. IEEE Int. Conf. Comput. Vis. (ICCV), 2015, pp. 1520–1528.

[18] V. Badrinarayanan, A. Kendall, R. Cipolla, SegNet: a deep convolutional encoder-decoder architecture for image segmentation, IEEE Trans. Pattern Anal. Mach. Intell. 39 (12) (2017) 2481–2495, https://doi.org/10.1109/TPAMI.2016.2644615.

[19] F. Milletari, N. Navab, S.-A. Ahmadi, V-Net: fully convolutional neural networks for volumetric medical image segmentation, Fourth International Conference on 3D Vision (3DV), 2016. http://arxiv.org/abs/1606.04797.

[20] O. Ronneberger, P. Fischer, T. Brox, U-Net: convolutional networks for biomedical image segmentation, in: Lect. Notes Comput. Sci., Proc. Int. Conf. Med. Imaging Comput. & Comput. Assist. Interven. (MICCAI), 9351, 2015, pp. 234–241. vol.

[21] T. Schlegl, S.M. Waldstein, H. Bogunovic, F. Endstraßer, A. Sadeghipour, A.-M. Philip, D. Podkowinski, B.S. Gerendas, G. Langs, U. Schmidt-Erfurth, Fully automated detection and quantification of macular fluid in OCT using deep learning, Ophthalmology 125 (4) (2018) 549–558, https://doi.org/10.1016/J.OPHTHA.2017.10.031.

[22] C.S. Lee, A.J. Tyring, N.P. Deruyter, Y. Wu, A. Rokem, A.Y. Lee, Deep-learning based, automated segmentation of macular edema in optical coherence tomography, Biomed. Opt. Express 8 (7) (2017) 3440–3448, https://doi.org/10.1364/BOE.8.003440.

[23] A.G. Roy, S. Conjeti, S.P.K. Karri, D. Sheet, A. Katouzian, C. Wachinger, N. Navab, ReLayNet: retinal layer and fluid segmentation of macular optical coherence tomography using fully convolutional networks, Biomed. Opt. Express 8 (8) (2017) 3627–3642, https://doi.org/10.1364/BOE.8.003627.

[24] S.J. Chiu, M.J. Allingham, P.S. Mettu, S.W. Cousins, J.A. Izatt, S. Farsiu, Kernel regression based segmentation of optical coherence tomography images with diabetic macular edema, Biomed. Opt. Express 6 (4) (2015) 1172–1194.

[25] F.G. Venhuizen, B. van Ginneken, B. Liefers, F. van Asten, V. Schreur, S. Fauser, C. Hoyng, T. Theelen, C.I. Sánchez, Deep learning approach for the detection and quantification of intraretinal cystoid fluid in multivendor optical coherence tomography, Biomed. Opt. Express 9 (4) (2018) 1545.

[26] F.G. Venhuizen, B. van Ginneken, B. Liefers, M.J.J.P. van Grinsven, S. Fauser, C. Hoyng, T. Theelen, C.I. Sánchez, Robust total retina thickness segmentation in optical coherence tomography images using convolutional neural networks, Biomed. Opt. Express 8 (7) (2017) 3292–3316, https://doi.org/10.1364/BOE.8.003292.

[27] J. De Fauw, J.R. Ledsam, B. Romera-Paredes, S. Nikolov, N. Tomasev, S. Blackwell, H. Askham, X. Glorot, B. O'Donoghue, D. Visentin, G. van den Driessche, B. Lakshminarayanan, C. Meyer, F. Mackinder, S. Bouton, K. Ayoub, R. Chopra, D. King, A. Karthikesalingam, C.O. Hughes, R. Raine, J. Hughes, D.A. Sim, C. Egan, A. Tufail, H. Montgomery, D. Hassabis, G. Rees, T. Back, P.T. Khaw, M. Suleyman, J. Cornebise, P.A. Keane, O. Ronneberger, Clinically applicable deep learning for diagnosis and referral in retinal disease, Nat. Med. (2018) 1, https://doi.org/10.1038/s41591-018-0107-6.

[28] Ö. Çiçek, A. Abdulkadir, S.S. Lienkamp, T. Brox, O. Ronneberger, 3D U-Net: learning dense volumetric segmentation from sparse annotation in: Lect. Notes Comput. Sci., Proc. Int. Conf. Med. Imaging Comput. & Comput. Assist. Intervent. (MICCAI), vol. 9901, 2016, pp. 424–432, https://doi.org/10.1007/978-3-319-46723-8_49.

[29] C. Tomasi, R. Manduchi, Bilateral filtering for gray and color images, Proc. IEEE Int. Conf. Comput. Vis. (ICCV), 1998, pp. 839–846.

[30] A. Chambolle, An algorithm for total variation minimization and applications, J. Math. Imaging Vis. 20 (1–2) (2004) 89–97.

[31] M.K. Garvin, M.D. Abramoff, X. Wu, S.R. Russell, T.L. Burns, M. Sonka, Automated 3-D intraretinal layer segmentation of macular spectral-domain optical coherence tomography images, IEEE Trans. Med. Imaging 28 (9) (2009) 1436–1447.

[32] L. Fang, D. Cunefare, C. Wang, R.H. Guymer, S. Li, S. Farsiu, Automatic segmentation of nine retinal layer boundaries in OCT images of non-exudative AMD patients using

deep learning and graph search, Biomed. Opt. Express 8 (5) (2017) 2732–2744, https://doi.org/10.1364/BOE.8.002732.

[33] X. Chen, M. Niemeijer, L. Zhang, K. Lee, M.D. Abramoff, M. Sonka, Three-dimensional segmentation of fluid-associated abnormalities in retinal OCT: probability constrained graph-search-graph-cut, IEEE Trans. Med. Imaging 31 (8) (2012) 1521–1531.

[34] X. Xu, K. Lee, L. Zhang, M. Sonka, M.D. Abramoff, Stratified sampling Voxel classification for segmentation of intraretinal and subretinal fluid in longitudinal clinical OCT data, IEEE Trans. Med. Imaging 34 (7) (2015) 1616–1623.

[35] J. Wang, M. Zhang, A.D. Pechauer, L. Liu, T.S. Hwang, D.J. Wilson, D. Li, Y. Jia, Automated volumetric segmentation of retinal fluid on optical coherence tomography, Biomed. Opt. Express 7 (4) (2016) 1577–1589, https://doi.org/10.1364/BOE.7.001577.

[36] J. Novosel, K.A. Vermeer, J.H. de Jong, Z. Wang, L.J. van Vliet, Joint segmentation of retinal layers and focal lesions in 3-D OCT data of topologically disrupted retinas, IEEE Trans. Med. Imaging 36 (6) (2017) 1276–1286, https://doi.org/10.1109/TMI.2017.2666045.

[37] A. Montuoro, S.M. Waldstein, B.S. Gerendas, U. Schmidt-Erfurth, Joint retinal layer and fluid segmentation in OCT scans of eyes with severe macular edema using unsupervised representation and auto-context, Biomed. Opt. Express 8 (3) (2017) 182–190, https://doi.org/10.1364/BOE.8.001874.

[38] Z. Tu, X. Bai, Auto-context and its application to high-level vision tasks and 3D brain image segmentation, IEEE Trans. Pattern Anal. Mach. Intell. 32 (10) (2010) 1744–1757.

[39] F. Shi, X. Chen, H. Zhao, W. Zhu, D. Xiang, E. Gao, M. Sonka, H. Chen, Automated 3-D retinal layer segmentation of macular optical coherence tomography images with serous pigment epithelial detachments, IEEE Trans. Med. Imaging 34 (2) (2015) 441–452.

[40] Z. Sun, H. Chen, F. Shi, L. Wang, W. Zhu, D. Xiang, C. Yan, L. Li, X. Chen, An automated framework for 3D serous pigment epithelium detachment segmentation in SD-OCT images, Sci. Rep. 6 (2016), https://doi.org/10.1038/srep21739.

[41] M. Wu, W. Fan, Q. Chen, Z. Du, X. Li, S. Yuan, H. Park, Three-dimensional continuous max flow optimization-based serous retinal detachment segmentation in SD-OCT for central serous chorioretinopathy, Biomed. Opt. Express 8 (9) (2017) 4257, https://doi.org/10.1364/BOE.8.004257.

[42] M. Wu, Q. Chen, X. He, P. Li, W. Fan, S. Yuan, H. Park, Automatic subretinal fluid segmentation of retinal SD-OCT images with neurosensory retinal detachment guided by enface fundus imaging, IEEE Trans. Biomed. Eng. 65 (1) (2018) 87–95.

[43] G. Quellec, K. Lee, M. Dolejsi, M.K. Garvin, M.D. Abramoff, M. Sonka, Three-dimensional analysis of retinal layer texture: identification of fluid-filled regions in SD-OCT of the macula, IEEE Trans. Med. Imaging 29 (6) (2010) 1321–1330.

[44] D.S. Kermany, M. Goldbaum, W. Cai, C.C.S. Valentim, H. Liang, S.L. Baxter, A. McKeown, G. Yang, X. Wu, F. Yan, J. Dong, M.K. Prasadha, J. Pei, M.Y.L. Ting, J. Zhu, C. Li, S. Hewett, J. Dong, I. Ziyar, A. Shi, R. Zhang, L. Zheng, R. Hou, W. Shi, X. Fu, Y. Duan, V.A.N. Huu, C. Wen, E.D. Zhang, C.L. Zhang, O. Li, X. Wang, M.A. Singer, X. Sun, J. Xu, A. Tafreshi, M.A. Lewis, H. Xia, K. Zhang, Identifying medical diagnoses and treatable diseases by image-based deep learning, Cell 172 (5) (2018). 1122–1131.e9.

[45] C.S. Lee, D.M. Baughman, A.Y. Lee, Deep learning is effective for classifying normal versus age-related macular degeneration OCT images, Ophthalmol. Retina 1 (4) (2017) 322–327, https://doi.org/10.1016/J.ORET.2016.12.009.

[46] P.L. Vidal, J. de Moura, J. Novo, M.G. Penedo, M. Ortega, Intraretinal fluid identification via enhanced maps using optical coherence tomography images, Biomed. Opt. Express 9 (10) (2018) 4730–4754, https://doi.org/10.1364/BOE.9.004730.

[47] P. Seeböck, S.M. Waldstein, S. Klimscha, H. Bogunovic, T. Schlegl, B.S. Gerendas, R. Donner, U. Schmidt-Erfurth, G. Langs, Unsupervised identification of disease marker candidates in retinal OCT imaging data, IEEE Trans. Med. Imaging 38 (4) (2019) 1037–1047, https://doi.org/10.1109/TMI.2018.2877080.

[48] P. Vincent, H. Larochelle, Y. Bengio, P.-A. Manzagol, Extracting and composing robust features with denoising autoencoders, Proceedings of the 25th International Conference on Machine learning (ICML), 2008, pp. 1096–1103, https://doi.org/10.1145/1390156.1390294.

[49] T. Schlegl, P. Seeböck, S.M. Waldstein, U. Schmidt-Erfurth, G. Langs, Unsupervised anomaly detection with generative adversarial networks to guide marker discovery, Proc. Int. Conf. Inform. Process. Med. Imaging (IPMI), vol. 10265, LNCS, Springer, Cham, 2017, pp. 146–147.

[50] I.J. Goodfellow, J. Pouget-Abadie, M. Mirza, B. Xu, D. Warde-Farley, S. Ozair, A. Courville, Y. Bengio, Generative adversarial networks, Proc. Adv. Neural Inform. Process. Syst. (NIPS), 2014.

[51] J. Wu, A.-M. Philip, D. Podkowinski, B.S. Gerendas, G. Langs, C. Simader, S.M. Waldstein, U. Schmidt-Erfurth, Multivendor spectral-domain optical coherence tomography dataset, observer annotation performance evaluation, and standardized evaluation framework for intraretinal cystoid fluid segmentation, J. Ophthalmol. (2016), https://doi.org/10.1155/2016/3898750.

[52] H. Bogunović, F. Venhuizen, S. Klimscha, S. Apostolopoulos, A. Bab-Hadiashar, U. Bagci, M.F. Beg, L. Bekalo, Q. Chen, C. Ciller, K. Gopinath, A.K. Gostar, K. Jeon, Z. Ji, S.H. Kang, D.D. Koozekanani, D. Lu, D. Morley, K.K. Parhi, H.S. Park, A. Rashno, M. Sarunic, S. Shaikh, J. Sivaswamy, R. Tennakoon, S. Yadav, S.D. Zanet, S.M. Waldstein, B.S. Gerendas, C. Klaver, C.I. Sánchez, U. Schmidt-Erfurth, RETOUCH—the retinal OCT fluid detection and segmentation benchmark and challenge, IEEE Trans. Med. Imaging 38 (8) (2019) 1858–1874, https://doi.org/10.1109/TMI.2019.2901398.

[53] U. Chakravarthy, D. Goldenberg, G. Young, M. Havilio, O. Rafaeli, G. Benyamini, A. Loewenstein, Automated identification of lesion activity in neovascular age-related macular degeneration, Ophthalmology 123 (8) (2016) 1731–1736.

[54] O. Russakovsky, J. Deng, H. Su, J. Krause, S. Satheesh, S. Ma, Z. Huang, A. Karpathy, A. Khosla, M. Bernstein, A.C. Berg, L. Fei-Fei, ImageNet large scale visual recognition challenge, Int. J. Comput. Vis. 115 (3) (2015) 211–252, https://doi.org/10.1007/s11263-015-0816-y.

[55] C. Szegedy, V. Vanhoucke, S. Ioffe, J. Shlens, Z. Wojna, Rethinking the inception architecture for computer vision, Proc. IEEE Int. Conf. Comput. Vis. Pattern Recogn. (CVPR), 2016, pp. 2818–2826, https://doi.org/10.1109/CVPR.2016.308.

[56] M. Treder, J.L. Lauermann, N. Eter, Automated detection of exudative age-related macular degeneration in spectral domain optical coherence tomography using deep learning, Graefe's Arch. Clin. Exp. Ophthalmol. 256 (2) (2018) 259–265, https://doi.org/10.1007/s00417-017-3850-3.

[57] K. Simonyan, A. Zisserman, Very deep convolutional networks for large-scale image recognition, http://arxiv.org/abs/1409.1556, 2014.

[58] P. Prahs, V. Radeck, C. Mayer, Y. Cvetkov, N. Cvetkova, H. Helbig, D. Märker, OCT-based deep learning algorithm for the evaluation of treatment indication with anti-vascular

endothelial growth factor medications, Graefe's Arch. Clin. Exp. Ophthalmol. 256 (1) (2018) 91–98, https://doi.org/10.1007/s00417-017-3839-y.

[59] C. Szegedy, W. Liu, Y. Jia, P. Sermanet, S. Reed, D. Anguelov, D. Erhan, V. Vanhoucke, A. Rabinovich, Going deeper with convolutions, Proc. IEEE Int. Conf. Comput. Vis. Pattern Recogn. (CVPR), IEEE, 2015, pp. 1–9, https://doi.org/10.1109/CVPR.2015.7298594.

[60] M.D. Zeiler, R. Fergus, Visualizing and understanding convolutional networks, Proc. Eur. Conf. Comput. Vis. (ECCV), 2014, pp. 818–833.

[61] Y.-Y. Liu, M. Chen, H. Ishikawa, G. Wollstein, J.S. Schuman, J.M. Rehg, Automated macular pathology diagnosis in retinal OCT images using multi-scale spatial pyramid and local binary patterns in texture and shape encoding, Med. Image Anal. 15 (5) (2011) 748–759, https://doi.org/10.1016/j.media.2011.06.005.

[62] P.P. Srinivasan, L.A. Kim, P.S. Mettu, S.W. Cousins, G.M. Comer, J.A. Izatt, S. Farsiu, Fully automated detection of diabetic macular edema and dry age-related macular degeneration from optical coherence tomography images, Biomed. Opt. Express 5 (10) (2014) 3568, https://doi.org/10.1364/BOE.5.003568.

[63] F.G. Venhuizen, B. van Ginneken, F. van Asten, M.J.J.P. van Grinsven, S. Fauser, C.B. Hoyng, T. Theelen, C.I. Sánchez, Automated staging of age-related macular degeneration using optical coherence tomography. Invest. Ophthalmol. Vis. Sci. 58 (4) (2017) 2318–2328, https://doi.org/10.1167/iovs.16-20541.

[64] S. Farsiu, Dataset for classification of ophthalmic SD-OCT images of normal, diabetic macular edema, and dry age-related macular degeneration subjects, 2014. http://people.duke.edu/ sf59/Srinivasan_BOE_2014_dataset.htm. Accessed 10 November 2018.

[65] D. Kermany, K. Zhang, M. Goldbaum, Large dataset of labeled optical coherence tomography (OCT) and chest X-ray images. 2018. https://doi.org/10.17632/rscbjbr9sj.3. Available from: https://data.mendeley.com/datasets/rscbjbr9sj/3, (Accessed November 10, 2018).

[66] U. Schmidt-Erfurth, H. Bogunovic, A. Sadeghipour, T. Schlegl, G. Langs, B.S. Gerendas, A. Osborne, S.M. Waldstein, Machine learning to analyze the prognostic value of current imaging biomarkers in neovascular age-related macular degeneration, Ophthalmol. Retina 2 (1) (2018) 24–30, https://doi.org/10.1016/j.oret.2017.03.015.

[67] B.S. Gerendas, H. Bogunovic, A. Sadeghipour, T. Schlegl, G. Langs, S.M. Waldstein, U. Schmidt-Erfurth, Computational image analysis for prognosis determination in DME, Vis. Res. 139 (2017) 204–210, https://doi.org/10.1016/j.visres.2017.03.008.

[68] W.-D. Vogl, S.M. Waldstein, B.S. Gerendas, T. Schlegl, G. Langs, U. Schmidt-Erfurth, Analyzing and predicting visual acuity outcomes of anti-VEGF therapy by a longitudinal mixed effects model of imaging and clinical data, Invest. Ophthalmol. Vis. Sci. 58 (10) (2017) 4173, https://doi.org/10.1167/iovs.17-21878.

[69] H. Bogunovic, S.M. Waldstein, T. Schlegl, G. Langs, A. Sadeghipour, X. Liu, B.S. Gerendas, A. Osborne, U. Schmidt-Erfurth, Prediction of anti-VEGF treatment requirements in neovascular AMD using a machine learning approach. Invest. Ophthalmol. Vis. Sci. 58 (7) (2017) 3240–3248, https://doi.org/10.1167/iovs.16-21053.

[70] F.L. Ferris, A. Kassoff, G.H. Bresnick, I. Bailey, New visual acuity charts for clinical research, Am. J. Ophthalmol. 94 (1) (1982) 91–96.

[71] U. Schmidt-Erfurth, S.M. Waldstein, G.G. Deak, M. Kundi, C. Simader, Pigment epithelial detachment followed by retinal cystoid degeneration leads to vision loss in treatment of neovascular age-related macular degeneration, Ophthalmology 122 (4) (2015) 822–832, https://doi.org/10.1016/j.ophtha.2014.11.017.

[72] N.M. Laird, J.H. Ware, Random-effects models for longitudinal data, Biometrics 38 (1982) 963–974.

[73] W.-D. Vogl, S.M. Waldstein, B.S. Gerendas, U. Schmidt-Erfurth, G. Langs, Predicting macular edema recurrence from spatio-temporal signatures in optical coherence tomography images, IEEE Trans. Med. Imaging 36 (9) (2017) 1773–1783, https://doi. org/10.1109/TMI.2017.2700213.

[74] G. Verbeke, G. Molenberghs, Linear Mixed Models for Longitudinal Data, Springer-Verlag, New York, 2009.

[75] B. Efron, R.J. Tibshirani, An Introduction to the Bootstrap, CRC Press, Boca Raton, FL, 1994.

[76] S. Nakagawa, H. Schielzeth, A general and simple method for obtaining R^2 from generalized linear mixed-effects models, Methods Ecol. Evol. 4 (2) (2013) 133–142.

[77] P.C.D. Johnson, Extension of Nakagawa & Schielzeth's R2GLMM to random slopes models, Methods Ecol. Evol. 5 (9) (2014) 944–946.

[78] D. Bates, M. Mächler, B. Bolker, S. Walker, Fitting linear mixed-effects models using Lme4, J. Stat. Softw. 67 (1) (2015) 1–48, https://doi.org/10.18637/jss.v067.i01.

[79] G.K. Robinson, That BLUP is a good thing: the estimation of random effects, Stat. Sci. 6 (1991) 15–32.

[80] A. Rokem, Y. Wu, A.Y. Lee, Assessment of the need for separate test set and number of medical images necessary for deep learning: a sub-sampling study, https://doi. org/10.1101/196659, 2017.

[81] J. Fujimoto, E. Swanson, The development, commercialization, and impact of optical coherence tomography, Invest. Ophthalmol. Vis. Sci. 57 (9) (2016), https://doi.org/10.1167/ iovs.16-19963.

Retinal biomarkers and cardiovascular disease: A clinical perspective

15

Carol Yim-lui Cheung[a], Posey Po-yin Wong[a], Tien Yin Wong[b]

[a]Department of Ophthalmology and Visual Sciences, The Chinese University of Hong Kong, Shatin, Hong Kong
[b]Singapore Eye Research Institute, Singapore National Eye Center, Singapore, Singapore

1 Introduction

Cardiovascular disease (CVD), comprising mainly coronary heart disease and stroke, remains a major cause of morbidity, disability and mortality worldwide [1, 2]. Current guidelines in the primary prevention of CVD recommend approaches to classify individuals as high, intermediate, or low risk using CVD risk prediction models based on the traditional risk factors such as age, gender, race, hypertension, diabetes, dyslipidemia and history of cigarette smoking. However, the risk prediction equations derived from cohorts established in the last century (e.g., Framingham risk score model, Pooled Cohort Equations) may not be useful in contemporary populations, resulting in undertreatment or overtreatment of CVD risk factors [3–6]. Newer cardiovascular biomarkers (e.g., C-reactive protein) have only provided modest improvements in predictive accuracy [3]. Therefore, new biomarkers that can improve risk prediction and stratification are needed.

It is recognized that small vessel or microvascular pathology play a major role in processes leading to the development of CVD events and its risk factors [7–9]. However, the microcirculation has been difficult to access, so robust microvascular biomarkers have yet to be developed. The retinal vasculature, which is noninvasively accessible, is a unique biological model to study microvascular abnormalities and pathology associated with CVD [10–12]. Numerous large population-based studies have provided evidence that retinal vascular changes are associated with CVD events (e.g., stroke, heart disease and CVD mortality) independent of traditional risk factors. These studies support a concept that changes seen in the retinal vasculature (e.g., retinal arteriolar narrowing, arterio-venous nicking) likely reflect similar changes in the systemic peripheral, cerebral and coronary microcirculation (e.g., vasoconstriction, intimal thickening). Thus, studying retinal vascular changes may provide additional insights into the structure and function of the systemic microcirculation that are important in the development of CVD. Furthermore, retinal vascular

Computational Retinal Image Analysis. https://doi.org/10.1016/B978-0-08-102816-2.00016-2

changes may be biomarkers of CVD and may thus be potentially useful to improve CVD risk prediction and stratification.

This chapter aims to review our current understanding of the relationship between retinal vascular changes and CVD in a clinical perspective.

2 The concept of retinal vascular imaging

As the retina and other end organs (e.g., brain, heart) share similar anatomical features and physiological properties (e.g., nonanastomotic end-arteries, blood-brain and blood-retina barrier), the retinal vessels, measuring 100–300 µm in size, offer a unique and easily accessible "window" to study the health and disease of the human microcirculation [11]. While this concept is well known [13], it is only with the introduction of digital retinal photography in the last two decades that retinal vascular changes could be easily imaged, objectively measured and regularly monitored in a precise manner.

Retinal vascular changes can be classified as qualitative and quantitative [14]. Panel 1 summaries the glossary of retinal vascular changes measured from retinal photographs. Qualitative retinal vascular changes can be further classified into classic retinopathy signs (usually considered to be related to hypertension or diabetes) and retinal arteriolar wall signs (traditionally thought to be more related to atherosclerosis). Retinopathy signs include microaneurysm, retinal hemorrhages, hard exudates and cotton wool spots while retinal arteriolar wall signs include focal arteriolar narrowing, arteriovenous nicking and opacification of arteriolar wall [15, 16]. Fig. 1 shows examples of qualitative retinopathy and Fig. 2 shows examples of retinal arteriolar wall signs.

With advancements in image processing technologies, quantitative retinal vasculature analysis from digital retinal photographs can be further measured with computer software and standardized photographic protocols. Earlier software such as the Retinal Analysis (RA; University of Wisconsin, Madison, WI) and Integrative Vessel Analysis (IVAN; University of Wisconsin, Madison; WI) were widely used for measuring retinal arteriolar caliber and retinal venular caliber from digital retinal photographs in numerous large population-based studies [17, 18]. Standardized protocols including measuring retinal vessels coursing through a specified area of a standardized grid (0.5–1.0 disc diameter from the disc margin), and converting individual vessels into summary variables. The revised Knudtson-Parr-Hubbard formula is widely used to summarize the retinal arteriolar and venular calibers of the large six arterioles and venules as central retinal artery equivalent (CRAE) and central retinal vein equivalent (CRVE) respectively [19].

Subsequent research has focused on assessment of other retinal vasculature including branching and geometry. It is known that the branching pattern of vascular networks develops to minimize the energy required to maintain efficient blood flow, based on Murray's principle [14, 20–22]. Deviations or alterations from optimal architecture are speculated to result in impaired microcirculatory transport, reduced

Panel 1 Glossary of retinal vascular changes measured from retinal photographs and used in studying CVD.

	Parameters measured from retinal imaging	Descriptions of the parameters
Retinopathy signs	Hemorrhages	Red deposits with dot, blot or flame shaped caused by exudation of blood
	Exudates	White or yellow deposits with distinct margin caused by exudation of lipids
	Cotton-wool spots	Fluffy white lesions caused by ischemia of nerve fiber layer
Retinal arteriolar wall signs	Focal arteriolar narrowing (FAN)	Focal narrowing or constriction of retinal arterioles
	Arteriovenous nicking/nipping (AVN)	Compression of the venules by arterioles at arteriovenous crossing
	Opacification of arteriolar wall (OAW)	Silver or copper wiring of retinal arterioles
Quantitative retinal vascular parameters	Central retinal artery equivalent (CRAE)	A summary index reflecting the average width of retinal arterioles
	Central retinal venule equivalent (CRVE)	A summary index reflecting the average width of retinal venules
	Fractal dimension	A measure of a fractal structure, that exhibits the property of self-similarity, characterizing the distribution of the branching retinal vasculature
	Tortuosity	A measure of the straightness/curliness of the retinal vessels
	Branching angle	An angle measure defined as the first angle subtended between two daughter vessels at each vascular bifurcation
	Branching coefficient	A measure of the ratio of the branching vessel widths to trunk vessel width
	Length-diameter-ratio	A measure of the ratio of the length between 2 branching points to trunk vessel width

efficiency and thereby, a greater risk of vascular damage, providing additional CVD risk information to enable better predictive ability of cardiovascular outcomes. Newer retinal branching geometric parameters such as tortuosity, fractal dimension, branching angles and vascular length-to-diameter ratio were thus subsequently defined to quantify the optimal state of retinal vasculature in recent computer software systems (e.g., SIVA (Singapore I Vessel Assessment) software and VAMPIRE software

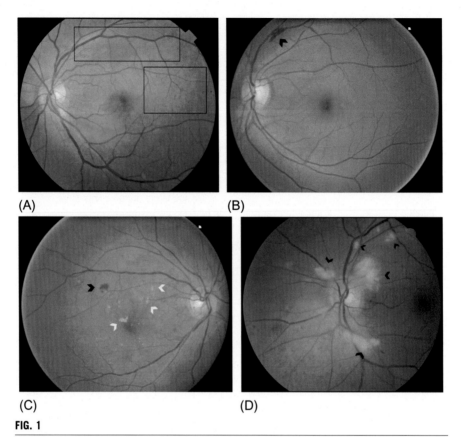

FIG. 1

Examples of retinopathy. Panel A shows microaneurysms *(black box)*. Panel B shows a flame shaped retinal hemorrhage *(black arrow)*. Panel C shows a blot shaped retinal hemorrhage *(black arrow)* and hard exudates *(white arrows)*. Panel D shows cotton wool spots (black arrows).

(Vascular Assessment and Measurement Platform for Images of the REtina)) measured from a wider measured area. Fig. 3 shows the measurement of retinal vascular caliber and retinal geometric branching parameters quantitatively from retinal photograph using SIVA software.

Table 1 summaries the general population-based studies of the association between retinal vascular changes with CVD.

3 Retinal vascular changes and heart disease

There is evidence that retinal vascular changes are predictive of clinical coronary artery disease events [24, 25, 43–45], and retinal vascular changes are also associated with prevalent heart failure [46] and multiple markers of subclinical atherosclerotic

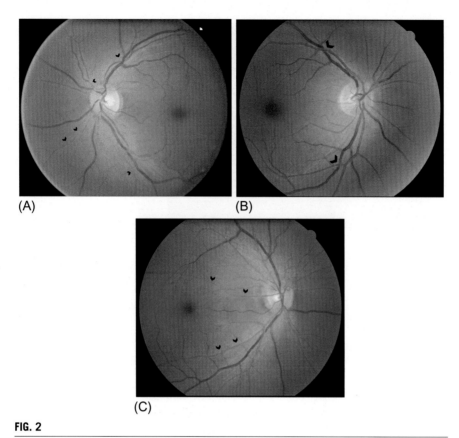

(A)   (B)

(C)

FIG. 2

Examples of retinal arteriolar wall signs. Panel A focal narrowing *(black arrows)*. Panel B shows arteriovenous nicking *(black arrows)*. Panel C shows opacification (silver or copper wiring) of arteriolar wall *(black arrows)*.

diseases, including coronary artery calcification [47], aortic stiffness [48], left ventricular hypertrophy [49] and carotid intima-media thickness [50]. A meta-analysis of six population-based studies provide robust evidence to confirm that changes in retinal vascular caliber (wider venules and narrower arterioles) are associated with an increased risk of coronary artery disease in women but not in men [51]. The links between retinal vascular branching geometry and heart disease have been reported by the Australian Heart Eye Study recently, a cross-sectional study surveyed 1680 participants presenting to a tertiary referral hospital for the evaluation of potential coronary artery disease by coronary angiography. They found that straighter retinal arterioles and venules (lower vascular curvature) are associated with coronary artery disease extent and severity as measured from coronary angiography quantitatively using Extent and Gensini scores [52]. They also observed that lower fractal dimension, indicating a sparser retinal microvascular network, is associated with greater

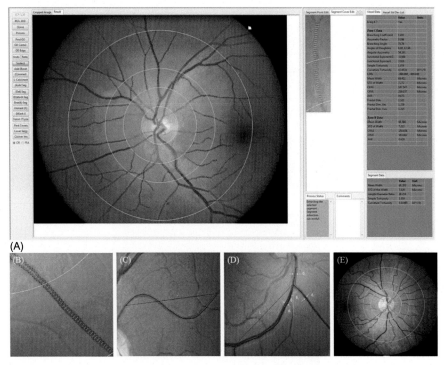

FIG. 3

Retinal photographs assessed quantitatively with SIVA software (A). Arterioles are in red and venules are in blue. The measured area is standardized and defined as the region 0.5–2.0 disc diameters away from the disc margin. SIVA measures a spectrum of retinal vascular parameters included (B) caliber; (C) tortuosity; (D) bifurcation; and (E) fractal dimension.

likelihood of atrial fibrillation [53]. These studies support the integral role of microvascular disease in the pathogenesis of heart disease.

4 Retinal vascular changes and stroke

4.1 Clinical stroke

Numerous large population-based studies have reported the strong link between retinal vascular changes and clinical stroke, both in cross-sectional and prospective studies. The Atherosclerosis Risk in Communities (ARIC) study firstly showed that persons with retinal vascular changes at baseline were more likely to develop an incident clinical stroke [23]. The ARIC study further demonstrated that persons who had both cerebral MRI lesions and retinopathy signs were at substantially higher risk of incident clinical stroke than those without either abnormality [54]. Subsequent

Table 1 General population-based studies of the association between retinal vascular changes with CVD.

Study	Ethnicity	Retinal vascular caliber changes	Outcomes	References
Atherosclerosis Risk in Communities Study (ARIC), USA	White, Black	Arteriolar narrowing	Incident clinical stroke	[23]
		Arteriolar narrowing	Incident coronary heart disease (in women only)	[24]
		Retinopathy	Incident congestive heart failure	[25]
		Arteriolar narrowing, venular widening and arteriolar walls signs	Incident lacunar stroke	[26]
		Arteriolar narrowing and venular widening	Long-term incident ischemic stroke and coronary heart disease (in women only)	[27]
Beaver Dam Eye Study (BDES), USA	White	Arteriolar narrowing	Cardiovascular mortality	[28]
		Arteriolar narrowing and venular widening	Coronary heart disease and stroke mortality	[29]
		Decreased retinal arteriolar tortuosity, increased arteriolar length:diameter ratio and impaired bifurcation optimality	Coronary heart disease and stroke mortality	[30]
Blue Mountains Eye Study (BMES), Australia	White	Arteriolar narrowing and venular widening	Coronary heart disease and stroke mortality	[29]
		Retinopathy	Coronary heart disease mortality	[31]
		Retinopathy	Incident stroke and stroke mortality	[32]
Cardiovascular Health Study (CHS), USA	White, Black	Arteriolar narrowing and venular widening	Incident coronary heart disease	[33]
		Venular widening	Incident stroke	[33]

(Continued)

Table 1 General population-based studies of the association between retinal vascular changes with CVD.—cont'd

Study	Ethnicity	Retinal vascular caliber changes	Outcomes	References
European Prospective Investigation into Cancer (EPIC) study-Norfolk Eye Study, UK	British	Increased arteriolar tortuosity	Prevalent stroke	[34]
Multi-Ethnic Study of Atherosclerosis (MESA), US	White, Chinese, Black, and Hispanic	Arteriolar narrowing, retinopathy	Incident stroke and stroke mortality	[35]
National Health and Nutrition Examination Survey (NHANES), US	Non-Hispanic white, non-Hispanic black, Mexican American	Retinopathy	Cardiovascular mortality (in persons with chronic kidney disease)	[36]
Rotterdam Study, Netherlands	White	Venular widening	Incident stroke	[37, 38]
Singapore Malay Eye Study (SiMES), Singapore	Malay	Venular widening	Incident stroke	[39]
		Arteriolar narrowing & retinopathy	Incident CVD in diabetics	[40]
		Diabetic retinopathy	CVD mortality	[41]
Singapore Prospective Study Program (SP2), Singapore	Chinese, Indian, Malay	Venular widening	Incident CVD in diabetics	[40]
UK-based triethnic population-based cohort, UK	Europeans, South Asians, and African Caribbeans	Retinopathy, arteriolar narrowing, fewer symmetrical arteriolar bifurcations, higher arteriolar optimality deviation, and higher venular tortuosity	Prevalent strokes/infarcts and white matter hyperintensities	[42]

studies consistently reported that persons with retinal vascular changes at baseline were more likely to develop stroke, even after controlling for traditional risk factors [26, 32, 35, 37, 39].

With respect to retinal vascular caliber, several studies consistently reported that retinal venular widening was related to an increased risk of stroke and stroke mortality [26, 29, 35, 37–39, 55], which was confirmed by a meta-analysis including data from 20,798 participants [56]. Alternations in the new retinal geometric branching parameters (e.g., decreased fractal dimension and increased tortuosity) have also been linked to stroke and stroke mortality [30, 34, 39, 42, 57–60]. The addition of retinal vascular imaging to existing models of stroke can improve stroke risk stratification, beyond that of established risk factors [39, 56].

Further studies have demonstrated that retinal vascular changes vary according to different stroke subtypes [57, 58, 61–66]. For example, retinal arteriolar narrowing was associated with lacunar stroke [59, 61], while retinal hemorrhages were linked with cerebral hemorrhages [64]. These studies suggest that retinal vascular changes reflect specific cerebral microvasculopathy and may allow more accurate sub-typing of stroke, or even differentiate stroke from other causes of focal neurologic deficits. Interestingly, a study showed that retinal vascular changes were similarly associated with both large-artery stroke and lacunar infarcts, suggesting that structural changes in retinal vessels not only reflect small vessel pathology, but may also result from downstream effects of large artery pathology in the retinal and cerebral circulations [59]. In addition, in a recent study, Zhuo et al. also found that retinal vascular changes are different between patients with recurrent stroke and with noncurrent stroke (e.g., patients with recurrent stroke are likely to have wider retinal vascular caliber and narrower branching angle), suggesting that retinal vasculature may provide information for recurrent stroke risk estimation [67].

4.2 Subclinical stroke

Several clinic-based and population-based studies have also shown associations between retinal vascular changes and subclinical cerebral changes. Lacunar infarcts, have been linked to different retinal vascular changes including retinopathy, retinal arteriolar wall signs, retinal arteriolar narrowing, retinal venular widening and increased retinal vascular fractal dimension, both in population-based studies [68–71] and in patients with stroke [57, 61, 72]. Numerous cross-sectional and prospective studies have also shown that white matter lesion (WML) and WML progression were associated with retinopathy, retinal arteriolar wall signs, changes in retinal vascular caliber (retinal arteriolar narrowing and venular widening), and suboptimal retinal bifurcation [42, 54, 58, 62, 65, 68, 69, 73–76]. For example, prospective data from the ARIC study showed that retinal vascular changes are associated with incident cerebral atrophy, incident cerebral infarct, incident lacunar infarct and white matter lesion incidence and progression, independent of traditional risk factors [69, 77]. Cerebral microbleeds have been suggested as another manifestation or marker of cerebral small vessel disease associated with stroke [78]. Hilal et al. have also reported that decreased retinal arteriolar fractal dimension and increased arteriolar tortuosity were associated with cerebral microbleeds, independent of vascular risk factors and other cerebral markers such as WML and lacunes, suggesting that these retinal vascular measures may be an early manifestation of cerebral small vessel disease [79]. These data provide strong evidence that retinal vascular changes mirror pre-clinical structural changes in the cerebral microcirculation, and support the hypothesis that retinal vascular changes provide insights into the microvascular structure and function in the cerebral microcirculation.

5 Retinal vascular changes and CVD mortality

Retinal vascular changes have also been shown to correlate with increased risk of CVD mortality, coronary heart disease mortality and stroke mortality, in both clinic-based and population-based studies [28–30, 41, 80, 81]. For example, in the Blue Mountains Eye Study, persons with retinopathy signs were more likely to die from coronary heart disease than persons without this sign, with an equivalent risk similar to that of diabetes [31]. In the Singapore Malay Eye Study, persons with diabetic retinopathy are associated with CVD mortality [41]. In the Hoorn study, retinopathy is associated with CVD mortality in both diabetic and nondiabetic subjects [82]. In the National Health and Nutrition Examination Survey (NHANES), persons with presence of both retinopathy and chronic kidney disease is associated with a more than 2-fold increase in CVD mortality, compared with individuals with neither retinopathy nor chronic kidney disease [36]. Also, in the Ibaraki Prefectural Health Study with 87,890 individuals, both hypertensive and non-hypertensive subjects with mild retinopathy signs were more likely to die from CVD mortality, independent of traditional cardiovascular risk factors [83].

6 Clinical implications

The above studies support the concept that common pathophysiologic processes may underlie both micro- and macrovascular disease and changes in retinal microvasculature may reflect subclinical pathological changes prior to the development of CVD. Exact mechanisms underlying the above associations are largely unknown, but potential explanations include microvascular damage associated with aging, hypertension, atherosclerosis, and other vascular and endothelial changes that might be present in the retina and other vascular beds such as the brain, and heart. The presence of retinal vascular changes may thus convey additional prognostic information than other risk measures of CVD. There are several clinical implications of retinal vascular imaging for CVD potentially.

6.1 Retinal vascular imaging as a tool to stratify CVD

Consistent large epidemiological studies demonstrated the relationship between retinal vascular changes and risk of CVD (as mentioned above). However, whether retinal assessment can provide incremental benefit on CVD prediction or stratification, in addition to traditional risk factors, has not been well-established. Recent studies tried to address this gap by performing incremental usefulness analysis (calibration, discrimination and reclassification) of adding retinal vascular parameters for CVD prediction. For example, recent data from the ARIC study with an average 16-year follow-up of 10,470 asymptomatic adults show that narrower retinal arterioles and wider venules confer a greater risk of CVD events in women and provide incremental value beyond the Pooled Cohort Equations risk score variables [27]. Furthermore, a recent prospective diabetic cohort study also provided evidence to show that the addition of retinal vascular changes add significant incremental value in discriminating and reclassifying CVD risk, beyond established risk factors and biochemical markers of high-sensitivity C-reactive protein and estimated glomerular filtration rate [40]. These data further validate the clinical utility of retinal vascular imaging for CVD risk prediction and risk stratification. Additional work is needed to optimize the risk-prediction algorithm, to determine how it may influence in clinical decision making, to identify the most appropriate subgroup of patients, and to estimate the cost-effectiveness and acceptability to patients in different settings for translating retinal vascular imaging as a clinical tool of daily routine.

6.2 Retinal imaging for clinical trials and outcome monitoring for CVD

Treatment of hypertension is associated with important reductions in risk of CVD. Studies have demonstrated regression of retinal vascular changes in response to blood pressure reduction and that regression are different in response to different antihypertensive regimens (e.g., ACE inhibitors appear to have a more favorable effect on the retinal vasculature) [84–87]. Furthermore, in the ENVIS-ion study, which aims to determine the effectiveness of low-dose aspirin in reducing the development of white-matter lesion and silent brain infraction, is also validating retinal vascular changes as potential treatment outcomes [88]. Changes in retinal vasculature, may act as therapeutic targets and capable to reflect the effectiveness of therapeutic response to medical intervention. Nevertheless, data is still largely lacking. There needs to be more studies to demonstrate regression of retinal vascular changes via interventions. Further prospective controlled trials are also required to clarify whether specific reduction of retinal vascular damage also reduces the morbidity and mortality associated with CVD.

7 New advances in retinal vascular imaging

The area of retinal vascular imaging has been continuing to develop rapidly due to the transparent nature of the eye which allows for an easy optical assessment. The recent new advances in retinal vascular imaging offer a great opportunity to further utilize the state-of-the-art technologies to explore retinal biomarkers for assessing CVD.

7.1 Retinal imaging with artificial intelligence

Currently, retinal vascular chances are either manually or semi-automated assessed in reading centers, following standardized grading protocols. Such manual assessment hinders the retinal vascular changes to be incorporated into current risk models additionally for refining the CVD risk stratification, beyond established risk factors. Medical image interpretation using artificial intelligence (AI), in particular deep learning with convolutional neural network (CNN), have been being developed rapidly in different fields such as ophthalmology, radiology, pathology and dermatology. It is shown that the performance of automated classification for retinal diseases [89–92] by deep learning systems is equal to or better than board-certified specialists. For example, Gulshan et al. and Ting et al. have developed and validated deep learning systems for automated detection of diabetic retinopathy using retinal photographs from multi-ethnic populations with diabetes [89, 91]. Furthermore, Poplin et al. have demonstrated that multiple CVD risk factors, including age, gender, blood pressure, body mass index, smoking and HbA_{1c}, can be predicted quantitatively using deep learning [93]. These studies underscore the ability of automated image interpretation using AI for detection of retinal vascular changes related to CVD is promising, further validate the clinical utility of retinal vascular imaging for CVD risk prediction and risk stratification.

7.2 Imaging of the choroidal vasculature

The choroid, a vascular layer of the eye with one of the highest blood flow of any tissue in the body, develops from two embryonic tissues: the mesoderm and cranial neural crest cells. In addition to retinal layers, choroidal layer can now be evaluated and quantified reliably using enhanced depth imaging OCT (EDI-OCT) and swept-source OCT (SS-OCT) (Fig. 4), providing another noninvasive assessment of vascular status in the body. Recent studies observed that in patients with coronary artery disease and heart failure have thinner choroidal thickness, compared with

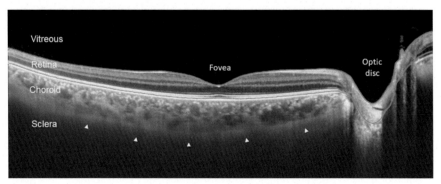

FIG. 4

Imaging of choroidal vasculature using swept-source optical coherence tomography.

healthy controls, demonstrating that imaging of the choroidal vasculature provides new opportunities for understanding of relationship between outer retinal health and systemic cardiovascular health. [33, 94]

7.3 Imaging of the retinal capillary network

Optical coherence tomography-angiography (OCT-A), based on mapping erythrocyte movement over time by comparing sequential OCT B-scans (motion contrast) at a given cross-section, has been developed to provide depth-resolved visualization of the retinal capillary network without the use of exogenous intravenous dye injection (Fig. 5) [95, 96]. Furthermore, new image analysis methods have been developed to quantify the capillary network from OCT-A images, and have been shown its role in identifying microvascular abnormalities [95, 97, 98]. Recently, Takayama et al. found a correlation between quantitative OCT-A metrics and hypertensive retinopathy scores, suggesting OCT-A might be a novel objective method to evaluate the progression of systemic hypertension from an early stage [99]. Chua et al. also found correlations between quantitative OCT-A metrics and systemic vascular risk factors in adults with treated systemic hypertension [100]. These findings highlight the potential role of OCT-A to study early microvascular changes in capillary level.

7.4 Ultra-widefield retinal imaging

Although the assessment of retinal changes from retinal photography has been used in numerous large population-based epidemiological studies, such assessment in these studies are based on a relatively narrow view of the retina area (30–50° of the retina). The latest ultra-widefield retinal imaging, based on the principle of confocal laser scanning microscopy combined with a concave elliptical mirror, has the ability to capture up to 200° of the retina in a single image without pupil dilation for assessment of peripheral lesions (Fig. 6). It is likely that assessment of the retina more peripherally (e.g., including smaller peripheral vessels) can provide a better representation of the retinal structure, and correlates better with the body [101].

8 Conclusions

The retinal vasculature is a unique biological model to study microcirculation abnormalities in CVD. Advanced retinal vascular imaging technologies have been developed to allow a more objective and precise assessment of retinal vascular changes. Further automated development of retinal vascular analyses and evaluation of the clinical utility of retinal vascular imaging in stratifying CVD, will allow the translation of retinal vascular imaging as a tool to improve the management of CVD in clinical practice.

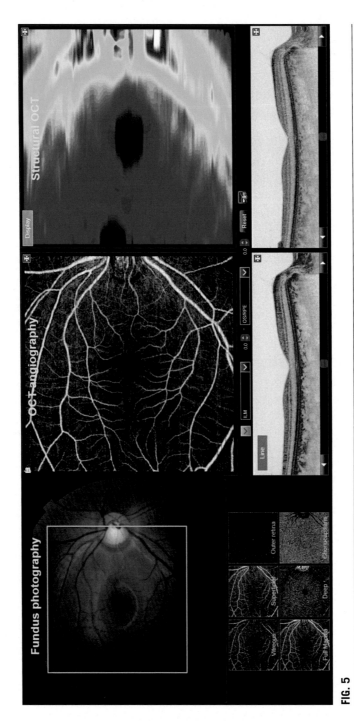

FIG. 5

Imaging of retinal capillary network using optical coherence tomography angiography.

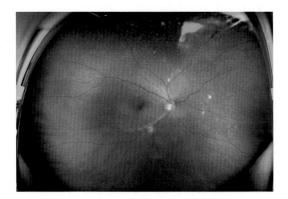

FIG. 6

Imaging of peripheral retinal vasculature using ultra-wide field retinal imaging.

References

[1] Writing Group M, D. Mozaffarian, E.J. Benjamin, et al., Executive summary: heart disease and stroke statistics—2016 update: a report from the American Heart Association, Circulation 133 (4) (2016) 447–454.

[2] G.A. Roth, C. Johnson, A. Abajobir, et al., Global, regional, and National Burden of Cardiovascular Diseases for 10 causes, 1990 to 2015, J. Am. Coll. Cardiol. 70 (1) (2017) 1–25.

[3] I.A. Scott, Evaluating cardiovascular risk assessment for asymptomatic people, BMJ 338 (2009) a2844.

[4] P. Brindle, J. Emberson, F. Lampe, et al., Predictive accuracy of the Framingham coronary risk score in British men: Prospective Cohort Study, BMJ 327 (7426) (2003) 1267.

[5] M. Al Rifai, M. Cainzos-Achirica, A.M. Kanaya, et al., Discordance between 10-year cardiovascular risk estimates using the ACC/AHA 2013 estimator and coronary artery calcium in individuals from 5 racial/ethnic groups: comparing MASALA and MESA, Atherosclerosis (2018).

[6] X. Yang, J. Li, D. Hu, et al., Predicting the 10-year risks of atherosclerotic cardiovascular disease in Chinese population: the China-PAR project (prediction for ASCVD risk in China), Circulation 134 (19) (2016) 1430–1440.

[7] G.A. Lanza, F. Crea, Primary coronary microvascular dysfunction: clinical presentation, pathophysiology, and management, Circulation 121 (21) (2010) 2317–2325.

[8] D.D. Gutterman, D.S. Chabowski, A.O. Kadlec, et al., The human microcirculation: regulation of flow and beyond, Circ. Res. 118 (1) (2016) 157–172.

[9] W.D. Strain, P.M. Paldanius, Diabetes, cardiovascular disease and the microcirculation, Cardiovasc. Diabetol. 17 (1) (2018) 57.

[10] T.Y. Wong, R. McIntosh, Systemic associations of retinal microvascular signs: a review of recent population-based studies, Ophthalmic Physiol. Opt. 25 (3) (2005) 195–204.

[11] C.Y. Cheung, M.K. Ikram, C. Sabanayagam, T.Y. Wong, Retinal microvasculature as a model to study the manifestations of hypertension, Hypertension 60 (5) (2012) 1094–1103.

[12] T.Y. Wong, R. Klein, B.E. Klein, et al., Retinal microvascular abnormalities and their relationship with hypertension, cardiovascular disease, and mortality, Surv. Ophthalmol. 46 (1) (2001) 59–80.

[13] R.M. Gunn, Ophthalmoscopic evidence of (1) arterial changes associated with chronic renal diseases and (2) of increased arterial tension, Trans. Ophthalmol. Soc. U. K. 12 (1982) 124–125.

[14] C.Y. Cheung, W.T. Tay, P. Mitchell, et al., Quantitative and qualitative retinal microvascular characteristics and blood pressure, J. Hypertens. 29 (7) (2011) 1380–1391.

[15] J.J. Wang, P. Mitchell, H. Leung, et al., Hypertensive retinal vessel wall signs in a general older population: the Blue Mountains Eye Study, Hypertension 42 (4) (2003) 534–541.

[16] S. Kaushik, A.G. Tan, P. Mitchell, J.J. Wang, Prevalence and associations of enhanced retinal arteriolar light reflex: a new look at an old sign, Ophthalmology 114 (1) (2007) 113–120.

[17] T.Y. Wong, M.D. Knudtson, R. Klein, et al., Computer-assisted measurement of retinal vessel diameters in the Beaver Dam Eye Study: methodology, correlation between eyes, and effect of refractive errors, Ophthalmology 111 (6) (2004) 1183–1190.

[18] L.D. Hubbard, R.J. Brothers, W.N. King, et al., Methods for evaluation of retinal microvascular abnormalities associated with hypertension/sclerosis in the Atherosclerosis Risk in Communities Study, Ophthalmology 106 (12) (1999) 2269–2280.

[19] M.D. Knudtson, K.E. Lee, L.D. Hubbard, et al., Revised formulas for summarizing retinal vessel diameters, Curr. Eye Res. 27 (3) (2003) 143–149.

[20] C.Y. Cheung, Y. Zheng, W. Hsu, et al., Retinal vascular tortuosity, blood pressure, and cardiovascular risk factors, Ophthalmology 118 (5) (2011) 812–818.

[21] S. McGrory, A.M. Taylor, E. Pellegrini, et al., Towards standardization of quantitative retinal vascular parameters: comparison of SIVA and VAMPIRE measurements in the Lothian birth cohort 1936, Transl. Vis. Sci. Technol. 7 (2) (2018) 12.

[22] A. Perez-Rovira, T. MacGillivray, E. Trucco, et al., VAMPIRE: vessel assessment and measurement platform for images of the REtina, in: Conf. Proc. IEEE Eng. Med. Biol. Soc. 2011, 2011, pp. 3391–3394.

[23] T.Y. Wong, R. Klein, D.J. Couper, et al., Retinal microvascular abnormalities and incident stroke: the Atherosclerosis Risk in Communities Study, Lancet 358 (9288) (2001) 1134–1140.

[24] T.Y. Wong, R. Klein, A.R. Sharrett, et al., Retinal arteriolar narrowing and risk of coronary heart disease in men and women. The Atherosclerosis Risk in Communities Study, JAMA 287 (9) (2002) 1153–1159.

[25] T.Y. Wong, W. Rosamond, P.P. Chang, et al., Retinopathy and risk of congestive heart failure, JAMA 293 (1) (2005) 63–69.

[26] H. Yatsuya, A.R. Folsom, T.Y. Wong, et al., Retinal microvascular abnormalities and risk of lacunar stroke: Atherosclerosis Risk in Communities Study, Stroke 41 (7) (2010) 1349–1355.

[27] S.B. Seidelmann, B. Claggett, P.E. Bravo, et al., Retinal vessel calibers in predicting long-term cardiovascular outcomes: the Atherosclerosis Risk in Communities Study, Circulation 134 (18) (2016) 1328–1338.

[28] T.Y. Wong, R. Klein, F.J. Nieto, et al., Retinal microvascular abnormalities and 10-year cardiovascular mortality: a Population-Based Case-Control Study, Ophthalmology 110 (5) (2003) 933–940.

[29] J.J. Wang, G. Liew, R. Klein, et al., Retinal vessel diameter and cardiovascular mortality: pooled data analysis from two older populations, Eur. Heart J. 28 (16) (2007) 1984–1992.

[30] N. Witt, T.Y. Wong, A.D. Hughes, et al., Abnormalities of retinal microvascular structure and risk of mortality from ischemic heart disease and stroke, Hypertension 47 (5) (2006) 975–981.

[31] G. Liew, T.Y. Wong, P. Mitchell, et al., Retinopathy predicts coronary heart disease mortality, Heart 95 (5) (2009) 391–394.

[32] P. Mitchell, J.J. Wang, T.Y. Wong, et al., Retinal microvascular signs and risk of stroke and stroke mortality, Neurology 65 (7) (2005) 1005–1009.

[33] H. Altinkaynak, N. Kara, N. Sayin, et al., Subfoveal choroidal thickness in patients with chronic heart failure analyzed by spectral-domain optical coherence tomography, Curr. Eye Res. 39 (11) (2014) 1123–1128.

[34] C.G. Owen, A.R. Rudnicka, R.A. Welikala, et al., Retinal vasculometry associations with cardiometabolic risk factors in the European Prospective Investigation of Cancer-Norfolk Study, Ophthalmology (2018).

[35] R. Kawasaki, J. Xie, N. Cheung, et al., Retinal microvascular signs and risk of stroke: the Multi-Ethnic Study of Atherosclerosis (MESA), Stroke 43 (12) (2012) 3245–3251.

[36] A.C. Ricardo, J.E. Grunwald, S. Parvathaneni, et al., Retinopathy and CKD as predictors of all-cause and cardiovascular mortality: National Health and Nutrition Examination Survey (NHANES) 1988–1994, Am. J. Kidney Dis. 64 (2) (2014) 198–203.

[37] M.K. Ikram, F.J. de Jong, M.J. Bos, et al., Retinal vessel diameters and risk of stroke: The Rotterdam study, Neurology 66 (9) (2006) 1339–1343.

[38] R.G. Wieberdink, M.K. Ikram, P.J. Koudstaal, et al., Retinal vascular calibers and the risk of intracerebral hemorrhage and cerebral infarction: the Rotterdam study, Stroke 41 (12) (2010) 2757–2761.

[39] C.Y. Cheung, W.T. Tay, M.K. Ikram, et al., Retinal microvascular changes and risk of stroke: the Singapore Malay Eye Study, Stroke 44 (9) (2013) 2402–2408.

[40] H. Ho, C.Y. Cheung, C. Sabanayagam, et al., Retinopathy signs improved prediction and reclassification of cardiovascular disease risk in diabetes: a Prospective Cohort Study, Sci. Rep. 7 (2017). 41492.

[41] R.G. Siantar, C.Y. Cheng, C.M. Gemmy Cheung, et al., Impact of visual impairment and eye diseases on mortality: the Singapore Malay Eye Study (SiMES), Sci. Rep. 5 (2015). 16304.

[42] A.D. Hughes, E. Falaschetti, N. Witt, et al., Association of retinopathy and retinal microvascular abnormalities with stroke and cerebrovascular disease, Stroke 47 (11) (2016) 2862–2864.

[43] E.L. Michelson, J. Morganroth, C.W. Nichols, H. MacVaugh III, Retinal arteriolar changes as an indicator of coronary artery disease, Arch. Intern. Med. 139 (10) (1979) 1139–1141.

[44] B.B. Duncan, T.Y. Wong, H.A. Tyroler, et al., Hypertensive retinopathy and incident coronary heart disease in high risk men, Br. J. Ophthalmol. 86 (9) (2002) 1002–1006.

[45] N. Cheung, J.J. Wang, S.L. Rogers, et al., Diabetic retinopathy and risk of heart failure, J. Am. Coll. Cardiol. 51 (16) (2008) 1573–1578.

[46] K. Phan, P. Mitchell, G. Liew, et al., Association between retinal arteriolar and Venule Calibre with prevalent heart failure: a Cross-Sectional Study, PLoS One 10 (12) (2015). e0144850.

[47] T.Y. Wong, N. Cheung, F.M. Islam, et al., Relation of retinopathy to coronary artery calcification: the multi-ethnic study of atherosclerosis, Am. J. Epidemiol. 167 (1) (2008) 51–58.

[48] N. Cheung, A.R. Sharrett, R. Klein, et al., Aortic distensibility and retinal arteriolar narrowing: the multi-ethnic study of atherosclerosis, Hypertension 50 (4) (2007) 617–622.

[49] N. Cheung, D.A. Bluemke, R. Klein, et al., Retinal arteriolar narrowing and left ventricular remodeling: the multi-ethnic study of atherosclerosis, J. Am. Coll. Cardiol. 50 (1) (2007) 48–55.

[50] R. Kawasaki, N. Cheung, F.M. Islam, et al., Is diabetic retinopathy related to subclinical cardiovascular disease? Ophthalmology 118 (5) (2011) 860–865.

[51] K. McGeechan, G. Liew, P. Macaskill, et al., Meta-analysis: retinal vessel caliber and risk for coronary heart disease, Ann. Intern. Med. 151 (6) (2009) 404–413.

[52] S.B. Wang, P. Mitchell, G. Liew, et al., A spectrum of retinal vasculature measures and coronary artery disease, Atherosclerosis 268 (2018) 215–224.

[53] B. Gopinath, S.B. Wang, G. Liew, et al., Retinal vascular geometry and the prevalence of atrial fibrillation and heart failure in a clinic-based sample, Heart Lung Circ. (2018).

[54] T.Y. Wong, R. Klein, A.R. Sharrett, et al., Cerebral white matter lesions, retinopathy, and incident clinical stroke, JAMA 288 (1) (2002) 67–74.

[55] T.Y. Wong, A. Kamineni, R. Klein, et al., Quantitative retinal venular caliber and risk of cardiovascular disease in older persons: the Cardiovascular Health Study, Arch. Intern. Med. 166 (21) (2006) 2388–2394.

[56] K. McGeechan, G. Liew, P. Macaskill, et al., Prediction of incident stroke events based on retinal vessel caliber: a systematic review and individual-participant meta-analysis, Am. J. Epidemiol. 170 (11) (2009) 1323–1332.

[57] N. Cheung, G. Liew, R.I. Lindley, et al., Retinal fractals and acute lacunar stroke, Ann. Neurol. 68 (1) (2010) 107–111.

[58] F.N. Doubal, T.J. MacGillivray, N. Patton, et al., Fractal analysis of retinal vessels suggests that a distinct vasculopathy causes lacunar stroke, Neurology 74 (14) (2010) 1102–1107.

[59] Y.T. Ong, D.A. De Silva, C.Y. Cheung, et al., Microvascular structure and network in the retina of patients with ischemic stroke, Stroke 44 (8) (2013) 2121–2127.

[60] R. Kawasaki, M.Z. Che Azemin, D.K. Kumar, et al., Fractal dimension of the retinal vasculature and risk of stroke: a Nested Case-Control Study, Neurology 76 (20) (2011) 1766–1767.

[61] R.I. Lindley, J.J. Wang, M.C. Wong, et al., Retinal microvasculature in acute lacunar stroke: a Cross-Sectional Study, Lancet Neurol. 8 (7) (2009) 628–634.

[62] M.L. Baker, J.J. Wang, G. Liew, et al., Differential associations of cortical and subcortical cerebral atrophy with retinal vascular signs in patients with acute stroke, Stroke 41 (10) (2010) 2143–2150.

[63] M.L. Baker, P.J. Hand, G. Liew, et al., Retinal microvascular signs may provide clues to the underlying vasculopathy in patients with deep intracerebral hemorrhage, Stroke 41 (4) (2010) 618–623.

[64] M.L. Baker, P.J. Hand, T.Y. Wong, et al., Retinopathy and lobar intracerebral hemorrhage: insights into pathogenesis, Arch. Neurol. 67 (10) (2010) 1224–1230.

[65] F.N. Doubal, R. de Haan, T.J. MacGillivray, et al., Retinal arteriolar geometry is associated with cerebral white matter hyperintensities on magnetic resonance imaging, Int. J. Stroke 5 (6) (2010) 434–439.

[66] L.N. Vuong, P. Thulasi, V. Biousse, et al., Ocular fundus photography of patients with focal neurologic deficits in an emergency department, Neurology 85 (3) (2015) 256–262.

[67] Y. Zhuo, H. Yu, Z. Yang, et al., Prediction factors of recurrent stroke among Chinese adults using retinal vasculature characteristics, J. Stroke Cerebrovasc. Dis. 26 (4) (2017) 679–685.

[68] M.K. Ikram, F.J. de Jong, E.J. Van Dijk, et al., Retinal vessel diameters and cerebral small vessel disease: the Rotterdam Scan Study, Brain 129 (2006) 182–188. Pt 1.

[69] N. Cheung, T. Mosley, A. Islam, et al., Retinal microvascular abnormalities and subclinical magnetic resonance imaging brain infarct: a Prospective Study, Brain 133 (2010) 1987–1993. Pt 7.

[70] V.I. Kwa, J.J. van der Sande, J. Stam, et al., Retinal arterial changes correlate with cerebral small-vessel disease, Neurology 59 (10) (2002) 1536–1540.

[71] L.S. Cooper, T.Y. Wong, R. Klein, et al., Retinal microvascular abnormalities and MRI-defined subclinical cerebral infarction: the Atherosclerosis Risk in Communities Study, Stroke 37 (1) (2006) 82–86.

[72] G. Liew, M.L. Baker, T.Y. Wong, et al., Differing associations of white matter lesions and lacunar infarction with retinal microvascular signs, Int. J. Stroke 9 (7) (2014) 921–925.

[73] M. Haan, M.A. Espeland, B.E. Klein, et al., Cognitive function and retinal and ischemic brain changes: the Women's Health Initiative, Neurology 78 (13) (2012) 942–949.

[74] W. Longstreth Jr., E.K. Larsen, R. Klein, et al., Associations between findings on cranial magnetic resonance imaging and retinal photography in the elderly: the Cardiovascular Health Study, Am. J. Epidemiol. 165 (1) (2007) 78–84.

[75] C. Qiu, M.F. Cotch, S. Sigurdsson, et al., Microvascular lesions in the brain and retina: the age, gene/environment susceptibility-Reykjavik Study, Ann. Neurol. 65 (5) (2009) 569–576.

[76] A. Tirsi, H. Bruehl, V. Sweat, et al., Retinal vessel abnormalities are associated with elevated fasting insulin levels and cerebral atrophy in nondiabetic individuals, Ophthalmology 116 (6) (2009) 1175–1181.

[77] R. Kawasaki, N. Cheung, T. Mosley, et al., Retinal microvascular signs and 10-year risk of cerebral atrophy: the Atherosclerosis Risk in Communities (ARIC) Study, Stroke 41 (8) (2010) 1826–1828.

[78] S. Akoudad, M.L. Portegies, P.J. Koudstaal, et al., Cerebral microbleeds are associated with an increased risk of stroke: the Rotterdam Study, Circulation 132 (6) (2015) 509–516.

[79] S. Hilal, Y.T. Ong, C.Y. Cheung, et al., Microvascular network alterations in retina of subjects with cerebral small vessel disease, Neurosci. Lett. 577 (2014) 95–100.

[80] J.J. Wang, G. Liew, T.Y. Wong, et al., Retinal vascular calibre and the risk of coronary heart disease-related death, Heart 92 (11) (2006) 1583–1587.

[81] A. Juutilainen, S. Lehto, T. Ronnemaa, et al., Retinopathy predicts cardiovascular mortality in type 2 diabetic men and women, Diabetes Care 30 (2) (2007) 292–299.

[82] M.V. Van Hecke, J.M. Dekker, G. Nijpels, et al., Retinopathy is associated with cardiovascular and all-cause mortality in both diabetic and nondiabetic subjects: the Hoorn Study, Diabetes Care 26 (10) (2003) 2958.

[83] T. Sairenchi, H. Iso, K. Yamagishi, et al., Mild retinopathy is a risk factor for cardiovascular mortality in Japanese with and without hypertension: the Ibaraki Prefectural Health Study, Circulation 124 (23) (2011) 2502–2511.

[84] A.D. Hughes, A.V. Stanton, A.S. Jabbar, et al., Effect of antihypertensive treatment on retinal microvascular changes in hypertension, J. Hypertens. 26 (8) (2008) 1703–1707.

[85] B. Dahlof, S. Stenkula, L. Hansson, Hypertensive retinal vascular changes: relationship to left ventricular hypertrophy and arteriolar changes before and after treatment, Blood Press. 1 (1) (1992) 35–44.

[86] S. Thom, C. Stettler, A. Stanton, et al., Differential effects of antihypertensive treatment on the retinal microcirculation: an Anglo-Scandinavian Cardiac Outcomes Trial Substudy, Hypertension 54 (2) (2009) 405–408.

[87] P.R. Antonio, P.S. Marta, D.D. Luis, et al., Factors associated with changes in retinal microcirculation after antihypertensive treatment, J. Hum. Hypertens. 28 (5) (2014) 310–315.

[88] C.M. Reid, E. Storey, T.Y. Wong, et al., Aspirin for the prevention of cognitive decline in the elderly: rationale and design of a neuro-vascular imaging study (ENVIS-ion), BMC Neurol. 12 (2012) 3.

[89] D.S.W. Ting, C.Y. Cheung, G. Lim, et al., Development and validation of a deep learning system for diabetic retinopathy and related eye diseases using retinal images from multiethnic populations with diabetes, JAMA 318 (22) (2017) 2211–2223.

[90] J. De Fauw, J.R. Ledsam, B. Romera-Paredes, et al., Clinically applicable deep learning for diagnosis and referral in retinal disease, Nat. Med. (2018).

[91] V. Gulshan, L. Peng, M. Coram, et al., Development and validation of a deep learning algorithm for detection of diabetic retinopathy in retinal fundus photographs, JAMA 316 (22) (2016) 2402–2410.

[92] Z. Li, Y. He, S. Keel, et al., Efficacy of a deep learning system for detecting glaucomatous optic neuropathy based on color fundus photographs, Ophthalmology 125 (8) (2018) 1199–1206.

[93] R. Poplin, A.V. Varadarajan, K. Blumer, et al., Prediction of cardiovascular risk factors from retinal fundus photographs via deep learning, Nat. Biomed. Eng. 2 (3) (2018) 158–164.

[94] M. Ahmad, P.A. Kaszubski, L. Cobbs, et al., Choroidal thickness in patients with coronary artery disease, PLoS One 12 (6) (2017) e0175691.

[95] Y. Jia, S.T. Bailey, T.S. Hwang, et al., Quantitative optical coherence tomography angiography of vascular abnormalities in the living human eye, Proc. Natl. Acad. Sci. U. S. A. 112 (18) (2015) E2395–E2402.

[96] R.F. Spaide, J.G. Fujimoto, N.K. Waheed, et al., Optical coherence tomography angiography, Prog. Retin. Eye Res. (2017).

[97] F.Y. Tang, D.S. Ng, A. Lam, et al., Determinants of quantitative optical coherence tomography angiography metrics in patients with diabetes, Sci. Rep. 7 (1) (2017) 2575.

[98] C.Y. Cheung, J. Li, N. Yuan, et al., Quantitative retinal microvasculature in children using swept-source optical coherence tomography: the Hong Kong Children Eye Study, Br. J. Ophthalmol. (2018).

[99] K. Takayama, H. Kaneko, Y. Ito, et al., Novel classification of early-stage systemic hypertensive changes in human retina based on OCTA measurement of Choriocapillaris, Sci. Rep. 8 (1) (2018). 15163.

[100] J. Chua, C.W.L. Chin, J. Hong, et al., Impact of hypertension on retinal capillary microvasculature using optical coherence tomographic angiography, J. Hypertens. (2018).

[101] C.Y. Cheung, W. Hsu, M.L. Lee, et al., A new method to measure peripheral retinal vascular caliber over an extended area, Microcirculation 17 (7) (2010) 495–503.

Vascular biomarkers for diabetes and diabetic retinopathy screening

16

Fan Huang[a], Samaneh Abbasi-Sureshjani[a], Jiong Zhang[b], Erik J. Bekkers[c], Behdad Dashtbozorg[d], Bart M. ter Haar Romeny[a]

[a]*Department of Biomedical Engineering, Eindhoven University of Technology, Eindhoven, The Netherlands*
[b]*Keck School of Medicine, University of Southern California, Los Angeles, CA, United States*
[c]*Department of Mathematics and Computer Science, Eindhoven University of Technology, Eindhoven, The Netherlands*
[d]*Department of Surgery, Netherlands Cancer Institute, Amsterdam, The Netherlands*

1 Introduction

The worldwide spread of diabetes is explosive and epidemic. It concerns mostly diabetes mellitus 2 (DM2), where cells no longer respond to insulin. Especially in China, where in 2016 a staggering 11.6% of people have diabetes [1]. The rise is almost linear from 1980, when diabetes was hardly present, till today, and no signs of leveling off can be perceived. The reasons for China to have such high prevalence are not clear but it may be due to Asian genetic predisposition and an unprecedented fast change in life style over the last two decades.

High glucose peaks lead to damage on the vessel wall, especially for the microvasculature. An especially vulnerable tissue is the retina, as this is the most oxygen-using tissue in our body, equipped with even two blood supplies, the inner retinal and outer choroidal vasculature. Retinal damage may lead to blindness, and it is expected that 4% of all diabetes patients may eventually go blind. The development of diabetes, and its accompanying diabetic retinopathy (DR) can be very gradual, and many people do not know that they have diabetes until more serious complaints bring them to medical inspection. Very early signs of microvascular damage (microaneurysms, morphological vessel changes, leak deposits) can be seen by analysis of high resolution (4–12 megapixels) optical images of the fundus with a very low-cost acquisition. The need for screening for DR is widely recognized, and today retinal imaging is a modality receiving much attention, due to its high information content at high resolution, and high volumes of big data for AI applications. As the retina is brain tissue, so is the microvasculature, with a similar blood-brain barrier. This chapter describes automated quantitative vascular biomarkers for screening for early warning of retinal damage.

Computational Retinal Image Analysis. https://doi.org/10.1016/B978-0-08-102816-2.00017-4

1.1 The Sino-Dutch collaboration project RetinaCheck

To expand their market in China, Philips Healthcare started a collaboration with Neusoft Medical Systems, the largest medical imaging industry in China, located in Shenyang, Liaoning Province, Northeast China. Together with two universities, Eindhoven University of Technology (TU/e, Eindhoven, the Netherlands) and Northeastern University (NEU, Shenyang, China), they founded a new Biomedical and Information Engineering School (BMIE, now around 1000 students) to generate skilled labor force and start biomedical research.

In 2014, the large Chinese He Vision Group (HVG, Shenyang, China) asked BMIE and TU/e for help to set up a retinal screening program in Liaoning Province. The first goal was to develop automated and quantitative image analysis software to find early signs of DR from fundus images and to validate the effectiveness of the biomarkers with Chinese and Western diabetes patients and healthy subjects.

A consortium was formed, with partners TU/e, NEU, HUEH, and i-Optics, a Dutch company developing innovative scanning laser ophthalmoscopes (SLOs). Funding was acquired from the Netherlands Organization for Scientific Research (NWO), the European Foundation for the Study of Diabetes (EFSD), the EU Marie Curie ITN Program, and the partners, and the project RetinaCheck was started.

1.2 Vascular analysis-specific biomarkers for early detection and screening

The classical biomarkers for early detection of DR are described in the Guidelines of the International Ophthalmology Council [2]. The earliest signs are microaneurysms. These can be detected easily by human experts, but this is a time-consuming process, and given the huge number of images in screening, automation is required. Another crucial reason for the development of a computer-aided diagnosis (CAD) system is that morphological changes in the microvasculature, like changes in tortuosity (curvature), branching deviations, and fractal dimensions, can hardly be discriminated by ophthalmologists, and definitely not quantified. Computer analysis can quantify these vascular biomarkers precisely, detecting changes earlier, and giving accurate measures to assist in following the effectiveness of treatment.

We decided to focus on the development of an accurate and quantitative analysis of the retinal microvasculature in four categories: vessel width, vessel tortuosity, vessel bifurcations, and vessel fractal dimensions. This requires a pipeline of processing, described in Section 2 (see Fig. 1).

1.3 Layout of this chapter

The chapter is organized as follows: As our group in particular exploits brain-inspired methods, we justify its use, and explain the physiological inspiration and current state-of-the-art in geometric models of visual perception. In Section 3, we explain

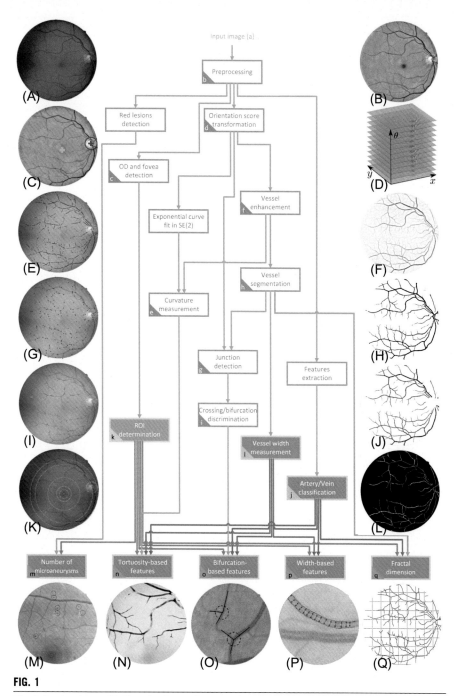

FIG. 1

The infrastructure with the pipelines of processing steps; (A) original fundus image, (B) normalized image, (C) OD and fovea locations, (D) orientation scores, (E) curvature map, (F) vessel probability map, (G) junctions, (H) vessel binary map, (I) bifurcations and crossings, (J) artery/vein classes, (K) regions of interest, (L) vessel caliber map, (M) microaneurysm detection, and (N–Q) assessment of biomarkers including global tortuosity, bifurcation features, width, and fractal dimension.

From B. Dashtbozorg, S. Abbasi-Sureshjani, J. Zhang, F. Huang, E.J. Bekkers, B.M. ter Haar Romeny, Infrastructure for retinal image analysis, in: Proceedings of the Ophthalmic Medical Image Analysis Second International Workshop, OMIA 2016, Held in Conjunction With MICCAI 2016, Athens, Greece, October 17, 2015, Iowa Research Online, 2016, pp. 105–112.

the preprocessing steps, such as background normalization, crossing-preserving vessel enhancement, denoising, and vessel completion. The description of the validation studies is given in Section 3.4. Section 4 is the core of the chapter, describing the vascular biomarkers *vessel width*, vessel *tortuosity*, several *vessel bifurcation measures*, and several *fractal dimensions*. The full processing pipeline is described in Section 5, the clinical validation in Section 6. The chapter ends with a discussion, and future outlook.

2 Brain- and vision-inspired computing

Our visual system is the best-studied part of the brain. The mathematics of our methodology is based on geometric models of functional circuits in the early visual system. The so-called simple cells in the primary visual cortex (V1) can be modeled as multiscale differential operators to high order [4], which are now default in computer vision for robust differential geometry calculations. The characteristic multiorientation pinwheel structure of the cortical hypercolumns enables the modeling of contextual operations, such as vessel completion and vessel enhancement. The visual system exploits a cascade of processing steps, now modeled with great success in deep learning convolutional neural networks.

2.1 The mathematics of V1: Sub-Riemannian geometry in *SE*(2)

A well-studied mathematical model for the primary visual cortex (V1) is that of sub-Riemannian geometry on the Lie group *SE*(2) of rotations and translations [5–7]. Two main components of this model are

1. organizing visual information based on positions and local orientations; and
2. quantifying notions of alignment between such "oriented pixels" via a sub-Riemannian geometry.

The first component is inspired by the observations of Hubel and Wiesel [8] who found that the primary visual cortex exhibits simple cells which are orientation sensitive and whose orientation sensitivity varies smoothly over the surface of the brain. These cells cluster spatially in radial pinwheel structures that encode for all orientated stimuli at a certain location in the retina. We follow a similar approach and generally do not process 2D images directly, but instead *lift* the image data to the space of positions and orientations.

The second component models both the Gestalt principles of "good continuation" [9, 10] in visual perception and the observations by Bosking et al. [11] who found that simple cells excite each other whenever they are "aligned." The mathematical modeling of this alignment requires an identification of the space of positions and orientations with the Lie group *SE*(2) and a definition of a suitable geometrical structure. In the next section, the essential mathematical notions are introduced.

2.2 Orientation scores

We lift image data to the space of positions and orientations $\mathbb{R}^2 \times S^1$ by filtering the input image f with orientation sensitive wavelets ψ in the following way:

$$U_f(\mathbf{x}, \theta) = (\overline{\mathbf{R}_\theta(\psi)} \star f)(\mathbf{x}) = \int_{\mathbb{R}^2} \overline{\psi(\mathbf{R}_\theta^{-1}(\mathbf{y} - \mathbf{x}))} f(\mathbf{y}) d\mathbf{y}, \tag{1}$$

where $\mathbf{R}_\theta = \begin{pmatrix} \cos\theta & -\sin\theta \\ \sin\theta & \cos\theta \end{pmatrix}$ is the 2D counter-clockwise rotation matrix over angle θ,

the overline denotes the complex conjugate, and $\star$ represents the correlation operator. The resulting function U_f on $\mathbb{R}^2 \times S^1$ is what we call an *orientation score (OS)* [12]. For a specific choice of wavelet ψ describes an *invertible OS transform*. The cake wavelet[1] is such a wavelet and it allows for exact reconstruction of the image via an inverse OS transform [13, 14]. The invertibility property is essential in our analysis as it ensures that no information is lost during the process of lifting 2D data to position orientation space.

2.3 A moving frame of reference

The space $\mathbb{R}^2 \times S^1$ is not a flat geometry, there exists a notion of "forward," "sideways," and "above" which changes as you move through this space (in particular along the vertical orientation axis). As such, it is essential that we do not do our processing in a standard Cartesian $\{\partial_x, \partial_y, \partial_\theta\}$ frame, but rather with a moving frame of reference. For this we rely on group theory and identify the space of positions and orientations with the special Euclidean motion group $SE(2)$. The group $SE(2) = \mathbb{R}^2 \rtimes SO(2)$ is the semidirect product of the group of planar translations $\mathbb{R}^2$ and rotations $SO(2)$ and it describes how to combine two "roto-translations" into a net roto-translation via the following group product

$$g \cdot g' = (\mathbf{x}, \mathbf{R}_\theta) \cdot (\mathbf{x}', \mathbf{R}_{\theta'}) = (\mathbf{R}_\theta \mathbf{x}' + \mathbf{x}, \mathbf{R}_{\theta+\theta'}), \tag{2}$$

with group elements $g = (\mathbf{x}, \theta)$, $g' = (\mathbf{x}', \theta') \in SE(2)$. The group structure provides a way to construct a moving frame of reference. By roto-translating the standard frame at the origin ($\{\partial_x, \partial_y, \partial_\theta\}$), we can assign the following frame to each location $g = (\mathbf{x}, \theta) \in SE(2)$:

$$\{\partial_\xi|_g, \partial_\eta|_g, \partial_\theta|_g\} := \{\cos\theta\partial_x + \sin\theta\partial_y, -\sin\theta\partial_x + \cos\theta\partial_y, \partial_\theta\}. \tag{3}$$

For convenience we will often omit the dependency of the frame on its location in $SE(2)$ and, for example, simply write ∂_ξ instead of $\partial_\xi|_g$. The collection of all frames defines a set of so-called *left-invariant vector fields*, which we can use as differential operators (instead of axis-aligned Cartesian derivatives) in image analysis pipelines.

---

[1] These filters originate as inverse transforms of an angular segment in the Fourier domain, which looks like a "piece of cake."

2.4 Sub-Riemannian geometry

In our processing, we want to take notions of alignment into account. For example in vessel enhancement, we prefer to smooth intensities in orientation scores along the vessel path rather than perpendicular to it. This means that we will define our smoothing operators in terms of blurring along the forward ∂_ξ direction and a small blur in the ∂_θ direction to encode some uncertainty in the orientation estimates. Another example is in the construction of tree structures where we would like to connect vessel segments when they are aligned. A notion of alignment can now be quantified using our moving frame of reference where we construct metrics in terms of distance traveled along the forward direction ∂_ξ and change in orientation (along ∂_θ) to get from one point to the other.

In both examples, motion or blurring in the orthogonal direction ∂_η is undesirable. A blood vessel follows a smooth path in which its orientation varies gradually, it does not make sudden jumps to the side. Therefore, in our processing, we strictly forbid any flow of information directly along the ∂_η direction. The correct geometric structure to use then is that of a *sub-Riemannian geometry* in $SE(2)$ in which distances and differential operators are defined only in terms of ∂_ξ and ∂_θ. Here, we will not formally define all mathematical details, but refer to Refs. [15–17] and the references given in the following sections for further details.

2.5 Application: Brain inspired image analysis

One of the key advantages of processing image data via orientation scores is that crossings do not exist in position orientation space: crossing lines are disentangled due to their difference in orientation. In our OS processing approach, we thus do not suffer from classical image processing problems at crossings (e.g., the widely used Frangi vesselness filter fails at crossings due to a lack of anisotropy there) which allowed us to develop successful crossing-preserving vessel enhancement [18–20] and tracking algorithms [21, 22]. In particular in tracking [22, 23] and perceptual grouping of vessel segments [24, 25], it is the combination of a sub-Riemannian geometry with OS processing that solves fundamental problems in curve analysis; it solves the problem of "short cuts" in optimal path algorithms caused by dominant nearby (or parallel) vessels and by construction allows control over the smoothness of the curves.

Image analysis via orientation scores also enables unique ways to robustly extract vessel biomarkers directly from the image data. For example, vessel curvature, a notoriously difficult parameter to measure, can now be deduced by analyzing the change of orientation along the vessel in the orientation score.

Finally, OS methods are not limited to vessel analysis. The OS provides an excellent representation to learn descriptors of key anatomical landmarks such as the optic nerve head and the fovea. Based on this principle, we developed a fast state-of-the-art retinal landmark detector in Ref. [26] and crossing and bifurcation detector in Ref. [27]. In recent work, we expanded these machine learning-based techniques to the context of deep learning in which our brain-inspired group theoretical approach lifts conventional methods to new levels of performance using $SE(2)$ group convolution networks [28].

3 Preprocessing

3.1 Denoising in the *SE*(2) space

Due to nonideal image acquisition conditions, retinal images are often affected by nonuniform luminosity, contrast variability, and noise. It is important to attenuate these artifacts at early stages and prevent performance reductions in the analysis.

In the first step, we apply the luminosity and contrast normalization technique proposed by Foracchia et al. [29], which only enhances the background part of the retinal images and does not affect the vessels or lesions. In next step, we enhance the blood vessels and attenuate the noise in the *SE*(2) space. By using the directional cake wavelets for the OS transformation, elongated structures (vessels) get high responses in this domain at their corresponding orientation, while nonelongated structures including background and noise get low responses at all orientations. Then applying an appropriate nonlinearity leads to attenuating the low OS responses while enhancing the high values (corresponding to the vessels). We propose to use the gamma transform as $\overset{\triangledown}{U}_f = \alpha |U_f|^{\gamma}$. Because of the quadratic property of cake wavelets, the absolute value $|U_f|$ of the OS (which is phase invariant) is used for gamma correction. α is determined by the sign of the real part $\text{Re}(U_f)$ of the OS. By setting the γ parameter to a value larger than 1 (typically we use $\gamma = 1.5$), the blood vessels get enhanced while the noise is suppressed. The image after applying the gamma correction in *SE*(2) is reconstructed by summation of the OS stack (see also Eq. 10). This transformation is highly effective in denoising both RGB and SLO images. The reader is referred to Abbasi-Sureshjani et al. [30] for more details (Fig. 2).

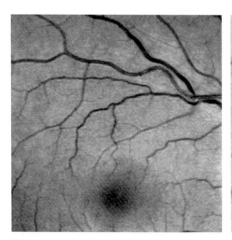 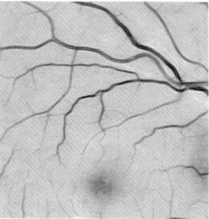

FIG. 2

Left: Retinal RGB image with background normalization. *Right*: Same image, denoised with a nonlinear multiorientation transform.

From S. Abbasi-Sureshjani, I. Smit-Ockeloen, J. Zhang, B.M. ter Haar Romeny, Biologically-inspired supervised vasculature segmentation in SLO retinal fundus images, in: International Conference Image Analysis and Recognition, Lecture Notes in Computer Science, vol. 9164, Springer, New York, 2015, pp. 325–334.

3.2 Vessel segmentation

Retinal vessel segmentation is an essential prestep for further geometrical and to-pological analysis on retinal vessel structures. An automatic and accurate vessel segmentation method [19, 31, 32] can largely reduce the workload of manually labeling by experts and improve the efficiency of diagnosis in particular to large-scale screening programs. In our previous work, vessel-enhancing filters, including the multiscale left-invariant derivative (LID) filters and the locally adaptive derivative (LAD) filters [19, 31], on orientation scores have been shown to robustly enhance and segment a complete retinal vessel network. The multiscale LID filters are set up based on the left-invariant rotating frame of reference using second-order operators perpendicular to the vessel direction. The LID filter is written as

$$\Phi_{\eta,\text{norm}}^{\sigma_s,\sigma_o}(U_f) := -\mu^{-2}\partial_\eta^2 G_{\sigma_s,\sigma_o} * U_f, \tag{4}$$

where the LID frame of reference is defined by Eq. (4). The Gaussian kernel with scale $\frac{1}{2}\sigma_s^2$ in the spatial direction and scale $\frac{1}{2}\sigma_o^2$ in the angular direction is used to smooth the orientation scores before applying the rotating operators. We use a conversion factor μ with physical unit 1/length to balance the units difference between angular and spatial directions.

With proper scale samples S, the orientation scores of multioriented vessel structures are enhanced using the LID filters at different scale levels. This ensures that both large and small vessels with multiple orientations are preserved properly. The final 2D enhanced vessel map $\Upsilon(f)(\mathbf{x})$ is obtained via imposing maximum intensity projection of filter responses over all orientations per position $\mathbf{x} = (x, y)$, which is denoted by

$$\Upsilon(f)(\mathbf{x}) := \max_{\theta_i \in \frac{\pi}{No}\{1,\dots,No\}} \left\{ \sum_{\sigma_s \in S} \Phi_{\eta,\text{norm}}^{\sigma_s,\sigma_o}(U_f)(\mathbf{x},\theta_i) \right\}, \tag{5}$$

where we define No as the number of orientations, and each orientation sample θ_i as $i\frac{\pi}{No}$.

The LAD filters [19] solve the limitation that the LID filters are not always perfectly aligned with local orientations in the scores. When the total amount of orientation samplings is reduced to a limited number, it becomes difficult for the LID filters to achieve optimal vessel enhancement results on multioriented structures. Hence, the LAD filters are set up based on the well-established LAD frame $\{\partial_a, \partial_b, \partial_c\}$ which owns the best alignment to each position and orientation of the data. The LAD filters are defined by taking the second-order partial derivatives ∂_b^2 based on the LAD frame in the direction perpendicular to the vessels. An efficient way for calculating the ∂_b^2 derivatives is to project the Hessian matrix onto the direction vector $\mathbf{e}_b$ via

$$\partial_b^2 U_f = \mathbf{e}_b^T(\mathcal{H}U_f)\mathbf{e}_b, \tag{6}$$

where the Hessian matrix in the orientation score domain is defined by $\mathcal{H}U_f$ given by

$$\mathcal{H}U_f = \begin{pmatrix} \partial_\xi^2 U_f & \partial_\xi \partial_\eta U_f & \partial_\theta \partial_\xi U_f \\ \partial_\xi \partial_\eta U_f & \partial_\eta^2 U_f & \partial_\theta \partial_\eta U_f \\ \partial_\xi \partial_\theta U_f & \partial_\eta \partial_\theta U_f & \partial_\theta^2 U_f \end{pmatrix}. \tag{7}$$

The scale-normalized LAD filters which has the best alignment to local structures can be written as

$$\Phi_{b,\text{norm}}^{\sigma_s, \sigma_o}(U_f) := -\mu^{-2} \partial_b^2 G_{\sigma_s, \sigma_o} * U_f. \tag{8}$$

In Fig. 3, we show an example of enhancing the elongated tubular structures in orientation scores using the LAD filters. The reconstruction from the processed score $\Phi(U_f)$ to the processed image $\Upsilon(f)$ is given by

$$\Upsilon(f)(\mathbf{x}) := \max_{\theta_i \in \frac{\pi}{N_o}\{1,\ldots,N_o\}} \left\{ \sum_{\sigma_s \in \mathcal{S}} \Phi_{b,\text{norm}}^{\sigma_s, \sigma_o}(U_f)(\mathbf{x}, \theta_i) \right\}. \tag{9}$$

The binary vessel map is obtained by applying a proper threshold value on the filtered image. See two typical segmentation examples from the STARE [33] and CHASE_DB1 [34] datasets in Fig. 4. For more details, please refer to Zhang et al. [19].

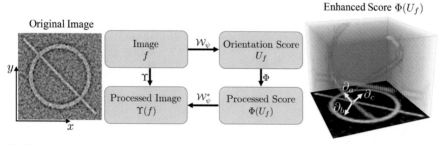

FIG. 3

The whole routine of achieving elongated structure enhancement operation Υ via left-invariant operation Φ based on the locally adaptive frame $\{\partial_a, \partial_b, \partial_c\}$. The exponential curve fit provides the LAD frame with full alignment to local structures. An orientation score $U_f := \mathcal{W}_\psi f$ can be constructed from a 2D image f to an orientation score U_f via wavelet-type transform $\mathcal{W}_\psi$, where we choose cake wavelets [13, 21] for ψ.

From J. Zhang, B. Dashtbozorg, E. Bekkers, J.P.W. Pluim, R. Duits, B.M. ter Haar Romeny, Robust retinal vessel segmentation via locally adaptive derivative frames in orientation scores, IEEE Trans. Med. Imaging 35 (12) (2016) 2631–2644. © 2016 IEEE.

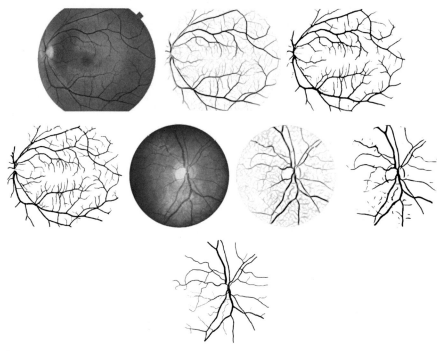

FIG. 4

Examples of vessel segmentation by the LAD algorithm on images from the STARE dataset (Se = 0.8317, Sp = 0.9792, Acc = 0.9609, and MCC = 0.8181) and the CHASE_DB1 dataset (Se = 0.8643, Sp = 0.9623, Acc = 0.9546, and MCC = 0.7319). From Column 1 to 4: original color images, vessel enhancement result, hard segmentation result, and ground truth.

Adapted from J. Zhang, B. Dashtbozorg, E. Bekkers, J.P.W. Pluim, R. Duits, B.M. ter Haar Romeny, Robust retinal vessel segmentation via locally adaptive derivative frames in orientation scores, IEEE Trans. Med. Imaging 35 (12) (2016) 2631–2644.

3.3 Vessel completion

In retinal vessel segmentation tasks, a challenging issue that often appears is the existence of interrupted segments in the extracted vessel structures [35] like the example shown in Fig. 5. There are many disconnections in vessel segments and crossings in the binary segmentations. The main reasons for causing such problems are the presence of nonuniform illumination, contrast variations, and local occlusions in retinal fundus images. The quantitative analysis of retinal vessels requires the extraction of a more complete vessel network for biomarker measurements. Missing/disconnecting retinal vessel segments may easily cause less reliable biomarker calculations and disease predictions in CAD tasks.

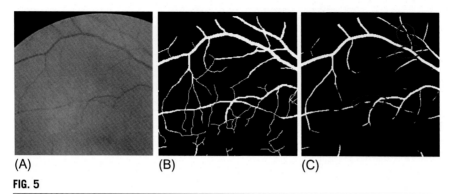

(A)   (B)   (C)

FIG. 5

Segmentation in retinal images with the presence of interruptions. (A) The original patch, (B) the ground truth, and (C) the segmentation results were obtained from the methods by Soares et al. [36].

From J. Zhang, E.J. Bekkers, D. Chen, T.J.M. Berendschot, J. Schouten, J.P.W. Pluim, Y. Shi, B. Dashtbozorg, B.M. ter Haar Romeny, Reconnection of interrupted curvilinear structures via cortically inspired completion for ophthalmologic images, IEEE Trans. Biomed. Eng. 65 (5) (2018) 1151–1165. © 2018 IEEE.

In our pipeline, we employ the automatic gap reconnection method proposed by Zhang et al. [35]. The method uses the stochastic contour completion process, that is, mathematical modeling of the directional process with iterative group convolutions in the roto-translation group $SE(2)$ to enforce line propagation along vessel structures for gap filling purpose. In this process, 2D vessel structures are firstly lifted into a 3D space of position and orientations via the orientation score framework (see Section 2.2). Afterward, interrupted vessel segments are reconnected by applying the $SE(2)$ group convolution between the contour completion kernel and orientation scores, which is defined by

$$\left(R_{\alpha,k}^{\mathbf{D},\mathbf{a}} *_{SE(2)} U_f\right)(\mathbf{x},\theta)$$
$$= \int_{\mathbb{R}^2}\int_0^{2\pi} R_{\alpha,k}^{\mathbf{D},\mathbf{a}}(\mathbf{R}_{\theta'}^{-1}(\mathbf{x}-\mathbf{x}'),\theta-\theta')U_f(\mathbf{x}',\theta')\mathrm{d}\theta'\,\mathrm{d}\mathbf{x}', \tag{10}$$

where $R_{\alpha,k}^{\mathbf{D},\mathbf{a}}$ represents the double-sided completion kernel obtained from Zhang et al. [35]. Fig. 6B and C shows the $SE(2)$ convolution between orientation scores of the image and the 3D completion kernel.

In Fig. 7, we show examples of applying the gap reconnection technique on artificially interrupted segments of retinal vessels. We can see the missing segments in all the gaps are successfully recovered after the reconnection process. The presented method is critical to obtain more complete curvilinear structures in ophthalmologic images. It also provides better topological and geometric connectivities for further analysis.

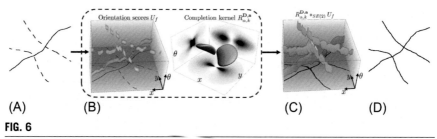

FIG. 6

The proposed pipeline for bridging the interrupted retinal vessel segments via completion process in *SE*(2). (A) Original skeleton, (B) data representation and kernel in *SE*(2), (C) *SE*(2) group convolution, (D) segment-wise thinning.

From J. Zhang, E.J. Bekkers, D. Chen, T.J.M. Berendschot, J. Schouten, J.P.W. Pluim, Y. Shi, B. Dashtbozorg, B.M. ter Haar Romeny, Reconnection of interrupted curvilinear structures via cortically inspired completion for ophthalmologic images, IEEE Trans. Biomed. Eng. 65 (5) (2018) 1151–1165. © 2018 IEEE.

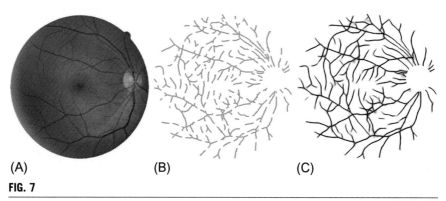

FIG. 7

Examples of applying our method on interrupted retinal vessels of a DRIVE image (565 × 584). (A) Original images; (B) skeletons with gap size 15 × 15; and (C) 2D projections after reconnection in orientation scores.

From J. Zhang, E.J. Bekkers, D. Chen, T.J.M. Berendschot, J. Schouten, J.P.W. Pluim, Y. Shi, B. Dashtbozorg, B.M. ter Haar Romeny, Reconnection of interrupted curvilinear structures via cortically inspired completion for ophthalmologic images, IEEE Trans. Biomed. Eng. 65 (5) (2018) 1151–1165. © 2018 IEEE.

3.4 **Validation studies**

For the validation studies in the RetinaCheck project, we developed a close collaboration with two major hospitals. In the Netherlands, we partnered with the Maastricht Study [37], the World's largest (funded by a 30 M€ Dutch government grant) phenotyping study to the interrelations of many parameters in diabetes. The longitudinal study includes a cohort of 5000 healthy subjects and 5000 diabetes patients, and runs for 10 years. We had access to the ophthalmology data. In China, we partnered with the Endocrinology Department of Shengjing Hospital of China Medical University, the largest hospital in Shenyang, where we built a dedicated acquisition room for retinal fundus images and relevant clinical metadata of the Chinese diabetes in-patients [38].

---

4 Vascular biomarkers

Changes in vessels' morphological and topological structure might reflect changes in blood flow and blood pressure in vessels. To detect even the tiniest early changes, we introduce multiple vascular biomarkers for quantitative blood vessel analysis: vessel width, vessel tortuosity, bifurcation-based features, and fractal dimension.

4.1 Vessel width

Many clinical studies have shown that changes in retinal vessel caliber are associated with the progress of a variety of systemic diseases. In DR, the narrowing on arterioles and the widening on venules are observed, which result in a lower arteriolar-to-venular diameter ratio (AVR) [39, 40]. Moreover, a decrease in generalized arteriolar diameter is associated with a higher risk of developing hypertension [41], and an increase on venular diameter is associated with renal failure, systemic inflammation, and stroke [40].

We developed a method for automatic vessel caliber measurement [42]. An enclosed and deformable contour is initialized using the extracted centerline pixels of a segmented blood vessel. We exploit the geodesic active contour model proposed in Ref. [43] for solving a global optimization problem [42, 44]. Afterward, the surface is iteratively deformed to fit a smooth boundary over the vessel segment.

Vessel caliber is then estimated using the evolved contour. The contour is split into left and right edges by removing the control points at the two ends of the vessel segments. For each control point on one side of the vessel, a corresponding nearest point is found on a B-spline-interpolated curve of two nearest points on the other side. The Euclidean distance between each two points is computed and converted to micrometer (μm) using the pixel size of each image. We estimate the pixel size by taking the ratio between the general optic disc diameter (1800 μm) and the diameter in pixels measured by the method described in Ref. [45]. The measured distances with extreme values are eliminated to prevent outliers and vessel width is calculated as the average of the remaining measurements. Then, the contour is evolved iteratively and fitted to the boundaries of the vessel. Finally, the vessel caliber is measured by computing the distance from one detected vessel edge to the other one. The stages are summarized in Fig. 8.

The results of vessel width measurement are used to estimate the central retinal arterial equivalent (CRAE) and the central retinal venous equivalent (CRVE) (see Fig. 9). The central artery and central veins are the vessels hidden behind the optic disc, where the retinal arteries and veins in the image originated from. The caliber

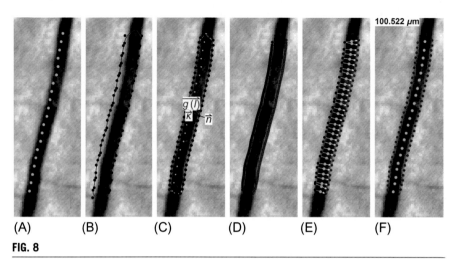

FIG. 8

The stages of the proposed automatic width measurement technique: (A) Centerline detection; (B) contour initialization; (C) active contour segmentation; (D) obtaining the left and right edges; (E) Euclidean distance calculation; and (F) vessel caliber estimation.

From F. Huang, B. Dashtbozorg, A.K.S. Yeung, J. Zhang, T.J.M. Berendschot, B.M. ter Haar Romeny, A comparative study towards the establishment of an automatic retinal vessel width measurement technique, in: Fetal, Infant and Ophthalmic Medical Image Analysis, Springer, 2017, pp. 227–234.

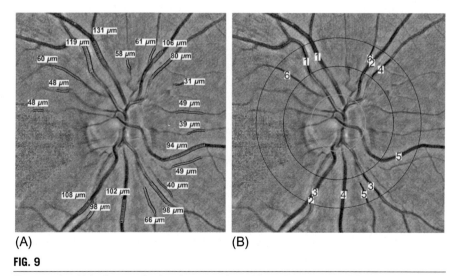

FIG. 9

The vessels within the standard region are selected for calculating the CRAE and CRVE values: (A) The widths of selected vessel are measured by the proposed method and indicated per segment in µm; (B) the six largest arteries and veins are then selected for the calculation of CRAE, CRVE, and AVR values.

From F. Huang, B. Dashtbozorg, A.K.S. Yeung, J. Zhang, T.J.M. Berendschot, B.M. ter Haar Romeny, A comparative study towards the establishment of an automatic retinal vessel width measurement technique, in: Fetal, Infant and Ophthalmic Medical Image Analysis, Springer, 2017, pp. 227–234.

of the central artery and vein, and the ratio between them, has been shown to have significant association to cardiovascular disease progression [46]. The two blood vessels cannot be observed in the retinal image, but can be estimated through two revised formulas for arteries and veins, respectively: first, the optic disc center and diameter are obtained using the super-elliptical convergence filters proposed in Ref. [45]. Then, the vessels within the standard area of 0.5–1.0 disc diameter around the optic disc center are selected and the width values are fed to Knudtson's revised formulas [47]. Finally, the AVR value is defined as the ratio between CRAE and CRVE.

4.2 Vessel tortuosity

Curvature-based metric is defined as the integration of curvature along a curve. In mathematics, the curvature is the second-order derivative along the arc, which is the (infinitesimal) gradient change per increment in path length. A curve can be viewed as the travel path taken by a moving point (x, y). At each time t, the point is located at $(x(t), y(t))$. So the curve (the path of $(x(t), y(t))$) can be formulated as a function of time $C(t) = (x(t), y(t))$. Then, the curvature of the curve C at time t is calculated as:

$$\kappa(t) = \frac{x'(t)y''(t) - x''(t)y'(t)}{(x'(t)^2 + y'(t)^2)}. \tag{11}$$

Eq. (12) is derived by taking the derivative of the tangential angle ϕ to the arc-length s. The formula can be better understood by considering an osculating circle, which is parameterized by $x = r\cos t$ and $y = r\sin t$, passing the point $(x(t), y(t))$ on curve C. Then, Eq. (12) can be simplified into:

$$\kappa(t) = \frac{x'(t)y''(t) - x''(t)y'(t)}{(x'(t)^2 + y'(t)^2)} = \frac{r^2}{r^3} = \frac{1}{r(t)}, \tag{12}$$

where $r(t)$ is the radius of the osculating circle passing point $(x(t), y(t))$ on C. Eq. (13) shows that the curvature at point p on curve is equivalent to the inverse of radius for the osculating circle that touches p. The curvature-based metric τ_C is calculated by integrating $\kappa(t)$ in the interval $[t_0, t_1]$:

$$\tau_C = \int_{t_0}^{t_1} \kappa(t)dt. \tag{13}$$

And the squared curvature metric is

$$\tau_{SC} = \int_{t_0}^{t_1} \kappa(t)^2 dt. \tag{14}$$

4.2.1 Single-vessel tortuosity

The curvature-based metric introduced in last section measures the tortuosity of continuous differentiable functions. However, the vasculature in retinal images is discretized as pixels. In order to perform the best tortuosity measurement on discrete vessel center points, it is necessary to convert it into a continuous curve. One of several possible methods is to construct a B-spline interpolation function for the discrete samples. A B-spline curve is defined as:

$$C(u) = \int_i^m B_{i,k}(u)P_i,$$ (15)

where m is the number of data points D_k, $B_{i,k}(u)$ is the B-spline basis function at degree k, and $0 \leq u \leq 1$ is the ith control point at the curve. However, the continuous curve reconstructed by the above equation is sensitive to outliers' points, because it uses the data points as control points. In other words, it forces the reconstructed curve to pass through every data point $D_k = C(t_k)$. In this case, the reconstructed curve is oscillating instead of smooth. To overcome this issue, Wong [47a] proposed a modified B-spline function in which the curve is not restricted to fit every sample point but only the start and end points, $D_0 = C(t_0)$ and $D_m = C(t_m)$. The curve does not pass data point D_k but a point near it, $D(k) \neq C(t_k)$. A cost function is derived as:

$$f(P_0,...,P_h) = \sum_{h-1}^{k} \left| Q_k - \sum_{h-1}^{i} B_{i,k}(u)P_i \right|^2,$$ (16)

where $Q_k = D_k - B_{0,k}(u)P_0 - B_{h,k}(u)P_h$ and $P_0, ..., P_h$ are the control points of the B-spline curve. Minimizing Eq. (17) yields the optimal set of control points for blood vessel reconstructions. Putting the control points into Eq. (16) yields a smooth curve function for the discrete data points. An illustration of the B-splines curve is shown in Fig. 10, where the red points are the discrete data points, the green curve is the B-spline curve, and the blue points are the optimal control points. Subsequently, the local curvature values τ_C and τ_{SC} of the reconstructed vessel are quantified analytically using Eq. (13).

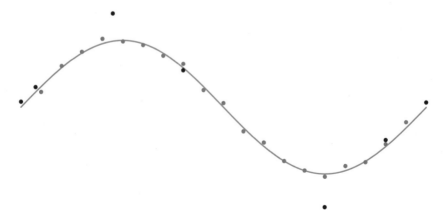

FIG. 10

A smooth B-spline curve created by the modified B-spline interpolation method. The *red points* are the initial discrete data points (i.e., the coordinates of vessel centerline pixels), the *blue points* are the optimal control points, and the *green curve* shows the B-spline curve.

4.2.2 Global tortuosity

The previous section introduced the tortuosity measurement for a single vessel. However, in order to compare the overall tortuosity difference for two retinal photographs, it is necessary to derive a global value representing the tortuosity of the whole vascular network instead of a single vessel or a few vessels. Several tortuosity techniques were proposed to measure the whole vessel tree. Onkaew et al. [48] used the sum of tortuosity values of all vessel segments, but the number of compared vessels must be the same for both images to yield an accurate outcome. Sasongko et al. [49] took 6 largest arteries and veins, 12 vessels in total, from both vascular trees to compare the tortuosity in between. Thus they neglected the sensitivity of small vessels to transmural pressure changes. Hart et al. [50] used the mean of curvature of all vessel segments to represent global tortuosity. This method overcomes the issues of the former two methods so the number of vessels of two vascular trees does not need to be the same, and all vessels are taken into account.

In practice, we compute the mean, standard deviation, minimum, median, and maximum of tortuosity of all vessels, arteries only and veins only, within different regions of interest.

4.3 *SE*(2) tortuosity

The tortuosity measurement introduced in previous section is the regular vessel tortuosity pipeline, which includes blood vessel segmentation, morphological thinning to obtain centerlines, splitting the vessels into segments by removing junction points and tortuosity measurement [50–53]. In such pipelines, errors might be introduced in each processing step, which propagate and accumulate to influence the final result of tortuosity, which makes the measurement unstable and unreliable. Alternatively, based on the theory of best exponential curve fits in *SE*(2) [54, 55], Bekkers et al. [56] proposed a reduced pipeline which does not rely on explicit segmentation of the blood vessels, but instead it computes the tortuosity directly from the retinal image. It computes the curvature of a curve in the orientation scores space.

4.3.1 Exponential curves in SE(2)

A planar curve $\gamma_{2D}(t) = (x(t), y(t))$ can be naturally lifted to position orientation space via $\gamma_{SE(2)}(t) = (x(t), y(t), \theta(t))$, with $\theta(t) = \arg \dot{x}(t) + i\dot{y}(t)$ the orientation of the tangent vector $\dot{\gamma}_{2D}(t)$ of the curve. The orientation $\theta(t)$ of such naturally lifted curves is thus related to the tangent vector of its 2D planar projection. From the previous sections, we know that curvature can be computed by analysis of the *second-order* derivative of the 2D curve (looking at the change in tangent direction). In our *SE*(2) approach, we can directly compute the curvature from *first-order* derivative of the lifted curve $\gamma_{SE(2)}$. When we describe the tangent vector $\dot{\gamma}_{SE(2)}(t)$ in our moving frame of reference

$$\dot{\gamma}_{SE(2)}(t) = c^\xi(t)\mathbf{e}_\xi(\gamma_{SE(2)}(t)) + c^\eta(t)\mathbf{e}_\eta(\gamma_{SE(2)}(t)) + c^\theta(t)\mathbf{e}_\theta(\gamma_{SE(2)}(t)), \tag{17}$$

where we identify $\{\mathbf{e}_\xi(g), \mathbf{e}_\eta(g), \mathbf{e}_\theta(g)\} \Leftrightarrow \{\partial_\xi|_g, \partial_\eta|_g, \partial_\theta|_g\}$ to indicate that now we adopt a geometric viewpoint rather than a differential geometric/algebraic viewpoint, then the curvature of its 2D projection is simply computed via the ratio between the change in orientation and spatial motion:

$$\kappa_{SE(2)}(t) = \frac{c^\theta(t)\text{sign}(c^\xi(t))}{\sqrt{|c^\xi(t)|^2 + |c^\eta(t)|^2}}. \tag{18}$$

Now we know how to compute the curvature if we have description of our curve in $SE(2)$. In this section, we consider a particular type of curves, namely exponential curves. An exponential γ_c is a curve in $SE(2)$ whose tangent vector components $\mathbf{c} = (c^\xi, c^\eta, c^\theta)$ expressed in the rotating frame (cf. Eq. 18) remain constant. In this sense, they can be considered the "straight lines" in the curved geometry of $SE(2)$. The exponential curves actually form circular spirals in $SE(2)$ due to the fact the moving frame of reference (cf. Eq. 4) can rotate with a constant speed proportional to c^θ. Exponential curves can be efficiently fitted to data in orientation scores, this is discussed in following sections.

4.3.2 Fitting the best exponential curve in the orientation scores

In medical image analysis, a common approach to determine the local tangent vector is to compute the direction of the minimal principal curvature, obtained via eigenanalysis of the Hessian matrix (as discussed in Ref. [57]). This essentially boils down to locally fitting a straight line (an exponential curves in $\mathbb{R}^2$) to the data along which variation in the image is minimized. Similarly, we can fit "straight lines" (the exponential curves in $SE(2)$) in orientation scores. We do this via analysis of the $SE(2)$ Hessian which we compute via LIDs (cf. Eq. 4):

$$\mathcal{H}U_f = \mathbf{M}_{\mu^{-2}} \begin{pmatrix} \partial_\xi^2 U_f & \partial_\xi\partial_\eta U_f & \partial_\theta\partial_\xi U_f \\ \partial_\xi\partial_\eta U_f & \partial_\eta^2 U_f & \partial_\theta\partial_\eta U_f \\ \partial_\xi\partial_\theta U_f & \partial_\eta\partial_\theta U_f & \partial_\theta^2 U_f \end{pmatrix} \mathbf{M}_{\mu^{-2}}, \tag{19}$$

with $\mathbf{M}_{\mu^{-2}} = \text{diag}(\mu, \mu, 1)$ and with μ an intrinsic parameter that balance spatial and orientation distances and make $\mathcal{H}U_f$ dimensionless. In addition, since the eigenanalysis requires a symmetric Hessian matrix, while $\mathcal{H}U_f$ is not, we symmetrize it via $\mathcal{H}_\mu U_f = \mathbf{M}_\mu (\mathcal{H}U_f)^T \mathbf{M}_{\mu^2} (\mathcal{H}U_f)\mathbf{M}_\mu$. Based on $\mathcal{H}_x U_f$, we compute the eigenvectors $M\mu\mathbf{c}^*$ which provides the solution to the optimization problem for finding the best exponential fitting at local oriented structures:

$$\mathbf{c}^*(g) = \arg\min_{\mathbf{c}\in\mathbb{R}^3, \|\mathbf{c}\|=1} \left\{ \left| \frac{d}{dt}(\nabla U(\gamma_\mathbf{c}^g(t)))|_{t=0} \right|_\mu^2 \right\}, \tag{20}$$

where $\nabla U = \mathbf{M}_\mu^{-2}(\partial_\xi U, \partial_\eta U, \partial_\theta U)$ is the left-invariant gradient operator, and $\|\mathbf{c}\|_\mu^2 = \mu^2|c^\xi|^2 + \mu^2|c^\eta|^2 + |c^\theta|^2$ computes the dimensionless arc-length of the exponential curve γ_c.

4.3.3 Global tortuosity measurement via the exponential curvature

The above procedure describes a way to obtain the tangent vector components of an exponential curve that best fits the data. From these components, we compute the curvature via Eq. (19). Since the Hessian can be computed for every position and orientation, we can assign to every voxel in our orientation score a curvature value $\kappa_{SE(2)}(g)$. These curvature values can be averaged to give a global tortuosity score. To do so we compute a weighted average and standard deviation, where weighting is done using the vessel confidence measure $\Phi_{\eta,\mathrm{norm}}^{\sigma_s,\sigma_o}(U_f)$. We compute the following global scores:

$$\mu_{|\kappa|} = \frac{1}{\Phi_{\mathrm{total}}} \int\limits_{-\infty}^{\infty} \int\limits_{0}^{\pi} |\kappa(\mathbf{x},\theta)| \Phi_{\eta,\mathrm{norm}}^{\sigma_s,\sigma_o}(U_f(\mathbf{x},\theta)) \mathrm{d}\mathbf{x}\, \mathrm{d}\theta, \qquad (21)$$

$$\sigma_{|\kappa|} = \sqrt{\frac{1}{\Phi_{\mathrm{total}}} \int\limits_{-\infty}^{\infty} \int\limits_{0}^{\pi} (|\kappa(\mathbf{x},\theta)| - \mu_{|\kappa|})^2 \Phi_{\eta,\mathrm{norm}}^{\sigma_s,\sigma_o}(U_f(\mathbf{x},\theta)) \mathrm{d}\mathbf{x}\, \mathrm{d}\theta}, \qquad (22)$$

where $\Phi_{\mathrm{total}} = \int\limits_{-\infty}^{\infty} \int\limits_{0}^{\pi} \Phi_{\eta,\mathrm{norm}}^{\sigma_s,\sigma_o}(U_f(\mathbf{x},\theta)) \mathrm{d}\mathbf{x}\, \mathrm{d}\theta$ is the integration of $\Phi_{\eta,\mathrm{norm}}^{\sigma_s,\sigma_o}$ for normalization

purpose. The features $\mu_{|\kappa|}$ and $\sigma_{|\kappa|}$ measure the weighted average and standard deviation of the absolute exponential curvatures.

The method gives excellent results, see, for example, Fig. 13H.

4.4 Bifurcations

The motivation for analyzing possible changes in vessel bifurcations due to pathology is that the branching pattern is governed by optimality principles. The vascular circulation system is not a totally random network but has developed under some optimum physical principles. Due to the natural selection in biological evolution, the circulation network must have achieved an optimum arrangement such that every vessel is developed with the least possible biological work, that is, the minimum friction between blood flow and vessel wall, the optimal heart rate to achieve proper blood supply, the shortest transport distances, etc.

We extract several biomarkers from vessel branches, including blood vessel diameters ratio and bifurcation angles, using the approach proposed by Al-Diri et al. [58].

4.4.1 Murray's law

For over a century, physiologists have been investigating the optimal conditions that should be held during mammalian circulation system development [59–61]. Murray et al. [60] stated in 1926 that the cube of the radius of a parent vessel should be equal to the sum of the cubes of the radii of its daughter vessels. Using this law, we can identify diseased retinal vasculature from healthy vasculature, where the optimal condition is not hold anymore.

Murray proposed that in a healthy circulation network, blood flow in every vessel segment is achieved with the least possible biological work. Two power terms (energy per second) are taken into account in the flow cost measurement: the power P_f to overcome viscous drag in a fluid as described by Poiseuille's law (the resistance R to a flow in a rigid tube is inversely proportional to the fourth power of the tube radius, and proportional to the tube length $R \propto L / r^4$), and the power P_m to maintain the volume of the blood and vessel tissue involved in achieving the flow. These two power terms are related to the vessel radius in an opposite way. The larger the radius is, the smaller resistance the fluid would have, thus costing less power P_f. However, a larger radius will lead to an increased power cost P_m to maintain the volume of the blood and vessel wall tissue. Therefore, the vessel radius must be an optimal value that minimizes the total power cost: $P_t = P_t + P_t$. This leads to the definition of junction exponents:

$$r_0^3 = r_1^3 + r_2^3, \tag{23}$$

where r_0 is the radius of parent vessel lumen (i.e., $d = 2r$ (diameter)) and r_1 and r_2 are the radii of the two daughter vessel lumina.

4.4.2 Bifurcation biomarkers

The bifurcations of a vasculature are detected using the orientation-score-based technique proposed by Abbasi et al. [27]. This method utilizes the orientation score of a 2D image, in which a pixel has multiple orientation values indicating its local directions. By analyzing the orientation profile of each pixel, one can recognize a vessel structure (two maxima), bifurcation (three maxima), and crossover (four maxima). After obtaining the location of the bifurcations, we extract the bifurcation-based biomarkers proposed by Al-Diri et al. [58] based on Eq. (24), formulated as follows:

(1) Area ratio: $\beta = \dfrac{(d_1^2 + d_2^2)}{d_0^2}$,

(2) Bifurcation index: $\lambda = \dfrac{d_2}{d_1}$,

(3) Diameter ratios: $\lambda_1 = \dfrac{d_1}{d_2}$ and $\lambda_2 = \dfrac{d_2}{d_0}$,

(4) Bifurcation angles: $\cos\theta_1 = \dfrac{\lambda_1^{-4} + 1 - \lambda^4}{2\lambda_1^{-2}} \cos\theta_2 = \dfrac{\lambda_1^{-4} + \lambda^4 - 1}{2\lambda^{-2}\lambda_1^{-2}}$ and $\theta = \theta_1 + \theta_2$,

where d_0 is the diameter of a parent vessel, d_1 and d_2 are the diameters of its two daughter vessels, and θ, θ_1, and θ_2 are the bifurcation angles as shown in Fig. 11.

4.5 Fractal dimension

Another vascular biomarker that describes changes in microvasculature due to disease progression is the fractal dimension (FD). The theory of FD was first introduced by Mandelbrot in 1983 [62]. He proposed a set of mathematical definitions for a

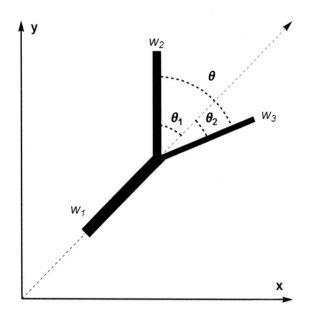

FIG. 11

The bifurcation biomarkers are calculated based on the vessel diameters (d_i) and bifurcation angles (θ, θ_1, θ_2).

"self-similar" object, where a same pattern with different sizes can be observed at different scales. Examples are trees, snowflakes, and river systems. A noninteger number is used to describe the dimension of this typically highly irregular shape. In 1989, the fractal was first introduced into ophthalmology by Family et al. [63] because the retinal vascular network can be considered as a fractal object over certain scales. After that there has been a growing interest in studying the association between the fractal dimension of the retinal vasculature and the disease severity and progression [64–68].

The self-similar property can be described by the formula:

$$N(r) = r^{-D}, \tag{24}$$

where $N(r)$ is a measurement applied on the complicated pattern of the object at a scale r, D is the fractal dimension that implies how many new similar patterns are observed as the resolution magnification (scale) decreases or increases. According to the definition, a fractal object is self-similar; therefore, the comparison of two measurements in various scales should yield the same results. This implies that the fractal dimension D can also be calculated by comparing the measurements between any two scales:

$$D \approx -\frac{\log N(r_n) - \log N(r_{n-1})}{\log r_n - \log r_{n-1}}. \tag{25}$$

In our study, we studied three fractal methods that are widely used in the literature: the *box dimension D_B*, the *information dimension D_I*, and the *correlation dimension D_C*, which measure different properties (different $N(r)$) of the self-similar pattern of the object, respectively.

Box dimension (D_B) is the most simple and popular method for estimating the FD of fractal objects proposed by Liebovitch and Toth [69]. It is the direct implementation of the Hausdorff dimension in mathematics [70]. The box dimension is defined as the real number D_B, such that the number $N(r)$ of balls with radius r that is needed to cover an object grows with $(1/r)^{D_B}$ as $r \to 0$. In other words, D_B is calculated via:

$$D_B = \lim_{r \to 0} \frac{\log N(r)}{\log 1/r}. \tag{26}$$

So in the image domain, the measurement $N(r)$ in Eq. (27) is the number of boxes with side-length r that overlap with the vessel segmentation. When dealing with discrete problems, taking the limit $r \to 0$ is not possible.

Based on the above relation between measurements in different scales, a box-counting method is introduced to do a simple, fast estimation of the fractal dimension D. In this method, the full space is firstly covered by squared boxes with side-length r_n. And then measurements are done in the boxes that are overlapping with the objects. This step will be repeated multiple times with different box side-lengths. Finally, the size of the box and the corresponding measurement are plotted in a log-log plot. The estimated fractal dimension is the slope of the regression line that fit to these data points.

Information dimension (D_I) is inspired from information theory. Entropy is the measure of the uncertainty of a random event. The less likely a random event is to happen, the more informative it is, thus the larger entropy it has. Conversely, if an event happens very often, it provides less information, implying lower entropy. The information dimension [71, 72] is defined as:

$$D_I = \lim_{\delta \to 0} \frac{-\sum_N^{i=1} p_i \log p_i}{\log 1/\delta}, \tag{27}$$

where N is the number of boxes with size δ overlapped with the object, the numerator $-\sum_{i=1}^{N} p_i \log p_i$ is the first-order Shannon entropy, $p_i = n_i/M$ is the probability for finding a part of the object in the ith box, M is the total mass of it, and n_i is the part of the object in the box. The limit of Eq. (28) is estimated as the slope of the regression line of the logarithmic points.

Correlation dimension (D_C) estimates the FD via the relationship between two pixels inside a region. A correlation integral is defined via the Heaviside step function for counting the pair of points in a region with size r_k, and can be approximately expressed in terms of the probability density:

$$C_k = \frac{1}{N^2} \sum_N^{\substack{i=1 \\ j=1 \\ i \neq j}} \Theta(r_k - \mathbf{x}_i - \mathbf{x}_j) \approx \sum_{N_k}^{j=1} p_{jk}^2, \tag{28}$$

where $\Theta(x)$ is the Heaviside step function, $\mathbf{x}_i$ is the ith pixel belonging to an object, $p_{jk} = n_{jk}/M$ is the probability density of the object with mass M in the jth box with size r_k. The correlation dimension D_C is defined via the relationship between C_k and r_k as $D_C = \lim_{r_k \to 0} \dfrac{\log C_k}{\log r_k}$.

5 The processing pipeline

The assessment of the characteristics of the retinal vascular network provides important information for an early diagnosis and prognosis of many systemic and vascular diseases. Current digital image processing techniques proposed in the literature still cannot ensure a 100% accuracy on segmentation, classification, and biomarkers extraction, each of which might introduce errors into the full pipeline. Therefore, manual analysis is still a necessary step for reviewing the automatic results and improving the automatic system.

In this section, we describe an efficient retinal health information and notification system (acronym RHINO) developed by Dashtbozorg et al. [3, 73]. It chains all the introduced image analysis techniques into a processing pipeline (see Fig. 1 how different modules interact with each other). It provides a user-friendly interface for human observers to review the automatic results and the extracted vascular biomarkers. In addition, it allows the user to manually correct the automatic results, such as artery/vein labels, the position and the boundary of the optic disc and fovea, and vessel centerlines to ensure a reliable analysis for a clinical research and application.

5.1 RHINO software and graphical user interface

The graphical user interface is developed in Matlab R2016b using the App Designer. The main interface and the generated reports are shown in Fig. 12. The software firstly checks the quality of each image, and determines if it as an optic disc-centered image or a fovea-centered image based on the location of optic disc. Afterward, the left panel shows a selected category of vascular biomarker measurement and the right panel illustrates the corresponding biomarker maps, see Fig. 13.

When errors are found, such as a miss-detected optic disc center, wrong vessel segmentation, or artery/vein labels, the user can activate the manual correction tool by switching the annotation button to "on," enter the manual correction module (see Fig. 14) and correct the inaccurate part and save the manual results. To add a vessel centerline to the binary segmentation, the human observer clicks a start point and an end point on a vessel segment, then a shortest path is generated forming a new vessel centerline. At last, an active contour will grow and fit to the boundary of the vessel (see Fig. 14A). To change the A/V label of a vessel, the human observer left clicks on a vessel and its label will be switched between "artery," "vein," and "not a vessel" (see Fig. 14B). To modify the center of the optic disc, the observer clicks on the image to determine the new position. And to determine a new optic disc boundary, the observer clicks 6/10 points on the boundary, then a circular shape is fitted to the clicked points (see Fig. 14C). After manual corrections, the updated results

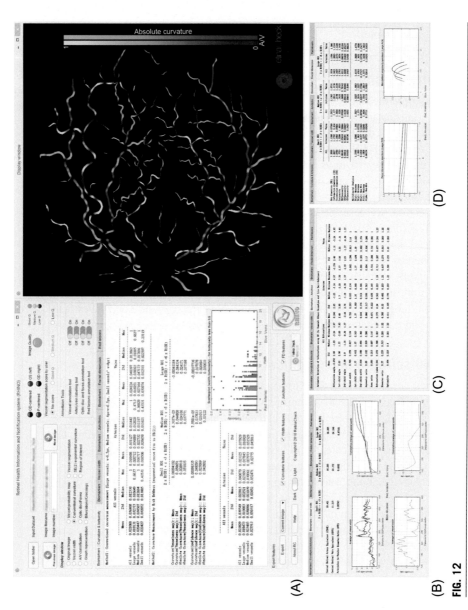

FIG. 12

Top row: (A) The main user interface of RHINO and the generated reports. *Bottom row:* (B) Vessel width biomarkers, (C) bifurcation biomarkers, and (D) fractal dimension biomarkers.

From B. Dashtbozorg, J. Zhang, S. Abbasi-Sureshjani, F. Huang, B.M. ter Haar Romeny, Retinal health information and notification system (RHINO), in: SPIE Medical Imaging, vol. 1013437, International Society for Optics and Photonics, 2017, 10.1117/12.2253839.

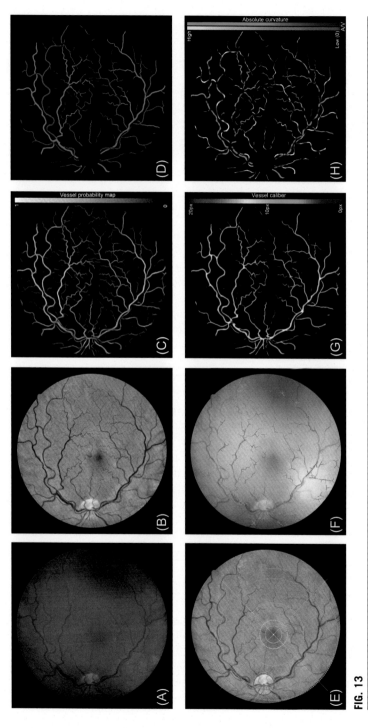

FIG. 13

RHINO displays: (A) Original fundus image, (B) normalized image, (C) vessel probability map, (D) artery/vein labels, (E) optic disc and fovea locations and regions of interest, (F) bifurcations and crossings, (G) vessel caliber map, and (H) curvature map. *Caption bars indicate the displayed ranges.*

From B. Dashtbozorg, J. Zhang, S. Abbasi-Sureshjani, F. Huang, B.M. ter Haar Romeny, Retinal health information and notification system (RHINO), in: SPIE Medical Imaging, vol. 1013437, International Society for Optics and Photonics, 2017, 10.1117/12.2253839.

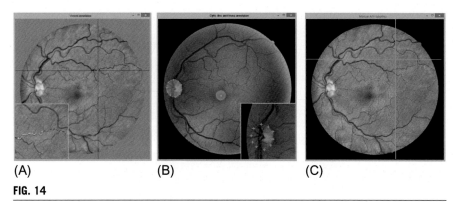

(A)   (B)   (C)

FIG. 14

Three RHINO annotation modules: (A) Artery/vein manual labeling, (B) optic disc and fovea delineation, and (C) vessel centerline annotation.

From B. Dashtbozorg, J. Zhang, S. Abbasi-Sureshjani, F. Huang, B.M. ter Haar Romeny, Retinal health information and notification system (RHINO), in: SPIE Medical Imaging, vol. 1013437, International Society for Optics and Photonics, 2017, 10.1117/12.2253839.

are immediately saved and shown in the main display panel. In order to increase interactivity and usability, additional features and tools are available, that is, the visualization of intermediate results and the generation of reports in PDF, XLSX, and CSV formats.

Only a few broad-range retinal image analysis systems for retinal vascular study have been developed previously. They are often semiautomated and restricted to a single area of analysis (e.g., vessel segmentation, vessel width measurement, or artery/vein labeling). The RHINO software presented in this section is based on the retinal image analysis algorithms developed by the RetinaCheck group. It provides quantitative biomarkers for accurate assessment of retinal vasculature geometry and manual correction on the automated results, which makes it useful for both research, general clinical applications, and screening. The software is aimed to be part of daily clinical practice, in both central hospitals and local clinics, as a stand-alone product or as an additional tool in ophthalmology devices.

6 Clinical validation studies

6.1 The Shengjing study

The details of the statistical study can be found in the paper of Zhu et al. [38]. In summary, Zhu et al. found that the DR patients generally had older age, longer duration of diabetes, higher baPWV, higher SBP, higher DBP, and were more likely to have higher retinal vascular tortuosity values (both mean and standard deviation). On the other hand, no significant difference was found between the two groups in terms of the glycated hemoglobin, BMI, cholesterol, fasting glucose, urine albumin/creatinine ratio, triglyceride, LDL, HDL, thrombosis, high blood pressure, smoking, and drinking (see Table 1 in [38]).

Older age, longer diabetes duration, higher baPWV, and diagnosed with high blood pressure, thrombosis, and the presence of DR were significantly associated with higher mean and standard deviation tortuosity (all P values <.05). Moreover, they found that higher urine microalbuminuria and urine albumin/creatinine ratio significantly correlated with both higher tortuosity measures (all P values <.05). For the multivariable-adjusted linear regression analysis, in model 1, patients with older age or longer duration of diabetes had significantly higher tortuosity values both in the mean and the standard deviation of tortuosity (all P values <.05), after the adjustment for LDL, HDL, and diagnosed high blood pressure.

In model 2, the factors related kidney failure and DR were added to the variables based on model 1. It was found that higher tortuosity values were still significantly associated with older age, longer duration, higher urine albumin/creatinine ratio (all P values <.05), while LDL was found negatively correlated with tortuosity. These associations remained even after excluding the factor of DR in model 3.

We can conclude that, on Chinese hospitalized type 2 diabetic patients, higher vascular tortuosity is independently associated with older age, longer diabetic duration, and higher urine albumin/creatinine ratio, after adjusting for the influence of DR (using model 3). This finding suggests that the vascular tortuosity is a highly interesting biomarker for diabetes detection, as it is significantly associated with multiple risk factors of diabetes. In addition, it is further supported by the finding using model 3, where we removed the factor of DR, which means: before DR appears on the retina of diabetic patients, the tortuosity has already changed.

6.2 The Maastricht study

We investigated the association between the caliber biomarkers and the diabetes status, using multivariate regression analysis [74]. The results are shown in Fig. 15 as a box plot. The horizontal axis represents the diabetes status and different models, and the vertical axis represents the difference in vessel caliber regarding to NGM (i.e., β_{preDM} and β_{T2DM}). Note that the unit of the vertical axis is μm, but it is not the actual width value but the difference with the normal ones. To give a better demonstration for the comparison, we add a small bar for the NGM while its value is zero. The plots show that, after adjusting for the effects of risk factors, both prediabetes patients and diabetes patients have generally larger CRAE and CRVE versus healthy (normal glucose metabolism). As we can see from the box plot, the arterioles are seriously affected by the hyperglycemia.

In prediabetes patients, with all risk factors adjusted (model 3), the difference in CRAE values is slightly less than 1.0, and in type 2 diabetes patients, the difference is above 3.0. It reveals that the prediabetes stage does not affect the arterioles too much, while the influence dramatically grows when the patients step into the diabetes stage. In addition, the box plots of models 1, 2, and 3 are similar to each other, suggesting that cardio risk factors do not affect arterioles very much.

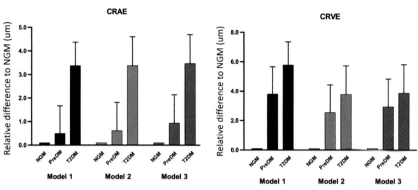

FIG. 15

The box plots of multivariable-adjusted difference analysis on retinal microvascular diameters between prediabetes and T2DM patients against NGM subjects. Model 1: adjusted by age and gender; model 2: additionally adjusted by the cardiovascular risk factors; model 3: additionally adjusted by eGFR, albuminuria, and prior CVD.

From W. Li, M. Schram, T.J.M. Berendschot, J. Schouten, A. Kroon, C. van der Kallen, R. Henry, A. Koster, P. Dagnelie, N. Schaper, et al., Prediabetes and diabetes are associated with wider retinal arterioles and venules: the Maastricht study, Diabetologia 61 (2018) S532–S533.

For the venules, after all the risk factors were adjusted, the difference between prediabetes and diabetes subjects is about 3.0 and 4.0, respectively. It shows that the influence of hyperglycemia on the venules is less than on arterioles, because as the hyperglycemia duration being longer, the increment of vein caliber is very small. In addition, we can see that after adjusting for a set of risk factors (i.e., models 2 and 3), the differences are slightly decreased, which means these risk factors might affect the venous vessels. At last, for prediabetes patients, the vein calibers have already shown a great difference compared to NGM, which suggests that the influence of impaired glucose metabolism on venules might begin in the very early stage and might be a powerful biomarker for early diabetes detection.

This study on investigating the association between diabetes status and vascular caliber suggests that prediabetes and diabetes are independently associated with both wider retinal arterioles and venules, in a predominantly Caucasian population. These findings support the concept that the microvascular dysfunction is an early phenomenon in disturbed glucose metabolism.

7 Discussion

In this chapter, we presented a set of clinically effective and robust retinal vascular biomarkers. The algorithms for segmentation, crossing-preserving enhancement, closing gaps, and quantifying bifurcations and widths were developed with innovative brain-inspired geometrical methods. The multiscale approach leads to regularized Gaussian differential operators, while the multiorientation approach allows for the construction of orientation scores, where sub-Riemannian methods give a rich repertoire of contextual directional operations, like oriented diffusion for vessel completion and enhancement. Many classical challenges, like the proper calculation of vessel tortuosity, crossing-preserving denoising, gap closure, and tracking parallel vessels, could be solved by this approach.

Humans are not good at judging early changes on the vasculature, while it is known that these changes occur before clinical symptoms occur. Also it is hard for experts to quantify the geometrical and topological vascular measures, for example, for longitudinal changes. Together with the expected large-scale application, these biomarkers may play a crucial role in early warning screening.

The retina is brain tissue, so inspection of the microvasculature of the retina may also give insight in the status of the microvasculature of the brain. If, for example, a significant correlation can be established between MRI-detected microbleeds in the brain and retinal microaneurysms/microbleeds, retinal imaging may offer a particularly cost-effective early detection system.

The prospects of deep learning are excellent, where the operators are learned from huge sets of data. It may be especially efficient when the clinically effective vascular biomarkers as discussed in this chapter can be learned during the training process. Retinal imaging has the specific advantage that huge datasets are readily available. However, the intrinsic mechanism of how deep learning works is still largely a black box. Cross-fertilizing the worlds of modern physiology and imaging of human vision at cellular functional level and modern progress in artificial neural networks will prove highly effective to understand both the human and the machine vision mechanisms.

The next phase of the RetinaCheck project will be as a start-up, now entering the clinical phase of large-scale detection and early warning in China. In this way, the analysis methods inspired by our visual system are now applied to prevent vision loss: *vision for vision.*

References

[1] Y. Xu, L. Wang, J. He, et al., Prevalence and control of diabetes in Chinese adults, JAMA 310 (9) (2013) 948–959, https://doi.org/10.1001/jama.2013.168118.

[2] International Ophthalmology Council, ICO Guidelines for Diabetic Eye Care, 2017. www.icoph.org/downloads/ICOGuidelinesforDiabeticEyeCare.pdf.

[3] B. Dashtbozorg, S. Abbasi-Sureshjani, J. Zhang, F. Huang, E.J. Bekkers, B.M. ter Haar Romeny, Infrastructure for retinal image analysis, in: Proceedings of the Ophthalmic Medical Image Analysis Second International Workshop, OMIA 2016, Held in Conjunction With MICCAI 2016, Athens, Greece, October 17, 2015, Iowa Research Online, 2016, pp. 105–112.

[4] B.M. ter Haar Romeny, Front-End Vision and Multi-S-cale Image Analysis, CIV, vol. 27, Springer, Berlin, 2003. https://doi.org/10.1007/978-1-4020-8840-7.

[5] J. Petitot, Y. Tondut, Vers une neurogéométrie. Fibrations corticales, structures de contact et contours subjectifs modaux, Math. Inf. Sci. Humaines 145 (1999) 5–102.

[6] A. Citti, G. Sarti, A cortical based model of perceptual completion in the roto-translation space, J. Math. Imaging Vis. 24 (3) (2006) 307–326.

[7] R. Duits, U. Boscain, F. Rossi, Y. Sachkov, Association fields via cuspless sub-Riemannian geodesics in *SE*(2). J. Math. Imaging Vis. 49 (2) (2013) 384–417, https://doi.org/10.1007/s10851-013-0475-y.

[8] D.H. Hubel, T.N. Wiesel, Receptive fields of single neurons in the cat's striate cortex, J. Physiol. 148 (1959) 574–591.

[9] K. Koffka, Principles of Gestalt Psychology, Routledge, New York, 1935.

[10] D. Field, A. Hayes, R.F. Hess, Contour integration by the human visual system: evidence for a local "association field", Vis. Res. 33-2 (1993) 173–193.

[11] W.H. Bosking, Y. Zhang, B. Scho, D. Fitzpatrick, Orientation selectivity and the arrangement of horizontal connections in tree shrew striate cortex, J. Neurosci. 6 (17) (1997) 2112–2127.

[12]. R. Duits, Perceptual Organization in Image Analysis (Ph.D. thesis), Department of Biomedical Engineering, Eindhoven University of Technology, The Netherlands, 2005.

[13] R. Duits, M. Duits, M. van Almsick, B. ter Haar Romeny, Invertible orientation scores as an application of generalized wavelet theory, Pattern Recogn. Image Anal. 17 (1) (2007) 42–75.

[14] R. Duits, M. Felsberg, G. Granlund, B.M. ter Haar Romeny, Image analysis and reconstruction using a wavelet transform constructed from a reducible representation of the Euclidean motion group, Int. J. Comput. Vis. 72 (1) (2007) 79–102.

[15]. E.J. Bekkers, Retinal Image Analysis Using Sub-Riemannian Geometry in SE(2) (Ph.D. thesis), Department of Biomedical Engineering, Eindhoven University of Technology, 2017.

[16] R. Duits, U. Boscain, F. Rossi, Y. Sachkov, Association fields via cuspless sub-Riemannian geodesics in SE(2), J. Math. Imaging Vis. 49 (2) (2014) 384–417.

[17] G. Citti, A. Sarti, A cortical based model of perceptional completion in the roto-translation space, J. Math. Imaging Vis. 24 (3) (2006) 307–326.

[18] J. Hannink, R. Duits, E.J. Bekkers, Crossing-preserving multi-scale vesselness. in: P. Golland, N. Hata, C. Barillot, J. Hornegger, R. Howe (Eds.), Medical Image Computing and Computer-Assisted Intervention—MICCAI 2014, Lecture Notes in Computer Science, vol. 8674, Springer International Publishing, 2014, pp. 603–610, https://doi.org/10.1007/978-3-319-10470-6_75.

[19] J. Zhang, B. Dashtbozorg, E. Bekkers, J.P.W. Pluim, R. Duits, B.M. ter Haar Romeny, Robust retinal vessel segmentation via locally adaptive derivative frames in orientation scores, IEEE Trans. Med. Imaging 35 (12) (2016) 2631–2644.

[20] S. Abbasi-Sureshjani, I. Smit-Ockeloen, J. Zhang, B.M. ter Haar Romeny, Biologically-inspired supervised vasculature segmentation in SLO retinal fundus images. in: M. Kamel, A. Campilho (Eds.), Image Analysis and Recognition, Lecture Notes in Computer Science, vol. 9164, Springer, 2015, pp. 325–334, https://doi.org/10.1007/978-3-319-20801-5_35.

[21] E.J. Bekkers, R. Duits, T.J.M. Berendschot, B.M. ter Haar Romeny, A multi-orientation analysis approach to retinal vessel tracking, J. Math. Imaging Vis. 49 (3) (2014) 583–610.

[22] E.J. Bekkers, R. Duits, A. Mashtakov, G.R. Sanguinetti, A PDE approach to data-driven sub-Riemannian geodesics in SE(2), SIAM J. Imaging Sci. 8 (4) (2015) 2740–2770, https://doi.org/10.1137/15M1018460.

[23] G. Sanguinetti, E. Bekkers, R. Duits, M. Janssen, A. Mashtakov, J. Mirebeau, Sub-Riemannian fast marching in SE(2). in: A. Pardo, J. Kittler (Eds.), Progress in Pattern Recognition, Image Analysis, Computer Vision, and Applications, Lecture

Notes in Computer Science, vol. 9423, Springer, 2015, pp. 366–374, https://doi.org/10.1007/978-3-319-25751-8_44.

[24] E.J. Bekkers, D. Chen, J.M. Portegies, Nilpotent approximations of sub-Riemannian distances for fast perceptual grouping of blood vessels in 2D and 3D, J. Math. Imaging Vis. 60 (6) (2018) 882–899, https://doi.org/10.1007/s10851-018-0787-z.

[25] S. Abbasi-Sureshjani, M. Favali, G. Citti, A. Sarti, B.M. ter Haar Romeny, Connectivity analysis of curvilinear retinal vessels by a cortically-inspired spectral clustering, in: IEEE International Symposium on Biomedical Imaging (ISBI), Melbourne, Australia, 2016, p. 189.

[26] E. Bekkers, M. Loog, B.M. ter Haar Romeny, R. Duits, Template matching via densities on the roto-translation group, IEEE Trans. Pattern Anal. Mach. Intell. 99 (2017) 1–14, https://doi.org/10.1109/TPAMI.2017.2652452.

[27] S. Abbasi-Sureshjani, I. Smit-Ockeloen, E.J. Bekkers, B. Dashtbozorg, B.M. ter Haar Romeny, Automatic detection of vascular bifurcations and crossings in retinal images using orientation scores, IEEE 13th International Symposium on Biomedical Imaging (ISBI), Prague, 2016, pp. 189–192, https://doi.org/10.1109/ISBI.2016.7493241.

[28] E.J. Bekkers, M.W. Lafarge, M. Veta, K.A. Eppenhof, J.P. Pluim, Roto-translation covariant convolutional networks for medical image analysis, in: MICCAI 2018, vol. 11070, 2018, pp. 440–448.

[29] M. Foracchia, E. Grisan, A. Ruggeri, Luminosity and contrast normalization in retinal images, Med. Image Anal. 9 (3) (2005) 179–190.

[30] S. Abbasi-Sureshjani, I. Smit-Ockeloen, J. Zhang, B.M. ter Haar Romeny, Biologically-inspired supervised vasculature segmentation in SLO retinal fundus images, in: Lecture Notes in Computer Science, International Conference Image Analysis and Recognition, vol. 9164, Springer, New York, 2015, pp. 325–334.

[31] J. Zhang, Robust and fast vessel segmentation via Gaussian derivatives in orientation scores, in: Proceedings of the International Conference on Image Analysis and Processing (ICIAP 2015), Lecture Notes in Computer Science, vol. 9279, 2015, pp. 537–547.

[32] J. Zhang, Retinal vessel delineation using a brain-inspired wavelet transform and random forest, Pattern Recogn. 69 (2017) 107–123.

[33] A. Hoover, V. Kouznetsova, M. Goldbaum, Locating blood vessels in retinal images by piecewise threshold probing of a matched filter response, IEEE Trans. Med. Imaging 19 (3) (2000) 203–210.

[34] C.G. Owen, A.R. Rudnicka, R. Mullen, S.A. Barman, D. Monekosso, P.H. Whincup, J. Ng, C. Paterson, Measuring retinal vessel tortuosity in 10-year-old children: validation of the computer-assisted image analysis of the retina (CAIAR) program, Invest. Ophthalmol. Vis. Sci. 50 (5) (2009) 2004–2010.

[35] J. Zhang, E.J. Bekkers, D. Chen, T.J.M. Berendschot, J. Schouten, J.P.W. Pluim, Y. Shi, B. Dashtbozorg, B.M. ter Haar Romeny, Reconnection of interrupted curvilinear structures via cortically inspired completion for ophthalmologic images, IEEE Trans. Biomed. Eng. 65 (5) (2018) 1151–1165, https://doi.org/10.1109/TBME.2017.2787025.

[36] J. Soares, J. Leandro, R. Cesar Jr., H. Jelinek, M. Cree, Retinal vessel segmentation using the 2-D Gabor wavelet and supervised classification, IEEE Trans. Med. Imaging 25 (9) (2006) 1214–1222.

[37] M.T. Schram, S.J.S. Sep, C.J. van der Kallen, P.C. Dagnelie, A. Koster, N. Schaper, R.M.A. Henry, C.D.A. Stehouwer, The Maastricht Study: an extensive phenotyping study on determinants of type 2 diabetes, its complications and its comorbidities, Eur. J. Epidemiol. 29 (6) (2014) 439–451.

[38] S. Zhu, M. van Triest, M. Tong, T. Lamers, P. Han, W. Qian, B.M. ter Haar Romeny, Retinal vascular tortuosity in hospitalized patients with type 2 diabetes and diabetic retinopathy in China, J. Biomed. Sci. Eng. 9 (2016) 143–154, https://doi.org/10.4236/jbise.2016.910B019.

[39] T.T. Nguyen, T.Y. Wong, Retinal vascular changes and diabetic retinopathy, Curr. Diabetes Rep. 9 (4) (2009) 277–283.

[40] C. Sun, J.J. Wang, D.A. Mackey, T.Y. Wong, Retinal vascular caliber: systemic, environmental, and genetic associations, Surv. Ophthalmol. 54 (1) (2009) 74–95.

[41] A.S. Neubauer, M. Luedtke, C. Haritoglou, S. Priglinger, A. Kampik, Retinal vessel analysis reproducibility in assessing cardiovascular disease, Optom. Vis. Sci. 85 (4) (2008) E247–E254.

[42] F. Huang, B. Dashtbozorg, J. Zhang, A. Yeung, T.J.M. Berendschot, B.M. ter Haar Romeny, Validation study on retinal vessel caliber measurement technique, in: European Congress on Computational Methods in Applied Sciences and Engineering, Springer, 2017, pp. 818–826.

[43] V. Caselles, R. Kimmel, G. Sapiro, Geodesic active contours, Int. J. Comput. Vis. 22 (1) (1997) 61–79.

[44] F. Huang, B. Dashtbozorg, A.K.S. Yeung, J. Zhang, T.J.M. Berendschot, B.M. ter Haar Romeny, A comparative study towards the establishment of an automatic retinal vessel width measurement technique, in: Fetal, Infant and Ophthalmic Medical Image Analysis, Springer, 2017, pp. 227–234.

[45] B. Dashtbozorg, J. Zhang, F. Huang, B.M. ter Haar Romeny, Automatic optic disc and fovea detection in retinal images using super-elliptical convergence index filters, in: Image Analysis and Recognition, Lecture Notes in Computer Science, vol. 9730, Springer, 2016, pp. 697–706.

[46] T.Y. Wong, A. Shankar, R. Klein, B.E. Klein, L.D. Hubbard, Prospective cohort study of retinal vessel diameters and risk of hypertension, Br. Med. J. 329 (7457) (2004) 79.

[47] M.D. Knudtson, K.E. Lee, L.D. Hubbard, T.Y. Wong, R. Klein, B.E.K. Klein, Revised formulas for summarizing retinal vessel diameters, Curr. Eye Res. 27 (3) (2003) 143–149.

[47a] S.M. Wong, Retinal Vessel Curvature and Tortuosity (Master thesis), Eindhoven University of Technology, 2012.

[48] D. Onkaew, R. Turior, B. Uyyanonvara, N. Akinori, C. Sinthanayothin, Automatic retinal vessel tortuosity measurement using curvature of improved chain code, in: International Conference on Electrical, Control and Computer Engineering (INECCE), IEEE, 2011, pp. 183–186.

[49] M.B. Sasongko, T.Y. Wong, T.T. Nguyen, C.Y. Cheung, J.E. Shaw, J.J. Wang, Retinal vascular tortuosity in persons with diabetes and diabetic retinopathy, Diabetologia 54 (9) (2011) 2409–2416.

[50] W.E. Hart, M. Goldbaum, B. Côté, P. Kube, M.R. Nelson, Measurement and classification of retinal vascular tortuosity, Int. J. Med. Inform. 53 (2–3) (1999) 239–252.

[51] C.M. Wilson, K.D. Cocker, M.J. Moseley, C. Paterson, S.T. Clay, W.E. Schulenburg, M.D. Mills, A.L. Ells, K.H. Parker, G.E. Quinn, Computerized analysis of retinal vessel width and tortuosity in premature infants, Invest. Ophthalmol. Vis. Sci. 49 (8) (2008) 3577–3585.

[52] C.Y. Cheung, E. Lamoureux, M.K. Ikram, M.B. Sasongko, J. Ding, Y. Zheng, P. Mitchell, J.J. Wang, T.Y. Wong, Retinal vascular geometry in Asian persons with diabetes and retinopathy, J. Diabetes Sci. Technol. 6 (3) (2012) 595–605.

[53] A.A. Kalitzeos, G.Y.H. Lip, R. Heitmar, Retinal vessel tortuosity measures and their applications, Exp. Eye Res. 106 (2013) 40–46.

[54] E.M. Franken, R. Duits, Crossing-preserving coherence-enhancing diffusion on invertible orientation scores, Int. J. Comput. Vis. 85 (3) (2009) 253–278.

[55] R. Duits, M.H.J. Janssen, J. Hannink, G.R. Sanguinetti, Locally adaptive frames in the roto-translation group and their applications in medical imaging, arXiv:1502.08002v5 math.GR (2015).

[56] E.J. Bekkers, J. Zhang, R. Duits, B.M. ter Haar Romeny, Curvature-based biomarkers for diabetic retinopathy via exponential curve fits in SE(2), in: Proceedings of the Ophthalmic Medical Image Analysis Second International Workshop, OMIA 2015, Held in Conjunction With MICCAI 2015, Munich, Germany, October 9, 2015, Iowa Research Online, 2015, pp. 113–120.

[57] A.F. Frangi, W.J. Niessen, K.L. Vincken, M.A. Viergever, Multiscale vessel enhancement filtering, in: Medical Image Computing and Computer-Assisted Intervention—MICCAI'98: First International Conference Cambridge, MA, USA, October 11–13, 1998 Proceedings, vol. 1496, Springer, 1998, pp. 130–137.

[58] B. Al-Diri, A. Hunter, Automated measurements of retinal bifurcations, World Congress on Medical Physics and Biomedical Engineering, September 7–12, 2009, Munich, Germany, Springer, 2009, pp. 205–208.

[59] T.F. Sherman, On connecting large vessels to small. The meaning of Murray's law, J. Gen. Physiol. 78 (4) (1981) 431–453.

[60] C.D. Murray, The physiological principle of minimum work I. The vascular system and the cost of blood volume, Proc. Natl. Acad. Sci. USA 12 (3) (1926) 207–214.

[61] N. Chapman, G. Dell'omo, M.S. Sartini, N. Witt, A. Hughes, S. Thom, R. Pedrinelli, Peripheral vascular disease is associated with abnormal arteriolar diameter relationships at bifurcations in the human retina, Clin. Sci. 103 (2) (2002) 111–116.

[62] B.B. Mandelbrot, The Fractal Geometry of Nature, vol. 173, WH Freeman, New York, NY, 1983.

[63] F. Family, B.R. Masters, D.E. Platt, Fractal pattern formation in human retinal vessels, Phys. D Nonlinear Phenomena 38 (1) (1989) 98–103.

[64] N. Cheung, K.C. Donaghue, G. Liew, S.L. Rogers, J.J. Wang, S.-W. Lim, A.J. Jenkins, W. Hsu, M.L. Lee, T.Y. Wong, Quantitative assessment of early diabetic retinopathy using fractal analysis, Diabet. Care 32 (1) (2009) 106–110.

[65] J.W.Y. Yau, R. Kawasaki, F.M.A. Islam, J. Shaw, P. Zimmet, J.J. Wang, T.Y. Wong, Retinal fractal dimension is increased in persons with diabetes but not impaired glucose metabolism: the Australian Diabetes, Obesity and Lifestyle (AusDiab) study, Diabetologia 53 (9) (2010) 2042–2045.

[66] J. Grauslund, A. Green, R. Kawasaki, L. Hodgson, A.K. Sjølie, T.Y. Wong, Retinal vascular fractals and microvascular and macrovascular complications in type 1 diabetes, Ophthalmology 117 (7) (2010) 1400–1405.

[67] R. Broe, M.L. Rasmussen, U. Frydkjaer-Olsen, B.S. Olsen, H.B. Mortensen, T. Peto, J. Grauslund, Retinal vascular fractals predict long-term microvascular complications in type 1 diabetes mellitus: the Danish Cohort of Pediatric Diabetes 1987 (DCPD1987), Diabetologia 57 (10) (2014) 2215–2221.

[68] B. Aliahmad, D.K. Kumar, M.G. Sarossy, R. Jain, Relationship between diabetes and grayscale fractal dimensions of retinal vasculature in the Indian population, BMC Ophthalmol. 14 (1) (2014) 152–157.

[69] L.S. Liebovitch, T. Toth, A fast algorithm to determine fractal dimensions by box counting, Phys. Lett. A 141 (8) (1989) 386–390.

[70] K. Falconer, Fractal Geometry: Mathematical Foundations and Applications, John Wiley & Sons, New York, NY, 2004.

[71] A. Rényi, On the dimension and entropy of probability distributions, Acta Math. Acad. Sci. Hung. 10 (1–2) (1959) 193–215.

[72] D. Harte, Multifractals: Theory and Applications, CRC Press, Cleveland, 2001.

[73] B. Dashtbozorg, J. Zhang, S. Abbasi-Sureshjani, F. Huang, B.M. ter Haar Romeny, Retinal health information and notification system (RHINO), in: SPIE Medical Imaging, vol. 1013437, International Society for Optics and Photonics, 2017, pp. 1–6. https://doi.org/10.1117/12.2253839.

[74] W. Li, M. Schram, T.J.M. Berendschot, J. Schouten, A. Kroon, C. van der Kallen, R. Henry, A. Koster, P. Dagnelie, N. Schaper, Prediabetes and diabetes are associated with wider retinal arterioles and venules: the Maastricht study, Diabetologia 61 (2018) S532–S533.

Image analysis tools for assessment of atrophic macular diseases

17

Zhihong Jewel Hu[a], Srinivas Reddy Sadda[a,b]

[a]*Doheny Eye Institute, Los Angeles, CA, United States*
[b]*Department of Ophthalmology, University of California—Los Angeles,*
Los Angeles, CA, United States

1 The clinical need for automatic image analysis tools in retinal disease

Retinal diagnostic technologies are evolving at a rapid pace. Recent advances in the last several years include ultra-widefield imaging devices [1], higher speed optical coherence tomography (OCT) technologies such as swept source OCT [2], OCT angiography [3], quantitative fundus autofluorescence [4], fluorescence lifetime imaging ophthalmoscopy [5], color autofluorescence [6], macular pigment optical density [7], and adaptive optics-based imaging [8] to name only a few. Concomitant with these technologic advances is a dramatic increase in the amount of data encoded within these images. This vast stream of data presents a major challenge for ophthalmologists to cope with in clinical practice. This is particularly problematic as the growth in the overall population and epidemic increases in certain retinal diseases such as diabetic retinopathy, threaten to overwhelm the healthcare system. Further compounding this problem is that many of these newer diagnostic technologies are relatively unfamiliar to clinicians who have been in practice for many years. Accurate and reliable interpretation of images from these new technologies can require extensive training and experience which may be out of reach for many practitioners. These demands have created a great need for automated retinal image analysis tools to assist in accurate diagnosis as well as to improve the efficiency of clinical practice. The use of automated analysis tools also offers the prospect for a more precise and quantitative assessment of disease severity and monitoring of disease progression over time. In addition to applications in clinical practice, these image analysis tools may have important applications in clinical research and clinical trials. As image-based biomarkers are commonly used as primary and secondary endpoints in such trials, automated image analysis tools present an opportunity to reduce the costs of these studies and facilitate the development of new therapeutics. To illustrate the potential value of retinal image analysis tools in clinical practice and research, this chapter highlights the application of these tools to a major blinding disease, age-related macular degeneration (AMD).

2 Overview of analysis tools of atrophic AMD and risk factors for progression to atrophy

Geographic atrophy (GA), with the loss of the retinal pigment epithelium (RPE) and photoreceptors, is a manifestation of the advanced or late-stage of AMD. AMD is the leading cause of blindness in people over the age of 65 in the western world [9]. GA is increasingly the main cause of vision loss in AMD patients. Clinically, GA is identified by the presence of depigmentation, sharply demarcated borders, and increased visibility of the underlying choroidal vessels [9, 10]. Typically, the atrophic areas initially appear in the extrafoveal region of the macula [11], with eventual growth and expansion into the fovea, resulting in vision loss and ultimately legal blindness. Although GA accounts for one third of the cases of late AMD and is responsible for 20% of the cases of severe visual loss due to the disorder, it currently lacks effective treatment, whereas antiangiogenic therapies have been shown to be successful in managing the other form of late AMD, namely choroidal neovascularization [9, 10]. A number of potential agents are currently in clinical investigations to determine if they are of benefit in preventing the development and growth of these atrophic lesions. Techniques to rapidly and precisely quantify atrophic lesions would appear to be of value in advancing the understanding of the pathogenesis of GA lesions and the level of effectiveness of these putative therapeutics.

Color fundus photography has been the historical gold standard method for documenting and measuring the size of GA lesions. Although GA lesions can be readily identified and delineated in high quality color images with good stereopsis, the borders may be more difficult to identify in monoscopic images of lower quality. Recently, fundus autofluorescence (FAF), obtained by confocal scanning laser ophthalmoscopy (CSLO) imaging, has emerged as a useful imaging technique to provide a high contrast for the identification of GA lesions. FAF imaging is a noninvasive, in vivo 2-D imaging technique for metabolic mapping of naturally or pathologically occurring fluorophores (e.g., in lipofuscin) of the ocular fundus [12]. FAF signals are reliable markers of lipofuscin in RPE cells. Abnormally increased lipofuscin accumulations, which produce hyper-fluorescent FAF signals, occur in earlier stages of AMD. However, when atrophy ensues, RPE cells are lost, resulting in the depletion of the fluorophores and a reduction in the autofluorescence signal. The FAF signal from that region becomes hypo-fluorescent or dark. Well-demarcated hypo-fluorescence is the FAF hallmark of GA. Spectral domain OCT (SD-OCT) [13, 14], however, is the most frequently used imaging tool in clinical practice as it provides useful 3-D depth-encoded information and is more comfortable for patients than FAF imaging. A consensus definition for atrophy on OCT was recently reported by the Classification of Atrophy Meetings (CAM) group. It was based on three criteria: a

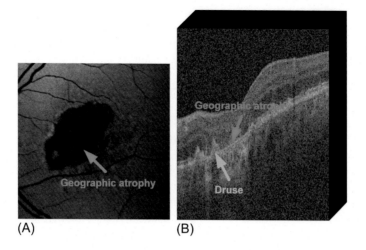

(A)   (B)

FIG. 1

Example illustration of the geographic atrophy on a FAF image and a B-scan of a SD-OCT volume image. (A) The green arrow of the hypo-reflective region in the FAF image indicates the geographic atrophy. (B) The green arrow of the hyper-reflective region in the B-scan of the SD-OCT image indicates the geographic atrophy. The orange arrow indicates a druse.

Credit: Z. Hu, G.G. Medioni, M. Hernandez, A. Hariri, X. Wu, S.R. Sadda, Segmentation of the geographic atrophy in spectral-domain optical coherence tomography and fundus autofluorescene images, Invest. Ophthalmol. Vis. Sci. 54 (13) (2013) 8375–8383, PMID: 24265015.

contiguous zone of choroidal hypertransmission of at least 250 μm in size, a defect in the RPE band of at least 250 μm in size, and thinning of the overlying retina [15]. Fig. 1 is an illustration of atrophy associated with AMD in FAF and SD-OCT images.

The reproducibility of measuring GA lesions by experienced human graders has been shown to be excellent [16]. However, the manual delineation of GA is tedious, time-consuming, and still prone to some degree of inter- and intra-observer variability by less experienced graders and clinicians in practice. Automatic detection and quantification of GA could be of value for identifying GA and monitoring disease progression, both in practice and in clinical research. A few groups have tackled this problem. For example, Schmitz-Valckenberg et al. [17] developed a region-growing approach (Heidelberg RegionFinder) to identify GA lesions in FAF images. Chen et al. [18] developed a geometric active contour model for segmenting GA in SD-OCT images. Hu et al. [19] reported a level set (implicit active contours) approach to segment GA lesions in SD-OCT and FAF images. All of the above approaches, however, were semiautomatic, thereby decreasing the overall efficiency and utility. Ramsey et al. [20] further reported a fuzzy c-means clustering algorithm which could detect GA lesions in a fully automated way. However, due to a well-known issue of over-segmentation with such an approach, the users needed to define the region(s) of interest (ROIs) in each image to achieve good algorithm performance. Such an approach was effectively "semiautomatic" due to the human interaction required for each image.

Automated approaches without human interaction to be able to batch process the image sets could potentially save users' time, an attribute of particular importance for analyzing large datasets. Machine learning is an analysis approach which begins with observations or existing data to look for patterns and then applies this training to automatically make determinations in previously unseen data [21–24]. With wider availability of "big data" that can serve as a source of training, machine learning is becoming the preferred technique for image segmentation and analysis. For instance, Hu et al. developed an automated GA segmentation approach using k-nearest neighbor (k-NN) classification, a traditional machine learning algorithm [25]. However, such an approach utilized hand-crafted filters to extract image features, which required operator expertise and presented a potential danger that the algorithm might not generalize to the large variations of ophthalmic image data in the general population. In contrast, artificial intelligence (AI) deep learning-based algorithms, e.g., deep convolutional neural networks (CNNs), automatically learn relevant image features which can yield a high level of image processing accuracy and may be more capable of generalization [26–39]. Recently Hu et al. developed an AI deep learning-based approach for automated GA segmentation using the LeNet [34] model of deep CNNs [35]. This initial approach, however, was based on sliding windows and included some fully connected layers, and thus was slow and less efficient in algorithm training and testing. Ji et al. reported a classic auto-encoder algorithm for automated GA segmentation which was composed of an encoder (downsampling) and a decoder (upsampling) [38]. But the linear compression of the input led to a bottleneck that did not transmit all features. More recently, Wang et al. developed a U-Net approach (an auto-encoder like algorithm) [39], which used deconvolutional units to overcome the bottleneck limitation of the classic auto-encoder by adding skip connections which concatenated the higher resolution features from the downsampling portion with the upsampled features, resulting in highly accurate algorithm performance for GA segmentation. Section 3 will review two typical semiautomated GA segmentation algorithms, followed by a review of a few advanced machine learning-based approaches in Section 4.

Over the last two decades, great interest has emerged in the identification of biomarkers and risk factors in early and intermediate AMD eyes which may predict a higher risk for progression to late AMD, and in particular GA. Through several studies from a large number of researchers, several OCT-based risk factors for progression to late AMD have been defined [40–60]. Recently, Lei et al. combined four of these factors into a simple, categorical (binary: feature present or absent) scoring system that could potentially be used to stage patients in a clinic setting [61]. The four OCT-derived high-risk factors incorporated into this scoring system were: intraretinal hyper-reflective foci (HRF), hyporeflective drusen (hD), subretinal drusenoid deposits (SDD), and drusen volume ≥ 0.03 mm^3 within a 3 mm circle centering on the fovea. Their analysis confirmed that each of four features was independent risk factor for progression to atrophy, with HRF > hD > SDD > drusen volume (≥ 0.03 mm^3) in terms of level of risk. However, such a system was based on only a simple qualitative assessment of the presence or absence of each risk factor in the entire OCT volume.

The precision of the system could be improved by quantification of risk factors from individual OCT scans (A-, B-, and C-scans), by manual or semiautomated approaches. Such an approach, however, is invariably tedious, time-consuming, and consequently expensive. An AI deep learning construct to objectively and automatically learn and quantify the most important risk factors would be of potentially significant value. As a pilot study, Saha et al. developed an AI deep learning-based system for the binary classification of the AMD risk factors based on individual B-scans. Schmidt-Erfurth also proposed a method for predicting disease conversion in early AMD based on automated volumetric segmentation of the outer neurosensory layers and RPE, as well as drusen and hyperreflective foci in OCT [62]. However, such an approach based on the quantification of individual lesions was not time-efficient and did not consider the risk of SSD. Instead, the approach by Saha et al. was based on individual OCT scans, ensuring a higher efficiency for detecting AMD risk factors and saving time. Section 5 will provide a review of such an approach.

3 Semiautomated segmentation of atrophic macular diseases

3.1 Heidelberg RegionFinder for atrophic AMD segmentation in FAF images

The RegionFinder [17] is a commercial software embedded in the Heidelberg Spectralis device (Heidelberg Engineering, Heidelberg, Germany), which provides a semiautomated segmentation of atrophic regions (or GA regions) on FAF images. The method was reported in detail by Schmitz-Valckenberg et al. in 2011 and was applied to digital FAF images with a resolution 768×768 pixels in a 30° by 30° frame, with one pixel roughly corresponding to 11 μm. The RegionFinder used a region-growing technique, a simple region-based image segmentation method. It involved the selection of initial seed point(s) within an atrophic region (hypo-fluorescent or dark) by the user, followed by growth to the lesion border, by progressively including all pixels with a signal intensity below a certain threshold. This threshold was defined by a parameter referred to as "growth power." The higher the growth power, the larger the enclosed area of the atrophic region. By adjusting the growth power, the operator was able to segment the atrophic region.

3.2 Level set approach for atrophic AMD segmentation in OCT and FAF images

Overview: Hu et al. reported a level-set-based algorithm for GA segmentation from SD-OCT en face images [19], derived from SD-OCT volumes with dimensions of 2 mm (depth) $\times$ 6 mm (A-scans) $\times$ 6 mm (B-scans) (Cirrus OCT; Carl Zeiss Meditec, Inc., Dublin, USA) and a scan pattern of $1024 \times 512 \times 128$ voxels. Level set is a numerical method for tracking the evolution of contours and surfaces [63, 64]. The central idea of the level set is to represent the evolving contour using a signed function, where its zero level corresponds to the actual contour. Level set is an implicit deformable model, also called implicit active contours, which can model arbitrarily complex shapes and topological changes. GA is a varied disease such that the progression could be of any arbitrarily irregular shape. The level set strategy is well suited for the detection of GA regions. More specifically, to identify the GA regions in SD-OCT en face images, three retinal surfaces consisting of the internal limiting membrane (ILM), RPE/Bruch's membrane (BM) complex, and the choroid-sclera junction are first segmented in SD-OCT volumes using a double-surface graph search scheme [65, 66]. An OCT en face map was created based on the OCT slab layer between the RPE/BM complex and the choroid-sclera junction, i.e., the choroid. Because increased transmission of light into the choroid occurs in areas with absent or depigmented RPE, the choroid in areas of atrophy appears much brighter than adjacent areas of choroid underlying intact RPE. The level set algorithm was then applied on the choroidal hypertransmission evident in en face maps to identify the GA regions (brighter regions). A flowchart of the GA segmentation system in SD-OCT images is provided in Fig. 2 and the details of the system are provided in the following sections.

Construction of OCT 2-D choroidal en face map: Prior to construction of en face maps at the choroid layer level, the choroidal layer needed to be segmented. Graph search was first applied to simultaneously segment the ILM surface and the surface of the RPE/BM complex using a double-surface graph search scheme. A penalty to the cost function was applied at certain distances above the segmented surface of the RPE/BM complex. The surfaces of the RPE/BM complex and the choroid-sclera junction were then simultaneously segmented using the same double-surface graph search technique.

The 2-D OCT en face map was then obtained by averaging the intensity value between the surfaces of the RPE/BM complex and choroid-sclera junction in the z-direction (depth). It should be noted that the original SD-OCT volume was not isotropic with 1024 (depth) $\times$ 512 (A-scans) $\times$ 128 (B-scans) voxels. To facilitate subsequent GA segmentation, an isotropic en face map was generated by linear interpolation of the B-scans (y-direction) to enlarge the image resolution to 512 (A-scans) $\times$ 512 (B-scans) pixels. Fig. 3 illustrates the segmentation of the three surfaces and the generation of an OCT en face map from the choroid layer.

Geographic atrophy segmentation: The underlying principle of GA detection on an OCT en face map using the level set approach is to represent the GA contour C by the zero level set of a higher dimensional embedding function $\emptyset$, defined as the signed distance function (SDF). Inside the GA region, the function has a value of $\emptyset > 0$ and outside the GA region, the function has a value of $\emptyset < 0$. Thus, on the GA contour, the function has a value of $\emptyset = 0$ and hence called the zero level set. Fundamentally, rather than directly evolving the GA contour C, the algorithm evolves the level set function $\emptyset$. The level set evolution is governed by a partial differential equation (PDE) as shown in Eq. 1

$$\frac{d}{dt}\emptyset \propto -\alpha P(x,y)|\nabla\emptyset| + \beta K(x,y)|\nabla\emptyset| \tag{1}$$

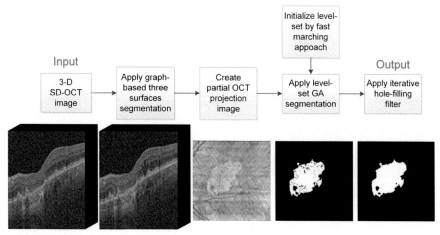

FIG. 2

Flowchart of GA segmentation in SD-OCT images. Specifically, three retinal surfaces of internal limiting membrane (ILM), RPE/BM complex, and the choroid-sclera junction, were first segmented in the volumetric OCT images using a double-surface graph search scheme. An OCT en face map was created by averaging the intensity value between the surfaces of the RPE/BM complex and the choroid-sclera junction. A level set approach was applied to segment the GA in the OCT en face map with the initialization by a fast marching approach. An iterative hole filing filter was then applied to refine the GA segmentation.

Credit: Z. Hu, G.G. Medioni, M. Hernandez, A. Hariri, X. Wu, S.R. Sadda, Segmentation of the geographic atrophy in spectral-domain optical coherence tomography and fundus autofluorescene images, Invest. Ophthalmol. Vis. Sci. 54 (13) (2013) 8375–8383, PMID: 24265015.

where $P(x, y)$ represents a propagation speed term; $K(x, y)$ represents a curvature term; α and β are the weights reflecting the different influences of the propagation speed and curvature over the contour evolution. The evolving GA contour C was then obtained by extracting the zero level set.

The level set segmentation generally starts with an initial contour and gradually evolves to the zero level set representing the desired boundary/surface. Intuitively, if the initial contour is closer to the detected contour, the evolution will be faster and more efficient. The fast marching approach [63], a simple version of the level set approach in which the level set evolution was only controlled by the propagation speed, was used to generate the initial model. More specifically, the algorithm first obtained a propagation speed image from the input OCT en face map, by the mapping of the gradient magnitude of the OCT en face map, in which the high contrast regions had low speeds and the homogeneous regions had high speeds. A sigmoid function was used for the mapping of the gradient magnitude.

Seed/Seeds (a seed is defined as any pixel/point inside the GA region) and an estimated GA region related to each seed were used as the initial inputs for the fast

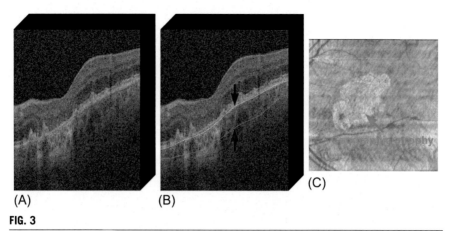

FIG. 3

Example illustration of three retinal layer segmentation in a SD-OCT volume and the OCT en face map creation. (A) A B-scan in a SD-OCT volume. (B) The B-scan overlapping with three segmented surfaces, where the red, yellow, and green color represent the ILM, RPE/BM complex, and the choroid-sclera junction, respectively. (C) The OCT en face map created by the choroid layer indicated by the blue arrows in (B). Note that the green arrow highlighted region with increased penetration indicates the GA.

Credit: Z. Hu, G.G. Medioni, M. Hernandez, A. Hariri, X. Wu, S.R. Sadda, Segmentation of the geographic atrophy in spectral-domain optical coherence tomography and fundus autofluorescene images, Invest. Ophthalmol. Vis. Sci. 54 (13) (2013) 8375–8383, PMID: 24265015.

marching algorithm. Propagation then started from the seeds and traveled with the speed in the speed image. The fast marching yielded a time-crossing map, which indicated for each pixel, the time required for the contour to reach the pixel. This outcome was then used as an initial shape model for the level set GA segmentation.

The putative GA regions in the OCT en face maps were noted to be hyper-reflective relative to adjacent nonatrophic regions. The propagation term in Eq. (1) was modeled based on the intensity of the GA region as shown in Eq. 2

$$P(x,y) = \begin{cases} I(x,y) - L, if\ I(x,y) < (U-L)/2 + L \\ U - I(x,y), \qquad\qquad otherwise \end{cases} \tag{2}$$

where $I(x,y)$ represents the GA image intensity at position (x,y); U and L are the upper and lower threshold of the estimated intensity region of GA. The above equation resulted in a positive propagation term when a pixel has an intensity value within the threshold and negative term outside the threshold. The curvature term in Eq. (2) was assigned a significantly lower weight than the propagation term due to the arbitrary shape of the GA region.

Fig. 4B illustrates a typical level set GA segmentation result. As a postprocessing step, a hole-filling filter was applied to fill in the holes evident in Fig. 4B. The hole-filling filter iteratively converted the background pixels into the foreground when the number of foreground pixels was a majority of the neighbors until no further pixel

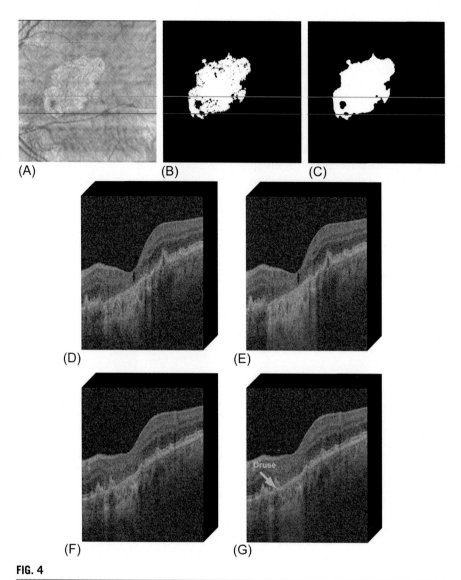

FIG. 4

Example illustration of GA segmentation in a SD-OCT image. (A) OCT en face map. (B) Level set GA segmentation result. (C) GA segmentation result after hole-filling. (D) A SD-OCT B-scan corresponding to the location indicated by the green line in (A) and (E) the GA segmentation (green) overlapping on that. (F) A SD-OCT B-scan corresponding to the location indicated by the purple line in (A) and (G) the GA segmentation (purple) overlapping on that. Note that under the druse (orange arrow), the GA was not present.

Credit: Z. Hu, G.G. Medioni, M. Hernandez, A. Hariri, X. Wu, S.R. Sadda, Segmentation of the geographic atrophy in spectral-domain optical coherence tomography and fundus autofluorescene images, Invest. Ophthalmol. Vis. Sci. 54 (13) (2013) 8375–8383, PMID: 24265015.

changes occurred. Fig. 4C shows the result of the hole-filling filter. The segmented 2-D GA region was then projected to the 3-D SD-OCT image as shown in Fig. 4E and G to find the 3-D location.

In addition, the same level set algorithm was also applied to identify the GA region in the corresponding FAF images (Spectralis HRA+OCT, Heidelberg Engineering, Heidelberg, Germany) with a specified intensity threshold region corresponding to the hypo-autofluorescent property of the atrophy in FAF images. Note that the original FAF images had a broader field of view than the SD-OCT images. The FAF images were registered to the corresponding OCT en face maps using a manual approach based on identifying multiple corresponding points between images (generally vessel crossings). The FAF images were then cropped to the same size as the OCT en face maps. Fig. 5C–E illustrates the registration and GA segmentation result in a FAF image.

Compared to the RegionFinder approach reported by Schmitz-Valckenberg et al. [17], the major advantage of the level set approach was that the capability of the speed function could be positive in some places and negative in others, so that the front could move forwards in some places and backwards in others. This capability

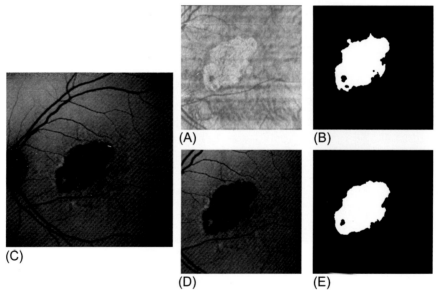

FIG. 5

Example illustration of GA segmentation in an OCT en face map and its corresponding FAF image. (A) OCT en face map. (B) GA segmentation in the OCT en face map. (C) Original FAF image. (D) Registered FAF image. (E) GA segmentation in the registered FAF image. Note that the GA segmentation in OCT and FAF images presents a similar performance.

Credit: Z. Hu, G.G. Medioni, M. Hernandez, A. Hariri, X. Wu, S.R. Sadda, Segmentation of the geographic atrophy in spectral-domain optical coherence tomography and fundus autofluorescene images, Invest. Ophthalmol. Vis. Sci. 54 (13) (2013) 8375–8383, PMID: 24265015.

enhanced its ability to segment objects of irregular shape and recognize GA contours better than RegionFinder which grew the region only forwards.

4 Automated segmentation of atrophic macular diseases

4.1 Supervised classification for atrophic AMD segmentation in FAF images using a traditional machine learning algorithm

Overview: Supervised classification has been reported as an effective automated approach for the detection of AMD lesions [25]. Recall that supervised classification is a machine learning task which can be divided into two phases: the learning (training) phase and the classification (testing) phase [21]. The training data consisted of a set of training samples. Each sample is a pair consisting of the feature vectors and a label. In the training phase, the supervised classification algorithm analyzes the labeled training data and produces classification rules. In the testing phase, the previously unseen new test data are classified into classes (labels) based on the generated classification rules. The classified labels are then compared with the labeled test data to validate the performance of the supervised classification. Fig. 6 is an overview of the supervised classification.

The k-NN classification is a supervised pixel-wise classification approach for traditional machine learning with hand-engineered images features designed based on specific questions. Hu et al. reported a k-NN approach for GA segmentation on FAF images (Spectralis HRA+OCT, Heidelberg Engineering, Heidelberg, Germany). The image resolution is 512×512 pixels and the physical dimensions as provided by the camera system are 6mm×6mm. The hand-crafted image features for their approach included region-wise intensity (mean and variance) measures, gray level

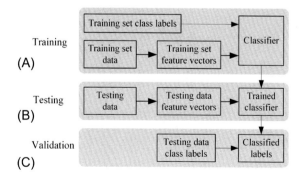

FIG. 6

Overview of supervised classification.

Credit: Z. Hu, G.G. Medioni, M. Hernandez, S.R. Sadda, Automated segmentation of geographic atrophy in fundus autofluorescene images using supervised pixel classification, J. Med. Imag. 2 (1) (2015) 014501, https://doi.org/10.1117/1.JMI.2.1.014501, PMID: 26158084.

co-occurrence matrix measures (angular second moment, entropy, and inverse difference moment) [22, 67], and Gaussian filter banks.

Feature extraction: The size of GA lesions varies considerably with two typical configurations—the uni- and multifocal GAs. Commonly, uni-focal GA lesions tend to be larger and multifocal GA lesions tend to be smaller as shown in Fig. 7. To be able to segment both uni- and multifocal GA lesion patterns, for a FAF gray value image $I(x, y)$ with size $X * Y$, the image feature extraction was performed on the underlying regions with a sliding window of varying sized $s_x * s_y = 2n * 2n, n \in \{1,,2,,...7\}$ pixels. Such a convention was applied on the intensity and gray level co-occurrence matrix measures. For the Gaussian filter banks, the filter sizes are defined by different Gaussian scales.

Specifically, the intensity level measures included the region-wise mean intensity and intensity variance which were extracted from the original gray value images $I(x, y)$. The sizes of the regions were defined by the sliding windows. The mean intensity value measured the image brightness and the intensity variance measured the image contrast.

A gray level co-occurrence matrix $P(i, j)$ with size $I * J$ describes the spatial relationships that the intensity tones have to one another. It is defined by specifying an offset vector $d = (dx, dy)$ and counting all pairs of pixels separated by the offset d which have gray values i and j. In the case of obtaining the gray-level co-occurrence matrices from a FAF image, the gray values of the original FAF image $I(x, y)$ were first converted from 0–255 to the range 0–15, resulting in 16 Gy levels from 0 to 15. All the pixel pairs having the gray value i in the first pixel and the gray value j in the second pixel separated by the offset $d = (dx, dy)$ were counted. The offsets were defined by varying values $(dx, dy) \in \{(1, 1), (3, 3), (5, 5), ..., (15, 15)\}$ pixels when they were within the sizes of the regions. Since the converted gray values had 16 levels, the resulted gray level co-occurrence matrices—a set of resulted $P(i, j)$ matrices satisfying the specified offsets, had the size of 16×16.

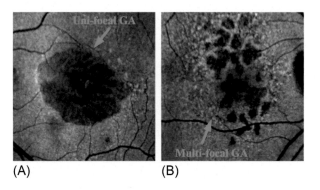

(A)   (B)

FIG. 7

Illustration of the geographic atrophy. (A) Uni-focal GA pattern. (B) Multifocal GA pattern.

Credit: Z. Hu, G.G. Medioni, M. Hernandez, S.R. Sadda, Automated segmentation of geographic atrophy in fundus autofluorescene images using supervised pixel classification, J. Med. Imag. 2 (1) (2015) 014501, https://doi.org/10.1117/1.JMI.2.1.014501, PMID: 26158084.

The gray level co-occurrence matrices are important because they can capture the spatial dependence of gray-level values through the resulted texture features. More specifically, three textural features, i.e., angular second moment, entropy, and inverse difference moment, are extracted from each gray-level co-occurrence matrix.

The angular second moment is a strong measure of the gray level uniformity.

$$\text{Angular second moment} = \sum_i \sum_j P^2(i,j) \tag{3}$$

The entropy measures the randomness of gray level distribution.

$$\textit{Entrophy} = \sum_i \sum_j P(i,j) \log P(i,j) \tag{4}$$

The inverse difference moment measures the local homogeneity.

$$\text{Inverse difference moment} = \sum_i \sum_j \frac{1}{1+(i-j)^2} P(i,j) \tag{5}$$

These features are important because they reflect the changes of image texture in GA regions from normal regions, which can help distinguish GA regions from the background.

A Gaussian filter bank with 8 Gaussian scales at $\sigma = 8n$, $n \in \{1, 2, ...8\}$ pixels was applied to blur the original gray value image $I(x,y)$. The Gaussian filters were applied only in the x- and y-direction. The different Gaussian scales define the different filter sizes and the sliding windows are not applied to the Gaussian feature extraction. In addition to the above features, the original gray value intensity image $I(x,y)$ was also included in the image feature space. Fig. 8 is an illustration of a few randomly selected image features. After extracting the image features, each feature vector was normalized to zero mean and unit variance.

k-NN classification: The supervised pixel classification includes a training phase and a testing phase which are performed on the training and test datasets, respectively. The entire dataset was split into two subsets with equal image numbers. The two subsets may be used interchangeably as training and test sets. To reduce the bias of the classification, the two subsets were shuffled as described in Experimental approach to obtain 8 training sets and 8 corresponding testing sets. At the training stage, the image feature vectors were obtained from each training image and combined to obtain the feature vectors for the entire training set. Each sample/pixel in the training set was labeled as two classes of "GA" or "non-GA" to serve as the ground truth for the training. The testing was performed on each individual image in the testing set. Similarly, each sample/pixel in the testing set was also labeled as two classes of "GA" or "non-GA" as the ground truth for the testing.

The *k*-NN classifier [68] is a supervised classifier which classifies each sample/pixel on an unseen test image based on a similarity measure, e.g., distance functions with the training samples. A sample/pixel was classified as "GA" or "non-GA" by a majority vote of its k ($k = 31$) neighbors in the training samples being identified as "GA" or "non-GA." To reduce execution time, in this work, the searching of the nearest

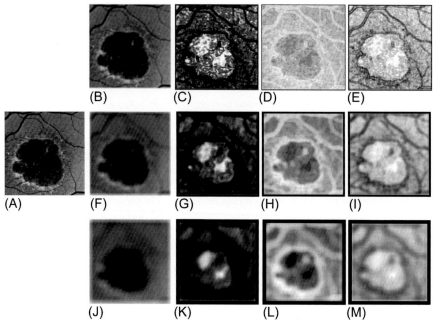

FIG. 8

Illustration of varying size image features. (A) Original FAF image. (B–E) Images features with a sliding window size of $s_x * s_y = 2 * 2$ pixels with (B) mean intensity, (C) angular second moment, (D) entropy, and (D) inverse difference moment extracted from gray level co-occurrence matrix with $(\Delta_i, \Delta_j) = (3, 3)$. (F–I) Images features with a sliding window size of $s_x * s_y = 6 * 6$ pixels with (B) mean intensity, (C) angular second moment, (D) entropy, and (D) inverse difference moment extracted from gray level co-occurrence matrix with $(\Delta_i, \Delta_j) = (5, 5)$ pixels. (J–M) Images features with a sliding window size of $s_x * s_y = 12 * 12$ pixels with (B) mean intensity, (C) angular second moment, (D) entropy, and (D) inverse difference moment extracted from gray level co-occurrence matrix with $(\Delta_i, \Delta_j) = (7, 7)$ pixels.

Credit: Z. Hu, G.G. Medioni, M. Hernandez, S.R. Sadda, Automated segmentation of geographic atrophy in fundus autofluorescene images using supervised pixel classification, J. Med. Imag. 2 (1) (2015) 014501, https://doi.org/10.1117/1.JMI.2.1.014501, PMID: 26158084.

neighbor training samples/pixels for each query sample/pixel was implemented using an approximate-nearest-neighbor approach [69], with a tolerance of a small amount of error, i.e., the searching algorithm could return a point that may not be the nearest neighbor, but is not significantly further away from the query sample/pixel than the true nearest neighbor. The error bound ϵ was defined such that the ratio between the distance to the found point and the distance to the true nearest neighbor was $< 1 + \epsilon$ and the ϵ was set to 0.1. Based on the obtained k nearest neighbor training samples/pixels, each query sample/pixel in the test image was assigned to a soft label p_{GA}:

$$p_{GA} = n / k \qquad (6)$$

where n is the number of the training samples/pixels labeled as "GA" among the k nearest neighbor training samples/pixels. The soft label represents the posterior probability of that query sample/pixel belonging to the GA lesion. The results in a GA probability map, representing the likelihood that the image pixels belong to GA. In the GA probability map, there were some small GA regions mis-classified as background (referred as holes). As a postprocessing step, a voting binary hole-filing filter [70] was applied to fill in the small holes. More specifically, centered at a pixel, in its neighborhood $\frac{R_x}{2}$ by $\frac{R_y}{2}$ pixels, the hole-filing filter iteratively converted the background pixels into the foreground until no pixels were being changed or until it reached the maximum number of iterations. The rule of the conversion is that a background pixel is converted into a foreground pixel if the number of fore-ground neighbors surpasses the number of background neighbors by a majority value ($\frac{R_x * R_y - 1}{2}$ + majority) in that neighborhood. By the observation of the "hole" sizes, the neighborhood was set to size of 7×7 pixels, the majority value was set to 2 and the iteration was set to 5. Fig. 9 provides some GA segmentation results using the automated k-NN classification for both uni- and multifocal patterns.

4.2 Supervised classification for age-related and juvenile atrophic macular degeneration using an AI deep learning approach

Method: Although the k-NN classification approach is automated and yields good algorithm performance for GA segmentation, such an approach uses hand-crafted filters to extract image features, which may not be applicable with large variations in ophthalmic image data. AI deep learning-based approaches with automated design of image features are highly desirable. U-Net is a state-of-the-art AI algorithm for semantic segmentation [30]. It relies on an encoder-decoder type network architecture and consists of a contracting path to capture context and an expansive path to enable precise localization. It is based on fully convolutional networks and does not require sliding windows [35], which naturally performs a data augmentation to use the annotated samples more efficiently and hence allows a much smaller training dataset and still maintains high algorithm performance.

Wang et al. reported a U-Net-based algorithm applied to FAF images for both atrophic AMD (or GA) and atrophic juvenile macular degeneration (JMD) (or Stargardt) respectively [39]. More specifically, the U-Net was first trained and tested on the FAF data with atrophic AMD. The basic structure of the U-Net was similar to the one by Ronneberger et al. [30], which was composed of downsampling layers of convolutional operation, max pooling, rectified linear units (ReLu) activation; and upsampling layers of transpose convolutional operation, ReLu, concatenation, and convolutional operation. Note that each convolutional layer was followed by a nor-malization operation. Dropout layers were also added in the downsampling process to avoid overfitting.

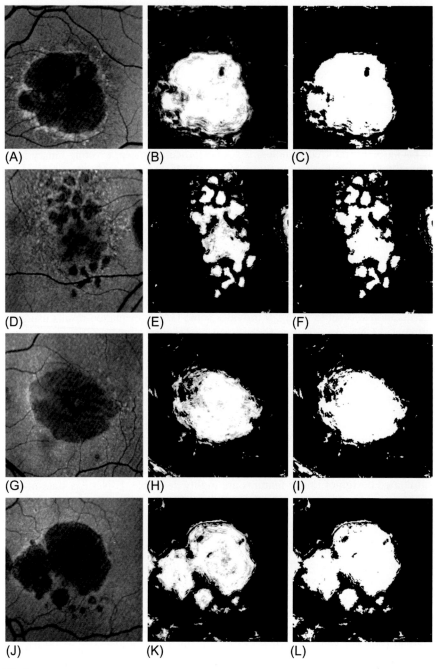

FIG. 9

Illustration of GA segmentation results. Left, middle, and right columns indicate the original FAF images, GA segmentation result, and the GA segmentation after hole-filing, respectively. The proposed algorithm can be applied to both uni- and multifocal GA detection and classification. Note the false positives from the blood vessels in the segmented images of row 3 and row 4.

Credit: Z. Hu, G.G. Medioni, M. Hernandez, S.R. Sadda, Automated segmentation of geographic atrophy in fundus autofluorescene images using supervised pixel classification, J. Med. Imag. 2 (1) (2015) 014501, https://doi.org/10.1117/1.JMI.2.1.014501, PMID: 26158084.

In the training of the original U-Net [30], the classical stochastic gradient descent (SGD) was used to interactively update network weights. However, in the training of the U-Net by Wang et al. [39], they used a more effective training optimization approach—adaptive moment estimation (Adam) for the two moment estimates (m_t, v_t) [71] with the following formulas to update the weights W_{t+1} in iteration $t+1$ for each component i.

$$(m_t)_i = \beta_1 (m_{t-1})_i + (1-\beta_1)(\nabla L(W_t))_i \tag{7}$$

$$(v_t)_i = \beta_2 (v_{t-1})_i + (1-\beta_2)(\nabla L(W_t))_i^2 \tag{8}$$

and

$$(w_{t+1})_i = (w_t)_i - \alpha \frac{\sqrt{1-(\beta_2)_i^t}}{1-(\beta_1)_i^t} \frac{(m_t)_i}{\sqrt{(v_t)_i} + \varepsilon} \tag{9}$$

Where $\nabla L(W_t)$ is the gradient of weights in iteration t. α is the learning rate or step size, reflecting how much the weights of the network are updated with respect the gradient. β_1 and β_2 are the decay rates of the first and second moment estimates for decaying the running average of the gradient and the running average of the square of gradient. ε is a small number to prevent division by zero.

The training of U-Net was driven by a loss function (also known as error, cost, or objective function) as in many machine learning algorithms. A loss function specifies the goal of training by mapping the current network weights to a scalar value specifying the "badness" of these network weights. Hence, the goal of training is to find a setting of the weights that minimizes the loss function. The loss function used by Wang et al. [39] was sigmoid cross-entropy loss (binary cross-entropy loss)—a sigmoid activation over the final feature map plus a cross-entropy loss. Unlike a softmax loss, it is independent on each class, meaning that the loss computed for every class is not affected by other classes. It's called binary cross-entropy loss because it sets up a binary classification problem between classes for every class. For a two-class classification (e.g., the classification of a pixel on a FAF image as atrophic AMD or background; or atrophic JMD or background), the formulas of the binary cross-entropy loss can be written as:

Sigmoid activation:

$$f(S_i) = \frac{1}{1+e^{S_i}} \tag{10}$$

Cross-entropy loss:

$$CE = -t_1 \log(f(S_1)) + (1-t_1)\log(1-f(S_1)) \tag{11}$$

where S_i and t_i are the algorithm resulted class score/probability and the ground truth label respectively.

Table 1 Results of automated segmentation of eyes with atrophic AMD and JMD

	DSC	OR	Algorithm area (mm²)	Manual area (mm²)	Area difference ration
Atrophic AMD	0.94±0.04	0.89±0.06	16.65±3.77	15.53±3.77	0.07±0.31
Atrophic JMD	0.87±0.13	0.78±0.17	5.31±3.99	4.59±3.90	0.16±0.31

Credit: Z. Wang, S. Sadda, Z. Hu, Deep learning for automated screening and semantic segmentation of age-related and juvenile atrophic macular degeneration, in: Proceedings of SPIE Medical Imaging 2019: Computer-Aided Diagnosis (in press).

Experimental approach and results: As a preliminary investigation, Wang et al. applied their U-Net algorithm to two FAF image datasets (Spectralis HRA+OCT, Heidelberg Engineering) with AMD and JMD respectively [39]. The AMD dataset has 320 FAF images with GA and the JMD data has 100 images with Stargardt-related atrophy. The FAF image resolution varied from 496×596 pixels to 1536×1536 pixels with a physical size of $8.85 \, mm \times 8.85 \, mm$. All the images were re-sized to a consistent dimension. To train and evaluate the U-Net atrophy segmentation, each pixel on each FAF image of the two datasets was marked as nonatrophy or atrophic AMD; or nonatrophy or atrophic JMD. To prevent the overfitting and yield better generalization of the trained U-Net model, they further augmented the training data via a number of random transformations, including rotation, vertical and horizontal translation, shearing transformations, zooming, and horizontal flipping. The U-Net-based GA segmentation demonstrated a very high agreement with the manual ground truth as shown in Table 1 and Fig. 10, representing the best algorithm accuracy of the automated GA segmentation on FAF images to date in the reported literature. This highly robust system offers the great potential to facilitate large scale atrophic AMD and JMD clinic trials, clinical research, and translation to clinical practice.

5 Automated binary classification of OCT risk factors for progression from intermediate AMD to atrophy using an AI deep learning approach

As a pilot study, Saha et al. (from Z. Hu and S. Sadda's group of Doheny Eye Institute) developed an AI deep learning-based supervised classification approach to detect risk factors for progression to atrophy. Since the Cirrus advanced RPE analysis already included FDA cleared drusen volume analysis, they focused on the detection of the three other prespecified risk factors, i.e., the hD, HRF, and SDD as shown in Fig. 11. The AI-based approach performed a binary classification on each individual OCT B-scan of an OCT volume as containing or not containing a prespecified risk factor.

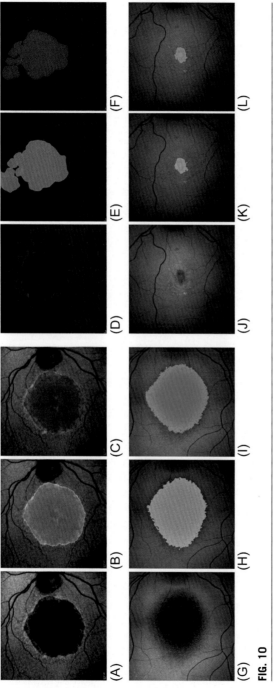

FIG. 10

Example illustration of the segmentation system results. Upper rows: atrophic AMD segmentation (A) and (D) FAF images, (B) and (E) U-Net segmentation, (C) and (F) manual delineation. Lower rows: atrophic JMD segmentation (G) and (J) FAF images, (H) and (K) U-Net segmentation, (I) and (L) manual delineation. Note that image D has very low image contrast, and image G and J have very different size of atrophic JMD profiles but the algorithm segmentation still presents high similarity as the manual gradings.

Credit: Z. Wang, S. Sadda, Z. Hu, Deep learning for automated screening and semantic segmentation of age-related and juvenile atrophic macular degeneration, in: Proceedings of SPIE Medical Imaging 2019: Computer-Aided Diagnosis (in press).

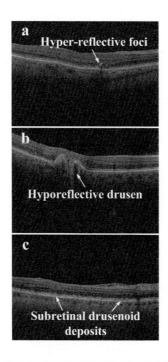

FIG. 11

Examples of prespecified high risk factors (A) HRF, (B) hD, and (C) SDD.

The residual connections [31] and Inception architecture [32] are arguably the most groundbreaking concepts in the deep leaning field in recent years. Network depth is of crucial importance in neural network architectures, but deeper networks are more difficult to train. The residual networks (ResNet) [31] can ease the training of deep networks by using the residual connection. Inception networks (i.e., GoogLeNet) [32] tend to have very deep architecture with complex network layers. Naturally, using residual connections to replace the filter concatenation stage of the Inception networks can ease the training of the expensive Inception networks and still retain its computational efficiency [33]. They compared the three state-of-the-art networks, ResNet, Inception, and the combination of the ResNet and Inception, i.e., Inception-ResNet [33]. All three networks demonstrated promising results with the combined Inception-ResNet slightly performing better than the Inception and ResNet.

The Inception-ResNet was then applied on a SD-OCT dataset from 153 patients with early AMD at baseline and followed for progression to atrophy at follow-up. Each SD-OCT volume included 128 B-scans. To simplify the training process, the classification was separately performed for each risk factor for presence or absence in each individual B-scan. Training a completely new neural network often requires an extremely large training dataset which usually has millions of weights to learn. Transfer learning is a technique which utilizes the cumulative knowledge trained from other datasets and is applied to a new neural network. The transfer learning [72, 73] was applied on the training of the Inception-ResNet by taking advantage of the ImageNet model pretrained from millions of general images and then the general features learned from the ImageNet data [74, 75] was applied to the Inception-ResNet. This allowed the Inception-ResNet model to be highly accurate even with a relatively small training dataset. In the pilot study, Saha et al. were able to achieve a classification accuracy >86% for all three risk factors of interest.

With the automated identification of risk factors on each individual 2-D OCT scan, there are several potential strategies one can take to produce a risk score. One simple approach would be to compute the percentage of B-scans in each volume which contain each risk factor. For example, in an eye with a macular OCT volume of 128 B-scans, if HRF is detected on 20 B-scans among the 128 B-scans, we can assign a risk score of $20/128 \approx 0.16$—this could be performed for each risk factor and the points could be totaled to assign a total score for each eye. Central drusen volume could also be integrated into such a system, though the drusen volume would need to be scaled to this "point system" with only volume over the previously established threshold (0.03 mm^3 within a 3-mm circle centering on the fovea) being considered. The main point to emphasize here, however, is that this "simple" approach is limited in that it presumes each risk factor (especially those other than drusen volume) are of equal importance in terms of risk, which is almost certainly not correct. Ultimately, the scaling system for each risk factor will need to be weighted based on the longitudinal outcome data.

6 Summary

The explosion of new retinal imaging technologies and the exponential growth in the size and complexity of retinal imaging datasets have fueled a demand for automated retinal image analysis tools. One disease where image analysis tools are of particular importance is AMD. Image analysis approaches to identify and quantify atrophy associated with AMD have evolved from semiautomatic approaches requiring extensive manual input to more automated approaches using prespecified or custom-crafted features, to fully automated AI-deep learning approaches where image features are learned automatically. In addition, similar approaches appear to be applicable for the automated identification and quantification of risk factors in early/intermediate AMD eyes which may be associated with risk for progression to late AMD. This may allow the design of novel therapeutic trials aimed at intervention early in the disease process.

Acknowledgments

The Association for Research in Vision and Ophthalmology as the copyright holder for reference [19] as described in Section 3.2. The international society for optics and photonics

(SPIE) as the copyright holder for reference [25] as described in Section 4.1. The international society for optics and photonics (SPIE) as the copyright holder for reference [39] as described in Section 4.2.

References

[1] A. Nagiel, R.A. Lalane, S.R. Sadda, S.D. Schwartz, ULTRA-WIDEFIELD FUNDUS IMAGING: a review of clinical applications and future trends, Retina 36 (4) (2016) 660–678.

[2] C.S. Tan, J.C. Chan, K.X. Cheong, W.K. Ngo, S.R. Sadda, Comparison of retinal thicknesses measured using swept-source and spectral-domain optical coherence tomography devices, Ophthal. Surg. Lasers Imaging Retina 46 (2) (2015) 172–179.

[3] T. Hirano, S. Kakihara, Y. Toriyama, M.G. Nittala, T. Murata, S. Sadda, Wide-field en face swept-source optical coherence tomography angiography using extended field imaging in diabetic retinopathy, Br. J. Ophthalmol. 102 (9) (2018) 1199–1203.

[4] J. Orellana-Rios, S. Yokoyama, J.M. Agee, N. Challa, K.B. Freund, L.A. Yannuzzi, R.T. Smith, Quantitative fundus autofluorescence in non-neovascular age-related macular degeneration, Ophthal. Surg. Lasers Imaging Retina 49 (10) (2018) S34–S42.

[5] C. Dysli, R. Fink, S. Wolf, M.S. Zinkernagel, Fluorescence lifetimes of drusen in age-related macular degeneration, Invest. Ophthalmol. Vis. Sci. 58 (11) (2017) 4856–4862.

[6] E. Borrelli, M.G. Nittala, N.S. Abdelfattah, J. Lei, A.H. Hariri, Y. Shi, W. Fan, M. Cozzi, V. Sarao, P. Lanzetta, G. Staurenghi, S.R. Sadda, Comparison of short-wavelength blue-light autofluorescence and conventional blue-light autofluorescence in geographic atrophy. Br. J. Ophthalmol. (2018), pii: bjophthalmol-2018-311849. https://doi.org/10.1136/bjophthalmol-2018-311849.

[7] J.F. Korobelnik, M.B. Rougier, M.N. Delyfer, A. Bron, B.M.J. Merle, H. Savel, G. Chêne, C. Delcourt, C. Creuzot-Garcher, Effect of dietary supplementation with lutein, zeaxanthin, and ω-3 on macular pigment: a randomized clinical trial, JAMA Ophthalmol. 135 (11) (2017) 1259–1266.

[8] X. Xu, X. Liu, X. Wang, M.E. Clark, G. McGwin Jr., C. Owsley, C.A. Curcio, Y. Zhang, Retinal pigment epithelium degeneration associated with subretinal drusenoid deposits in age-related macular degeneration, Am. J. Ophthalmol. 175 (2017) 87–98.

[9] R. Klein, B.E. Klein, K.E. Lee, K.J. Cruickshanks, R.E. Gangnon, Changes in visual acuity in a population over a 15 year period: the Beaver Dam Eye Study, Am J. Ophthalmol. 142 (2006) 539–549.

[10] C.J. Blair, Geographic atrophy of the retinal pigment epithelium: a manifestation of senile macular degeneration, Arch. Ophthalmol. 93 (1975) 19–25.

[11] J.P. Sarks, S.H. Sarks, M.C. Killingsworth, Evolution of geographic atrophy of the retinal pigment epithelium, Eye 2 (1988) 552–577.

[12] S. Schmitz-Valckenberg, F.G. Holz, A.C. Bird, R.F. Spaide, Fundus autofluorescence imaging: review and perspectives, Retina 28 (2008) 385–409.

[13] D. Huang, E.A. Swanson, C.P. Lin, J.S. Schuman, W.G. Stinson, W. Chang, M.R. Hee, T. Flotte, K. Gregory, C.A. Puliafito, J.G. Fujimoto, Optical coherence tomography, Science 254 (5035) (1991) 1178–1181. 1957169. PMC4638169.

[14] J.G. Fujimoto, B. Bouma, G.J. Tearney, S.A. Boppart, C. Pitris, J.F. Southern, M.E. Brezinski, New technology for high-speed and high-resolution optical coherence tomography, Ann. N. Y. Acad. Sci. 838 (1998) 95–107. 9511798.

[15] S.R. Sadda, et al., Consensus definition for atrophy associated with age-related macular degeneration on OCT. Classification of Atrophy Report 3. Ophthalmology (2017), https://doi.org/10.1016/j.ophtha.2017.09.028.

[16] A.A. Khanifar, D.E. Lederer, J.H. Ghodasra, S.S. Stinnett, J.J. Lee, S.W. Cousins, S. Bearelly, Comparison of color fundus photographs and fundus autofluorescence images in measuring geographic atrophy area, Retina 32 (9) (2012) 1884–1891.

[17] S. Schmitz-Valckenberg, C.K. Brinkmann, F. Alten, P. Herrmann, N.K. Stratmann, A.P. Göbel, M. Fleckenstein, M. Diller, G.J. Jaffe, F.G. Holz, Semiautomated image processing method for identification and quantification of geographic atrophy in age-related macular degeneration, Invest. Ophthalmol. Vis. Sci. 52 (10) (2011) 7640–7646.

[18] Q. Chen, L. de Sisternes, T. Leng, L. Zheng, L. Kutzscher, D.L. Rubin, Semi-automatic geographic atrophy segmentation for SD-OCT images, Biomed. Opt. Express. 4 (12) (2013) 2729–2750, https://doi.org/10.1364/BOE.4.002729.eCollection.

[19] Z. Hu, G.G. Medioni, M. Hernandez, A. Hariri, X. Wu, S.R. Sadda, Segmentation of the geographic atrophy in spectral-domain optical coherence tomography volume scans and fundus autofluorescene images, Invest. Ophthalmol. Vis. Sci. 54 (13) (2013) 8375–8383.

[20] D.J. Ramsey, J.S. Sunness, P. Malviya, C. Applegate, G.D. Hager, J.T. Handa, Automated image alignment and segmentation to follow progression of geographic atrophy in age-related macular degeneration, Retina 34 (7) (2014) 1296–1307, https://doi.org/10.1097/IAE.0000000000000069.

[21] M. Mohri, A. Rostamizadeh, A. Talwalkar, Foundations of Machine Learning, in: The MIT Press, 2012.

[22] R. Jain, R. Kasturi, B.G. Schunck, Machine Vision, McGraw-Hill, Inc, 1995.

[23] Pellegrini, et al., Machine learning of neuroimaging for assisted diagnosis of cognitive impairment and dementia: a systematic review, Alzheimer's Dementia: Diagnos. Assess. Dis. Monitor. 10 (2018) P519–P535.

[24] F.G. Venhuizen, B. van Ginneken, F. van Asten, M. van Grinsven, S. Fauser, C.B. Hoyng, T. Theelen, C.I. Sanchez, Automated staging of age-related macular degeneration using optical coherence tomography, Invest. Ophthalmol. Vis. Sci. 58 (2017) 2318–2328.

[25] Z. Hu, G.G. Medioni, M. Hernandez, S.R. Sadda, Automated segmentation of geographic atrophy in fundus autofluorescene images using supervised pixel classification, J. Med. Imag. 2 (1) (2015), 014501. https://doi.org/10.1117/1.JMI.2.1.014501. 26158084.

[26] V. Gulshan, L. Peng, M. Coram, et al., Development and validation of a deep learning algorithm for detection of diabetic retinopathy in retinal fundus photographs, JAMA 316 (22) (2016) 2402–2410, https://doi.org/10.1001/jama.2016.17216. 27898976.

[27] Y. Jia, E. Shelhamer, J. Donahue, S. Karayev, J. Long, R. Girshick, S. Guadarrama, T. Darrell, Caffe: convolutional architecture for fast feature embedding, in: Proceedings of the 22nd ACM International Conference on Multimedia, vol. 9, 2014, pp. 675–678.

[28] J. Long, E. Shelhamer, T. Darrell, Fully convolutional networks for semantic segmentation, Computer Vision and Pattern Recognition (CVPR), IEEE (2015).

[29] W. Shen, M. Zhou, F. Yang, C. Yang, J. Tian, Multi-scale convolutional neural networks for lung nodule classification, Inf. Process. Med. Imaging 24 (2015) 588–599. 26221705.

[30] O. Ronneberger, P. Fischer, T. Brox, U-Net: convolutional networks for biomedical image segmentation, in: International Conference on Medical Image Computing and Computer-Assisted Intervention, Springer, Cham, 2015, pp. 234–241.

[31] K. He, X. Zhang, S. Ren, J. Sun, Deep residual learning for image recognition, in: IEEE Conference on Computer Vision and Pattern Recognition (CVPR), 2016.

[32] C. Szegedy, W. Liu, Y. Jia, P. Sermanet, S. Reed, D. Anguelov, D. Erhan, V. Vanhoucke, A. Rabinovich, Going deeper with convolutions, in: 2015 IEEE Conference on Computer Vision and Pattern Recognition (CVPR), 2015, https://doi.org/10.1109/CVPR.2015.7298594.

[33] C. Szegedy, V. Vanhoucke, S. Loffe, J. Shlens, Z. Wojna, Rethinking the inception architecture for computer vision. in: 2016 IEEE Conference on Computer Vision and Pattern Recognition (CVPR), 2016, https://doi.org/10.1109/CVPR.2016.308.

[34] Y. LeCun, Y. Bengio, Convolutional networks for images, speech, and time-series, in: M.A. Arbib (Ed.), The Handbook of Brain Theory and Neural Networks, MIT Press, 1995.

[35] Z. Hu, Z. Wang, S. Sadda, Automated segmentation of geographic atrophy using deep convolutional neural networks, in: Proceedings Volume 10575, SPIE Medical Imaging 2018: Computer-Aided Diagnosis, 2018, p. 1057511, https://doi.org/10.1117/12.2287001.

[36] Z. Hu, Z. Wang, N. Abdelfattah, J. Sadda, S. Sadda, Automated Geographic Atrophy Segmentation in Infrared Reflectance Images Using Deep Convolutional Neural Networks, ARVO, 2018.

[37] U. Schmidt-Erfurth, A. Sadeghipou, B.S. Gerendas, S.M. Waldstein, H. Bogunović, Artificial intelligence in retina, Progr. Retinal Eye Res. 67 (2018) 1–29. https://www.doi.org/10.1016/j.preteyeres.2018.07.004.

[38] Z. Ji, Q. Chen, S. Niu, T. Leng, D.L. Rubin, Beyond retinal layers: a deep voting model for automated geographic atrophy segmentation in SD-OCT images, Transl. Vis. Sci. Technol. 7 (1) (2018) 1, https://doi.org/10.1167/tvst.7.1.1.eCollection. PMC5749649 29302382.

[39] Z. Wang, S. Sadda, Z. Hu, Deep learning for automated screening and semantic segmentation of age-related and juvenile atrophic macular degeneration, in: Proc. SPIE 10950, Medical Imaging 2019: Computer-Aided Diagnosis, 109501Q, March 13, 2019, https://doi.org/10.1117/12.2511538.

[40] M.D. Davis, R.E. Gangnon, L.L.-Y. al, The age-related eye disease study severity scale for age-related macular degeneration: AREDS report no. 17, Arch. Ophthalmol. 123 (2005) 1484–1498.

[41] F.L. Ferris, M.D. Davis, T.E. Clemons, et al., A simplified severity scale for age-related macular degeneration: AREDS report no. 18, Arch. Ophthalmol. 123 (2005) 1570–1574.

[42] N.S. Abdelfattah, H. Zhang, D.S. Boyer, et al., Drusen volume as a predictor of disease progression in patients with late age-related macular degeneration in the fellow eye, Invest. Ophthalmol. Vis. Sci. 57 (2016) 1839–1846.

[43] Y. Ouyang, F.M. Heussen, A. Hariri, et al., Optical coherence tomography-based observation of the natural history of drusenoid lesion in eyes with dry age-related macular degeneration, Ophthalmology 120 (2013) 2656–2665.

[44] R.P. Finger, Z. Wu, C.D. Luu, et al., Reticular pseudodrusen: a risk factor for geographic atrophy in fellow eyes of individuals with unilateral choroidal neovascularization, Ophthalmology 121 (2014) 1252–1256.

[45] B.S. MarsigliaM, S. Bearelly, et al., Association between geographic atrophy progression and reticular pseudodrusen in eyes with dry age-related macular degeneration, Invest. Ophthalmol. Vis. Sci. 54 (2013) 7362–7369.

[46] Q. Zhou, E. Daniel, M.G. Maguire, et al., Pseudodrusen and incidence of late age-related macular degeneration in fellow eyes in the comparison of age-related macular degeneration treatments trials, Ophthalmology 123 (2016) 1530–1540.

[47] M.A.B. Filho, A.J. Witkin, Outer retinal layers as predictors of vision loss, Rev. Ophthalmol. (2015).

[48] P.A. Keane, S. Liakopoulos, K.T. Chang, M. Wang, L. Dustin, A.C. Walsh, S.R. Sadda, Relationship between optical coherence tomography retinal parameters and visual acuity in neovascular age-related macular degeneration, Ophthalmology 115 (2008) 2206–2214. 18930551. PMC5340147.

[49] J.K. Sun, M.M. Lin, J. Lammer, S. Prager, R. Sarangi, P.S. Silva, L.P. Aiello, Disorganization of the retinal inner layers as a predictor of visual acuity in eyes with center-involved diabetic macular edema, JAMA Ophthalmol. 132 (2014) 1309–1316. 25058813.

[50] R.F. Spaide, C.A. Curcio, Anatomical correlates to the bands seen in the outer retina by optical coherence tomography: literature review and model, Retina 31 (2011) 1609–1619. 21844839. PMC3619110.

[51] Y. Mitamura, S. Mitamura-Aizawa, T. Katome, T. Naito, A. Hagiwara, K. Kumagai, S. Yamamoto, Photoreceptor impairment and restoration on optical coherence tomographic image, J. Ophthalmol. 2013 (2013) 518170. 23691278. PMC3649344.

[52] S. Saxena, K. Srivastav, C.M. Cheung, J.Y. Ng, T.Y. Lai, Photoreceptor inner segment ellipsoid band integrity on spectral domain optical coherence tomography, Clin. Ophthalmol. 8 (2014) 2507–2522. 25525329. PMC4266419.

[53] S. Aizawa, Y. Mitamura, A. Hagiwara, T. Sugawara, S. Yamamoto, Changes of fundus autofluorescence, photoreceptor inner and outer segment junction line, and visual function in patients with retinitis pigmentosa, Clin. Exp. Ophthalmol. 38 (6) (2010) 597–604. 20456441.

[54] T. Wakabayashi, Y. Oshima, H. Fujimoto, Y. Murakami, H. Sakaguchi, S. Kusaka, Y. Tano, Foveal microstructure and visual acuity after retinal detachment repair: imaging analysis by Fourier-domain optical coherence tomography, Ophthalmology 116 (2009) 519–528. 19147231.

[55] K.I. Hartmann, M.L. Gomez, D.U. Bartsch, A.K. Schuster, W.R. Freeman, Effect of change in drusen evolution on photoreceptor inner segment/outer segment junction, Retina 32 (2012) 1492–1499. 22481478. PMC3792858.

[56] S. Mrejen, T. Sato, C.A. Curcio, R.F. Spaide, Assessing the cone photoreceptor mosaic in eyes with pseudodrusen and soft drusen in vivo using adaptive optics imaging, Ophthalmology 121 (2014) 545–551. 24183341. PMC3946613.

[57] C.A. Curcio, J.D. Messinger, K.R. Sloan, G. McGwin, N.E. Medeiros, R.F. Spaide, Subretinal drusenoid deposits in non-neovascular age-related macular degeneration: morphology, prevalence, topography, and biogenesis model, Retina 33 (2013) 265–276. 23266879. PMC3870202.

[58] R.R. Pappuru, Y. Ouyang, M.G. Nittala, H.D. Hemmati, P.A. Keane, A.C. Walsh, S.R. Sadda, Relationship between outer retinal thickness substructures and visual acuity in eyes with dry age-related macular degeneration, Invest. Ophthalmol. Vis. Sci. 52 (9) (2011) 6743–6748. 21685337.

[59] E. Pilotto, E. Benetti, E. Convento, F. Guidolin, E. Longhin, R. Parrozzani, E. Midena, Microperimetry, fundus autofluorescence, and retinal layer changes in progressing geographic atrophy, Can. J. Ophthalmol. 48 (5) (2013) 386–393. 24093185.

[60] M. Inoue, S. Morita, Y. Watanabe, T. Kaneko, S. Yamane, S. Kobayashi, A. Arakawa, K. Kadonosono, Inner segment/outer segment junction assessed by spectral-domain optical coherence tomography in patients with idiopathic epiretinal membrane, Am J. Ophthalmol. 150 (2010) 834–839. 20719295.

[61] J. Lei, S. Balasubramanian, N.S. Abdelfattah, M.G. Nittala, S.R. Sadda, Proposal of a simple optical coherence tomography-based scoring system for progression of age-related macular degeneration, Graefes Arch. Clin. Exp. Ophthalmol. 255 (8) (2017) 1551–1558, https://doi.org/10.1007/s00417-017-3693-y (Epub 2017 May 22).

[62] U. Schmidt-Erfurth, S.M. Waldstein, S. Klimscha, A. Sadeghipour, X. Hu, B.S. Gerendas, A. Osborne, H. Bogunović, Prediction of individual disease conversion in early AMD using artificial intelligence, Invest. Ophthalmol. Vis. Sci. 59 (8) (2018) 3199–3208, https://doi.org/10.1167/iovs.18-24106. 29971444.

[63] J.A. Sethian, Level Set Methods and Fast Marching Methods, Cambridge University Press, 1996.

[64] S. Chen, R.J. Radke, Level set segmentation with both shape and intensity priors, in: IEEE Conference on Computer Vision, 2009, pp. 763–770.

[65] Z. Hu, X. Wu, A. Hariri, S. Sadda, Multiple layer segmentation and analysis in three-dimensional spectral-domain optical coherence tomography volume scans, J. Biomed. Opt. 18 (7) (2001) 076006, https://doi.org/10.1117/1.JBO.18.7.076006. 23843084.

[66] Z. Hu, M.D. Abràmoff, Y.H. Kwon, K. Lee, M.K. Garvin, Automated segmentation of neural canal opening and optic cup in 3D spectral optical coherence tomography volumes of the optic nerve head, Invest. Ophthalmol. Vis. Sci. 51 (11) (2010) 5708–5717. PMC3061507.

[67] N. Sharma, A.K. Ray, S. Sharma, K.K. Shukla, S. Pradhan, L.M. Aggarwal, Segmentation and classification of medical images using texture-primitive features: application of BAM-type artificial neural network, J. Med. Phys. 33 (3) (2008) 119–126, https://doi.org/10.4103/0971-6203.42763.

[68] R. Duda, P. Hart, D. Stork, Pattern Classification, second ed., John Wiley and Sons, New York, 2001.

[69] S. Arya, D. Mount, N. Netanyahu, R. Silverman, A. Wu, An optimal algorithm for approximate nearest neighbor searching in fixed dimensions, J. ACM 45 (6) (1998) 891–923.

[70] Luis Ibàñez, Will Schroeder, Lydia Ng, Josh Cates, and the Insight Software Consortium, The ITK Software Guide, second ed., http://www.itk.org. 2005.

[71] D.P. Kingma, J. Ba, Adam: a method for stochastic optimization, in: Proceedings of the 3rd International Conference for Learning Representations (ICLR), San Diego, 2015.

[72] J. West, D. Ventura, S. Warnick, Spring Research Presentation: A Theoretical Foundation for Inductive Transfer, Brigham Young University, College of Physical and Mathematical Sciences, 2007. Archived from the Original on 2007-08-01. Retrieved 2007-08-05.

[73] S. Thrun, L. Pratt, Learning to Learn, Springer Science & Business Media, ISBN: 978-1-4615-5529-2, 2012.

[74] J. Deng, W. Dong, R. Socher, L.-J. Li, K. Li, L. Fei-Fei, ImageNet: a large-scale hierarchical image database, in: 2009 Conference on Computer Vision and Pattern Recognition, 2009.

[75] O. Russakovsky*, J. Deng*, S. Hao, J. Krause, S. Satheesh, S. Ma, Z. Huang, A. Karpathy, A. Khosla, M. Bernstein, A.C. Berg, F.-F. Li, (* = equal contribution) ImageNet Large Scale Visual Recognition Challenge, IJCV, 2015.

Artificial intelligence and deep learning in retinal image analysis

18

Philippe Burlina*,a,b, Adrian Galdran*,c, Pedro Costac, Adam Cohena,b,
Aurélio Campilhoc,d

aThe Johns Hopkins University Applied Physics Lab, Laurel, MD, United States
bJohns Hopkins School of Medicine, Baltimore, MD, United States
cINESC TEC—Institute for Systems and Computer Engineering, Technology and
Science, Porto, Portugal
dFaculty of Engineering, University of Porto, Porto, Portugal

1 Introduction

Age-related macular degeneration (AMD), diabetic retinopathy (DR), and glaucoma are among the leading global causes of human blindness [1–3]. AMD and DR produce lesion of the retina and macula that can lead to visual impairment and blindness. Image analysis is integral to the detection, management, and monitoring of these conditions. Although real-time optical inspection (i.e., via fundus imaging or optical coherence tomography [OCT]) is the current diagnostic cornerstone of these diseases, this approach is immensely resource-intensive, which greatly limits ophthalmic care access to varied populations. Thus, new approaches to ophthalmic care are needed that would allow for lower cost and broader access to care. In this light, automated retinal image analysis (ARIA) has gained increasing importance. In addition to ophthalmic disease applications, it has also become relevant to neurological and nonophthalmic disorders because many of such conditions may have specific retinal signatures, revealing useful disease biomarkers.

AMD, a retinal disease, is one of the leading causes of blindness and visual impairment for people over 50 years of age. It is a leading cause of irreversible central vision loss [1, 4–7]. Over one hundred million people in the United States alone above the age of 50 are at risk, and an estimated 1.75–3 million people are afflicted with some form of the disease [1], with possible resultant serious loss of function from severe visual loss. Its devastation stems from the retinal location it affects—the macula. The macula contains the greatest number and density of light-sensing elements relevant to high-resolution visual discrimination (i.e., cones) as compared to the rest of the retina. The primary measure of visual discrimination, visual acuity, is reduced in macular diseases like AMD.

---

* Both authors have equally contributed to this work.

Computational Retinal Image Analysis. https://doi.org/10.1016/B978-0-08-102816-2.00019-8

Like AMD, DR produces functionally relevant visual loss because it also affects the macula (in addition to other parts of the retina). It occurs after years of metabolic disregulation in the setting of long-standing diabetes (mellitus), a disease of glucose disregulation [3]. After chronic exposure to elevated blood glucose levels (i.e., hyperglycemia), patients with diabetes develop pathological changes of the blood vessels of the eye, brain, heart, kidney, and limbs. This leads to diabetic retinopathy, stroke, myocardial infarction, kidney failure, and limb-threatening ischemic conditions, among other conditions.

Unlike AMD and DR, glaucoma is not a retinal pathology. It results from chronic exposure to raised intraocular pressure, which in turn damages the ocular portion of the optic nerve. The optic nerve is a collection of retinal nerve fibers that transmit visual information from the light-sensing retinal cells to the brain. When exposed to abnormally high intraocular pressure, the anterior portion of the optic nerve within the eye (optic nerve head, also known as optic disc) fails. The pathology begins with the peripheral portion of the disc, but slowly progresses centrally. Clinically, peripheral visual field loss precedes central visual field loss. While patients with AMD and DR are typically aware of early-onset disease because central vision is involved from the start, glaucoma patients commonly remain unaware of their disease until late in its course because the disease first affects peripheral vision.

Relevant to these three conditions, two current diagnostic modalities, utilized by ARIA, have seen wide deployment and usage in clinical practice: fundus photography and optical coherence tomography (OCT). Both are noninvasive, high-resolution imaging techniques capable of capturing the fine anatomical structure and lesions within the retina. Fundus photography offers views of the visible surface of the retina, when viewed through the pupil. OCT, also obtained through pupillary access, provides cross-sectional retinal images, allowing analysis of the varied retinal layers, anterior optic nerve (including the optic disc), and the highly vascular structure under the retina, the choroid.

These two imaging modalities are the mainstay of ophthalmic diagnostics and are used to detect and manage most retinal and optic nerve diseases. Of note, additional modalities can provide other anatomic and pathological information, including fluorescein angiography, electroretinogram, orbital ultrasound, computed tomography of the orbit, and magnetic resonance imaging of the orbit. The last three modalities provide fairly gross ophthalmic views and aren't suitable for resolution of the fine details of retinal anatomy and pathology. Instead, they may be useful for gross ocular and optic nerve pathologies.

As mentioned earlier, retinal imaging may also provide insights related to nonophthalmic diseases, including various neurological diseases [8–10]. These diseases include stroke and neurodegenerative conditions such as multiple sclerosis, Parkinson's disease, and Alzheimer's disease [8–10]. ARIA-related work in these fields holds potential to provide new biomarkers for such conditions, particularly for those that currently lack objective markers for early diagnosis, prognosis, disease monitoring, and response to treatment.

ARIA-related applications to ophthalmic and nonophthalmic conditions have made great strides in recent years, mainly secondary to the increasing size and availability of relevant data sets. Additionally, there has been steady progress with use of more advanced machine learning and machine vision techniques allowing for higher accuracy and efficiency algorithms. Advances in artificial intelligence (AI) approaches, too, such as deep learning (DL), have recently significantly improved performance of algorithms and therefore greatly expanded the potential for impact of medical imaging (e.g., [11]). This has enabled better means to detect patients with DR, AMD, and other retinal affects using fundus images [12] or OCT [13].

In this chapter, we offer an overview—by no means exhaustive—of relevant work connecting ARIA with artificial intelligence, with a prominent focus on deep learning techniques. For more reviews with a broader medical imaging scope, the reader is also referred to several other valuable resources and recent surveys of the state of the art in AI applications to medical imaging including: Litjens' and colleagues summary of DL applications on general medical imaging [14] which summarizes over 300 relevant publications or Carneiro et al.'s chapter [15] which provides a thorough and sweeping review on DL methods in several imaging modalities including mammography, cardiology, and microscopy. A host of other notable review papers can be found and should also provide useful information including Ker et al. [16], Razzak et al. [17], and Shen et al. [18].

In ophthalmic image analysis in particular, several other relevant papers offer detailed and useful reviews. The work in Jordan et al. [19] presents a survey of traditional image processing and machine learning techniques, whereas Schmidt-Erfurth et al. [20] offers a comparison of classical machine learning and deep learning techniques for different clinically relevant tasks covering an array of retinal diseases. A more recent review of the state of the art of AI in ophthalmology is Hogarty et al. [21], which scours MEDLINE and SCOPUS databases for AI and various eye diseases, including AMD, diabetic retinopathy, and glaucoma, among others. For a more clinical perspective, a recent discussion on the benefits and limitations of applying DL in ophthalmology can be found in Grewal et al. [22]. Finally, Ting et al. offers also a good review [23] of recent AI applications to modern retinal image analysis for DR, AMD, glaucoma, and other conditions.

2 Fundamentals of deep learning

Since DL is the main AI technical approach recently used for ARIA this section provides an introduction to the concepts and techniques of DL.

Machine learning allows for tasks such as classification or regression without explicit programming and via the use of *models* that map, for example input images (e.g., retinal images) into corresponding labels (e.g., retinal disease type). DL allows the combination of processing units that enable the generation of such *models* that can be put to use for different computer vision tasks such as classification or segmentation. The fundamentals of DL methods are reviewed next using mathematical notations. For other introductions that may be more amenable to the clinical reader of this topic, we also refer to the above cited review papers.

2.1 Fundamentals of neural networks

Neural networks (NNs), or deep neural networks, are defined by hierarchical compositions of simple transformations. Given an input data sample $\mathbf{x} \in \mathbb{R}^n$, the output of a NN $\mathbf{U}\theta$ parameterized by weights θ is given by:

$$\mathbf{U}_{\theta}(\mathbf{x}) = (\mathcal{A}^L \circ \cdots \circ \mathcal{A}^j \circ \ldots \mathcal{A}^2 \circ \mathcal{A}^1)(\mathbf{x}), \tag{1}$$

where $\mathcal{A}^j$ is an operator to be specified below. The typically high dimensionality of $\mathbf{x}$ is reduced by the intermediate mappings defining each layer of $\mathbf{U}\theta$, effectively compressing it into a lower-dimensional representation that retains its most salient aspects.

Training $\mathbf{U}\theta$ amounts to learning a mapping from an input to a target space. For this, we consider a dataset $\mathbf{S}_{train} = (\mathbf{D}_{train}, \mathbf{T}_{train})$ of examples $\mathbf{x} \in \mathbf{D}_{train}$ and associated targets $\mathbf{y} \in \mathbf{T}_{train}$. In order to optimize the weights θ, we consider a loss function $\mathcal{L}_{\theta}(\mathbf{y}, \hat{\mathbf{y}})$ that measures the deviation of the prediction $\hat{\mathbf{y}} = \mathbf{U}_{\theta}(\mathbf{x})$ from its corresponding target $\mathbf{y}$. This function models the problem to be solved (e.g., classification, regression, segmentation), and the training process determines which is the most relevant information in the data that best serves its minimization. This represents one of the major advantages of NNs: they can bypass feature engineering, the process of manually defining relevant aspects of the data for each particular problem.

The standard algorithm to optimize weights θ so that the value of $\mathcal{L}_{\theta}$ over the training set is reduced is called *back-propagation*. Back-propagation proceeds by first carrying out a forward-pass for a given data sample $\mathbf{x}$ in order to compute a prediction $\hat{\mathbf{y}}$ and the corresponding error $\mathcal{L}_{\theta}(\mathbf{y}, \hat{\mathbf{y}})$. This error is then propagated backwards through $\mathbf{U}\theta$ by applying the chain-rule to the composition of functions defining its different layers. This provides estimates of the loss function's gradient for each layer's weights. The process is then iterated over all samples of the training set so as to minimize the loss function.

Early NNs, known as fully connected NNs, define the operators in Eq. (1) to be $(\mathcal{A}^j(\mathbf{x}) = s(A^j \cdot \mathbf{x} + b^j)$, that is, an affine transformation of the input followed by a nonlinear point-wise scalar mapping s (also called an *activation function*). However, in this case A^j are dense matrices, connecting every component of the input of a given layer to its output. This results in a large number of parameters (weights) that need to be learned. In addition, the composition of nonlinear functions in Eq. (1) turns $\mathbf{U}\theta$ into a very expressive nonlinear model, but also leads to highly nonconvex loss functions that are hard to minimize. Moreover, the input data dimensionality must be reduced so that the problem of minimizing such loss is numerically tractable. For this reason, application of this model occurs typically after a manual feature extraction step to encode the data into a low-dimensional set of descriptors, as shown in Fig. 1. Early applications of this approach on retinal images can be found for instance in Yun et al. [24] and García et al. [25].

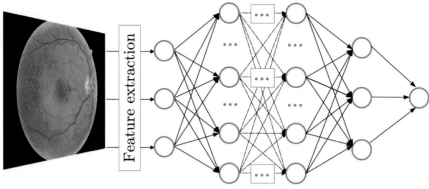

FIG. 1

AI for retinal image analysis. A prototypical use of a fully connected neural network architecture for processing retinal images. As can be seen all nodes in one layer of the network are connected to all nodes in the previous layer. A retinal image can be used as input from which visual features are derived. These features are then used as input and processed via the fully connected network. These are mapped to a target output, for example, a number, that is sort of confidence, for a label signifying the type of retinal disease.

Recently, several factors have made deep learning and the use of neural nets significantly outperform their early implementations. This has included the advent of efficient parallel computing processors, coupled with an increasing amount of available training data, and more advanced network architectures that substantially reduce the number of trainable parameters to be optimized. These advances have enabled researchers to fully leverage the promised potential of deep NNs. A key architectural design to achieve such reduction of weights while keeping predictive accuracy are convolutional neural networks (CNNs) also referred to as deep convolutional neural networks (or DCNNs).

2.2 Deep convolutional neural networks

CNNs are a particular kind of neural network where the weights are learned for the application of a series of convolutions on the input image, being the filter weights shared across the same convolutional layer. This design and related learning mechanisms are discussed in detail throughout this section.

CNNs replace fully connected affine layers $\mathcal{A}$ in Eq. (1) by operators $\mathcal{C}$ defined by small convolution kernels. This localizes computations, effectively reducing the number of parameters in $\mathbf{U}\theta$. The resulting network is defined as:

$$\mathbf{U}_{\theta}(\mathbf{x}) = (\mathcal{C}^{f^{L}} \circ \cdots \circ \mathcal{C}^{f^{j}} \circ \ldots \mathcal{C}^{f^{2}} \circ \mathcal{C}^{f^{1}})(\mathbf{x}). \tag{2}$$

Convolutional layer j is determined by a set $f^{j} = \{f_{1}^{j}, \ldots, f_{j+1}^{j}\}$ of such kernels, and accepts as input a tensor $\mathbf{x}^{j}$ of dimension $h_{j} \times w_{j} \times c_{j}$. Convolving $\mathbf{x}^{j}$ with each of these $j + 1$ filters and stacking the output results in a tensor $\mathbf{x}^{j+1}$ of dimension $h_{j} \times w_{j} \times c_{j+1}$.

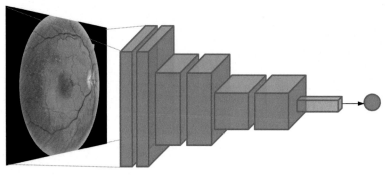

FIG. 2

AI for retinal image analysis. Prototypical convolutional neural network architecture. An input image is mapped to an output (e.g., a classification label). In this case processing layers use convolutions. Many deep neural networks use a combination of convolutional and fully connected layers.

Each of these convolutional layers is followed by a nonlinear pointwise function, and the spatial size $h_j \times w_j$ of the output tensor is decreased by means of a pooling operator $\mathcal{P}^j : \mathbb{R}^{h_j \times w_j} \to \mathbb{R}^{h_{j+1} \times w_{j+1}}$. In a CNN, learnable weights lie in convolution kernels, and the training process leads to finding the optimal way of filtering the training data so that irrelevant information is discarded and the error (loss) in the training set is decreased as much as possible, as shown in Fig. 2.

From the above fundamental setting, a number of algorithmic improvements have been proposed in recent years. For instance, the implementation of so-called 1 × 1 convolutions facilitated the design of a special kind of convolution layer called *inception block*, which was the key for the success of the Inception architecture [26]. In addition, skip connections represented another step toward improving the training dynamics of deep CNNs, resulting in a key architecture called ResNet [27]. In both cases, the goal was to allow practitioners to train CNNs composed of a large number of layers while avoiding problems related to the error's gradient vanishing during its backpropagation. These two CNN architecture designs paradigms have become default choices for the Computer Vision community, and also in retinal image analysis, quickly advancing the state of the art in image-based automatic diagnosis.

2.3 CNNs for semantic image segmentation

The use of CNNs as described earlier for retinal image analysis typically consists of mapping input images onto output scalar values. This approach can help solving a binary classification problem (e.g., referable DR vs. nonreferable/control DR), a multiclass classification problem (such as fine-grained classification of the severity of AMD), or a regression problem, where an input retinal image is mapped into 5-year risk (a probability value) for the imaged retina to develop the advanced form

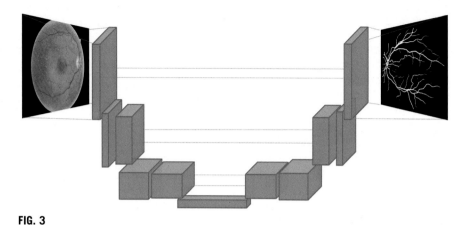

FIG. 3

AI for retinal image analysis. Prototypical U-Net architecture, which is akin to an autoencoder with additional skip connections across levels of similar spatial resolution.

of AMD or DR disease. In all these cases, the input image is mapped into a single output value (in the previous examples, either the classification label or the regressed value of risk). Another possibility is to map the input image via two connected CNNs to an output image. This kind of architecture first encodes an image into a low-dimensional representation. Next, this representation is fed to a "reversed" CNN that repeatedly upsamples and convolves it until it reaches the same dimensionality of the input. The output can be a semantic map on which each pixels encodes a label, resulting in a model that can perform pixel-wise segmentation. In this case, the loss to be minimized captures the segmentation accuracy of the entire autoencoder model. Fig. 3 shows such an architecture for retinal vessel segmentation.

Examples of successful recent autoencoder-like CNN architectures include DenseNet [28, 29]. Instead of processing data serially (each layer operating solely upon the output of the previous layer), DenseNet passes the output features of each layer as inputs to each subsequent layer. This construction allows information (i.e., features) extracted in the early layers to flow through the network without being modified by intermediate layers. Directly passing feature maps from early to downstream layers also has benefits with regard to efficient training via backpropagation.

Another relevant architecture is U-Net [30], which also directly propagates a subset of features maps via skip layers. These intralayer connections are somewhat less abundant relative to DenseNet (only one step forward skip layers). U-Net also features an autoencoder-like network, using down-sampling and up-sampling paths, and results in less connections between nonsubsequent layers than DenseNet.

It is worth mentioning that typically autoencoder-like CNNs are followed by additional postprocessing, which can have different goals: one could be to smooth out the output labels, such postprocessing can include the application of conditional random fields (CRFs) or Gaussian processes (GP) as was done in Pekala et al. [31].

3 Deep learning applications to retinal disease analysis

In the next sections we review the application of deep learning techniques to various analysis tasks focused on primarily retinal diseases and fundus imagery, including applications to diabetic retinopathy (DR), age-related maculopathy (AMD), and retinopathy of prematurity (ROP).

3.1 Deep learning for diabetic retinopathy

Diabetic retinopathy (DR) is one of the leading causes of blindness in the working age population. It affects more than 25% of the estimated 425 million diabetic patients in the world [32]. Further, the prevalence of diabetes is expected to grow to an estimate of 642 million diabetic patients by 2040 [33]. Due to the importance of early detection of DR, and since early stages of DR do not show any symptoms, screening programs have been created in many countries. Most existing DR screening programs use retinal fundus images, manually reviewed by experts, to detect retinal disease in diabetic patients.

The International Clinical Diabetic Retinopathy severity scale categorizes DR into five different groups: (0) no DR, (1) mild DR, (2) moderate nonproliferative DR, (3) severe nonproliferative DR, and (4) proliferative DR. Patients with no or mild DR are not referred for treatment. Therefore, in the context of screening programs the main goal is to detect patients with grade 2 or higher, also known as referable DR, in order to refer to clinicians for monitoring and possibly begin relevant treatment.

Deep learning methods for DR detection gained attention from the scientific community after a 2015 Kaggle competition for DR grading where all winning teams used end-to-end CNNs. In this competition, 35, 126 retinal fundus images with grade annotations were provided for training and 53,576 images for testing. This new dataset and the ideas from winning architectures spurred the development of novel deep learning methods for DR detection.

As an example, Quellec et al. based their work [34] in this Kaggle's competition dataset and its winning architecture. They used a modification to the backpropagation algorithm in order to create saliency maps (heatmaps) showing pixels locations that have the highest influence in the model decision, which ideally would coincide with lesions associated to DR. During backpropagation, the derivative of the output classification with respect to the input pixels was computed as a means of generating such heatmap. The rationale behind this is that these maps should be very sparse since DR lesions are usually small and occupy a small percentage of the image pixels. In order to enforce the sparsity constraint, the L1-norm of the heatmap is minimized along with the classification loss. Since the heatmap is computed from the network's first-order derivatives, second-order derivatives need to be computed before updating the model's parameters. The authors reported results on referable DR on the Kaggle dataset, achieving an area under the ROC curve (AUC) of 0.95, and on the E-ophtha dataset (see Table 3), achieving an AUC of 0.94, in line with the result of the same network trained without the sparsity constraint. Even though their method did not improve image level results, lesion detection performance was improved. The sparsity constraint was shown to improve lesion detection results also on the DiaretDB1 dataset, even outperforming some competing methods that were trained using lesion segmentation information.

In 2016, Gulshan et al. [35] trained an Inception v3 model on a large, richly annotated private dataset and reported results comparable to a panel of seven certified ophthalmologists. The authors trained an ensemble of 10 pretrained Inception v3 networks [26] to simultaneously solve four binary classification problems: (1) detect moderate, severe, and proliferative DR; (2) detect severe and proliferative DR; (3) detect referable diabetic macular edema; and (4) image quality assessment. On the referable DR problem, the authors report 0.99 AUC on EyePACS-1, with 97.5% sensitivity and 93.4% specificity, and 0.99 AUC on Messidor-2, with 96.1% sensitivity and 93.9% specificity.

In the same year, Abràmoff et al. [36] proposed an alternative approach to solve the problem of grading and referable DR detection. The authors trained several CNN models to detect the presence of different lesions, such as hemorrhages, exudates, and neovascularization, as well as the location of normal anatomical landmarks, such as optic disc and fovea—the center of the macula. Different CNN architectures were used for different lesion detectors and trained on a private dataset. The choice of the network architecture depended on the availability of data for each particular task, with architectures inspired by AlexNet [37] being favored for smaller datasets while architectures inspired by VGG [38] were used on larger datasets. The trained models were used on an entire patient examination consisting of four retinal fundus images (two images per eye) and, finally, feature vectors were formed from these CNN detectors and provided to two random forests' fusion algorithms that output the final DR grade and the quality of the examination. The authors reported an AUC of 0.98 on the problem of referable DR, achieving a sensitivity of 96.8% and specificity of 87.0%.

Gargeya and Leng [39] addressed the problem of detecting DR, distinguishing between healthy retinas from retinas with any pathology, including mild DR. This represents a substantially more difficult setting, since the only indication of this stage of DR is the presence of microaneurysms, which are visually hard to detect due to their small size. A residual CNN [27] was trained on a subset of the publicly available EyePACS dataset, containing 75,137 color retina fundus images. This CNN was used to extract a feature map of dimension $8 \times 8 \times 1024$ from 512×512 images. Subsequently, these features were supplied to a global average pooling layer followed by a fully connected layer with a Softmax activation function to classify the image. After optimizing the CNN model on the training dataset, the authors used the output of the global average pooling layer as a 1024-dimensional feature vector. Finally, the field of view of the input image and its pixel height and width were concatenated with the extracted feature vector, and a gradient boosted tree classifier was trained to form the final DR classifier. The authors reported an AUC of 0.97 on their dataset using fivefold cross-validation, with a threshold point yielding 94% sensitivity and 98% specificity. The method was also tested on Messidor-2 achieving

0.94 AUC, with 93% sensitivity and 87% specificity, and on E-ophtha achieving 0.95 AUC, with 90% sensitivity and 94% specificity. Additionally, the authors provided a heatmap that highlighted the regions of the input image that were more likely to contain abnormalities. They implemented class activation mapping (CAM) [40], a technique that simply performs a dot product between the weights of the last fully connected layer that correspond to the DR class and each of the 1024-dimensional feature vectors that are given to the global average pooling layer. This operation resulted in a 8 × 8 matrix, where higher values corresponding to regions with higher likelihood of containing DR-related lesions.

In 2017, Ting and colleagues [41] proposed a DL approach to DR detection using CNNs to classify referable versus not referable DR in fundus images, specifically using VGG-19 deep convolutional networks [38] with transfer learning. The method was applied to a number of datasets, most of which were sourced from healthcare systems in Singapore and Asia, resulting in AUCs ranging from 0.88 to 0.98. Specifically results on the largest datasets used included SIDRP (71,896 images) with AUC of 0.94, sensitivity of 90.5% and specificity of 91.6%, and Guangdong (15,798 images) with AUC of 0.95 and sensitivity and specificity of 98.7% and 81.6%.

3.2 Deep learning for age-related macular degeneration

Age-related macular degeneration (AMD) is one of the main causes of blindness in the world [2, 4]. AMD affects millions of adults in the United States alone and is the main cause of irreversible central vision loss in the United States and in developed countries in people over 50. Intermediate stage AMD often goes undetected, as it typically produces no noticeable visual symptoms. Nevertheless, it is best practice to identify at-risk individuals since choroidal neovascular AMD, an AMD subset, is treatable if detected before the disease progresses to advanced stages when vision loss occurs. This has inspired several studies to develop automatic detection methods for AMD using fundus images.

Age-related macular degeneration (AMD) is caused by macular damage, which is associated with the presence of drusen. Drusen are deposits of collagen and phospholipid vesicles located between the basement membrane of the retinal pigment epithelium (RPE) and the remainder of Bruchs membrane. The intermediate stage AMD—often causing no visual deficit—is marked by the occurrence of many medium-sized drusen with a greatest linear dimension ranging from 63 μ up to 125 μ, or at least one large drusen greater than 125 μ, or geographic atrophy (GA) of the RPE not involving the fovea. The intermediate stage of AMD often leads to the advanced stage, where more significant damage to the macula happens via either choroidal neovascular (CNV) or wet advanced form, or GA involving the center of the macula (dry advanced form). Advanced stage AMD, if untreated, often leads to damage with loss of central vision and visual acuity. This has dramatic deleterious effects on daily activities like reading or recognizing faces. Taken together, these visual consequences cause functional visual decline, consequently leading to substantial societal burden.

While AMD currently has no definite cure, especially for GA, the Age-Related Eye Disease Study (AREDS) has suggested that there are benefits of specific dietary supplements for slowing AMD progression. Additionally, vision loss due to CNV can be slowed by anti-VEGF intravitreous injections. This motivates the goal to identify individuals with the intermediate stage AMD and refer them to an ophthalmologist for regular monitoring and possible treatment.

It is worth noting that manual screening of the entire at-risk population of individuals over 50 (over 100 million in the United States only) is not realistic. Further, it is not feasible in many US healthcare environments to perform such screening because of poor access to health care. Such issues can be more pronounced in low and middle income countries. Therefore, automated AMD diagnostic algorithms are critical part of the strategy to augment retinal screening and management.

In the above context, ARIA has recently shown particular promise to automatically detect patients with referable AMD from fundus images [12, 42]. It has also shown promise for fine-grained severity classification in AMD and assessment of 5-year risk of progression to the advanced forms of disease [43, 44]. This progress has developed in parallel with applications of DL to DR that were discussed in the previous section.

Datasets for AMD have been less plentiful than for DR (e.g., MESSIDOR, EyePacs). One exception to this is the NIH public dataset which was developed under the AREDS (Age-Related Eye Disease Study). AREDS [45] images were procured from 4613 individuals over a 12-year study and had approximately 130,000 field-2 stereoscopic color fundi. Quantitative grading was performed by graders. Grades include multiple scaling systems including 4-step, 5-step (so-called simplified scale), and 9-step scales, which can be used as reference standard. The 4-step scale classification had been used to categorize participants at the time of AREDS enrollment. This scale was not based on an analysis of outcome data, and it differentiated between no AMD (AMD-1), early AMD (AMD-2), intermediate AMD (AMD-3), and advanced AMD (AMD-4) [45]. This scale was first employed in DL studies in Refs. [42, 46]. In Burlina et al. [42] it was used directly for 4-class classification and also reduced to a three and also a two-class nonreferable AMD (AMD-1 and AMD-2) versus referable AMD (AMD-3 and AMD-4) problems. That study in particular considered the ability to perform AMD classification using CNNs with a first implementation using transfer learning and CNN universal features [42]. Using a subset of AREDS that consisted of about 5000 high quality fundus images, performance analysis resulted in accuracies of 79.4%, 81.5%, and 93.4%, respectively, for the 4-, 3-, and 2-class classification problems, and linear kappa values of 0.696, 0.722, and 0.848. This performance was shown to be consistent with physician performance. A problem that was further refined in Burlina et al. [12] was the binary classification consisting of discerning between referable and nonreferable. Those studies used the full AREDS dataset. The 4-step scale was again reduced to a 2-class classification into nonreferable AMD (AMD-1 and AMD-2) versus referable AMD (AMD-3 and AMD-4). This reflected the fact that the case of AMD-3 (intermediate) was particularly of interest given that individuals could present no obvious signs of having it in terms of visual acuity loss, yet be at the threshold of developing the advanced form which could entail irremediable visual loss. In that work, using CNNs (AlexNet) and employing nearly the full 130,000 images from AREDS, and considering various data partitioning schemes, resulted in classification accuracies between 88.4% and 91.6%, and AUC between 0.94 and 0.96, and kappa between 0.764 and 0.829.

As a follow up to the work performed in Burlina et al. [12], the study in Burlina et al. [44] considered again referability of AMD, and used AREDS as the training dataset. This work used an approach that solved first a 4-class problem that was fused down to the 2-class problem and ResNet CNNs, for which the study obtained an AUC of 0.972. This was also compared to an approach that directly used ResNet which resulted in an AUC of 0.970, in both cases improving on Burlina et al. [12].

The aforementioned AMD studies using AREDS have included individuals that are predominantly white participants. Another previously mentioned study that was conducted for DR referability in Ting et al. [47] also included AMD referability as a goal and was performed on datasets including a large population consisting of more varied ethnic groups (three ethnic groups comprising Malays, Chinese, and Indian subpopulations). In that study, using a dataset developed at the Singapore Eye Research Institute and including 35,948 images, and using VGG-19, AMD referability classification results were found to yield an AUC of 0.932 and sensitivity and specificity, respectively, of 93.20% and 88.70%.

More complex and granular AMD severity classification problems using 9 and 12 classes of severity were considered in Burlina et al. [43] as well as Grassmann et al. [48]. In particular, Burlina et al. [43] addressed the 4-class classification problem and the detailed AREDS 9-step severity scale, using ResNet. It resulted in a performance measured via linearly weighted kappa equal to 0.77 for the 4-class problem, and a 9-class detailed severity performance with linear kappa of 0.74.

The same study then looked at the challenge of doing prognosis. This second aim was to predict the probability of a 5-year risk for the eye to move to the more severe forms of advanced neovascular or nonneovascular stage of the disease. That work used three different methods. Two methods performed 9-class classification and soft or hard mapping of these classes into probabilities of developing the advanced forms of the disease by exploiting results from epidemiology studies. As an alternative, this work also used a regression CNN to directly map fundus images into 5-year risk probabilities. With regard to predicting the probability for advancing to the severe stage of AMD within 5 years, the probability error was (averaging across all 9 classes) 3.47%.

In Grassmann et al. [48] a similar work was done with different data partitioning and using over 120,000 manually graded color fundus images from 3654 patients in the AREDS dataset to perform a 12-class classification problem (including the 9-step scale and 3 steps for the advance neovascular or nonneovascular forms) and an additional 13th class corresponding to nongradable images due to insufficient quality, and using various CNNs (AlexNet, VGG-19, ResNet) and ensembles of CNNs. Performance evaluation led to a linear kappa value of 0.83, quadratic weighted kappa of 0.92, and accuracy of 63.3%. Generalizability was also tested by testing the DL models developed on AREDS with another dataset (Augsburg Study KORA dataset) and led to linear kappa values of 0.58, when evaluated for individuals over 55.

Overall, these studies show the promise of DL algorithms for public screening applications. This is particularly important considering that the number of individuals in the population at risk of intermediate or advanced AMD is expected to increase to 2.4 billion worldwide by 2050 [2]. The ability to monitor such individuals for possible progression to advanced AMD and administration of AREDS-like supplements to reduce risk of progression to advanced AMD is and will remain for the near future a very important goal to pursue via DL methods.

3.2.1 Deep learning for retinopathy of prematurity and glaucoma

Retinopathy of prematurity (ROP) is a retinal disease that affects premature infants. Given the advances in neonatal care, an increased number of premature babies are surviving, which has increased the prevalence of this disease. It is one of the main preventable causes of blindness in children [49] and can be effectively treated with laser photocoagulation of the retina if detected early.

In Brown et al. [50], deep learning was used to automatically diagnose ROP from retinal photographs using a CNN. This study used 5511 retinal images. Three experts generated a reference standard for each image. A fivefold cross-validation was used for testing on 100 images. All images were obtained from eight academic institutions and the ROP detection was evaluated against eight ROP experts with more than 10 years of clinical experience. An AUC of 0.94 was obtained for the diagnosis of normal versus affected (preplus disease or plus disease), and an AUC of 0.98 for the diagnosis of plus disease (vs normal or preplus disease). The machine outperformed six out of the eight retinal experts. The approach used two networks, one for performing vessel segmentation and the second for doing classification.

In Worrall et al. [49], a study reported performance of two main tasks: first, fine tuning of a CNN (GoogLeNet) was used to perform a binary classification of ROP. Second, to aid the physician in interpretation and assessment, a second CNN was used to generate a feature map to help visualizations of the pathology.

In Hu et al. [51], two separate CNNs were used, one performing binary classification, and a second to assess a severity grade. Using over 500 cases, the study obtained 96.62% and 99.32% for binary classification. For grading, it had sensitivity and specificity of, respectively, 88.46% and 92.31%.

In other diseases, and glaucoma for example, relatively less work in the application of deep learning exists when compared to DR and AMD. For example, the work in Ting et al. [41] addresses glaucoma and uses a binary classification for finding cases suspected for glaucoma using as criteria vertical cup to disc ratio and the presence of any glaucomatous disc changes. Using CNNs (VGG-19) and a dataset (SiDRP) including 71,896 images resulted in an AUC of 0.942 and sensitivity and specificity of 96.4% and 93.20%. In another study of glaucoma, CNNs were used for detecting glaucomatous optic neuropathy on a dataset of 48,116 images and resulted in AUC of 0.986 and sensitivity and specificity of 95.6% and 92.0%.

3.3 Deep learning applications in OCT segmentation

Optical coherence tomography (OCT) has become in recent years an essential ophthalmic imaging modality. It is a noninvasive, high-resolution retinal imaging technique capable of capturing micron-scale structure within the human retina. Further, unlike traditional imaging of the retina, it does not require pharmacological dilation of the pupil (by a care provider). The retina is organized into several layers and the qualitative and quantitative analyses of its structure aids in diagnosing many ophthalmic diseases. In particular, it has become one of the key diagnostic and monitoring tools for diabetic retinopathy and AMD. In addition to retinal diseases, retinal structure changes detected by OCT may also be associated with neurological diseases such as multiple sclerosis, Parkinson's disease, and Alzheimer's disease [52]. Although these neurological disease produce progressive thinning of the retinal nerve fiber layer (RNFL) on OCT [52], this imaging modality has not become part of the standard clinical evaluations for these conditions. Various ophthalmic and neurological diseases affect different layers of the retina in various forms. Therefore, automatic and accurate OCT semantic segmentation can be crucial for facilitating scientific investigation and possibly future diagnosis and monitoring of these conditions.

Traditionally, work in automatic OCT segmentation has focused on the use of graph-based methods [53–60]. For example in Chiu et al. [61], a seven-layer OCT segmentation using kernel regression (KR)-based classification was developed to estimate diabetic macular edema (DME). It also estimated OCT layer boundaries, a method that was then combined with an approach using graph theory and dynamic programming. This was validated on ultrasound (110 B-scans) and 10 patients with severe DME pathology, yielding DICE coefficient of 0.78. Other contributions from academia and industry include the following algorithms: Spectralis 6.0 [55], IOWA Reference Algorithm [56], Automated Retinal Analysis Tools (AURA) [57], Dufour's (Bern) algorithm [58], and OCTRIMA3D [59]. For a more extensive recent review of the state of the practice for OCT segmentation, see Refs. [59, 60].

Next, we describe briefly, and in a nonexhaustive way, some more recent studies of OCT segmentation that have utilized CNNs. A recent study [62] used a cascaded U-Net architecture [30] and compared performance to that of a classical approaches based on random forests. Fang et al. [63] used a hybrid ConvNets and graph-based method to identify OCT boundary layers. Additional efforts at the University of Miami [53] have also taken steps to develop publicly available OCT datasets with clinical gold standards for comparing performance among various methods, including a number of OCT segmentation algorithms of record. In Pekala et al. [31], an OCT segmentation method utilizing fully convolutional networks and using the DenseNet architecture and Gaussian processes was used. That study did a performance comparison both with methods of record that used graph-based methods and human showing performance close to a human annotator and with a performance which compared favorably against other methods of record. This comparison was done using the publicly available Miami dataset [53].

The work in Roy et al. [64] was applied for both retinal layers and fluid segmentation. The architecture used was also related to the encoder and decoder structure of U-Nets. One particular aspect of this approach included using a modified loss function that included also the DICE coefficient in the loss. The method was evaluated on the Duke OCT dataset. The dataset included 110 annotated SD-OCT B-scans of 512×740 images from 10 patients. The segmentation was done on seven layers and included one additional class for the fluid labeling. The study demonstrated improvement over baseline versions of FCNs including U-Nets. Distances in pixels from ground truth for the methods ranged from 0.16 to 0.34 for different zones in the retina, and compared favorably to the other methods. DICE metrics using leave one out experiments performed on eight patients resulted in values from 0.77, for the fluid segmentation, to 0.99, for several other layers.

The work in Devalla et al. [65] utilized a U-Net-based architecture to segment the optic nerve head in OCT. This study included 100 patients from the Singapore National Eye Center, including 40 healthy patients and 60 glaucoma patients. This algorithm achieved a DICE value of 0.84. The algorithm performed better when compensated images were used for training. Adaptive compensation is a postprocessing technique used to remove effects of light attenuation and was shown to remove various artifacts, such as blood vessel shadows.

Finally, the study [66] used ConvNets and a U-Net-based networks to delineate intraretinal fluid on OCT. The CNN obtained a maximal cross-validated DICE of 0.911 when evaluated on 1289 OCT images. The intraoperator error and error measured between experts and CNN were found to be on par.

4 Deep learning for retinal biomarker extraction

Besides the tasks of eye disease diagnosis or semantic segmentation, as was reported in the previous sections, retinal biomarker extraction is an area of interest for the application of deep learning methods. In addition to ophthalmic and retinal diseases being of interest, the eye, and the retina in particular, are a window to the human body, allowing a direct noninvasive detection and diagnosis of several systemic diseases beyond diabetes, for example, hypertension, cardiovascular and brain diseases like Alzheimer, Parkinson, and other age-related impairments. These are often related with some specific biomarkers that can be extracted from retinal images, usually amounting to the detection and segmentation of the main anatomical regions as the retinal vasculature (including the arteriolar and venular networks), the optic disc, the macular region, and fovea. These landmarks can then be used for the characterization of higher-level retinal biomarkers, namely arteriovenous nicking, retinal arteriolar constriction, vascular calibers, vascular tortuosity, arteriolar-venular ratio (AVR), optic disc/optic cup ratio, etc. These are the base for computation of several biomarkers for systemic diseases as hypertension, diabetic retinopathy, cardiovascular diseases, and glaucoma.

Deep learning approaches have consistently improved previous performance on the task of locating, segmenting, and/or analyzing the aforementioned retinal biomarkers. It is beyond the limits of this work to provide a detailed overview of every recent method leveraging deep neural networks for such tasks, but we believe it is worth to introduce a concise summarization of most relevant recent advances. Most of them are related to either retinal vasculature or optic disc extraction and analysis. Accordingly, and in order to offer a compact view of these two groups of problems, we provide two tables and refer the reader to recent surveys of the state of the art in these topics like [67] or [68] for further information.

Table 1 provides an overview of a selection of recent papers describing the use of DL-based techniques for solving the task of vasculature segmentation and the related goal of artery/vein classification, whereas in Table 2, the detection and segmentation of the optic disc are addressed.

Table 1 AI for retinal image analysis.

Method	Task	Observations
Liskowski et al. [69]	Vessel segmentation	Standard CNN architecture Patch-center pixel classification
Li et al. [70]	Vessel segmentation	U-Net-like autoencoder architecture Full-patch prediction and reconstruction
Maninis et al. [71]	Vessel segmentation	Base CNN + two auxiliary side layers Joint vessel and optic disc segmentation
Fu et al. [72]	Vessel segmentation	Multiscale CNN + auxiliary side layer Conditional random field (CRF) refinement
Mo et al. [73]	Vessel segmentation	U-Net-like autoencoder architecture (FCN) Auxiliary classifiers and transfer learning
Zhao et al. [74]	Vessel segmentation	GANs for training data synthesis Independent second trained model
Lin et al. [75]	Vessel segmentation	U-Net-like autoencoder architecture (FCN) Holistic integration of CNN and CRFs
Yan et al. [76]	Vessel segmentation	U-Net-like autoencoder architecture Pixel-wise and segment-wise balancing loss
Wu et al. [77]	Vessel segmentation	Concatenation of two CNNs Probability map followed by refinement
Yan et al. [78]	Vessel segmentation	U-Net-like autoencoder architecture Thick/thin vessel segmentation + fusion
Welikala et al. [79]	Artery/vein classification	Standard CNN architecture Vessel centerline pixel classification
Meyer et al. [80]	Artery/vein classification	U-Net-like autoencoder architecture Studies optimal color representation
Xu et al. [81]	Artery/vein segmentation	U-Net-like autoencoder architecture Weighted cross-entropy loss
Galdran et al. [82]	Artery/vein segmentation	U-Net-like autoencoder architecture Takes into account label uncertainty

Notes: Overview of recent DL-based techniques for retinal vasculature analysis.

Table 2 AI for retinal image analysis.

Method	Task	Observations
Fu et al. [83]	OD/cup segmentation	Multiscale network, multilabel loss Application in glaucoma screening
Zilly et al. [84]	OD/cup segmentation	Improved entropy-based sampling Unsupervised graph-cut refinement
Gu et al. [85]	OD segmentation	Pretrained resnet + atrous convolutions Multiscale spatial pyramid pooling
Liu et al. [86]	OD segmentation	U-Net-like autoencoder architecture Patch-level adversarial module
Sun et al. [87]	OD segmentation	Faster R-CNN for OD detection Bounding box mapped to ellipse
Fu et al. [88]	OD/cup segmentation	Hierarchical ensemble of four networks Application in glaucoma screening
Sedai et al. [89]	OD/cup segmentation	Semisupervised variational autoencoder Supervised training on few examples
Sedai et al. [90]	Fovea segmentation	Coarse-to-fine approach F-CNNs for localization + segmentation
Al-Bander et al. [91]	OD/fovea localization	Standard CNN architecture Problem formulated as regression
Meyer et al. [92]	OD/fovea localization	U-Net-like autoencoder architecture Bi-distance map regression
Araujo et al. [93]	OD/fovea localization	Combination of Yolo and U-Net Optional OD segmentation

Notes: Overview of selected DL-based techniques for several retinal image analysis tasks for retinal biomarker extraction.

4.1 Automatic retinal biomarker discovery

The ability of deep learning models to automatically extract relevant information from retinal images may lead to the possibility of training such algorithms to identify patterns in these images related to clinical findings that practitioners could not be able to discern. Research in this direction has only recently started to appear. Most notably, in Ref. [94] the authors manage to predict several cardiovascular risk factors (as age with an MAE = 3.26 years, gender, AUC = 0.97, smoking status, AUC = 0.71, systolic blood pressure, MAE = 11.23 mmHg) and major adverse cardiac events, AUC = 070. The model trained for this was relatively standard (Inception V3), and it was trained on retinal images from 48,101 patients from the UK Biobank and 236,234 patients from EyePACS. The performance of this model was close to that of other cardiovascular risk calculators requiring blood sample analysis. This new and exciting research venue may result in the understanding and association with of retinal findings to other cardiovascular or neurodegenerative diseases.

5 Datasets

For the application of DL to retinal image analysis (and medical imaging in general), it is crucial to operate on a large-scale data scenario. A characteristic feature of DL models is that their complexity is orders of magnitude greater than that of previous machine learning approaches. For this reason, if they are trained on a fewer examples they will tend to memorize the training data and become useless. Having this into account, we provide here a review of existing retinal image analysis datasets, sorted by the task they are useful for. For a more compact overview, we focus on publicly available datasets, and consider only the largest ones or the more richly annotated, see Table 3. A website has been created to register datasets described below and others that were not presented due to space constraints. This website will remain up-to-date, including datasets that may become available for the research community in the future. The reader is referred to the following URL for further details: https://github.com/agaldran/retinal_datasets, where download instructions and links for the different datasets links are also offered.

6 Conclusion

This chapter has discussed recent advances in the application of AI and deep learning to the analysis of retinal images with emphasis on the main causes of blindness including diabetic retinopathy and age-related macular degeneration and focus on tasks such as diagnostics and segmentation.

Table 3 AI for retinal image analysis.

Method	Task	Observations
Eyepacs (Kaggle)	DR Grading	35,126 train to 53,576 test images; 5 classes ~3000 × 2000 pixels resolution
AREDS (NIH)	AMD Grading	About 130k fundi; 4/5/9 classes Includes other medical/genetic data
Messidor-2 [95]	DR and AMD Grading	1748 Images, different resolutions Subsumes Messidor-1, 4 DR/3 AMD grades
DRi-DB [96]	DR grading Retinal lesions	50 Images, 720 × 576 pixels resolution Multiple expert annotations
DR HAGIS [97]	Multidisease Detection	39 Images, different resolutions DR, AMD, glaucoma, hypertension
IDRID [98]	DR and AMD Retinal lesions	516 Images, 5 classes, Indian population Pixelwise lesions, OD, and fovea locations
REFUGE	Glaucoma Assessment	1200 Images, 2121 × 2056 pixels resolution Pixelwise OD, cup, and fovea locations

Table 3 AI for retinal image analysis—cont'd

Method	Task	Observations
PALM	Pathologic Myopia	400 Images, 1444 × 1444 pixels resolution Myopia analysis/lesion detection
DiaRetDB 0/1 [99]	DR detection Retinal lesions	130/89 Images, 1500 × 1152 pixels resolution 50 degrees FOV, macula-centered
ROC challenge [100]	Microaneurysm Detection	50/50 Images, different resolutions Hidden test set: 343 microaneurysms
E-Ophtha MA/EX [101]	Lesion segmentation	82/381 Images, different resolutions Microaneurysm/exudate annotations
DRIVE/RITE [102]	Vessel/A-V segmentation	40 Images, 768 × 584 pixels resolution 45 degrees FOV, macula-centered
STARE [103]	Clinical findings Vessel segmentation	400 Images, 605 × 700 pixels resolution 40 Labeled for vessel segmentation
HRF [104]	DR and glaucoma Vessel segmentation	45 Images, 3504 × 2336 pixels resolution Contains vessels and OD annotations
LES-AV [105]	Artery-vein segmentation	22 Images, 1444 × 1620 pixels resolution 45 degrees FOV, OD-centered

Notes: Overview of publicly available datasets for retinal fundus image analysis. See https://github.com/agaldran/retinal_datasets for download links.

References

[1] N.M. Bressler, Age-related macular degeneration is the leading cause of blindness, JAMA 291 (15) (2004) 1900–1901.

[2] R. Velez-Montoya, S.C.N. Oliver, J.L. Olson, S.L. Fine, H. Quiroz-Mercado, N. Mandava, Current knowledge and trends in age-related macular degeneration: genetics, epidemiology, and prevention, Retina 34 (3) (2014) 423–441.

[3] R. Lee, T.Y. Wong, C. Sabanayagam, Epidemiology of diabetic retinopathy, diabetic macular edema and related vision loss, Eye Vis. 2 (1) (2015) 17.

[4] R. Klein, B.E.K. Klein, The prevalence of age-related eye diseases and visual impairment in aging: current estimates, Invest. Ophthalmol. Vis. Sci. 54 (14) (2013) ORSF5–ORSF13.

[5] A.C. Bird, N.M. Bressler, S.B. Bressler, I.H. Chisholm, G. Coscas, M.D. Davis, P.T. de Jong, C.C. Klaver, B.E. Klein, R. Klein, An international classification and grading system for age-related maculopathy and age-related macular degeneration, Surv. Ophthalmol. 39 (5) (1995) 367–374.

[6] Age-Related Eye Disease Study Research Group, Potential public health impact of age-related eye disease study results: {AREDS} Report No. 11, Arch. Ophthalmol. 121 (11) (2003) 1621.

[7] Age-Related Eye Disease Study Research Group, A randomized, placebo-controlled, clinical trial of high-dose supplementation with vitamins {C} and {E}, beta carotene, and zinc for age-related macular degeneration and vision loss: {AREDS} Report No. 8, Arch. Ophthalmol. 119 (10) (2001) 1417.

[8] V.K. Ramanan, A.J. Saykin, Pathways to neurodegeneration: mechanistic insights from GWAS in Alzheimer's disease, Parkinson's disease, and related disorders, Am. J. Neurodegener. Dis. 2 (3) (2013) 145.

[9] K.G. Schmidt, H. Bergert, R.H.W. Funk, Neurodegenerative diseases of the retina and potential for protection and recovery, Curr. Neuropharmacol. 6 (2) (2008) 164–178.

[10] E.M. Lad, D. Mukherjee, S.S. Stinnett, S.W. Cousins, G.G. Potter, J.R. Burke, S. Farsiu, H.E. Whitson, Evaluation of inner retinal layers as biomarkers in mild cognitive impairment to moderate Alzheimer's disease, PLoS ONE 13 (2) (2018) e0192646.

[11] A. Esteva, B. Kuprel, R.A. Novoa, J. Ko, S.M. Swetter, H.M. Blau, S. Thrun, Dermatologist-level classification of skin cancer with deep neural networks, Nature 542 (7639) (2017) 115–118.

[12] P. Burlina, N. Joshi, M. Pekala, K. Pacheco, D.E. Freund, N.M. Bressler, Automated grading of age-related macular degeneration from color fundus images using deep convolutional neural networks, JAMA Ophtalmol. 135 (11) (2017) 1170–1176.

[13] C.S. Lee, D.M. Baughman, A.Y. Lee, Deep learning is effective for classifying normal versus age-related macular degeneration OCT images, Ophthalmol. Retina 1 (4) (2017) 322–327.

[14] G. Litjens, T. Kooi, B.E. Bejnordi, A.A.A. Setio, F. Ciompi, M. Ghafoorian, J.A.W.M. van der Laak, B. van Ginneken, C.I. Sánchez, A survey on deep learning in medical image analysis, Med. Image Anal. 42 (2017) 60–88.

[15] G. Carneiro, Y. Zheng, F. Xing, L. Yang, Review of deep learning methods in mammography, cardiovascular, and microscopy image analysis, in: Deep Learning and Convolutional Neural Networks for Medical Image Computing, 2017, pp. 11–32. https://doi.org/10.1007/978-3-319-42999-1_2.

[16] J. Ker, L. Wang, J. Rao, T. Lim, Deep learning applications in medical image analysis, IEEE Access 6 (2018) 9375–9389.

[17] M.I. Razzak, S. Naz, A. Zaib, Deep Learning for Medical Image Processing: Overview, Challenges and the Future, Springer, Cham, 2018, pp. 323–350.

[18] D. Shen, G. Wu, H.-I. Suk, Deep learning in medical image analysis, Annu. Rev. Biomed. Eng. 19 (2017) 221–248.

[19] K.C. Jordan, M. Menolotto, N.M. Bolster, I.A.T. Livingstone, M.E. Giardini, A review of feature-based retinal image analysis, Expert Rev. Ophthalmol. 12 (3) (2017) 207–220.

[20] U. Schmidt-Erfurth, A. Sadeghipour, B.S. Gerendas, S.M. Waldstein, H. Bogunović, Artificial intelligence in retina, Prog. Retin. Eye Res. 67 (2018) 1–29.

[21] D.T. Hogarty, D.A. Mackey, A.W. Hewitt, Current state and future prospects of artificial intelligence in ophthalmology: a review, Clin. Exp. Ophthalmol. 47 (2019) 128–139.

[22] P.S. Grewal, F. Oloumi, U. Rubin, M.T.S. Tennant, Deep learning in ophthalmology: a review, Can. J. Ophthalmol. 53 (4) (2018) 309–313.

[23] D.S.W. Ting, L.R. Pasquale, L. Peng, J.P. Campbell, A.Y. Lee, R. Raman, G.S.W. Tan, L. Schmetterer, P.A. Keane, T.Y. Wong, Artificial intelligence and deep learning in ophthalmology, Br. J. Ophthalmol. 103 (2) (2019) 167–175.

[24] W.L. Yun, U. Rajendra Acharya, Y.V. Venkatesh, C. Chee, L.C. Min, E.Y.K. Ng, Identification of different stages of diabetic retinopathy using retinal optical images, Inf. Sci. 178 (1) (2008) 106–121.

[25] M. García, C.I. Sánchez, M.I. López, D. Abásolo, R. Hornero, Neural network based detection of hard exudates in retinal images, Comput. Methods Programs Biomed. 93 (1) (2009) 9–19.

[26] C. Szegedy, V. Vanhoucke, S. Ioffe, J. Shlens, Z. Wojna, Rethinking the inception architecture for computer vision, in: 2016 IEEE Conference on Computer Vision and Pattern Recognition (CVPR), IEEE, 2016, pp. 2818–2826, https://doi.org/10.1109/CVPR.2016.308.

[27] K. He, X. Zhang, S. Ren, J. Sun, Deep residual learning for image recognition, in: IEEE Conference on Computer Vision and Pattern Recognition (CVPR), 2016.

[28] S. Jégou, M. Drozdzal, D. Vazquez, A. Romero, Y. Bengio, The one hundred layers tiramisu: fully convolutional DenseNets for semantic segmentation, in: 2017 IEEE Conference on Computer Vision and Pattern Recognition Workshops (CVPRW), IEEE, 2017, pp. 1175–1183.

[29] G. Huang, Z. Liu, K.Q. Weinberger, L. van der Maaten, Densely connected convolutional networks, in: Proceedings of the IEEE Conference on Computer Vision and Pattern Recognition, 2017, pp. 4700–4708.

[30] O. Ronneberger, P. Fischer, T. Brox, U-net: convolutional networks for biomedical image segmentation, in: Medical Image Computing and Computer-Assisted Intervention MICCAI 2015, Springer, Cham, 2015, pp. 234–241, https://doi.org/10.1007/978-3-319-24574-4_28.

[31] M. Pekala, N. Joshi, D.E. Freund, N.M. Bressler, D.C. DeBuc, P.M. Burlina, Deep learning based retinal OCT segmentation, arXiv preprint arXiv:1801.09749 (2018).

[32] L.M. Ruta, D.J. Magliano, R. Lemesurier, H.R. Taylor, P.Z. Zimmet, J.E. Shaw, Prevalence of diabetic retinopathy in type 2 diabetes in developing and developed countries, Diabet. Med. 30 (4) (2013) 387–398, https://doi.org/10.1111/dme.12119.

[33] K. Ogurtsova, J.D. Rocha, Y. Huang, U. Linnenkamp, L. Guariguata, IDF diabetes atlas: global estimates for the prevalence of diabetes for 2015 and 2040, Diabetes Res. Clin. Pract. 128 (2017) 40–50, https://doi.org/10.1016/j.diabres.2017.03.024.

[34] G. Quellec, K. Charrière, Y. Boudi, B. Cochener, M. Lamard, Deep image mining for diabetic retinopathy screening, Med. Image Anal. 39 (2017) 178–193, https://doi.org/10.1016/j.media.2017.04.012.

[35] V. Gulshan, L. Peng, M. Coram, M.C. Stumpe, D. Wu, A. Narayanaswamy, S. Venugopalan, K. Widner, T. Madams, J. Cuadros, R. Kim, R. Raman, P.C. Nelson, J.L. Mega, D.R. Webster, X. Zhang, R. Raman, R. Chakrabarti, M.D. Abràmoff, M.R.K. Mookiah, Y. LeCun, S. Ioffe, C. Szegedy, E. Decencière, G. Quellec, L. Giancardo, K. Solanki, G. Quellec, G.H. Bresnick, J. Dean, O. Russakovsky, R. Caruana, A. Krizhevsky, C.J. Clopper, S. Philip, L. Verma, J.G. Elmore, J.G. Elmore, Development and validation of a deep learning algorithm for detection of diabetic retinopathy in retinal fundus photographs, JAMA 304 (6) (2016) 649–656, https://doi.org/10.1001/JAMA.2016.17216.

[36] M.D. Abràmoff, Y. Lou, A. Erginay, W. Clarida, R. Amelon, J.C. Folk, M. Niemeijer, Improved automated detection of diabetic retinopathy on a publicly available dataset through integration of deep learning, Invest. Ophthalmol. Vis. Sci. 57 (13) (2016) 5200–5206, https://doi.org/10.1167/iovs.16-19964.

[37] A. Krizhevsky, I. Sutskever, G.E. Hinton, ImageNet classification with deep convolutional neural networks, in: F. Pereira, C.J.C. Burges, L. Bottou, K.Q. Weinberger (Eds.), Advances in Neural Information Processing Systems, vol. 25, Curran Associates, Inc., 2012, pp. 1097–1105. http://papers.nips.cc/paper/4824-imagenet-classification-with-deep-convolutional-neural-networks.pdf.

[38] K. Simonyan, A. Zisserman, Very deep convolutional networks for large-scale image recognition, CoRR abs/1409.1556 (2014).

[39] R. Gargeya, T. Leng, Automated identification of diabetic retinopathy using deep learning, Ophthalmology 124 (7) (2017) 962–969, https://doi.org/10.1016/j. ophtha.2017.02.008.

[40] B. Zhou, A. Khosla, A. Lapedriza, A. Oliva, A. Torralba, Learning deep features for discriminative localization, in: Proceedings of the IEEE Conference on Computer Vision and Pattern Recognition, 2016, pp. 2921–2929, https://doi.org/10.1109/ CVPR.2016.319.

[41] D.S.W. Ting, C.Y.-L. Cheung, G. Lim, G.S.W. Tan, N.D. Quang, A. Gan, H. Hamzah, R. Garcia-Franco, I.Y. San Yeo, S.Y. Lee, Development and validation of a deep learning system for diabetic retinopathy and related eye diseases using retinal images from multiethnic populations with diabetes, JAMA 318 (22) (2017) 2211–2223.

[42] P. Burlina, K.D. Pacheco, N. Joshi, D.E. Freund, N.M. Bressler, Comparing humans and deep learning performance for grading {AMD}: a study in using universal deep features and transfer learning for automated {AMD} analysis, Comput. Biol. Med. 82 (2017) 80–86.

[43] P.M. Burlina, N. Joshi, K.D. Pacheco, D.E. Freund, J. Kong, N.M. Bressler, Use of deep learning for detailed severity characterization and estimation of 5-year risk among patients with age-related macular degeneration, JAMA Ophthalmol. 136 (12) (2018) 1359–1366.

[44] P. Burlina, N. Joshi, K.D. Pacheco, D.E. Freund, J. Kong, N.M. Bressler, Utility of deep learning methods for referability classification of age-related macular degeneration, JAMA Ophthalmol. 136 (11) (2018) 1305–1307.

[45] Group, Age-Related Eye Disease Study Research, The Age-Related Eye Disease Study system for classifying age-related macular degeneration from stereoscopic color fundus photographs: the Age-Related Eye Disease Study Report Number 6, Am. J. Ophthalmol. 132 (5) (2001) 668–681.

[46] P. Burlina, D.E. Freund, N. Joshi, Y. Wolfson, N.M. Bressler, Detection of age-related macular degeneration via deep learning, in: 2016 IEEE 13th International Symposium on Biomedical Imaging (ISBI), IEEE, 2016, pp. 184–188.

[47] D.S.W. Ting, Y. Liu, P. Burlina, X. Xu, N.M. Bressler, T.Y. Wong, AI for medical imaging goes deep, Nat. Med. 24 (5) (2018) 539.

[48] F. Grassmann, J. Mengelkamp, C. Brandl, S. Harsch, M.E. Zimmermann, B. Linkohr, A. Peters, I.M. Heid, C. Palm, B.H.F. Weber, A deep learning algorithm for prediction of age-related eye disease study severity scale for age-related macular degeneration from color fundus photography, Ophthalmology 125 (9) (2018) 1410–1420.

[49] D.E. Worrall, C.M. Wilson, G.J. Brostow, Automated retinopathy of prematurity case detection with convolutional neural networks, in: Deep Learning and Data Labeling for Medical Applications, Springer, 2016, pp. 68–76.

[50] J.M. Brown, J.P. Campbell, A. Beers, K. Chang, S. Ostmo, R.V.P. Chan, J. Dy, D. Erdogmus, S. Ioannidis, J. Kalpathy-Cramer, Automated diagnosis of plus disease in retinopathy of prematurity using deep convolutional neural networks, JAMA Ophthalmol. 136 (7) (2018) 803–810.

[51] J. Hu, Y. Chen, J. Zhong, R. Ju, Z. Yi, Automated analysis for retinopathy of prematurity by deep neural networks, IEEE Trans. Med. Imaging 38 (1) (2018) 263–279.

[52] A. London, I. Benhar, M. Schwartz, The retina as a window to the brain from eye research to CNS disorders, Nat. Rev. Neurol. 9 (1) (2013) 44–53.

[53] J. Tian, B. Varga, E. Tatrai, P. Fanni, G.M. Somfai, W.E. Smiddy, D.C. DeBuc, Performance evaluation of automated segmentation software on optical coherence tomography volume data, J. Biophoton. 9 (5) (2016) 478–489.

[54] D.C. DeBuc, A review of algorithms for segmentation of retinal image data using optical coherence tomography, in: Image Segmentation, InTech, 2011.

[55] Heidelberg Engineering GmbH, Spectralis HRA+OCT User Manual Software, 2014.

[56] K. Lee, M.D. Abramoff, M. Garvin, M. Sonka, The Iowa Reference Algorithms (Retinal Image Analysis Lab, Iowa Institute for Biomedical Imaging, IA), 2014.

[57] A. Lang, A. Carass, M. Hauser, E.S. Sotirchos, P.A. Calabresi, H.S. Ying, J.L. Prince, Retinal layer segmentation of macular {OCT} images using boundary classification, Biomed. Opt. Express 4 (7) (2013) 1133–1152.

[58] P.A. Dufour, L. Ceklic, H. Abdillahi, S. Schroder, S. De Dzanet, U. Wolf-Schnurrbusch, J. Kowal, Graph-based multi-surface segmentation of {OCT} data using trained hard and soft constraints, IEEE Trans. Med. Imaging 32 (3) (2013) 531–543.

[59] J. Tian, B. Varga, G.M. Somfai, W.-H. Lee, W.E. Smiddy, D.C. DeBuc, Real-time automatic segmentation of optical coherence tomography volume data of the macular region, PLoS ONE 10 (8) (2015) e0133908.

[60] A. Breger, M. Ehler, H. Bogunovic, S.M. Waldstein, A.M. Philip, U. Schmidt-Erfurth, B.S. Gerendas, Supervised learning and dimension reduction techniques for quantification of retinal fluid in optical coherence tomography images, Eye 31 (2017) 1212–1220.

[61] S.J. Chiu, M.J. Allingham, P.S. Mettu, S.W. Cousins, J.A. Izatt, S. Farsiu, Kernel regression based segmentation of optical coherence tomography images with diabetic macular edema, Biomed. Opt. Express 6 (4) (2015) 1172–1194.

[62] Y. He, A. Carass, Y. Yun, C. Zhao, B.M. Jedynak, S.D. Solomon, S. Saidha, P.A. Calabresi, J.L. Prince, Towards topological correct segmentation of macular OCT from cascaded FCNs, in: Fetal, Infant and Ophthalmic Medical Image Analysis, Springer, 2017, pp. 202–209.

[63] L. Fang, D. Cunefare, C. Wang, R.H. Guymer, S. Li, S. Farsiu, Automatic segmentation of nine retinal layer boundaries in {OCT} images of non-exudative AMD patients using deep learning and graph search, Biomed. Opt. Express 8 (5) (2017) 2732–2744.

[64] A.G. Roy, S. Conjeti, S.P.K. Karri, D. Sheet, A. Katouzian, C. Wachinger, N. Navab, ReLayNet: retinal layer and fluid segmentation of macular optical coherence tomography using fully convolutional networks, Biomed. Opt. Express 8 (8) (2017) 3627–3642.

[65] S.K. Devalla, K.S. Chin, J.-M. Mari, T.A. Tun, N.G. Strouthidis, T. Aung, A.H. Thiéry, M.J.A. Girard, A deep learning approach to digitally stain optical coherence tomography images of the optic nerve head, Invest. Ophthalmol. Vis. Sci. 59 (1) (2018) 63–74.

[66] C.S. Lee, A.J. Tyring, N.P. Deruyter, Y. Wu, A. Rokem, A.Y. Lee, Deep-learning based, automated segmentation of macular edema in optical coherence tomography, Biomed. Opt. Express. 8 (7) (2017) 3440–3448.

[67] S. Moccia, E. De Momi, S. El Hadji, L.S. Mattos, Blood vessel segmentation algorithms review of methods, datasets and evaluation metrics, Comput. Methods Prog. Biomed. 158 (2018) 71–91, https://doi.org/10.1016/J.CMPB.2018.02.001.

[68] N. Thakur, M. Juneja, Survey on segmentation and classification approaches of optic cup and optic disc for diagnosis of glaucoma, Biomed. Signal Process. Control 42 (2018) 162–189, https://doi.org/10.1016/J.BSPC.2018.01.014.

[69] P. Liskowski, K. Krawiec, Segmenting retinal blood vessels with deep neural networks, IEEE Trans. Med. Imaging 35 (11) (2016) 2369–2380, https://doi.org/10.1109/TMI.2016.2546227.

[70] Q. Li, B. Feng, L. Xie, P. Liang, H. Zhang, T. Wang, A cross-modality learning approach for vessel segmentation in retinal images, IEEE Trans. Med. Imaging 35 (1) (2016) 109–118, https://doi.org/10.1109/TMI.2015.2457891.

[71] K.K. Maninis, J. Pont-Tuset, P. Arbeláez, L. Van Gool, Deep retinal image understanding, in: Lecture Notes in Computer Science (including subseries Lecture Notes in Artificial Intelligence and Lecture Notes in Bioinformatics), LNCS, vol. 9901, Springer, Cham, 2016, pp. 140–148, https://doi.org/10.1007/978-3-319-46723-8_17.

[72] H. Fu, Y. Xu, S. Lin, D.W. Kee Wong, J. Liu, DeepVessel: Retinal Vessel Segmentation via Deep Learning and Conditional Random Field, Springer, Cham, 2016, pp. 132–139, https://doi.org/10.1007/978-3-319-46723-8_16.

[73] J. Mo, L. Zhang, Multi-level deep supervised networks for retinal vessel segmentation, Int. J. Comput. Assist. Radiol. Surg. 12 (12) (2017) 2181–2193, https://doi.org/10.1007/s11548-017-1619-0.

[74] H. Zhao, H. Li, S. Maurer-Stroh, Y. Guo, Q. Deng, L. Cheng, Supervised segmentation of un-annotated retinal fundus images by synthesis, IEEE Trans. Med. Imaging 38 (1) (2019) 46–56, https://doi.org/10.1109/TMI.2018.2854886.

[75] Y. Lin, H. Zhang, G. Hu, Automatic retinal vessel segmentation via deeply supervised and smoothly regularized network, IEEE Access (2018) 1, https://doi.org/10.1109/ACCESS.2018.2844861. 1.

[76] Z. Yan, X. Yang, K.-T.T. Cheng, A three-stage deep learning model for accurate retinal vessel segmentation, IEEE J. Biomed. Health Inform. (2018) 1, https://doi.org/10.1109/JBHI.2018.2872813. 1.

[77] Y. Wu, Y. Xia, Y. Song, Y. Zhang, W. Cai, Multiscale Network Followed Network Model for Retinal Vessel Segmentation, Springer, Cham, 2018, pp. 119–126, https://doi.org/10.1007/978-3-030-00934-2_14.

[78] Z. Yan, X. Yang, K.-T. Cheng, Joint segment-level and pixel-wise losses for deep learning based retinal vessel segmentation, IEEE Trans. Biomed. Eng. 65 (9) (2018) 1912–1923, https://doi.org/10.1109/TBME.2018.2828137.

[79] R.A. Welikala, P.J. Foster, P.H. Whincup, A.R. Rudnicka, C.G. Owen, D.P. Strachan, S.A. Barman, Automated arteriole and venule classification using deep learning for retinal images from the UK Biobank cohort, Comput. Biol. Med. 90 (2017) 23–32, https://doi.org/10.1016/J.COMPBIOMED.2017.09.005.

[80] M.I. Meyer, A. Galdran, P. Costa, A.M. Mendonça, A. Campilho, Deep convolutional artery/vein classification of retinal vessels, in: Lecture Notes in Computer Science (including subseries Lecture Notes in Artificial Intelligence and Lecture Notes in Bioinformatics), LNCS, vol. 10882, Springer, Cham, 2018, pp. 622–630, https://doi.org/10.1007/978-3-319-93000-8_71.

[81] X. Xu, R. Wang, P. Lv, B. Gao, C. Li, Z. Tian, T. Tan, F. Xu, Simultaneous arteriole and venule segmentation with domain-specific loss function on a new public database, Biomed. Opt. Express 9 (7) (2018) 3153, https://doi.org/10.1364/BOE.9.003153.

[82] A. Galdran, M.I. Meyer, P. Costa, A.M. Mendonça, A. Campilho, Uncertainty-aware retinal vessel classification on retinal images, International Symposium on Biomedical Engineering, 2019.

[83] H. Fu, J. Cheng, Y. Xu, D.W.K. Wong, J. Liu, X. Cao, Joint optic disc and cup segmentation based on multi-label deep network and polar transformation, IEEE Trans. Med. Imaging 37 (7) (2018) 1597–1605, https://doi.org/10.1109/TMI.2018.2791488.

[84] J.G. Zilly, J.M. Buhmann, D. Mahapatra, Boosting Convolutional Filters with Entropy Sampling for Optic Cup and Disc Image Segmentation From Fundus Images, Springer, Cham, 2015, pp. 136–143, https://doi.org/10.1007/978-3-319-24888-2_17.

[85] Z. Gu, P. Liu, K. Zhou, Y. Jiang, H. Mao, J. Cheng, J. Liu, DeepDisc: Optic Disc Segmentation Based on Atrous Convolution and Spatial Pyramid Pooling, Springer, Cham, 2018, pp. 253–260, https://doi.org/10.1007/978-3-030-00949-6_30.

[86] Y. Liu, D. Fu, Z. Huang, Optic disc segmentation in fundus images using adversarial training, IET Image Process. 13 (2) (2018) 375–381. https://digital-library.theiet.org/content/journals/10.1049/iet-ipr.2018.5922.

[87] X. Sun, Y. Xu, W. Zhao, T. You, J. Liu, Optic disc segmentation from retinal fundus images via deep object detection networks, in: 2018 40th Annual International Conference of the IEEE Engineering in Medicine and Biology Society (EMBC), IEEE, 2018, pp. 5954–5957, https://doi.org/10.1109/EMBC.2018.8513592.

[88] H. Fu, J. Cheng, Y. Xu, C. Zhang, D.W.K. Wong, J. Liu, X. Cao, Disc-aware ensemble network for glaucoma screening from fundus image, IEEE Trans. Med. Imaging 37 (11) (2018) 2493–2501, https://doi.org/10.1109/TMI.2018.2837012.

[89] S. Sedai, D. Mahapatra, S. Hewavitharanage, S. Maetschke, R. Garnavi, Semi-Supervised Segmentation of Optic Cup in Retinal Fundus Images Using Variational Autoencoder, Springer, Cham, 2017, pp. 75–82, https://doi.org/10.1007/978-3-319-66185-8_9.

[90] S. Sedai, R. Tennakoon, P. Roy, K. Cao, R. Garnavi, Multi-stage segmentation of the fovea in retinal fundus images using fully convolutional neural networks, in: 2017 IEEE 14th International Symposium on Biomedical Imaging (ISBI 2017), IEEE, 2017, pp. 1083–1086, https://doi.org/10.1109/ISBI.2017.7950704.

[91] B. Al-Bander, W. Al-Nuaimy, B.M. Williams, Y. Zheng, Multiscale sequential convolutional neural networks for simultaneous detection of fovea and optic disc, Biomed. Signal Process. Control 40 (2018) 91–101, https://doi.org/10.1016/J.BSPC.2017.09.008.

[92] M.I. Meyer, A. Galdran, A.M. Mendonça, A. Campilho, A pixel-wise distance regression approach for joint retinal optical disc and fovea detection, in: Lecture Notes in Computer Science (including subseries Lecture Notes in Artificial Intelligence and Lecture Notes in Bioinformatics), LNCS, vol. 11071, Springer, Cham, 2018, pp. 39–47, https://doi.org/10.1007/978-3-030-00934-2_5.

[93] T. Araújo, G. Aresta, A. Galdran, P. Costa, A.M. Mendonça, A. Campilho, UOLO—Automatic Object Detection and Segmentation in Biomedical Images, Springer, Cham, 2018, pp. 165–173, https://doi.org/10.1007/978-3-030-00889-5_19.

[94] R. Poplin, A.V. Varadarajan, K. Blumer, Y. Liu, M.V. McConnell, G.S. Corrado, L. Peng, D.R. Webster, Prediction of cardiovascular risk factors from retinal fundus photographs via deep learning, Nat. Biomed. Eng. 2 (3) (2018) 158.

[95] E. Decencière, X. Zhang, G. Cazuguel, B. Laÿ, B. Cochener, C. Trone, P. Gain, J.R. Ordóñez-Varela, P. Massin, A. Erginay, B. Charton, J.C. Klein, Feedback on a publicly distributed image database: the Messidor database, Image Anal. Stereol. 33 (3) (2014) 231–234, https://doi.org/10.5566/ias.1155.

[96] P. Prentasic, S. Loncaric, Z. Vatavuk, G. Bencic, M. Subasic, T. Petkovic, L. Dujmovic, M. Malenica-Ravlic, N. Budimlija, R. Tadic, Diabetic retinopathy image database (DRiDB): a new database for diabetic retinopathy screening programs research, in: 2013 8th International Symposium on Image and Signal Processing and Analysis (ISPA), IEEE, 2013, pp. 711–716, https://doi.org/10.1109/ISPA.2013.6703830.

[97] S. Holm, G. Russell, V. Nourrit, N. McLoughlin, DR HAGIS—a fundus image database for the automatic extraction of retinal surface vessels from diabetic patients, J. Med. Imaging (Bellingham, Wash.) 4 (1) (2017) 014503, https://doi.org/10.1117/1.JMI.4.1.014503.

[98] P. Porwal, S. Pachade, R. Kamble, M. Kokare, G. Deshmukh, V. Sahasrabuddhe, F. Meriaudeau, Indian diabetic retinopathy image dataset (IDRiD): a database for diabetic retinopathy screening research, Data 3 (3) (2018) 25, https://doi.org/10.3390/data3030025.

[99] T. Kauppi, V. Kalesnykiene, J.K. Kamarainen, L. Lensu, I. Sorri, A. Raninen, R. Voutilainen, H. Uusitalo, H. Kalviainen, J. Pietila, The DIARETDB1 diabetic retinopathy database and evaluation protocol, in: Proceedings of the British Machine Vision Conference 2007, British Machine Vision Association, 2007, pp. 15.1–15.10, https://doi.org/10.5244/C.21.15.

[100] M. Niemeijer, B. van Ginneken, M.J. Cree, A. Mizutani, G. Quellec, C.I. Sanchez, B. Zhang, R. Hornero, M. Lamard, C. Muramatsu, X. Wu, G. Cazuguel, J. You, A. Mayo, Q. Li, Y. Hatanaka, B. Cochener, C. Roux, F. Karray, M. Garcia, H. Fujita, M.D. Abramoff, Retinopathy online challenge: automatic detection of microaneurysms in digital color fundus photographs, IEEE Trans. Med. Imaging 29 (1) (2010) 185–195, https://doi.org/10.1109/TMI.2009.2033909.

[101] E. Decencière, G. Cazuguel, X. Zhang, G. Thibault, J.C. Klein, F. Meyer, B. Marcotegui, G. Quellec, M. Lamard, R. Danno, D. Elie, P. Massin, Z. Viktor, A. Erginay, B. Laÿ, A. Chabouis, TeleOphta: machine learning and image processing methods for teleophthalmology, IRBM 34 (2) (2013) 196–203, https://doi.org/10.1016/J.IRBM.2013.01.010.

[102] J. Staal, M.D. Abramoff, M. Niemeijer, M.A. Viergever, B. van Ginneken, Ridge-based vessel segmentation in color images of the retina, IEEE Trans. Med. Imaging 23 (4) (2004) 501–509, https://doi.org/10.1109/TMI.2004.825627.

[103] A.D. Hoover, V. Kouznetsova, M. Goldbaum, Locating blood vessels in retinal images by piecewise threshold probing of a matched filter response, IEEE Trans. Med. Imaging 19 (3) (2000) 203–210, https://doi.org/10.1109/42.845178.

[104] A. Budai, R. Bock, A. Maier, J. Hornegger, G. Michelson, Robust vessel segmentation in fundus images, Int. J. Biomed. Imaging 2013 (2013) 154860, https://doi.org/10.1155/2013/154860.

[105] J.I. Orlando, J. Barbosa Breda, K. Van Keer, M.B. Blaschko, P.J. Blanco, C.A. Bulant, Towards a glaucoma risk index based on simulated hemodynamics from fundus images, in: International Conference on Medical Image Computing and Computer-Assisted Interventions, 2018, pp. 65–73.

AI and retinal image analysis at Baidu

19

Yehui Yang[a], Dalu Yang[a], Yanwu Xu[a], Lei Wang[a], Yan Huang[a], Xing Li[b], Xuan Liu[c], Le Van La[b]

[a]*Artificial Intelligence Innovation Business (AIIB), Baidu, Beijing, China*
[b]*Baidu Research Institute (BRI), Baidu, Sunnyvale, CA, United States*
[c]*Artificial Intelligence Group, Baidu, Beijing, China*

Abbreviations

AMD	age-related macular degeneration
AOI	area of interest
DR	diabetic retinopathy
GC	glaucoma
IQA	image quality assessment

1 Baidu: Mission, products, and next-steps

Baidu, China's largest search engine provider, was founded in 2000 by internet pioneer, Robin Li. Li was the creator of Hyperlink Analysis, the visionary search technology. Li founded Baidu with the mission of providing people with optimum information access and connection to services.

1.1 The Baidu mission

Over the past decade, Baidu has fulfilled its original mission by listening carefully to its users' needs and wants. There are tens of billions of queries entered into Baidu's search platform every day. In order to provide intelligent, relevant search results for these queries, Baidu's engine utilizes state-of-the-art technology, optimized for local tastes and preferences. Baidu's deep and nuanced understanding of Chinese language and culture is central to its success, creating search technology tailored to individual users. Baidu aims to make a complex world simpler through technology.

Baidu provides users with multiple channels to connect with information and services. In addition to its core web-search product, there are several popular community-based products. These include: Baidu PostBar, the world's first and largest Chinese-language, query-based, searchable online community platform; Baidu

Knows, the world's largest Chinese-language, interactive, knowledge-sharing platform; and Baidu Encyclopedia, the world's largest, user-generated, Chinese-language encyclopedia. Beyond these marquee products, Baidu also offers dozens of popular vertical search-based products, such as Maps, Image Search, Video Search, News Search, and more.

"AI is the key technology and new productive force of the fourth industrial revolution," says Haifeng Wang, the Senior Vice President of Baidu. *"It is integrating into all walks of life and affecting every aspect of people's lives."*

1.2 AI in Baidu

Baidu has been closely involved with AI development since its founding in 2000. The company was the first technology giant in China to investigate the use of AI in services such as Natural Language Processing (NLP), voice and machine learning, image processing, and more. Now, with nearly twenty years of development experience, Baidu's core search algorithm has become a large and complex AI system with a comprehensive suite of services. In early 2012, Baidu applied deep-learning technology to speech recognition. Since then, Baidu has established several specialty AI workgroups, including the Institute of Deep Learning (2013); the Silicon Valley AI Lab (2014); the Big Data Lab (2014); the Augmented Reality Laboratory (2017); and the AI Group (2017).

Baidu has received numerous awards for this development. Baidu's AI technology has also been selected as one of MIT's "Top Ten Breakthrough Technologies" for three consecutive years, from 2016 to 2018.

Additionally, Baidu leads the field in reading comprehension technology. In 2015, Baidu became the first company globally to release a neural-network, machine-translation system. With billions of entities and hundreds of billions of facts, Baidu has acquired potentially the largest knowledge base regarding Chinese culture ever compiled. Baidu's machine reading comprehension technology was recognized as a breakthrough and received first place in the MS MARCO ranking list for releasing the largest Chinese reading comprehension data set.

1.3 Baidu Brain

Building on years of accumulated technology and business practice, Baidu has started an ambitious move toward Baidu Brain, where a wide range of cutting-edge AI technologies—computer vision, speech, natural language processing, knowledge graph, deep learning—are seamlessly integrated into an open AI platform. Since its first release in September 2016, Baidu Brain has upgraded from version 1.0 to 3.0 with continuous and significant improvements, and has become the synthesizer of Baidu's comprehensive AI technologies and services.

The latest iteration of Baidu Brain 3.0 announced a new phase of innovation in which multiple categories of data (e.g., text, sound, pictures, videos, etc.) are integrated to provide a comprehensive and multidimensional understanding of information. As Haifeng Wang stated: "Multimodal deep semantic understanding can not only make the machine hear and see clearly, but also comprehensively understand the meaning and the real world behind it, which can better support various applications."

The technology of data semantics transforms the immense and multielement sources of information in the physical world, human society, and cyberspace into a holistic semantic network containing hundreds of billions of nodes and trillions of relationships. It can then summarize rules, refine knowledge, and discover values to promote the development of economy and society.

1.3.1 Visual semantic AI

Visual semantics allow the machine to understand videos from the perspective of a viewer and extract structured semantic knowledge. From this semantic knowledge, it automates interpretation, such as collection of highlights or statistical analysis of data. Visual semantic technology can transform digitized video into structured semantic knowledge by recognizing people, movements, items and associated time series.

1.3.2 Speech semantic AI

Baidu Brain has developed an innovative speech recognition architecture that leverages and integrates multigrained acoustic and semantic features, which breaks through the limitations of traditional big data analysis methods. Baidu Brain also developed the first end-to-end, online, Chinese-speech synthesis engine based on Bi-LSTM models, which utilize over 100 h of voice recordings from a single speaker and comprise the largest speech library available. These techniques have been implemented for the purpose of far-field speech recognition and the so-called "endless conversation" in the DuerOS service.

1.3.3 Natural language AI

Speech semantic integration and natural language processing technology can enable machines to accurately identify and understand verbal communication and achieve a natural human-machine dialogue.

With the aid of natural language processing technology, Baidu Brain has read hundreds of billions of articles, equivalent to the collection of 60,000 Chinese National Libraries. Therefore, it holds the accumulated knowledge of billions of entities and hundreds of billions of facts.

Baidu Brain has also established a comprehensive infrastructure supporting the research and development of the aforementioned AI technologies. The infrastructure is made available to the general public with a set of open-source software, training materials, and computing platforms at different levels, spanning from hardware to deep learning frameworks and application solutions. PaddlePaddle (see website http://www.paddlepaddle.org/) is an open-source deep-learning framework that was independently developed by Baidu. As the key foundation of Baidu Brain, PaddlePaddle is a groundbreaking technology that enables developers and companies to safely and quickly implement their AI ideas. Baidu Brain 3.0 was the first to incorporate a GPU chip, known as "Kunlun," into the technical system, which enabled it to have greater capacity to integrate software with hardware. Kunlun was specifically optimized for speech, natural language and image processing. It reduced cost by 10 times and increased ease of use while maintaining performance. This innovation has the potential to drive explosive growth of Baidu Brain.

Thus far, we have established the exciting evolution of Baidu Brain's comprehensive AI layout (Fig. 1). The ever-available Baidu Brain benefits countless users and is accessed over 400 billion times a day. This access is provided in accordance with the Chinese maxim: "Give a man a fish and you feed him for a day. Teach a man to fish and you feed him for a lifetime." As such, Baidu Brain's users include novices without prior AI knowledge, as well as AI engineers and a broad variety of industries and enterprises that utilize AI to innovate and transform their businesses.

As AI integrates into the capillaries of various industries and becomes a worldwide trend, Baidu will continue to strive toward its mission of making a complex world simpler through technology. In the words of Robin Li, the CEO of Baidu, "We hope that no matter where you are, no matter who you are today, you can get AI ability through Baidu equally and conveniently."

In the healthcare sector, Baidu has released three evidence-based AI medical products, including an AI fundus screening device, a clinical decision support system, and an intelligent triage system. These AI medical products can augment the knowledge of less-experienced clinicians, enabling them to make decisions comparable to those of highly-skilled physicians in leading hospitals and research institutions. Baidu aims to expand high-quality medical services to underdeveloped areas, enabling everyone to achieve equal access to healthcare. In the following sections we present an overview of Baidu's AI technology for retinal image analysis, including the algorithm architecture, the real-world use cases, and an outlook of the technology.

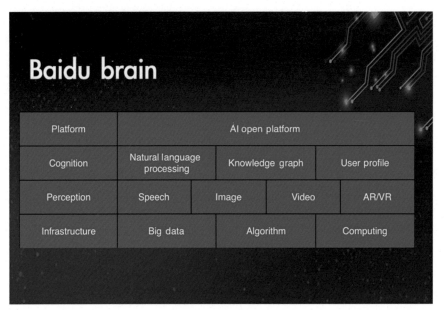

FIG. 1

Baidu Brain's comprehensive AI layout.

2 General architecture of AI retinal image analysis

The general architecture of Baidu's AI retinal algorithm (shown in Fig. 2) consists of three main modules:

1. *Image quality assessment module.* Images of the fundus typically come from different types of retinal cameras under various conditions. As a result, the images may contain undesirable artifacts (e.g., background noise), lack focus, exhibit uneven illumination or under-/overexposure, etc. Image quality plays a critical role in retinal image analysis during clinical examination [1]. Baidu utilizes an image quality assessment module to automatically evaluate the quality of a fundus image. The module strives to assess whether input images are suitable for follow-up AI algorithms to detect eye diseases. In the event the input image fails to pass this assessment module, the patient will be requested to take a new picture.

2. *Disease detection module.* This module describes several eye-disease detection algorithms, which assess whether an input image has the target diseases. The disease detection algorithms are developed in parallel. To date, AI algorithms for detecting diabetic retinopathy (DR), glaucoma (GC), and age-related macular degeneration (AMD) have been developed.

3. *Interpretation module.* A medical report relies on reliable interpretation of an AI-based disease conclusion. Therefore, this module is designed to provide

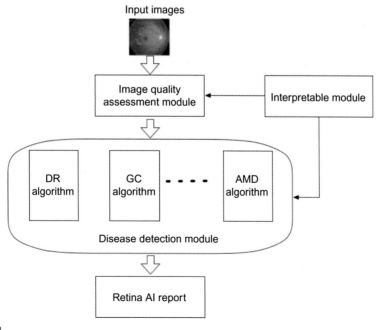

FIG. 2

Baidu's AI retinal algorithm architecture. DR, GC and AMD refer to diabetic retinopathy, glaucoma and age-related macular degeneration, respectively.

evidentiary support for the disease-detection module. As most eye diseases are determined based on the type of lesion at specific areas in the retina, the interpretation module conducts lesion detection (e.g., differentiating micro-aneurysms, hemorrhage, exudates, etc.) and critical area of interest (AOI) extraction (e.g., optical disk & cup, macular region, blood vessels, etc.) from the retinal images. This module is embedded in both quality assessment and disease detection modules, which align clinical experiences with massive data-driven features to make each module more interpretable and more confident.

The remainder of this chapter will provide details for each of the aforementioned modules.

4. Image quality assessment (IQA) module.

A separate, automated image quality assessment module is necessary for the following reasons:

1. The complex image acquisition process makes low-quality images very prevalent in screening projects.
2. The photographer seldom has sufficient knowledge and training to assess whether the image is gradable.
3. The disease classification and lesion detection AI algorithms are developed from clean images; consequently, their analysis of variable types of low-quality images is undefined.

In most experimental settings, retinal image quality can be described using several criterion: focus and clarity, illumination, dirt and other lens artifacts, and visibility of macular and optic disk [2]. Fig. 3 illustrates images of various low-quality criteria. Each individual criterion indicates a specific problem with image acquisition, thereby informing the photographer how to retake the image to improve quality.

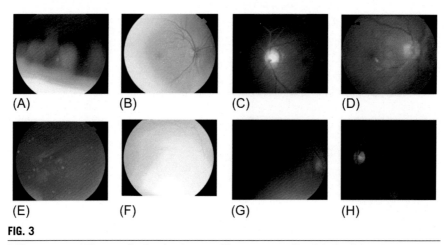

(A)   (B)   (C)   (D)

(E)   (F)   (G)   (H)

FIG. 3

Different types of low-quality fundus images. The corresponding labels of the above images are summarized in Table 1.

Table 1 Label of example fundus images in Fig. 3.

Image	In-focus	Normal brightness/ contrast	Even illumination	DR gradable	AMD gradable	Glaucoma gradable
a	No	No	No	No	No	No
b	Yes	Yes	No	Yes	No	Yes
c	Yes	Yes	No	No	No	Yes
d	No	Yes	Yes	Yes	Yes	No
e	No	Yes	Yes	No	No	No
f	No	No	No	No	No	No
g	No	No	No	No	No	Yes
h	Yes	No	Yes	Yes	No	Yes

Considering a real application scenario, image quality problems are more complicated. For instance, retaking the fundus image may not be enough to resolve a problem even if the source of the problem can be identified. This could result from environmental illumination limitations, low patient cooperation, small pupil size in older patients, inexperienced photographers, etc. Therefore, many images are only partially gradable.

Further, the gradability definitions for different diseases may vary (e.g., an image with a clear optic disk and a completely obscured macula is fully gradable for glaucoma but ungradable for AMD). Thus, to maximize the overall screening service efficiency, the IQA module must allow partially gradable images to be utilized.

Baidu's proposed IQA module has the following features:

1. Descriptive IQA: Identifies image quality in terms of brightness/contrast, focus, and illumination. This enables the photographer to adjust accordingly to improve image quality.
2. Disease-Specific IQA: Determines if an image is gradable for different diseases. The IQA module provides a unique gradability score for each disease classification and lesion detection task.

The Descriptive IQA and the Disease-Specific IQA modules were developed separately. Results from each module are combined with an "OR" operator to determine the final image quality result (fully, partially, or nongradable). Fig. 4 briefly illustrates the relationship between proposed IQA modules.

2.1 Descriptive IQA

To describe image quality, several processing techniques were developed for each criterion. This process involves three key assessment tasks [2]:

2.1.1 Focus and clarity assessment

The input fundus image is first converted to greyscale. A 3×3 and 5×5 moving average filter is then applied to generate two filtered images. This step is important

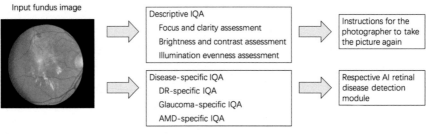

FIG. 4

Proposed image quality assessment algorithm structure. IQA, DR, and AMD refer to image quality assessment, diabetic retinopathy and age-related macular degeneration, respectively.

as a low-pass filter will affect a "focused" retinal image more than a "blurred" one.

To quantify the difference between the filtered image and the original image, Sobel operators are applied to the aforementioned images (i.e., the greyscale version of the original image, the 3×3 filtered image, and the 5×5 filtered image). The Sobel filter is a gradient operator that captures focus information [2]. For each image, four Sobel operators (as shown in Fig. 5) are used and the resulting four gradient maps are added to produce a single map. The mean of the resulting feature map describes the focus information of the corresponding image. At this point, three numbers (i.e., the sum of the Sobel feature maps of nonfiltered, 3×3 filtered, and 5×5 filtered) are generated for each fundus image. The difference between these three numbers is used to ascertain whether the image is in focus.

2.1.2 Brightness and contrast assessment

To ensure image brightness is normal, mean, maximum, and minimum brightness values are computed for the images labeled too-bright, too-dark, and normal. These values establish brightness index mappings for dark, normal, and bright images. Mean values of the index mappings are then used to determine if the image is too dark, too bright, or normal.

Image contrast assessment utilizes local standard deviation of image patches at different scales as the contrast measure [3]. Scales of nonoverlapping patches range in 1/8, 1/4, and 1/2 of the fundus image radius. The standard deviation of pixel values within each patch is computed, and the minimum standard deviation values from each scale serve as the contrast feature for the entire image.

$$
\begin{array}{ccc}
1 & 2 & 1 \\
0 & 0 & 0 \\
-1 & -2 & -1
\end{array}
\qquad
\begin{array}{ccc}
-1 & -2 & -1 \\
0 & 0 & 0 \\
1 & 2 & 1
\end{array}
\qquad
\begin{array}{ccc}
1 & 0 & -1 \\
2 & 0 & -2 \\
1 & 0 & -1
\end{array}
\qquad
\begin{array}{ccc}
-1 & 0 & 1 \\
-2 & 0 & 2 \\
-1 & 0 & 1
\end{array}
$$

FIG. 5

Sobel operators used for gradient map. The arrows indicate the direction of gradient calculated by the corresponding operators.

2.1.3 Illumination evenness assessment

Image illumination information is captured by converting the original image from RGB to HSV. Several illumination measures on the "value" channel of the HSV image are then computed [2]:

Mean of value channel: $M = \frac{1}{n}\sum_{i=1}^{n} V_i$, where V_i is the ith pixel value of the value channel.

Variance of value channel: $Var = \frac{1}{n}\sum_{i=1}^{n}(V_i - M)$.

Submean variance: $Var1 = \frac{1}{n}\sum_{i=1}^{n}(V_i - M)$, for all $V_i < M$.

Super-mean variance: $Var2 = \frac{1}{n}\sum_{i=1}^{n}(V_i - M)$, for all $V_i > M$.

M, Var, $Var1$, and $Var2$ are combined together as a measure of the illumination evenness.

2.2 Disease-specific IQA

Aside from the generic descriptive IQA, it is important to determine whether the image is gradable for different diseases. This relies primarily on a deep learning method to account for all the image variables without explicitly extracting predefined features from the images.

Our Disease-Specific IQA system is subdivided into three modules, each performing a binary classification task for a specific disease—DR, AMD, or GC. The three binary classification models are based on ResNet [4], a deep learning architecture balanced between model size and performance. It was determined that the original model input resolution (224×224) is adequate for the IQA task—all images are resized to 224×224, with a fixed aspect ratio and adaptive cropping and padding to ensure the fundus regions are approximately the same size. Since most fundus image preprocessing techniques are designed to "enhance" image quality, no preprocessing (except resizing and cropping) is used for the Disease-Specific IQA. Overfitting is avoided by employing common standardization and augmentation techniques. Each resulting model is evaluated based on the area under the ROC curve (AUC), sensitivity and specificity.

2.3 Discussion

For real-world applications, high sensitivity is a desired property as it ensures the following disease detection modules only receive images of high quality (and thus provide more reliable results). The 1-specificity value, or false positive rate, measures how often the photographer retakes an image that is of adequate quality. This can have impacts on the operating costs of a screening center.

Given suitable data, there are alternative ways to evaluate descriptive IQA performance besides sensitivity and specificity measures. Descriptive IQA modules are designed to inform the photographer how he/she should adjust image acquisition parameters or instruct the patient. Thus, descriptive IQA module performance can be evaluated by the reduction in frequency of picture retakes, as compared to a quality assessment procedure without instructions.

A potential drawback to the proposed IQA module is that, at non-100% sensitivity, the low-quality images passed on to the following disease detection modules can cause undefined behaviors. One possible solution to this problem is building a ternary classifier (i.e., classifying the image as disease A vs. no disease A vs. disease A ungradable). The classifier is trained on both clean data for the specific disease and low-quality image data. This may improve the confidence level for any input. Alternatively, the problem may be solved by forcing the IQA module to manage health information. The IQA module will first do a binary classification (i.e., healthy AND high-quality vs. the rest). Images filed with the "rest" class will cycle through the normal disease detection modules. If none of the diseases appear positive, the image can be sent for analysis by an experienced clinician.

2.4 Diabetic retinopathy detection algorithm

In this section, details of the proposed two-stage model for DR binary classification is presented. Fig. 6 illustrates the main pipeline of the algorithm. The input fundus images are preprocessed to enhance the appearance of lesions and to standardize the field of view and resolution. A deep neural network is then used to perform binary classification on the preprocessed images. Finally, any ambiguous cases (classified as nonreferable but with a prediction score close to 0.5) will go through a lesion detection pipeline to confirm the result.

2.4.1 Preprocessing

Lesion enhancement is conducted by mixing the original image and its Gaussian filtered results as follows [5, 6]:

$$I = \alpha I_{raw} + \beta G(\theta) \circ I_{raw} + \gamma$$

where I_{raw} is the original fundus image, and I denotes the corresponding output image after preprocessing. $G(\theta)$ is a Gaussian kernel with scale θ. In our experiment, θ is set as 7. $\circ$ is the convolution operator. α, β, and γ are weight coefficients for the raw image and the Gaussian filtered image. We set $\alpha=4$, $\beta=-4$, and $\gamma=128$. Fig. 7 illustrates

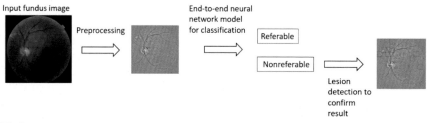

FIG. 6

Workflow of referable DR detection algorithm.

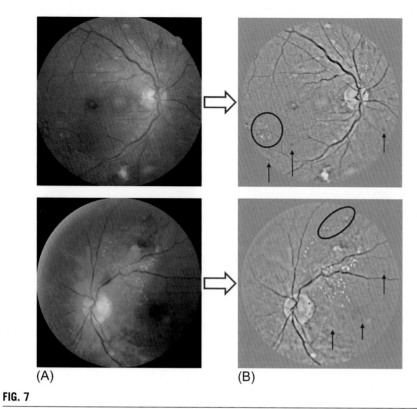

FIG. 7

Illustration of the effectiveness of the preprocessing method. (A) Raw fundus images.
(B) Corresponding images after preprocessing.

examples of raw fundus images and their preprocessed versions. Underlying lesions, including exudates and hemorrhages, are more distinguishable after preprocessing.

To balance computational complexity with the level of image details, an image input size of 512×512 is used for the neural network model. Since the images have different margin widths, the radius of the fundus region is computed for each lesion-enhanced image and resized accordingly. Finally, the resized images are padded to maintain a 1:1 aspect ratio.

2.4.2 Data augmentation

This module relies on the implementation of standard online augmentation, which dynamically transforms the input images in each epoch while training. Random rotation and color jittering are used for the augmentation. Random rotation serves to maintain a certain degree of lesion location invariance. Random color jittering helps reduce the coloring effect from different fundus camera manufacturers. The augmentation is not randomly cropped or scaled because the appearance of certain lesions as well as its size are decisive of referable/nonreferable DR.

2.4.3 Classification model

A deep neural network is used to perform a binary classification for referable/non-referable DR. The neural network is based on DenseNet-121 [4], which is a popular network architecture proposed in recent years. The layers and dimensions of the model are similar to the "vanilla" version described in [4] with two major differences. First, the input dimension of our model is 512×512, thus making the dimensions of the feature map before the average pooling layer 16×16. Second, the ReLU activation function is changed in the DenseNet to Leaky ReLU with a slope of 0.5. To reduce the unbalanced class problem, the loss function is a standard cross-entropy loss with weights equal to the ratio of the number of samples.

For faster convergence of the DenseNet [7] model, pretrained model weights (https://www.kaggle.com/pytorch/densenet121#densenet121.pth) were used for initialization of all layers except the first convolutional layer due to the dimension mismatch. The preprocessed images are standardized according to the mean and standard deviation of RGB channels from all training images to provide a highly stable training process. The AUC measure on the validation set is tracked. If the AUC change is less than 0.001 between two consecutive epochs, the training process is stopped.

2.5 Glaucoma detection algorithm

Nowadays, an increasing number of people are affected by glaucoma, which can lead to irreversible blindness without early intervention [8]. Researchers typically detect glaucoma using clinical features, such as the optic cup-to-disc ratio (CDR), retinal nerve fiber layer (RNFL), peripapillary atrophy (PPA), etc. [9].

Baidu's algorithm uses both the CDR and an end-to-end classifier for glaucoma detection from fundus images. The CDR plays an important role when predicting whether the input image exhibits glaucoma or not. However, quantitatively extracting glaucoma-related retinal features (e.g., RNFL, PPA, etc.) is not trivial work. An end-to-end classifier is used to automatically learn the underlying data-driving features.

A multitask algorithm to locate and segment the optic disc (OD) and optic cup (OC) jointly, while simultaneously providing the probability of glaucoma risk, has been proposed. As shown in Fig. 8, the architecture of Baidu's method consists of two cascading parts. First, the optic disc region is detected by an object detection model. Faster-RCNN [1] is used in our practice; however, the detector can be any state-of-the-art detection algorithm. Second, during the multitask algorithm, two parallel models are employed to increase the confidence level of the result. In one model, the optic disc region is placed into an end-to-end classifier to determine whether the input fundus has glaucoma. Simultaneously, a segmentation model is used to extract the optic cup out of the optic disc region. The maximum inscribed bounding ellipse of the Faster-RCNN bounding box is obtained as the optic disc ellipse. The two parts are aligned by the joint loss as per:

$$\mathcal{L}\left(pred_{cdr}, prob_{y=1}\right) = \min \sum_i \left(pred_{cdr}^{(i)} - gt_{cdr}^{(i)}\right)^2 + \lambda_1 \sum_i \left(prob_{y=1}^{(i)} - gt_{y=1}^{(i)}\right)^2 + \lambda_2 \sum_j \frac{pred_{cdr}^{(j)}}{prob_{y=1}^{(j)}}$$

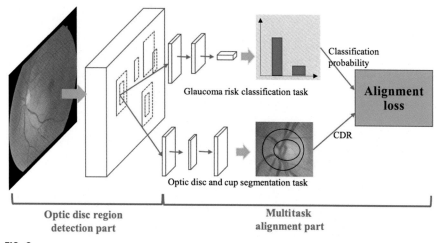

Glaucoma risk classification task

Optic disc and cup segmentation task

Optic disc region
detection part

Multitask
alignment part

FIG. 8

The architecture of multitask glaucoma detection algorithm.

where $pred_{cdr}^{(i)}$ refers to the predicted CDR of the ith sample. $gt_{cdr}^{(i)}$ is the corresponding ground truth CDR, and $gt_{y=1}^{(i)} = 1$ if the ith image is a positive sample otherwise $gt_{y=1}^{(i)} = 0$. The first term on the right-hand side forces the correctness of the predicted CDR. The second term is constructed to align the CDR and end-to-end glaucoma classifier. When the CDR is big, the probability of glaucoma $pred_{cdr}^{(i)}$ should get bigger simultaneously, and vice versa. λ is a super-parameter to control the weight of the two parts. By applying the above alignment loss, the classification task and segmentation task can be jointly learned for more precise and fine-grained glaucoma detection.

2.6 Age-related macular degeneration detection (AMD) algorithm

AMD is a leading cause of blindness in the elderly, worldwide [5]. The type of lesion present in the macular region helps classify AMD into two categories:

1. *Dry AMD:* Confirmed through the detection of yellow or white deposits, called drusen, in the macular region (as shown in Fig. 9B). Dry AMD is classified by the severity of drusen and further subdivided into early, intermediate and advanced stages.
2. *Wet AMD:* Confirmed through the presence of neovascularization, or abnormal blood vessel formation, under the retina (as shown in Fig. 9C). Dry AMD, at any severity stage, can progress into wet AMD.

Our aim is to automatically differentiate referable AMD (intermediate or worse AMD) from nonreferable AMD under various situations. To that extent, a multiscale algorithm to exploit both global information and local details for AMD detection was proposed. Workflow of the AMD detection algorithm is shown in Fig. 10.

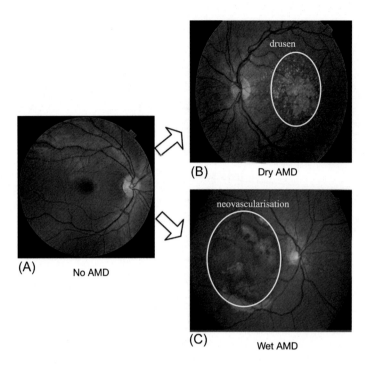

FIG. 9

The typical observation of retina with (A) no AMD, (B) dry AMD, and (C) wet AMD.

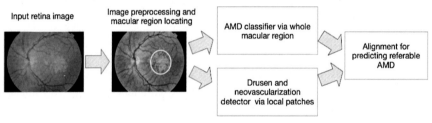

FIG. 10

Workflow of our referable AMD detection algorithm.

A given input retina image is first preprocessed to highlight specific information (e.g., lesions). The macular area of interest (AOI) extraction method is then used to remove the region out of the macular area as it could generate artifact noise. The next step is to conduct two scale prediction methods: (1) end-to-end AMD classification of the entire macular region and (2) drusen and neovascularization detection via local patches. The two scale components are subsequently aligned to predict if the input images have referable or nonreferable AMD.

The end-to-end classifier analyzes the global structure of the macular region to distinguish if the AMD is referable or not. The lesion detector analyzes the image on a local scale; presence of typical lesions in the macular region of the input image increases the probability that the input image has referable AMD. Notably, the two scale components are complementary and improve performance of the AMD detection algorithm.

We will now discuss how to: (1) determine the macular AOI; (2) construct the global AMD classifier; and (3) detect lesions.

2.6.1 Macular AOI location

Since AMD is characterized by abnormal degeneration around the macular region, we extract the macular AOI to gain specific information about the region and limit background noise where possible.

The macula is an oval-shaped, pigmented area near the center of the retina [8]. It is difficult to locate the macula in a fundus image as it does not have a clearly demarcated or observable boundary. Additionally, the fovea (center of the macula) is often occluded by retinal lesions, making the macula increasingly challenging to detect. Resultantly, the location of the optic disc, which is easier to detect (refer to Fig. 11), is used to determine the AOI.

The optic disc appears as a light oval in a fundus image. Suppose the vertical axis and horizontal axis of the optic disc are d_v and d_h, respectively; then, the optical disc diameter is defined as $ODD = (d_v + d_h)/2$. According to Levels [9], the horizontal distance between the fovea and the optic disc (shown in Fig. 11A) is $a = 2.5 \times ODD$, and the vertical distance (shown in Fig. 11B) is $b = 0.35 \times ODD$. As illustrated in Fig. 11, the average of the included angle is $\theta = 6.47° \pm 2.76°$.

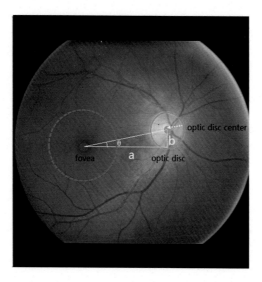

FIG. 11

The relationship between fovea and optic disc, and the area in the blue dashed circle is the macular AOI.

As a result, once the optic disc has been located (x_{fovea}, y_{fovea}), the coordinates of the fovea can be calculated as:

$$\text{(1) } x_{fovea} = \begin{cases} x_{disc} - 2.5^* \left(d_h + d_v \right) / 2; if & x_{disc} \geq width_{image} / 2 \\ x_{disc} + 2.5^* \left(d_h + d_v \right) / 2; if & x_{disc} < width_{image} / 2 \end{cases}$$

$$\text{(2) } x_{fovea} = y_{disc} + \tan(6.47) * 2.5^* (d_h + d_v)/2 = y_{disc} + 0.28^* (d_h + d_v)/2$$

The macular AOI is the circular region centered at (x_{fovea}, y_{fovea}) with a diameter of $2 \times ODD$ (refer to the blue circle in Fig. 11).

The next challenge which needs to be solved is detecting the optic disc. Baidu's algorithm employs Faster-RCNN [4] to find the optic disc. With the overlap between the target detection result and the ground truth set to 0.75, both the recall and precision of optic disc detection among fundus images crosses 0.98, passing the quality assessment module.

In some cases, however, the optic disc cannot be located accurately. To overcome this challenge, the distribution of macular AOI locations and size are calculated to correct the false negative of the optic disc detector. In general, if the optic disc cannot be detected, or the macular AOI predicted via disc information deviates significantly from the distribution, the statistic value of the distribution is used to extract the macular AOI. Fig. 12 illustrates the distribution of the macular AOI among the fundus from a *Topcon NW 400* retina camera.

2.6.2 End-to-end referable AMD classifier

The macular AOI of the input fundus is only used to train an end-to-end classifier. Some state-of-the-art deep nets, such as ResNet [4], DenseNet [7] and Inception-V3 [10] are fine-tuned to construct the ensemble classifier. In our experiment, ResNet gives the best performance on both the accuracy and classification time. The main structure of ResNet-34 is formed by stacking multiple residual blocks (see Fig. 13).

The details for training our referable AMD classifier are as follows. First we resize the macular AOI to 224 × 224 resolution. Then, in order to increase the robustness of the model, we performed data augmentation, including adding noises, horizontal flipping, and image rotation, etc. We applied focal loss for the sample imbalance problem [11]. The focal loss parameters are set as $\alpha = 0.25$, $\gamma = 2$ when training begins, and $\alpha = 0.5$, $\gamma = 4$ after 100 epochs. During training, we used a starting learning rate of 0.01 and a momentum of 0.9. We used 5-fold cross-validation to ensure stable generalization performance.

2.6.3 Drusen and neovascularization detector

Faster-RCNN is used to simultaneously detect drusen, neovascularization, and the optic disc. Since the observation of these three target objects is quite different, detection performance is improved by using single Faster-RCNN model by multiple output.

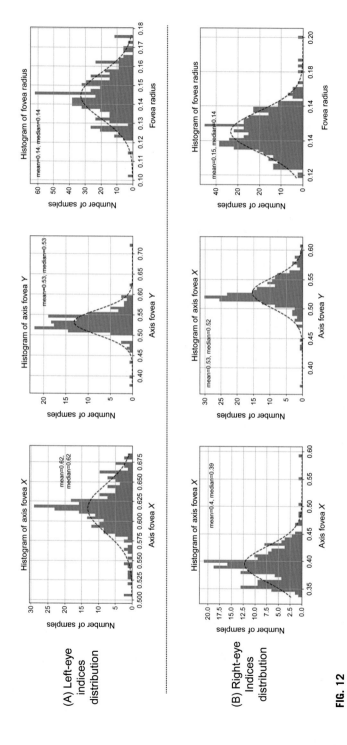

FIG. 12

Distributions of key indices of the macular AOI in *Topcon NW400* retina camera. (A) and (B) record the histogram of left and right eyes' fundus, respectively. The horizontal axis denotes the relative value according to the width and height of the original retina image. The vertical axis refers to the samples of the histogram. The first, second and third columns present the distributions of the x, y locations, and the macular AOI radius of left and right eyes, respectively.

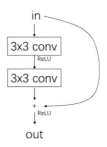

FIG. 13

Residual block unit for constructing ResNet.

2.7 Interpretation module

This module analyzes eye diseases in a fine-grain scale and provides convincing evidence for disease detection. Notably, this module is embedded in each aforementioned disease detection algorithms, including DR lesion detection (shown in Fig. 3), AMD drusen and neovascularization detection, and GC optic disc/cup segmentation. Additionally, key structure (e.g., optic disc region, macular region, blood vessels, etc.) extraction can also be included in the interpretation module, providing valuable information for image quality assessment.

Lesion detection currently takes into consideration microaneurysms, hemorrhage, hard/soft exudates, drusen and neovascularization. All lesions are indicated with patches and detection strategies vary depending on the lesion type. For instance, for lesions with distinguishable features and proper size, state-of-the-art detection algorithms (e.g., Fast-RCNN) can be used to drive favorable performance. However, existing state-of-the-art detection algorithms remain unable to detect certain tiny lesions, such as microaneurysms, which are so small they cannot be spotted with ease by trained professionals. In these circumstances, a novel algorithm for small object detection is used. The details of this algorithm are beyond the scope of this chapter. Interested readers can review this work once the submission is accepted and the paper becomes open access.

Future directions include enabling the interpretation module to detect more lesions, such as vein beading, microvascular abnormality, etc., in order to improve retina analysis. Furthermore, pixel-wise prediction may be incorporated, if necessary.

2.8 Experimental results and real-world application

To evaluate the effectiveness of our algorithms, experimental results and real-world application performance is provided.

All the training dataset are annotated by at least three Licensed ophthalmologists. The final label of each image is determined only if the three annotators give the same decision. Otherwise, a discussion will be held and a more senior expert will join the discussion to achieve a unanimous annotation.

2.8.1 Image quality assessment

30,000 fundus images were used. Each image is assessed for overall image quality (fully gradable, partially gradable or nongradable) and gradability (gradable/nongradable) for DR/AMD/GC. If the overall image quality was graded as low or medium, the grader was asked to further provide label information about brightness/contrast (poor or normal), focus (in or out-of focus), and illumination (even or uneven). The gradability of DR, AMD, and GC are each assessed by a domain expert for the disease.

The descriptive IQA can be viewed as several binary classification tasks. The corresponding sensitivity, specificity, and AUC are listed in Table 2.

Each disease-specific IQA is a binary classifier. The corresponding sensitivity, specificity, and AUC are listed in Table 3.

The performance results of fully gradable vs. partially-/nongradable classification by combining all the IQA submodules is listed in Table 4.

2.8.2 Diabetic retinopathy

A total of 62,912 macula-centered retinal fundus images were used. The images are assigned into five DR stages (i.e., none, mild, moderate, severe, or proliferative). In the binary DR classification task, moderate, severe, and proliferative DR are considered as referable DR, while none and mild are deemed nonreferable.

Table 2 Performance evaluation of descriptive IQA classifiers.

IQA classifiers	Sensitivity	Specificity	AUC
Normal versus poor brightness and contrast	92.5%	87.2%	0.955
In versus out-of focus	94.2%	84.5%	0.921
Even versus uneven illumination	96.0%	83.4%	0.949

Table 3 Performance evaluation of descriptive IQA classifiers.

IQA classifiers	Sensitivity	Specificity	AUC
DR gradable versus ungradable	90.3%	88.7%	0.962
Glaucoma gradable versus ungradable	91.5%	89.0%	0.967
AMD gradable versus ungradable	91.3%	84.3%	0.934

Table 4 Performance of overall IQA.

IQA	Sensitivity	Specificity	AUC
Gradable versus partial-/nongradable	99.6%	73.0%	0.922

The dataset is split into training and testing sets at a 4:1 ratio. The ROC curve for the testing set is shown in Fig. 14A. Quantitative performance evaluation found AUC=0.984, sensitivity=0.924, and specificity=0.945.

2.8.3 Glaucoma

To train and test the glaucoma classifier, a large fundus image dataset was collected from several partner hospitals. Each image is labeled as a suspicious glaucoma case or a nonsuspicious glaucoma case. This dataset is subdivided into three parts: the training set (11,048 suspicious cases and 53,142 nonsuspicious cases), the validation set (3801 suspicious cases and 7279 nonsuspicious cases) and the testing set (3723 suspicious cases and 7286 nonsuspicious cases). The algorithm achieved an AUC=0.990, sensitivity=0.920, and specificity=0.993. The ROC curve is shown in Fig. 14B.

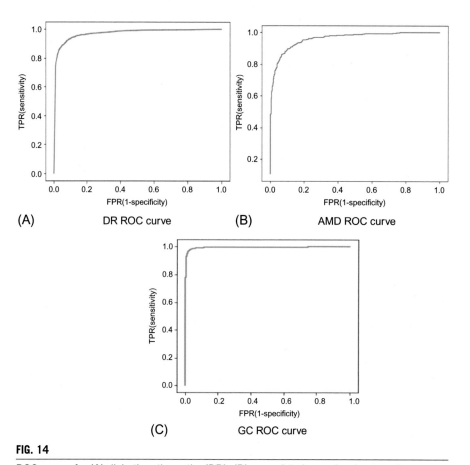

FIG. 14

ROC curves for (A) diabetic retinopathy (DR); (B) age-related macular degeneration (AMD); and (C) glaucoma (GC) algorithms, respectively.

2.8.4 Age-related macular degeneration

The dataset contains 5719 images, including 3054 AMD images and 2665 non-AMD images. Using five-fold cross validation, the AMD algorithm achieved mean values of AUC = 0.960, sensitivity = 0.913, and specificity = 0.904. The ROC curve is shown in Fig. 14C.

2.8.5 Real-world application

In November 2018, Baidu release AI *Retina Screening All-in-One Machine* which integrated all the above algorithms into one machine which can automatically generate the retina report within 10 s, and the results given by the machine have been confirmed by experts in top hospitals.

Validated by hundreds of people in several high-level activities, such as Baidu World Conference 2018,[1] Beijing, China, China Central Television AI exhibition,[2] NeualIps 2018 exhibition,[3] Montreal, Canada etc., the *All-in-One Machine* has achieved wide influence in intelligent health in both academic and industry region.

Additionally, Baidu AI *Retina Screening All-in-One Machine* has been utilized in several hospitals in Guangdong province, China. The real-world application introduces several challenges to the robustness of Baidu's algorithm due to camera device discrepancy. For example, some of the images from the screening centers are captured by handheld fundus cameras, which exhibit a very distinct color tone and noise pattern with the training set. Additionally, not enough well annotated samples from the handheld fundus cameras exist to fine-tune the model.

Despite these complications, the DR algorithm achieves over 90% on both sensitivity and specificity measures. The sensitivity and specificity results from the real-world screening centers, which apply Baidu's algorithm, is anticipated to be 92.1% and 90.3%, respectively.

The application of Baidu's AI algorithm in real-world scenarios creates a positive feedback loop for improving both the algorithm performance and the data collection process. The algorithm can improve if more training data is available. Similarly, data collection is made easier if the algorithm performs well and can expand to more application scenarios. Baidu remains optimistic that novel AI algorithms with better performance are under development and will soon emerge on the market.

2.9 Outlook of Baidu retina system

Currently, Baidu has established automatic detection of DR, AMD, and GC in retinal image analysis. Future directions include detection of all diseases that can be detected early by retinal imaging. To achieve this goal, Baidu is extending its collaborations to more hospitals and ophthalmologists. A large-scale fundus image tagging system for more objective clinical annotation is also under development.

---

1   http://ai.baidu.com/support/news?action=detail&id=586.
2   http://rmbjb.jyrmb.com/?id=83E.
3   https://www.jiqizhixin.com/articles/2018-12-05-4.

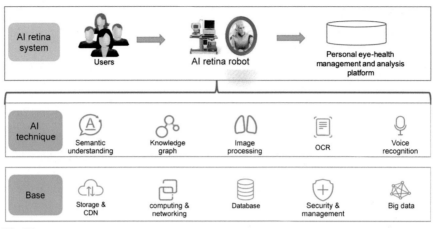

FIG. 15

The outlook of AI retina system.

Baidu is an international company with leading AI technology and platforms. Our retinal algorithms focus not only on inputting an image and outputting several eye-disease risks, but also building a powerful AI retina system that integrates all related AI capacity to provide better service and enhance the end-user experience.

As shown in Fig. 15, the base component guarantees big data storage, processing, and security capacity. The AI technique component will integrate various Baidu AI technologies for reinvigorating retinal imaging, including knowledge graph, voice recognition, face recognition, etc. These extra technologies dramatically enhance the user experience and facilitate the incorporation of the AI retinal image analysis algorithms into an AI retina robot.

The AI retina system aims to build a personal eye-health management and analysis platform for each user. Baidu's mission is to use AI to defend people's eyes and global health.

Acknowledgments

The authors would like to thank Qinpei Sun, Xu Sun in *Baidu AI Innovation Business (AIIB)* department, and Tiantian Huang in *East China Normal University* for proving some valuable materials and suggestions for this chapter.

References

[1] A. Galdran, T. Araújo, A.M. Mendonça, A. Campilho, Retinal image quality assessment by mean-subtracted contrast-normalized coefficients, in: J.M.R.S. Tavares, R.M. Natal Jorge (Eds.), *VipIMAGE* 2017. Lecture Notes in Computational Vision and Biomechanics, Springer International Publishing, Cham, 2018, pp. 844–853.

[2] J.M. Dias, C.M. Oliveira, L.A. da Silva Cruz, Retinal image quality assessment using generic image quality indicators, Inform. Fus. 19 (2014) 73–90.

[3] P. Reinagel, A.M. Zador, Natural scene statistics at the center of gaze, Netw. Comput. Neural Syst. 10 (1) (1999) 38–70.

[4] K. He, X. Zhang, S. Ren, J. Sun, Deep residual learning for image recognition, in: 2016 IEEE Conference on Computer Vision and Pattern Recognition (CVPR), IEEE, 2016, pp. 770–778.

[5] M.J.J.P. van Grinsven, B. van Ginneken, C.B. Hoyng, T. Theelen, C.I. Sanchez, Fast convolutional neural network training using selective data sampling: application to hemorrhage detection in color fundus images, IEEE Trans. Med. Imaging 35 (5) (2016) 1273–1284.

[6] Y. Yang, T. Li, W. Li, H. Wu, W. Fan, W. Zhang, Lesion detection and grading of diabetic retinopathy via two-stages deep convolutional neural networks, in: 2017 Medical Image Computing and Computer Assisted Intervention (MICCAI), Springer, 2017, pp. 533–540.

[7] G. Huang, Z. Liu, L. van der Maaten, K.Q. Weinberger, Densely connected convolutional networks, in: 2017 IEEE Conference on Computer Vision and Pattern Recognition (CVPR), IEEE, 2017, pp. 2261–2269.

[8] V. Gulshan, L. Peng, M. Coram, M.C. Stumpe, D. Wu, A. Narayanaswamy, S. Venugopalan, K. Widner, T. Madams, J. Cuadros, R. Kim, R. Raman, P.C. Nelson, J.L. Mega, D.R. Webster, Development and validation of a deep learning algorithm for detection of diabetic retinopathy in retinal fundus photographs, J. Am. Med. Assoc. 316 (22) (2016) 2402–2410.

[9] E.T. Levels, International Clinical Diabetic Retinopathy Disease Severity Scale Detailed Table, 2002.

[10] C. Szegedy, V. Vanhoucke, S. Ioffe, J. Shlens, Z. Wojna, Rethinking the inception architecture for computer vision, in: 2016 IEEE Conference on Computer Vision and Pattern Recognition (CVPR), IEEE, 2016, pp. 2818–2826.

[11] T.Y. Lin, P. Goyal, R. Girshick, K. He, P. Dollár, Focal loss for dense object detection, IEEE Trans. Pattern Anal. Mach. Intell. (2018).

The challenges of assembling, maintaining and making available large data sets of clinical data for research

20

Emily R. Jefferson[a], Emanuele Trucco[b]

[a]Health Informatics Centre, University of Dundee, Dundee, United Kingdom
[b]VAMPIRE Project, Computing (SSEN), University of Dundee, Dundee, United Kingdom

1 Introduction

Medical images, of which retinal images are a special class, are widely used for clinical and research purposes, for example machine learning [1], computer vision methods for biomarker extraction [2, 3], genotype-phenotype associations [4], disease progression [5, 6], examining early/preclinical diagnosis [7], development of risk profiles [8, 9], discovery and classification of disease types [10] and personalized medicine [11]. However, access to clinical images for research purposes presents a number of challenges that may not always be obvious to computer science and image analysis researchers. This chapter provides an overview of the landscape and different approaches to address the challenges. Although examples will be frequently drawn from the radiological domain, generating large volumes of clinical data, the discussion applies to every type of clinical images and data.

The topics we will review include:

- Sources of clinical images: collected specifically for a research project or collected through routine clinical care
- The law covering access to patient data and when patient consent is required
- Obtaining the appropriate data governance applications
- Controls on the handling of sensitive data
- Anonymization of clinical imaging data and other linked data
- Secure access to clinical images through the use of Safe Havens/Trusted Research Environments

Computational Retinal Image Analysis. https://doi.org/10.1016/B978-0-08-102816-2.00021-6

Our findings are based on our experience of providing clinical images collected during routine care linked to other health data for research purposes at the Health Informatics Centre (HIC) at the University of Dundee, where the first author is Director. HIC leads work to enable clinical images, especially radiological data, captured at the point of care across Scotland to be made securely available at scale for research. This data is population-wide, including over 5.4 million people, and over 30 million series of images collected from 2006.

2 Sources of images and associated data

In this section we outline the different sources of image data for research and the main characteristics and constraints/challenges of working with each type of data.

2.1 Research collected images

Historically most AI/Medical Image Analysis/Deep Learning research has taken place on research-grade images which have been captured under stringent conditions using a specific machine with constrained environmental factors (such as contrast agent and at high resolution). Images were generally collected for a specific research project where consent was obtained from the participants prior to collection. Most studies tend to be in the order of hundreds or a few thousand images. There are several challenges when using such sources of images, including:

- *Limited generalizability:* The resulting algorithm/method may not generalize to a real-world clinical environment as it was not trained using data from a clinical setting (where the environmental factors are not constrained, and images are collected using many different machine types).
- *High cost:* The collection of images for a specific research project is generally expensive and constrains the scale of many studies.

2.2 Routinely collected images

Alternatively, routinely collected images, which are generated as part of clinical care, can be obtained and used for the secondary purpose of research. These images are often highly heterogeneous as they can be captured using varying technical specifications from a range of machines sourced from different vendors. Even images captured on identical machines may have significant variations in metadata due to differing operational conventions. It is often infeasible to obtain individual patient consent to use such imaging data. Larger volumes of images (than research collected images) may be available, in the order of tens/hundreds of thousands of images.

Challenges of using this alternative source of data for research include:

- *Large datasets:* Larger volumes of patient images are required to train algorithms/methods which can handle the heterogeneity of the data, compared to research studies. This leads to challenges in processing time, storage capacity and scalability.

- *Data governance constraints:* Using unconsented, routinely collected data requires additional data governance approvals and processes which, although varying with countries, are generally complex and time-consuming. To gain approval, additional constraints on the way the data is processed and securely managed may be enforced.
- *Data anonymization:* Anonymizing such heterogeneous data can be challenging.

2.3 Sources of ground truth data

From a machine learning perspective, the most important requirement for supervised learning is the availability of ground truth data to train algorithms. Ground truth data is the classification information associated with the data. This could be a simple binary label to indicate the presence of a particular feature within the pixel data; for example, whether or not an MRI image contains a lung nodule or coronary artery calcification, or a retinal scan contains sufficient signs of diabetic retinopathy for patient referral. Alternatively, the ground truth could be a detailed image feature, for example, a tumor boundary is marked up on the image.

There are several potential sources of ground truth data. For research collected images, other relevant clinical data is often collected at the time of scan, e.g., clinical diagnosis. For routinely collected images, the ground truth data many be captured within the specific image metadata (e.g., within the DICOM tag information) or within other databases containing details of the procedure (e.g., within a clinical report, most common in ophthalmology as images are not often saved in DICOM format).

In many instances, however, the ground truth data required is not captured either routinely during clinical care or at the time of a research collected scan, and trained individuals may have to annotate each image creating the ground truth information. Such hand curated data is often referred to as "gold standard" as taken as the most accurate result achievable. However, the preparation of such data is extremely labor intensive and furthermore, possibilities of re-use may be severely limited by data governance or IP constraints. We refer the reader to the chapter on validation in this book for further discussion on these points.

2.4 Linking clinical data to imaging data

The power of imaging data is increased when linked to other datasets. Data linkage is performed by obtaining different datasets relating to the same patient, from various data sources and data controllers. Examples of such data include:

- Patient clinical information
- Prescription data
- Hospital admissions
- Primary care data

- Birth and death records
- Disease registry data
- Genomic data
- Biobank data

In many instances these records have been captured over several decades and capture a longitudinal picture of the patient. Such linked longitudinal data provides, crucially, the potential for large-scale retrospective studies, which should theoretically be more cost-effective and efficient than prospective studies, especially when large data sets are required. For example, rather than training on clinical diagnosis of dementia at the time of a brain or retinal scan, the longitudinal health records could be used to see if a patient received a dementia diagnosis within 3 years of the scan.

3 Data governance

Regardless of whether images have been collected in a research setting or routinely, the imaging data (and any linked data) must be managed securely in a manner that maintains the data subject's privacy. Any applications to collect and use imaging data must explain how the research project will achieve such security and patient confidentiality. Understanding the landscape in which health care data is collected, shared, and utilized can help navigation through an increasingly complex system.

3.1 Key data protection terminology and concepts

The General Data Protection Regulation (GDPR) came into force across Europe in May 2018. However, each country also has its own data protection legislation and so each European country has incorporated the legal requirements of GDPR into their own country's laws. The rules of GDPR, therefore, sit alongside the legislation of each country so that researchers have to adhere to GDPR legislation and also any other relevant legislation of their specific state. For example, when ensuring legal compliance within the UK, both the GDPR legislation and also English or Scots law on confidentiality need to be considered. GDRP legislation will still apply in the UK after Brexit [12].

Key legislation in the US is the Health Insurance Portability and Accountability Act of 1996 (HIPAA) [13]. A significant difference between EU and US legislation is the GDPR's 'right to erasure' for which there is no comparable concept in HIPAA [14].

Key terminology used in Data Protection is given below. Although these terms are the wording of GDPR, other legislations across the world use similar terminology and key concepts.

Data Subject—A data subject is any 'identifiable natural person'. Patients are considered as data subjects about which clinical data is collected for a specified purpose.

Personal/Sensitive Data—Article 4 of GDPR categorizes certain types of data about patients as 'personal' or 'sensitive' including racial or ethnic origin, political opinions, religious or philosophical beliefs, or trade union membership, and the processing of genetic data, biometric data and health data. Whilst limitations generally exist on processing such data, research institutions are exempt and may capture such data as required, as per Article 9 of GDPR.

Anonymization—the removal of identifiable data from a data collection to make it irreversibly and fully anonymous. As per recital 26 of GDPR, fully anonymized data is not subject to data protection considerations as they apply only 'to any information concerning an identified or identifiable natural person'.

Pseudonymization—the reversible process of substitution of identifiable data fields (e.g., name, address, date of birth) from a data collection with a newly generated pseudonym key. The identifying data associated with the pseudonym key is held securely and separately from the non-identifying pseudonymized data collection itself. The pseudonym key can be used to link or join different data sets that have been subjected to the same pseudonymization process in a non-identifiable way. Because it is potentially reversible, personal data which have undergone pseudonymization is subject to data protection considerations as per recital 26, as 'it is considered to be information on an identifiable natural person'.

Implicit or Explicit consent—Patient agreement or 'consent' may be needed to get their approval for sharing of their patient data with other third parties. Article 4 of GDPR defines explicit consent as 'any freely given, specific, informed and unambiguous indication of the data subject's wishes by which he or she, by a statement or by a clear affirmative action, signifies agreement to the processing of personal data relating to him or her'. Under GDPR, where patient data is shared with others involved in the direct provision of care of that patient, consent is considered to be 'implicit' and already granted by the patient.

Secondary use for research purposes is specifically addressed in Article 5 of GDPR. It states that 'further processing for archiving purposes in the public interest, scientific or historical research purposes or statistical purposes shall, in accordance with Article 89 [1], must not be considered to be incompatible with the initial purposes.' Sharing of anonymized data to support health auditing or research initiatives is considered to be a public health interest and consistent with the provision of care to the patient more generally and consent is therefore implicitly granted.

Children under 16 are treated as a special category and where consent is needed it should happen via a guardian with parental responsibility for the child.

Primary Data Controllers—Data controllers have responsibility for handling all requests for shared access to data and for ensuring a 'lawful basis for processing' of that data [15]. A data controller must have a legitimate 'need' for using the data (provision of patient care for example) and the information contained in the data should be appropriate to support that need only.

Secondary Data Processors—Data can be shared with secondary parties for aggregation and further analysis for secondary research purposes [16]. Secondary parties do not have direct responsibility for the collection and maintenance of the shared patient data itself. Examples of secondary processing bodies for conducting national research within the UK include NHS Digital [17], the Clinical Practice Research

Datalink (CPRD) [18], the Secure Anonymized Information Linkage (SAIL) in Wales [19, 20], and the electronic Data Research and Innovation Service (eDRIS) in Scotland [21]. Other secondary processors include disease specific research registries or commercial initiatives such as insurers or solicitors. Patient data held in the 'cloud' on their behalf by a third party is also considered to be shared with a secondary data processor (the 'cloud' provider).

Lawful basis for processing—The lawful basis for holding patient data is to directly provide care to the patient. However, a lawful basis for processing also includes ensuring that appropriate technical steps have been taken to ensure security, privacy and integrity of data. For research the lawful basis normally is in the "public interest".

Third Country Transfers—GDPR covers transfers of data to countries that are external to the European Union including the United States of America (USA). The EU publishes a list of countries that it classifies as having equivalent data protection legislation to allow for third country transfer of data and this includes the USA.

Data protection by design—GDPR expects that data controllers be demonstrably open and proactive in their documented approach to data protection. Best practice encourages open communication with patients about the use of their data and sharing of that data. This may take the form of prominently displayed notice boards or statements on the practice website explaining how data is confidentially held for patients and when medical records might be shared for purposes other than direct patient care.

Data breach notification—In the event of unexpected disclosure of data to third parties as a result of accidental or malicious breaches, GDPR specifies that data controllers must notify their data protection supervisory authority of those data breaches within 72 hours where there is a risk to the data protection rights of the individuals concerned. In the UK the supervisory authority is the Information Commissioners Office (ICO) [22].

Administrative sanctions—GDPR provides for more significant penalties for blatant infringements of the regulation. Financial penalties can be imposed of up to £17 m (€20 m) or 4% of global turnover.

3.2 Applications to access data for research

In practical terms, to access data for research several approvals are required before data is provided. For example, within the UK this is often in the form of ethical and Caldicott approval for access to health data. A 'Caldicott guardian' is the data controller for each National Health Service (NHS) board. In addition to these, other documents can be required such as data sharing agreements and privacy impact assessments.

Regardless of the specific differences in the application processes within different regions and states, all research projects need to consider several key aspects of data protection when designing any research study using patient data. Although the precise wording and structure of application forms to access data may differ, they are generally pertaining to:

- How will patient confidentially be protected?
- What controls will be in place around the release of data?

- Who will have access?
- What data security controls will be in place?
- Who is the data controller? Are there any secondary data processors?
- Is the project research in the public interest?

As described above, data controllers are responsible for the security of their data and there can be considerable associated costs if they do not implement appropriate controls, such as those under GDPR. It is, therefore, understandable that data controllers may be hesitant to share their data for research as it represents an additional risk. Therefore, any application requesting data for research should consider the risks to the data controllers and explain how these risks will be mitigated. The controls can be classed into three key areas: safe data, safe people and safe access. Each of these is discussed below and need to be considered when designing a data management plan and completing data governance applications.

4 Controls

4.1 Safe data

4.1.1 Identifying information

Removing any uniquely identifying information (e.g., name, email address, phone number) for all individuals ensures the anonymity of a data set—there is no way of identifying or re-identifying the individual. However, rather than removing all unique identifying information, it is possible to encrypt or substitute an individual's unique ID with a pseudonym, creating a pseudonymized data set. A patient's pseudonym can be replicated across all datasets to use for data linkage. This allows future datasets containing the same individuals to be linked over time. There also exist indirect identifying variables in datasets (sometimes called *quasi-identifiers*) [23]. Such variables represent a risk of identification if someone knows the background information of an individual beforehand which means that they can identify the individual from the characteristics in the dataset, e.g., gender, age, location, job, diagnosis.

A statistical approach to test for identifying information is for two members of the research team, who know the data and the study population, to classify the variables independently as an identifier or not an identifier. A measure of agreement, such as Cohen's kappa, can then be calculated [24]. If the value of kappa is over 0.8 then this is generally accepted as overall agreement and a discussion can be held to resolve any of the disagreements. If the kappa is <0.8 then it is recommended that a larger group of individuals meet to reach a consensus.

4.1.2 Acceptance threshold for re-identification

There will always be some risk of re-identification in a data set, so it is sensible to specify a threshold where the risk level is acceptable [25]. One simple method is to set a minimum size for a 'cell' in a table, i.e., the minimum frequency of individuals appearing within all combinations of values for all variables; for instance, the number of males aged 33 with Type 2 diabetes in a database with the quasi-identifiers gender, age and diabetic status [26]. Commonly this size is set to 5 (a control to be agreed with the data controllers) but there is no agreed standard. When choosing a threshold, the security and privacy practices in place, the sensitivity of the data, and the motives and capacity of the research team to re-identify the data [27] all need to be considered. Once an acceptable threshold has been determined, the probability of re-identification is measured on the dataset [28]. If this probability is higher than the threshold then transformation of the data should be performed to take this probability below the threshold.

4.1.3 Transformation of data

With regards to quasi-identifiers, there are a number of ways to transform a dataset to reduce the probability of re-identification. Such methods should minimize the changes to the data while ensuring that the probability is below the threshold. Four different techniques are recommended and a combination of these can be applied in practice [29]:

1. *Generalization:* This is when the value of a variable is changed to a more general value. For example, a date of birth or date of diagnosis can be generalized to a month and year of birth.
2. *Suppression:* This involves removing specific values from a dataset (i.e., induced missingness).
3. *Randomization:* This is a method of adding noise to a variable. The noise can come from a uniform or some other distribution. For example, a date of birth may be shifted a number of days backward or forward.
4. *Subsampling:* A random subset of the dataset is released to the research team rather than the full dataset. This decreases the probability of re-identification. However, it also can potentially reduce the power/impact of the research.

4.1.4 Considerations when anonymizing pixel data

Images can be highly identifiable. It is good practice for clinicians who are carrying out research to use anonymized data for their research even though they can see identifiable data in their clinical role. As well as fulfilling the required rules of data governance when using data for a different purpose than clinical care, this reduces the chance of the clinician biasing their research. Unfortunately, due to the nature of imaging data, the identity of a patient can be very obvious to clinicians given a particular scan if they have treated that patient directly through their clinical role. Hence it is advisable for such studies that, where possible, researchers on the team who have not directly treated the patients view or annotate these particular images.

For certain types of scans it can be possible to combine images into a three dimensional (3D) representation. For example, for head MRI or CT scans, the 3D image can be highly identifiable upon re-construction as it will display the 3D face of a person. Most researchers who view these images do not know the individual patients and cannot, therefore, identify them, but the potential risk should be considered. Different methods, like anatomical surface modification [30], obscure the patient's identity and prevent facial recognition when rendering medical resonance images of the head in 3D [31]. This is increasingly important as data sets are provided for AI-based projects, with a higher risk of facial recognition.

4.1.5 Software to anonymize DICOM images

DICOM (Digital Imaging and Communications in Medicine) is a standard for storing imaging data which contains the pixel data along with >5000 metadata tags which include text data about the image. Identifiable data can be held within text-based tags and also within the pixel data itself. Some machines, e.g., ultrasound, burn unique identifiers on the image pixels.

There are many software tools available which will anonymize DICOM files. Examples include XNAT [32, 33], Clinical Trials Processor - CTP [34] and DICOM Confidential [35, 36]. Another option for anonymizing imaging data is to convert images into another standard format such as NIFTI (Neuroimaging Informatics Technology Initiative). NIFTI stores image data as a single 3D image (.nii file) rather than separate image files for each slice of the scan as per the DICOM standard. The NIFTI format only stores pixel data and metadata related to the image itself, excluding the patient and study information, unlike a DICOM image. Therefore, converting a DICOM file to NIFTI format is one method of anonymizing DICOM files.

4.2 Safe people and organizations

This section outlines how organizational design and operating procedures can improve data security.

4.2.1 Indexing and linking

General principles of good data governance include only providing the minimum amount of data to fulfill the specified role, and that data should be anonymized where possible. If data required for research analysis are to be provided from a single data controller then the anonymization process can be reasonably straight forward: the data controller replaces the identifiable data with pseudo-IDs for the particular study and transfers the data for access (see access models below) by the research team. However, when data is required from multiple data controllers the data has to be linked prior to research analysis. There are recognized methods for carrying out linkage where no single organization needs to see both the descriptive and identifiable data from another organization through separation of Indexer and Linker roles.

The Guiding Principles for Data Linkage [13] defines an *Indexer* as an "Individual (or body) who receives personal data from one or more Data Controller and determines which records in each dataset relate to the same individual (or entity). The Indexer then creates a unique reference for each individual (or entity) and a corresponding key to allow the data from the different sources to be joined". A *Linker* is defined as an "Individual (or body) who receives datasets from Data Controllers and links them together using a key created by the Indexer".

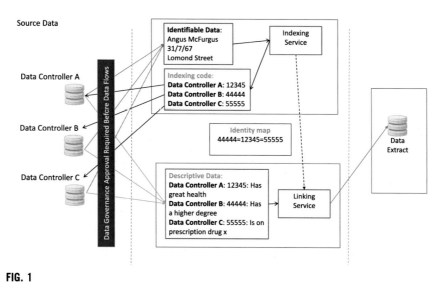

FIG. 1

Example of the separation of indexer and linker functions.

Fig. 1 provides an example of how the separation of Indexer and Linker can support the anonymization process where linkage between datasets from three different organizations is required.

In the example, each data controller organization sends the indexing service the identifiable data they have about Angus (such as Name, Address and Data of Birth) without any of the descriptive data which they also hold. The indexing service then returns a unique code/number (a pseudonym) to refer to Angus. This is different for each data controller organization to prevent cross-organizational linkage. The data controller organizations then prepare a data extract which includes the descriptive data and the unique code/number for each person within the cohort, without including the identifiable data. In the example for Angus above, Data Controller A would prepare a data extract about Angus which would only contain 12,345 (the unique code) linked to "has great health", not including anything about the fact that this information is for a person called Angus, of Lomond Street, DOB 31/7/67. Each data extract from each organization is then given to the linking service who then combines the records using the unique/code mapping from the identity map provided by the indexing service.

Using such a method, no single organization ever gets to see the linked identifiable data of another organization. The indexing service can only see the identifiable data without any descriptive data. The linking service can only see the descriptive data without any associated identifiable data. Each data controller organization can only see their own descriptive data linked to identifiable data and cannot see any other organization's data. Researchers can only see the anonymized linked extract provided by the linking service with a completely new pseudonym.

It can be challenging and time-consuming to coordinate this process afresh for each research project, though there are organizations that provide support for data linkage from multiple sources. This process can also be automated if it is to be performed many times to support numerous research projects (each of which would use different identifiers).

4.2.2 Trusted third parties

To support the anonymization of data, trusted third parties can be used. These can provide either the role of Indexer or the role of Linker as in the example above.

Alternatively, in some instances, data controllers are content that a single trusted third party carries out both roles of Indexer and Linker, i.e., there is no separation of roles. In this instance, the trusted third party receives all of the identifiable data and descriptive data from different sources and then uses the identifiable data to link and anonymize the information before providing an extract for a research project.

This method can be considerably less time consuming but it is technically complex and increases the risk to the data controller in terms of data protection. So other controls can be put in place to mitigate these risks. If data is to be transferred to a trusted third party, then data sharing agreements need to be in place and the trusted third party also have other legal obligations.

4.2.3 Who will be accessing the research data

Researchers who are given access to clinical data for research may be required to complete data governance training before they are given access to the data. They may also be required to sign non-disclosure agreements and other relevant documentation.

The organization which is carrying out the research can also be important. For example, academic researchers who are associated with a university or a public body may have fewer constraints on access to sensitive data for research than a person carrying out research on behalf of a commercial organization. It may be that a commercial organization could commission a research group to carry out a piece of research on their behalf. Individuals from the commercial organization do not see the data directly but do see the results from the research itself.

4.3 Safe access

4.3.1 Transferring data

How data will be transferred between organizations should also be considered within the controls. Transfer of sensitive data (even if anonymized) via email attachments, for example, is not a safe mechanism as it is generally not encrypted during flight. Secure transfer such as SSH File Transfer Protocol (sFTP) should be considered.

4.3.2 Data hosted on a researcher managed environment

Data leaving the control of a data controller and being hosted within a different environment, brings a new set of associated risks to the data controller. There are many examples of anonymized clinical datasets. These are held on university managed servers under the control of the research groups who access the data through access permissions. This is often the case for data from a consented research project. Whilst such environments can be made secure, for example through adherence to standards such as ISO27001 [37], copies of the data could theoretically be made and transferred to other individuals/organizations/environments without the knowledge of the data controller organization. Legally binding constraints and data sharing agreements can be put in place to mitigate this risk but many data controllers feel that the risk is too high to accept, especially for non-consented research projects using routinely collected data.

4.3.3 Safe Havens/trusted research environments

Increasingly, environments called *Safe Havens* or *Trusted Research Environments* have been utilized to support the secure analysis of patient data. These environments are often ISO 27001 certified [37] and host the data under the control of the data controllers, enabling access to be revoked at any time. Many Safe Havens are virtual environments where researchers log on to a virtual machine to run their analysis on the data. Other safe havens require access from a physical location where there might be additional security such as CCTV (for access to highly sensitive data). Generally, patient-level data cannot be exported from the environment. There is a disclosure control process where any output from a research group's analysis is checked by the Safe Haven staff for potentially individual-level data prior to release. For instance, graphs of trends are allowed to be exported whilst tables containing cells with patient numbers <5 are not (as per Section 4.1.2). Access to the internet is often limited within the environment to prevent data export. Software tools, such as statistical analysis packages, are provided for researchers to analyze the data. It is sometimes possible to install software applications developed by research groups.

Many Safe Havens also require other controls for access, e.g., safe people (signed non-disclosure and data sharing agreements, only access to researchers from public bodies) and safe data (all data governance approvals are in place, only the minimum amount of data is provided to answer a specific question, data is anonymized, etc.).

Many Safe Havens provide not only the virtual environment for researcher access but also other functions to support the provisioning of data for research, such as acting as the trusted third party for linkage or carrying out the anonymization of data.

4.3.4 Federated or distributed analysis

An alternative to accessing data within Safe Haven environments is *federated* or *distributed analysis*. Using this model, researchers can analyze data but never view or extract it. Algorithms can be run in real-time remotely on the data held in each location, and the aggregated results are returned. Data controllers maintain full control of the data and its access permissions, safeguarding the intellectual property, governance procedures and data disclosure concerns of the data controller. An example of this methodology for text-based data is DataSHIELD [38].

Federated learning [39] is a class of distributed machine learning algorithms aimed to train a reliable centralized model with training data distributed over a network of clients having possibly slow network connections. For example, clients can compute locally updated model and send them to a central server in charge of aggregation and global model updating. For an example of algorithm see for instance Federated Averaging [40].

4.3.5 Challenges of assembling large quantities of clinical data within data governance controls

There are additional practical considerations when accessing clinical imaging data in this new era of "big data." Imaging data required for deep learning can be petabytes in size and thus the generation of separate copies for each research project is impractical. In addition, hundreds of GPUs and fast data access are ideally required for large-scale deep learning analysis. Researchers need to be able to develop their own software and train algorithms on the data. These factors push the boundaries of traditional Safe Haven environments, which have historically been adequate for text-based "small" data analysis such as for longitudinal epidemiological research.

Safe Havens provided by public organizations are evolving to meet these demands for access to large volumes of images backed by significant computational resources. Environments are becoming available which support researchers installing their own tools and developing software and AI within the environments themselves whilst still hosting the data securely.

Looking forward, Safe Havens environments are likely to move to secure cloud environments rather than being provisioned by public bodies from their own managed servers as a private cloud. There are also several examples of industry also developing environments where researchers can securely access data and develop tools; examples include Google Deepmind and IBM Watson.

5 Conclusions

We have introduced a range of issues associated with obtaining imaging data for research. In practice, there are many experts trained to help guide researchers through this landscape, providing practical support. Within most research organizations there are data governance experts who understand the processes and the legal constraints and can support the completion of data governance and ethical applications. Most health care providers (as data controllers) are also able to direct researchers to data governance experts who can guide researchers through their processes for access to routinely collected images and linked datasets. If the health care provider does not have the suitable processes in place or suitable data they should be able to direct you to other providers such as secondary processors or National data providers.

Many of the controls listed here are enforced by data controllers or secondary data processors as a matter of course and researchers are often not required to implement such controls from scratch themselves. It is just helpful to understand why the controls are in place and to adhere to them.

Looking forward it is likely that access to routinely collected, annotated clinical images become more easily available for research purposes and that the data governance application processes become more streamlined. It is an exciting time for the field with many public bodies and industry recognizing the potential of training AI using clinical images and endeavoring to build the required infrastructures and processes to support secure access at scale, backed by appropriate hardware.

References

[1] C. Parmar, P. Grossmann, J. Bussink, P. Lambin, H.J.W.L. Aerts, Machine learning methods for quantitative radiomic biomarkers, Sci. Rep. 5 (2015) 13087.

[2] C. Shen, Z. Liu, M. Guan, J. Song, Y. Lian, S. Wang, et al., 2D and 3D CT radiomics features prognostic performance comparison in non-small cell lung cancer, Transl. Oncol. 10 (6) (2017) 886–894.

[3] R.J. Gillies, P.E. Kinahan, H. Hricak, Radiomics: images are more than pictures, they are data, Radiology 278 (2) (2015) 563–577.

[4] E. Rios Velazquez, C. Parmar, Y. Liu, T.P. Coroller, G. Cruz, O. Stringfield, et al., Somatic mutations drive distinct imaging phenotypes in lung cancer, Cancer Res. 77 (14) (2017) 3922.

[5] P. Kickingereder, U. Neuberger, D. Bonekamp, P.L. Piechotta, M. Götz, A. Wick, et al., Radiomic subtyping improves disease stratification beyond key molecular, clinical, and standard imaging characteristics in patients with glioblastoma, Neuro Oncol. 20 (6) (2018) 848–857. https://doi.org/10.1093/neuonc/nox188.

[6] A. Chaddad, C. Desrosiers, M. Toews, B. Abdulkarim, Predicting survival time of lung cancer patients using radiomic analysis, Oncotarget 8 (61) (2017) 104393–104407.

[7] P.J. Snyder, L.N. Johnson, Y.Y. Lim, C.Y. Santos, J. Alber, P. Maruff, et al., Nonvascular retinal imaging markers of preclinical Alzheimer's disease, Alzheimer's Dement. 4 (2016) 169–178.

[8] S.D. McGarry, S.L. Hurrell, A.L. Kaczmarowski, E.J. Cochran, J. Connelly, S.D. Rand, et al., Magnetic resonance imaging-based radiomic profiles predict patient prognosis in newly diagnosed glioblastoma before therapy, Tomography 2 (3) (2016) 223–228.

[9] W. Yu, C. Tang, B.P. Hobbs, X. Li, E.J. Koay, I.I. Wistuba, et al., Development and validation of a predictive radiomics model for clinical outcomes in stage I non-small cell lung cancer, Int. J. Radiat. Oncol. Biol. Phys. 102 (2018) 1090–1097.

[10] C.-Y. Hsu, M. Doubrovin, C.-H. Hua, O. Mohammed, B.L. Shulkin, S. Kaste, et al., Radiomics features differentiate between normal and tumoral high-Fdg uptake, Sci. Rep. 8 (1) (2018) 3913.

[11] J. Atutornu, C.M. Hayre, Personalised medicine and medical imaging: opportunities and challenges for contemporary health care, J. Med. Imag. Radiat. Sci. 49 (4) (2018) 352–359.

[12] UK Government, Data Protection Act, Available from: http://www.legislation.gov.uk/ukpga/2018/12/pdfs/ukpga_20180012_en.pdf, 2018.

[13] The Scottish Government, Joined-up Data for Better Decisions—Guiding Principles for Data Linkage, 2012.

[14] S.A. Tovino, The HIPAA privacy rule and the EU GDPR: illustrative comparisons, Seton Hall Law Rev. 47 (2016) 973.

[15] British Medical Association, GPs as Data Controllers, [19/12/2017]. Available from: https://www.bma.org.uk/advice/employment/ethics/confidentiality-and-health-records/gps-as-data-controllers, 2016.

[16] A. Burgun, E. Bernal-Delgado, W. Kuchinke, T. van Staa, J. Cunningham, E. Lettieri, et al., Health data for public health: towards new ways of combining data sources to support research efforts in Europe, Yearb. Med. Inform. 26 (1) (2017) 235–240.

[17] NHS Digital, Data and Information, Available from: https://digital.nhs.uk/article/191/Find-data-and-publications.

[18] Clinical Practice Research Datalink, Clinical Practice Research Datalink, Available from: https://www.cprd.com.

[19] NHS Wales Informatics Service, Secure Anonymised Information Linkage (SAIL), Available from: https://saildatabank.com/.

[20] D.V. Ford, K.H. Jones, J.P. Verplancke, R.A. Lyons, G. John, G. Brown, et al., The SAIL databank: building a national architecture for e-health research and evaluation, BMC Health Serv. Res. 9 (2009) 157.

[21] ISD Scotland, Electronic Data Research and Innovation Service (eDRIS), Available from: http://www.isdscotland.org/Products-and-Services/eDRIS/.

[22] Data Linkage Western Australia, Available from: https://www.datalinkage-wa.org.au/.

[23] S.L. Garfinkel, De-Identification of Personal Information, National Institute of Standards and Technology Internal Report, 2015. Available from: https://nvlpubs.nist.gov/nistpubs/ir/2015/NIST.IR.8053.pdf.

[24] J. Cohen, A coefficient of agreement for nominal scales, Educ. Psychol. Meas. 20 (1) (1960) 37–46.

[25] Institute of Medicine (IOM), Sharing Clinical Trial Data: Maximizing Benefits, Minimizing Risk, The National Academies Press, Washington, DC, 2015.

[26] L. Sweeney, k-Anonymity: a model for protecting privacy, Int. J. Uncertain. Fuzziness Knowl. Based Syst. 10 (5) (2002) 557–570.

[27] M. Eekdfvrrtl, Evaluating patient re-identification risk from hospital prescription records, Can. J. Hosp. Pharm. 62 (4) (2009) 307–319.

[28] K. El Emam, Methods for the de-identification of electronic health records for genomic research, Genome Med. 3 (4) (2011) 25.

[29] K. El Emam, L. Arbuckle, Anonymizing Health Data: Case Studies and Methods to Get You Started, O'Reilly Media, Sebastopol, CA, 2013.

[30] M. Milchenko, D. Marcus, Obscuring surface anatomy in volumetric imaging data, Neuroinformatics 11 (1) (2013) 65–75.

[31] F. Budin, D. Zeng, A. Ghosh, E. Bullitt, Preventing facial recognition when rendering MR images of the head in three dimensions, Med. Image Anal. 12 (3) (2008) 229–239.

[32] D. Abbott, What Is Digital Curation? Digital Curation Centre, Edinburgh, 2014. Available from: http://www.dcc.ac.uk/resources/briefing-papers/introduction-curation/what-digital-curation.

[33] D.S. Marcus, A.F. Fotenos, J.G. Csernansky, J.C. Morris, R.L. Buckner, Open access series of imaging studies: longitudinal MRI data in nondemented and demented older adults, J. Cogn. Neurosci. 22 (12) (2010) 2677–2684.

[34] K.Y.E. Aryanto, A. Broekema, M. Oudkerk, P.M.A. van Ooijen, Implementation of an anonymisation tool for clinical trials using a clinical trial processor integrated with an existing trial patient data information system, Eur. Radiol. 22 (1) (2012) 144–151.

[35] DICOM Confidential Wiki, Available from: https://sourceforge.net/p/privacyguard/wiki/Home/.

[36] D. Rodríguez González, T. Carpenter, J.I. van Hemert, et al., An open source toolkit for medical imaging de-identification, Eur. Radiol. 20 (2010) 1896.

[37] IOS. ISO/IEC 27000 Family—Information Security Management Systems: International Organization for Standardization; Available from: https://www.iso.org/isoiec-27001-information-security.html.

[38] R.C. Wilson, O.W. Butters, D. Avraam, J. Baker, J.A. Tedds, A. Turner, et al., DataSHIELD—new directions and dimensions, Data Sci. J. 16 (2017) 21.

[39] J. Konecny, H.B. MacMahan, Y. F, P. Richtarik, A.T. Suresh, D. Bacon, Federated learning: strategy to improve communication efficiency, in: Proceedings of the 29th Conference on Neural Information Processing Systems (NIPS 2016), Barcelona, Spain, 2016.

[40] H.B. MacMahan, E. Moore, B. Agüera y Arcas, Federated Learning of Deep Networks Using Model Averaging, https://uk.arxiv.org/abs/1602.05629v1, 2016.

Technical and clinical challenges of A.I. in retinal image analysis

21

Gilbert Lim[a], Wynne Hsu[a], Mong Li Lee[a], Daniel Shu Wei Ting[b], Tien Yin Wong[b]

[a]*School of Computing, National University of Singapore, Singapore, Singapore*

[b]*Singapore Eye Research Institute, Singapore National Eye Centre, Singapore, Singapore*

1 Introduction

Artificial intelligence (A.I.) has been playing an increasingly important role in retinal image analysis [1]. This is a natural progression of the field in as much of retinal image analysis has essentially been on automating processes that are traditionally performed by clinicians and other trained human experts, with a view towards duplicating their results as closely as possible. In this sense, such retinal image analysis methods can be understood as attempts to replicate human intelligence, albeit within a narrowly specialized domain.

The present revolution in retinal image analysis is focused on a particular subset of A.I., namely *machine learning*. While A.I. can broadly be described as either mimicking or augmenting human intelligence, machine learning specifically requires that the A.I. system *learn by itself* from the data. This important distinction can perhaps best be explained through a concrete case study, on the evolution of the detection of a particular disease condition, diabetic retinopathy, from retinal images.

Diabetic retinopathy (DR) is a complication of diabetes mellitus and DR is a leading cause for acquired visual loss in working aged adults globally, affecting more than 100 million people [2, 3]. DR manifests itself through capillary wall dilatation, leakages and ruptures, leading to microaneurysms, edema/exudates and hemorrhages respectively [4]. Typically, DR is classified into five stages as none, mild, moderate, severe and proliferative DR (Fig. 1). Importantly, early detection, appropriate referral of more severe stages of DR and subsequent treatment can prevent up to 98% of visual loss [2]. Therefore, it is widely recommended that all patients with diabetes are regularly screened for DR, and referred for treatment when necessary [5].

Conventionally, a retinal examination can only be conducted in the clinics by specialist physicians—ophthalmologists. More recently, teleretinal screening using retinal photography with measurement of DR signs by human assessors has been shown to be a cost-effective method to screen populations with diabetes, especially for those living in remote areas [6]. Such DR screening using retinal photography, however, requires trained human assessors. However, given the rising diabetes prevalence and

Computational Retinal Image Analysis. https://doi.org/10.1016/B978-0-08-102816-2.00022-8

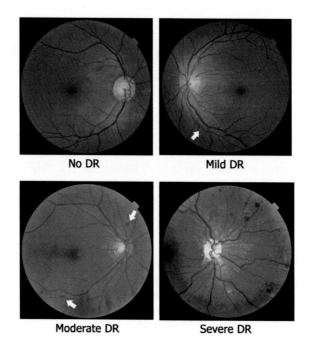

FIG. 1

Examples of retinal photographs exhibiting increasing levels of diabetic severity.

ageing population, the manpower required for retinal imaging screening may be unsustainable. For example, it has been estimated that even in a small country like Singapore, it will require significant resources to screen the estimated 400,000 diabetes patients annually [6a]. These factors, based on the significant clinical and public health need, the ability to use a focused technology (retinal photography) to impact on care, A.I. using deep learning may be a potential solution to rectify the long-term manpower shortage issue. While such a concept is elegant, there are significant technical and clinical challenges [7]. This chapter will focus on some of these challenges.

Common forms of retinal image analysis can broadly be divided into:

- *Classification.* In classification, the retinal images are considered to be sufficient to be indicative of certain medical diagnoses (e.g., presence of mild or severe DR), possibly in conjunction with other patient data. The goal of an automated system has then essentially been to replicate the grades assigned by reference human graders following a chosen scheme, as accurately as possible.
- *Segmentation.* In segmentation, the goal is to identify different areas or regions of interest in the retinal image (e.g., microaneurysms or hard exudates at the macula). These regions often correspond to anatomical features such as the optic disc, macula, and blood vessels. Segmentation is closely related to object detection, where the exact region boundaries may not be required.

- *Registration.* In registration, multiple views of the same image data are transformed and aligned to fit the same coordinate system (e.g., determine if there is an increasing or decreasing number of microaneurysms in a particular area of the retina in patient which has been imaged over time). This is useful when imaging cannot capture the entire region of interest in a single instance, and when the data is to be mapped to an atlas.
- *Enhancement & Restoration.* In enhancement, image data is processed to more clearly highlight salient characteristics. In restoration, artifacts introduced by the imaging source or during storage and transmission (e.g., due to compression) are repaired. They are often employed as preprocessing steps before other forms of primary analysis are applied.
- *Modeling.* In modeling, image data is used to infer features about the underlying population, or the data itself. This may be exploited to generate further synthetic image data both to support the inferences made, as well as used in combination with other markers to estimate associations with risk factors [8, 8a].

2 Progression of A.I. in retinal imaging

Retinal image analysis is often A.I. by definition, when the objective of the analysis is to replicate an existing human workflow. Take for instance DR screening, where best-practice diagnostic procedure has been formalized for clinical practitioners. Here, to classify an image, graders adhere to various recognized retinal image grading schemes such as the International Clinical Diabetic Retinopathy Disease Severity Scale (ICDRSS), the Early Treatment Diabetic Retinopathy Study Scheme (ETDRS), the Scottish Diabetic Retinopathy Grading Scheme, etc.

The earliest A.I. systems for DR screening date from the early 1980s, and were implemented in a handcrafted manner, with researchers manually decomposing the problem into multiple subtasks within a predefined workflow. Some of these subtasks could then be performed by an A.I. module, depending on what computational capabilities were available. For example, Akita and Kuga [9] studied loop-composable sets on thinned binary blood vessels, and Laÿ et al. [10] applied mathematical morphology to detect microaneurysms. In both these cases, the features to the A.I. (line loops and morphological regions respectively) were explicitly defined by the researchers, usually aided by domain knowledge (e.g., the hexagonal raster in [10] was set to have a minimum value of 4–7 pixels, derived from the average expected capillary width). The output of these features was likewise processed by explicit rules, following the *expert system* methodology prevalent at the time. Therefore, while these systems could qualify as A.I., because they sought to perform tasks (e.g., counting microaneurysms) that a human did, they did not involve machine learning since all of the underlying logic was designed by hand.

Although this expert system approach performed acceptably in certain medical settings such as computer-aided diagnosis from symptoms, signs and labs [11], the imaging modality posed special challenges. A fundamental issue was that of articulating "obvious" visual appearances to an A.I. system. For instance, a description of "microaneurysms" as "fluorescent spots" [12] in angiogram images would be quickly understood by human students, especially when provided with a few examples, aided by an intuitive understanding of biology. However, imparting this definition to an A.I. is not straightforward. Morphological or filter-based approaches might encode the basic idea of picking up small regions which are darker than their surroundings, but they would tend towards false positives that humans would generally never commit—points at the junction of or within blood vessels may fulfil the basic definition of a microaneurysm as programmed, for example.

For a period, the answer to this was to engage in increasingly involved *feature engineering*, with researchers trying to design and utilize more-strongly discriminative features [13], and combine them with more-specific rules [14]. To ignore microaneurysm false positives at vessel junctions, additional validation involving connectivity, intensity and contrast features may be considered [15]. Good feature engineering however relies heavily on domain knowledge [16], and can be difficult to scale in a principled manner. This was less of an issue when both training and validation data was relatively scarce, but its limitations became apparent as imaging became increasingly digitized.

The attraction of introducing machine learning to undertake at least part of the reasoning process was evident, and the transition began with formerly human-determined thresholds being quantitatively optimized from available data. For example, the choice of pixel inclusion criteria was an important decision in region growing for lesion detection. Earlier work such as [14] would define rules such as:

$$i \geq i_p - x\left(i_p - i_b\right) \tag{1}$$

where i is the gray-level of the pixel being considered, i_p is the gray-level of the seed pixel for the region, and i_b is the gray-level of the background. x was then a parameter that could be adjusted, to control region growth. The authors informally noted that a value of x between 0.50 and 0.75 achieved reasonable compromise between accurate segmentation and overgrowth, and chose $x = 0.50$ to obtain their results. Such free parameters would gradually be more-rigorously *learned* from data (e.g., [17]).

It was gradually realized that retinal image analysis could be framed as a machine learning problem, with statistical classifiers such as Bayesian, Mahalanobis and k nearest-neighbor (kNN) classifiers being applied to the generated region/lesion candidates [18]. This hybrid approach combined handcrafted computer vision expert systems with machine learning methods and reduced the influence of ad hoc rules. For example, Niemeijer et al. [19] built on the previously described morphological method by Spencer and Frame [14, 20] by classifying red lesion candidates with kNN, with the k parameter determined from the training set. Under this general framework, increasingly-sophisticated machine learning classifiers such as neural networks [21], support vector machines [22] and random forests [23] have been explored, alongside concurrent development in feature extraction that has involved Gaussian filters [24], matched filters [25], clustering [16], eigensystems [26], wavelet transforms [27], maximally stable extremal regions [28], splats [29] and fuzzy image processing [30], among other methods. Alongside the above hybrid approaches, end-to-end machine learning—where even the intermediate features were automatically learnt—had actually been tried as early as 1996, with a single hidden layer neural network trained directly on the pixels of 20×20 image tiles, to classify the tile as containing hemorrhages, exudates or vessels [31]. However, such end-to-end learning for retinal imaging would largely be abandoned for a long period, with rare exceptions (e.g., [32]). Neural networks generally reverted to being utilized as a classifier on predefined or preprocessed features, e.g., summary statistics from primary component analysis (PCA), or candidate features such as size, shape and hue [21, 33–35]. A more comprehensive review of these advances may be found in Ref. [36].

Machine learning directly on image representations would only return much later with deep convolutional neural networks [37], and would thereafter be reported to attain human-level classification performance on full retinal fundus photographs [38–40, 40a]. This broad shift from hybrid towards end-to-end machine learning was not limited to classification, with various retinal structure detection [41] and pixel-level retinal image segmentation [42–45] tasks also increasingly handled with deep architectures such as the U-Net [46]. This mirrors a similar trend observed in general medical imaging [1].

The key drivers of retinal image analysis moving from custom feature-based A.I. to end-to-end machine learning are threefold: increase in quantity of digitized image data, fundamental technical advances in deep neural network architectures and training procedures, and the exploitation of dedicated graphics processing units (GPUs) for large-scale model learning. It is the recent confluence of these factors that has led to the explosion in popularity of end-to-end machine learning in the field. However, this has also brought with it some new and unique challenges, which shall be discussed in the following section.

3 Technical challenges

For a long time, the main technical challenge of A.I. in retinal image analysis has resided in good *feature engineering*, which lay at the heart of earlier rule-based and hybrid systems. Without good features, training models with low generalization error is not possible in general [47]. The choice and design of these features were heavily influenced by both what the researchers thought was relevant to the task from experience and prior literature, and what was practical to implement. The most prevalent features tended to satisfy both conditions. For example, since microaneurysms are dot-like with a profile that could be modeled by a 2D Gaussian in theory, Gaussian filter responses were obvious features to use [48]. This was of course not as straightforward where the conditions were more varied in appearance (e.g., hemorrhages) or were difficult to enunciate (e.g., the difference between a hemorrhage and the macula, or a vessel crossover segment).

One popular approach is to begin with a large set of plausible features and extract a subset or combination of informative features through experimentation (a process known as *feature selection*). Abràmoff et al. [49] for example begins by constructing a collection of features, which are determined to be "more" (e.g., Gabor wavelets), "somewhat" (e.g., Gaussian filters) or "less" (e.g., edge detector outputs) physiologically plausible. From an initial total of 253 features, they computed the most discriminant twelve features with sequential forward-floating search. Interestingly, other than two a priori probability features, nine of the ten remaining most-discriminative features are some flavor of Gaussian. The direct implication is therefore that features thought by human experts to be the most appropriate, may not in actuality be so. As such, feature engineering has been recognized as being as much of an art as a science, and automatically learning good features has been proposed to be desirable [50].

This automatic learning of intermediate features is exactly what happens with end-to-end machine learning, most notably deep learning. Consider a convolutional neural network taking retinal images as the input, and a disease classification as the output. Other than the number of, and spatial dimensions of, the network filterbanks, there need not be any further hints about what the network model should watch out for; the model *learns* what is necessary to classify retinal images on its own, by adjusting its weights according to gradient descent.

It should be remembered that while deep learning has proven to be a successful approach to medical image analysis, it is not a "silver bullet" that is appropriate for all imaging tasks. Some of its limitations will be discussed in the next subsections. Practitioners should keep in mind that A.I. is a means to an end, and simpler models may be better preferred over heavyweight cutting-edge models, under the right circumstances. Furthermore, due to the highly-empirical nature of deep learning research at present, it is advisable to extensively validate model performance on diverse datasets [40].

Technical challenges pertaining to A.I. in retinal imaging broadly revolve around two themes—data and models. We inspect each of these in turn.

3.1 Quantity of data

The availability of a large amount of data has been a fundamental prerequisite of successful end-to-end machine learning. This makes sense in that the data is all that the model has to work with—by definition, there is minimal preconceived (feature) knowledge programmed into the model. For illustration, early work such as that by Laÿ et al. [10] tended to involve just a few dozen images, which allowed results on individual retinal images to be listed. Major contemporary studies however train and validate on hundreds of thousands of images [39, 40].

It is important to recognize that the quantity of data depends on the task at hand. For example, for pixel-level semantic segmentation of retinal structures such as the optic disc and cup and blood vessels, the relevant model input unit can be a relatively small tile, and not the entire retinal image [43]. This is because the immediate neighborhood of these relatively-small structures is generally sufficient to determine their identity. As such, a single retinal image may contain tens of thousands of relevant (if correlated) inputs for these segmentation tasks, whereas for classification tasks that may depend on a single abnormality [39, 40], each retinal image would be considered as a single independent input.

The increased amount of data can therefore be considered as a driving force behind the rise of end-to-end machine learning methods, as opposed to hybrid methods, in that there is a lower bound to the amount of data required for intermediate features to be reliably learnt. Without sufficient data, these intermediate features are likely to be overfitting, and not be representative of the "true" data distribution. Gulshan et al. [39] reports a specificity of below 40% with 208 training images relative to the specificity with over 50,000 images, as an indicator of performance loss.

However, obtaining a large amount of retinal image data is often difficult (refer to the later discussion on clinical challenges). This shortage has been mitigated in various ways. One common approach is the use of pretrained models. Pretrained models have their intermediate features already learnt from a suitable large dataset such as ImageNet. These models may then be used for transfer learning as *feature extractors*, where the intermediate features are unchanged, and a further classifier is learnt on the outputs of the pretrained model [51].

Alternatively, the intermediate features can be *fine-tuned* with the retinal image data. This allows smaller-scale features such as corners and edges to be retained, while larger-scale domain-specific features are adapted. The exact details, such as which network layers to freeze, are usually empirically determined. Tajbakhsh et al. [52] suggests that fine-tuning pretrained deep neural networks matches or outperforms training from scratch on randomly initialized weights, on several medical imaging tasks, and that this effect is strongest when there is a relative lack of training data.

In the common case where there exists a large amount of raw but mostly unannotated image data, one approach would be to first train a bootstrap model using a subset of image data for which good ground truth is available, and then use this bootstrap model to classify the full dataset. The bootstrap model's classification can then be regarded as an artificial ground truth, which is then used to train the actual model. Another approach is to divide the end-to-end classification into a segmentation step followed by a classification step, to allow more direct adaptation of the classification model to smaller datasets, as explored on OCT images by De Fauw et al. [53].

A lack of data may also be addressed by generating additional data. However, this is nontrivial because the underlying true data distribution is necessarily unknown. Despite that, a simple method is to generate new data by applying minor transformations to the actual training data. For retinal images, it is intuitive that image transforms such as rotation, flipping, limited scaling and limited elastic deformation should still result in a valid (and slightly different) retinal image from the original. Of course, the variability of images generated by this way would remain heavily constrained by the available data. Still, its ease of application and lack of obvious downsides have seen it as a common preprocessing step.

There has been some progress on generating synthetic retinal images. Fiorini et al. [54] generates the optic disc and retinal background, which is dependent on high-quality vascular tree data. The vascular tree is itself simulated by Bonaldi et al. [55], considering characteristics such as texture, bifurcations and width variation. Costa et al. [56] presents end-to-end retinal image synthesis, using an adversarial autoencoder to generate vascular trees, which are themselves then used to train a generative adversarial network, from which retinal images can be sampled. The authors however acknowledge limitations again relating to the available quantity of image data, particularly for rarer pathological cases.

3.2 Quality of data

Other than quantity, addressing image quality issues is also a major challenge with retinal image analysis. Here, image quality is understood as how visually similar the actual image is, as compared to an ideal image (the retina itself). Since automated analysis operates on digitized images, image resolution is a first influence on effective image quality—if the resolution is too low, certain small indicators such as microaneurysms may not be visible. On the other hand, higher image resolutions require more processing effort.

A resolution of about 3000×3000 pixels and field of view (FOV) of 30–50° is now common with specialized digital fundus cameras, and significantly higher resolutions are limited by the optics of the eye [57]. Though other imaging techniques such as OCT may allow for better depth resolution [58], fundus photography remains the most widely used modality for retinal imaging. The raw resolution may however be compromised by image compression, which is often used to reduce the image file size to facilitate transmission and storage in telemedicine. Prior studies have suggested that retinal images may be compressed with a JPEG compression rate of 1:28 without human-discernible loss in image quality [59], but this is perhaps less of a concern nowadays given advances in bandwidth and storage devices. Resolutions of 512×512 and lower have been demonstrated to be sufficient for human-level diabetic retinopathy classification [39, 40].

Other than image resolution, retinal photography in practice produces images of varying quality, due to environmental variables such as operator experience and patient behavior. Out-of-focus blurred images and other imaging artifacts may be observed. Camera operator behavior on poor quality images may not take into account the needs of an A.I. system. For example, it may be assumed that the grader knows to ignore ungradable images, which is not necessarily the case for an A.I.; as such, it is important for an A.I. system to take image quality into account, minimally by recognizing ungradable images [60]. Future directions may include automated restoration of minor quality issues [56].

3.3 Heterogeneous data

A third major technical challenge for A.I. in retinal imaging is *data heterogeneity*. Heterogeneity may manifest itself in many ways, both technological and methodological.

Firstly, images in a dataset may be heterogeneous due to equipment and differing image capture standards. For example, images from various sources may have been

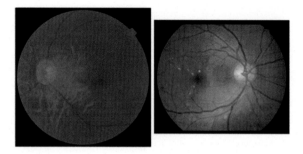

FIG. 2

Example of retinal photographs that may be expected to be classified with the same model.

saved with different compression algorithms and compression ratios, as discussed above. Similarly, images taken by different camera models may be trivially distinguished from each other due to features such as tabs at the edge of the retinal circle, and the presence of borders at the top and bottom (Fig. 2). Cameras with the same major specifications (such as resolution and FOV) may in fact retain subtle differences in image capture. Even cameras that are of the exact same manufacturer make may be differentiated by features such as minute scratches and artifacts.

Secondly, images in a dataset may be heterogeneous because of the underlying distribution of the subjects. For example, the image data may be composed almost entirely of subjects of a certain ethnicity, gender or age (Fig. 3). There may be further hidden environmental variables, such as room lighting and the time of day.

The technical significance of these observations is that popular neural network architectures are extremely sensitive to image details, and are capable of learning features that are not discernible by humans, from the evidence of adversarial images [61]. Therefore, data heterogeneity may cause the model to learn spurious relationships. For example, consider researchers testing a hypothesis as to whether a particular medical condition is predictable by a machine learning model from retinal fundus photographs. It may be that very good performance is achieved on the available training and validation data, but only because of technological (e.g., all images from one class are uncompressed, while all images from the other class have very minor compression artifacts) or methodological (e.g., all images from one class are of one ethnicity, while all images from the other class are from another ethnicity) biases.

Data heterogeneity is ideally mitigated by ensuring that the training set used is of as similar a distribution as that of the actual application, as possible. For example, a model to be used at a particular site is usually best trained or fine-tuned on data from that site. However, this may not always be possible. In these cases, the impact of heterogeneity may be reduced by principled sampling according to known variables. For example, it may be that for a particular rare condition, there exist 500 images each from Ethnicity A and B. However, for normal retina images, there are ten thousand images from Ethnicity A, but only 200 images from Ethnicity B. Then, if a model is trained to detect the rare condition without taking the underlying ethnic

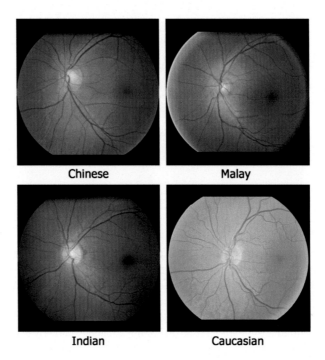

Chinese · Malay · Indian · Caucasian

FIG. 3

Example of retinal photographs from subjects of different ethnicities.

distribution into consideration, it is possible that the model would ultimately classify for ethnicity, rather than for the target condition. This may not even be realized during validation, if the validation data set maintains the same data distribution as the training set. Preprocessing may also be undertaken to reduce heterogeneity, before the retinal images are input to the actual model. Techniques such as color and contrast normalization eliminate the most obvious image variation. Adaptation to new data distributions may be attempted by additional classifier training on model outputs, given a sample of the new distribution. A simple realization would be adjustable score thresholds [40].

3.4 Unbalanced data

Data balance is a concern in tasks where there are multiple classes involved, such as classification and segmentation. Although there may seem to be a large quantity of data overall, model performance is generally also limited by the quantity of data available for each individual class of interest. For example, consider a dataset with a million normal retinal images, but only ten abnormal retinal images. Broadly speaking, an A.I. classifier would probably be better off with ten thousand normal retinal images, and a thousand abnormal retinal images. While there is a much greater *absolute quantity* of data in the first case, the balance of data is much better in the second case, since additional examples of the rarer (abnormal) class would be more useful to a classifier in learning to discriminate between them.

Unfortunately, in retinal image analysis, abnormal images are in practice usually far harder to come by. As such, it is common to oversample rare classes (or alternatively, undersample the common normal class) during model training. Recent research in general image classification with convolutional neural networks suggests that oversampling rare classes, such that all classes have the same input frequency without discarding any data, is recommended [62]. Another possible approach to the unbalanced data challenge is to frame the task as a one-class classification problem. Here, instead of being provided examples of both the normal class and the abnormal class(es), the idea is to learn the essence of what constitutes a normal retinal image from data—perhaps with autoencoders or GANs—and thereby be able to detect abnormal retinal images as being *different* from the normal image model. The advantage of this approach is that it possibly identifies rare conditions, which may not even be represented in the training data. The drawback is however that modeling retinal images is nontrivial, especially where structural details are concerned [56].

3.5 Incomplete data

A.I. models are often trained and optimized for a specific configuration. For example, a model may assume two particular retinal fundus photograph views as input. There has also been increasing interest in incorporating nonimage patient features such as age and medical history, inspired by the rising interest in precision medicine [63].

However, the more such features are used by a model, the more likely some features may not be available. There may be only one photograph available from a particular source, and another source may have only partial demographic information. In such cases, the model should have some way of handling missing features. A straightforward approach is to assume average values for missing features. Alternatively, if the number of features is small, separate models may be trained for each feature combination.

3.6 Private data

Due to patient privacy and other relevant regulations, medical data such as retinal photographs are often not readily transferrable between different research groups. However, as explained in the previous subsections, data quantity and diversity is critical to learning good A.I. models.

There have been various methods used to overcome data sharing problems. A simple approach is to share only the separately-trained A.I. models for analysis. The underlying image data remains private, since neural network-based A.I. models are generally irreversible. If the models are targeted towards the same task, these separately-trained models should produce similar results. The model outputs can therefore be ensembled, and any serious disagreements flagged for review. However, there is likely to remain some performance loss as compared to a model trained with all available image data.

More complex solutions include distributed model training and model encryption schemes. In distributed model training, the A.I. models are rotated between multiple institutions for training on their own private data. Chang et al. [64] suggests that cyclical weight transfer, where a deep neural network model is trained for a fixed number of epochs by an institution before being passed to the next institution, can produce a final model that has performance comparable to that from a model that is trained on all available retinal images. This would however necessitate strong cooperation and coordination between participating institutions, from model selection to timely model transfer. Model encryption on the other hand attacks the problem from a different angle, by enabling the sharing of encrypted image data. As such, patient privacy is not compromised. Homomorphic encryption then enables model architectures such as CryptoNets [65] to be trained and validated on encrypted image data. Therefore, unlike distributed model training, there would be no coordination issues after the encrypted image data is shared. There are however some tradeoffs with processing time and performance.

3.7 Model generalizability

As discussed in the section on heterogeneous data, a key practical concern is whether an A.I. model is generalizable to unseen image data. While humans may naturally understand the "big picture" and adapt accordingly, this is not necessarily the case for A.I. models.

In fact, models may not generalize well even where the data distribution accurately reflects the true distribution. Since training of machine learning models is often stochastic, there may still be sampling biases especially for rare classes. One approach to mitigate this is by training multiple models and examining the variance of their performance metrics. As an additional incentive, these models can further be ensembled, which generally improves overall performance.

There are also particular generalizability concerns with certain model architectures. Generative adversarial networks are for instance known to be vulnerable to mode collapse, where the network becomes focused on modeling only a subset of the image data, e.g., one particular ethnicity. Technical solutions include minibatch discrimination [66] and unrolling [67], as well as training separate models for each target class.

3.8 Model interpretability

A general concern with end-to-end machine learning models is that their internal workings are effectively a "black box." Unlike earlier feature-based methods, the thought process behind the model's decisions are not directly expressible with reference to human-comprehensible features (e.g., a microaneurysm having a certain level of similarity with a fixed template). This has led to reluctance on using A.I. in clinical settings [68]. Fortunately, a number of techniques have been developed to visualize neural network models, generally by producing a *saliency map* (Fig. 4) that

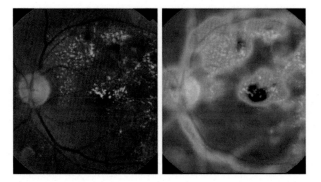

FIG. 4

Example of saliency map displaying regions contributing most strongly to a referable diabetic retinopathy image-level classification.

indicates which parts of the image contributed most significantly to the classification output [69, 70]. Such methods have been used to demonstrate that a model's classifications are derived from plausible retinal image regions [8, 38, 71]. However, such visualizations are passive in that they are a by-product of the classification process, and have no effect in practical deployment without explicit human oversight.

Some forms of interpretability may be designed into A.I. systems. For example, it is possible to model diabetic retinopathy screening mostly as a lesion segmentation problem [28, 37], possibly with semantic segmentation on pixel-level data. If so, the part of the model that involves classification according to a retinal image grading scheme becomes directly interpretable, in that the quantity of each type of lesion in the retinal image is revealed. The drawback is the requirement for lesion data to be labeled, which is not usually part of the grading workflow.

3.9 Model maintainability

An often-understated challenge with A.I. systems is their amenability to being updated with new image data. Since the collection of image data is often an ongoing process, decisions will have to be taken about whether to, and when to, create an updated model. In general, it is difficult to selectively update end-to-end machine learning models. Neural networks are in particular susceptible to *catastrophic forgetting*, where the updated model remembers the new data most strongly upon retraining, while neglecting what it had previously learnt [71a]. Their training process is therefore time and resource intensive, especially given that full re-validation should be undertaken after each re-training to ensure that intended model behavior has not deviated.

3.10 Model deployability

Deep neural network models are heavily resource-intensive, all the more when ensembles of multiple models are involved. Each retinal image may take seconds to analyze, including preprocessing steps, even with GPUs available. Given that many retinal images may need to be analyzed for each patient, possibly for multiple conditions requiring different models, the total time required adds up quickly. This has implications when turnaround timings are mandated. Commercial server hosting may moreover be prohibited due to security concerns, resulting in high upfront startup costs. Remote hosting of models may also be entirely infeasible in less-developed environments. In such circumstances, lightweight compressed models may be appropriate [72].

4 Clinical challenges

In addition to technical challenges, there have historically been a number of clinical factors that prevent simple adoption and usage of A.I. for retinal imaging, despite widespread uptake in other technological directions such as telemedicine [73]. We discuss some of the issues below.

4.1 Variation in DR classification systems and reference standards

Many DR classification systems are currently adopted in different countries, including International Clinical Diabetic Retinopathy Severity Scales (ICDRSS), Modified Airlie House Classification, English National Health Service Classification, Scottish DR classification system and Multi-ethnic Study of Atherosclerosis (MESA) system. These classification systems have slight variation on each of the DR severity scales. Some of these classification systems may be convertible between each other, but others may not. Because of this, an A.I. model developing by using one DR classification system may not perform as expected when tested on a dataset graded using a different classification system, despite both systems ostensibly measuring the same medical phenomena. Therefore, it is important to ensure the standardization of the ground truth between the training and testing datasets, to ensure the robustness of the A.I. models being developed.

In addition to the choice of classification system, determining who, or what, should be the reference standard remains a challenge. For example, how many reference standards do we need to ensure the quality of the ground truth? Different A.I. papers in retinal imaging have reported their results using different reference standards, with ground truth obtained from a variety of retinal specialists, general ophthalmologists, professional graders and optometrists. Does a senior professional grader who has worked more than 20 years in DR grading necessarily perform less well than a newly minted retinal specialist who has done just three years of ophthalmology residency followed by two years of retinal fellowship, despite nominally ranking below the retinal specialist? Also, is clinical examination by retinal specialists the best way to ascertain the ground truth, in the first place? This is not a fair comparison when the deep learning system only has access to single-field (macula-centered) or two-field (optic disc- and macula-centered) images. These are just some of the questions about which there is no consensus thus far.

4.2 Disagreement in clinical ground truth

Separate from the existence of multiple reference standards, a further complication lies in the existence of different opinions even when operating under the same classification framework, such as agreement among professional retinal image graders (*inter-grader agreement*). More recently, Krause et al. [74] reports very high specificity (99%) in diagnosing referable DR by retinal specialists against an adjudicated consensus, although their sensitivity ranged from a more modest 74.4–82.1%. Indeed, it has been long recognized that graders may not even always agree with their own previous classifications (*intra-grader agreement*).

Ideally, images for which discrepant ground truth is observed are reviewed by the individual graders until consensus is reached or arbitrated by a senior clinician. If this is not possible, a majority vote may be applied. Alternatively, the individual graders may be independently modeled using their respective ground truth, which has been shown to improve classification performance upon weighted ensembling [75].

4.3 Integration into clinical workflows

The integration of A.I. systems into existing clinical workflows can be complicated. Since patient well-being is paramount, the integration process should not have any negative effects on outcomes. Although early image analysis can be done separately and offline (i.e. parallel to clinical care), there will eventually have to be a transition period in which the A.I. system is introduced to the actual clinical workflow. This would entail a temporary increase in clinician workload, as the A.I. system operates alongside the existing practice.

4.4 Privacy and data collection

Existing A.I. systems require large quantities of patient image data to train and validate. Patient confidentiality in turn requires there to be established procedures in place, for the de-identification and anonymization of the image data (e.g., according to the Health Insurance Portability and Accountability Act, in the U.S.A.). If these regulations mandate that image data stay on-site or in a secured location, there would be additional infrastructural costs associated with A.I. systems. Furthermore, such regulations would severely complicate data-sharing collaborations, which are often necessary for a sufficient quantity and diversity of image data to be collected. This is without even mentioning the effort needed to clean and reconcile image data from different insular sources [76]. Some technical solutions to this issue have been explored in the previous subsection on private data.

4.5 Assignment of liability

A longstanding challenge with A.I. in medicine is the assignment of liability. With A.I. in the pipeline, the burden of decision-making is shared between human clinicians and the A.I. system. Disentangling responsibility for misdiagnoses under such a complicated regime is not easy, but it has profound legal and insurance implications. There already remain serious unresolved legal uncertainties surrounding telemedicine and state law, for example [77]. Given the custom and nonstandardized nature of A.I. in specific domains such as retinal imaging, there are likely to be legal and regulatory obstacles surrounding actual uptake.

4.6 Patient and physician acceptance of "black box" models

As discussed in the previous subsection on model interpretability, there has been reluctance by stakeholders (physicians, patients and healthcare regulators) to accept "black box" models whose internal workings cannot easily be understood, scrutinized, regulated and monitored. Instead, more-conventional rule-based models have been preferred over neural network models, despite offering poorer performance [68], in part because post hoc analysis (i.e. the effect of changing a single factor) is possible with rule-based models [78]. Efforts have been made to mitigate this lack of interpretability with saliency map methods, but these are also ultimately retrospective, as previously mentioned.

One possible observation on "black box" A.I. models in retinal image analysis, is that such a lack of interpretability has actually been present from well before the current shift to end-to-end models. Hybrid models, where a manually designed feature selection step precedes input to a machine learning classifier, has generally employed poorly interpretable classifiers as well. As such, stakeholders are now seemingly faced with a trade-off: consult a "black box" model with high accuracy, or settle for a simpler, interpretable model with poorer accuracy.

A large part of the aversion to reliance on "black box" models may be attributed to the types of mistakes that such models can make. In particular, despite possibly achieving an aggregated performance that is comparable to, or even better than, that of human experts, A.I. models may still be vulnerable to occasional "obvious" mistakes that it would be unreasonable for a human to make. As such, the generally-excellent and absolutely repeatable performance of A.I. models can get heavily discounted by such rare errors [79].

If the goal is to maximize clinical care and obtain best patient outcome, however, it is important to overcome unwarranted fear of "black box" models. Taking a concrete example, if an interpretable model with 90% accuracy is preferred over a "black box" model with 95% accuracy, the number of misdiagnosed patients may be twice as high as it could have been. Of course, this has to be balanced against the possibility of general failure, perhaps due to data heterogeneity in training. It is therefore important for "black box" models to be heavily and extensively validated against real-world and out-of-set data [40], and accompanied by common-sense "sanity checks" where possible.

4.7 Expectation management

Finally, despite the growing and increasingly substantiated promise of A.I. in retinal image analysis, there exists a danger of over-inflated expectations from all parties involved [80]. For example, computer scientists may become overconfident about the ability of deep learning to solve any problem given enough data, without appreciating the many clinical nuances involved. Conversely, clinicians may also underestimate the difficulty of producing robust and reliable models and have overly-high expectations of what is possible, given present-day A.I. technology and resources. Likewise, health administrators may primarily be concerned about savings in manpower and costs, while patients may unrealistically expect perfect diagnosis. If these expectations are not properly balanced and tempered beforehand, A.I. solutions may be abandoned prematurely, as has arguably happened to computer-aided diagnosis in mammography [81].

5 Conclusion

We have surveyed a number of technical and clinical challenges facing the use of A.I. in retinal image analysis and discussed how these challenges are being—or can be—addressed. On the technical end, much current development has been driven by the rise of deep learning. Such end-to-end models however impose many prerequisites, mostly relating to data quantity and distribution, which directly impact model performance and generalizability. Deep neural network models are moreover not directly interpretable. In addition, practical concerns relating to maintaining and deploying A.I. models are often overlooked.

On the clinical side, unsupervised A.I. systems remain rare in medical application, given the complexity and holistic nature of the field. Acceptance and integration of A.I. into existing workflows is to be expected, if clinicians do not trust the behavior of the A.I. system—especially when they bear ultimate responsibility for the results. The data-hungry nature of modern A.I. models also raises difficulties with data collection, particularly in a regulatory environment where patient privacy is being emphasized.

A.I. models also raise difficulties with data collection, particularly in a regulatory environment where patient privacy is being emphasized. For all these challenges, however, we remain confident that A.I. is the future of retinal image analysis, due to its obvious potential to produce reliable, repeatable and rapid diagnosis, which would in turn free clinicians to focus only on the most complex cases, and thus provide better care for the population as a whole.

References

[1] G. Litjens, T. Kooi, B.E. Bejnordi, A.A.A. Setio, F. Ciompi, M. Ghafoorian, et al., A survey on deep learning in medical image analysis, Med. Image Anal. 42 (2017) 60–88.

[2] T.Y. Wong, G.C. Cheung, M. Larsen, S. Sharma, R. Simó, Diabetic retinopathy, Nat. Rev. Dis. Primers 2 (2016) 16012.

[3] J.W. Yau, S.L. Rogers, R. Kawasaki, E.L. Lamoureux, J.W. Kowalski, T. Bek, et al., Global prevalence and major risk factors of diabetic retinopathy, Diabetes Care 35 (3) (2012) 556–564.

[4] N. Cheung, P. Mitchell, T.Y. Wong, Diabetic retinopathy, Lancet 376 (9735) (2010) 124–136.

[5] T.Y. Wong, J. Sun, R. Kawasaki, P. Ruamviboonsuk, N. Gupta, V.C. Lansingh, et al., Guidelines on diabetic eye care: the international council of ophthalmology recommendations for screening, follow-up, referral, and treatment based on resource settings, Ophthalmology (2018).

[6] J.K.H. Goh, C.Y. Cheung, S.S. Sim, P.C. Tan, G.S.W. Tan, T.Y. Wong, Retinal imaging techniques for diabetic retinopathy screening, J. Diabetes Sci. Technol. 10 (2) (2016) 282–294.

[6a] H.V. Nguyen, G.S.W. Tan, R.J. Tapp, S. Mital, D.S.W. Ting, H.T. Wong, et al., Cost-effectiveness of a national telemedicine diabetic retinopathy screening program in Singapore, Ophthalmology 123 (12) (2016) 2571–2580.

[7] T.Y. Wong, N.M. Bressler, Artificial intelligence with deep learning technology looks into diabetic retinopathy screening, JAMA 316 (22) (2016) 2366–2367.

[8] R. Poplin, A.V. Varadarajan, K. Blumer, Y. Liu, M.V. McConnell, G.S. Corrado, et al., Prediction of cardiovascular risk factors from retinal fundus photographs via deep learning, Nat. Biomed. Eng. 2 (3) (2018) 158–164.

[8a] D.S. Ting, C.Y. Cheung, Q. Nguyen, C. Sabanayagam, G. Lim, Z.W. Lim, et al., Deep learning in estimating prevalence and systemic risk factors for diabetic retinopathy: a multi-ethnic study, npj Digit, Med. 2 (1) (2019) 24.

[9] K. Akita, H. Kuga, A computer method of understanding ocular fundus images, Pattern Recogn. 15 (6) (1982) 431–443.

[10] B. Laÿ, C. Baudoin, J.-C. Klein, Automatic detection of microaneurysms in retinopathy fluoro-angiogram, in: Proceedings of SPIE, vol. 0432, 1984, pp. 165–173.

[11] R.A. Miller, H.E. Pople Jr., J.D. Myers, Internist-i, an experimental computer-based diagnostic consultant for general internal medicine, N. Engl. J. Med. 307 (8) (1982) 468–476.

[12] G.H. Bresnick, M.D. Davis, F.L. Myers, G. de Venecia, Clinicopathologic correlations in diabetic retinopathy. II. Clinical and histologic appearances of retinal capillary microaneurysms, Arch. Ophthalmol. 95 (7) (1977) 1215–1220.

[13] T. Spencer, R.P. Phillips, P.F. Sharp, J.V. Forrester, Automated detection and quantification of microaneurysms in fluorescein angiograms, Graefes Arch. Clin. Exp. Ophthalmol. 230 (1) (1992) 36–41.

[14] T. Spencer, J.A. Olson, K.C. McHardy, P.F. Sharp, J.V. Forrester, An image-processing strategy for the segmentation and quantification of microaneurysms in fluorescein angiograms of the ocular fundus, Comput. Biomed. Res. 29 (4) (1996) 284–302.

[15] A.M. Mendonça, A.J. Campilho, J.M. Nunes, Automatic segmentation of microaneurysms in retinal angiograms of diabetic patients, in: Proceedings of the 10th International Conference on Image Analysis and Processing, 1999, pp. 728–733.

[16] W. Hsu, P. Pallawala, M.L. Lee, K.-G.A. Eong, The role of domain knowledge in the detection of retinal hard exudates, in: Proceedings of the IEEE Computer Society Conference on Computer Vision and Pattern Recognition, IEEE, 2001.

[17] G. Yang, L. Gagnon, S. Wang, M.-C. Boucher, Algorithm for detecting micro-aneurysms in low-resolution color retinal images, in: Proceedings of Vision Interface, 2001.

[18] B.M. Ege, O.K. Hejlesen, O.V. Larsen, K. Møller, B. Jennings, D. Kerr, D.A. Cavan, Screening for diabetic retinopathy using computer based image analysis and statistical classification, Comput. Methods Prog. Biomed. 62 (3) (2000) 165–175.

[19] M. Niemeijer, B. Van Ginneken, J. Staal, M.S. Suttorp-Schulten, M.D. Abràmoff, Automatic detection of red lesions in digital color fundus photographs, IEEE Trans. Med. Imaging 24 (5) (2005) 584–592.

[20] A.J. Frame, P.E. Undrill, M.J. Cree, J.A. Olson, K.C. McHardy, P.F. Sharp, J.V. Forrester, A comparison of computer based classification methods applied to the detection of microaneurysms in ophthalmic fluorescein angiograms, Comput. Biol. Med. 28 (3) (1998) 225–238.

[21] A. Hunter, J. Lowell, J. Owens, L. Kennedy, D. Steele, Quantification of diabetic retinopathy using neural networks and sensitivity analysis, in: Artificial Neural Networks in Medicine and Biology, Springer, 2000, pp. 81–86.

[22] A. Osareh, M. Mirmehdi, B. Thomas, R. Markham, Comparative exudate classification using support vector machines and neural networks, in: Proceedings of the International Conference on Medical Image Computing and Computer-Assisted Intervention, Springer, 2002, pp. 413–420.

[23] R. Casanova, S. Saldana, E.Y. Chew, R.P. Danis, C.M. Greven, W.T. Ambrosius, Application of random forests methods to diabetic retinopathy classification analyses, PLoS One 9 (6) (2014) e98587.

[24] M.J. Cree, J.A. Olson, K.C. McHardy, P.F. Sharp, J.V. Forrester, A fully automated comparative microaneurysm digital detection system, Eye 11 (5) (1997) 622–628.

[25] A. Hoover, V. Kouznetsova, M. Goldbaum, Locating blood vessels in retinal images by piece-wise threshold probing of a matched filter response, IEEE Trans. Med. Imaging 19 (3) (2000) 203–210.

[26] P. Pallawala, W. Hsu, M.L. Lee, S.S. Goh, Automated microaneurysm segmentation and detection using generalized eigenvectors, in: Proceedings of the 7th IEEE Workshop on Applications of Computer Vision, vol. 1, IEEE, 2005, pp. 322–327.

[27] G. Quellec, M. Lamard, P.M. Josselin, G. Cazuguel, B. Cochener, C. Roux, Optimal wavelet transform for the detection of microaneurysms in retina photographs, IEEE Trans. Med. Imaging 27 (9) (2008) 1230–1241.

[28] G. Lim, M.L. Lee, W. Hsu, Constrained-mser detection of retinal pathology, in: Proceedings of the 21st International Conference on Pattern Recognition, IEEE, 2012, pp. 2059–2062.

[29] L. Tang, M. Niemeijer, J.M. Reinhardt, M.K. Garvin, M.D. Abràmoff, Splat feature classification with application to retinal hemorrhage detection in fundus images, IEEE Trans. Med. Imaging 32 (2) (2013) 364–375.

[30] S.S. Rahim, V. Palade, J. Shuttleworth, C. Jayne, Automatic screening and classification of diabetic retinopathy and maculopathy using fuzzy image processing, Brain Inform. 3 (4) (2016) 249–267.

[31] G.G. Gardner, D. Keating, T.H. Williamson, A.T. Elliott, Automatic detection of diabetic retinopathy using an artificial neural network: a screening tool, Br. J. Ophthalmol. 80 (11) (1996) 940–944.

[32] A. Starita, A. Sperduti, A neural-based system for the automatic classification and follow-up of diabetic retinopathies, in: Artificial Neural Networks in Biomedicine, Springer, 2000, pp. 233–247.

[33] A. Osareh, M. Mirmehdi, B. Thomas, R. Markham, Automated identification of diabetic retinal exudates in digital colour images, Br. J. Ophthalmol. 87 (10) (2003) 1220–1223.

[34] C. Sinthanayothin, J.F. Boyce, T.H. Williamson, H.L. Cook, E. Mensah, S. Lal, D. Usher, Automated detection of diabetic retinopathy on digital fundus images, Diabet. Med. 19 (2) (2002) 105–112.

[35] D. Usher, M. Dumskyj, M. Himaga, T.H. Williamson, S. Nussey, J. Boyce, Automated detection of diabetic retinopathy in digital retinal images: a tool for diabetic retinopathy screening, Diabet. Med. 21 (1) (2004) 84–90.

[36] G. Lim, Automated Methods for Retinopathy and Glaucoma Screening, (Doctoral Dissertation), National University of Singapore, 2015.

[37] G. Lim, M.L. Lee, W. Hsu, T.Y. Wong, Transformed representations for convolutional neural networks in diabetic retinopathy screening, in: Proceedings of the AAAI Workshop on Modern Artificial Intelligence for Health Analytics (MAIHA), AAAI, 2014, pp. 34–38.

[38] R. Gargeya, T. Leng, Automated identification of diabetic retinopathy using deep learning, Ophthalmology 124 (7) (2017) 962–969.

[39] V. Gulshan, L. Peng, M. Coram, M.C. Stumpe, D. Wu, A. Narayanaswamy, et al., Development and validation of a deep learning algorithm for detection of diabetic retinopathy in retinal fundus photographs, JAMA 316 (22) (2016) 2402–2410.

[40] D.S.W. Ting, C.Y. Cheung, G. Lim, G.S.W. Tan, N.D. Quang, A. Gan, et al., Development and validation of a deep learning system for diabetic retinopathy and related eye diseases using retinal images from multiethnic populations with diabetes, JAMA 318 (22) (2017) 2211–2223.

[40a] V. Bellemo, Z.W. Lim, G. Lim, Q.D. Nguyen, Y. Xie, M.Y.T. Yip, et al., Artificial intelligence using deep learning to screen for referable and vision-threatening diabetic retinopathy in Africa: a clinical validation study, Lancet Digit. Health 1 (1) (2019) e35–e44.

[41] F. Calimeri, A. Marzullo, C. Stamile, G. Terracina, Optic disc detection using fine tuned convolutional neural networks, in: 2016 12th International Conference on Signal Image Technology & Internet-based Systems (SITIS), IEEE, 2016, pp. 69–75.

[42] H. Fu, J. Cheng, Y. Xu, D.W.K. Wong, J. Liu, X. Cao, Joint optic disc and cup segmentation based on multi-label deep network and polar transformation, IEEE Trans. Med. Imaging 37 (7) (2018) 1597–1605.

[43] G. Lim, Y. Cheng, W. Hsu, M.L. Lee, Integrated optic disc and cup segmentation with deep learning, in: Proceedings of the 27th IEEE International Conference on Tools with Artificial Intelligence, IEEE, 2015, pp. 162–169.

[44] K.-K. Maninis, J. Pont-Tuset, P. Arbeláez, L. Van Gool, Deep retinal image understanding, in: Proceedings of the International Conference on Medical Image Computing and Computer-Assisted Intervention, Springer, 2016, pp. 140–148.

[45] A. Sevastopolsky, Optic disc and cup segmentation methods for glaucoma detection with modification of u-net convolutional neural network, Pattern Recogn. Image Anal. 27 (3) (2017) 618–624.

[46] O. Ronneberger, P. Fischer, T. Brox, U-net: convolutional networks for biomedical image segmentation, in: International Conference on Medical Image Computing and Computer-Assisted Intervention, Springer, 2015, pp. 234–241.

[47] L. van der Maaten, E. Postma, J. Van den Herik, Dimensionality reduction: a comparative review, J. Mach. Learn. Res. 10 (2009) 66–71.

[48] B. Zhang, X. Wu, J. You, Q. Li, F. Karray, Detection of microaneurysms using multiscale correlation coefficients, Pattern Recogn. 43 (6) (2010) 2237–2248.

[49] M.D. Abràmoff, W.L. Alward, E.C. Greenlee, L. Shuba, C.Y. Kim, J.H. Fingert, Y.H. Kwon, Automated segmentation of the optic disc from stereo color photographs using physiologically plausible features, Invest. Ophthalmol. Vis. Sci. 48 (4) (2007) 1665–1673.

[50] P. Domingos, A few useful things to know about machine learning, Commun. ACM 55 (10) (2012) 78–87.

[51] P. Burlina, K.D. Pacheco, N. Joshi, D.E. Freund, N.M. Bressler, Comparing humans and deep learning performance for grading AMD: a study in using universal deep features and transfer learning for automated AMD analysis, Comput. Biol. Med. 82 (2017) 80–86.

[52] N. Tajbakhsh, J.Y. Shin, S.R. Gurudu, R.T. Hurst, C.B. Kendall, M.B. Gotway, J. Liang, Convolutional neural networks for medical image analysis: Full training or fine tuning? IEEE Trans. Med. Imaging 35 (5) (2016) 1299–1312.

[53] J. De Fauw, J.R. Ledsam, B. Romera-Paredes, S. Nikolov, N. Tomasev, S. Blackwell, et al., Clinically applicable deep learning for diagnosis and referral in retinal disease, Nat. Med. 24 (9) (2018) 1342–1350.

[54] S. Fiorini, L. Ballerini, E. Trucco, A. Ruggeri, Automatic generation of synthetic retinal fundus images, in: Eurographics Italian Chapter Conference, 2014, pp. 41–44.

[55] L. Bonaldi, E. Menti, L. Ballerini, A. Ruggeri, E. Trucco, Automatic generation of synthetic retinal fundus images: vascular network, Procedia Comput. Sci. 90 (2016) 54–60.

[56] P. Costa, A. Galdran, M.I. Meyer, M. Niemeijer, M.D. Abràmoff, A.M. Mendonça, A. Campilho, End-to-end adversarial retinal image synthesis, IEEE Trans. Med. Imaging 37 (3) (2018) 781–791.

[57] E. Trucco, A. Ruggeri, T. Karnowski, L. Giancardo, E. Chaum, J.P. Hubschman, et al., Validating retinal fundus image analysis algorithms: issues and a proposal, Invest. Ophthalmol. Vis. Sci. 54 (5) (2013) 3546–3559.

[58] S. Hariri, A.A. Moayed, A. Dracopoulos, C. Hyun, S. Boyd, K. Bizheva, Limiting factors to the oct axial resolution for in-vivo imaging of human and rodent retina in the 1060nm wavelength range, Opt. Express 17 (26) (2009) 24304–24316.

[59] R.H. Eikelboom, K. Yogesan, C.J. Barry, I.J. Constable, M.-L. Tay-Kearney, L. Jitskaia, P.H. House, Methods and limits of digital image compression of retinal images for telemedicine, Invest. Ophthalmol. Vis. Sci. 41 (7) (2000) 1916–1924.

[60] J.M.P. Dias, C.M. Oliveira, L.A. da Silva Cruz, Retinal image quality assessment using generic image quality indicators, Inform. Fus. 19 (2014) 73–90.

[61] I.J. Goodfellow, J. Shlens, C. Szegedy, Explaining and harnessing adversarial examples, in: Proceedings of the International Conference on Learning Representations, 2015.

[62] M. Buda, A. Maki, M.A. Mazurowski, A Systematic Study of the Class Imbalance Problem in Convolutional Neural Networks, 2017. arXiv preprint arXiv:1710.05381.

[63] R. Mirnezami, J. Nicholson, A. Darzi, Preparing for precision medicine, N. Engl. J. Med. 366 (6) (2012) 489–491.

[64] K. Chang, N. Balachandar, C. Lam, D. Yi, J. Brown, A. Beers, et al., Distributed deep learning networks among institutions for medical imaging, J. Am. Med. Inform. Assoc. (2018).

[65] R. Gilad-Bachrach, N. Dowlin, K. Laine, K. Lauter, M. Naehrig, J. Wernsing, Cryptonets: applying neural networks to encrypted data with high throughput and accuracy, in: Proceedings of the International Conference on Machine Learning, 2016, pp. 201–210.

[66] T. Salimans, I. Goodfellow, W. Zaremba, V. Cheung, A. Radford, X. Chen, Improved techniques for training gans, in: Advances in Neural Information Processing Systems, 2016, pp. 2234–2242.

[67] T. Che, Y. Li, A.P. Jacob, Y. Bengio, W. Li, Mode regularized generative adversarial networks, in: Proceedings of the International Conference on Learning Representations, 2017.

[68] R. Caruana, Y. Lou, J. Gehrke, P. Koch, M. Sturm, N. Elhadad, Intelligible models for healthcare: predicting pneumonia risk and hospital 30-day readmission, in: Proceedings of the 21th ACM SIGKDD International Conference on Knowledge Discovery and Data Mining, ACM, 2015, pp. 1721–1730.

[69] R.R. Selvaraju, M. Cogswell, A. Das, R. Vedantam, D. Parikh, D. Batra, Grad-cam: visual explanations from deep networks via gradient-based localization, in: Proceedings of the IEEE Conference on Computer Vision and Pattern Recognition, 2017, pp. 618–626.

[70] K. Simonyan, A. Vedaldi, A. Zisserman, Deep inside convolutional networks: visualising image classification models and saliency maps, in: Proceedings of the International Conference on Learning Representations, 2014.

[71] G. Quellec, K. Charrière, Y. Boudi, B. Cochener, M. Lamard, Deep image mining for diabetic retinopathy screening, Med. Image Anal. 39 (2017) 178–193.

[71a] R.M. French, Catastrophic forgetting in connectionist networks, Trends Cogn. Sci. 3 (4) (1999) 128–135.

[72] A.G. Howard, M. Zhu, B. Chen, D. Kalenichenko, W. Wang, T. Weyand, et al., Mobilenets: Efficient Convolutional Neural Networks for Mobile Vision Applications, 2017. arXiv preprint arXiv:1704.04861.

[73] D.S.W. Ting, G.S.W. Tan, Telemedicine for diabetic retinopathy screening, JAMA Ophthalmol. 135 (7) (2017) 722–723.

[74] J. Krause, V. Gulshan, E. Rahimy, P. Karth, K. Widner, G.S. Corrado, et al., Grader variability and the importance of reference standards for evaluating machine learning models for diabetic retinopathy, Ophthalmology 125 (8) (2018) 1264–1272.

[75] M.Y. Guan, V. Gulshan, A.M. Dai, G.E. Hinton, Who said what: modeling individual labelers improves classification, in: Proceedings of AAAI, 2018.

[76] A. Flanders, Medical image and data sharing: are we there yet? Radiographics 29 (5) (2009) 1247–1251.

[77] J.S. Allain, From jeopardy to jaundice: the medical liability implications of Dr. Watson and other artificial intelligence systems, Louis. Law Rev. 73 (2012) 1049–1079.

[78] F. Cabitza, R. Rasoini, G.F. Gensini, Unintended consequences of machine learning in medicine, JAMA 318 (6) (2017) 517–518.

[79] B.J. Dietvorst, J.P. Simmons, C. Massey, Algorithm aversion: people erroneously avoid algorithms after seeing them err, J. Exp. Psychol. Gen. 144 (1) (2015) 114–126.

[80] J.H. Chen, S.M. Asch, Machine learning and prediction in medicine—beyond the peak of inflated expectations, N. Engl. J. Med. 376 (26) (2017) 2507–2509.

[81] A. Kohli, S. Jha, Why cad failed in mammography, J. Am. Coll. Radiol. 15 (3) (2018) 535–537.

Index

Note: Page numbers followed by *f* indicate figures and *t* indicate tables.